1974

W9-ACP-449
Heinrich Heine
3 0301 00033380 3

Yale Germanic Studies, 3

Heinrich Heine, The Elusive Poet

BY JEFFREY L. SAMMONS

New Haven and London, Yale University Press, 1969

LIBRARY
College of St. Francis
JOLIET, ILL.

Copyright © 1969 by Yale University.

All rights reserved. This book may not be
reproduced, in whole or in part, in any form
(except by reviewers for the public press),
without written permission from the publishers.

Library of Congress catalog card number: 74-81429,

Designed by John O. C. McCrillis,
set in Baskerville type,
and printed in the United States of America by
The Colonial Press Inc., Clinton, Massachusetts.
Distributed in Great Britain, Europe, Asia, and
Africa by Yale University Press Ltd., London; in
Canada by McGill University Press, Montreal; and
in Latin America by Centro Interamericano de Libros
Académicos, Mexico City.

Published with assistance from
the Louis Stern Memorial Fund.

831.75
S189

FOR CHRISTA

68492

Preface

Although the study of Heinrich Heine continues to be plagued, as it always has been, both by the puzzling difficulties inherent in the subject and by distractions that are basically of a political nature, a process of reinterpretation and, to some extent, consolidation, is now evidently and thankfully in motion. Eventually we may hope to achieve a genuinely sound understanding of a career and a reputation of almost unparalleled significance in the history of European letters. This book is meant to belong to the now well-established beginning phase of the process, for the state of Heine scholarship is not yet such that comprehensive interpretations of more or less permanent validity can be offered with any confidence. My study is avowedly a pile of bricks and a certain amount of mortar for an edifice yet to be built, not an edifice itself. It is for others to judge the soundness of the materials and use them or discard them as their strength may warrant upon further testing. The nature of this book, which is determined by the present state of scholarship, in turn determines one or two of its peculiarities that perhaps require some defense.

I hope the reader will not find the extensive apparatus of references and notes unwieldy. In the first place, Heine is so problematical and self-contradictory a writer and puts such a strain on the memory that it seems best to deal with him by, as it were, ostensible definition; it is extraordinarily difficult to discuss him reliably without laying out his text before the reader almost line by line. Secondly, it has struck me in my studies that, for a variety of reasons, the scholarly dialogue broke down some considerable time ago and has not yet been wholly restored. The last serious attempt to debate with the scholarship as a whole was Ernst Elster's annotation to his unfinished second edition of Heine's works in 1924. Since then, knowledge and interpretation have often not accumulated; they have merely been stored. Today it is only a slight exaggeration to say that the West Germans and the

East Germans do not listen to each other, that neither listens to the French, English, and Americans, and that nobody listens to the Scandinavians, the Netherlanders, and the Italians, not to mention writers in other, less accessible languages. Now the ideal of studying everything of potential significance that has been written about Heine conflicts seriously with the, I believe, natural desire to complete one's own study within a predictable life span. I have tried to cover a substantial portion of the literature, and in order to make this labor of some value to others, I have included several hundred references to secondary sources in the hope that they may serve as a guide to other students of Heine and help to reconvene the scholarly dialogue. To spare the patience of the reader somewhat, notes that contain text references or collateral support have been put at the back of the book, those containing additional comments or observations at the bottom of the page.

The appended bibliography is a record of my own experience in the literature about Heine and is meant to serve no other purpose; it pretends to be neither an exhaustive compilation of important studies on Heine nor a basic guide for any other student. It contains many items that are significant in a negative way, and knowledgeable Heine scholars may well detect and disapprove of an omission here and there. Heine is one of the best-served writers in German literature in point of bibliography. The *Heine-Bibliographie* of Gottfried Wilhelm and Eberhard Galley (2 vols. Weimar, 1960) contains some six thousand items of primary and secondary material through 1953; the *Heine-Jahrbuch,* published in Düsseldorf since 1962, has closed the gap and continues to maintain a very thorough running account. An excellent working bibliography of basic Heine studies will be found in S. S. Prawer's *Heine: The Tragic Satirist* (Cambridge, Eng., 1961), pp. 302–07.

A word about Prawer's book is probably in order here. It may seem odd that out of the vast plethora of Heine studies a single work is referred to with such frequency in these pages. But Prawer's book is, in my view, the very best that has ever been written on Heine's poetry, and integrity requires me to acknowledge my pervasive indebtedness to it. I certainly would not propose to compete with it. In method, however, I differ from Prawer in that, on the whole, I deal with books as Heine published them rather than with works as he wrote them. This method has its disadvantages, especially with regard to depth in the interpretation of poetry, but for my purposes it has the advantage of comprehending Heine's whole career in a relatively unitary way. My study assumes Prawer's and proposes to supplement it, not to supersede it.

Thanks are due the editors of the *Heine-Jahrbuch* and of the *German Quarterly* for gracious permission to include revised and expanded versions of papers as Chapter 4 and the first part of Chapter 11 respectively. Full references to the original articles will be found under my name in the bibliography.

I have a lively sense of gratitude toward Richard Gilbert of the Yale Class of 1968, who meticulously assisted me in checking references. For my wife's literally limitless patience and encouragement, her penetrating suggestions and labors of assistance, and particularly the Fowleresque rigor with which she helped me in my effort to keep my sentences honest, no words can express my feelings.

I am grateful to Yale University for granting me a Morse Fellowship that provided me with the necessary leisure for my studies. I wish to thank Dr. Eberhard Galley and Dr. Franz Finke, who cheerfully tolerated me underfoot for several months in the cramped quarters of the *Heine-Archiv* in Düsseldorf and offered me every kind of assistance. Finally, I owe a special debt of gratitude to Hermann J. Weigand, who taught me more of fundamental importance about Heine in nine months than I have been able to learn for myself in the nine years or so since; although he is now totally blind and his time, as a consequence, is extremely precious, he permitted me to read to him my entire manuscript; he made many valuable suggestions and raised my spirits with even more valuable encouragement.

Jeffrey L. Sammons

New Haven, Connecticut
Spring 1968

Contents

List of Abbreviations

When a work is quoted more than once in the notes to the same chapter the full reference is given for the first occurrence and short titles are used thereafter.

E	*Heinrich Heines Sämtliche Werke,* ed. Ernst Elster, 7 vols. Leipzig and Vienna, [1887–90].
E²	*Heinrich Heines Werke,* ed. Ernst Elster, 4 vols. (incomplete), Leipzig, [1924].
Hirth	*Heinrich Heines Briefe,* ed. Friedrich Hirth [and Claire Hartgenbusch], 6 vols. Mainz, 1950–51.
Houben	*Gespräche mit Heine,* ed. H. H. Houben, Frankfurt am Main, 1926.
Prawer, *TS*	S. S. Prawer, *Heine The Tragic Satirist: A Study of the Later Poetry, 1827–1856,* Cambridge, England, 1961.
W	*Heinrich Heines Sämtliche Werke,* ed. Oskar Walzel, Jonas Fränkel, Ludwig Krähe, Albert Leitzmann, and Julius Petersen, 10 vols. Leipzig, 1910–15; index vol., Leipzig, 1920.

CHAPTER 1

Introduction: The Elusive Birthdate

La chose la plus importante,
c'est que je suis né.

—HEINE

Heinrich Heine was born on December 13, 1797—as nearly as we can tell with any assurance. And thereby hangs a tale that will serve as well as any for an introduction to this study. It has been often told, and I propose to offer no new solutions and only one new factual observation. But it is fair to question whether the most fruitful interpretation has ordinarily been put on the whole muddle surrounding Heine's birthdate. The problem itself is of minor importance, except as a curiosity to pique scholars—for it is admittedly a little maddening that the birthdate of a writer of international fame, born in a European city little more than a century and a half ago, should be so difficult to determine. But this datum does not matter very much after all, and such psychological interpretations as have accrued to the discussion in the past have turned out to be grounded in untenable assumptions. The issue, however, is paradigmatic for the larger problem of coping with the phenomenon of Heine effectively, and there are some methodological conclusions to be drawn from it that are basic to the interpretation to be pursued in this book.

In the chronology of Heine's life the question of his birthdate does not become troublesome until the time of his doctoral degree and baptism—when he was twenty-seven years old—for, with a single exception,* all the evidence up to that time points at least

* The protocol of the *Akademisches Gericht* at the University of Bonn in 1819, recording the investigation of a patriotic demonstration, reads as follows: "Der vorgerufene *studiosus juris* Harry Heine aus Düsseldorf, 19 Jahr alt." The full text will be found in Hermann Hüffer, "Heine vor dem Bonner Universitäts-Gericht," in *Heinrich Heine, Gesammelte Aufsätze,* ed. Ernst Elster (Berlin, 1906), p. 54. This

roughly to the date now generally assumed to be correct. In 1821 Heine indicated 1797 as the year of his birth in response to a request for biographical data.* His boyhood friends, Friedrich Steinmann,[1] Johann Baptist Rousseau,[2] and Joseph Neunzig,[3] all agree that Heine was born in 1797, which is significant because age differences among children are particularly noticeable. It has been shown that Heine attended school classes for which he would have been too young had he been born later than 1797 or early 1798.[4] A Prussian government report on Heine in 1843 also gives the year 1797, although the source of this information is not known.[5] In 1809 the Rabbi of Jülich-Berg, Judah Löb Scheuer, was asked to give the names and birthdates of all Jewish children born in Düsseldorf between 1797 and 1808; since the circumcision records had been destroyed, he was obliged to rely upon his memory, and gave the date of "Hery" Heine's birth as February 1798.[6] An article by Philipp F. Veit, which will concern us again presently, suggests that this may be more correct than the earlier date generally assumed by Heine scholars, and also that Rabbi Scheuer may be more correct about the birth years of Heine's brothers and sister than the usual sources.[7] This is far from certain, however: Rabbi Scheuer would probably have been thinking in terms of the Jewish calendar, and the year of Heine's birth, 5588 (September 21, 1797, to September 11, 1798), includes both dates.

The difficulties really begin in 1825. During that year, on his application for admission to his doctoral examination, Heine wrote: "Natus sum mense Decembri anni 1779 Dusseldorpii ad Rhenum" (Hirth, *1*, 203). One may, if one likes, look upon this as a combination of nervousness and the familiar numerical error of transposition,[8] but the sequel suggests something more complex. His baptismal certificate gives the date of his birth as December 13, 1799,[9] two months later than that on his doctoral

---

may be a singular instance, because Heine, not yet matriculated and already in trouble, may have wanted to impress the court with his youth, especially as he was a good deal older than most students and because the other sources for 1799 or 1800 all appear after 1825.

* To Friedrich Rassmann, Oct. 20, 1821; Hirth, *1*, 31. Heine here says that he is twenty-four, although he must in fact have been twenty-three. Rassmann assumed that he meant 1797. Cf. E, *1*, 515.

application, and from that point on, for the rest of Heine's life, there is nothing but confusion. His passport from England, dated August 14, 1827, gives his age as twenty-eight, which, if one assumes that December is the correct month, indicates 1798, not, as Friedrich Hirth claims, 1799.* On his passport to Italy, dated August 8, 1828, his age is also given as twenty-eight, over which Hirth again stumbles, for this indicates 1799 and not 1800.[10]

The year 1800, however, appears elsewhere with some frequency. It appears first in a joke in *Die Bäder von Lucca* of 1829:

> "Und wie alt sind Sie, Dottore?"
> "Ich, Signora, bin in der Neujahrsnacht Achtzehnhundert geboren."
> "Ich habe Ihnen ja schon gesagt," bemerkte der Markese, "es ist einer der ersten Männer unseres Jahrhunderts." (E, *3*, 316)

This is clearly nothing more than a bit of humorous dialogue with Heine's poetic persona acting as his own straight man. But Heine apparently thought it was good enough to perpetuate. In 1835 he wrote to Philarète Chasles[11] that he had been born in 1800; Chasles, in turn, printed this,[12] and for many years the date 1800 was the common assumption in France.

Heine published in the spring of 1836 a poem beginning: "Ich bin nun fünfunddreißig Jahr' alt,"† and his marriage license, issued August 31, 1841, gives the date December 31, 1799.‡ In the preface to the French edition of the *Reisebilder* in 1853, he says that he was "né au commencement du XIXe siècle" (E, *4*, 621); a similar statement appears in the *Geständnisse* of 1854.[13] When Maria Embden-Heine, the daughter of Heine's sister Charlotte, added another volume to the family tradition of misinforma-

* Hirth, *4*, 151. There is a surprising amount of inaccuracy in the calculation of Heine's age by scholars who forget that he was presumably born in December.

† This piece of evidence is undoubtedly valueless and may be pure fiction, for when Heine first offered the poem to Laube for publication in November 1835, it apparently began: "Ich bin nun drey und dreyßig Jahr alt." (Hirth, 2, 104)

‡ Elster, "Zu Heines Biographie," *Vierteljahrschrift für Litteraturgeschichte, 4* (1891), p. 466. The date "31" instead of "13" may be a slip of the pen, possibly influenced by the date of the license, or a concession to a superstition of Mathilde's or, conceivably, a recurrence of the fiction of the "first man of the century."

tion, she repeated the fiction from *Die Bäder von Lucca;*[14] Heine's brother Maximilian, however, gave official family approval to the date December 13, 1799.[15]

At this point in the story one is indeed entitled to wonder what the reason for all this might be. Heine himself offers a solution in a letter of November 3, 1851 to Saint-René Taillandier. He admits that the birthdates in his various biographical notices are not exact and goes on to say: "Entre nous soit dit, ces inexactitudes semblent [!] provenir d'erreurs volontaires, qu'on a commises en ma faveur lors de l'invasion prussienne, pour me soustraire au service de Sa Majesté le roi de Prusse . . . En regardant mon acte de baptême, je trouve le 13 décembre 1799 comme date de ma naissance" (Hirth, *3*, 333).[16] This explanation has struck a number of people as plausible. But it has some troublesome features, quite apart from its demonstratively indefinite tone and the reference to the baptismal certificate. First, because of the information Heine had given to Chasles some years before, one would think that the discrepancy referred to here is that between 1800 and 1799, not that between 1799 and 1797.[17] Veit objects, reasonably enough, that this would only be a difference of three weeks,[18] but the fact remains that 1800 was the date prevalent in French sources, and that Heine is here proposing to offer the correct information; he could not give 1799 as a correction of 1797 if his argument is that previously he had made himself *younger*. Secondly, it is most ironic that in Heine's application for his doctoral examination—the same document in which he gives 1779 as his birthdate—he claims that, along with his classmates in Düsseldorf, he had volunteered *for* the Prussian campaign *against* Napoleon.[19] It is not known whether this is true or not, but obviously this statement and that to Saint-René Taillandier of 1851 cannot both be true. Now Heine's practice of planting in publications statements he thought would be advantageous to himself is notorious, and it was not farfetched to argue that, after having acquired a certain reputation as an admirer of Louis-Philippe, he was now anxious to remind Louis Napoleon and the current leadership of France of his original Bonapartism.[20] Indeed, in the very next sentence of the letter he calls attention to his poem *Die Grenadiere,* "qui vous fera voir que tout mon culte d'alors était l'empereur." Finally, apparently no one has troubled to inquire whether Heine actually would have been liable to conscription. It seems unlikely. According to the Prussian *Wehrgesetz* of 1814, Heine would have been eligible for the draft at age twenty, that is, effectively, in 1818.[21] Thus there would have been no need for Heine to have been made younger at the time of the Prussian invasion, and if this was done to avoid the draft at a later date, it certainly had nothing to do with the Napoleonic wars, as Heine intimated in his letter. In any case, by that time Heine was no longer a resident of Prussia but lived in the city-state of Hamburg.*

Dissatisfaction with the "draft dodger" theory has led scholars to search for some other explanation. The nature of Heine's relations to his Uncle Salomon, the fact that the muddle about the birthdate was perpetuated and even further confused by Heine's family after his death, and a few rather cryptic remarks by Heine himself, encouraged Walter Wadepuhl [22] and Hirth[23] to engage in elaborate biographical speculations in order to demonstrate that Heine was born some weeks before his parents' wedding and that the subsequent hocus-pocus was an attempt to obscure the illegitimacy of his birth and to protect his mother. The implausibility of such a violation of strict moral code by an eighteenth-century Jewish couple while they were engaged in a rather difficult negotiation for acceptance by the community does not seem to have struck either Wadepuhl or Hirth. In any case, we do not need to examine their arguments in detail, for the whole theory has been laid to rest. Veit, by means of convincing computations with the Jewish calendar, has established beyond reasonable doubt that Heine's parents were married on February 1, 1797, and thus that Heine was legitimately born.† Veit then falls back on the "draft

* For these reasons, the theory that Heine made himself two years younger in order to be able to go to Hamburg in 1816 to seek a career without making it appear that he was avoiding the Prussian military service is without foundation. It was proposed by Hüffer, "Wann ist Heinrich Heine geboren?", *Heinrich Heine: Gesammelte Aufsätze,* ed. Ernst Elster (Berlin, 1906), pp. 250–52.

† Veit first presented this conclusion in "Heine's Birth: Illegitimate or Legitimate," *Germanic Review, 33* (1958), 276–84. This article, unfortunately, is rather difficult to follow because of a number of misprints in dates, which are, after all, the most important part of the argument. Veit took up the matter again in his article in the

dodger" hypothesis; but, for the reasons I have mentioned, I think that there is only an outside chance it is correct. We are left, consequently, with no explanation at all for a most prominent peculiarity of Heine's presentation of himself to the public and to posterity. This situation is worth meditating upon a little longer.

The most important document bearing on the problem, apart from the letter to Saint-René Taillandier, is one to Heine's sister, Charlotte Embden, of July 16, 1853. It contains biographical information supplied for some unknown purpose. Here Heine writes, *to his sister,* be it noted:

> Was das Datum meiner Geburt betrifft, so bemerke ich Dir, daß ich laut meinem Taufschein den 13. Decbr. 1799 geboren bin. . . . Da alle unsere Familienpapiere durch die Feuersbrünste in Altona und in Hamburg zu Grunde gegangen und in den Düsseldorfer Archiven das Datum meiner Geburt nicht richtig angegeben seyn kann, aus Gründen, die ich nicht sagen will, so ist obiges Datum allein authentisch, jedenfalls authentischer als die Erinnerungen meiner Mutter, deren alterndes Gedächtniß keine verloren gegangene Papiere ersetzen kann. Bey dieser Gelegenheit bemerke ich Dir, liebes Lottchen, daß Du vielleicht viel jünger bist als die Mutter glaubt, da Du viele Jahre nach mir zur Welt gekommen. (Hirth, *3,* 475).

This letter is an astonishing, not to say impertinent, performance. It makes Heine's baptismal certificate (a document of no demonstrative force) a higher authority than possible civil records and his mother's memory concerning the year of her first-born child's birth. In order to maintain this argument, Heine tells Charlotte

---

Heine-Jahrbuch 1962, presenting essentially the same argument with respect to the marriage date and then adding his doubts as to whether Heine was not in fact born in February 1798. This article is, unfortunately again, defective, for Veit neglected to include in it the account of Rabbi Scheuer's deposition, although he refers back to it twice ("Die Rätsel um Heines Geburt," p. 19; p. 24, n. 22). This carelessness is regrettable because here, as elsewhere, Veit has made significant contributions toward cleaning up the litter left behind in Heine studies by Hirth. Hugo Bieber made an independent computation in refutation of Wadepuhl and came up with February 2, 1797, for the marriage date, in "Recent Literature on Heine's Attitude Toward Judaism," *Historia Judaica, 10* (1948), 176. Veit's date of February 1, however, is the correct one.

that she herself does not know how old she is.* It permits neither of the major hypotheses concerning Heine's reasons: as Veit has pointed out, it is hardly likely that, if Heine's birth had been illegitimate, Charlotte would have had to be warned against their mother insisting it was;[24] as for the "draft dodger" hypothesis, there is little reason why Heine should have kept so obsolete an issue secret from his own sister in 1853 when he had admitted it to a French journalist in 1851.

While we cannot extract from this document any solution to the problem as it is ordinarily posed, its style, like that of Heine's other statements on the matter, does permit two further conclusions of a different kind: we are not to know Heine's reasons for obscuring his birthdate—and we are to know that we are not to know them. It is not only the secretiveness that is striking, but the ostentation of it. Heine is denying to all and sundry any access to his private person. At first this may seem paradoxical, for Heine has always figured as one of the most subjective of writers, without regard for propriety, humility, or consistency. Let us consider for a moment, however, some of the things we do not know about Heine.

His childhood, compared, let us say, with that of Goethe, is very unclear. An anecdote here and there throws a little light on the circumstances of his boyhood, but these tales do not coalesce into biography. That Heine idealized his parents and the quality of life in his home when he wrote about them has been generally recognized.[25] We know very little about his religious education or the quality of religious life in his home. Perhaps we could have learned more from Heine's memoirs—another problem in his biography that defies solution—but if the fragment that has been retained is any indication, we should not have been much better off, for the most exciting part of it, the story of Red Sefchen, is quite obviously a fiction influenced by Heine's reading in folklore. How easily he transported anecdotes into the realm of fiction

* I am prepared neither to accept nor reject Veit's willingness to believe that there might be something to this ("Die Rätsel um Heines Geburt," *Heine Jahrbuch 1962*, pp. 21–22). His argument with respect to Maximilian Heine's birthdate, that Rabbi Scheuer would not have confused a two-year-old with a five-year-old, is certainly solid. But if all this is so, we are still at a loss for a satisfactory explanation for such an elaborate family effort.

is apparent from a passage in *Die Stadt Lucca* where Lady Mathilde describes a childhood experience that Heine had originally written down, although not published, as one of his own.[26] On the years from age sixteen to twenty-one, when he was being prepared for a commercial career, Heine maintained an almost unbroken and quite ominous silence; the only trace of these years, apart from an occasional vague allusion, is his implacable hatred for everything having to do with finance and the merchant ethos. Yet these years must have been full of experiences worth the telling—certainly they are vital years in the development of a man and a poet—and their loss is very damaging to our effort to understand Heine. He does not really begin to come into focus until he is twenty-two years old, when the unbroken sequence of his preserved correspondence begins. Before that there are only two distraught Sturm-und-Drang letters to Christian Sethe of 1816, which do, to be sure, shed some light on his emotional state at that time.

We know about interesting events in Heine's life of which he tells little or nothing. A notorious example is his visit to Goethe in the fall of 1824, about which he remained notably vague. On his journey to Munich in 1827, he appears to have been arrested in Heidelberg and expelled from Württemberg,[27] yet of this undoubtedly exciting adventure he says nothing at all. Problems persist in the Paris years. Despite his carefully fostered reputation as a libertine in the early 1830s, Heine is in fact quite uncommunicative about the details of his private life up to his association with Mathilde, and most of what has been written about it is speculation. E. M. Butler has pointed out how little Heine has to report in a concrete way of his associations with the Saint-Simonians or of his subsequent disenchantment with them,[28] although this was a vital aspect of his initial experience of France. On the other hand, one wonders whether Heine was as much a public figure in Paris as he is often said to have been and sometimes suggested himself; Dresch has commented on the remarkable silence upon Heine in the memoirs and histories of the eminent Frenchmen with whom he was acquainted.[29]

For all his notorious and often shameless self-display, Heine was in some important respects a reticent man. Throughout his life it was difficult to extract from him significant biographical information. In 1838 and 1839 his friend Heinrich Laube wrote him letter after letter requesting information for a biographical sketch; Heine promised and put him off, but never sent anything.[30] Often he led people around by the nose; this was noted in Heine's young manhood by Eduard Wedekind, in his middle age by Philibert Audebrand—who reported how Heine, in a conversation with Chasles, created biographical fiction in full view of his auditor—and in his latter years by Maximilian Heine, who described how his brother would satanically supply curious visitors with pure canards.[31] Heine's more acute acquaintances sensed that he was not inclined to bare his soul with complete candor. The musician Ferdinand Hiller, for example, made one of the more sensible contemporary comments about Heine's late religious return: "ich weiß nicht, was er glaubt—aber wenn ich auch glaube, daß er es weiß, so glaube ich doch nicht, daß er so leicht hierüber irgend jemanden ganz reinen Wein einschenkt." [32]

Heine's intellectual equipment is also often difficult to determine. There is no way to discover, it seems to me, how much and how well Heine actually studied philosophy, how much he learned from secondary sources, and how many of his insights derive from more or less accurate instinct. From *Zur Geschichte der Religion und Philosophie in Deutschland,* one gets the impression that he must have read a good deal of Kant and Fichte. But his mind was not rigorous, as he admitted on the first page of that work: "Und doch habe ich weder die Subtilitäten der Theologie, noch die der Metaphysik so tief ergründet, daß ich im stande wäre, dergleichen nach den Bedürfnissen des französischen Publikums, ganz einfach und ganz kurz zu formulieren" (E, *4,* 163). This problem becomes acute in the matter of Hegel. Considerable claims have been made for the influence of Hegel upon Heine's mode of thinking, and there are passages that read very much like an application of Hegelian dialectic to a real situation.* On the other hand, the better one becomes acquainted with Heine and the rather rigid structure of his fundamental ideas, the less likely it seems that he could possibly have understood that most awesomely difficult of philosophers; indeed, he himself said that he rarely had.[33] Cer-

* An example is Heine's discussion of the development of revolution out of the disharmony of institutions with the present state of the nation: E, *5,* 92.

tainly it seems so to a philosopher: Benedetto Croce has written that one should read Lichtenberger's *Henri Heine penseur* (Paris, 1905), "to convince one's self of the opposite of what the title says and the thesis intends, namely of a Heine *non penseur,* whose concepts are neither original nor coherent." [34] But if this judgment is just, a great deal of Heine's philosophical commentary and dialectical analysis of historical and current events remains unexplained. He must have learned something, but he does not let us know with any clarity just what he knew and how he went about studying it.

What one might call Heine's blatant reticence concerning himself, of which the confusion surrounding the birthdate is a paradigmatic example, has not always been clearly seen. More obvious has been the related and irritating fact that in his statements about himself Heine was not a truthful man. One wonders whether it is of ironical significance that, on the occasion of his doctoral examination, Heine defended the thesis: "Ex jurejurando non nascitur obligatio" (E, 7, 528). He once accused his brother Gustav of "Emanzipazion von der Wahrheit" (Hirth, *3,* 427), but the phrase applies to Heine himself with at least equal force. The student of Heine quickly falls into the habit of doubting almost everything he says unless there is some corroborating evidence. This indifference to literal truth extends to almost every aspect of Heine's life, and particularly to his presentations of and apologies for his own character. One cannot read his letters or his essays and numerous prefaces without becoming painfully aware of this.

Heine was, in fact, a mass of contradictions. Despite his posture as the eternal brokenhearted victim, Walzel remarked quite fairly that he was "trotz seiner seelischen Unruhe und Überbeweglichkeit, eine robuste, zähe Natur von starken, fast primitiven Instinkten. Von der Widerstandsschwäche des Dekadenten hat er sehr wenig an sich." [35] When Heine is in a stupendous nervous fury he congratulates himself for his calm; when he is about to play a particularly sly trick on Julius Campe, he gives lengthy assurances of the sacrifices he makes because he has only his publisher's interests at heart; an outright political tergiversation is usually signaled by firm claims of unalterable principle; as he is thrashing about wildly trying to find out what people are writing and saying about him, he asserts his total indifference to critical opinion; when he is driven to frightened distraction by the real and imagined machinations of his enemies, he insists that he regards them with Olympian pity. Because of these mannerisms, which he rarely abandons, it is extraordinarily difficult to discover what he in fact thinks or believes about anything, and it is frequently all but impossible to get to the bottom of real events. This feature of Heine is especially noticeable and troublesome in his political writings; the more one studies, for example, *Französische Zustände* or *Börne,* the less one understands; practically every passage contains the seeds of its own contradiction.

That Heine's behavior is the result of fairly severe psychological disturbance, aggravated by the genuinely difficult conditions under which he subsisted during most of his life, is evident to the naked eye. Heine's psychological instability is so apparent that the ancient and tiresome issue of his "character" really is moot. During his lifetime and afterwards, it was common to attack him on grounds of character and morality. These excoriations, however, have as a rule been no more honest than the poet was himself; by and large they are merely an expression in moral terms of conservative or reactionary resentments. For whatever the inner weaknesses of Heine's political attitudes and his general behavior, "objectively," as the Marxists like to say, he was a symbol of libertarianism, antinationalist cosmopolitanism, and steadfast opposition to feudal remnants and plutocratic usurpations in European society. Most of the time it is this symbol that is actually under attack when the issue of Heine's character is raised.

One might reasonably expect that this aspect of Heine criticism would have passed away with the Third Reich. Remarkably, this is not so, and even more remarkably, it is not a scholar in Germany, but one in the United States, Norbert Fuerst, who has revived the old saws about Heine's character and has come to the startling conclusion that his "greatest contemporaries," like Metternich, turn out to have been right about him.[36] It is instructive to compare Fuerst's belief that Heine's works were suppressed on exclusively moral, not political, grounds with Metternich's own blunt admission that the ban of 1835 was necessary to preserve "das politische Gebäude des Staates." [37]

Characteristic of Fuerst's revival of the old libels is an appreciation of Heine's poetry strictly limited to its more brilliant and superficial aspects—"cookies suddenly complete with bromo," as he elegantly characterizes it—combined with a conviction that Heine is, after all, fundamentally inferior to writers in the conservative canon. Somewhat more modern, although grounded in the same set of assumptions, is the effort to pretend that the critic is confronting the poet solely in aesthetic terms; but the very language used is that of a rigidly conservative idealism:

> art is not composite like life; art is personal only at its sources; its aims and its criteria must be collective: aspirations of humanity. And in that respect, Heine had a bad character. Not because of his private personality have Gundolf and Karl Kraus and Hofmannsthal considered him the worst influence in German literature, but because he cheapened poetry: because he was a blight; because he taught that (in art) the way down was as good as the way up.[38]

As long ago as 1870, an English writer, Bulwer-Lytton's son Owen Meredith, understood far better the relationship of Heine's manner of writing to the "aspirations of humanity"; he wrote: "Heine is the poet of the profane vulgar; and it is the exceptional merit of him to have uplifted into the sacred sphere of poesy the consciousness of what is vulgar and profane in our experience of ourselves. He did not withhold his pearls from the swine's snout; for he knew that his audience dwell not so much in a paradise as in a piggery."[39] We will do well to desist from making stuffy judgments upon Heine's character—or upon what little of it we can bring into focus—and attempt to understand him a little better in intrinsic terms.

For observers who are, in one way or another, fascinated by the Hegelian view of reality, Heine appears to personify the dialectic strains that are supposedly endemic in the modern consciousness. This view of Heine has more than a little merit, but the question needs to be posed in a more precise and individualistic way; for in characterizing Heine it is of some importance to inquire why the dialectic should have become lodged in this single person. Part of the answer lies, of course, in his odd position as a Rhenish Jew and—consequently?—as an engaged writer. But part of it certainly lies in what, in an ordinary person, we should be inclined to call qualities of immaturity. For it was Heine's nature always to want everything both ways. He wanted to be loved without himself being obliged to love. He wanted to be a Romantic without sharing any of the presuppositions that supply German Romanticism with its peculiar energy. He wanted to be a poet when the occasion suited him, and an antipoet when the claims of other matters of importance to him conflicted with the view of poetry he shared with his age. He wanted to be both a sensualist and a spiritualist, when in fact he lacked the daring for the moral and emotional freedom of the former and the inner quietude of the latter. He wanted to be both a German and a European—read: Frenchman—and both a German and a Jew, at a time when the majority of his contemporaries regarded these categories as mutually exclusive. Within them, he wanted to be a German without any enthusiasm for German national unity, a European (Frenchman) without sympathy for revolutionary gloire, and a Jew without obeying the Law. He wanted to be both an aristocrat of the intellectual-artistic life and a bourgeois, and both a bourgeois and a champion of the proletariat, but he had no notion of making the sacrifices of pride required to fight one's way into the real aristocracy, as most of his relatives did, no enthusiasm for the ethic of the bourgeoisie, and no taste for the rough-and-tumble of the proletariat as it actually lived. In the latter part of his life, he wanted to believe in God without drawing any binding consequences from such a belief. From beginning to end, he wanted to be his own man—and be paid for it. But he did so because of the one accurate and stable element of his self-knowledge: he knew that he was a genius of extraordinary gifts, despite the perversity and stupidity of a world that withheld the rich rewards due him.

This conviction of his preeminent poetic vocation combines with his fundamental instability to make of Heine a personality who continually eludes our grasp. From the establishment of basic biographical facts to the definition of his intellectual attitudes, we find ourselves constantly puzzled by lacunae, contradictions, sleight of hand, and misdirection. It is as though the man were hiding behind a veritable cascade of self-assertion. He appears to invite biographical interpretation while simultaneously making it all but impossible. Observers who are obsessed with Heine's moral character and with idealistic assumptions about the nature of poetry cannot cope with this aspect of the man. Fuerst writes: "Heine is so unwilling to leave the realm of the impurely personal that he forces us back continually upon biographical considerations. . . . The fellow was so much bigger than his works that he remains visible behind their every corner, no matter how we look at them." [40] I submit that this proposition is totally mistaken, and that we shall never come to any understanding of Heine upon its assumptions. The most spectacular example of the futility of approaching Heine in this way is the matter of the experience of unrequited love that inspired his early poetry.

The poems of *Buch der Lieder* appear to have been inspired by a devastating and enduring emotional catastrophe about which we know very little. That they may in fact not be so inspired has been suggested by several modern critics; Laura Hofrichter has argued that rather than being too close to experience, the early poems are too disciplined;[41] and William Rose, to whom we shall return presently, has cast much doubt on the biographical origins of Heine's pervasive theme of unrequited love.[42] Yet it seems hardly credible that this poetic motor should have run so intensely and without intermission for eight or ten years on a single theme fueled only by the creative imagination. One difficulty is that there is something of a tendency to look upon the bulk of Heine's early poems as all versions of the same poem. This does too little justice to the wealth of *Buch der Lieder*; the theme is persistent, but the variations are innumerable, and it is the variety of tensions with and within the theme that ought to occupy our critical attention. The reason for the kind of revisionism offered by Hofrichter and others is that earlier Heine scholarship has left us with a very unsatisfactory legacy.

It would not necessarily be irrelevant to know something about the development of Heine's emotional life from his teens through his mid-twenties. Wilhelm Bölsche was right when, in a remarkably clever, unusually cautious, and now rather forgotten study of 1888, he observed that there are issues "die mit dem Biographischen eng verwachsen sind und deren Nichtbeachtung sein Werk in der Wurzel bereits unheilbar schädigt." * But the fact is that we do not know very much, for Heine's reticence on this fundamental experience is nothing short of spectacular. The positivistic *Literaturwissenschaft* of seventy-five years ago was unwilling to tolerate such ignorance and, obsessed by Goethe's mode of *Erlebnisdichtung,* was unable to make very clear distinctions between real experiences and their fictional transforms. Thus was reconstructed, out of flimsy materials, the romance of Heine's tragic infatuation with his cousin Amalie. Added to that, because of some chronological difficulties and a hint here and there, was the supposed transference of this infatuation to Amalie's sister Therese. How much of this is sheer conjecture has been amply demonstrated by William Rose. Amalie is not referred to or hinted at as many as a half-dozen times in Heine's letters, and then always in a most circumspect and sometimes periphrastic way. In the nearly one thousand pages of conversations with Heine collected by Houben, Amalie is mentioned only once, and there it is Heine's conversational partner who mentions her without getting any response whatever.[43]

The older criticism regarded the poems and early prose writings as a faithful record of the experience and then pieced out the biography on the basis of these materials.† Why the German critics of that age, presumably trained in philosophical rigor, were not able to see that this procedure is a vicious circle that begs the question from the very beginning is one of the mysteries of the history of criticism. If we do not know what the original experience was, we do not know what kinds of transformations it has undergone in its conversion into literature and thus we cannot argue back from the literary record to biography. The number of verifiable events from which we can study Heine's procedures of

* Wilhelm Bölsche, *Heinrich Heine. Versuch einer ästhetisch-kritischen Analyse seiner Werke und seiner Weltanschauung* (Leipzig, 1888), p. 3. This book should be restored to the canon of a basic Heine library. The right word for it was found by Jules Legras, *Henri Heine Poète* (Paris, 1897), p. 26, n. 1: "délicieux."

† The admirable Adolf Strodtmann, Heine's first and, in many respects, still his best biographer, demonstrated his usual soundness by warning against this procedure. See *H. Heine's Leben und Werke* (3d ed. Hamburg, 1884), *I*, 51. Subsequent scholars would have done well to heed him.

poetic transformation are few indeed. There is, furthermore, a rather embarrassing problem of chronology. Heine's poems are notoriously difficult to date, but Rose argues that most of the early ones were composed at least five years after Heine's rejection by Amalie and at least two-and-a-half years after he could last have seen her.[44] Indeed, in a letter to Varnhagen von Ense of October 19, 1827, Heine makes light of the rumor that he had been in love with Amalie, claiming that he had not seen her in eleven years,[45] which in turn is not credible but just another burst of the smoke screen. Several years before, Heine had explicitly warned his friend Karl Immermann against interpretation from his personal history: "Nur etwas kann mich aufs Schmerzlichste verletzen: wenn man den Geist meiner Dichtungen aus der Geschichte (Sie wissen, was dieses Wort bedeutet), aus der Geschichte des Verfassers erklären will . . . Und wie wenig ist oft das äußere Gerüste unserer Geschichte mit unserer wirklichen, inneren Geschichte zusammenpassend! Bey mir wenigstens paßte es *nie*" (Hirth, *1,* 85). As early as 1822, he had referred to Amalie as "ein weiblicher Schatten, der jetzt nur noch in meinen Gedichten lebt" (Hirth, *1,* 37). Rose concludes: "Most of Heine's love poetry was probably composed when his erotic feeling was not strongly affected by any woman in particular" and "a close study of the available data indicates that in this particular aspect of Heine's life and writings there has been much building with unsound materials. Most of the biographers and commentators of the present century have, in fact, been content to erect a not unimportant part of their edifice on a framework prefabricated by their predecessors." [46]

This is not to say that Heine in his late teens did not fancy himself violently in love with Amalie; indeed, a not very kindly poem written for Amalie's daughter in 1844 puts it beyond any reasonable doubt that he did,[47] and I think it is even possible that for a time he showed interest in Therese; such hints as we have of this are few, but one or two, such as the anagram *Resede* in Chapter 7 of *Das Buch Le Grand* [48] and an unpublished poem,[49] are rather suggestive, as is Heine's comment in a letter to his uncle on the occasion of Therese's marriage.[50] Heine, after all, did not exactly exhibit indifference to his Uncle Salomon's wealth, and the two girls shared the attractive characteristic of being heiresses to that fortune. Nor do I doubt very seriously that the relationship with Amalie lies at the beginning of the emotional state out of which the poems of *Buch der Lieder* developed. Like Rose, I do not believe the poems are about a love affair in present time; I do not think myself that they are primarily about a love affair at all, but that they are about something else. This is a distinction that we may approach by one more roundabout path.

It is noteworthy that both Marxist critics and most contemporary interpreters in the West are disinclined to take cognizance of Heine's probable psychological state in these years. In the case of the former this is due to the traditional Communist distrust of the whole science of psychology as it is practiced in the West, while Western critics have for good reason become suspicious of psychologizing criticism. It is difficult enough to gain a true psychological understanding of a living, breathing person in our own presence, as anyone who has experienced analysis or therapy knows all too well; how much more doubtful is analysis on the basis of written records of a person long since dead. The attempts to apply "scientific" psychological categories to literary phenomena, with a few exceptions done with caution and a humble appreciation of the intrinsic limitations, have usually led to criticisms of a rather low order.* Nor do I propose to attempt any such thing here. But it does seem inescapably obvious that Heine in his youth was a problem-ridden neurotic personality and that he was in emotional difficulties with regard to sex. Whether it is true or not that *Buch der Lieder* is the record of a struggle with an irrational, hopeless, self-destructive, and humiliating infatuation with his pretty but trivial cousin—and I believe it is such a record—the fact that a young man should write poems for ten years on the subject of unrequited love, not to mention the reprise of the theme in *Neuer Frühling,* suggests irresistibly that he had a long and hard time in overcoming what today we should call his adolescence; Heine was, after all, twenty-nine years old when the second *Nordsee* cycle appeared. The playwright Christian Dietrich

* A study such as Gustav Jung's "Der Erotiker Heinrich Heine," *Zeitschrift für Sexualwissenschaft, 11* (1924), 113–28, does not help; it is vague, imprecise, and written as though Freud had never happened.

Grabbe, a neurotic of a different sort who thought highly of his own libido, wrote scornfully of Heine's celibacy in his Berlin years,[51] and despite Grabbe's notorious bad mouth, it may well be true.

We will not comb Heine's works for evidence of neurosis; it is there for anyone to see. But there is one recurring image in the early poems of *Buch der Lieder* that is in itself very striking and not easily integrated with the fabric of the work—the image of the mother as avenging witch. This image appears in *Traumbilder* 7, in *Romanzen* 5 (as grandmother), *Romanzen* 8, and the original version of *Romanzen* 14, where the mother will comfort the dying poet and drag the guilty beloved by the hair to see his corpse.[52] In connection with this one might also look at the two totally undistinguished and strangely unreal sonnets Heine addressed to his mother in *Buch der Lieder*. In the second of these the poet asserts that he had returned to his mother's love after fruitlessly searching for love elsewhere: "Das war die süße, langgesuchte Liebe" (E, *1*, 57). It is well known that throughout his life Heine was a model Jewish son, treating his mother, who outlived him by three years, with affection and respect and in his latter years shielding her from the complete knowledge of his catastrophic illness.* No critical conclusions are to be drawn from these observations, but they are nevertheless suggestive. It is also true that in his early years in Paris, when his sex life took a decided turn for the better, Heine became, for a time, considerably more cheerful. He also just about stopped writing lyrical verse.

Even without the assistance of specific details, a general, although somewhat abstract, picture begins to emerge. Young Heine found himself apparently unattractive, maladroit, rejected, as well as quite seriously alienated from his environment. He was helplessly infatuated with a girl he did not even like, much less respect;

* Martin Greiner has some interesting observations on this problem in *Zwischen Biedermeier und Bourgeoisie: Ein Kapitel deutscher Literaturgeschichte im Zeichen Heinrich Heines* (Leipzig, 1954), pp. 125, 136, 286–87. Strodtmann, in "Die Mutter H. Heine's, nach ihren Jugendbriefen geschildert," *Deutsche Rundschau, 12* (1877), 90, stressed that at twenty-four Heine's mother insisted she did not want to marry, and she did not until she was thirty. The frightening mother recurs in the late poetry: the unsympathetic mother of *Der Mohrenkönig* in *Romanzero* (E, *1*, 361) and the witch Uraka in *Atta Troll*.

being very intelligent, he may have suspected that this passion was in some degree autonomous and divorced from its object, making it all the more self-perpetuating. All in all it was a demeaning situation, and a sense of embarrassed shame crops out here and there in *Buch der Lieder,* as in *Romanzen* 13:

> Als schimpflich muß er betrachten
> Die eigne Liebespein (E, *1,* 48).

It was the sort of situation to feed neurotic self-contempt. It is clear in general that Heine found his own emotions suspect. In a revealing remark to Moses Moser, he reports sentimental feelings toward his friend and says that he would therefore have said many rude things had his friend been present.[53]

Heine's affects were tangled and tumultuous. But his pride was fierce and unquenchable; he had genius and he knew it. There is no evidence that at any time in his life he consciously doubted this, even though his protestations of it and his immoderate reaction to adverse criticism may indicate secret anxieties. Throughout his life he pictured himself with images of power and sovereignty: poet, knight, king. It is not difficult to imagine how painful the contrast must have been between this vision of the grandeur of his inner, true self, and the prostrate, whining, contemptible, and self-indulgent posture into which his emotional vulnerability had led him. The solution was to draw on his strength, and his strength was his poetic genius. In one of the sonnets to August Wilhelm Schlegel not included in *Buch der Lieder,* Heine gives a rare direct account of his plight:

> Der schlimmste Wurm: des Zweifels Dolchgedanken,
> Das schlimmste Gift: an eigner Kraft verzagen,
> Das wollt' mir fast des Lebens Mark zernagen;
> Ich war ein Reis, dem seine Stützen sanken. (E, *2,* 61).

The remainder of the sonnet suggests that his salvation was to be found in that poetic effort in which Schlegel had encouraged him.

Buch der Lieder is thus not essentially an account of an unhappy love, but a display of poetic powers. The undignified grief is stylized and ultimately ironized. The poetic persona, the strongest part of the inner man, is developed and to a large extent fictionalized, and is displayed to us in the process of gaining sovereignty over an emotional state without abandoning the pleasure in the bittersweet sorrows of defeat in love. The young poet gave himself a fictionalized and pathetic history, just as he remarked in his review of J. B. Rousseau's poems in 1823: "Der Jüngling will eine Geschichte haben" (E, *7*, 218). The much discussed "subjectivity" of Heine's poetry is an oversimplification. Heine certainly was aware of the problem and wished to achieve a measure of objectivity; he adverts to the matter from time to time, perhaps most succinctly in the depressed mood of *Über die französische Bühne,* where he remarks: "Ein Schriftsteller darf sich nicht seiner Subjektivität ganz überlassen, er muß alles schreiben können, und sollte es ihm noch so übel dabei werden" (E, *4*, 513).[54] Heine's basic emotional state is indeed subjective if not almost solipsistic, but its projection into a poetic fiction that gradually takes on a life and logic of its own is a process of objectification. Bölsche was closer to understanding this than most critics of his age when he remarked (of *Lyrisches Intermezzo*) that, "indem er dieselben Motive immer neu dreht und wendet, erreicht er unwillkürlich jene Objektivität, die eine freiere künstlerische Behandlung ermöglicht." [55] But the word "unwillkürlich" is gratituous and betrays Romantic ideas of the creative process. Strodtmann had already argued perceptively that Heine's poetry gave an objective picture of his subjective feeling, which remains perhaps the best view of all.[56] There is no reason to suppose that Heine, slow, meticulous, and constantly revising writer that he was, did not write these poems with an increasing consciousness of what he was about. One of Heine's acquaintances in the mid-1820s, Ludwig Freiherr von Diepenbrock-Grüter, noted in his diary: "Er [Heine] sprach . . . von seiner Anschauungsweise seiner selbst als Objekts. 'Wäre ich so glücklich, jetzt noch eine unglückliche Liebe erschwingen zu können, so wäre ich ein gemachter Mann,' sagte er! Wohin dieses 'zur Sache machen seiner Selbst' ihn führen wird, weiß der Himmel." [57]

The conclusion we must draw from all this is that we cannot extort from the elusive poet the ultimate logic of his true self. We can, however, examine his works and study the poetic persona, the first-person narrator, to see how he displays himself and gains mastery over his troubles and his materials, in order to achieve a poetic attitude that, among other things, puts the demons back in their bottles and the girls in their place. It would not be misleading to say that the creation of a surrogate persona, achieved with such energy in the years of *Buch der Lieder* and the *Reisebilder,* became a habit with Heine throughout most of the rest of his public and private life.

The realization that Heine created a fictive persona and propelled it into the foreground of his works is not new; it was recognized, with greater or less clarity, by many of the best interpreters. One of Heine's more acute friends, François Wille, said of the poet's manner in 1843: "Es war mit einem Wort die Persönlichkeit in dem Schriftsteller aufgegangen." [58] Even Charles Andler, who in one place made the remarkable claim that Heine is the least professional of poets and must be interpreted out of the circumstances of his life, elsewhere remarked more perceptively: "Il a toujours eu cette faculté de vivre ainsi d'une double vie, dont la seconde imposait des images hallucinatoires à son moi réel." [59] Again Bölsche was as clear as any critic of his generation:

> Heines eigene Aussprüche über sein Leben sind . . . stets sehr wertvoll, aber auch nur mit der Kritik zu benutzen, die aus der bekannten Thatsache entspringt, daß dem phantasiereichen Dichter sein eigenes Bild stets unter der Feder zur Romanfigur wird, hier freilich mit romanhaften Ergänzungen, die, wenn nicht wahr, doch wenigstens durchweg charakterisch sind." [60]

Lion Feuchtwanger reacted to Heine's elusiveness with frustration: "Man kann den Schriftsteller Heine aufblättern wie eine Zwiebel. Unter jeder Maske ist eine neue. Wo stößt man auf dieses Mannes wirkliches Gesicht?" [61] Ewald Boucke, not unreasonably, detected in Heine's procedure a form of solipsism:

> Überhaupt besteht Heines Denkverfahren weniger in einem ruhigen Anschauen und planvollen Ordnen der Dinge durch den zielbewußt wählenden Geist, als in einem *Projizieren* des problematischen, veränderlichen Selbst in die bunte

> Mannigfaltigkeit der Erscheinungen. *Die Welt wird zum Tropus des Ichs,* und die Vorgänge der Außenwelt erscheinen als Ausstrahlungen dieses Ichs, die mit seinen Leiden und Freuden in geheimer Sympathie mitschwingen.*

Older critics, however, were seldom able to draw comfortable conclusions from these observations; they continually attempted to pin down Heine by means of biographical data or with the help of intellectual categories. But, as Walter A. Berendsohn has pointed out, it is hopeless to attempt to expose "die innere Seelengeschichte des Menschen Heine." [62] Modern critical techniques of concentration upon literary works as self-revealing structures have made it easier to cope with the phenomenon of Heine, by turning attention primarily to the works themselves and subordinating extraneous considerations as far as it is feasible to do so. Some very good results have been achieved by applying more or less hermeneutic methods of interpretation to Heine. It is at least partly in the light of current critical theory that this study attempts to confront directly the problem of Heine's fictive persona and its development.

The so-called New Criticism, to be sure, is no longer new, and at present it is growing increasingly subject to substantial revision for a number of weighty reasons.[63] While it offers techniques and guidelines for approaching so complex a phenomenon as Heine, I do not believe that the hermeneutic method in its purest form is appropriate to this writer. For one thing, whereas minute analysis of individual poems and prose passages may be instructive with respect to Heine's style, I find, at least for the purposes of my topic, that it is more fruitful to treat Heine's publications as units, even if to do so sometimes violates chronological considerations. This is particularly true of Heine's poetry; Legras observed seventy years ago that while Goethe's poems may be enjoyed individually, the value of Heine's poems lies very much in their aggregation.[64] His prose works have rarely been treated as whole,

* Ewald Boucke, "Heine im Dienste der 'Idee,'" *Euphorion, 16* (1909), 116. Cf. Boucke's observation that Heine's Francophilia was also "ein Kokettieren mit einem '*alter ego,*' das er von seinem wirklichen Selbst abgespalten hatte, und das schließlich, wie der Schatten in Andersens Märchen, eine Art Eigenleben führte und sich als Herr gebärdete," in his edition of *Heines Werke* (Berlin, [1928–30]), *9,* 358.

organized structures, but it will appear in some of what follows that there are good reasons for doing so. Secondly, the persona is tantalizingly related to the genuine Heine and to substantial perceptions of hard reality. My effort will be to steer a course between a mode of interpretation that shuts itself off entirely from external referents and one that fails to do justice to the inner autonomy of art that Heine himself so jealously defended—when he was not denying it. Nor will I attempt to force my theory of the fictive persona to within an inch of its life, but rather I would wish to use it as a general guideline for a set of interpretations the procedures of which are determined by the nature of the various topics.

I should like to stress, however, that even if this study were to live up to its purposes without flaws and weaknesses, which is hardly likely, I would not regard it as a total interpretation of Heine. Many aspects of him are not comprehended by it. I will touch upon the complexities of his political and social writing, by and large, only as regards the problem of the fictive persona; I will advert to Heine's studies in Jewish history and in European folklore only when necessary; and I will almost totally avoid his very extensive writings on art, music, and literature. Above all, I have left the sociological aspect almost entirely out of consideration. This is not because I have any fundamental prejudice against the study of literature from the sociological point of view; indeed, I believe that the defensive campaign being waged against it in some academic quarters is ill-advised. Literature, after all, does occur in the real world and we have much to learn from those who, unlike myself, are equipped to examine the interrelations of literature and society.[65] This is true of Heine *par excellence,* and we will not get a good biography of him or a comprehensive interpretation of his career until the sociological aspects of his life and work are elucidated in scholarly detail.

At the moment, however, it seems to me that the present state of the art is not well advanced, and it is constantly necessary for the critic to remind the sociologist that great literature is something more than a socio-political artifact. It is inevitable that considerations of class and society are the dominant theme in East German criticism; although an occasional contribution of great value appears in East Germany,* the level of scholarship there is frequently depressing (see Appendix I). But in West Germany, too, literary sociology seems to be almost exclusively in the hands of Marxists and/or neo-Hegelians, who often approach literary phenomena with discouraging obtuseness. When Theodor W. Adorno writes that Heine's poetry is the application of the industrial technique of mass production to Romantic archetypes, or that his colloquial style is assimilationist and "der nachahmende Übereifer des Ausgeschlossenen," or that Heine's theme of unrequited love is not what it seems at all but rather a simile for his rootlessness in society, which in turn has become the rootlessness of us all under capitalism,† then the literary critic must stand up and say, with all due respect for Adorno's great intellectual gifts and achievements, that this is absurd and tends to bring the sociological enterprise into disrepute.

We must know what literary texts are before we can draw sociological conclusions from them.‡ With Heine this is particu-

* Indeed, the very best book about the interrelationship of Heine and his times came out of the DDR: Martin Greiner's study mentioned above (p. 18n.). Greiner makes a genuine effort to think through the problem of Heine where Communists have uncritical praise and Western idealists scorn and condemnation; he makes a perceptive observation upon the striking mediocrity of Heine's emotional and experiential fundament (p. 329), and then tries to connect this feature of Heine to his poetic strengths and the generation of the fictive persona:

> Heine ist der schöpferische Durchschnittsmensch; das Normale, Durchschnittliche, Banale, erhält in ihm eine schöpferische Qualität, es wird seiner selbst bewußt und damit fähig, sich selbst darzustellen. Seine ungeheure Überlegenheit über die anderen beruht auf dem Wissen, daß es so ist, und seine ständige geheime Sorge beruht darauf, es die anderen nicht wissen zu lassen, daß es so ist. Das ist das Geheimnis seines Scharlatanismus (ibid.).

We are not obliged to believe this as it stands, but it is the sort of argument that could play an honorable role in working out some synthesis of the conflicting perspectives of literary critic and sociologist of literature.

† Theodor W. Adorno, "Die Wunde Heine," *Noten zur Literatur, I* (Frankfurt am Main, 1958), 147–49, 151, 152. The same volume contains a subtle and fascinating essay on the interrelationship of societal contexts and lyric poetry: "Rede über Lyrik und Gesellschaft," ibid., *I*, 73–104. But when it comes to Heine, more than one outstanding intellect has had trouble maintaining sensitive nuances.

‡ This would seem to be a self-evident truism hardly worth mentioning, but in fact it apparently needs to be defended. Professor Jost Hermand, who has been systematically mounting an attack upon the introverted aestheticism of contemporary criticism, took the occasion of a book review to speak rather harshly of Barker Fairley's critical contribution to our understanding of Heine's poetry and

larly the case because he is so very elusive. He covered his tracks and barricaded his inner self to an extraordinary degree. He literally obliges us to concentrate on his poetic creations, and the coquettishness with which he causes himself to appear and disappear at will only serves to draw attention to his desire to be comprehended as a poet who is master of his own image. The following interpretations, it is hoped, will be a contribution toward understanding the development of this remarkable poetic self-creation.

---

to treat the translation of Fairley's book into German as instantly obsolete (*Germanistik,* 7/4 [Oct., 1966], 620). Here one must register a protest. For one thing, the German scholarly tradition has not yet altogether caught up with the achievements of Heine interpretation in foreign countries and it is well that books like Fairley's are translated; for another, sociological criticism will ignore the essence and dynamics of the texts with which it deals only at its peril.

68492

LIBRARY
College of St. Francis
JOLIET, ILL.

CHAPTER 2

The Struggle for a Poetic Attitude: *Buch der Lieder*

Angreifend für das Herz . . .
ist auch das Närrischste.
—THOMAS MANN

Heine's international fame rests to a large extent on *Buch der Lieder*. According to one estimate, poems from this collection have been set to music some 2,750 times,[1] surely a record for Western literature. It is without doubt the most renowned book of German poetry in the world, and for many decades Heine's verse was widely imitated, both in German and in other languages, although not usually with complete understanding. Since the discovery by more recent criticism of the great significance of the later poetry, there has been a tendency to devaluate *Buch der Lieder* and to see its canonical status as grounded in a misunderstanding. This is partly due to the rather unhealthy influence it exerted on later writers of lesser gifts. S. S. Prawer calls its influence on German literature disastrous because Heine's imitators lacked the complexity of his character, missed his ambivalence, and misunderstood his irony.[2] Friedrich Sieburg, in an essay on the perpetuated artificiality of the German literary language, argues that Heine's style offered a model for nondescript and trivial poetry: "Erleichtert wurde nicht nur der Weg vom Stammtisch zur blauen Blume, sondern auch das Dichten der schwärmenden Knaben und Verliebten, die auf der Suche nach Bildern und Reimen den Weg des scheinbar geringsten Widerstandes wählten."[3] Adorno, from his sociological point of view, has claimed that in Heine's wake poetry was dragged down into the language of journalism and commerce, and as a consequence Heine lost his reputation around 1900 among the intellectually responsible.[4] Michael Hamburger shows how far this process of devaluation has come when he bluntly asserts, as though it were truism, that "Heine's lyrical poetry has been discredited." [5] In one of the very best recent books on Heine, Laura Hofrichter sees *Buch der Lieder* as a wrong direction for him altogether and argues that the important effort of Heine's career was the struggle to get away from "song." * Prawer points out further that really outstanding German men of letters have apparently not been much impressed by Heine's most widely popular achievement; when thirty outstanding writers and critics, including Thomas Mann, his son Golo, Hermann Hesse, Martin Buber, and Emil Staiger, were asked in 1953 to name their favorite poems, not one of Heine's was mentioned.† [6] But, given the history of Heine's reputation, the reasons for this probably go beyond considerations of disinterested critical taste, as the preceding chapter suggests.

In the process of our critical reevaluation of Heine's total career, it would be most unfortunate and unreasonable to fall into an attitude of snobbery toward *Buch der Lieder*. If we are to take Heine seriously as one of the great poets of his time, it will not do to dismiss this compendium of some ten years of poetic achievement and seventeen years more of intermittent revision and reorganization as a flawed youthful work. Even in 1837, when Heine's attitude toward lyric poetry had changed considerably, he called it "mein Hauptbuch" (Hirth, 2, 183). It is in fact a book of fascinating wonders. As the case of a poet like Eduard Mörike proves, literary quality will often maintain its status and hold the attention of readers even when the works in question are misunderstood or apparently admired for bad reasons. They wait for us to try to understand them properly. Heine himself, in his very important conversations on poetics with Eduard Wedekind

* Laura Hofrichter, *Heinrich Heine* (Oxford, 1963). This is one of the most stimulating studies of Heine to be published for some time, and the untimely death of the author is greatly to be lamented. It does tend, however, to be somewhat rigid and over-argued, and I frequently find myself obliged to take issue with it.

† Golo Mann seems to have been made a little uncomfortable by this; in 1956 he published a rather labored explanation and as a compensation reprinted eleven Heine poems and Caput 27 of *Deutschland. Ein Wintermärchen* in *Deutsche Rundschau*, 82 (1956), 1300–09.

in 1824, is said to have given a warning against taking his poems to be as simple as they at first appear: "Studieren . . . sollte man sie eigentlich auch, denn sie sind nicht so ganz leicht zu verstehen" (Houben, p. 63). Indeed they are not, and we shall have to proceed cautiously in our effort to understand the collection better than it generally has been in the past.

With only a handful of exceptions, the nearly 240 poems of *Buch der Lieder* are about unrequited love. This concentration upon a single theme is in itself extraordinary, and in Germany one would have to go back to the *Minnelieder* of the classical Middle Ages to find a comparable phenomenon; Prawer justly calls *Buch der Lieder* the "greatest set of variations in German verse since the days of Reinmar von Hagenau." [7] The first mistake that is often made in trying to locate Heine's achievements historically is to assume that unrequited love is a Romantic theme. It is not in fact a major topic in German Romantic poetry. There are, of course, poems about it—one thinks of Brentano and particularly of Wilhelm Müller, to whom Heine was much indebted—but by and large in the Romantic world, love is an uplifting experience of yearning or fulfillment, not one of unrelieved misery. Furthermore, the steady concentration upon a single emotional state is quite alien to the universal pretensions of Romanticism. To say this is not to deny that Heine's development in the years of these poems was one of overcoming, or trying to overcome, Romantic lyricism in matters of style, rhythm, and image. In Heine's generation the music of Romantic poetry seemed to be the epitome of poetry per se in the German language; the sound of it was firmly lodged in his sensitive ear, and his struggle with it was long, difficult, and only partly successful,* so that for some time after the years of *Buch der Lieder* he despaired of poetry altogether. But the logic of the struggle arises out of thematic considerations, and the results of the discussion in the preceding chapter indicate that we can best illuminate these by examining the details of the growth of the fictive persona in *Buch der Lieder*.

The first group of poems in the collection, the *Traumbilder* of

* It has been shown that Heine's vocabulary definitely belongs to the so-called "Kunstperiode" he himself endeavored to supersede, and not to the age of realism.[8]

Junge Leiden, has not, on the whole, had a good press. Despite the colorful imagery and language of these poems, they are generally seen as immature works dependent upon the "Gothic" conventions of late Romanticism and exploiting the Romantic cliché of the dream situation without inner urgency.[9] It is interesting, however, that Hofrichter sees these poems, because of the strength of their imagery, as *pre-Romantic* and regards Heine's subsequent verse as a retrogressive lapse into the Romantic style.[10] It is true that the poems do not exhibit the style for which *Buch der Lieder* is famous; they are longish and lack the intense compression of the later verses, and there are many clearly derivative elements. The loss of salvation in *Traumbilder* 6, for example, is not characteristic of the problems confronting the poetic persona, and ultimately, like dozens of poems in the Romantic period, this one is dependent upon Bürger's *Lenore* (1773). The witches' sabbath of *Traumbilder* 7 also operates with literary materials, although it does point ahead to Heine's later considerable interest in German legends. But, on the other hand, it is not without significance that Heine allowed these poems to stand with only stylistic revisions through seven editions, whereas several of the second group, originally called *Minnelieder,* were rejected. There are a number of ways in which the *Traumbilder* quite adequately serve as an introduction to *Buch der Lieder.*

Paul Beyer, in his valuable study of the young Heine, draws particular attention to the passive posture of the poetic persona in the earliest delineations of the love situation: "Es findet eine Zusammenkunft mit der Geliebten statt, angeregt niemals durch den willenlosen Träumer, sondern durch den willensstärkeren weiblichen Teil, verbunden zunächst mit angenehmen Empfindungen; der Ausgang aber ist niemals befriedigend, er bringt Verderben, Leid oder Tod, direkt oder indirekt durch die Geliebte herbeigeführt." [11] This passivity of the helpless victim is a prominent feature of the *Traumbilder.* One of the most significant characteristics of *Buch der Lieder* as a whole is the long curve from the passivity of the persona in the dream situation to the activism and energy of that in the first *Nordsee* cycle, so that, in terms of development, the *Traumbilder* present the initial arrangement of the thematic elements which bind the collection together.

Although dreams are a prominent feature of Romantic writing, Heine does something different with them.[12] Whereas for a writer like Novalis the dream establishes contact with a mystically intuited metaphysical universe, Heine's dream sequences are individualistically conceived and penetrate into a specific situation;* unlike Romantic dreams, they do not illuminate a wider and greater general reality, but arouse the sensual elements of a pathological state that has been incompletely buried in the memory. This is not to say that Heine's *Traumbilder* are genuine dreams, such as one actually experiences, any more than the Romantic allegories are. (This is true also of the dream sequences in Heine's prose. See, for example, the peroration of *Börne*.†) While the fiction of the dream does permit symbolic events to be treated as experiences and events that follow upon one another in an associative rather than cause-and-effect sequence, Heine's dreams are stylized and rationally organized; they are not so much dreams as dramas of the ordered imagination. This apparent incongruence of irrational dream and rational order is significant for the thematic development of *Buch der Lieder*; the extent to which this is true will become clearer if we take a closer look at the first of the *Traumbilder,* which was originally separated out as a prologue with the title *Zueignung*.

The poem (E, *1,* 13) begins: "Mir träumte einst von wildem Liebesglühn." Thus not only is the love situation of the past revived by the dreams, but the dreams themselves—dreams that "Ich einst gegossen hab' in weiche Reime"—are seen retrospectively in the poems. We are dealing here with a remarkable and

* Maria Anna Bernhard, *Welterlebnis und gestaltete Wirklichkeit in Heinrich Heines Prosaschriften* (Stuttgart, 1961), p. 74, makes a perceptive point when she argues that Heine's dream-poems are "Reservate für noch nicht gelöste Probleme." She beclouds the contrast with the Romantics, however, by arguing that the dreams are repetitions of reality (ibid., pp. 73–74).

† E, *7,* 145. A most idiosyncratic interpretation of this matter will be found in Jacques Bousquet, *Les thèmes du rêve dans la littérature romantique (France, Angleterre, Allemagne). Essai sur la naissance et l'évolution des images* (Paris, 1964), pp. 30–34. This bizarre attack on psychological theory argues that the history of images can be an exact science (pp. 13–16) and that dreams are not a product of the unconscious but a phenomenon of the waking state (pp. 37–44); thus literary dreams are the most true (p. 48); on this basis Bousquet can argue that Heine's reported dreams must be genuine.

to some extent ironically complex time situation in the narrative. What is in the foreground of this poem is not the love situation, nor even the dreams, but the poem. It is the poem that is sent to seek the dream and revive it:

> Du bliebst, verwaistes Lied! Verweh jetzt auch,
> Und such das Traumbild, das mir längst entschwunden.

This is more than a tricky conceit. The primacy of the poet is established here in no uncertain terms; the situation that provides the content of the poems is revived at will, illustrated in carefully constructed pseudo-dreams, and the result presents itself, not as a lament, nor as a dream, but as a poem. The poem is seen here as so substantially and independently existent that it is activated in the process of reviving the dreams. The character of the poems as poems is reiterated at many places in *Buch der Lieder* and is so important that Barker Fairley entitled a section of his well-known study "Song Within Song." [13] These verses, to use the terms of a Heine quip from another context, imply the versifex. One critic has recently argued that the dream situation provides merely a background for "die Besinnung des Dichters auf sich selbst," and that, as a result, "das Traumgedicht wird umfunktionalisiert als Reflexionsgedicht" because past and present are not allowed to flow into each other; the *Traumbilder* end with an unmerciful awakening.[14] Nevertheless, the dream situation is not "umfunktionalisiert" out of existence; it provides a context for the passivity of the narrator and also the opportunity to create a tension within the poetic situation, for as the epilogue (*Traumbilder* 10) stresses, the dream memories are more easily called to the surface than sent back into limbo. Thus we see the poet not in control of the emotional situation, but *trying to be.* There is already some embryonic irony in these first indications of narrative distance, and even more in the concluding line of the first of the *Traumbilder*: "Dem luft'gen Schatten send' ich luft'gen Hauch." The shades of the past, however, turn out to be more substantial than that, and the poems, too, will have to become more substantial than "luft'ger Hauch" if the poet is to cope with his haunted condition.

The *Traumbilder* proper call up a series of images characterizing the situation that has been revived in the memory. *Traumbilder* 2 is a tightly organized tripartite narrative that has the form of a Romantic *Kunstmärchen*. In its language the poem is a veritable pastiche of Romantic clichés (the variant readings show that this feature was much more pronounced in the original version), but they are treated with an unconventional bitterness that places them in a different perspective. The Romantic landscape is described in tones that would have embarrassed Eichendorff:

> Es zwitscherten die Vögelein
> Viel muntre Liebesmelodei'n;
> Die Sonne rot, von Gold umstrahlt,
> Die Blumen lustig bunt bemalt. (E, *1*, 14)

The giveway word here is "bemalt." Heine has often been criticized by those who measure all things by the standards of Romantic verse for presenting the Romantic scene as stage-dressing; this is supposed to be evidence of his shallowness. The more critical reader will easily see what Heine is doing: the twittering birds, the gay flowers, the stock marble fountain, are all tinsel when compared to the desolate landscape of the poet's own heart. In this fake setting appears a girl from the depths of Romantic subliterature:

> Die Wänglein süß, die Äuglein mild,
> Ein blondgelocktes Heil'genbild;
> Und wie ich schau', die Maid ich fand
> So fremd und doch so wohlbekannt. (E, *1*, 14)

And what is this paragon of holy female purity doing? She is reciting magic folk-incantation while washing linen, chopping down an oak, and digging a grave. She is preparing the accoutrements for the poet's burial.

The poem is programmatic for the initial situation of *Buch der Lieder*. Already it shows the beginnings of a fusion of the emotional problem with the poetic problem. The girl, to put it bluntly, will be the poet's death. He devaluates the girl by describing her and her surroundings in meaningless Romantic clichés. Heine generally had little respect for girls (quite apart from his respect for *women*, like Rahel Varnhagen, Princess

Belgioioso, or George Sand), and he finally married—and loved —a girl he did not have to respect. We know too little of Heine's inner life to speculate whether this contempt is a form of aggression arising out of neurosis and frustrations, or whether it is a primary attitude connected with his elitist view of himself. Doubtless it was a complex, an interacting and self-generating combination of both. For the poetic persona, however, the contempt is primary, and it is part of the humiliation in the situation that the poet must be trapped in frustrated infatuation for an inferior creature. By portraying the girl as an unreal doll with no more than a subliterary existence, the poet satirizes her and ironizes himself. At the same time he seeks control over the situation by impressing upon it a strict form and structure. The four-foot iambic verses are more strictly alternating than the folk song model or than Heine's own more subtle rhythms soon to appear. The incantations of the girl ring with the deathless charm of folk magic, and the three stages of the confrontation, borrowed from the *Märchen* structure, are developed with some subtlety: the washing of the linen appears in all innocence; the chopping of the oak adds a more dangerous and aggressive aspect, and even the *Grube* is not clearly stated to be a *Grab* until the second-last stanza. It is not a great poem, but the poet knows what he is about.

Certainly the most interesting of the poems in this group is *Traumbilder* 8, in which the poet engineers a clever and amusing scene in a graveyard.* Here the poet-persona, still in an undeveloped stage, is split into two: the poet-narrator, plunged into "Wahnsinn und Mitternachtgraus" (E, *1*, 23) by his unhappy love, sees the *Spielmann* rise out of the grave and conduct a performance of the dead in which each apparition tells of the sort of love that has been his ruin. Heine claimed the poem was quite early,[15] and later on he would possibly have combined the roles of narrator and minstrel into one. The minstrel is a surviving remnant of Romantic medievalism, and indeed the whole poem is constructed like a late medieval morality play, in which each character appears in turn and recites in more or less epigrammatic form the details

* It shows a remarkable, and, it would seem, hardly accidental resemblance to a poem by Burns. See Rudolf Zenker, "Heines achtes Traumbild und Burns' Jolly Beggars," *Zeitschrift für vergleichende Litteraturgeschichte,* n.s. 7 (1894), 245-51.

of his special case. The poem is conceived in part as a metrical tour de force full of literary reminiscences. It begins in *Knittelvers,* then switches into a *Lied* form in stanzas four and six. The first two lines of stanzas seven are in Baroque dactyls:

> So heult es verworren, und ächzet und girrt,
> Und brauset und sauset, und krächzet und klirrt, (E, *1,* 23)

and are clearly a parodistic rendering of lines from Goethe's *Hochzeitslied* of 1802:

> Da pfeift es und geigt es und klinget und klirrt,
> Da ringelt's und schleift es und rauschet und wirrt.[16]

The minstrel introduces the series of apparitions in an irregular *Moritat* style, and each section is separated by a rhymed dactylic couplet serving as a sardonic chorus. Each of the self-presentations is in a different scheme of rhyme and meter, and the second and third of them advert explicitly to pathetic scenes from Schiller.

All this is clever and amusing, but the poem lacks thematic unity. Heine has not managed to concentrate on the theme that informs *Buch der Lieder.* Of the six apparitions, the first, third, and sixth find their doom because of unrequited love; the fourth and fifth, however, come to grief because their loves conflict with the society around them; they thus belong in the tradition of romance. The case of number two, the most bitterly ironic of the group, is unclear in this regard: having confused himself with the heroes of trivial adventure novels and especially with Schiller's "Carlo Moor" (a rather heavy-handed literary jibe), and even more absentminded because of his love, he picks his neighbor's pocket:

> Und ich seufzte auch und girrte;
> Und wenn Liebe mich verwirrte,
> Steckt' ich meine Finger rasch
> In des reichen Nachbars Tasch'.
>
> Doch der Gassenvogt mir grollte,
> Daß ich Sehnsuchtsthränen wollte
> Trocknen mit dem Taschentuch,
> Das mein Nachbar bei sich trug. (E, *1,* 25)

The sardonic self-accusation in these lines and implied in the poem as a whole is as harsh as anywhere in *Buch der Lieder.* The sighs, postures, and catastrophes of the unhappy lover are seen here in a highly sarcastic light. While no one ever dreamed a dream as ordered and refined as this one, the laughter that howls through the poem has a nightmarish quality. It has in addition a double implication, suggesting on the one hand the unforgivable absurdity of these pathetic situations, and on the other, the complete absence of warmth and sympathy in the environment surrounding the suffering lover. When the six apparitions have finished, the minstrel himself, the poet-persona of this poem (for the narrator has disappeared altogether), expresses himself with more dignity and subtlety, suggesting a deeper suffering, in what is now becoming the familiar image of the song itself as the vehicle and symbol of love:

> Ich hab' mal ein Liedchen gesungen,
> Das schöne Lied ist aus;
> Wenn das Herz im Leibe zersprungen,
> Dann gehen die Lieder nach Haus! (E, *1,* 27)

But even less quarter is given to the higher poetic sensitivity: "Und das tolle Gelächter sich doppelt erhebt" (E, *1,* 27). Like the prologue to the group, *Traumbilder* 8 is one of the key poems of *Buch der Lieder,* despite its eclectic satire. It places the emotional situation in the context in which it must be overcome. It has not been overcome, but a step has been taken in the direction of self-knowledge and poetic distance.

The epilogue shows, however, that there is a hard road ahead. Borrowing, one suspects, from Goethe's *Der Zauberlehrling,* the poet finds he cannot send his dream-images back to where they came from:

> Da hab' ich viel blasse Leichen
> Beschworen mit Wortesmacht;
> Die wollen nun nicht mehr weichen
> Zurück in die alte Nacht.
>
> Das zähmende Sprüchlein vom Meister
> Vergaß ich vor Schauer und Graus;

Nun ziehn die eignen Geister
Mich selber ins neblichte Haus. (E, *1,* 29)

In the next stanza there is a hint that if the poet could escape his haunted past, there would be new joys to be found in a life of reality:

Laßt ab, ihr finstern Dämonen.
Laßt ab, und drängt mich nicht!
Noch manche Freude mag wohnen
Hier oben im Rosenlicht. (E, *1,* 29)

But the remainder of the poem is a steady slide into the original passive despair; the longings for the lost love reassert themselves, the poet is willing to yield to the ghostly realm, and he ends babbling puerile Romantic diminutives and a wistful plea:

Feins Liebchen, nun bin ich gekommen;—
Feins Liebchen, liebst du mich? (E, *1,* 29)

The section of *Junge Leiden* originally entitled *Minnelieder* caused Heine the most trouble. Of the original seventeen poems, he threw five out of *Buch der Lieder* altogether, moved four to other sections, and added one from another section, giving a final total in *Lieder* of nine.[17] What is left is still not particularly impressive. As early as the summer of 1820, in his essay *Die Romantik,* Heine had begun his attack on the conventions to which he himself was so frustratingly bound; Beyer observed of this essay: "Heine geht hier ins Gericht nicht nur mit seinem eigenen schemenhaften Minnesängertum von anno dazumal, seinen mittelalterlichen Magedeins und seiner . . . 1819 als unzeitgemäß verworfenen frommen Minne, sondern auch mit denen, die ihn voreinst mit jenem dichterischen Spielzeug bekannt gemacht hatten, in erster Linie Fouqué." [18] The coquettish *Minnelieder* that Heine threw out in 1827 include a variation on Goethe's *Heidenröslein,* although with the distinctly non-Goethean address to the plucked flower, "Ich bin so krank wie du" (E, *2,* 6), and a short, six-line echo of Schiller's ode *An die Freude* (E, *2,* 61). The remaining *Lieder* for the most part show the persona in a prostrate posture, flirting with death and, especially in *Lieder* 8, just barely enduring the pain. The most famous of them, partly due to Schumann's setting, is the Hamburg poem, *Lieder* 5, beginning "Schöne Wiege meiner Leiden." But this is an example, of which there are myriads to be found in poetic literature everywhere, of a poem the inspiration of which begins and ends with a happy opening line or two. *Lieder* 7 picks up an element from the *Traumbilder* —the identification of the beloved with the Romantic landscape —and combines it with a theme that is to be heavily worked in *Lyrisches Intermezzo*—resentful accusation of the beloved. It is a Rhine-song, a familiar Romantic genre, but it uncharacteristically stresses the treacherousness of that seemingly peaceful river:

> Doch ich kenn' ihn, oben gleißend,
> Birgt sein Innres Tod und Nacht.
>
> Oben Lust, im Busen Tücken,
> Strom, du bist der Liebsten Bild!
> Die kann auch so freundlich nicken,
> Lächelt auch so fromm und mild. (E, *I*, 33).

A first hint of the renowned *Loreley* is audible in these verses.

Since the topic of resentment has been raised, perhaps this is the place to mention the three "ich grolle nicht" poems, which were originally included in this group but in *Buch der Lieder* were moved to *Lyrisches Intermezzo* (17, 18, 19), where they fit in much better. These three poems, the second of which was given a magnificent setting by Schumann, live within a triangular tension of self-control, resentment, and self-delusion. The three elements are present in all three poems, but each stresses one of them: the transparent effort at self-control and sour forgiveness that is denied by the language itself in *Lyrisches Intermezzo* 17:

> Grolle nicht ob dem Verrat;
> Trag es, trag es, und entschuldig' es,
> Was die holde Thörin that; (E, *I*, 72)

resentment generated by self-pity in No. 18:

Ich grolle nicht, und wenn das Herz auch bricht (E, *I*, 72); and the self-delusion about the supposed secret misery of the beloved in No. 19, where the sixfold repetition of the word "elend" cannot mask the fact that assuming the beloved's present misery is a flimsy construct:

> Wohl seh' ich Spott, der deinen Mund umschwebt,
> Und seh' dein Auge blitzen trotziglich,
> Und seh' den Stolz, der deinen Busen hebt,—
> Und elend bist du doch, elend wie ich.
>
> Unsichtbar zuckt auch Schmerz um deinen Mund,
> Verborgne Thräne trübt des Auges Schein,
> Der stolze Busen hegt geheime Wund',—
> Mein Lieb, wir sollen beide elend sein. (E, *I*, 73)

It is not surprising that these poems were moved into *Lyrisches Intermezzo.* Not only are they superior to any of the other original *Minnelieder,* but in their layers of transparency, in which the poet displays and exposes the desperate delusions of the persona, they belong to a later stage in the process of achieving some semblance of unity of feeling and attitude.

Similarly to the epilogue poem of *Traumbilder,* the last of the *Lieder* (No. 9) speaks of the as yet unsuccessful effort to incapsulate the sufferings of the poet in the songs and bury them once and for all. The failure, thus far, of time to do its healing work is indicated by the two meanings of "einst" in stanzas three and four; in stanza three, the ambivalent word refers to the "Lavastrom" of the past that generated these poems; in stanza four, "einst" refers to their propensity in time future, when "der Liebe Geist" reasserts itself, to revive the old heat (E, *I*, 34). The poet has gained little strength thus far; the group ends on a melancholy and despairing note.

The *Romanzen* are related by genre to the narrative ballad of the Classical-Romantic period, but usually in Heine's case they are much shorter and more compressed; with the exception of the tripartite *Der arme Peter* (No. 4) and the long *Don Ramiro* (No. 9), they concentrate on a single scene that implies an emotional situation or relationship. It is in the nature of the genre that there should be a switch here into third-person personae, but this distinction is not usually a meaningful one with Heine; on the contrary, the new personae are projections of the role that is being worked out in *Buch der Lieder*. Rather than encouraging more objectivity or sovereignty over situations, the switch into the third person may permit even greater self-indulgence, as it does in the first of the *Romanzen, Der Traurige,* where both girls and nature notice the sadness of the "bleicher Knabe" (E, *1*, 35). This lachrymose poem was probably composed with the *Minnelieder* and should have been left there.

The horseman of *Bergstimme* (No. 2) riding tearfully into his grave is an element of the ballad tradition and becomes a prototype for the knight-persona that plays such a large part in Heine's works. This persona appears again in *Die Botschaft* (No. 7), which is even closer to the ballad tradition and is related verbally to Bürger's *Die Entführung*; another version is the tragic, urbane cavalier of *Don Ramiro,* who after his death haunts the wedding of his faithless beloved. This last, which exists in two widely differing versions, is composed in the meter of one of Heine's earliest known poems, the entertaining schoolboy spoof *Wünnebergiade* (E, *2*, 53–56), and of some of the greatest achievements of later years such as *Atta Troll* and *Jehuda ben Halevy*—the four-beat, so-called Spanish trochees, here with irregular and sometimes quite impure assonance. As Beyer has pointed out,[19] the poem operates with a good many materials from the *Volkslied,* but adapts them to the theme of *Buch der Lieder*. Unlike the more compressed *Romanzen,* the poem spins out the situation into a complete narration with genuine dialogue; here it is the girl who speaks of self-mastery, and with oblivious insensitivity, she invites Don Ramiro to her wedding:

> Rüttle ab den dumpfen Trübsinn;
> Mädchen gibt es viel auf Erden,
> Aber uns hat Gott geschieden.
>
> Don Ramiro, der du mutig
> So viel Mohren überwunden,
> Überwinde nun dich selber,—
> Komm auf meine Hochzeit morgen. (E, *1*, 42)

A difference from the original version of 1817 is that there Donna

Clara exculpates herself on the grounds that her father has forced her into this marriage, whereas in the version of *Buch der Lieder* she is content with a stereotype reference to fate:

> . . . der Spruch der Sterne,
> Die da spotten meines Willens. (E, *1*, 42)

Although Don Ramiro has in fact died, apparently by his own hand, at noon on this wedding day, it is clear at the end that his apparition is merely Donna Clara's dream or hallucination. She consequently emerges as the rueful beloved, an experimental fiction that we have noted before. The poem turns out to be the most thoroughly developed wish-dream of the secret sensitivity of the beloved to the poet persona's pathetic state.

Der arme Peter, in the first of its three parts, tries a different tack: it looks at the ridiculous side of the poet's sufferings. Here the characters of the wedding-day tragedy are reduced to common folk, and Peter has no claim to the knightly dignity of Don Ramiro or the hero of *Die Botschaft:*

> Der Hans und die Grete tanzen herum,
> Und jauchzen vor lauter Freude.
> Der Peter steht so still und stumm,
> Und ist so blaß wie Kreide. (E, *1*, 37)

Peter exhibits his desperation by biting his nails, and at the end of the first part he unheroically subordinates his suffering to his common sense:

> Ach! wenn ich nicht gar zu vernünftig wär',
> Ich thät' mir was zuleide. (E, *1*, 37)

In the remainder of the poem, Peter resumes the by now conventional posture of the pale lad wasting away from love and catching the sympathetic attention of the other girls. In *Die Fensterschau* (No. 12), however, Heine gives this ghostly state of affairs a witty turn. The pale lad, here called Heinrich, perhaps not only to alliterate with his Hedwig, languishes, as in other places in the work, under his beloved's window; but this time the girl, too, is struck with "Liebesweh," and ultimately they put the witching hours to more cheerful use:

> Bald aber lag sie in Heinrichs Arm,
> Allnächtlich zur Zeit der Gespenster. (E, *1,* 48)

The poem itself is, of course, slight, but it is of interest in the total context of *Buch der Lieder,* because it is involved in the process of wrenching both the persistent Romantic clichés and the prostrate emotional attitude onto new ground, where the passions are flattened out to a manageable level and sex is relieved of its spookiness. This process is not a straight line, but progresses as through a maze, taking innumerable wrong turnings, and it is continually forced back to the starting point to begin anew.

Two items in the *Romanzen, Die Grenadiere* (No. 6) and *Belsatzar* (No. 10), seem like foreign bodies in this collection, and it is no accident that they are the most famous of the group; they are the first poems among the few in *Buch der Lieder* that have nothing to do with the love situation. They are difficult to date, but they are clearly early[20] and are the best evidence in Heine's youthful poetry that here was a genius of the first order. Although both the quasi-revolutionary Napoleonic soldier and the monarch fuse with the poetic persona at later stages in Heine's career, there is no such fusion here, and, in *Belsatzar,* the evil king has nothing to do with the persona even by anticipation. An interpretation of these remarkable achievements does not, therefore, really belong in this discussion. Despite their excellences, especially in terms of concentration of scene and rhythmic characterization, we must regretfully leave them aside, with only the remark that they are intrinsically more worthy of attention than any of the other poems of this group.

Two other poems among the *Romanzen* bear some notice. One is the *Gespräch auf der Paderborner Heide* (No. 18), a subtle variant of the traditional German theme of Philistinism. Heine's dialogue is a confrontation of Romantic fantasy with unimaginative realism; the narrator transforms the sounds and sights of the heath into apperceptions of "poesy," while his companion retranslates them into reality: the dance music is the squealing of piglets and grunting of hogs; the *Waldhorn* and *Schalmeien* are the swineherd driving his sows home; it is not church bells that are ringing, but cowbells; it is not the vision of the beloved they see, but the old hag of the forest. In parallel to these poetic delusions, the poet mentions finally his unhappy love, although here he receives no answer:

> Nun, mein Freund, so magst du lachen
> Über des Phantasten Frage!
> Wirst du auch zur Täuschung machen,
> Was ich fest im Busen trage? (E, *1*, 54)

The poem is a trap for the unwary reader. The companion may be an unpleasant stick, but he is also right. The poet may be sad and sensitive, but he is also out of touch with reality. The third line of the last stanza, incidentally, was originally a statement and thus more aggressive: "Kannst doch nicht zur Täuschung machen" (E, *1*, 514).[21] By transforming the line into a question, the whole depressing dialectic is left open. That the question receives no answer indicates the stage the poetic attitude has reached: the poet is not prepared to let go of his melancholy emotions, but he is aware, or at any rate suspects, that they fall into the same category as his bucolic falsifications.

This awareness finds sobering and quite sour expression in the epilogue to the group, entitled *Wahrhaftig* (No. 20):

> Wenn der Frühling kommt mit dem Sonnenschein,
> Dann knospen und blühen die Blümlein auf;
> Wenn der Mond beginnt seinen Strahlenlauf,
> Dann schwimmen die Sternlein hintendrein;
> Wenn der Sänger zwei süße Äuglein sieht,
> Dann quellen ihm Lieder aus tiefem Gemüt;—
> Doch Lieder und Sterne und Blümelein,
> Und Äuglein und Mondglanz und Sonnenschein,
> Wie sehr das Zeug auch gefällt,
> So macht's doch noch lang' keine Welt. (E, *1*, 55)

"Sooner or later," writes Prawer of this poem, "he had to assume a poetic self different from that so often mocked by his uncomfortable 'Doppelgänger.' "[22] It will be later rather than sooner, but the problem is sharply stated in these verses. The unresolved tension in the poem lies in the words "aus tiefem Gemüt"; whereas Heine believed in the depth of his sensitivity and had some reason to do so—whence would the songs otherwise have come?—he turns the phrase into a suspect cliché by putting it in context with the persistent diminutives of worn-out Romantic diction. Where is the world, indeed? But before a world can be perceived and mastered, the perceiver must put himself into some sort of tolerable relationship to himself, and that will take some time as yet.

A brief word may be inserted here about the sonnets. Discussing the *Fresko-Sonette* addressed to Christian Sethe, E. M. Butler speaks of the "extreme virtuosity . . . in which satire and savage irony run rough-shod over the highly sophisticated form."[23] Heine does not ordinarily seem to have been comfortable in the sonnet form,[24] and Strodtmann interpreted the ruggedness of the *Fresko-Sonette* as a sign of the rebellious spirit.[25] They are the most clearly narrative of the first-person poems, and in *Buch der Lieder* they seem like a kind of catching of breath, a retrospective brooding on the emotional situation, accompanied by a temporary abandonment of lyricism. But perhaps this contrast has encouraged interpreters to overrate these poems somewhat. They are savage enough, but the colloquial diction seems self-conscious, and, although the title indicates that the broad brushstrokes will fracture the delicate sonnet form, they do not really do so; the rugged diction sits uncomfortably within a strictly maintained form. The last tercet of No. 3, to be sure, has gained some currency as a statement of the characteristic Heinean attitude:

> Und wenn das Herz im Leibe ist zerrissen,
> Zerrissen, und zerschnitten, und zerstochen,—
> Dann bleibt uns doch das schöne gelle Lachen. (E, *1*, 59)*

But the formulation has often been grist for the mills of Heine's detractors and does not adequately represent what is happening in *Buch der Lieder*. Number 4 is of interest because of the way in which it analyzes the stages of the love situation: in the first quartet the girl is presented in Romantic terms as a *Märchen* figure: "Ein wunderschönes zartes Mägdelein" (E, *1*, 59). In the second quartet it is discovered that she is, in fact, loveless and frosty; in the first tercet the songs ring in the poet's head to the

* One is easily reminded of the reiterated, bitter "ich lache" in Heine's letter to Heinrich Straube of ca. February-April 1821.[26]

background of the girl's giggling, and in the final lines the poet fears for his reason, yet would be glad to keep it. This cool résumé of the situation in *Junge Leiden* is the best and most instructive of the sonnets. The last of them, No. 9, is a riot of self-pity and self-contempt; the poet writhes on the floor, losing the battle to overcome his broken heart, longing for the fantasy realm where his love can still be imagined and dreamed of. It is time, surely, for a new beginning and a new effort, and this is what we find in the next group of poems.

With *Lyrisches Intermezzo,* we come to the poems for which Heine is most remembered. They are characterized by strict compression—most of them are composed in a few four-line stanzas—and a deceptive simplicity of diction that, in contrast to Heine's prose, has largely jettisoned the adjectival style so prominent in Romantic writing. In this group Heine really gets to work on establishing the poetic persona. *Lyrisches Intermezzo,* like its successor, *Die Heimkehr,* is a remarkable display of the testing of the validity of feelings by language; at the same time, it questions the adequacy and genuineness of language by questioning the adequacy and genuineness of the feelings expressed by it. So thoroughgoing and ultimately serious is this process that it is difficult to think of these poems, as some contemporary critics do, as existing exclusively on the surface of language and as representing merely a display of poetic skill. It would be more accurate to say that a pure poetic fiction is the *goal* of the undertaking, not the initial situation.

We know from Heine's correspondence that he was much concerned about the order of his poems, and the interpreters, too, have encouraged us to think of them in cycles. "Heine sucht im 'Buch der Lieder' um der künstlerischen Abrundung eines Werkes willen," writes Helene Herrmann, "namentlich im 'Intermezzo' und in der 'Heimkehr,'' fragmentarisch erlebtes Liebesgeschick zu ganzen Romanen in Liedern zu gestalten." [27] Whether the experience was as "fragmentarisch erlebt" as Hermann thought it was is doubtful. Although it is not possible to extract a coherent narrative from the cycle, it is obvious that *Lyrisches Intermezzo,* in a vague way, tells a story. Belart described the pattern of the group by means of a mechanical but not unconvincing division into six groups, with three intermezzi, a postscript, and an epilogue, all turning on two main axes; others have suggested different divisions.[28] Since, however, we are here less concerned with the romance itself than the poetic attitude toward it, we will let the efforts at structuring rest on their own merits. The procedure here will show a much less clear line; the poetic posture probes solutions and drops them, only to take them up again, and vacillates between strength and weakness. The poems of *Lyrisches Intermezzo* are, on the average, so good, within the poet's self-imposed limitations, that it is a temptation to take them up one by one and interpret the special qualities of each. Such an effort in this context would quickly become unmanageable. Instead, we will take a walk through this thorny garden of verses, keeping our eyes open for the movements and gestures of the persona dwelling in it.

The prologue, which, except for the last three lines, appears also in the tragedy *Almansor*,[29] establishes the portrait of a knight who resembles Offa, the male Cinderella of Old Norse legend, so maladroit and lost in his sad dreams that the flowers and the girls giggle as he goes by. An erotic dream of his beloved fills him with fire, but when he awakens, he is thrust back into his gloomy reality —as a poet:

> Der Ritter sitzt wieder ganz einsam zu Haus,
> In dem düstern Poetenstübchen. (E, *1*, 66)

Then, beginning with the late addition *Im wunderschönen Monat Mai*, the cycle proper gets into motion: some light and harmless love songs build up the situation. But already in the last two lines of No. 4 there is a surprising turn:

> Doch wenn du sprichst: Ich liebe dich!
> So muß ich weinen bitterlich. (E, *1*, 67)

The meaning of this unexpected phrase is not clear; it may be that the girl's asseverations of love are not to be trusted; the phrase may also raise the question of whether this love is something the poet really wants and is able to endure, or whether it is not rather a frustrating situation that provides safety and perverse pleasure.

This last interpretation seems to be supported in No. 6, where the sense of longing continues despite the embrace:

> Und wenn dich mein Arm gewaltig umschließt—
> Sterb' ich vor Liebessehnen! (E, v, 68)

In Nos. 8, 9, and 10 there is a brief experiment with Romantic language. Number 8 plays with combining two disparate Romantic motifs: the secret language of nature—here of the stars—and the science of linguistics, which was also born in the Romantic era:

> Sie sprechen eine Sprache,
> Die ist so reich, so schön;
> Doch keiner der Philologen
> Kann diese Sprache verstehn.
>
> Ich aber hab' sie gelernet,
> Und ich vergesse sie nicht;
> Mir diente als Grammatik
> Der Herzallerliebsten Gesicht. (E, *I*, 68)

The "unpoetic" words "Philologen" and "Grammatik" are part of an attack, here just hinted at, upon Romanticism with its own materials. Number 9, *Auf Flügeln des Gesanges,** [30] and No. 10 are brief excursions into Romantic Orientalism, although in No. 10 the lotus is nothing more than an exotic prop in a German Romantic setting.

In Nos. 12–15 there appears a new tone altogether, which Elster and others, commenting on some similar poems of *Die Heimkehr,* called "niedere Minne." [31] The reference is to a style of medieval poetry introduced by Walther von der Vogelweide and carried on by others, most notably the sardonic and programmatically offensive Neidhart von Reuental; and the comparison is appropriate insofar as here, too, there is an attempt to break away from the stylization of an unreal love situation by writing of more casual relationships in which there is no emotional drain. The disapproval of Wilhelminian scholars for Heine's abandonment of perpetual high tension in love poetry is not appropriate.[32] In

* For an interpretation that tries to rescue this poem from its own banalities, see Prawer, *Heine: Buch der Lieder,* pp. 11–13.

the context of *Buch der Lieder* it is a part of the hunting about for exits, or for a lower level where the persona can stand taller. In this sense, the poems of "niedere Minne" in *Lyrisches Intermezzo* point to an important feature of the ultimate solution, although here, to be sure, they communicate more tension than confidence; the assertions of indifference to the lack of love in the beloved—

> Du liebst mich nicht, du liebst mich nicht,
> Das kümmert mich gar wenig (E, *1*, 70)

—are in a state of tension with the still urgent longing, which is brought directly into the poetic context in No. 14:

> Auf meiner Herzliebsten Äugelein
> Mach' ich die schönsten Kanzonen.
> Auf meiner Herzliebsten Mündchen klein
> Mach' ich die besten Terzinen.
> Auf meiner Herzliebsten Wängelein
> Mach' ich die herrlichsten Stanzen.
> Und wenn meine Liebste ein Herzchen hätt',
> Ich machte darauf ein hübsches Sonett. (E, *1*, 71)

Such a poem is an expression of crisis. The self-conscious insistence upon the poetic mastery, which turns the details of the love experience into strict forms, is negated by the self-contemptuous use of puerile diminutives; yet this insubstantial posing is, of course, not sufficient to trivialize the lament in the last two lines. Here emotion not only has the upper hand over poetry, but threatens to destroy it altogether. The "ich grolle nicht" poems, which were moved from *Lieder* and inserted into *Lyrisches Intermezzo* at this point, are sounder poetry, but still maintain the tension of crisis. Between the two groups is a poem (No. 16) that vaguely attempts to deal with the relationship between poesy and reality. In the first stanza, it is asked whether the beloved is not a "Traumgebild" produced by the poet's overheated imagination; in the second stanza this is denied, since such sweet beauty is not within the poet's power to create, and the third would have it that the poet's imagination is only adequate to myths of terror:

Basilisken und Vampire,
Lindenwürm' und Ungeheu'r,
Solche schlimme Fabeltiere,
Die erschafft des Dichters Feu'r. (E, *1*, 71)

The poem then turns sharply around in the fourth stanza, where, with double-edged hyperbole, both the beauty and the faithlessness of the beloved are placed beyond the poet's reach:

Aber dich und deine Tücke,
Und dein holdes Angesicht,
Und die falschen frommen Blicke—
Das erschafft der Dichter nicht. (E, *1*, 72)

The poem is of significance not primarily because of this trick, nor for the edgy restatement of the lament, but because the question of the reality of the beloved versus the poet's capacity to capture her in images is raised.

In connection with the theme of "niedere Minne," it is worth calling attention to a poem that was originally included as No. 36 in *Lyrisches Intermezzo* but was removed from the second edition of *Buch der Lieder* of 1837. It is the only place in the original cycle where the poet clearly indicates that he has had a successful sexual experience (although another poem, absent from the first edition of *Buch der Lieder,*[33] hints at the same thing). In it the poet pretends to a voluptuous and self-confident cynicism:

Den Leib möcht' ich noch haben,
Den Leib, so zart und jung;
Die Seele könnt ihr begraben,
Hab' selber Seele genung. (E, *2*, 10)

Early commentators were inclined to believe that this poem and one or two similar ones were removed because they bordered too closely on the obscene.[34] But in 1837 Heine was still in his aggressive Parisian mood concerning the equal claims of body and soul, and he could not have objected to the sentiment of the poem as such. Heine probably removed it because of its clumsy rhymes and because it is misplaced in the cycle (thematically it belongs with Nos. 12–15). Moreover, it expresses an attitude more advanced than that being developed in *Lyrisches Intermezzo*; it is as though Heine, meticulous reviser that he was, thought the cycle had not progressed far enough in the solution of the original problem to permit the inclusion of such a poem.

In No. 24, along with a complaint of slander, there is the first hint of the poet's awareness of his undignified posture since *Romanzen* 13:

> Das Schlimmste und das Dümmste,
> Das trug ich geheim in der Brust. (E, *1*, 75)

This slight admission stands on the edge of a partial solution in irony, which in turn has the potential of strengthening the poetic posture, so that in Nos. 25–28 a more ironic and at the same time more accusatory tone becomes audible; Heine begins to operate with his famous devastating last lines. Number 28, for example, adverts again to the marriage and trivializes the beloved with conventional French phrases, while cracking the rhythm of the last lines to pieces:

> Das Menschenvolk mich ennuyieret,
> Sogar der Freund, der sonst passabel;—
> Das kömmt, weil man Madame titulieret
> Mein süßes Liebchen, so süß und aimabel. (E, *1*, 76)

In No. 29, an insult to the bridegroom, in the form of the conventional student invitation to a duel—"Als Bräut'gam den dümmsten der dummen Jungen" (E, *1*, 76)—combines with a feeble attempt at a new tack: the poet suggests that it is he who has abandoned the beloved:

> Daß ich von solchem Lieb konnt' weichen
> War der dümmste von meinen dummen Streichen.

But this idea is dropped in the next few poems in which a pathetic gesture of joining the beloved in the grave is combined with increased resentment.

The central poem of the cycle, No. 33, with its famous image of the spruce tree, standing in the North "auf kahler Höh" (E, *1*, 78)*

* See Houben, p. 751, for an account of how this poem came to be written; it is

and the unreachable palm in the East, resumes the fiction of the unhappy beloved. The image is at the same time an embryonic symbol of the poet's chill, lonely dignity. Rose observes that it is "one of the only three poems of the cycle in which there is no direct mention of [the poet's] own feeling or of the object of his love (the others are Nos. 10 and 59). The objective image of the pine and the palm is a metaphor of hopeless separation." † This observation, though irrefutable, does not seem to me to be quite to the point, and it is characteristic of the obsession of modern critics with Heine's movement toward objective imagery. But *Lyrisches Intermezzo* is a poetic fugue the ultimate substance of which is not the perpetual recapitulation of feeling but the overcoming of emotional prostration. What is important about the poem in its place in the cycle is not the image of separation, a feature of the situation long since established, but its relative location on the scale of development: a step forward in symbolizing the suffering dignity of the persona, a step backward in reverting to the fiction of the unhappy beloved.

Andler has argued, according to his Hegelian postulates, that the cycle moves at this point from one thesis to another, from joys to sadnesses.[35] But matters are by no means so specific; Rose observes that after the midpoint the cycle seems to lack consistent development,[36] and it is true that from here through No. 46 there is a turn to a more sentimental and gentler tone. The poet rings the changes on his loneliness; even his songs do not bridge the now hopeless gap (No. 36):

---

a good example of a poem that undoubtedly has nothing whatever to do with the Amalie experience (and indeed very little to do with the experience recounted in Houben), but which is fit carefully into the context of *Lyriches Intermezzo.* Dietrich Weber, " 'Gesetze des Standpunkts' in Heines Lyrik," *Jahrbuch des Freien Deutschen Hochstifts 1965,* p. 381, points out that instead of the usual feminine *Fichte,* Heine uses the unusual masculine form *Fichtenbaum,* and comments, "der Gegenstand erscheint nicht von einem anwesenden Ich-Subjekt fingirt, sondern fiktiv als er selbst."

* Rose, *Early Love Poetry,* pp. 33–34. For a history of the image after Heine, see Richard M. Meyer, "Motiv-Wanderungen," *Deutsche Dichtung, 25* (1898–99), 25–28. The image occurs in the Mishnah, although it is unlikely that Heine knew this. See E[2], *1,* 450 and Claude Owen, "Heinrich Heines Kenntnisse der Weltliteratur ohne Berücksichtigung der deutschen Literatur. Ein bibliographisches Verzeichnis" (M.A. thesis, University of Alberta, 1961), pp. 42–43.

Aus meinen großen Schmerzen
Mach' ich die kleinen Lieder;
Die haben ihr klingend Gefieder
Und flattern nach ihrem Herzen.

Sie fanden den Weg zur Trauten,
Doch kommen sie wieder und klagen,
Und klagen, und wollen nicht sagen,
Was sie im Herzen schauten (E, *1*, 79)

Yet there is an effort at ironic discipline in No. 39, where the poet is the loser in a chain of unrequited loves:

Es ist eine alte Geschichte,
Doch bleibt sie immer neu;
Und wem sie just passieret,
Dem bricht das Herz entzwei. (E, *1*, 80)

The effort to extract some pride from this situation, however, turns gradually to anger, which becomes ambivalently bitter in No. 50, *Sie saßen und tranken am Teetisch.* This poem has been often quoted, although it is not easy to understand completely. The description of the Philistine tea party, where the bourgeois types talk stuffily of love, points ahead to the development of Heine's satiric poetry in his middle period; Prawer suggests that these characters, flirting in their constipated way with the subject of passion, are in fact a portrait of Heine's audience, whose sentimentality gives his poetry a "double edge," and Prawer calls attention also to the variety of absurd rhymes that gradually became a hallmark of Heine's verse: "Teetisch / ästhetisch"; "platonisch / ironisch"; "Mund weit / Gesundheit." [37] But what of the final stanza?

Am Tische war noch ein Plätzchen,
Mein Liebchen, da hast du gefehlt,
Du hättest so hübsch, mein Schätzchen,
Von deiner Liebe erzählt. (E, *1*, 85)

Taken out of the context of *Lyrisches Intermezzo,* the ending might suggest that the girl's love was more active and that she was absent from the conversation because she was with the poet—an indirect version of "niedere Minne"; but, in the context, it seems more likely that the statement is an angry slander on the beloved, indicating that she, too, would have taken part in the stupid palaver. Since the context in Heine's cycles is never airtight, it is difficult to decide.[38]

In the midst of a group of satirical and to some extent self-lacerating poems, as though in explanation of them, is placed the familiar No. 51, *Vergiftet sind meine Lieder.* Placed as it is, this poem marks a stage in the development of the poetic attitude. On the one hand, a certain amount of independence is being asserted through satire and hostility, but on the other, the beloved is charged with having poisoned the poet's songs, so that he has been driven into a defensive position that he would not have chosen himself; there is still the wish that the sentimentality corresponded to something real.

Numbers 52, 54, 55, and 56 pick up the dream motif again and are a sort of reprise of the *Traumbilder,* although now compressed into the compact forms of the *Lyrisches Intermezzo.* The lachrymose No. 55 suggests a good deal of emotional confusion: in the first stanza, the poet weeps because he has dreamed that his beloved is in her grave; in the second, he weeps at the dream that she has left him, and in the third, he dreams that she has remained well-disposed toward him, but:

> Ich wachte auf, und noch immer
> Strömt mein Tränenflut. (E, *1,* 87)

The weeping, no doubt, results from the contradiction between dream and reality, but there is a hint that the inner suffering is not subject to ease even by the realization of love and, paradoxically, that it is in some sense autonomous and isolated within the persona. Number 56, with its unfortunate line, "Zu deinen süßen Füßen," which reportedly set the Berlin circle of Elise von Hohenhausen a-roaring, to Heine's great chagrin,[39] is nevertheless interesting because of its last stanza:

> Du sagst mir heimlich ein leises Wort,
> Und gibst mir den Strauß mit Cypressen.
> Ich wache auf, und der Strauß ist fort,
> Und das Wort hab' ich vergessen. (E, *1,* 87)

The poem reverts to the fiction of the suffering beloved, and the finality of the loss of love is stressed by the bouquet of cypress, the symbol of mourning. Most important is the forgotten word of love, for in the verbal context of poetry, this loss, despite the elegiac tone, suggests a certain achieved distance.

In the autumnal mood at the end of the cycle, the dreams themselves become ambivalent and uncertain; in No. 58, in which the poet has revived the persona of the rider—a transform of the knight—the oak tree mocks him as he pretends to be riding to his waiting beloved:

> Es säuselt der Wind in den Blättern,
> Es spricht der Eichenbaum:
> Was willst du, thörichter Reiter,
> Mit deinem thörichten Traum? (E, *1*, 88)

In No. 60, Heine takes up again the abandoned form of the *Traumbilder,* but the poem exhibits new insights. The dream-god brings the poet into a Romantic death-palace of knights and maidens, in which he becomes very anxious and seeks to escape; but he finds the exit blocked by the vision of the beloved, here elevated into mythic proportions—she reminds one, rather inappropriately, of Athena. The poem is the clearest expression of the problem at this point: the escape from the imprisoning Romantic visions requires somehow a circumvention of the vision of the beloved. Number 64 treats another aspect of these anxieties. The poet lies in his grave; his emotions are dead. The beloved wants to arouse him on the Day of Judgment and promises him love, but it is too late; the wounds are too deep, and when he tries to arise, he falls back, not into the grave, but into the waking state. This emotional exhaustion, coupled with the specifically poetic insight of No. 60, shows some promise that the prerequisites for a solution are being developed.

The epilogue, No. 65, in which the poet wants to bury "Die alten, bösen Lieder" (E, *1*, 92), is similar to the epilogue of the *Lieder*. This is not surprising, as it is one of Heine's earliest published poems, having appeared in *Der Gesellschafter* in January 1822, where it was the sad year 1821 that was to be buried.[40] These poems, as well as the epilogue to *Die Heimkehr,* have the same function: they express a desire to overcome sufferings and consign them to the past. What is particularly notable about No. 65 is the studied hyperbole of the images. The coffin in which the bad dreams are to be buried must be larger than the Heidelberg Cask; the bier, longer than the bridge at Mainz; the pallbearers, giants stronger than St. Christopher (a most curious association here); and the burial place, the sea,

> Denn solchem großen Sarge
> Gebührt ein großes Grab. (E, *1*, 92)

This Titanic vastness, the last stanza points out, corresponds to the size and weight of the poet's love and pain. It is clear that this hyperbole expresses a carefully constructed pride in the importance and the dimensions of his suffering. It is upon this pride that the ultimate poetic posture will be founded.

Die Heimkehr 47

> Du bist wie eine Blume
> So hold und schön und rein;
> Ich schau' dich an, und Wehmut
> Schleicht mir ins Herz hinein.
>
> Mir ist, als ob ich die Hände
> Aufs Haupt dir legen sollt'.
> Betend, daß Gott dich erhalte
> So rein und schön und hold. (E, *1*, 117–18)

Any evaluation of the poetry of Heine's first period must stand or fall on the interpretation of a poem like this. Our reading of it will decide whether we take Heine seriously or not, whether we respect his poetic judgment and his intelligence, or whether, as admirers or detractors, we view him as an entertaining, though rather mannered rhyme-smith. Adolf Stahr reports that Heine told him in 1850 that this poem was the sort of thing which would remain valid in his works, and that he characterized it as one of "die reinen, von aller Opposition freien Lieder, die schon jetzt Volkslieder sind" (Houben, p. 745). There is no particular reason to suppose that Stahr's account is strictly accurate; if it is, there is very little reason to think that Heine was expressing more than a momentary opinion, and even less that Heine's opinions on his works are binding anyway. But we do need to be concerned about the implications of the poem for Heine's aesthetic judgment. Recently, a most able critic has dismissed Ford Madox Ford's admiring comments on the poem with summary justice as "maudlin trash." * [41] Such a judgment, of course, does not reflect on Ford as a writer of estimable novels, but if a moved response to it is maudlin or if the poem itself is trash, what are we to say of the poet who keeps it through seven printings with hardly a change and continues to speak well of it in later years?

Modern critics have begun to suspect that despite what one might call the urbane Romanticism that lies on the surface of this poem, all is not as it appears at first sight.[42] It will be useful to take a closer look at it to see whether, in the context of the development of the persona, we can extract from it anything other than mannered naïveté. The very first line is remarkable in more than one way. Its very simplicity is daring; it surprises us that the adder-tongued poet should address his beloved with so naïve a simile and that this *jongleur* of language should have no more specific word at his disposal than "Blume"; not even a particular flower is called upon to give a slight plasticity to an already worn out Romantic conceit. A Romantic line this certainly is, in that its meter is very much subordinated to its rhythm; with the exception of the two *schwa*-syllables, no syllable in the line has exactly the same stress as any other if read properly. It is Romantic lyrical prosody, and an adequate description of the line would be given not by a metrical scheme, but by a rising and falling curve: [curve]. Not so, however, in the second line, where the three monosyllabic stresses are as clear and strong as they can be. This is post-Romantic prosody, in which the lyrical Romantic effort to make words flow imperceptibly into one another is abandoned for stricter meter; individual words become prominent and important, and poetry becomes verbal again rather than musical. But what words they are that bear these heavy stresses! William

* A look at Ford's *The March of Literature* (New York, 1938), pp. 722–23, at which the barb is aimed, shows that the "maudlin trash" does not refer directly to this poem.

Rose remarks, somewhat unfairly, that *hold, schön, lieb,* and *süß* "almost exhaust [Heine's] vocabulary," [43] and here these worn-out and all but contentless words are certainly thrust under the nose of the reader. Rose seems to forget, however, how violently Heine expressed himself with regard to the word *hold* in his critique of Steinmann's verse; his disapproval of it is intense.[44] Among the older critics, Oskar Walzel came closest to an understanding of this diction when he observed: "Den Spott zu steigern, holt Heine abgebrauchte Worte des Preises weiblicher Schönheit heran." [45] Surely the prominence given to these empty words is an expression of contempt, in keeping with Heine's general view of the fair sex. The one Romantic conceit he does not abandon his whole career through is this comparison of girls with flowers, and the patronizing, unspecific expression "Blumengesichter" occurs repeatedly in his writing. Heine shared with most of the males of his century (although in notable contrast to the Young Germans and the tradition of which they are a part) the belief that girls are and ought to be meek doodlewits. This observation is important because this sense of male superiority is one of the pillars upon which the persona is finally built. It comes to the fore in this poem in the impudent location of three nearly meaningless complimentary attributes in metrically prominent position, not once, but twice.

The poet looks upon the beloved with sadness, but, as it turns out, it is not the misery and self-pity of previous poems. Rather, he slips into a reverie in which he imagines a gesture that both reduces the girl to relative inferiority and contains a veiled barb. The gesture of laying his hands on the girl's head and then praying (in a line that significantly slips into lilting dactyls) that God shall maintain these indefinable qualities is not only intentionally avuncular and supercilious, but implies also that these sweet qualities are not likely to be preserved and that degeneration and infidelity are what one is likely to expect from womanhood.

Even the structure of the poem is something of a trap. Since the first stanza begins with "Du," and the second with "Mir," it would seem at first glance that the poem is dialectically arranged, with the first stanza about the girl and the second about the poet. But it is not so. Through rhetorical tricks, the poet causes the girl to recede into insignificance and almost into invisibility. In fact both stanzas are about the poet; in the first he locates the girl in a manageable, that is to say, trivial perspective, and in the second he mulls a gesture that will act out his superiority and at the same time urbanely dismiss the girl's character, all the while assuming that the girl is so simple that she will take these things for compliments and lovemaking. Seen in these terms, the poem would not easily be imaginable in *Lyrisches Intermezzo*; it represents a more advanced stage in the developing self-assurance of the poetic persona. Pain and suffering are absent from the poem; what is left is amused disdain, and the very poem is a trap for the insensitive girl (as it has been, I fear, for many a reader*). It cannot be denied, moreover, that there is an element of arrogance and even of cruelty in the ultimate solution.

Die Heimkehr, despite its more programmatic title, is a more complicated and less unified group than *Lyrisches Intermezzo*; there is no clear line of development in it. At times there seems to be a serious retrogression into the maudlin self-indulgence of some of the earlier poems; elsewhere, as in *Du bist wie eine Blume,* there are steps forward to a new poetic attitude. Both Elster[46] and Belart,[47] in their efforts to organize the poems, divide them into nine groups—although not in the same way—and see these groups separated by what Elster calls "Einschnitte" and Belart "Intermezzi"; Legras divides them into seven groups separated by "Intermèdes." [48] These distinctions are not always easy to maintain, although there are some clear groupings, such as a section of "niedere Minne" (Nos. 69–78), and a group of North Sea poems (Nos. 7–14) that anticipate the final section of *Buch der Lieder.* On the whole, *Die Heimkehr* seems more expansive and varied: "Il est très en progrès sur l'*Intermezzo,*" writes Andler, "par l'aisance, par la multiplicité des thèmes, l'approfondissement de la réflexion poétique." [49]

It opens with three different, though related moods, and none

* Gustav Karpeles, in "Ein Gedicht von Heinrich Heine," *Unter Palmen* (Berlin, 1871), pp. 95–101, told a pretty story that the poem was inspired by an abandoned Polish-Jewish girl whom Rahel Varnhagen had taken in and with whom Heine had fallen in love. Walzel (W, *1,* 471) thought the story worth repeating; Elster (E[2], *1,* 459) dismissed it without saying why.

of them are really cheerful. Number 1, the prologue, speaks of the emotional state anterior to these poems:

> In mein gar zu dunkles Leben
> Strahlte einst ein süßes Bild;
> Nun das süße Bild erblichen,
> Bin ich gänzlich nachtumhüllt. (E, *1*, 95)

It is more than a recapitulation, however, for the poem is another of Heine's songs about his songs, and it states quite clearly that his verses are a form of whistling in the dark, with a considerable function in driving the spooks away:

> Ich, ein tolles Kind, ich singe
> Jetzo in der Dunkelheit;
> Klingt das Lied auch nicht ergötzlich,
> Hat's mich doch von Angst befreit

In No. 3, one of Heine's cleverest early poems, the despair is untouched by nature and a pleasant view: in five stanzas he paints a pretty picture of a peaceful Romantic landscape, ending with a red-coated soldier pacing in front of his sentrybox; this *Schönheitsfehler* in the scene, with its political undertone, allows the poem to end with a growl of self-pity:

> Er spielt mit seiner Flinte,
> Die funkelt im Sonnenrot,
> Er präsentiert und schultert—
> Ich wollt', er schösse mich tot. (E, *1*, 97)

Number 2, the renowned song of the Lorelei, presents special problems, for it has been wrenched out of its context by a persistently seductive, if third-rate, piece of music; it takes considerable concentration to read the poem without Friedrich Silcher's tune running irrepressibly through one's head.[50] Frustration with the aura that the poem has acquired was expressed with characteristic waspishness by Karl Kraus in his philippic against the Heine tradition: "Ist es Einsicht in den lyrischen Wert eines Gedichtes, was den Gassenhauer, den einer komponiert hat, populär werden läßt?"[51] Andler's comment is drier and less surly: "Le musicien médiocre, Silcher, qui a composé l'air trainant sur lequel on chante le poème, n'a pas réussi à en detruire complètement la magie." [52] The whole complex of feeling described in the poem has departed from us:

> Die Zeit vergeht. Man stirbt nicht mehr beim Schiffen,
> bloß weil ein blondes Weib sich dauernd kämmt,

wrote Heine's most convincing successor in Germany, Erich Kästner.[53] Heine's poem is probably best comprehended by references to other treatments of the motif in his time.[54] Although there is a sixteenth-century Flemish folksong that shows remarkable verbal similarities to Heine's poem,[55] the legend of the Lorelei seems indisputably to have been invented by Clemens Brentano, whose poem about it appeared in his novel *Godwi* (1801). In this version of the tale, the girl has been abandoned by a knight and is languishing in her suffering; Her allure traps three knights on the rock, from which they are unable to descend. She herself lives in horror of her power over men:

> Herr Bischof, laßt mich sterben,
> Ich bin des Lebens müd,
> Weil jeder muß verderben,
> Der meine Augen sieht.[56]

Finally she dies in a plunge from the rock.

In Eichendorff's *Waldgespräch,* the Lorelei is also repentant and in addition bears a grudge against men:

> "Groß ist der Männer Trug und List,
> Vor Schmerz mein Herz gebrochen ist,
> Wohl irrt das Waldhorn her und hin,
> O flieh! Du weißt nicht, wer ich bin!" [57]

Eichendorff's friend Otto von Loeben also based a poem on Brentano's version; in some ways it is closer to Heine's and is probably his immediate source:* the intoxicating allure of the

* This is the belief of Elster, both in E, *1,* 427–28 and E², *1,* 455–56. Mücke, *Beziehungen zum deutschen Mittelalter,* p. 95, thought both Loeben and Heine were dependent on Aloys Schreiber's version of the story in *Handbuch für Reisende am Rhein* (2d ed. 1818). Ehrenzeller-Favre, *Loreley. Enstehung und Wandlung einer Sage* (Flensburg, 1948), p. 125, and Krogmann, "Lorelei. Geburt einer Sage," *Rhenisch-westfälische Zeitschrift für Volkskunde, 3* (1956), p. 183, are both satisfied

"Zauberfräulein" is stressed more than the Romanticized Christian elements of Brentano and Eichendorff, and in the first stanza a rhyme occurs that Heine picked up in the third stanza of his poem:

> Da wo der Mondschein blitzet
> Ums höchste Felsgestein,
> Das Zauberfräulein sitzet
> Und schauet auf den Rhein . . .
>
> Sie singt dir hold zum Ohre,
> Sie blickt dich töricht an,
> Sie ist die schöne Lore,
> Sie hat dirs angetan.[58]

Heine's poem, however, is only incidentally narrative. In the first stanza, the content is relegated to the imagination, as a tale that will not leave the poet's mind. The Lorelei herself is described in high and dramatic colors, but appears to have no interest in or relation to the man she fascinates and destroys. The poem is bitter and accusatory, but a considerable distance has been opened up between the poet and the now mythologized object of his infatuation; thus the final stanza begins with the words "Ich glaube" (E, *1*, 96), which have the distinct effect of separating the poet-narrator from the boatman.

The actual return home that gives the cycle its name is suggested in No. 6—"Als ich auf der Reise zufällig / Der Liebsten Familie fand" (E, *1*, 98)—but these weak verses about loneliness and isolation in company yield to a group of poems (Nos. 7–14) that tell of a light flirtation with a fisherman's daughter and contain scenes and images of the sea which vaguely anticipate *Die Nordsee*.[59] These poems are among the calmest thus far in *Buch der Lieder*, and they give some hints of the solution that *Die Nordsee* will present. With access to a wilder nature, the poet is freed from the diminutive images of the semicultivated Romantic landscape, and this stronger imagery supports a new poetic self-assurance and self-esteem, as in the final stanza of No. 8:

---

that Loeben was the direct source. However, Elster (E^2, *1*, 455–56) points out that Heine undoubtedly knew *all* the sources.

Mein Herz gleicht ganz dem Meere,
Hat Sturm und Ebb' und Flut,
Und manche schöne Perle
In seiner Tiefe ruht. (E, *1*, 100)

This posture receives direct statement in the famous last two stanzas of No. 13, in which the pain and stature of the poet are put into an intentionally arrogant equation and expanded to suggest considerations of a public nature that transcend private melancholy:

Ich bin ein deutscher Dichter,
Bekannt im deutschen Land;
Nennt man die besten Namen,
So wird auch der meine genannt.

Und was mir fehlt, du Kleine,
Fehlt manchem im deutschen Land;
Nennt man die schlimmsten Schmerzen,
So wird auch der meine genannt. (E, *1*, 102)

But this attitude is temporary and far from stable in *Die Heimkehr;* it is just one facet contending with others. In the Hamburg poems, beginning with No. 16, all the old pain rushes to the surface again, although the elegiac mood of this group shows a certain amount of distance achieved. By far the most important in this group and one of the high points of *Buch der Lieder* is the famous No. 20:

Still ist die Nacht, es ruhen die Gassen,
In diesem Hause wohnte mein Schatz;
Sie hat schon längst die Stadt verlassen,
Doch steht noch das Haus auf demselben Platz.

Da steht auch ein Mensch und starrt in die Höhe,
Und ringt die Hände vor Schmerzensgewalt;
Mir graust es, wenn ich sein Antlitz sehe—
Der Mond zeigt mir meine eigne Gestalt.

Du Doppeltgänger! du bleicher Geselle!
Was äffst du nach mein Liebesleid,

Das mich gequält auf dieser Stelle,
So manche Nacht in alter Zeit? (E, *1*, 105)

This "division into an acting and a watching self," as Prawer has pointed out,[60] has some clear antecedents—in a letter of October 27, 1816, to Christian Sethe, where Heine asserts that the mournful letter has been written by a pale alter ego;[61] in the drama *William Ratcliff,* where the word *Doppelgänger* describes the tormenting ghost of Ratcliff's father,[62] and in *Lyrisches Intermezzo* 38:

Ich und mein Schatten selbander,
Wir wandelten schweigend einher. (E, *1*, 80) [63]

In *Die Heimkehr* 20 the poetic potential of the split persona is fully realized. Prawer speaks of the lost "naïveté of suffering" and of the poet's "grief over the lost simplicity of grief," [64] but combined with the grief there is also fear, scorn, and perhaps an implied release. It does not seem to have been noticed that there are actually *three* personae in this poem: the immature, love-tormented poet of yesteryear, the "Doppeltgänger" in the present scene, who "apes" the suffering postures of the old persona, and the speaker of the poem, who watches that scene. This distinction is important because it corresponds to three ascending levels of self-awareness in *Buch der Lieder.* The posturing of the old persona is stylized in a fashion that is just a little ludicrous and theatrical—"Und ringt die Hände vor Schmerzensgewalt." The "Doppeltgänger," who is engaged in a reprise of this posture, is nevertheless at a certain remove from it because he is "aping," that is, foolishly imitating a past situation rather than responding directly to a present one. And the observing self asks quite simply: "Why are you doing this?" It is characteristic of the ultimate poetic attitude that the pain of days gone was real, has left its marks, and is to be respected—in its past context. But it must not be allowed to penetrate perpetually into the present. At this point the poet is afraid of the spectre of his own self; why does it continue to go through these motions like a ghost that will not be laid to rest? The whole complex, after all, has lost its relevance; the beloved is no longer even physically present in this place.

Both the shock and the criticism are stages in the process of overcoming.

From here through a dozen poems or so, there is a continuing analysis of the poetic posture—a casting about for a formulation that is both prideful and expressive of pain. In No. 21, there is an edgy repudiation of the *Lenore*-motif, in which the dead knight hauls his beloved away into the grave; here the poet asserts that he is alive and stronger than any of the dead. The unexpectedly rhymeless No. 24, "Ich unglücksel'ger Atlas," takes the position of the proud heart that has lost the great gamble; what is significant in this context is the Titantism of the self-imagery, which points ahead to the first *Nordsee* cycle:

> Die ganze Welt der Schmerzen, muß ich tragen,
> Ich trage Unerträgliches . . . (E, *1*, 107)

Furthermore, there seems to be a conscious adversion to the fiction of the "ich grolle nicht" poems in which the proud beloved is said to be "elend"; here it is the poet's own proud heart that has chosen and found misery:

> Du stolzes Herz, du hast es ja gewollt!
> Du wolltest glücklich sein, unendlich glücklich,
> Oder unendlich elend, stolzes Herz,
> Und jetzo bist du elend.

Number 25, with its scornful and, to some readers, offensive last line, "Madame, ich liebe Sie!", is part of the process of denigrating the beloved, who, as Prawer points out, "has no ear for the language of feeling." [65] Numbers 30, 32, and 33 uncertainly introduce a new and rather shaky fiction: that the poet lost his beloved by not speaking up in time. But this is something of a red herring and does not grow into an important element of the new attitude.

It is rather difficult to explain why Heine introduced here several poems that not only are not his best but also completely shift the universe of discourse. They are poems that point beyond *Buch der Lieder* to *Neue Gedichte*. The two satirical poems about the devil (Nos. 35 and 36) are not strong: No. 35 is mildly witty, but that the devil is a charming and urbane diplomat had not been news from the underground since Marlowe's *Faust*; and No. 36 is trivial. Number 37 is a clumsy piece of Christian Romanticism, doubtless meant to be parody, and No. 38, although a not uninteresting autobiographical poem about Heine's childhood with his sister, has nothing to do with the development of the persona despite the stereotype lament about the passing of faith, love, and loyalty. Number 39 expresses hope for a little love in a godless world, a sentimental anticipation of Nietzsche:

> Gestorben ist der Herrgott oben,
> Und unten ist der Teufel tot . . . .
> Und wäre nicht das bißchen Liebe,
> So gäb' es nirgends einen Halt. (E, *1*, 114)

What this access of religion and reminiscence means is not clear, at least to me. Perhaps it is a test of the ability of the persona to comment poetically without reference to the old emotional burden. If so, the test is by and large a failure.

In general, the poetic picture is chaotic and wildly uncertain at this point; it is as though a persistent clinging to the past and a struggle for a way of escape were at war with one another. Number 41, a dream-poem, imagines the beloved, worn-out and weary with a load of children, being comforted and supported by the infinitely kind and self-effacing poet; Prawer summarily and not unfairly characterizes it as gross self-indulgence.[66] Numbers 42 and 45, on the other hand, turn devastating satire upon the poet's own insistence on his theme. Number 42 begins with "Teurer Freund," an occasional signal of Heine's that the poet is about to subject himself to criticism and scorn:

> Teurer Freund! Was soll es nützen,
> Stets das alte Lied zu leiern?
> Willst du ewig brütend sitzen
> Auf den alten Liebes-Eiern? (E, *1*, 116)

Number 45 contains the most absurd of all the personae, the legendary Indian king who lusts after a cow:

> O, König Wiswamitra,
> O, welch ein Ochs bist du,

Daß du so viel kämpfest und büßest,
Und alles für eine Kuh! (E, *1*, 117)

But this kind of self-denigration, amusing as it may be, holds no solution; it is simply another version of the prostrate posture combined with scornful resentment of the beloved. A new note is struck in No. 43, a kind of wistful hope for the revival of the spirit that points ahead to the title, though not the content, of *Neuer Frühling:*

Wartet nur, es wird verhallen
Dieses Echo meiner Schmerzen,
Und ein neuer Liederfrühling
Sprießt aus dem geheilten Herzen, (E, *1*, 116)

and in No. 46:

Herz, mein Herz, sei nicht beklommen,
Und ertrage dein Geschick.
Neuer Frühling gibt zurück,
Was der Winter dir genommen. (E, *1*, 117)

But it is not easy to maintain this hope, and in No. 44, one of the finest poems in *Buch der Lieder,* the poet recognizes the persistence of the emotional state while at the same time trying to put a little backbone into the posture by reviving the self-image of the knight:

Nun ist es Zeit, daß ich mit Verstand
Mich aller Thorheit entled'ge;
Ich hab' so lang als ein Komödiant
Mit dir gespielt die Komödie.

Die prächt'gen Kulissen, sie waren bemalt
Im hochromantischen Stile,
Mein Rittermantel hat goldig gestrahlt,
Ich fühlte die feinsten Gefühle.

Und nun ich mich gar säuberlich
Des tollen Tands entled'ge,
Noch immer elend fühl' ich mich,
Als spielt' ich noch immer Komödie.

Ach Gott! im Scherz und unbewußt
Sprach ich, was ich gefühlet;
Ich hab' mit dem Tod in der eignen Brust
Den sterbenden Fechter gespielet. (E, *I*, 116–17)

The persona here is far from clearly drawn. At one level in the poem there is a struggle between genuine feeling and pose; at another is the problem of what new pose the persona, perfectly clear in his mind about the elements of his poetic biography, may now succesfully take.

It is not without significance that *Du bist wie eine Blume* suggests something of a turning point here; the self-awareness and the irony become both clearer and less intense, as in No. 48:

Kind! es wäre dein Verderben,
Und ich geb' mir selber Mühe,
Daß dein liebes Herz in Liebe
Nimmermehr für mich erglühe.

Nur daß mir's so leicht gelinget,
Will mich dennoch fast betrüben,
Und ich denke manchmal dennoch:
Möchtest du mich dennoch lieben! (E, *I*, 118)

This love-situation is in fact a new one, but since it is in a sense a reprise (No. 55), the poet understands it better:

Glaub nicht, daß ich mich erschieße,
Wie schlimm auch die Sachen stehn!
Das alles, meine Süße,
Ist mir schon einmal geschehn. (E, *I*, 120)

He is aware of his own irrationality and thus maintains a rational control over it (No. 54):

Teurer Freund, du bist verliebt,
Und dich quälen neue Schmerzen;
Dunkler wird es dir im Kopf,
Heller wird es dir im Herzen. (E, *I*, 120)

The poet plays at jealousy (No. 56) and finds himself, with some amusement, trapped in his own flirtation (No. 63):

Wer zum ersten Male liebt,
Sei's auch glücklos, ist ein Gott;
Aber wer zum zweiten Male
Glücklos liebt, der ist ein Narr. (E, *1*, 123)

After a group of occasional poems, there is an erotic intermezzo from No. 69 to No. 77, the first extended indication of a lighter love without the heavy burden of pain. Of some interest here are three poems that Heine removed from *Die Heimkehr* after one appearance; in them an effort is made to treat the erotic experience cynically and even to reduce it to the level of an obscenity:

Himmlisch war's, wenn ich bezwang
Meine sündige Begier,
Aber wenn's mir nicht gelang,
Hatt' ich doch ein groß Pläsir. (E, *2*, 13)[07]

It was usually Heine's custom to remove such things from his own canon on second thought;* here perhaps he felt that they led away from the sense of the group, which is to explore the possibility of a love relationship without emotional torment. The poems are in a number of ways parodistic of the old posture. In No. 71, the poet sends the moon off to comfort some other unhappy lover. The inevitable parting will not be bitter for him, as he has acquired a certain capacity for living in the present (No. 73):

Und willst du mich morgen verlassen,
So bist du doch heute noch mein,
Und in deinen schönen Armen
Will ich doppelt selig sein. (E, *1*, 129)

The poet, to be sure, cannot sustain his own interest in so easy-going an affair, and, in anticipation of the *Verschiedene* in *Neue Gedichte,* he ends in boredom (No. 77):

Von den weißen, schönen Armen
Fest und liebevoll umschlossen,

* It is oddly characteristic of Heine that as late as the fifth edition of *Buch der Lieder,* he found it appropriate to change "Busen" to "Schulter" in *Die Heimkehr* 73 (E, *1*, 525).

Lieg' ich jetzt an ihrem Herzen
Dumpfen Sinnes und verdrossen. (E, *1*, 130)

Die Heimkehr peters out somewhat toward the end; one suspects that the batch of student poems was inserted here to bring the total number to an even multiple of eleven as in *Lyrisches Intermezzo.* Only at the very end does a more substantial tone appear, and, indeed, the cycle appears to have not one epilogue, but two, for Nos. 87 and 88, though both are summations, sum up in different ways. Number 87, the famous *Der Tod, das ist die kühle Nacht,* reverts to the dream situation in a gloomy equation of love, death, poetry, and night. The Romantic vision, however, is fading; with tired wistfulness the poet hears in his dream the nightingale singing of love; it seems no longer to touch him. We know No. 88 in a less mature form from a letter to Rudolf Christiani of September 4, 1824, in which it appears that Heine had written the poem to accompany a volume of *Tragödien nebst einem lyrischen Intermezzo* sent to his friend Heinrich Straube.[68] Heine thus thought of it as applicable to either cycle, and, like the epilogues to *Lieder* and *Lyrisches Intermezzo,* it speaks of interring the dead remnants of love in a book of poems. But in this case the tone is not so much painful as expressive of the drying up of emotion. The struggle of *Die Heimkehr* has not produced a stable surrogate for the irretrievably lost illusions of love:

Jene Flammen sind erloschen,
Und mein Herz ist kalt und trübe,
Und dies Büchlein ist die Urne
Mit der Asche meiner Liebe. (E, *1*, 134)

Attached to *Die Heimkehr* are five moderately long poems; they are more experiments in forms contrasting to that of *Lyrisches Intermezzo* and *Die Heimkehr* than completely successful accomplishments. The first two and the fifth go back to 1822 and, of these, the first two are clearly dependent on Byron, although in content they advert to the love-situation in *Buch der Lieder. Götterdämmerung,* written in regular but rhythmically uneven blank verse, is a rather confused poem because traditional and borrowed elements are mixed with Heine's characteristic themes; the poem is dependent on Byron's *Darkness.*[69] There are actually two axes of meaning: the first is a contrast between the bright, cheerful spring and the unhappy mood of the poet; the second is a treatment of the traditional theme of *Vergänglichkeit*—the conviction that the world has no substantiality and is receptive illusion. This implies a projection of the private feelings of the poet into the structure of the universe in a way that is not really justified. On the one hand, the poet is the "bleicher Träumer" (E, *1*, 135) who will not join the cheerful throng on a pleasant May day; on the other, he sees "Lug und Trug und Elend" (E, *1*, 136) in human society, denies the uprightness of men, and dwells upon the decomposition of the body after death, which makes vain the fertility of the spring. The title of the poem refers to a vision in which the human dwarfs storm and desecrate the heavens, bringing desperation upon "der bleiche Gott" (E, *1*, 137)—an echo of the self-image of the "bleicher Träumer"—but this cosmic disaster yields to a more personal vision, in which the poet's angel, filled with love, is overwhelmed by a black goblin, thus bringing the heavens down with a crash. Even the warmest admirers of Heine will not argue, I think, that the orchestration of themes is very successful here. The two axes of the poem are at cross-purposes.

Ratcliff, another blank verse effort that is again dependent on a poem of Byron's, *The Dream,*[70] is a slight improvement in that it is thematically more unified. It has nothing to do with the tragedy *William Ratcliff* beyond the names of the characters; rather, it combines familiar motifs from *Buch der Lieder:* the repentant former beloved, married miserably to a wooden husband, and the songs that communicate the poet's awareness of her misery:

> Wie wußtest du, daß ich so elend bin?
> Ich las es jüngst in deinen wilden Liedern. (E, *1*, 140)

These themes were tolerable in the earlier development of *Buch der Lieder,* but by now they have become tiresome, especially in this narrative context.

The next two poems, *Donna Clara* and *Almansor,* are experiments with the so-called "Spanish" trochees, in these cases with assonance. Both poems are among the few in Heine's early writing that are concerned specifically with his Jewish feelings and, with the unimportant exception of *Belsatzar,* they are the only appearance of Jewish motifs in *Buch der Lieder.* Heine made much of *Donna Clara,* as he was wont to do when something he had written had not worked out well. In a letter to his friend Moser in November 1823,[71] he claims that the poem, in which an urbane Sephardic knight seduces an anti-Semitic noblewoman, reflects a personal experience in the *Tiergarten* in Berlin; he does not mention that there was also a literary source, a ballad by Fouqué.[72] Heine also claims that the poem was to be the first of a trilogy; in the second part the hero would be scorned by his own son who does not know him, and in the third the son, now a Dominican friar, would have become a persecutor of the Jews. But with that characteristic manner Heine assumed when he was not likely to write something he though he should, he tells Moser that it will probably be a long time before he gets around to writing it.[73] In a letter to Ludwig Robert three weeks later,[74] Heine seems more aware of the weaknesses of the poem—that what he had intended as a serious, objective presentation, had turned out to be an extended *plaisanterie.* The poem has at least as much to do with the hostilities arising out of his love situation as with his Jewish feeling. The punishing story of seduction in *Donna Clara* was more important to him than the revenge taken on behalf of the Jewish people.

Almansor, which is closer to the tragedy of that name than *Ratcliff* is to its namesake, is a better poem and undoubtedly the best of this group. Whereas *Donna Clara* is composed throughout with o-assonance—although the dark vowel is not necessarily in harmony with the sprightly trick played by the rabbi's son—*Almansor* is divided into three parts in which the different assonances support the content. The first part, in u-assonance, describes the heavy richness of the Moorish mosque at Cordova, which has been converted into a cathedral, and the gloominess of Christian ritual is compared unfavorably with the church's former glories:

> Und das ist ein Drehn und Winden
> Vor den buntbemalten Puppen,
> Und das blökt und dampft und klingelt,
> Und die dummen Kerzen funkeln. (E, *1,* 143)

In the light of these pejorative observations, Almansor's baptism "mit heiterm Antlitz" (E, *1,* 144) is bitingly sardonic. With the a-assonance of the second part, the tone brightens; Almansor loses himself in the lively whirl of Spanish society, and, with self-amused ambiguity, perjures himself in his flirtations:

> Er versichert jede Dame,
> Daß er sie im Herzen trage;
> Und "so wahr ich Christ bin!" schwört er
> Dreißigmal an jenem Abend. (E, *1,* 145)

But with the i-assonance of the third part, the tone becomes more nervous and high-pitched. Although Almansor has won his Christian Donna Clara, in her embrace he dreams ruefully and with growing hostility of the desecrated mosque; in one of Heine's most violent stanzas, Almansor imagines himself, like Samson, bringing the roof down on the heads of the Christians:

> Und sie brechen wild zusammen,
> Es erbleichen Volk und Priester,
> Krachend stürzt herab die Kuppel,
> Und die Christengötter wimmern. (E, *1,* 146)

That Heine has deposited in this poem some of his feelings about his conversion to Christianity seems clear enough, although the dating of the poem is uncertain.[75] It is interesting that Almansor is never seen to rouse himself to any action; his hostility remains in his fantasy world, whereas in reality he continues to recline in the tearful embrace of his beloved. The persistent relevance of all issues to the love situation, which distinguishes Heine's early poetry from his later work, is evident here, as it is in the preceding poem.

Die Wallfahrt nach Kevlaar generally gives Heine's interpreters some trouble: it is not easy to tell why this exercise in Christian Romanticism should appear at this point. The poem is a product of what has been called his madonna period;[76] Heine is reported to have written to his friend J. B. Rousseau in August, 1822, that he had composed it to show "daß der Verfasser nicht bloß wild und sinnlich, sondern auch fromm und kindlich dichten könne" (Hirth, *1,* 45). In a note to the poem Heine asserts that its inspiration came from a boyhood acquaintance who had actually performed the pilgrimage here described.[77] Most critics have seen it as an exercise in the objective presentation of a mystical faith; Bölsche calls it a "vollkommen harmonische Verschmelzung des poetischen Gehaltes in der mystischen Weltbetrachtung der Religion mit dem klaren Lichte geläuterter Erkenntnis des Wirklichen." [78] But he has missed the point; the poem, in its rhymes and static tableaux is a parody of the popular *Moritat*.[79] Moreover, the Mother of God heals Wilhelm's broken heart by causing him to die. It is another version of the hyperbole we have seen elsewhere, calculated to make the sufferings of the heart appear as massive and incurable as possible. It is the sufferings of one more persona that are in the foreground, and the naïve piety is only a setting. But both chronologically and in content the poem seems slightly out of place.

"Thalatta! Thalatta!" Thus begins the second *Nordsee* cycle, with the cry of Xenophon's ten thousand Greeks, or what remained of them, when, after the harrowing and costly retreat from Persia, they once again caught sight of the familiar sea, the element of their survival and superiority. It is most extraordinarily appropriate to the mood of these poems, and might have been even more appropriate to *Nordsee I* had Heine thought of it in time; in the second edition of *Reisebilder I,* Heine set the reference to Xenophon as a motto for both cycles.[80] The *Nordsee* poems are remarkable in every respect, and, although the impact of Heine's first experience of the sea is evident in a letter to Moser,* very little in Heine's previous poetry reflects the depth of the response. The brief North Sea idyll described in *Die Heimkehr* 7–14 is in style and intent integrated with that cycle; except for the cheerful flirtation with the fisher maiden, there is little in those verses that points to the power and emancipation of this group. In the collected edition that Heine and Campe discussed fruitlessly for many years, Heine intended to separate the *Nordsee* cycles form *Buch der Lieder* and put them in a separate volume

* To Moser, August 23, 1823, Hirth, *1,* 102. Through the years Heine's response to the sea remained enthusiastic. Cf. to Moser, October 14, 1826, and August 6, 1829, Hirth, *1,* 286, 395–96.

along with the prose essay called *Nordsee III*.* Whether this is a good solution is doubtful, although it is understandable that Heine thought the poems should be separated. There is a qualitative difference that represents a significant breakthrough. These poems are unlike anything Heine ever wrote before; they have no models to speak of,† and Heine never wrote anything like them again. They are a unique achievement serving a unique purpose at a particular time.

Despite Germany's long northern coastline on the rugged North Sea and the moody Baltic, the sea, up to Heine's time, had not played a large part in modern German literature. It is not at all easy to say why. Perhaps it is because many German writers lived their lives without ever having seen the sea, or, if at all, then more likely the bluer and quieter waters of the Italian peninsula. The Romantic landscape was a pretty one, and the far north of Germany is not pretty; it is gray and sandy, rough and damp, and wide in its prospects. In prose it is the characteristic achievement of Theodor Storm (1817–88) to have exploited that landscape; it is Heine's achievement in poetry. It is true, as Prawer remarks, that Heine's seascapes are "mindscapes" [81]—that is, rather than writing poems about the sea and the island on which he experi-

* To Campe, Nov. 12, 1846; June 7, 1848; Mar. 18–22, 1852; Hirth, *3*, 90, 142, 368. There is apparently no intention to follow Heine's wishes in this respect in the forthcoming Düsseldorf edition. See Manfred Windfuhr, "Zu einer kritischen Gesamtausgabe von Heines Werken," *Heine-Jahrbuch 1962*, p. 82.

† Elster's references to Tieck and Ludwig Robert in "Das Vorbild der freien Rhythmen Heinrich Heines," *Euphorion, 25* (1924), 63–80, are far from convincing. Gerhard Hoppe, *Das Meer in der deutschen Dichtung von Friedrich L. Graf zu Stolberg bis Heinrich Heine* (Marburg, 1929), discusses these, along with Fritz Stolberg and Goethe, without diminishing Heine's uniqueness. Fritz Strich in *Deutsche Klassik und Romantik* (5th ed. Bern and Munich, 1962), pp. 157–59, compares poems about the sea by Goethe and Eichendorff. It is clear from the comparison how much more plastic Heine's poems are, where for Goethe and the Romantic poet the sea has largely allegorical significance. If models are to be sought anywhere, it is undoubtedly in Homer, which Heine studied on Norderney in 1826 (to Friedrich Merckel, ca. Aug. 16, 1826; Hirth, *1*, 277); cf. Lydia Baer, "Anklänge an Homer (nach Voß) in der *Nordsee* Heinrich Heines," *Journal of English and Germanic Philology, 29* (1930), 1–17. L. L. Hammerich calls these poems a first turn to Hellenism and argues that the rhythms "bestehen ausschließlich aus Cola antiker Metra," in "Trochäen bei Heinrich Heine. Zugleich ein Beitrag zum Werdegang eines alten Germanisten," *Formenwandel. Festschrift Zum 65. Geburtstag von Paul Böckmann* (Hamburg, 1964), p. 403.

enced it, he writes about the impact of the sea upon his poetic consciousness and shows the result of the experience in a re-formed and greatly strengthened fictive persona. But the sea is vastly present in most of these poems: as the vision and the environment are wider, so the words are bigger; the rolling trochaic and dactylic polysyllables give a more expansive, harder, and louder sound than the weeping, whining, or sour wit of many of the earlier poems.[82] Even where the poems are melancholy—and many of them are—the speaker has grown in stature, his sadness is more dignified, and he has more certain control over a more difficult medium.

Students sometimes ask why it is that, except for a few scattered late poems, Heine never wrote free verse again and why the manifestly successful style of *Die Nordsee* is exhausted in the twenty-two poems of the two cycles, plus the finally rejected *Seekrankheit* [83] and the fragment *Sonnenaufgang*.[84] It is the sort of question that does not allow of a certain answer. We know that Heine thought very seriously about matters of form; Eduard Wedekind reports from a conversation: "Heine hat mir selbst gesagt, daß er über die Form, in welcher er den Gegenstand dieser Gedichte habe darstellen wollen, lange nicht mit sich habe einig werden können." * The answer is perhaps twofold: first, the free-flowing, expansive form of these poems was uniquely appropriate to Heine's poetic development at this point and to the public posture of the persona; secondly, judging from his own scattered comments, Heine generally thought of questions of metrics and rhythm in a carefully limited, technical, and rather conservative way, perhaps because his considerable glibness and capacity for manipulating the surface features of language required the discipline of more strictly bound forms. In any case, *Die Nordsee* is unique and its poems mark a very clear boundary in Heine's literary career.

It is significant that the first poem of the first cycle, *Krönung*, begins with "Ihr Lieder" (E, *I*, 163), for the topic of poetry is central to this new process of settling accounts with himself. These

* Houben, p. 73. Wedekind mentions the *Nordsee* poems in this connection, but that cannot be right, as the conversation took place in 1824. Cf. Heine's humorous remark that the rhythms will make the public seasick in his letter to Karl Simrock of May 26, 1826; Hirth, *I*, 265–66.

songs are to have a new quality and a new function, and it is remarkable with what skill Heine here manages to make his language do two things at once. On the one hand, there is an energy, excitement, and gaiety in the rhythms unlike anything he had written earlier:

> Ihr Lieder! Ihr meine guten Lieder!
> Auf, auf! und wappnet euch!
> Laßt die Trompeten klingen,
> Und hebt mir auf den Schild
> Dies junge Mädchen,
> Das jetzt mein ganzes Herz
> Beherrschen soll, als Königin.
>
> Heil dir! du junge Königin! (E, *1*, 163)

On the other hand, the language is mannered and courtly, using poetry itself as a metaphor in a way that calls up recollections of medieval courtly lyric—there is a continual play with alliteration in this poem—and thus establishing by only slight indirection the knight-persona of the poet. The new energy is combined with a new irony and sovereign distance; the gesture is playacting, a pose. The poems of which the poet speaks here—the "steifgeputzten Sonetten, / Stolzen Terzinen und höflichen Stanzen"—do not seem to have a life of their own, as they do in some of the more Romantic "songs about the songs" in the earlier parts of *Buch der Lieder*; rather, they are objects in the hand of the poet, used for his own purposes at his own discretion, here to decorate the new beloved.* And when it comes time, as it must, to refer to the sorrows of the past, it is done with an amused and urbane gesture, which also has the effect of putting the new "queen" somewhat in her place:

> Und huld'gend, auf rotem Sammetkissen,
> Überreiche ich dir
> Das bißchen Verstand,

* Hofrichter, *Heinrich Heine*, p. 42, argues that in this poem the new queen of his heart is his new poetry, an example of the kind of bad interpretation to be found in this good book.

Das mir aus Mitleid noch gelassen hat
Deine Vorgängerin im Reich. (E, *1*, 164)

In the next two poems, the poet more clearly defines his relationship to the sea. In No. 2, *Abenddämmerung,* he makes a connection between himself and the sea by a kind of transferred epithet in the first line, in which he applies to the seashore an adjective often previously applied to his own countenance:

Am blassen Meerestrande
Saß ich gedankenbekümmert und einsam. (E, *1*, 164)

Out of the rolling rhythms of the waves come back basic memories of the folktales and friends of childhood, and, in a subtle reflective turn, he reproduces the child's perspective on "die großen Mädchen":

Rosengesichter,
Lächelnd und mondbeglänzt,

who are to bring him so much grief in later years. The poem seems to me less an elegy on the lost paradise of childhood than a kind of recapitulation of the sources of the poet's stiuation; the persona begins to have a past that reaches beyond the immediate origins of the love situation. In No. 3, *Sonnenuntergang,* the poet creates his own myth of the sun and moon (as he is to do again, in more sarcastic tones, in the second cycle). The sun and the moon are separated by intrigue, and the polarization of their characters is reflected in men's differing responses to them. The sun is praised "Von stolzen, glückgehärteten Menschen" (E, *1*, 165), whereas the melancholy moon belongs to love and poetry. In what seems to be a non sequitur, except insofar as it arises out of the poetic context of this completely original mythologizing, the contrast in the world of the cosmos teaches a kind of humility and absorbs the lamentation of the poet, while at the same time allowing him to remain in a pose of some pride:

Ich aber, der Mensch,
Der niedrig gepflanzte, der Tod-beglückte,
Ich klage nicht länger. (E, *1*, 166)

In connection with these two poems it is worth mentioning another poetic advance characteristic of the *Nordsee* cycles: a partial emancipation from direct statement. There are almost no poems in the earlier sections of *Buch der Lieder* of which the literal meaning is not immediately clear. In many of these "mindscapes," however, we must try to divine the contours of an attitude and to piece together a portrait that is being sketched out with the broad and suggestive strokes of an ink-brush. On the other hand, and in contrast to this more general outline, there is a new precision of language in the strong compound adjectives that are characteristic of the cycle. A word such as "glückgehärtet" speaks volumes about the poet's relationship to the world of normal men.

Number 4, *Die Nacht am Strande,* picks up the theme of the flirtation with the fisher maiden from *Die Heimkehr* 7–14. It is set up entirely as an action of the poet, who descends upon the girl, like Zeus upon Semele, in all his godly majesty. He keeps the initiative by taking upon himself his own self-mockery; he deflates himself back to the human level by asking for tea with rum to avoid a cold:

> Und, ich bitte dich, koche mir Tee mit Rum;
> Denn draußen war's kalt,
> Und bei solcher Nachtluft
> Frieren auch wir, wir ewigen Götter,
> Und kriegen wir leicht den göttlichsten Schnupfen
> Und einen unsterblichen Husten. (E, *1,* 168)

The planes of reality and of the poetic imagination are managed simultaneously and openly by the poet; he controls the contrast, and out of it arises a cheerful pride. It should be noted that none of these feelings are forced on the poet by his situation with the girl or his relationship with the outside world; they are self-generated: the mocking irony is turned on and off as the poet wishes, and the persona of the god is by no means merely a joke, but a presentation of himself in a position highly superior to that of the girl. This new self-estimate then permits a new self-awareness; in No. 5 (*Poseidon*), the poet places himself on speaking terms with the god of the sea, from whom, however, he gets his comeuppance:

> Fürchte dich nicht, Poetlein!
> Ich will nicht im g'ringsten gefährden

Dein armes Schiffchen,
Und nicht dein liebes Leben beängst'gen
Mit allzu bedenklichem Schaukeln.
Denn du, Poetlein, hast nie mich erzürnt,
Du hast kein einziges Türmchen verletzt
An Priamos' heiliger Feste,
Kein einziges Härchen hast du versengt
Am Aug' meines Sohns Polyphemos,
Und dich hat niemals ratend beschützt
Die Göttin der Klugheit, Pallas Athene. (E, *1*, 169)

The poet, it seems, lacks daring and wisdom, but what of it? He can still strike back and call Poseidon's Amphitrite "das plumpe Fischweib."

Number 6, *Erklärung,* is a key poem in the *Nordsee* group and also to a certain extent in *Buch der Lieder* as a whole. Nowhere in it is there any mention of unrequited love or of elegiac pain, not necessarily because this is a new and happier love situation, but because the poet's love and his expression of it have by now almost completely emancipated themselves from their object. The only direct reference we get in the poem to the beloved herself is the single apostrophe in the seventh line, "du holdes Bild" (E, *1*, 170), and it is significant that the word "Bild" is used here, for it seems that "Agnes" lives chiefly in the now massively comprehended poetic imagination. The poem, furthermore, is about poetry in a more extravagant way than we have yet seen. Amidst the wildness of the seashore, the poet inscribes his confession of love in the sand; but the sea washes it out, just as the experience of the sea, temporarily at any rate, has washed away the earlier, less substantial poetic manner. So the poet, "mit starker Hand," tears a pine from the northern forests, dips it into the fire of Mt. Etna, and inscribes his confession of love indelibly upon the sky. This Titanism reminds one strongly of the "Laura" poems of Schiller's youth. But here the images are less cosmic than they are literary. The pine tree is torn out of the forests of the Romantic North and dipped in the fire of the Classical South; by this action the poet completely spans the dichotomy of Classicism and Romanticism pondered so urgently by the literary minds of the eighteenth and nineteenth centuries. The inscription is written on the eternal heavens, and there it will remain forever:

> Jedwede Nacht lodert alsdann
> Dort oben die ewige Flammenschrift,
> Und alle nachwachsende Enkelsgeschlechter
> Lesen jauchzend die Himmelsworte:
> "Agnes, ich liebe dich!"

The message, then, is intended only incidentally for "Agnes," but primarily for the universal literary audience of posterity. The poet's awareness of his own stature as a literary giant dwarfs the details of the love situation altogether. While this consciousness of poetic greatness seems always to have been with Heine in embryonic form, this is one of the first clear expressions of it. The image the poet gives here of his own poetry—"die ewige Flammenschrift"—is the strongest expression in *Buch der Lieder* of the source from which the salvation of the persona comes.

In the next three poems, the poet defines more subtly and somewhat less self-assertively his relationship to the sea. In No. 7, *Nachts in der Kajüte,* with a series of hypnotic rhythms, repetitions, and alliterations, he mulls his love. The sting is out of love now because the girl has become insignificant relative to the greatness of the poet and his harmony with the vast seascape:

> Du kleines, junges Mädchen,
> Komm an mein großes Herz;
> Mein Herz und das Meer und der Himmel
> Vergehn vor lauter Liebe. (E, *I*, 171)

But, as in the address to Poseidon, the poet is not to indulge in these self-satisfied reveries without being cut down to size, for the cosmos is still larger than he:

> An die bretterne Schiffswand,
> Wo mein träumendes Haupt liegt,
> Branden die Wellen, die wilden Wellen;
> Sie rauschen und murmeln
> Mir heimlich ins Ohr:
> "Bethörter Geselle!

Dein Arm ist kurz, und der Himmel ist weit,
Und die Sterne droben sind festgenagelt
Mit goldnen Nägeln,—
Vergebliches Sehnen, vergebliches Seufzen,
Das beste wäre, du schliefest ein." (E, *1*, 172)

This insight plunges the poet back, in the final two stanzas, into a resurgence of the earlier self-pity; he dreams he is lying in his grave while the eyes of his beloved gleam lovingly out of the starry sky. Of course, he has put them there.

Despite this setback the poet maintains his dialogue with nature. In No. 8, *Sturm,* the poet, uneasy for his safety in the storm at sea, begs the sea, as the mother of beauty (Aphrodite) and the grandmother of love (Eros), for mercy on the grounds that his heart resounds in praise of beauty and is the plaything of Eros. But the sea does not respond:

Vergebens mein Bitten und Flehn!
Mein Rufen verhallt im tosenden Sturm,
Im Schlachtlärm der Winde.
Es braust und pfeift und prasselt und heult,
Wie ein Tollhaus von Tönen! (E, *1*, 173)

Nature is harsh. Though not unrelated to the poet, it does not reflect his inner concerns in a benign, Romantic way. In his journey into the wider cosmos, the poet has exposed himself in a thrilling but dangerous manner. In No. 9, in what seems to be a genre picture of the peaceful sailors on a calm day, the "Meeresstille" is broken, first by the captain, who snarls at the cabin boy for swiping a herring, and then by sudden death, as a gull plunges from the sky and snatches its prey from the water.

The last three poems of *Nordsee I* are a trilogy dealing, as it were, with the proper use of the sea. In No. 10 (*Seegespenst*), the poet is hypnotized by a Romantic vision of a city under the sea*—a vision concentrated around the now mythical, long yearned-for girl; in a series of short, rhythmic lines, the hypnotized poet is lured ever closer to the poetic vision and thus to dissolution until

* The sunken city recurs in Heine's writings in 1826, 1832, and 1833 (E, *3*, 102; E, *5*, 262; E, *4*, 115).[85]

the rough captain seizes him by the foot and calls him back to reality:

> Aber zur rechten Zeit noch
> Ergriff mich beim Fuß der Kapitän,
> Und zog mich vom Schiffsrand,
> Und rief, ärgerlich lachend:
> Doktor, sind Sie des Teufels? (E, *1*, 176–77)

The poet must resist his tendency to plunge helplessly into unreal and destructive reveries of the imagination. For it is not the depths of the sea with which he should concern himself, but its surface. In the next poem (*Reinigung*), he repudiates the "wahnsinniger Traum" (E, *1*, 177); he flings after it his pain, sins, foolishness, and, significantly, his hypocrisy, whereupon the wind comes up to carry the ship and his joyous, freed soul over the surface. To be sure, the awareness of the depth and the danger are still there, for, with one of those extraordinary adjective compounds characteristic of *Die Nordsee,* the sea over which the poet sails so joyously is a "stillverderbliche Fläche."

The last poem, called *Frieden,* has always been something of a puzzle and perhaps must be chalked up as a failure. It is again a vision, but this time of the Saviour in the heavens, stretching his hands in blessing over the land and sea below. This description of cosmic peace under benevolent governance seems generated by what has occurred in the two poems preceding, but Heine is always to be suspected when he does such things. The original version of the poem had an additional final section that he removed in *Buch der Lieder.* There the tone turns satirical and a little mean; the poet heaps scorn on the pious Philistines claiming that they could not have created this picture, thus relegating it to a poetic fiction. The language is rough and accusatory, and has something of a student quality, in that the treatment of an attitude toward the Philistines is taken over completely from the *Sturm-und-Drang* tradition. What it has to do with the content of *Nordsee I* is not clear, but the shorter, later version of the poem is even less clear, unless we are to sense an undercurrent of satire and see a display of poetic virtuosity in it. Even so, it seems a weak note on which to end the cycle.

The general tone of *Nordsee II* is not quite the same as that of the first cycle. Heine wrote to his friend Merckel that he felt much less cheerful on his second Norderney vacation than on the first,[86] and the difference is reflected in the atmosphere of the second cycle. Despite the high-hearted opening poem, *Meergruß*, the quality of euphoria—an important part of the mood of the first cycle—is considerably dampened in the second; darker notes are audible, as though a more realistic adjustment of attitude were in progress. But in a way, the realization of the poet-persona is firmer, precisely because it takes these gloomier perspectives into account. There is, however, nothing gloomy about the opening poem, which is entirely in the spirit of the first cycle. The equation of the persona with Xenophon's Ten Thousand (all of them!) establishes exactly the kind of heroic posture the poet is after:

> Sei mir gegrüßt . . . ,
> Wie einst dich begrüßten
> Zehntausend Griechenherzen,
> Unglückbekämpfende, heimatverlangende,
> Weltberühmte Griechenherzen. (E, *I*, 179)

The adjective "heimatverlangend" refers also to the poet's longing for the sea; in the third stanza he establishes a kind of "elective affinity" with the sea by remembering that it was the source of his pretty childhood playthings:

> Und alte Erinnrung erzählt mir aufs neue
> Von all den lieben, herrlichen Spielzeug,
> Von all den blinkenden Weihnachtsgaben,
> Von all den roten Korallenbäumchen,
> Goldfischchen, Perlen und bunten Muscheln. . . .

There is a change in the quality of his sorrows, too, for he describes the persecution by "des Nordens Barbarinnen" (E, *I*, 180) in terms that imply their pursuit of him rather than vice versa.

With No. 2 (*Gewitter*), the sea becomes darker and more threatening. The travails of a boat in a storm are watched from the shore and described with images from Greek mythology. The substance of the poem is the familiar and ancient allegory of life as a sea voyage. The stress is on danger, and the sailor barely manages to control the ship; as he watches the compass, he appeals to the twin patrons of mariners, Castor and Polydeuces. Despite the discipline and the Classical rhetoric of this poem, there are few others in *Buch der Lieder* that appear to penetrate so far behind the various personae to the personality of the poet himself. The generalized sense of threat and fear, emancipated from any specifics about the love situation, the feeling of being just barely in control of a stormy and threatened career, seem more basic than any of the usual poetic postures; in *Gewitter* we are looking at the thin edge of Heine's courage. In the next poem, *Der Schiffbrüchige,* the poetic posture is resumed, and it is a melancholy one indeed. The poet, with hope and love lost, is shipwrecked on the beach; before him is the wasteland of the water; behind him, misery; above him, a gray sky. The rain cycle, described mythologically, is useless, like his own life, and the memory of the lost beloved is called up in powerful tones. The poem ends in a gesture of total despair that is unlike anything in the first cycle:

> Schweigt, ihr Wogen und Möwen!
> Vorüber ist alles, Glück und Hoffnung,
> Hoffnung und Liebe! Ich liege am Boden,
> Ein öder, schiffbrüchiger Mann,
> Und drücke mein glühendes Antlitz
> In den feuchten Sand. (E, *I*, 183)

The demons are once again out of the box into which the poet tried to put them in his several epilogues.

The sardonic low-point of the cycle is reached with No. 5 (*Der Gesang der Okeaniden*). The poet-figure, here described in the third person, sits gloomily groaning at the sea. With great bitterness and what seems like a parody of his own Homeridic rhetoric in *Die Nordsee,* he praises his love in contrast to the bitter life of the gulls:

> Schwarzbeinigte Vögel,
> Mit weißen Flügeln Meer-überflatternde,
> Mit krummen Schnäbeln Seewasser-saufende,
> Und tranigtes Robbenfleisch-fressende,
> Eu'r Leben ist bitter wie eure Nahrung!
> Ich aber, der Glückliche, koste nur Süßes! (E, *I*, 185)

The fiction of the girl longing for him is aroused with heavy sarcasm:

> Sie liebt mich! sie liebt mich! die holde Jungfrau!
> Jetzt steht sie daheim am Erker des Hauses,
> Und schaut in die Dämmerung hinaus auf die Landstraß',
> Und horcht und sehnt sich nach mir—wahrhaftig!
> Vergebens späht sie umher und sie seufzet,
> Und seufzend steigt sie hinab in den Garten,
> Und wandelt in Duft und Mondschein,
> Und spricht mit den Blumen, erzählet ihnen,
> Wie ich, der Geliebte, so lieblich bin
> Und so liebenswürdig—wahrhaftig!
> Nachher im Bette, im Schlafe, im Traum,
> Umgaukelt sie selig mein teures Bild,
> Sogar des Morgens, beim Frühstück,
> Auf dem glänzenden Butterbrote,
> Sieht sie mein lächelndes Antlitz,
> Und sie frißt es auf vor Liebe—wahrhaftig!

Ruthlessly, with the sarcastic refrain "wahrhaftig!", the poet tears to shreds the occasionally recurring fiction-within-a-fiction in *Buch der Lieder*—that the beloved in fact longs for him—and throws onto the heap the remains of the newer fiction from *Nordsee I*—that he is himself attractive; by means of the language in the last lines of the stanza he manages also to work in an insult to the girl. The gulls merely giggle, but the Oceanids sing to him sympathetically; they acknowledge his right to suffering and take cognizance of his murdered hopes and petrified heart, although also observing that his boasting borders on insanity: he is a stubborn fool. The song of the Oceanids is the *first and only external objective recognition* of the persona in *Buch der Lieder* as the poet wants to project it, and because there is still such a residue of unwanted feelings, this recognition is arrived at with sardonic irony. The poet has been understood, and the (admittedly somewhat limping) equation of the persona with Prometheus acknowledges also his stubborn pride and god-like stature, battered though it may be. Having given this acknowledgment, the Oceanids, like

Oceanus in Aeschylus' *Prometheus Bound* (ll. 308–31), advise "Prometheus" to accept his burden and honor the gods. They disappear into the yawning night, but this first experience of objective sympathy releases the poet into tears and thus out of impenetrable grief.

Der Gesang der Okeaniden is the last key poem in *Buch der Lieder*. What follows is interesting, but serves only as an adjustment of the posture and the release achieved in No. 5. The following poem, *Die Götter Griechenlands,* named, no doubt, after Schiller's long poem of the same title, disregards the advice of the Oceanids and casts off the gods that have more or less accompanied the poet throughout the two cycles. It is a farewell to the Classical rhetoric from which the discipline of these poems has in part been drawn:

> Ich hab' euch niemals geliebt, ihr Götter!
> Denn widerwärtig sind mir die Griechen,
> Und gar die Römer sind mir verhaßt. (E, *1,* 188–89)

The gods are dethroned and mere ghosts of themselves, arousing only the pity of the mortal poet (the first indication of what Heine will have to say of the gods in his essay of 1853, *Die Götter im Exil*). The poem ends with the disappearance of the melancholy moon and an image of victorious calm:

> Also sprach ich, und sichtbar erröteten
> Droben die blassen Wolkengestalten,
> Und schauten mich an wie Sterbende,
> Schmerzenverklärt, und schwanden plötzlich.
> Der Mond verbarg sich eben
> Hinter Gewölk, das dunkler heranzog;
> Hoch aufrauschte das Meer,
> Und siegreich traten hervor am Himmel
> Die ewigen Sterne.

There is a last pessimistic note in No. 7 (*Fragen*) in which the poet puts to the sea the cosmic questions and receives no answer:

> "Sagt mir, was bedeutet der Mensch?
> Woher ist er kommen? Wo geht er hin?

Wer wohnt dort oben auf goldenen Sternen?"

Es murmeln die Wogen ihr ew'ges Gemurmel,
Es wehet der Wind, es fliehen die Wolken,
Es blinken die Sterne gleichgültig und kalt,
Und ein Narr wartet auf Antwort. (E, *1,* 190)

This reminds us strongly of some of Heine's very late poems, particularly the first of the group *Zum Lazarus* in *Gedichte 1853 und 1854*.[87] In this context its function seems to indicate both a sobering of the intellect and a gradual emancipation from the sea, which has become dumb now that it has served its poetic purpose. It is significant that the persona is described as a "Jüngling-Mann" (E, *1,* 190), as though the boundary between adolescence and manhood (Heine was nearly thirty!) had been reached.

If this interpretation of the *Nordsee* cycles thus far is at all correct, it must be said that No. 8 (*Der Phönix*) comes as a disappointment. It revives quite unexpectedly the fiction that the poet's love is secretly returned, and without any apparent irony or criticism. All that can be said is that the poem appears to be in the wrong place and that Heine's eye for order and arrangement failed him here.[88] It is placed where it is because the scene is supposed to have taken place on the deck of the ship on the way home, and thus it fits chronologically into the narration of the journey; but otherwise it is thematically jarring and, despite its pleasant rhythms and careful structure (it was originally two poems, one echoing the other), Heine probably would have done well to scrap it. The following poem, *Im Hafen,*[89] is, however, a genuine tour de force; with each succeeding stanza, the familiar concerns of the poet swim about ever more disjointedly in his increasing intoxication in the *Ratskeller* of Bremen. It is not, I hope, a violation of critical purity to point out that our amusement at this wryly cheerful poem is heightened by our knowledge that Heine was very temperate in his consumption of alcohol.

The *Epilog* is a quiet-spoken defense of love and poetry. It is significant, not so much for its content, which draws upon Romantic imagery and conventional disdain for the practical insensitives, but for its tone, which contrasts notably with the other epilogues of *Buch der Lieder*: here there is no agonized effort to bury past pains and lay persistent ghosts to rest; lyric poetry is gentle, pleasant, and controlled; it has lost its exacerbating urgency, which it is not to regain in Heine's career for many years to come.

What are we to say of this poetic performance of just about a decade? It seems hardly sufficient to dispose of it as Ludwig Marcuse does: "Heine's suffering was genuine and also a pose. By his parade of suffering he relieved his pain; he flaunted his suffering, and thereby mitigated it. This technique of alleviation by self-dramatization was also connected with his other method of relief by self-torment—by artificially increasing his distress, he actually dulled it."[90] There is truth in these remarks, but *Buch der Lieder* is rather more than an artificially self-lacerating, Rousseauistic confession in verse, and in any case we know too little about Heine's inner agonies to assume that they were less intense, in their own way, than the laments of the poetic persona. Purely as a literary phenomenon, *Buch der Lieder* is one of the most extraordinary poetic struggles in the history of letters. Out of the clay and stone and the worn and tarnished semiprecious gems of an inherited and borrowed language, with trembling strength, Heine formed and sculpted a figure, a poet as he should be. The road out of the slough of despond was full of traps, and the fictive persona fell into every one of them and struggled out again. Love and pain, weakness and self-indulgence, vanity and humiliation, all somehow had to be overcome and put into perspective. The vision had to be turned outward—and this is the great experience of the sea. Sovereignty and urbanity, gesture and pose, wit and intelligence, skill and mastery, and, above all, self-awareness, as opposed to resentment and undifferentiated self-pity, had to be molded by force into a public portrait somehow commensurate with the poetic genius out of which it was created. This achievement must have meant a very great deal to Heine. It certainly has to the generations that have come after.

CHAPTER 3

The Elusive Drama: *Almansor* and *William Ratcliff*

> Was helfen aber alle Künste des Talents, wenn aus einem Theaterstücke uns nicht eine liebenswürdige oder große Persönlichkeit des Autors entgegenkommt!
>
> —GOETHE

A frustrated fascination with the drama is a continuing motif in the history of German literature in the nineteenth century; many of the major post-Romantic writers wrestled with the genre, usually with disappointing results. Mörike, for example, whose gifts surely did not lie in this direction, struggled repeatedly with no success whatever;[1] and Gottfried Keller, who had made any number of fruitless efforts, responded to the honors tendered to him on his seventieth birthday by growling that it was absurd to praise a writer who had not even produced a good play.[2] Today one must look far and wide to find even the more substantial achievements of the age, the dramas of Hebbel and Grillparzer, actually performed.

The massive theoretical stature accorded the drama is epitomized by Hegel's aesthetics, climaxed by his spectacular definition of tragedy and the announcement that the drama was the highest form not only of literature but of all art.[3] The disappointing record of the nineteenth century in the drama indicates that the *Weltgeist* was perhaps not as thoroughly at home in Germany as Hegel may have thought. Certainly there were a number of political and sociological considerations in the German situation to which Hegel was relatively insensitive, but which no doubt had some part in preventing the most public of the literary arts from flourishing. However, apart from the pervasive example of Shakespeare, and whatever the workings of the *Weltgeist* may or may not have been, the wistful preoccupation with the drama probably is closely bound up with its public character. Among the motivations that impelled the writers of the time, one may suppose a desire for prestige and the urgent wish to achieve contact and communication with a wider segment of the population. Since the time of Lessing the interest in a national theater as an ideal substitute for the apparently unachievable German unity had occupied many literary minds. Goethe's career, so far as the public was aware of it, had begun with a great, sprawling drama, and it was to end with the completion of the most renowned dramatic poem in world literature; his best-known novel after *Werther* dealt largely with the life of the theater. Schiller, whose stature in the public mind was greater than Goethe's until well along in the century, became something of a national cult. Furthermore, in the course of time three liberal writers achieved their best successes in this branch of art—Karl Gutzkow with his entertaining and sometimes not uninteresting plays, and Heinrich Laube and Franz Dingelstedt as theater managers. How important the theater was as a channel to public attention can be seen from the early career of Ludwig Börne, who was obliged to write drama criticism in order to exercise any journalistic influence.

These or similar considerations may well have been in Heine's mind when he undertook to write tragedies. He was not to have any luck with them or with any of his other dramatic efforts. George Eliot's witty remark that with the two tragedies Heine had recovered from the "chicken-pox of authorship" [4] was not quite correct. Strodtmann tells us that Heine was continually plagued by the desire to write dramatic works,[5] but the efforts were all abortive. He apparently conceived and perhaps even worked on a tragedy in 1823 and 1824,[6] but the plan seems to have been dropped amid legal studies and preparations for *Der Rabbi von Bacherach*. In 1851, Heine mentions an operetta that was destroyed by fire and an opera that was lost.[7] To what extent any of these works existed is not known. Heine's comment to Laube in 1850, that he would have written one drama after the other if Laube had got the directorship of a theater fifteen years before,[8] is, undoubtedly, just talk. As for the completed tragedies, no one is ever likely to succeed in revising the low regard in which they have almost always been held, and no one but students of Heine need be obliged to read them. Nevertheless, for our purposes they merit some attention, for they reflect quite exactly the development of Heine's poetic consciousness at this stage in his career. Furthermore, the plays are very different from one another, and Heine himself had a very different view of each. After a good deal of initial enthusiasm,[9] he repudiated *Almansor* and its hypertonic diction for good and sound reasons.[10] He continued, however, perversely and somewhat inexplicably, to plug *William Ratcliff* until almost the end of his life.[11] Neither of these works is totally lacking in a certain rudimentary talent; Heine paid a good deal of attention to the theater, especially in Paris, and his friend Laube made some claims for Heine's sense of dramatic form.[12]

Almansor was written, with much labor and attention, in the summer of 1820 and the winter of 1820–21; thus it is contemporaneous with some of the *Romanzen* of *Junge Leiden* and the early poems of *Lyrisches Intermezzo,* as well as with the instruction in poetics Heine received from August Wilhelm Schlegel. *William Ratcliff* was written at one burst during the last days of January 1822, and is roughly contemporaneous with the remainder of *Lyrisches Intermezzo* and the earliest poems of *Die Heimkehr.* The tragedies come, therefore, at a crucial stage in the development of the poetic persona. Heine was quite voluble about the genesis of these works, and it is rather easier than usual to see what was on his mind while he was composing them. The most revealing document is an essay Heine wrote for a Berlin magazine in the summer of 1821 on a play called *Tassos Tod,* written by a casual friend, Wilhelm Smets. The essay is long, pompous, and not very well written; Weckmüller identified in it traces of an "academic" style soon to be abandoned.[13] It antedates the brilliant prose style of the *Reisebilder* and allows one to sense the embarrassment Heine must have felt at writing both justly and kindly of a friend's clearly indifferent achievement. Heine took the opportunity to expatiate at considerable length on general questions of dramaturgy: the piece touches upon Shakespeare versus the

French theater, the three unities, Greek tragedy, rhyme, and metrics, and it ends with some fairly muddled observations about the ethical import of the theater. The most interesting part of the essay contains remarks that clearly bear on Heine's own experience with *Almansor.*

Kurt Sternberg has argued that the essay sets out a dramaturgical program that *Almansor* fulfills.[14] In this he is certainly mistaken; as Mutzenbecher had observed some years before,[15] Heine's argument explains something about his reasons for his turn to the drama, but they imply a critique of his first effort. He begins by saying that the lyric is the most primitive form of poesy, and that as a poet matures he becomes concerned with objective clarity and finds his way to the epic and dramatic genres. This line of argument, which is meant to apply to the historical development of literature as well as to the development of the individual poet, is probably influenced by Herder, but it is significant in this context not only because of the concern with the problem of objectivity but because it is so early a prefiguration of the suspicion of poetry that was to trouble Heine in the 1830s. He goes on to say that the drama is more objective than the epic because the narrator is excluded. In this Heine is, on the whole, wrong, both theoretically and with respect to his own tragedies: a play, depending on its structuring of the dramatic problem and the relative grouping of the characters, can certainly have a subjective perspective similar to the narrative perspective of the novel; a classical case in point is Goethe's *Egmont.** Thus Heine's demand for "die allerstrengste Unterdrückung der hervorquellenden Subjektivität" (E, 7, 155) seems theoretically somewhat irrelevant. It is not irrelevant, however, to the urgent desire to objectify the poetic persona and gain some distance from it, a desire that seems to lie behind the whole dramatic undertaking. Heine takes off from the supposed subjectivity of the lyric to arrive at a critique of *Tassos Tod* that quite obviously applies also to *Almansor*; he objects that most of Smets's characters speak in the same tone, with the same lyrical language, and adds, "Das ist ein Fehler, dem fast

* I tried to show some of the consequences of this kind of perspective in "On the Structure of Goethe's *Egmont,*" *Journal of English and Germanic Philology,* 62 (1963), 241–51.

kein lyrischer Dichter in seinen dramatischen Erstlingen entging" (E, 7, 162). But the language, overwrought though it may be, is not really what is wrong with *Almansor*; *William Ratcliff* demonstratively avoids the lyricism of *Almansor*, but it is not a good play. Anyway, judging from a passage in *Über die französische Bühne* of 1837, Heine seems to have believed in the long run that dramatic diction should be declamatory and nonrealistic.[16] Heinz Seeger has pointed out, in contradiction to critics who have been too inclined to follow Heine's train of thought in this matter, that the inadequacy of his plays does not lie in the obtrusion of the lyric self, but in the lack of sustaining action.[17] This, in turn, is a problem of the characterization of the persona.

When Heine published the first fragments of *Almansor*, he called it a "dramatisches Gedicht" (E, 2, 517) rather than a tragedy, and the verses that serve as a motto call it a "Lied" (E, 2, 250). Thus Heine showed from the beginning his awareness of the lyrical quality of his style that he was eventually to regard as the major weakness of the play. But the lushness of the language is not necessarily inappropriate to the oriental setting and is in any case often not unattractive. Here and there the diction achieves genuine intensity, and there is not a reader today, I expect, who will fail to be struck by those uncannily prophetic lines of Hassan: "dort wo man Bücher / Verbrennt, verbrennt man auch am Ende Menschen" (E, 2, 259). Nor, when one thinks, for example, of *Romeo and Juliet*, is Heine's mannered lyricism entirely incongruent with the Shakespearean reminiscences that are inevitable in almost any serious German play of this period. There are, of course, quite a number in *Almansor*. Most notable among them is the similarity of the pair Diego and Enrique to Shakespeare's Iago and Roderigo; less felicitous is the completely unexpected appearance of the "ghost" of Almansor's father giving grim advice and even worse the lame attempt to explain this borrowing from *Hamlet* as a natural occurrence. Of general Shakespearean provenance, too, by way of Heine's well-developed sense of the absurd, is the finely comic figure of the recent Christian convert Pedrillo, who has difficulty in adjusting his mode of cursing to the symbols of the new religion. The Shakespearean inheritances, among which the expressive style ought perhaps to be numbered, do not weaken the play. The decisive failure of *Almansor* must be sought elsewhere: the play has two separate themes that Heine did not succeed in unifying. There is a little evidence in the play itself that he was aware of this.

Almansor is, first of all, a play of protest against Christianity—a polemical expression of Jewish resentment[18]—although it is considerably tempered by an effort to present positive, kindly representatives of Christianity in the figures of Aly and, to some extent, Zuleima. Heine's Spanish Moors, defeated, oppressed, forced to apostasy and helpless in their rage, reenact the situation of the Jews of Germany as Heine then felt it to be. But his treatment of the theme is emotional rather than critical, static rather than dramatic. It is, besides, continually being crowded out by the theme that genuinely preoccupied Heine in these years—his unrequited love. It is this situation in terms of which Almansor understands himself and that generates the poetry of the play; in turn, it is Heine's poetic sensibility that determines Almansor's attitude toward the Christians. Behind Heine's reflections on "objectivity" in the essay on Smets's *Tassos Tod* lies the desire to give the persona a wider and more meaningful context. The attempt failed because Heine had not yet developed the persona to the point where the love-despair had been sufficiently mastered. This is all too evident even in the mechanics of the play: Bölsche remarks in his plain-spoken way, "Zuleima—und das bricht den Stab über den ganzen 'Almansor'—stößt den Jugendgeliebten nicht kalt zurück, weil das Stück es notwendig fordert, sondern weil Amalie Heine ihren Vetter Heinrich Heine so behandelt hat." [19] We are still in the atmosphere of *Junge Leiden*; the persona does not yet have enough independence from his own demeaning reality.

But the process is observably in motion. In *Almansor,* as in *William Ratcliff,* Heine employs one of his chief methods of strengthening the stature of the persona, that of supplying him with manly and heroic courage, which in Heine's mind was generally synonymous with readiness to fight. Thus it happens that, at the very beginning, Almansor is obliged to fight the members of his household before the characters recognize one another—a clumsy application of a tiresome dramatic convention. But this heroic posture cannot be sustained in the play because the larger issue—the conflict of the Moors and the Christians—is constantly being upstaged by Almansor's amorous woe. Heine seems to be quite aware of this difficulty because early in the play he has Hassan call Almansor's attention to it.[20] But it is to no avail; Almansor's self-image lies wholly within the realm of love, as becomes apparent when he identifies himself with the hero of a medieval Persian love poem, a literary allusion that he repeats at the final catastrophe.[21] After the account of his exile, Almansor describes his appearance as changed beyond recognition by grief. It is not the exile itself that has brought this about, however, but his broken heart; it is the portrait of the persona of *Buch der Lieder* at its most self-pitying. His heroic stature is thus unconvincing. In his long monologue before Aly's palace he becomes aware of his own impotence;[22] his rhetoric avails nothing in the political context, and so the Sturm-und-Drang echoes sound feeble and tentative.

It follows from this—and here we are close to one of the most problematic characteristics of Heine's mind—that Almansor's aversion to Christianity is expressed in aesthetic terms and does not proceed from faith; his perspective remains within the limits of "poesy." Zuleima tries to bridge the gap between Almansor and Christianity with the concept of love, and this immediately captures Almansor's attention so that he is moved to accept the idea of conversion. But Christian love is of no interest to him; what he cares about is Zuleima's love, and since the real difficulty between them is not the incompatibility of religions but the fact that this is Zuleima's wedding day, the spell is abruptly broken and Almansor breaks out in a furious diatribe against her falsity; later he adopts a transparent pose of uncaring, sadistic lustfulness. All this corresponds exactly to the thrashing about of the persona in *Lyrisches Intermezzo.* After this turn of events Almansor is reduced to total inactivity and self-pity; the poetic metaphors of nature lose their beauty with the loss of love. Hassan tries to get him to concentrate on the larger atrocities, but Almansor's attention can only be mobilized around his personal loss. It is significant that in the abduction scene, Heine has Almansor babbling "Zuleima! Mahomet!" (E, 2, 304), as though to demonstrate the confusion of the two themes. At the end, however, the religious and historical context vanishes altogether; the suicide is a leap into the trappings of Heine's own love poetry: flowers, butterflies, and nightingales.

It is not only Hassan's running critique of Almansor that makes the work seem so uneasy. The basic problem is raised in what is the oddest feature of *Almansor*—the unexpected appearance of a chorus toward the end of the play. This ill-advised experiment is obviously related to the classicistic preoccupations that appear generally in the essay on Smets, particularly with regard to the dramatic unities. The experiment is an awkward failure; it is completely unclear who the chorus might be, and it has no structural function whatever in the drama. Abundantly clear, however, is that the chorus is an effort to revive by other means the perspective upon the external world that the main character himself is unable to keep in view. Eccentrically, the chorus produces a wild alienation effect by adverting anachronistically to Spanish political matters of the 1820s. Brecht, though, would not have approved, since there is no political relevance in the dramatic action to be pointed up by this device. The phenomenon does suggest, however, that the seam in Heine's artistic consciousness started to rip much earlier than is generally recognized; the incompatibility of "poesy" and politics is already beginning to be a problem in 1821.

Apart from this striking dissonance, there are traces of a critique of "poesy" elsewhere in *Almansor*. One example is the versified courting of Zuleima by the fraudulent Don Enrique, which, with its ludicrous rhyme "Strahlenkuniginne / Minne" (E, 2, 263), is reminiscent of the immature diction of Heine's earliest *Minnelieder*. The hollowness of Don Enrique's poetic languishing becomes even more apparent when confronted with Don Diego's Iago-like cynicism. It is interesting that Enrique-Roderigo, though a low-born swindler, does not share this cynicism; he is genuinely in love with Zuleima, and in yielding to his own poetic raptures appears quite stupid. It would seem that Heine is illuminating the problem of the persona and his dignity from a different, more sardonic perspective. Almansor's relationship to poetry also exhibits some problematic features. In his Romeo-like monologue under Zulemia's balcony, he finds that the metaphors of love poetry are simply not related to reality; the stars, which in the past he has apostrophized as messengers of love, have not delivered the message.[23] Here the persona seems annoyed and puzzled by this, but the recognition of the actual unresponsiveness of the elements of nature, so cavalierly manipulated by the love poet, anticipates the attitudes of the *Nordsee* poems *Sturm* and *Fragen*. Almansor's song in the same scene also strikes one oddly; it is a dreadful piece of Rococo verse, more mannered and precious than anything even the youthful Heine was accustomed to write. All these things combine to form an undertone that communicates an awareness of the weaknesses of *Almansor* and its persona in the play itself.

While few have ever really shared Heine's persistent view that *William Ratcliff* is a worthwhile piece of work, it has been rather generally agreed that it is a substantial improvement on *Almansor*. Elster, whose introduction to the tragedies in his second edition is one of his best pieces of criticism, calls *William Ratcliff* "dichterisch wertvoll," [24] and tries to defend the work, although he goes a little too far. It is true that Heine's second effort is theatrically more satisfying than his first. It is more compact and shorter by half (although, as Louis Untermeyer has said, "twice as unconvincing" [25]); and it avoids the long, lachrymose monologues that bring *Almansor* almost to a standstill. While in *Almansor* it takes Heine over three hundred lines to complete the exposition, in *William Ratcliff* he accomplishes this task in a little over half that space. The really substantial gain is in the diction, as might be expected from Heine's own dissatisfactions with *Almansor*. As the scenery is shifted from Moorish Spain to the Scottish Highlands, so the lush, orientalizing metaphorics are abandoned for a rugged, sometimes even harsh versification that is a refreshing contrast. A few lines of MacGregor will illustrate the new tone:

> Er sah Marie, und sah ihr in die Augen,
> Und sah dort viel zu tief, begann zu seufzen,
> Zu schmachten und zu ächzen,—bis Maria
> Ihm rund erklärte: daß er lästig sei.
> Die Liebe packt' er in den Korb und ging. (E, 2, 317)

This hardy tone dominates the style of the play.

In 1851, in the third edition of *Neue Gedichte,* Heine removed *Deutschland. Ein Wintermärchen* and replaced it with *William Ratcliff*; his preface is a last attempt to make a case for the play. His remarks are a curious mixture of good judgment and ex post facto interpretation. The tragedy, says Heine, with perfect justice, belongs as "eine bedeutsame Urkunde zu den Prozeß-Akten meines Dichterlebens" (E, 2, 522). He goes on to say that the play is a résumé of his Sturm-und-Drang period, which appears only incompletely in *Junge Leiden.* But Heine beclouds the point: "Der junge Autor, der hier [in *Junge Leiden*] nur träumerische Naturlaute lallt, spricht dort, im Ratcliff, eine wache, mündige Sprache und sagt unverhohlen sein letztes Wort." The reason Heine proceeds in this way is because now, in 1851, he wants to argue the social relevance of the play and congratulate himself for having raised "die große Suppenfrage" in the scene of the robbers' tavern. There follows a sentence that expresses more compactly than anywhere else Heine's effort to force a synthesis between "poesy" and political relevance: "Ein wunderliches Sonntagskind ist der Poet; er sieht die Eichenwälder, welche noch in der Eichel schlummern, und er hält Zwiesprache mit den Geschlechtern, die noch nicht geboren sind." Strodtmann remarks apropos of this, with unwonted scornfulness, that in the play "die große Suppenfrage" was derived from the purest accident, from the pleasure of a girl's whim.[26] It is clear that Heine's later effort to make the handful of lines in the robbers' tavern bear the whole burden of meaning of the play is illegitimate—the verses he added to presentation copies of the play at the time[27] make it plain that a dramatization of his love experience was foremost in his mind—but the total rejection by Strodtmann and others of the significance of the passage will not do either. Heine's striking division of mankind into two nations, the satiated and the starving,[28] exactly anticipates the formulations of two very different observers of the English scene more than twenty years later: Friedrich Engels' *Die Lage der arbeitenden Klassen in England* and Benjamin Disraeli's novel *Sibyl, or the Two Nations,* both published in 1845.[29] If Heine in 1851 wanted to claim that in 1822 his poetic sensitivity had perceived a sound of the future, no one can gainsay him. We cannot allow him, on the other hand, to identify this element as the meaning of *William Ratcliff*. In fact, it may be doubted whether the play has any sensible meaning at all.

Despite its weaknesses, *Almansor*, with its bitter religious conflict, is at least potentially about something humanly and historically important. *William Ratcliff*, despite its structural and stylistic improvements, is a lot of nonsense. First of all, from the point of view of literary influence, the play is the most outrageous performance of plagiaristic synthesis anywhere in Heine's works. The milieu is lifted from Sir Walter Scott, particularly from *The Black Dwarf* (1816). The play is full of echoes from Byron, particularly from *Manfred*.* [30] The ballad of Edward, made ubiquitously popular by Herder, dutifully appears. Ratcliff's own speeches and self-representation owe much to Schiller's *Räuber*; the Sturm-und-Drang elements of the play are a rather wearisome revival of a mode of writing that in 1822 was fifty years old. Secondly, *William Ratcliff* is modeled on a genre that should have been beneath Heine's serious attention: the popular tragedy of fate. The early nineteenth-century fate-tragedies may shed some light on aspects of the Romantic agony, but from any artistic point of view almost all of them are subliterary and trivial. Exceptions such as Zacharias Werner's *Der vierundzwanzigste Februar* (1810) or Grillparzer's *Die Ahnfrau* (1817) manage to be barely respectable because of qualities of atmosphere, language, and psychology, but by and large the plays of this type, because of the mechanistic operation of fate, which serves as a substitute for a principle of dramatic form, tend to be silly as well as dehumanized.

Of course Heine had enough taste and intelligence to realize this. In the classicistic mood of his essay on Smets, he had some harsh words about the modern use of fate as compared with that in Greek tragedy.[31] On December 30, 1821, Heine wrote a letter to Adolf Müllner, asking him for a favorable review of his first book of poems.[32] Müllner had written one of the most popular of the fate-tragedies, *Die Schuld* (1816), which for a reason not clear to me supplied the motto to *Das Buch Le Grand*.[33] This letter is throughout an impudent exercise in leg-pulling, which Heine

* One speech of Ratcliff's to Maria (E, 2, 341) is an almost verbatim translation of a passage from *Manfred*.

probably presumed Müllner would not have the wit to perceive; in it he says he had made a present of *Die Schuld* to his beloved, who scornfully challenged him to write something like it. Given Amalie's apparent level of poetic sensitivity, this compliment is, to say the least, seriously flawed. But if Heine had a negative view of the tragedy of fate, why did he undertake such an effort himself? When he offered the *Tragödien nebst einem lyrischen Intermezzo* for publication in 1823, he argued that the "Grundidee" of *William Ratcliff* was supposed to be "ein Surrogat für das gewöhnliche Fatum" (Hirth, *1*, 52), but in what sense this is true, if it is true at all, is unclear. The answer to the question seems to lie again in the unresolved problem of the persona.

Heine found it difficult to believe that Amalie rejected him because she did not like him well enough, and the projected persona does not entertain this possibility until *Das Buch Le Grand:* "Sie war liebenswürdig, und Er liebte Sie; Er aber war nicht liebenswürdig, und Sie liebte Ihn nicht" (E, *3*, 131). In *Buch der Lieder* all kinds of other explanations for the beloved's behavior are offered: libel, self-destructiveness, false-heartedness, and whatnot. The rejection of Ratcliff by Maria in the play is similarly obscure: her father's account is that Maria found him tiresome and sent him off; Ratcliff's is that she falsely showed him signs of love and then scornfully turned him down out of pure malice; Maria's is that he was too wild and frightening. What Heine achieves through the mechanisms of the fate tragedy is a release from any need to make sense out of these various motivations. Maria and Ratcliff are forced, for no reason inherent in their own beings, to play the roles prefigured for them by their parents, and to submit to the fate acted out by the ghosts of Schön-Betty and Edward Ratcliff, which appear to both of them. Thus the poet-persona is relieved of responsibility for his own wretchedness, and the apparent cruelty of the beloved finds an explanation.

That this resolution resolves nothing would be apparent to a child. As in almost all fate-tragedies, the whole action is made hollow and pointless by the motivating assumptions, and no amount of intense rhetoric can restore the dramatic substance. Apart from that, the problem of unrequited love is merely shifted back one generation; the question remains why Schön-Betty refused Edward. The explanation given, that Schön-Betty went into a pique at Edward and married another because Edward sang a line of a ballad at an inappropriate moment, is so foolish that it exposes the speciousness of the whole undertaking. Bogus means yield a counterfeit solution, and the play is a failure.

Heine's problems with the persona are evident in other features. *William Ratcliff* continues the effort of *Almansor* to strengthen the persona by supplying it with qualities of heroic pugnaciousness.[34] The fantasy projection of the self has many of the characteristics of the Sturm-und-Drang hero: brave, desperately careless of life, scrupulously chivalric (Ratcliff kills Maria's fiancés in equal combat and not by murder), and generous-hearted (Ratcliff risks his life to save that of the unknown, beleaguered Douglas on the road). All this is shallow enough, but Heine cannot even sustain it any more than he was able to sustain Almansor's heroic posture; the self-pity that the persona of *Buch der Lieder* must struggle so hard to overcome reasserts itself. In the combat we actually see on the stage, Ratcliff is not victorious but thoroughly whipped; that he has been beaten not in fair combat, but because the ghosts of his two victims have assisted Douglas, only reinforces his position as one who is outrageously abused. Ratcliff appears before Maria not as barbaric victor, but as wounded suppliant, an object of pity. Consequently his killing of Maria and himself makes an ugly impression. It might be pointed out that Maria is never given a chance to answer Ratcliff's demand that she flee with him, nor is it clear why their deaths finally reconcile the ghosts of the parents. Some deep and unpleasant layer of violent hatred and masochism in Heine is turned up in this play. Ratcliff has already evinced a high degree of self-hatred in his outbreak of rage after his defeat in the duel.

As in *Almansor,* there is in *William Ratcliff* an undertone of criticism of the persona. The function of Hassan is assumed in the second play, mutatis mutandis, by Ratcliff's companion Lesley, who makes fun of Ratcliff's overcharged rhetoric and amorous posturing, and reacts with icy indifference to Ratcliff's account of the rejection: "Das war ja ganz infam und niederträchtig" (E, 2,

327). As in the *Gespräch auf der Paderborner Heide,* the overwrought emotions of the persona are set off against the insensitivity of the normal man. There is also an incomplete effort to separate the persona from the helpless posture of the poet, for in the same scene with Lesley, Ratcliff distinguishes his brutal activism from the sentimentality of

Ein magenkrank schwindsüchtelnder Poet,
Der mit den Sternen Unzucht treibt, der Leibschmerz
Vor Rührung kriegt, wenn Nachtigallen trillern . . . (E, 2, 325)

This passage clearly belongs in the general context of the critique of "poesy."

Finally, it may be asked if there is not a second, embryonic persona in the play, namely Douglas. In a soliloquy he states that he does not love Maria and desires to marry her only for convenience. But he is in no sense the counterpart of the scoundrel Diego of *Almansor.* He makes it plain that he likes Maria and is kindly disposed to her. More importantly, he possesses in fact the brave qualities that Heine tried unsuccessfully to graft onto the protagonist: Douglas enthusiastically welcomes the challenge from Ratcliff and in the duel exhibits every characteristic of chivalry; he spares Ratcliff in gratitude for the latter's assistance in the ambush on the road. Of the main characters, he is the only one left alive at the end. It is tempting to see Douglas as a better solution to the problem of the persona than Ratcliff himself. Douglas is manly, masterful, and, above all, love-proof—qualities toward which the development of the persona is tending.

Heinrich Laube thought Heine was unable to create successful dramas because he lacked the ability to concentrate.[35] Others have believed that it was because he could not transcend the subjectivity he himself discusses in the essay on Smets. These strictures do not apply to Heine's tragedies; he worked long and hard on *Almansor,* and the problem of subjectivity tends to be overrated. Heine's skills were impressionistic, and it is likely that he lacked talent for dramatic composition. But *Almansor* and *William Ratcliff* do not prove this; their failure is too closely involved with the still vexatious problem of the poetic persona. Perhaps if Heine had ever found comfortable leisure and some relaxation of spirit, he might have managed a tolerably decent drama. As it was, he finally and characteristically blamed his failure on the genre and sighed: "Das Theater ist nicht günstig für Poeten" (E, 7, 414).

CHAPTER 4

Heine's Prose Art: *Die Harzreise*

Umsonst! Das ist nun einmal so,
Kein Dichter reist inkognito,
Der lustge Frühling merkt es gleich,
Wer König ist in seinem Reich.

—EICHENDORFF

When Erich Loewenthal in 1922 spoke of "die mehr oder weniger lockere Form der 'Reisebilder', denen es an einheitlicher Komposition durchaus fehlt," [1] he was expressing a judgment on Heine's prose fiction that has remained fairly constant from the time of the original reviewers; at best, artistic unity in Heine's prose is recognized only in the obtrusive presence of the first-person narrator and in linear verbal association. But the question may be seriously asked whether a prose art so described can lay claim to greatness and if it must really be said that Heine's greatest achievements lie exclusively in his lyric poetry. This question has largely been avoided due to the overwhelmingly biographical character of much Heine interpretation.

Despite the apparent presence of the author in his own person, however, a number of the *Reisebilder* are best approached as works of fiction. *Die Bäder von Lucca* (1829), *Die Stadt Lucca* (1829), *Der Rabbi von Bacherach* (1824–25, 1840), *Die Memoiren des Herren von Schnabelewopski* (1833), and the *Florentinische Nächte* (1836) are the only works of Heine that correspond in any strict sense to what we would normally regard as prose fiction. But even in these works, the disturbing factor in the fiction is the apparent presence of the author himself. If we think of the author's presence as the "essay aspect," as opposed to the "fiction aspect," it will be noted that the relationship between these two aspects varies widely in the *Reisebilder*. In the three pieces of the Italian set, for example, the *Reise von München nach Genua* is almost entirely essay, although it is not lacking in fictional anecdotes; *Die Bäder von Lucca,* although one of its chief elements of composition is the personal attack on Platen (see Chapter 6), is, through ten of its eleven chapters, narrative fiction; and in *Die Stadt Lucca* the two aspects interpenetrate in a dialogue placed in a fictional setting; by this means Heine objectifies some of his ambivalent feelings about religion, culminated by a straight essay in the last three chapters. The basic problem in understanding Heine's works—which may be simply stated as the presence of the author in his narration and, more exactly, as the interrelation of the fictional presentation and the first-person persona who relates it—tends thus to be considerably more complicated in the prose works than in the poetry. But the fiction aspect of these works has been traditionally neglected, and it will be useful to spend some time with several of the *Reisebilder* in this regard.

If the fiction aspect is genuinely significant in these works, then the issue of formal composition ought to be discussed; and I propose to focus on *Die Harzreise* just because it is the first and the least mature of the *Reisebilder.* Here and there it shows remnants of sophomoric wit from Heine's student environment, and its language, as has been shown,[2] remains largely restricted within the inherited diction of Heine's more conventional contemporaries. The vast fame of the work, therefore, and the frequency with which it is employed as an introduction for students to Heine's prose, is somewhat out of proportion to its relative stature. Heine himself seemed to be far from pleased with it, although whether he was as totally dismayed by the weaknesses of the work as he indicated to his friend Christiani[3] must be left open. But if certain disciplined binding forces can be discovered in this work, it will encourage us to apply ourselves similarly to the more complex structures of the later *Reisebilder.* Recently critics have begun to suspect a larger degree of artistic control than was seen in the past. Bernhard, for example, meets Heine at least half way when she remarks, "So leicht und flüssig, assoziativ und ungeformt gerade die Prosaschriften auch wirken mögen, Heine gestaltet sie ganz bewußt." [4] Near the end of *Die Harzreise,* Heine himself, in the person of his narrator, speaks of "die bunten Fäden, die so hübsch hineingesponnen sind, um sich im Ganzen harmonisch zu verschlingen" (E, *3*, 74), suggesting that it will be worthwhile to trace some of these threads. Here only the major outlines will be touched upon, leaving aside the minor interconnections that, in the very nature of Heine's style, reach down to the level of verbal association.

Die Harzreise, like so many of Heine's works, can be divided into three parts. They are: the departure from Göttingen and the journey as far as Goslar; the climb to the Brocken and the night spent there; and the descent, including the climb to the Ilsenstein as well as the final coda, which, it will appear, must be seen as an integral part of the work. This pattern of rise and descent is clearly significant: it relates to a pattern of transformations in the narrator's mood, for *Die Harzreise* is the story of a journey taken to release the poet-narrator from an oppressed and unpleasant state of mind. The release is achieved partly through the effect of nature, but even more through the workings of the poetic mind under the impulses of nature and the adventures of traveling. This healing effect of poetry is suggested in the motto quoted from, of all people, Ludwig Börne: "das Leben wäre ein ewiges Verbluten, wenn nicht die Dichtkunst wäre."[5] We find again, incidentally, that Wilhelm Bölsche, with unique instinct, grasped the nature of the case exactly: "Es ist, als arbeite der Erzähler sich selbst mit jedem Schritte mehr aus der Trivialität des Anfanges heraus und zu einer wahren Kunsthöhe empor."[6]

The opening mood in Göttingen is cramped and rather nasty; the scorn heaped upon the university town is ill-humored, and the undeniable wit of the opening passage (which demonstrably reflects traditional student lore that goes back as far as Lichtenberg[7]) is constantly threatened by lapses into mere crudity. The poem prefixed to this passage, however, points ahead to those things that will bring release: "die frommen Hütten" (E, *3*, 15) and the phenomena of nature. The first part consists mainly of a struggle by the narrator, developed in various ways, to gain control over his own spirits. Twice there is the symbolic gesture of lightening his pack. Repeatedly he engages in confrontations with other travelers, always gaining the upper hand due to his superior wit and understanding; the three versions of this in the first part, however, are juvenile and the first of them, at least, where he recommends the student prison as a hotel for a traveling family, is hardly more than a prank. The second shows his condescension toward the folk-singing "journeyman," and particular attention is drawn to the narrator's greater stamina.* The third confrontation, where the narrator responds to a tiresome table companion by relating nonsense, shows somewhat more refined presence of mind, but does not compare in quality to those that appear in the second part. The narrator's apparent high spirits, however, are contrasted with two dreams and the visit to the silver mine. The first dream, taking him back to the Göttingen library amid a cacophony of learned legal disputation, ends in flight to the images of Apollo and Venus, symbols of the poetry and love that restore him in the course of the journey. But the second, where the poet appears as a knight who attempts to free a charmed maiden from a deep well, ends in images of gloom and fear. This dream is motivated by the preceding visit to the silver mine, the low point, both physically and symbolically, of the journey. It is important that it carries him down to the origin of money, the basic substance of the Philistine world so hated by the poet. Although the descent into the earth is related as an interesting adventure with an attempt at a light tone, the imagery is anxious and oppressive to a degree hardly found elsewhere in Heine's early works. The narrator must crawl into the shaft "auf allen vieren"; in almost childish cadence he remarks, "das dunkle Loch ist so dunkel"; once in the mine, vapors rise from the earth and the miner's lamp grows pale. So strong is the sense of claustrophobic fear that the narrator yearns for the open space of a storm at sea.[8] This intensification of the inhibited, lacerated mood of the poet in the cavern where the ore for coinage is mined is one of the finest achievements of Heine's early prose.

From this point the first part of *Die Harzreise* continues in a pattern that has the quality of a fugue: the symbols and motifs alternate in such a way as to bind the following, otherwise un-

* E, *3*, 23–25. This scene has attracted a certain amount of attention, for the traveling merchant who pulled Heine's leg sufficiently to become the original for this character subsequently identified himself and gave an account of the confrontation (E, *3*, 6–9). This opportunity to compare a narration of Heine's with the actual event is just about unique in his career, and it provides a vital example of the kinds of fictive transformations Heine worked on his experiences.

connected experiences into a total picture of the narrator's present concerns until, at the end of the first part, some sort of resolution is achieved, as so often with Heine, in the ridiculous.

The narrator's emergence to the surface provides a temporary release from the terrors of the mine, but his highly interesting remarks about the personification of inanimate objects in folklore are followed by a Romantic disquisition on the situation of modern man, who is so divorced from the objects around him that he no longer has a living relationship with them; the sense of dissociation felt in the mine is reintroduced on another level. The images of fear from the mine—darkness and a stormy sea—recur in the dream of the knight who descends into the well, where he is eventually surrounded by ghosts and feels like a harlequin among the dead. The motif of death is picked up again in the story of the world-traveler returning home to Quedlinburg to be buried near his family—a moment of uncommon delicacy where the traveler, after relating the beauties of oriental burial, concludes, in implicit contradiction to the insensitive, rationalistic innkeeper, "alles sehr hübsch—wie weit hab' ich noch bis Quedlinburg?" (E, *3*, 37). This is immediately followed by a scene in which the narrator extorts a kiss from a pretty girl on the grounds that he will not pass that way again. This, he says, is the formula of the transient soldier. Thus the motif of the narrator as knight is taken up again with a slight transformation: now he is successful and controls the situation, but in a more insignificant context. The death motif resumes in a meditation on immortality, leading directly into a poetic assertion of the strength of his own love, in which the discouragement symbolized by the knight in the well seems somehow to have been relieved by his minor success with the girl in Goslar. All this culminates in the famous dream in which the rationalist Saul Ascher appears from the grave and proceeds to disprove the possibility of ghosts, thus combining the death-motif with an expanded version of the anti-poetic and inhuman rationalism of the innkeeper. The end result of this careful interweaving of motifs is a new situation for the poet, in which some of the edge has been taken off the pain of his unhappy love, and his anxiety and morbidity have dissolved in the comically absurd dream of the self-contradictory apparition. This resolution determines the new mood of the poet as he continues on his travels.

The second part is characterized by a more joyful response to nature and a more obvious inner and outer ease on the part of the narrator. His passive submission to nature is gradually transformed, first, into a sense of being accepted and appreciated by it —"Der Geist des Gebirges begünstigte mich ganz offenbar; er wußte wohl, daß so ein Dichtermensch viel Hübsches wieder erzählen kann" (E, *3*, 49); second, into an awareness of the superiority of his own receptivity over that of the Philistine who comments, "Wie ist die Natur doch im allgemeinen so schön!" (E, *3*, 56) (a point that was to be developed more thoroughly in *Die Bäder von Lucca*[9]); and finally, into a cheerful ability to take nature as it suits him, when he passes up the sunrise for the sake of his morning coffee. This progressive dissociation from dependence on nature runs parallel to an increasing independence of spirit. His treatment of tiresome persons displays a finer wit than the pranks of the first part: the vulgar, old-fashioned teleology of a traveler is reduced to absurdity, and the narrator takes his revenge upon his anti-Semitic roommate on the Brocken by announcing that he is a sleepwalker, thus frightening the man out of a night's rest. The idyllic evening in the mountains presents an admiring self-portrait of the poet even as he displays his virtuosity by turning the experience into verse. The portrait has some familiar features of the poet-persona: in an unmistakable parodistic treatment of the "Marthens Garten" scene in *Faust,* the girl notices the contrast between "Jenes böse, kalte Zucken" of the poet's lips and "Deiner Augen frommer Strahl" (E, *3*, 45), and she expresses her doubts as to his religious faith. He responds with what first appears to be a conventional confession of faith, which, however, by means of an adept juggling of words and their meanings, leaves the Christian ground altogether for something quite new.

This poem, which in *Buch der Lieder* is entitled *Berg-Idylle,*[10] obliges one to stop for a moment in the seductive flow of *Die Harzreise* and ponder, for, while it exploits themes that belong to the fugue of the narrative, it points beyond the apparent boundaries of the work to the significance of the *Reisebilder* as a whole. It is characteristic of Heine's turbulent aesthetics that this long *lyrical* insert should define the particular thrust of the *prose* that was to mean so much to many younger writers of his generation. There is a potential energy in *Die Harzreise* that breaks through the boundaries of its form, the account of a quasi-Romantic wandering. The sharp perception of real scenes that belong specifically to an identifiable sociological context and moment in historical time and the differentiation of types of people according to their status establish a contrast with the timeless landscapes and characters who are fundamentally alike regardless of status in the stories of wandering of, say, Tieck or Eichendorff. In *Die Harzreise* these more modern features are embedded in a pattern of perception that is inherited from the preceding generation, and indeed this continues to be so, in greater or lesser degree, in Heine's writing until his move to Paris and to some extent beyond. But Heine was engaged in an urgent effort to turn the elements of the heritage to a profoundly different direction. Intellectually, there is more than one way to look at this fundamental aspect of Heine's significance, but in the *Berg-Idylle* it can be described as an *action* of the poet-persona that displays the use he intends to make of the thematic considerations which inform *Die Harzreise*. Heine draws from Romantic medievalism his persona as knight, but this has nothing whatever to do with a retreat into a utopia of the past. Rather, the knight-image is one of power, and the power is exercised in transcending the terms of the heritage by giving them a new meaning. The poet-knight is the "Ritter von dem heil'gen Geist" (E, *3*, 46); as knight he is a defender of the faith; as poet, he is the herald of a new faith, a new holy spirit that promises liberty from the old repressive society and the release of love and gaiety:

> Dieser that die größten Wunder,
> Und viel größre thut er noch;
> Er zerbrach die Zwingherrnburgen,
> Und zerbrach des Knechtes Joch.
>
> Alte Todeswunden heilt er,
> Und erneut das alte Recht:

Alle Menschen, gleichgeboren,
Sind ein adliches Geschlecht.

Er verscheucht die bösen Nebel,
Und das dunkle Hirngespinst,
Das uns Lieb' und Lust verleidet,
Tag und Nacht uns angegrinst. (E, *3*, 46)

In these lines, which antedate Heine's Saint-Simonian experience by several years, the whole nature of that experience is fixed. Just as for the Young Germans, so for Heine liberty is on the one hand an issue to be treated in religious terms, and, on the other, one intimately bound up with the emancipation of love and pleasure from what he was later to think of as Nazarene restraint.

As a consequence, the release and relaxation achieved in the journey through the Harz is not as intimately bound up with the essence of nature and naive society that the poet experiences as it is in cases of Romantic wanderlust; the poet-persona, for all his nostalgic appreciation, is potentially superior to the implications of the landscape and its inhabitants. He does not react with humility to the simplistic faith of the girl in the mountains; he takes its terms and propels them into a definition that is far beyond her horizon. Similarly, in his capacity as poet, he almost violently arrogates to himself the imaginative sources of the folklore that the girl herself only recites out of a superstitious heritage. Although he himself had had anxieties about ghosts in the first part, here he stands infinitely above the girl's popular superstitions and expresses metaphorically his poet's magic, which transforms his surroundings and creates a world of wonder with a word. Folklore is no longer a mysterious depth into which the poet plunges in order to harmonize with a fundamental essence of things; instead, it is something that he himself makes and will turn to his own ends, for the poet-knight-persona is a beautiful and powerful prince: "Pauken und Trompeten huld'gen / Meiner jungen Herrlichkeit!" (E, *3*, 49). It is important to remember in *Die Harzreise* that, although wandering in nature and among the simple folk provides release from the stultified existence of the backward academe in Göttingen, the terms of the release are not intrinsic to the *ambiance* of the Harz, but located in the creative energy of the poet.

The visit to the Brocken itself does not provide the narrator much in the way of release, since the student world of Göttingen follows him there; but neither does it oppress him, for he maintains a position as a superior observer: he manages to involve the hotheads in arguments without being drawn into them himself, delivers the famous interpretation of the Berlin ballet as a political allegory, and describes with amusement the absurdity and final discomfiture of the two youths intoxicated with Romantic and Ossianic posturings. An example of the way in which his manner of narration reflects his sense of superiority is found in the scene in the observation tower, where he describes the surroundings; first he takes care to stress the complex nature of the feelings stimulated by the experience: "alle Seiten unseres Geistes empfangen neue Eindrücke, und diese, meistens verschiedenartig, sogar sich widersprechend, verbinden sich in unserer Seele zu einem großen, noch unentworrenen, unverstandenen Gefühl" (E, *3*, 54); then he proceeds with a sure hand to unravel the complexity by describing the Brocken as a symbol of Germany.

The chief new feature of the third section is the interpenetration of the poet's reaction to nature with his erotic sensibilities, about which more will be said presently. However, although the brief third part describes the descent from the Brocken, it reaches a new high point—in a sense the highest point of all—on the Ilsenstein, where the narrator, lost in his musings, grows suddenly dizzy and must take hold of the iron cross to prevent a fall. This scene, with its ironic and sheepish plea for forbearance, is usually interpreted as an apologetic reference to Heine's conversion to Christianity, and no doubt it is. In the manuscript, the train of thought generated by the cross is considerably expanded and develops into a set of ironic observations about the Jews.[11] Perhaps Heine dropped the passage for reasons of prudence. But perhaps also he felt that it was a misleading digression. We should like to know if there is any way the scene on the Ilsenstein can be accounted for within the pattern of *Die Harzreise* without reference to extraneous matters. It is possible to suggest that the narrator's vertigo is a symbol of his inability to remain permanently on such a high imaginative plane; it is not where he belongs. *Die Harzreise* is not a Romantic journey into an indeterminate yonder of sublime withdrawal; it is, in some ways like Eichendorff's *Taugenichts,* a journey *through* a Romantic landscape back to the solid ground of reality; the Romantic world of nature and poetry is not the goal, but rather the means by which the narrator achieves refreshment of spirit; thus the dreamy peak of the Ilsenstein is dangerous and uninhabitable, and the coda of the work takes him down to the valley and finally back to his permanent situation of unrequited love, but in an entirely different mood from that of his departure.

The theme of the persona bearing, in one way or another, the burden of unhappy love is subtly woven into the fabric of *Die Harzreise* and undergoes a series of transformations determined by the structural pattern. The very precondition, asserts the narrator, for a receptive appreciation of nature is that the wanderer have love in his heart,[12] a quality that the opening verses describe as missing in the people of Göttingen. But the love he carries with him from Göttingen is a torment, as is illustrated by the dream of the knight in the well. This awareness of his permanent situation, however, now begins to be punctuated with a series of casual, limited, but on the whole successful confrontations with pretty girls. The kiss stolen from the girl in Goslar is followed by a soliloquy that describes the poet's love as able to cross the distance to his beloved;[13] already the narrator's love has become an attitude that strengthens his own consciousness of self. His developing sense of poetic power unfolds fully in the idyll with the girl in the mountains, and on the following day a vision of the distant beloved appears in the midst of the poet's enjoyment of the high forest, with only mild symptoms of suffering: "ach, daß sie so schnell wieder verschwindet!" (E, *3,* 51). Particularly the girl he meets in the observation tower on the Brocken has a salutary effect, for he is able to enjoy her pleasant company without being aroused by strong emotion: "Ich liebe solche Gesichter, weil sie mein schlimmbewegtes Herz zur Ruhe lächeln" (E, *3,* 55); here the development of the persona runs parallel to that in *Nordsee I.* On the following day, before sunrise, the narrator produces a poem that repeats the theme of crossing the distance to the beloved, but its effect, like many of the later poems in *Buch der Lieder,* is one of a sadness largely overcome by its compression into verses and indeed into conventional imagery; the poet's wish to whisper into the sleeping beloved's ear, "Denk im Traum, daß wirs uns lieben, und daß wir uns nie verloren" (E, *3,* 67), is an expression of both resignation and distance.

By means of this alternation a certain emotional stability has been achieved. In the third part the complex is picked up in an entirely new pattern. The narrator is now in complete harmony with nature: "Unendlich selig ist das Gefühl, wenn die Erscheinungswelt mit unserer Gemütswelt zusammenrinnt" (E, *3,* 72). The phenomena of nature, particularly the river Ilse and its legendary associations, become erotically charged in an expansive way. The poem about *Prinzessin Ilse* describes a sort of *Venusberg* situation in which the narrator is invited to find solace from the torments of reality in Ilse's physical love, and his persona as knight is expanded to the point where he is urged to share the pleasures enjoyed by the emperor. The threads of the theme are pulled together through the coquettish personification of the three streams who oblige the narrator to judge their beauty. All three are yielding: the Selke requests him to write a poem about her; the Bode asks his love because he equals her in pride and pain; but, so typical for Heine, the prize goes to the least yielding, the Ilse, who looks at him "mit unwiderstehlicher Gleichgültigkeit" (E, *3,* 76).

What has happened is a shift from symbolic events to imaginative imagery in order to bring the problem to a resolution: the function performed in the first two parts by the girls encountered on the journey is now taken over by the streams that the narrator personifies; on the one hand, they establish his attractiveness by their compliments and interest; on the other, the Ilse, in this agreeable context, is constructed into a symbol for the nature of his love. This is all consciously done by the narrator; at the same time it exposes the quality of his poetic imagination; he has gained control. The result is evident in the concluding scene. The imagery is shifted once again: the narrator's heart is the flower of a rare plant with cutting leaves, bursting into bloom with great éclat once in a hundred years, but so high in the air that the beloved must get a stepladder if she wishes to look into it. With a single stroke the narrator establishes not only the rarity and beauty of his emotion, but also, with inimitable, studied arrogance, he places it beyond the reach of the beloved, the desired, but nevertheless inferior "Agnes"—the "real" counterpart of the river Ilse. We have come a long way from the petty irritability of the departure from Göttingen.

A word must be said here about the narrator's designation of *Die Harzreise* as a fragment. It would not be appropriate to suggest that the work is incomplete because it does not describe the remainder of Heine's journey through the Lower Harz or his visit to Goethe, even if Heine intended to continue it in that way; like fully half of the remaining pieces in the *Reisebilder, Die Harzreise* is not primarily an account of a journey but a piece of prose fiction, and for this reason Hofrichter's remark that it "was no more like life than Sunday was like a weekday" [14] seems to me to be off the point. Furthermore, Heine did write more of *Die Harzreise* than he published—a passage of several pages about Ilsenburg.[15] But it is digressive and does not fit at all into the structure as I have described it, and that Heine ultimately made no use of it tends to support my contentions about the formal unity of the work. The word "fragment" can be applied to Heine's works in at least three different senses. There are definitely unfinished works, such as *Der Rabbi von Bacherach,* which have foundered in their own narrative problems; there are incomplete undertakings like *Florentinische Nächte* and *Die Memoiren des Herren von Schnabelewopski,* which, though unfinished in terms of their total conception, contain smaller novellistic wholes; and thirdly, there are fragments in a sense ultimately deriving from Friedrich Schlegel, which by their very nature cannot be rounded off into a traditional well-made form; into this category fall such works as *Jehuda ben Halevy* and *Die Harzreise.* The major tension in the latter—the narrator's unrequited love—does not admit of a total solution, but it can be absorbed into an attitude he can manage. Heine overstates the case, however, when he asserts that "die bunten Fäden" (E, *3,* 74) have been abruptly cut. *Die Harzreise* has a distinct profile, structured by the stages of the journey; within the limits of this profile are ordered a set of mutually interconnected themes and symbols that develop in a clear and traceable movement from beginning situation to end situation. Many of the other individual elements of the work not mentioned here can be shown to have their place in the pattern. We should not take the word "fragment," which here refers to a concept of *Gehalt* implying a certain open-endedness in the narrator's situation and the difficulty of capturing complex emotional states perfectly, as an indication of formal incompleteness; *Die Harzreise* has indeed a beginning and an end, with a structural logic between them.

CHAPTER 5

Masterpiece: *Ideen: Das Buch Le Grand*

> To read it is like nothing so much as watching a conjurer pulling yards and yards of multicoloured ribbon from a tall top-hat. The whole stage is knee-deep in it; but he has not done yet—
>
> —E. M. BUTLER

From external appearances, Heine's life in the years following the completion of his studies seems vague, disparate, and full of problems. The sloppily acquired doctor's degree led nowhere, and Heine's affairs as he approached the age of thirty are characterized by drift. His father had been bankrupt since 1819, and Heine's trip to England in 1827 resulted in a broil with Uncle Salomon because Heine cashed a large draft that his uncle had meant to be conspicuous, but not for consumption. The whole ambiguous transaction, which resulted in Heine's unlucky and never forgotten remark that the best thing about Salomon Heine was that he bore Heinrich Heine's name, is thoroughly paradigmatic for the relationship between the oafish millionaire and his both needy and nervy nephew. Apart from the opaque period in the world of commerce, Heine did not acquire a paying position until he was thirty, and his performance in that job—the editorship of the *Politische Annalen* in Munich—did him little credit; after six months of not editing the journal for a substantial salary, he abandoned the valuable patronage of Baron Cotta in order to knock about Italy, while engaging in a totally quixotic effort to acquire a professorship at the University of Munich.

Nevertheless, the *Nordsee* poems in particular and the whole line of development of *Buch der Lieder* in general suggest that in these years Heine's inner firmness in his true vocation was much further developed than the state of his assimilation to the mundane world. The two prose works that follow immediately upon the experiences that inspired the *Nordsee* poems, *Nordsee III* and *Ideen: Das Buch Le Grand,* confirm this impression. Both works were composed in the latter part of 1826, immediately after the second summer on the island of Norderney, and were published in the second volume of the *Reisebilder,* which turned out to be, in terms of its immediate reception, one of Heine's most popular books.

Heine's turn to prose at this point in his career is not accidental and is only incidentally an indication that the lyrical vein from which he had mined the poems of *Buch der Lieder* had temporarily been worked out. Heine was at the beginning of a development to which he gave cryptic expression in the preface to the third edition of *Buch der Lieder* in 1839, which begins with a poem that retrospectively reverts to the tone of some of his earliest verse, followed by the remark: "Das hätte ich alles sehr gut in guter Prosa sagen können" (E, *1,* 9). Heine goes on to say that Apollo knows very well "warum die Flamme, die einst in brillanten Feuerwerkspielen die Welt ergötzte, plötzlich zu weit ernsteren Bränden verwendet werden mußte" (E, *1,* 10). The first stage of the consolidation of the poetic persona released Heine somewhat from his preoccupation with his inner emotional life and allowed him to turn his attention outward to the state of the world around him. That world, in many respects disturbing, discouraging, and even sinister, nevertheless seemed, for a while at least, pregnant with new and hopeful events incompatible with Romantic attitudes. Heine, in his own mind, was never really able to separate poetry—or, as he characteristically liked to call it, *Poesie*—from the context of the Romantic imagination, and thus, despite the havoc he wreaked within that context, he was less able to generate productive new directions for poetry than some of his less spectacular contemporaries like Platen and Mörike. It is logical therefore that his turn to new realities should be accompanied by a gradual turn from poetry to prose in the latter 1820s.

How conscious Heine was of this change is sufficiently indicated by the title of the interesting essay *Die Nordsee: Dritte Abteilung,* which relates a prose work to two poetical works; indeed, in the first edition of *Reisebilder II, Nordsee III* was immediately preceded by *Nordsee II*. This essay[1] is in a number of ways a prelude to Heine's thinking on matters that were to occupy him with increasing intensity until the middle of the 1830s, culminating in the ambitious studies of German literary, religious, and philosophical history. Thus present and future concerns are woven together in *Nordsee III*. The present concern is that which underlies both *Buch der Lieder* and *Das Buch Le Grand*—the definition of the poet's own self—here developed in terms of the fashionable concept of *Zerrissenheit,* which Heine was to appropriate so thoroughly for himself,[2] and accompanied by appearances of the suffering persona. The future concern is the effort to define the nature of the epoch in which Heine lived, developed primarily by means of characterizations of Goethe and Napoleon, the two great men of the age just past, whose heritage and its relevance were to occupy Heine's mind with varying intensity for the rest of his life. Thus *Nordsee III* consists largely of open-ended ruminations. Although it is composed with care,[3] it ends weakly with the shallow polemic epigrams contributed by Karl Immermann, out of which was to grow the brawl with Platen.

Ideen: Das Buch Le Grand is a different matter. This astonishing little work is by far the prose masterpiece of Heine's younger years, if not indeed of his whole career. Elster fairly called it a peak performance among all Heine's prose works.[4] Heine, whose judgment on his own works was far from reliable and sometimes not even serious, knew this time what he had done; his letters to his friends are full of enthusiastic satisfaction with his achievement in *Reisebilder II,*[5] and this enthusiasm refers in large part to *Das Buch Le Grand.* As an artistic accomplishment it ranks with the *Nordsee* poems, and its excellences derive from the same source: out of the unlovely chaos of his life and feelings Heine distilled a poetic persona of convincing contour and constructed its elements and their complex interrelation in a carefully balanced composition masquerading as an effortless capriccio. The result is breathtaking.

Or it ought to be. Again, however, the subtlety of Heine's art has turned out to be beyond the reach of many of his readers, and one can find over and over again the opinion that *Das Buch Le*

Grand is a collage of witty fancies lying wherever they happen to have fallen, despite Heine's own often reiterated convictions about the primacy of form.[6] It not infrequently happens that the contemporary newspaper criticism of Heine's works, even when it tends to be negative, makes better sense than the later analyses of more noted literati and scholars; Elster quotes a passage from a Hamburg newspaper in which the anonymous critic, with admirable perception, remarks: "Hier erhebt sich der Verfasser in Inhalt und Form zu einer Vollendung, welche ihn in die Reihe der ersten humoristischen Schriftsteller Deutschlands versetzt."[7] One of the few later critics to defend the form of the work was Léon Polak, who argued forcefully for the "absolute éénheid" of *Das Buch Le Grand* compared to Heine's other works.[8] But Elster himself originally called the work a "Tohuwabohu von bunten Einfällen,"[9] although he later changed his mind and spoke of it as a well-organized whole;[10] and even the playwright Ludwig Robert, whose connection to the work was, as we shall see, probably slightly more than casual, could see in it only a disorderly succession of ideas.[11] It is an entertaining situation. This work, with the word *Ideen* in its title and its brilliant persiflage of misapplied logical rigor (Chapters 8 and 14), is the best evidence that in dealing with Heine it is important not only to listen to what he says, but also to watch what he is doing.

The misapprehension concerning the artistic character of this and other prose works of Heine derives from two sources: the inherited unwillingness to see in Romantic prose and its aftermath artistically organized structures,* and the urge to expose the biographical substratum. With respect to the latter pastime, *Das Buch Le Grand* is particularly productive, for it presents biographical problems enough to occupy several generations of scholars. Of all these problems, few of which yield satisfactory solutions, the most troublesome has been the identification of the "Madame" to whom the *causerie* of the work is addressed, along with the question of whether she is identical with the "Evelina" to whom it is dedicated. Elster identified "Evelina" with Cousin

* A modest example of an attempt to extract a structural sense from a work that has been traditionally so regarded is my study *The Nachtwachen von Bonaventura: A Structural Interpretation* (The Hague, 1965).

Therese and saw the work as a whole as referring to that putative affair.[12] Elster always looks his worst when he gets on the subject of Therese, and it is rather sad to report that in his second edition he identified also the "Signora Laura" of the text not only with Therese,[13] but with Amalie as well.[14] In his first edition, Elster went so far as to identify "Madame" with the wife of Salomon Heine, offering the utterly mad suggestion that Heine's praise of learnedness (!) in the work was aimed at making him more respected and welcome as a prospective son-in-law in his uncle's house.* [15] It is clear that there is nothing to be accomplished on this path of inquiry. As to "Madame," Karl Hessel in 1892 presented a solution that, despite a number of doubtful features, remains our best answer.† Hessel's instincts with respect to *Das Buch Le Grand* led him in the right direction, although he could not free himself from biographical considerations: "Ganz sicherlich hat das Bedürfnis, das Publikum irrezuführen über seine Liebeserlebnisse, genau ebensoviel Antheil an dem Entschluß gehabt, ein Stück Selbstbiographie zu schreiben, wie das Bedürfnis, Aufklärungen über seine Vergangenheit zu geben." [16] Translated into more simple terms: the work is not a report to the public about Heine's love affairs. It will be worthwhile to follow Hessel a moment longer because his speculations lead to a useful result.

Hessel identifies "Madame" with the sister-in-law of Heine's valuable friend Rahel Varnhagen, Friederike Robert (1795–1832). She was the wife of Rahel's brother Ludwig Robert, a comic playwright of minor significance, whose relations with Heine deteriorated a good deal later on.[17] Friederike was a considerable beauty, and Heine flattered her, as was his custom, with that noncommittal gallantry toward unattainable women that sometimes

* Elster abandoned this absurd idea in his second edition (E², *1*, 53*–54*).

† Karl Hessel, "Heines 'Buch Legrand,'" *Vierteljahrschrift für Litteraturgeschichte, 5* (1892), 546–72. Léon Polak in "Heinrich Heines *Buch Legrand,*" *Neophilologus, 7* (1921/22) attacked Hessel and argued that "Madame" and Evelina must both be Therese (pp. 263–64) and the dead Veronika a symbol for the lost Amalie (p. 267). The debate was continued by H. Uyttersprot, "Nog eens Das Buch Le Grand," *Album Prof. Dr. Frank Baur* (Antwerp, Brussels, Ghent, and Leuven, 1948), *2*, 317–32, and Polak, "En nogmaals Heine's Buch Legrand," *Revue des Langues Vivantes, 15* (1949), 96–100. For all one's sympathy for Polak's complaint that his contribution had remained unnoticed for twenty-six years (ibid., p. 96), the debate ultimately yields little of value.

serves lonely bachelors as a vent for inner feelings.* Hessel brings a good deal of evidence to bear on his supposition. In his letter to Robert of March 4 and one to Friederike of October 12, 1825, Heine refers to her as a "Türkin," which fits very well with the description of the female figure in the painting.[18] The comments about the seriousness of Shakespeare's fools in Chapter 11 occur in very similar terms in the letter to Friederike.[19] Hessel also proposed an allusion to Robert's comedy *Der Pavian,* which Heine professed to admire.[20] The question of whether Friederike is also "Evelina" remains difficult, and Hessel was undecided.[21] It would seem reasonable, since the work ends in extravagant flattery of "Madame," that she should be identical with the dedicatee. The problem is complicated by the occurrence of "Evelina" in *Nordsee III,*[22] where she clearly appears to belong to the pathos of lost love that produces similar exclamations in the *Nordsee* poems. But it is purposeless to continue the speculation. The value of Hessel's suggestion lies elsewhere: if we can accept as a working hypothesis that "Madame" in fact does refer to Friederike Robert, then the question loses all interest even from a biographical point of view, since Friederike did not play a major role in Heine's life. The importance of "Madame" is thereby restricted to her fictional function in *Das Buch Le Grand,* about which more will be said shortly. The other problems of identification in the work—Signora Laura, the dead child Veronika, and so on—may by analogy be regarded as of the same order.*

To be sure, Heine himself described *Das Buch Le Grand* as an autobiographical fragment.[23] Furthermore, there is some reason to believe that the memoirs of which Heine spoke in 1824, if they ever existed,[24] supplied some of the material for the account of the narrator's childhood, especially for the Napoleon chapters.[25] But to come to an adequate understanding of *Das Buch Le Grand* it is necessary to see the autobiographical material as sublimated into an artistic structure, just as this was necessary in the case of

* Hirth, in his usual manner, turns this relationship into a passionate love affair (Hirth, *4,* 203, 209). Certainly he exaggerates the case.

* Hirth claimed to have found in the archives of the Princess Murat proof that the "heroine" of the work, as he misleadingly puts it, was indeed Friederike. See his *Heinrich Heine und seine französische Freunde* (Mainz, 1949), p. 10. But some doubt is cast upon his conclusions by Claire Hartgenbusch in Hirth, *6,* 86.

Buch der Lieder. We are dealing with the development of a literary personality; *Das Buch Le Grand* is the biography of the fictive persona and it is narrated by the fictive persona. The result demonstrates that Heine had good reason for going about it in this way.

Let us recapitulate for a moment the situation as it developed in *Buch der Lieder.* The poet succeeded in forcing the pathos of his suffering into a poetic perspective, so that gradually an entirely new figure arises, the poetic narrator who describes, relates, and orders the chaos of feeling and generates himself, as it were, in a context that becomes increasingly fictional. The weight of pathetic experience and recollection still bears on this figure; but he has freed himself from it to a relative degree by gaining control over the management of the self-image. The quality of strength characteristic of most of the *Nordsee* poems, therefore, has its source in the poetry itself. The strength of the poet lies in his art; in his existence in his art he seeks his salvation. Now the poet, in the role of his own persona, can give an account of himself, describe the elements of his own self-composition, and differentiate out of his experience materials for fresh perspectives and a new orientation of the persona. This is the content of *Das Buch Le Grand.*

The first chapter begins with a motto from, it is claimed, an "Altes Stück": "Sie war liebenswürdig, und Er liebte Sie; Er aber war nicht liebenswürdig, und Sie liebte Ihn nicht" (E, *3,* 131). That the "Altes Stück" is fictitious is both obvious and significant. It suggests from the very beginning that the context of the work is a literary one created exclusively by the poet—a point that, with Heine's familiar delayed-action technique, acquires, as we shall see, sudden importance in Chapter 2, where the poet's awareness of his own creativity saves his life. That the motto of his life, moreover, is claimed to be from a play also suggests distance achieved by a literary perspective. It is furthermore worth pointing out that Heine does not call this play an "Alte Tragödie," which he might have done a few years earlier when he was still impressed by the power of his feelings and tried, in his own plays, to set them into a tragic form. No, it is simply a "Stück," a play, for this is what Heine is determined to make out of it. The language of the "quotation" avoids all pathos and is content to express an unhappy fact; in the objectivity of the statement there is a form of acceptance, although there is no effort to deny that the fact is an unhappy one. Heine was not one to put disappointments and sufferings behind him; they echo in all the rooms and hallways of his growing literary edifice. The problem is to keep them from totally absorbing the present and stultifying the creative flow. Accompanying this effort to put the whole matter into the narrative past is an entirely new element: "Er aber war nicht liebenswürdig." The amiability of the beloved is intermittently denied in *Buch der Lieder,* and this denial is one of the blind alleys in the search for a workable attitude. The persona, on the other hand, is frequently presented as amiable indeed, for example, in the idylls of the *Nordsee* poems or of *Die Harzreise.* This entirely new statement and new self-estimate is another step forward in objectifying the persona.

Now the causerie, which is the narrative form of the work, begins: "Madame, kennen Sie das alte Stück? Es ist ein ganz außerordentliches Stück, nur etwas zu sehr melancholisch. Ich hab' mal die Hauptrolle darin gespielt" (E, *3,* 131). The silent role played by "Madame" in *Das Buch Le Grand* is an interesting one. The narrator chooses a charming and beautiful lady—a married lady, let it be noted—to listen to his recitation of the story of himself. He does not tell this story as he would to a friend or to an older mother figure like Rahel Varnhagen—one may search Heine's letters in vain for anything approximating the atmosphere and the kind of self-presentation of *Das Buch Le Grand.* He tells the story to charm, to entertain, to make an ironic though irresistible appeal for sympathy, and as though the whole thing were constructed for the sake of the gallantly hyperbolic flattery with which it ends. But now it is necessary for the health of the persona, as it were, that the melancholy features of the story be made as harmless as possible; to this end it is necessary that "Madame" not be taken too seriously and that she not be given full access to the darkest caverns of the narrator's heart, for there she would not be able to be of any help. This suits Heine's temperament perfectly, for when it came to women he was not usually inclined to accompany love and admiration with respect. So it is that "Madame" is treated throughout with delicate condescension. This appears, for example, in the rhetorical questions like the one that opens the work, to which the answer can always only be visualized as a bemused shake of the head. There are any number of passages in *Das Buch Le Grand* where the narrator's superiority and condescension for "Madame" are reinforced—for example, in Chapter 5, where, with an air of innocence, he assumes that she has read Franz Bopp's Indological studies; [26] by contrast, in Chapter 7, he asserts that she has no idea of how complicated Latin is,[27] which gives no great impression of her education; the same phrase, "you have no idea," occurs in a different context in Chapter 11.[28] In Chapter 14, with somewhat heavier irony, he asserts that his writings are sufficiently harmless that she may read them without fear.[29] In almost every direct address of "Madame" this undertone is audible.

The narrator begins his self-presentation, as I have said, in a literary context. The old play is "extraordinary," but "rather too melancholy." It is remarkable to see with what a sure hand Heine begins to construct the elements of the persona in the very first sentence. On the one hand, the experience of unhappy love is under no circumstances to be regarded as a bagatelle; on the other, it was admittedly overwrought, too melancholy. The narrator played the leading role and all the ladies wept, except one, and that was the point and the catastrophe of the whole piece. We are getting into the context of *Buch der Lieder,* but at a double literary remove, for the catastrophe that generated the poems is described as that of a *play*. And, sure enough, the connection to *Buch der Lieder* is made in the very next paragraph, where the narrator speaks of the *Lied* of the unwept tear. But this *Lied,* it seems, is whispered into the narrator's ear by Satan in order to destroy his soul; the melody is heard only in the Hell within. So the pathos of the unwept tear is dangerous to the soul—a recognition that from the point of view of the young Heine is of the utmost importance—and the narrator abruptly takes flight.

He does this by the technique of association that is his surface principle of composition. From Hell he comes to Heaven, and from Heaven to marriage—an association that reminds us of the love-wounded bachelor—and from marriage to food. Any reader of Heine knows that there are few thoughts that can touch off in him such fireworks of hyperbole as that of food, and his picture of roast geese flying about with saucedishes in their beaks is one of the most extraordinary descriptions of marriage ever written. It is not meant seriously, of course; it is only a capriccio that allows the narrator to draw back from the edge of the abyss. But it serves its purpose, for when he returns to the subject of Hell, his mind is quite differently attuned. "Madame," of course, can have no notion of Hell, and the narrator does not miss the opportunity to suggest by means of a reference to Don Juan, the triviality of her mind.[30] It is interesting, however, to hear him assert that of all the devils Amor is the smallest, for this is truly an admission. More important is that the narrator's description of Hell turns to satire. The elements of the satire—a caricature of the primitive Christian concept of Hell and a sour reference to the Christian insistence upon the baptism of the Jews, of which Heine himself had so recently been a victim—are less significant than the fact that the narrator has turned to matters that transcend his individual suffering. This dimension becomes widest at the point where Socrates is denied any right to an exception from the rule that all pagans must burn, and the passage gives a hint of Heine's pessimistic view of later years that the universe is inimical or indifferent to the good, the true, the wise, and the beautiful. Finally the narrator closes the circle: amidst all the cacophony of Hell the *Lied* of the unwept tear is audible. The temptation to pathos has not been overcome, but the personal suffering is allowed to combine with meta-personal considerations, and this will turn out to be of significance for the course of *Das Buch Le Grand.*

Because the circle has been closed, however, Chapter 2 must start once more from the beginning, and so the motto from the "Altes Stück" occurs again, and the narrator begins a new tack that will expand the fictional context a good deal. He starts by putting the reader—and "Madame"—on a false track, for this time he flatly says that the "Altes Stück" is a tragedy, which it certainly is not, as it turns out, and he hints as much with the important limitation that the hero is neither killed nor does he kill himself. And now he uses "Madame" for an interesting purpose in one of the key passages of *Das Buch Le Grand:*

> Die Augen der Heldin sind schön, sehr schön—Madame, riechen Sie nicht Veilchenduft?—sehr schön, und doch so scharfgeschliffen, daß sie mir wie gläserne Dolche durch das Herz drangen und gewiß aus meinem Rücken wieder herausguckten—aber ich starb doch nicht an diesen meuchelmörderischen Augen. Die Stimme der Heldin ist auch schön—Madame, hörten Sie nicht eben eine Nachtigall schlagen?—eine schöne, seidne Stimme, ein süßes Gespinst der sonnigsten Töne, und meine Seele ward darin verstrickt und würgte sich und quälte sich. (E, *3*, 133)

Here three elements are skillfully combined: the suffering of the hero, its Romantic expression, and the recognition that the suffering has not killed him. The third element relativizes the first, and the second is relativized by the combination of the language with which it is expressed and the use made of "Madame." The mode of expression is taken directly out of the earlier stages of *Buch der Lieder:* the mannered naïveté of the language ("schön, sehr schön") and the image of the beloved as, one might say, existentially destructive. But the rhetorical questions make it clear that it is "*Madame*" who is expected to react Romantically; the Romantic clichés—the aroma of violets and the song of the nightingale—are placed on her account. One is almost tempted to call this a sneaky trick. But it is important; the narrator is trying to shed a skin.

This is followed by another ingenious trick: the constructed persona constructs yet another persona. The self-identification of the constructed persona as the "Graf vom Ganges" not only visibly demonstrates the process of the fictive construction—perhaps we could call this the synthetic feature of the fictive construction—but also will allow the narrator to discard an element of this persona, in an analogy to the overcoming and leaving behind of an aspect of the original persona. This latter we can call an analytic feature; it will become clearer presently. That the hyper-persona, if one may so call it, of the "Graf vom Ganges" is a fiction is made immediately and purposefully evident, for though he claims to tell a story that took place in Venice, it is made clear that the location is actually Hamburg: the "Via Burstah" is a street in Hamburg, the "Strada San Giovanni" is the Johannisstrasse in that city, and "Signor Unbescheiden" is a Hamburg restaurateur whom Heine mentions again in an article on the Hamburg fire of 1842.[31] This is the sort of thing that has caused people to accuse Heine of being irrational and frivolous in his composition, but in fact it yields an interpretation without much difficulty. The partial fusion of Hamburg with Venice represents an effort to achieve distance and perspective, as is evident when one considers the extent to which the recollection of Hamburg was capable of roiling Heine's emotions for years after his unhappy experiences there. At the same time, the aesthetic principle of fictive self-creation is exposed. That the "Graf vom Ganges" is not located in his homeland, but far away from it, is connected with the analytic feature, which will fall into its proper place in a moment.

The "Graf vom Ganges," weary of the sufferings of unrequited love, decides to take his life. He buys his pistols in a "Galanterieladen" (E, *3*, 133), a shop of frippery and knickknacks. The effect is to trivialize the attempted suicide at the very outset. (Compare by contrast Büchner's *Woyzeck,* where the shabbiness and hostility of the Jew from whom Woyzeck buys the murder weapon points up the unrelieved dismalness of Woyzeck's situation.) Furthermore, the objects that catch his eye in the shop all have erotic associations—hearts on gold chains, cups "mit zärtlichen Devisen," portraits of famous objects of love or lust. Heine's vulgar epithet for Lucretia, "das dicke Tugendmensch" (E, *3*, 134), incidentally suggests the frustrated bitterness of the despairing lover. But it is of significance that, as the "Graf vom Ganges" prepares his suicide, his eye is caught by all these pretty things that are symbols of eros and life. Symbolic of the pleasures of life, also, is the delicate last meal of oysters and Rhine wine; that the narrator was unable to eat it is, for Heine, an indication of really serious emotional disturbance.

Now the analytic feature of the "Graf vom Ganges"-persona

comes into play, for the distance between Venice and India symbolizes the distance between the narrating person and the inner landscape of Romanticism. It is not always remembered outside of Germany that there was such a thing as Romantic scholarship, out of which grew a tradition more enduring than that of Romantic literature and philosophy; the fascination with language as the bridge between the life and spirit of the folk on the one hand and aesthetic transcendence on the other led to the founding of linguistic science, while, on a parallel track, the interest in exotic and presumably harmonious cultures solidified into the foundations of Indology. Since the study of European languages leads also to India, the whole complex, which is pursued consistently in *Das Buch Le Grand,* can serve Heine as a symbol for Romanticism. The inner landscape of Romanticism into which the "Graf vom Ganges" dreams his way in "Venice" is impossibly distant—it is three thousand miles away and three thousand years in the past. This is the analytic feature of the Indian persona: the element of Romantic suffering in the narrative persona, although it still echoes powerfully in his memory, is nevertheless a layer of his self that is separated out and forcibly put at a vast remove in time and space. The painful process of overcoming that is being demonstrated to us here, stage by stage, is similar to that of *Buch der Lieder.* Indeed, into the lost and distant landscape, rather than into the present situation, is introduced an important element from *Buch der Lieder*—the fiction of the remorseful beloved who has lost her chance.

That the tragedy was not to end in suicide we have already been told. Now we are to see how this comes about. The "Graf vom Ganges" assumes a theatrical pose—on a corner of the busy "Strada San Giovanni," be it noted—and recites the death-monologue from *Almansor.* This sudden collapsing together of the three personae—the author, the narrator, and the "Graf vom Ganges"—has in itself an irresistibly comic effect. But there is more to it than that, for the narrator goes on to observe, with the most urbane wit, that while ordinary folk are obliged to borrow Shakespeare's "To be or not to be" as a "Lebensabiturientenrede" (E, *3,* 135), it is a different matter for one who has written immortal tragedies of his own. "Jeder ist sich selbst der Nächste": Heine's persona quotes from Heine's works, and thereby saves his own life. For, first of all, the monologue, in the lush lyrical style of *Almansor,* is packed with references to the beauties of life and nature, and, secondly, it is observed, such lengthy monologues have the advantage that the would-be suicide gains time. So it happens that suddenly the lost beloved comes by and graces the "Graf vom Ganges" with a generous glance; the result is a resurgence of vital hope. It should be noted that nothing has changed in the actual situation of the "Graf vom Ganges"; the beloved goes her way without further ado, so that what has in fact saved his life is the recitation of the monologue. Thus the narrator's consciousness of his own poetic creation has contributed to his salvation, and the self-awareness of the poet as a poet—the bold comparison with Shakespeare—is expressed in such strong terms that the appearance of the beloved seems really only incidental. The parallel to *Buch der Lieder* is evident at once. Also evident is the irony with which this hyperbolic self-confidence is modified; for Heine knew perfectly well that *Almansor* was anything but immortal. The poetic persona comes to rest in a parallelogram of forces: memories of unhappy love, set in a context of Romantic imagery, pull in the direction of death and dissolution; pride in poetic genius inspires an ultimately invincible love of life. In the center resides the irony that allows a substantially healthy self-awareness.

In view of all this it is appropriate that Chapter 3 should expand into a vast relaxation, a set of variations on the importance of being alive. It is curious, though, that almost immediately after this topic has been opened, there is a sudden detour into an expression of what can only be called existential anxiety. It seems that, on the one hand, the recognition that disappointment in love does not kill releases a latent vitality and gaiety, but, on the other, it cannot lead to a totally affirmative view of life. The idea of life as an only partially rational dream of a drunken god that will be extinguished upon his awakening is unexpected at this juncture and opens up briefly a pessimistic cosmic perspective in the same way that the adversion to Socrates did in Chapter 1. But this is only an undertone, a hint at depths not deeply probed.

The remainder of the chapter is aggressively nonheroic and antitragic, and it is underpinned with a variety of literary references, including an explicit contradiction of the famous line from Schiller, "Das Leben ist der Güter höchstes *nicht*" (E, *3*, 136).[32] The programmatically untragic Goethe is also brought into the complex with a reference to the troublesome ending of *Egmont,* along with a full-length quotation of one of Heine's favorite passages in literature, that in the *Odyssey* where the dead Achilles expresses envy of the simplest living peasant. The anecdote of Israel Löwe, who refused a duel with the remark, "Ich will lieber ein lebendiger Hund sein, als ein toter Löwe" (E, *3*, 137), was maliciously picked up by the Republican Jacob Venedey in 1854 as an example of Heine's cowardly character,[33] which was absurd enough, since Venedey seems not to have noticed or cared that the pun is a paraphrase of a passage from the grouchy wisdom of Ecclesiastes (9:4): "For to him that is joined to all the living there is hope; for a living dog is better than a dead lion." *

The affirmation of life supported by these literary references is a Sturm und Drang of robust self-assurance that is closely related to the Titanism of *Nordsee I*. "In meinen Adern kocht das rote Leben" (E, *3*, 137), exults the narrator. And, in a phrase that has always been carefully misunderstood by Heine's small-souled detractors, "Jedes Weib ist mir eine geschenkte Welt"—a formulation that, far from suggesting Don Juanism, is the most generous view of the female sex anywhere in his works. The cosmic perspective echoes again briefly in a renunciation of immortality: the theme of this-worldliness, which plays an important part in the subsequent apotheosis of Napoleon, is here introduced. The Titanism of *Nordsee I* finally appears full-blown in the highly rhetorical peroration to Chapter 3: "o! dann durchbebt mich erst recht die rechte Lust, wie schmeichelnde Mädchen legen sich die Abendlüfte an mein brausendes Herz, und die Sterne winken, und ich erhebe mich und schwebe über der kleinen Erde und den kleinen Gedanken der Menschen." This hyperbole strikes one as overwrought and suggests troubled undercurrents that will oblige revision and moderation.

In Chapter 4, however, the narrator prefers to stick, for the

* In commenting on this point, Rudolf Schlösser surmised, correctly, as far as we know, that Löwe and Düvent are fictional figures. See Schlösser, "Kleinigkeiten aus dem Koheleth bei Klopstock und Heine," *Euphorion, 22* (1915), 89.

time being, with rhetorical pathos; he introduces what is in a sense a new persona: the self-projection into the future as the aged poet. The purpose of this projection is to deflect the always threatening self-pity into a new kind of vision, enabling the narrator to see his sufferings as a source of consolation for others through the medium of his poetry. This passage which, with its gentle, elegiac tone, contrasts so vividly with the trumpets of the preceding paragraph, prophesies the sentimental role Heine's poetry will play in the lives of young people of future generations and is unique in his works. The all-too-accurate prophecy of the isolation of Heine's latter years is moving, despite its sentimentality; it is as though he knew where the forces churning inside of him must necessarily take him, despite his desperate efforts to give his fate a different direction. This little chapter is another effort to justify the persona in a literary context. The song of the flowers of the Brenta—that is, of the lost love, for the love story of the secondary persona is located throughout in "Venice"—which the poet sings at the request of the young lads, is a song of the dreams of the poet's youth. The recollection of the youthful dreams is consolidated into poetry and thus carried across present reality into the future on a literary plane. Real time and poetic time are thereby distinguished from one another, and this distinction is part of the effort to overcome.

With that, the first section of *Das Buch Le Grand* comes to a close, for Chapter 5 gradually shifts into a different reality, what one might perhaps call a four-dimensional reality: the recollections of childhood and youth that are the theme of the next five chapters are enhanced by the Romantic dimension, which is both a Rhenish and a literary heritage. This shift begins with the piecemeal dismantlement of the secondary persona, the "Graf vom Ganges." "Madame," who cannot be expected to understand the subtleties of this tale, is informed that the narrator is not the "Graf vom Ganges." But, he insists, "ich stamme aus Hindostan" (E, *3*, 139)—that is, from the symbolic Romantic landscape, a matter that the narrator adumbrates for a while by means of a reference to the linguist Franz Bopp, whose lectures Heine had attended in Berlin when he was supposed to be doing other things. Here, too, the poetic context is carefully maintained. The *Maha-*

bharata, the narrator presumes, is a 200,000-line love letter from one of his ancestors to the other, and this love is told on the shores of the Pacific in the song of the nightingale. This lapse into Romantic exoticism is quickly brought up short by self-ironic hyperbole: the dedication to the god of love, says the narrator, is as long as all of Walter Scott's novels, and this comparison is finally devaluated by an allusion to the chatter of Aristophanes' *Birds.*

The persona of the "Graf vom Ganges" is now finally disposed of as the inner landscape of Hindustan is replaced by the real, though no less thematically significant, landscape of the Rhineland. The shift of scene is introduced by a peculiar digression: the first feature of the new landscape to be introduced is the "Berge der Thorheit"—that is, the vineyards of the Rhine—and the narrator amuses himself with the speculation that the foolishness he heard spoken at the table yesterday was bottled years before on the Johannisberg; he asserts that if he had the faith to move mountains he would have the Johannisberg follow him about. This apparent irrelevance seems to support the opinion that Heine strings his humorous associations together without regard to rational composition. But is it too recherché to point out that the Johannisberg, as was well known, was the property of the redoubtable adversary of Heine and all proponents of liberty, Prince Metternich? * Perhaps not, when we take a look at the next step: the narrator gives a résumé of the political conversation of the Rhenish burghers during his youth. The point is in the next sentence: "Ich habe mich nie um dergleichen Gespräche bekümmert und saß lieber bei den Mädchen" (E, *3,* 141). Here we are made aware of the two contrasting elements of the persona that are developed in *Das Buch Le Grand:* the Romantic sensibility, which is bound up with poetry and the tribulations of eros, and the alertness to present, particularly political, reality. This sentence stands at the beginning of a spiral into the depths of fictive memory, and it intimates that, at the stage now to be recounted, there was a definite predominance of the Romantic combination of poetry

* Heine made this connection repeatedly: E, *3,* 561, 570; E, *6,* 138. The Johannisberg came into Metternich's possession in 1816. It is about eighty-five miles from Düsseldorf as the crow flies and thus cannot belong to boyhood memories of the local landscape.

and eros over the sense of the political present. The account of the way in which this relationship shifted and the restless balance that was eventually achieved will fill the remainder of *Das Buch Le Grand;* this problem is so central to what is happening in the work that it can without exaggeration be called a principle of form.

There are three stages of this plunge into fictive recollection—fictive in the sense that there is no point in trying to attest the autobiographical reality of the events related, which have relevance only in this literary context. It is interesting that the three stages move progressively from a Romanticism of eros to a Romanticism of death. The first stage is a kind of fiction familiar from *Die Harzreise* and some moments of *Buch der Lieder:* the desirable young poet is adored by three different girls (who with their contrasting temperaments correspond very loosely to the three rivers at the end of *Die Harzreise*), but this experience is of only indifferent importance, for the narrator's relationship to eros is tense indeed: in a confessional outburst, similar to a later one in a poem of *Neue Gedichte, Clarissa* 2,[34] the narrator admits to "Madame," that "wenn man von mir geliebt sein will, muß man mich *en canaille* behandeln" (E, *3,* 142). His interest is held, rather, by the cousin of the three sisters, "die schöne Johanna." This figure, I would propose, is a distant relative of the famous "rotes Sefchen" of the *Memoiren,* but free of the latter's Gothic-novel characteristics. Both girls perform the same function: they open up to the narrator the realm of the Romantic imagination. Johanna tells the young poet-to-be the legends of the Rhineland, including that of the Loreley (the well-known literary provenance of the latter indicates that Johanna is also a literary creation); she is, moreover, mortally ill, and this characteristic is coupled with an intimation of a past history of love, now apparently sublimated into a magical, fragile, sensitivity. This nearness to death has a noetic quality, for she knows names the boy himself has forgotten, particularly that of the dead Veronika.

The dead child Veronika, whose story is here temporarily broken off, is one of the more difficult problems of interpretation in Heine's works. One suspects that she is related to the equally mysterious dead Maria of *Reise von München nach Genua,*[35] but this does not help us much, especially as Maria is a woman and not a child.[36] A closer correspondence to the dead Very of *Florentinische Nächte* is probable.* Heine has been accused of speculating here with Romantic clichés in order to achieve a shallow effect. While the continual recurrence of the dead Maria in *Reise von München nach Genua* does strike one as a little gratuitous and annoying, here the charge seems to me unfounded in view of the tense and serious way in which the problem of Romanticism is dealt with. Perhaps it would not be unreasonable to suggest that we have here symbolic materials toward a psychological understanding of the persona. It is quite obvious that this plunge into the depths of recollection passes through three stages of the relationship of eros and death. The three sisters who adored the narrator participate in eros only, but they are rejected. Johanna participates in both, but clearly tends in the direction of death. Veronika does not participate in eros at all, for she is a child; her beauty, of which much is made later on, belongs exclusively to the aesthetic fascination of death. If it is true that this descent into memory serves as a background to the love story around which *Das Buch Le Grand* is constructed, then the following solution presents itself: the misery of unrequited love is closely bound up with and finds its expression in the Romantic imagination (*Poesie*); the pursuit of the source of the Romantic imagination leads beyond and beneath eros to death. The love experience is doomed and threatens, as in Chapter 2, to lead back to death. Furious effort must be expended to make the turn to life within the context of poetry itself; for all the while, though life calls with a loud voice, death has lost none of its aesthetic fascination. The transcendence of poetry by means of poetry can take place only through the re-creation of the poet; at the same time, elements that turn away from death toward life, from the dissolving imagination to external reality, must be firmed in the persona, as is done gradually in *Das Buch Le Grand.* The bond with poetry must not be cut, for to it the persona owes his whole existence; on the other hand, it must not be permitted to haul the poet back to its deadly source. One good way to prevent this, if my metaphor will

* This was asserted by Julius Petersen (W, *4,* 507) and denied by Elster (E^2, *4,* 511).

stand the strain, is to loop the bond around something firm—like Napoleon. I do not insist upon this interpretation; I propose it as a hypothesis. It seems to suggest some possibilities for a more general interpretation of Heine than will be attempted in this book. It makes no assumptions about the level of consciousness at which Heine may have woven these connections together, but it makes a very considerable assumption about his depth and sensitivity as an artist.

However all this may be, it is apparent that once the dead Veronika has been briefly touched upon, there is an abrupt change in atmosphere in Chapter 6. The plunge into fictive memory is interrupted and a more substantial reality comes into focus. As the story becomes specifically localized in Düsseldorf, we are confronted with genuine childhood memories of the author, and here it becomes quite possible that Heine used materials originally intended for memoirs; for the first time in *Das Buch Le Grand,* we find researchable events out of Heine's childhood and youth. At no point, however, is the poet-persona abandoned or lost from view. The chapter begins with an ironic comparison with Homer: the poet identifies his place of birth in case seven towns should compete for the honor after his death. It is characteristic, of course, that the seven towns named should all be nondescript, including the hated Göttingen, and that the first should be Schilda, legendary locale of incurable foolishness, and the second Krähwinkel, symbol of the remotest provincialism; the shamelessness of the comparison with Homer is thereby ironized. From the background of the childhood milieu, the poet projects ahead to the time when green veiled Englishwomen will visit the house of his birth. It is interesting that in the midst of this banter more memories of death intervene, as though as an echo of the end of Chapter 5: first the mention of Heine's dead relatives on his respectable mother's side and his dead nurse, and then the recollection of the drowned "Wilhelm." * "Wilhelm's" drowning is described again twenty-five years later in the poem *Erinnerung* in *Romanzero;*[37] it must have made a strong impression on Heine, especially as he seems to have been in some sense the cause of the accident.

* Heine misremembered or altered the name of the victim, Fritz von Wizewski (E, *3*, 144, n. 1).

But the account of childhood is moving in a new direction, towards the other pole of *Das Buch Le Grand.* From the gastronomic delights of his childhood—his passion for apple tarts—the narrator moves to his passions of the present: "Liebe, Wahrheit, Freiheit und Krebssuppe" (E, *3,* 145), a catalogue of elements that make up the present persona: added to the familiar element of love and the intermediate one of sensual enjoyment are the more public one of truth and the political one of liberty. With refined elegance, the narrator does not let us forget here that what is being recounted is an inner struggle:

> Und wahrlich, nie würden Apfeltörtchen mich so sehr angereizt haben, hätte der krumme Hermann sie nicht so geheimnisvoll mit seiner weißen Schürze bedeckt—und die Schürzen sind es, welche—doch sie bringen mich ganz aus dem Kontext, ich sprach ja von der Reuterstatue, die so viel silberne Löffel im Leibe hat und keine Suppe, und den Kurfürsten Jan Wilhelm darstellt. (E, *3,* 145).

It is nothing short of amazing with what a light hand Heine controls the vital elements of the persona. He is on his way toward the description of a political *Urerlebnis,* when a verbal association threatens to revive the love-complex; but he notices in time that the skirts "bringen mich ganz aus dem Kontext," and he finds his way again. There are few passages in which Heine succeeded with such elegance in exposing the nature of the problem around which the persona is constructed. Only a careless reader will see here a display of capriciousness.

The statue of the Elector Jan Willem may be seen in Düsseldorf to this day; it stands on the Marktplatz in the *Altstadt* at the end of the Bolkerstrasse, where Heine was born and grew up. Heine quite appropriately uses it as a symbol of the absolutist order that the French Revolution and Napoleon were to shatter, at least temporarily. What Heine here describes, from the skillfully emulated perspective of a child, is the destruction of the tolerably well-ordered world of the eighteenth century, a historical upheaval from which Germany did not recover for a very long time and to some extent, at least emotionally, has not recovered yet. For, despite the Romantic notions about the medieval imperium that beclouded conservative minds in the nineteenth century, the restorative forces were in fact engaged in an effort to reinstitute the absolutism of the Frederician age. The libertarian ideas generated by the French Revolution and the modern world generally work against a predestined order of society in which each individual occupies a secure, unquestioned, and hierarchically determined place and lives and thinks in a way to preserve and maintain this order and not to upset it. German authority has never given up trying to reestablish this situation in some workable way, whether by means of the oppression of Metternich's system, the militarism of the Empire, the terror of Fascism, or, in a highly diluted and somewhat comic form, the "formierte Gesellschaft" of Ex-Chancellor Erhard. Any historical interpretation of Heine must proceed from the fact that the beginnings of this development coincide with his impressionable youthful years.

In this account of the abdication of Duke Wilhelm of Bavaria (Heine incorrectly calls him the Elector) and the introduction of the Napoleonic regime in the Duchy of Berg, it is the details that are significant. The common people react to the abdication with great pathos, and the boy is certain that the world has come to an end. On the next day it appears that the world is still there, but it has changed: it has become French. An element of Napoleonic heroism is introduced with the first mention of the French drum major. But Heine operates with two Düsseldorf folk characters to relativize this heroism: "der tolle Alouisius" rattles off the names of the French generals, and the drunken cripple Gumpertz lies in the gutter and sings *Ça ira.** [38] The genre picture of the boys climbing up on the statue of Jan Willem is desentimentalized with the information that one was later shot as a deserter and the other hanged as a thief. The boy himself is not free from restorative tendencies, for he grows dizzy on his perch and must cling to the statue of the Elector to keep from falling. Heine's aversion to the common people and his disinclination for radical democracy, which became increasingly pronounced over the years, is here anticipated.

* These are characters from local carnival songs. See Eugen Moos, *Heine und Düsseldorf. (Beiträge zur Kritik von Heines "Memoiren" und "Buch Le Grand")* (Marburg, 1908), p. 65.

On the next day it appears that the world has not been so thoroughly revolutionized after all, for school begins again. Chapter 7 is a satire that permits the narrator to emerge on a surface of witty writing. The chapter is about the education of the poet-persona, and its theme is the resistance of his mind not only to dry learning but also to rigorous thinking. The learning process is continually transposed into that process of association, particularly verbal association, which characterizes Heine's style; at the same time the value of the material learned is measured against its practical commonplace usefulness, corresponding to the persona's turn to external reality. Historical dates provide a mnemonic technique for remembering addresses and subtraction a rule of thumb for borrowing money. Charming is the excursion on the difficulty of Latin; the concern that it would have been shameful not to know the eight *i*-stems with accusative in *-im* on the occasion of the doctoral defense is a little learned joke, for it would be difficult to find Latin nouns as unlikely to occur in a dissertation on law as those for mustard, strength, plowshare, thirst, cough, pickle, carpenter's rule, and hemp. This succession of words connected only by an inflectional peculiarity may be seen as prototypical for Heine's technique of verbal association, while his remark that they had made "so viel Aufsehen in der Welt . . . , indem sie sich zu einer bestimmten Klasse schlugen und dennoch eine Ausnahme blieben" (E, *3*, 150–51) is probably also a reflection upon himself. A similar game is played with the Hebrew verb forms.*

"Indessen," continues the narrator, "von der deutschen Sprache begriff ich viel mehr" (E, *3*, 151); the development of the poet is not lost from sight, and after a brief disquisition on the difficulties of German, including a reference to Heine's notorious uncertainty in the use of dative and accusative, he provides an excellent formula for the progress of the present work: "Während ich in einem Zuge fortschrieb und allerlei dabei dachte" (E, *3*, 152). Meanwhile

* With the form "pokat" (E, *3*, 151), Heine must be referring to the verb *pakad*, "to visit." That he should write it with a *t* rather than a *d* suggests an aural memory rather than a visual one of the written form, influenced by German *Auslautsverhärtung*. This, in turn, would suggest some limits on the extent of his knowledge of Hebrew.

the political content of the chapters is expanding. While on the subject of geography, the narrator finds occasion to advert to the upheavals that are continually changing the map of Europe, although this train of thought is broken off for the moment by another self-ironic comment on style. A brief excursion on the study of Classical mythology permits, as is customary with Heine, an allusion to the sensualism of the ancient Greeks and a sour reference to "unserem jüdischen Eingötzentum" (E, *3*, 153). This latter topic reemerges in fugue-like fashion in the account of the French lessons, during which the narrator has got into trouble by insisting upon translating "der Glaube" as "le crédit" instead of "la religion." The French lessons have been tied in with political history, for it has already been mentioned that the learning of French requires "viel Getrommel" (E, *3*, 153); the narration is becoming a fabric of overlapping themes. All this—the political motif, with its related theme of liberated sensuality, and the continual awareness of poetic sensitivity—leads up to the figure of the drum major Le Grand.

Of Heine's relatively few fictional characters, only a handful remain vividly in the reader's memory: Gumpelino and Hirsch in *Die Bäder von Luca,* the dancing bear of *Atta Troll,* Simson in *Schnabelewopski,* "das rote Sefchen" in the *Memoiren*—and Le Grand. Of all these, Le Grand is the most brilliantly conceived symbolic figure. He is named for *la Grande Armée,* the grand Napoleon, and the grand cause whose arms he bears. He represents military might in the service of the Revolution, which is a very differently valued thing for Heine than the militarism of Prussia. In the narrator's boyhood he is a visible incarnation of the revolutionary impetus of youth and a connecting link to the deified figure of Napoleon. Heine expands the dimensions of this complex by making Le Grand a drum major.* The attribute of erotic attractiveness, which is traditionally associated with the drum major (compare again Büchner's *Woyzeck*) and which stands in clear contrast to the private miseries the narrator is fighting, is

* Heine seems to have told Camille Selden of the drum major who taught him French (Houben, p. 935). There may actually have been such a person frequenting Heine's house during the occupation. But, of course, we cannot tell whether Heine was reciting to the girl true recollections of boyhood or a version of his own fictions.

stressed in the first passing mention of Le Grand in Chapter 6 and makes the connection, so central for Heine, between sensualism and political liberty. Of even greater significance is the fact that Le Grand represents a possible connection between poetry and action. He communicates with the narrator, not through words (for he knows no German) but by means of his drumming—that is, by means of rhythm and meter. The drumming of the guillotine march communicates the Terror more effectively than the dry prosaic account of the execution of "hochdero" aristocrats and "allerhöchstdero" king (E, *3*, 155). The poetry of this drumming is transformed into political action, as the narrator illustrates with two apposite anecdotes. At table with a "menagerie" of aristocrats his feet began to drum the revolutionary march when he got nothing to eat; and his feet played him the same trick during a soporific lecture in which the reactionary Professor Schmalz argued against constitutionalism. Thus the stage is set for the confrontation of the poet with Napoleon.

The preoccupation with Napoleon is so important that one of the most interesting books ever written about Heine, Paul Holzhausen's *Heinrich Heine und Napoleon I.,** is entirely devoted to it. This is not the place to go into Holzhausen's detailed analysis of the various stages of Heine's Bonapartism. But it should be stressed at the outset that Heine's Napoleon is a literary, indeed, a mythical creation and not a portrait of the historical figure. Heine knew a great deal less about Napoleon than, say, a contemporary student of history, and, moreover, he knew a good many things that were not so. Holzhausen was not able to say exactly how much of the Napoleon literature Heine had read,[39] but it is to be assumed that, like most of Europe at that time, he avidly and uncritically consumed the various installments of the legend manufactured on St. Helena. Heine was not of a studious nature; even when he did engage in extensive studies, such as his researches into Jewish history in the 1820s,[40] or into folklore and the Faust legend later on, his tendency was to mine books rather than study them.

* (Frankfurt am Main, 1903). Wilhelm Hauff described the enthusiasm for Napoleon in the South and Southwest of Germany in his story *Das Bild des Kaisers*. See Kenneth C. Hayens, "Heine's Love of Country," *Journal of English and Germanic Philology*, *30* (1931), 74–79.

The chronology of events is also important. Heine was thirteen when he saw Napoleon with his own eyes, seventeen at the time of Waterloo, and twenty-three at the time of Napoleon's death. He was too young to have suffered in one of Napoleon's numberless armies or to have felt very severely the heavy burden of taxation or the deprivations caused by the continental system, and, of course, much too young to have sensed the burden of the first occupation after the French Revolution, upon which his mother in her time had remarked with despair.* The encounter with Napoleon came at the age of puberty, notoriously susceptible to heroic fantasies, and Napoleon's death and the flood of memoir literature occurred in the years when Heine was struggling for a definition of his own poetic personality. The explanation of Heine's enthusiasm for Napoleon should not be confined to the extrinsic reasons usually given for it. It is of course true that the Napoleonic regime achieved the emancipation of the Jews in the Duchy of Berg—Holzhausen points out that Napoleon actually inherited this feature of his policy from the Revolution†—and that Napoleonic rule brought the Rhineland a large number of political blessings, as did Napoleon's visit of 1811 to the city of Düsseldorf.[41] These things touched Heine personally and are one feature of the stylized image of Napoleon as representative of the libertarian Revolution. But Heine's poetic self-image had a strong elitist component. In the turn to the real world, the persona seeks a heroic, even authoritarian referent. Holzhausen points out that there was no such figure available in the stagnation of the restoration period;[42] the cynical Metternich, the fat, unheroic Louis XVIII, and the perjured Frederick William III were hardly up to the mark. The apotheosis of Napoleon in *Das Buch Le Grand* is a reflection of an effort to bind together in the persona two

* See Adolf Strodtmann, "Die Mutter H. Heine's, nach ihren Jugendbriefen geschildert," *Deutsche Rundschau, 12* (1877), 86–100. Strodtmann claims that in the six and a half years of the first French occupation after the Revolution, the French quartered the vast number of nearly three and a half million men and a half million horses on the Rhineland (p. 91).

† Holzhausen, p. 62. Napoleon's own policy toward the Jews and the developments in the occupied states were more dubious than the clear attitude of the French Revolution. See Ismar Elbogen and Eleonore Sterling, *Die Geschichte der Juden in Deutschland* (Frankfurt am Main, 1966), pp. 172–78.

rather heterogeneous elements—aristocratic poetic self-awareness and the passion for liberty. This characteristic dichotomy is evident throughout Heine's career. The figure of Napoleon in *Das Buch Le Grand* is one of the most ambitious of Heine's efforts to resolve it.

The narrator makes clear what the experience of Napoleon meant in terms of the development of the poetic persona: at the time Le Grand drummed the history of Napoleon, the boy had as yet no acquaintance with myrtle and laurel—that is, love and fame—but was intimate with the "Reseden, womit ich jetzt so schlecht stehe" (E, *3*, 158). It has been argued that this passage yields a meaning only if "Resede" (mignonette) is understood as an anagram for Therese,[43] which would then make the connection with the early love poetry. Perhaps it is so, but in any case it is the drumming of Le Grand that arouses the poet's excitement for Napoleon. The rhetorical swell of the naming of Napoleon's victories sets the stage for the apotheosis in Chapter 8. Although Napoleon's visit to Düsseldorf in 1811 actually took place in November, the scene is shifted to summer, for it is primarily a product of the poetic imagination, as the narrator has already made clear: "Denk ich an den großen Kaiser, so wird es in meinem Gedächtnisse wieder recht sommergrün und goldig, eine lange Lindenallee taucht blühend empor (E, *3*, 157). Chapter 8 itself reminds us more of Palm Sunday; the one true God rides through the Hofgarten in Düsseldorf, untouchable and all-powerful. The description of Napoleon in Düsseldorf is too famous to require a detailed account here; just a characteristic point or two needs mention. First, it is stressed that Napoleon's hands had tamed the anarchy of Europe and ordered the feuding nations; second, the chattering fool Alouisius and the drunken Gumpertz have almost the last word as they did in Chapter 6: the stress on order and the mistrust of the people is not submerged in the revolutionary intoxication. Nor need the highly rhetorical elegy in Chapter 9 detain us long; Holzhausen has shown that a number of quotations from Napoleon were woven into the curse against England and that the picture of the grave with its five weeping willows is a cliché of the St. Helena literature and far from original.[44] The studied blasphemy is maintained: Napoleon is the worldly saviour who suffered under Sir Hudson Lowe as written in the gospels of Las Cases, O'Meara, and Antommarchi.[45]

Of more interest for our purposes is Chapter 10, where the final knot between Le Grand, Napoleon, and the poetic persona is tied. The private suffering of the poet is confronted with the historical tragedy of the end of Napoleon's glory. The narrator describes himself as passing through Düsseldorf at a time when the love pathos has already passed its high point; what is left is nothing but "Mut und Gram" (E, *3*, 161), a combination of misery with, presumably, the courage of a new maturity. The tone of self-pity is still evident, however, and it is woven into a gloomy portrait of Düsseldorf in the restoration; the Philistine order has been re-established. The pathetic quality of the scene is compounded by the typical reaction of an adult returning to the place of his childhood; as in Thomas Mann's *Tonio Kröger,* everything seems smaller and less imposing than it was remembered. The old aristocracy, symbolized in the weary little baron, has become tired and worn-out. Memories from the context of *Buch der Lieder,* recollections of the dead Veronika and of a local Gothic legend obtrude. These melancholy musings are interrupted by a troop of French soldiers returning in wretched condition from Russian imprisonment. The lachrymose mood of the poet is perfectly attuned to the apprehension of a political reality in these circumstances. Nor is it accidental that the first response to the reappearance of Le Grand is a poetic one, a song from *Des Knaben Wunderhorn.* With melodramatic pathos, Le Grand drums the tragic story of the Russian campaign and dies; and, with an equally melodramatic gesture, the narrator destroys the drum, that it may never serve the enemies of freedom. Thus closes the second part of *Das Buch Le Grand.*

The course of the narration has led downwards into the depths of memory and upwards to enthusiastic apotheosis. Now it returns to the level of present reality with a bounce. Beginning with the sardonic mot Napoleon is said to have coined on the retreat from Moscow, "Du sublime au ridicule il n'y a qu'un pas" (E, *3*, 166), the narrator sets himself up for a display of gay tomfoolery. But, just as Napoleon was inspired to this comment in a black hour, so the narrator does not let us forget the melancholy background. From an observation on the function of Shakespeare's fools in the tragedies (which parallels a passage in a letter to Friederike Robert of October 12, 1825[46]), he proceeds to a rather dark view of the theatrum mundi, which is on the verge of collapse, interestingly enough, because of the economic inequality of the actors; life in it is made bearable only by the clowns. And here, on the threshold of present reality, the poet's thoughts turn to the miseries of the writer in the world as it was then constituted, and there follows the shortest and one of the most famous chapters in Heine's works, the four words "Die deutschen Zensoren . . . Dummköpfe" (E, *3,* 167) and ninety-some dashes representing the deletions of the censor. This statement may be called self-evident to an unusual degree, for the censors, in letting it pass, proved it.*

The next three chapters are concerned with the first part of Heine's title, *Ideen.* They are a concentrated attack of the poetic sensibility upon the more trivial products of the rational mind, a satire upon thoughtless rigor by means of the poetic technique of verbal association. At the beginning of Chapter 13 the narrator warns "Madame" not to suspect him of having been guilty of digressions thus far: "In allen vorhergehenden Kapiteln ist keine Zeile, die nicht zur Sache gehörte, ich schreibe gedrängt, ich vermeide sogar alles Überflüssige" (E, *3,* 167), and our interpretation thus far gives us some reason to believe that this is seriously meant. For what is to come in the short run, it is self-ironic, because the next two chapters are a pastiche of digressions. In the long run, however, these digressions are not only a display of verbal superiority, but also form a monologue that will end in considerations of surprising importance. For the moment the fireworks of verbal association are on display. From citations he comes to bad writers, and then to food; from food to the Jews; from the Jews to Tacitus and his absurd account of asses in the Holy of Holies in Jerusalem; from asses, by way of Balaam (with aggressive religious

* Once, for the fun of it, Heine even inserted some dashes in a text when he himself had deleted a passage for his own reasons, thus suggesting dangerous allusions that had never been there in the first place. See Hermann J. Weigand, "How Censorship Worked in 1831. Heine's Amusing Bickerings and Baitings, Sensationally Documented by an Unpublished Manuscript of the Kohut-Rutra Collection of Heineana," *Yale University Library Gazette, 10* (1935/36), 17–22.

indifference, the narrator asserts that he cannot give the citation because "the book" is not at hand) to famous people who have been in love, including "Henricum Heineum" (E, *3,* 171)—a gesture of relativizing self-irony directed against his own love story. What is astonishing about this compendium and the following list of famous men who have smoked or have run away from danger is, as we now know, that it was actually all copied out of one "scholarly" source, a volume of late Baroque encyclopedism gone mad: Adam Bernhard, *Kurtzgefaste Curieuse Historie derer Gelehrten* (Frankfurt am Main, 1718).[47] The satire, it seems, was not without a point. The chapter ends with an outline of the subdivisions of ideas, a caricature of German systematic philosophy.

Chapter 14 is a long catching of breath, which turns into a visible struggle of the narrator for a new posture. The chapter begins by demonstrating the gulf between the rigorous intellectual mind and the common understanding; the word "idea" has been reduced in normal usage to a vague concept, which the cabdriver ultimately defines as "alles dumme Zeug, was man sich einbildet" (E, *3,* 173), with that, it appears, the word is also defined for *Das Buch Le Grand.* The question of the persona's poetic talent is up for discussion, and though it is treated with much amusement, there is, I believe, a troubled undertone. Judging from the three-ring circus of ideas in the preceding chapter, rational rigor is not a characteristic of the narrator's mind or even a desideratum for him. In Chapter 14, the narrator derives his cleverness from his profane lack of piety, for, he argues, in an unconscious parody of Emerson, God compensates the impious for the loss of salvation with good ideas and worldly fame. This particular rapier has two edges, for the argument implies not only that the pious are stupid but that the poet's intellect is incompatible with peace of soul. This is no very comforting thought; it touches upon one of the most enduring and modern elements of the Romantic problem, and it is probably for this reason that the narrator switches abruptly to a more mundane consideration: that a writer who is to follow Horace's rule of *nonumque prematur in annum* should also be taught to go nine years without eating. But the more existential problem does not seem to come to rest, for Chapter 14 continues in confusion, although this is not immediately apparent.

The narrator tries to talk himself into a sense of security, but he undermines it at the very beginning with the assertion, "Der Philosoph Pangloß hat recht; es ist die beste Welt!" (E, *3*, 177), since the whole point of Voltaire's *Candide* is that Pangloss is most absurdly wrong. Had the narrator meant this assertion straightforwardly, he could have as easily referred to Leibniz. This fragile security is grounded in the belief that the world will never stop supplying material for the Romantic poet and satirist, in connection with which his assertion that the queen of his heart will never die seems, in the context of *Das Buch Le Grand,* like a dangerous regression. Most of the rest of the chapter is devoted to the famous and highly entertaining passage in which the narrator describes how he will earn his bread and his luxuries by satirical portrayals of the mean and despicable, of whom he knows so many. This display of dexterity in the satirical description of other human beings implies the narrator's superiority over his fellow man and in this respect is related to *Die Harzreise.* But the end of the chapter is curious: the narrator becomes so extravagant in the description of the goodies he will earn in this fashion that he spoils his digestion and must find his way back to sobriety: "Der Henker hole solche Schlemmerei!" (E, *3*, 182). Something is wrong.

The problem is identified in Chapter 15: the awkward position of the persona between the two warring parties of mankind, the rational and the irrational. The narrator claims to belong to the first, and the "Narren" of the second, as becomes increasingly clear, are the Romantics. The "Narren," however, claim that the narrator is by rights one of them—"Und da haben die Narren vollkommen recht" (E, *3*, 184). The private conflict—the effort to overcome the complex of *Buch der Lieder*—is tied into the stresses of the contemporary literary scene, for the narrator, with his "ausgezeichnet poetisches Talent" (E, *3*, 185), could easily and comfortably have remained in the camp of the "Narren," in what Heine was later to call the Romantic School. But, he continues, he has an unfortunate and unrequited passion for reason, and this assertion leads to a remarkable reinterpretation of *Buch der Lieder:*

> Und wie einst der jüdische König Salomon im Hohenliede die christliche Kirche besungen und zwar unter dem Bilde

> eines schwarzen, liebeglühenden Mädchens, damit seine Juden nichts merkten, so habe ich in unzähligen Liedern just das Gegenteil, nämlich die Vernunft, besungen, und zwar unter dem Bilde einer weißen, kalten Jungfrau, die mich anzieht und abstößt, mir bald lächelt, bald zürnt und mir endlich gar den Rücken kehrt. Dieses Geheimnis meiner unglücklichen Liebe, das ich niemanden offenbare, gibt Ihnen, Madame, einen Maßstab zur Würdigung meiner Narrheit (E, *3,* 186).

This unexpected interpretation is, in one sense, as illegitimate as the Christian interpretation of the Song of Songs, which is undoubtedly why the comparison is made. But, in another sense, if we think of the process of *Buch der Lieder* and the content of *Das Buch Le Grand,* the curious passage does suggest the true state of affairs: the struggle with the private love pathos—equated with Romanticism—and the turn of the strengthened poet to more substantial concerns. At this point the narrator combines his Titanism with hyperbolic self-persiflage: a flight of the self-aware poetic imagination to divine heights, combines with the concern that he is not striking the right tone, that the divine inspiration is not present. So the thread of the narration is to be picked up again at the death of Le Grand—after the symbolic final collapse of the politics of heroism there is a return to the plane of Romantic narration. The final section of the work is about to begin.

In the last five chapters "Madame" becomes more thoroughly integrated into the fabric of the narration. The reason for this is a subtle change in the content of the work. The complex self-presentation of the poetic persona, with which "Madame" has little to do and which presumably lies largely outside the range of her understanding, is by and large completed. The tense balance of elements—the partly overcome love-pathos, on the one hand, connected with Romanticism, *Poesie,* irrationality, and on the other the strengthened concern with the outside world, bound up with politics, liberty, the tragic-heroic figure of Napoleon, and reason, laboriously held together by the self-awareness of the poet—has been worked out. The real story has been told. Now the narrator turns, as he says at the end of Chapter 17, to what *for "Madame"* is the real story—the completed account of the wellsprings of Romantic sensibility and the "facts" of the unhappy love affair. Thus it is a sort of coda, composed on the relatively stable ground of poetic sovereignty and structured as an extravagant piece of flattery directed toward "Madame." Chapter 16, a gallant description of "Madame's" beauty, is entirely devoted to this purpose.

It is notable, however, that the theme of beauty automatically introduces the theme of death in the symbol of Veronika. This latter echoes briefly towards the end of Chapter 15. At the beginning of Chapter 17, as though with an attempted conscious repression, the narrator refuses to describe Veronika and returns to the homage to "Madame." But he comes back to a description of Veronika nonetheless, and when the question is raised of the source of her still beauty, the answer is: "Das thut der Tod" (E, *3*, 190). And now something occurs that is most significant: with visible effort the narrator tears himself out of these depths and, turning to the "Geschichte, die in diesem Buche vorgetragen werden sollte," places himself in Chapter 18 firmly on the ground of *Buch der Lieder:* in rhythmic, poetic prose the narrator, with sovereign control, tells the story of the slandered knight-persona whose confession of love to Signora Laura goes unheard. And "Madame," as she is supposed to do, weeps.

But we are not through yet. There is still to come another knotting up of the themes in Chapter 19, into which "Madame" herself is now to be integrated. First her own beauty is somewhat unexpectedly connected with the theme of death; the narrator wishes her a kind death and asserts that she is the reincarnation of the dead Veronika. Then she is set into the inner Romantic landscape: she is identified with the Sultana of Delhi in the painting. This leads back, by a process of association, to the poetic persona who can sing and dance despite the misery hidden in his breast. Death, love, Romanticism, the transposition onto a poetic plane, all are tied together; not a thread is left hanging.

Chapter 20 is the reckoning up. It begins with a reprise of the original motto and with a terse judgment on the poetic persona:

> Und wegen dieser dummen Geschichte haben Sie sich totschießen wollen? Madame, wenn ein Mensch sich totschießen will, so hat er dazu immer hinlängliche Gründe. Darauf kön-

> nen Sie sich verlassen. Aber ob er selbst diese Gründe kennt, das ist die Frage. Bis auf den letzten Augenblick spielen wir Komödie mit uns selber. (E, *3*, 194).

So, as we have suspected in connection with the dead Veronika, the misery of unrequited love is not primary; indeed, it is presented here as almost accidental. The misery, the inelegant but vivid "toothache in the heart" [48] is congenital: "ich habe dieses Elend mit mir zur Welt gebracht. Es lag schon mit mir in der Wiege" (E, *3*, 194). This observation threatens a resurgence of self-pity; the narrator is about to say that this indefinable misery exploded his heart. But the word "Herz" does not come; the narrator breaks off sharply on the edge of banality and turns to the froth of the *Briefe aus Berlin*.

Would Heine's mysterious, vanished memoirs have had the quality of *Das Buch Le Grand*? The fictional aspects of the fragmentary *Memoiren* suggest that it is possible. The prospect is breathtaking. But who would have understood them? Certainly not a public that was able to see only a treasonable apotheosis of Napoleon embedded in a confused mass of disconnected ironies, or a generation of *Literaturwissenschaftler* who expected the translation of autobiography into art to be as orderly and reliable as a police report. And perhaps not even Heine would have been capable of it. *Das Buch Le Grand* exhibits a high degree of nervous tension, and it is difficult to imagine so delicate an arabesque maintained for much longer. Moreover, *Das Buch Le Grand* is static; its content is not a sequence of events, but a state of being; events are absorbed into this state through various levels of memory. Thus they undergo the transformations that permit the narrator to keep all the elements of the persona more or less present all the time. When the quality of the love experience is probed, the awareness of external reality creates distance and generates irony. The political confession remains within the perspective of the poetic vision. The darker and more morbid impulses that are anterior to the Romantic pathos are never entirely lost from view. The persona is whole, but not completely steady; the synthesis is fragile. This fragility is the source of the aesthetic excitement in Heine's prose masterpiece.

CHAPTER 6

The Poet as Executioner: *Die Bäder von Lucca*

> Nur, schreit nicht dauernd wie am Spieß,
> was ihr für tolle Kerle wärt!
> Bloß weil ihr hintenrum verkehrt,
> seid ihr noch nicht Genies.
>
> —ERICH KÄSTNER

Of all the lapses from decorum and gentlemanliness in Heine's works that have nourished the scorn of his enemies and often caused even his warmest admirers to blush and look the other way, the attack upon August Graf von Platen-Hallermünde in *Die Bäder von Lucca* is one of the most notorious. For not only did Heine engage in a battle of wits with an unarmed man, but he made use of other weapons in a way that was, to say the least, far from sportsmanlike. No other work, with the exception of *Börne,* with its vile libel of Börne's friend Jeanette Wohl, raised such a cry of outrage or did more to undermine Heine's position and block access to his public in Germany.

The polemic against Platen was the ultimate result of a series of stupidities. In 1826 and early 1827, Heine, irritable and pugnacious from a succession of disappointments and the uncertainty of his situation, offered to his friends the pages of *Reisebilder II* as a forum for attacks on any prominent personalities they might wish to see excoriated.[1] None of his acquaintances responded to this outrageous suggestion but the loyal and tractable Karl Immermann, who delivered a set of *xenia,* that is, aphoristic verses attacking literary figures and fashions in imitation of a similarly questionable undertaking of Goethe and Schiller in 1796. Immermann's *xenia,* however, are not distichs, as were Goethe's and Schiller's, but quatrains of four feet in each line, printed so that they appeared as rhymed couplets. Most of them are weak and insignificant, as Heine no doubt very well knew, but, being in an aggressive mood, he duly appended them to *Nordsee III* in the second volume of the *Reisebilder,* which appeared in April 1827.

Several of these *xenia* referred to Platen; compared to what was to come, the most specific of them was both mild in its content and poetically unimpressive:

> "Ganz bewältigt er die Sprache"; ja, es ist, sich tot zu lachen,
> Seht nur, was für tolle Sprünge lässet er die arme machen.
> (E, *3,* 124)

More at the level the exchange was to reach is an epigramm directed against the poets who were exploiting Persian motifs and forms, of whom Platen was an outstanding example:

> Von den Früchten, die sie aus dem Gartenhain von Schiras stehlen,
> Essen sie zu viel, die Armen, und vomieren dann Ghaselen.
> (E, *3,* 123)

The most rational thing for Platen to have done would have been to take no notice of the matter, the course chosen by the rest of Immermann's "victims," particularly the gentle Rückert, who was implicitly included in the attack on Persian mannerisms. But Platen was pathologically touchy about his literary reputation and went into a rage; he did not approve of Immermann, anyway, and had begun to prepare an attack on him before the publication of *Reisebilder II.*[2] Of all the undesirable alternatives to the rational course, he chose by far the most foolish one: he embarked upon a literary offensive in the grand style. The result was a satirical drama, *Der romantische Oedipus* (1829), an attack on a broad front upon all the contemporary writers laboring in the wake of Romanticism, but particularly and explicitly upon Heine and Immermann, whom, as an example of the level of his wit, he called "Nimmermann."

The course Platen chose was foolish for three reasons. First of all, he was not very well acquainted with either Heine's or Immermann's works; indeed he had to beg information from his friends about them.[3] The whole ad hominem character of the exchange is exemplified by this fact. Heine, however, who had better sense, had, as subsequently appeared, made a thorough study of Platen's verse. This blunder of Platen's is one of the best examples in the history of literary feuds of the dangers of not knowing one's enemy. Had Platen read more of Heine, he would have had a clearer measure of his man and some notion of the satirical ruthlessness of which he was capable. Secondly, and related to this, was an unfortunate lack of self-knowledge and sense of his own limitations, which brought Platen much grief throughout his tormented career. Platen was Heine's inferior in alertness and adroitness of mind, but his intense need to regard himself as a man of greatness blinded him to caution. Platen's description of himself in a letter to a friend as "einen offenbar Größeren, der ihn [Heine] zerquetschen kann," [4] is, in view of the outcome, pathetic in the extreme, and indeed Platen has earned from posterity pity more than the admiration he so desperately sought. Thirdly, Platen had two egregious weaknesses that made him vulnerable to attack: his mania for extravagant self-praise, preempting the laurels the world would not grant him, and the homoerotic content of much of his poetry. Heine saw through the first of these postures without any difficulty:

> Ich habe Gründe zu vermuten, daß der Herr Graf an seine eigne Prahlerei nicht glaubt, und daß er, dürftig im Leben wie in der Litteratur, vielmehr für das Bedürfnis des Augenblicks sein eigner anpreisender Ruffiano sein mußte, in der Litteratur wie im Leben. Daher in beiden die Erscheinungen, von denen man sagen konnte, daß sie mehr ein psychologisches als ästhetisches Interesse gewährten, daher zu gleicher Zeit die weinerlichte Seelenerschlaffung und der erlogene Übermut, daher das klägliche Dünnethun mit baldigem Sterben und das drohende Dickthun mit künftiger Unsterblichkeit. (E, *3*, 360)

As for the second weakness, it is Heine's merciless exploitation of it that has made the book so unpalatable to the delicate-minded.

Der romantische Oedipus has spots that are moderately amusing in a baroque sort of way. But on the whole it is badly organized, inconsistent, and lacks a thematic center. Platen attempts to parody bad taste with worse and the presumed disorder of Romantic writing with genuine confusion. As Platen could have consigned Immermann's verses to oblivion by ignoring them, so *Der romantische Oedipus* would be nearly forgotten today if Heine had not taken up the gauntlet. Yet it is hard to see, given the circumstances, how Heine could have let the matter pass altogether, quite apart from the fact that he mistakenly preferred to think of Platen as the representative of a priestly-aristocratic cabal in Munich.* For Platen's treatment of Heine in his comedy is far from amusing. Being ignorant of the genuine weaknesses of his opponent, Platen resorted to an age-old recourse of ignorance —anti-Semitism. The few lines he devoted to Heine in the play turn exclusively on Heine's Jewishness, and in a manner so witless and vulgar that one can sympathize with Elster's stern judgment that the attack represents an ineradicable stain on Platen's character.† Horst Krüger[5] has argued that Heine knew an even nastier epigram by Platen:

An den Dichterling Heine
Täglich bedanke du dich im Gebet, o hebräischer Witzling,
Daß bei Deutschen und nicht unter Griechen du lebst:
Solltest du nackt dich zeigen im männlichen Spiel der Palästra,
Sprich, wie verstecktest du dann jenen verstümmelten Teil? [6]

Beyond these considerations, however, *Die Bäder von Lucca* is of prototypical significance for a very important aspect of Heine's self-image as a poet. He professed an almost magical belief in the

* Heine's letter to Immermann of Dec. 26, 1829, shows great confusion in this matter; he describes Platen as an enemy of the writer and minister Eduard von Schenk and a confederate of "Pfäffchen, Baronen und Pedrasten" (Hirth, *1*, 407). But Schenk was a rigid reactionary—whom Heine had praised and flattered in his dubious effort to get a professorship in Munich. Heine always maintained this position that the fight against Platen was really one against "Pfaffen" (see Houben, p. 490); possibly, as Elster suggested, he did not realize that Platen was acting alone (E[2], *4*, 241).

† It has been argued that Platen's anti-Semitism was not really as nasty as it appears in this instance. In Platen's satire upon fate-tragedy, *Die verhängnisvolle Gabel*, the chorus is a Jew named Schmuhl, who is represented by the author with complete good humor, as was attested by one of Heine's most sensitively Jewish admirers, Max Brod, in *Heinrich Heine: The Artist in Revolt* (New York, 1957), p. 248. Elster tried to defend Platen on the grounds that in his native Ansbach, he knew only uneducated and uncultured Jews, so that the whole idea of a Jewish poet and writer seemed absurd to him (E[2], *4*, 238–39).

power of the literary word as a weapon, and this belief compounds with Heine's understanding of courage as pugnaciousness and the elitist aspect of the persona as warrior to yield the character of the poet as executioner. Heine took on this role with increasing seriousness in the years following *Die Bäder von Lucca,* and in *Die Romantische Schule* he took the occasion to mount a defense of the polemics of Johann Heinrich Voss, which is simultaneously a defense of his own tendency to drag painful personal details into public attacks.[7] Heine's militant imagery in his role as executioner and avenger is familiar to any of his readers; one thinks particularly of the figure of the lictor in Capita 6 and 7 of *Deutschland: Ein Wintermärchen,* who carries out the condemnations uttered by the poet,[8] or the prose poem that probably dates around 1840, in which Heine, or his politically activist persona, announces: "Ich bin das Schwert, ich bin die Flamme" (E, 2, 166).[9] Heine was by no means alone in his time with his view of the force of published polemic. The Young Germans, particularly Gutzkow, seem to have been similarly convinced; Platen himself, with his talk of squashing Heine to death with a literary satire, showed that he shared these assumptions to an extent; and Varnhagen von Ense was certainly willing to appear as though he did when in an essay on Heine's behalf he said of *Die Bäder von Lucca*: "die Hinrichtung ist vollzogen, der Scharfrichter hat sein Amt als Meister ausgeübt, *der* Kopf ist herunter!" [10] Of course the written word is a weapon—the Holy Alliance would not have gone to such lengths to defuse it if this were not so—and the faith in its force was energetically revived decades later in the Expressionist movement.[11] Perhaps this conviction of Heine's goes some way to explain his current prominence in Communist countries; C. P. Snow has pointed out how Russians—Stalin, for example—have always had great respect for the practical efficacy of literature.[12] But of Heine it must be said that he overestimated the firepower of literary artillery, tended to be completely incapable of distinguishing between the pertinent and the impertinent, and was inclined to misjudge the effect of his attacks both upon his target and upon critical bystanders. Martin Greiner has said fairly that Heine, by turning such great violence upon Platen, missed him altogether.[13] Heine himself undoubtedly felt the futility of polemic from time to time; he remarked in *Die Stadt Lucca* that, after all, "Jeder ist selbst krank genug in diesem großen Lazarett" (E, *3*, 394) and that public polemic reminded him of a squabble among the dying he had witnessed in a Polish hospital. When he believed himself to be sitting on Platen's corpse, as he put it, he wrote to Immermann: "Wenn auch mahl das Ganze gedruckt wird, wird auch der Herr Graf, wie sich gebührt, aus dem Buche hinausgeschmissen" (Hirth, *1*, 407, 406). But he never did so, and, indeed, he could not have very effectively, for the polemic against Platen is too thoroughly integrated into the whole work to permit its removal without thoroughly altering the sense of the piece.*

This claim may strike the reader as extravagant. It has always been believed, as H. G. Atkins put it, that "anyone reading the work for the first time feels that these Platen chapters, which form nearly half the book, are deliberately dragged in, without any artistic necessity, and with a transition that is somewhat artificially effected. As a matter of fact they were only added when the book was already being printed." [14] The history of publication of the work seems at first to support Atkins' view. *Reisebilder III* began to go to press in early October 1829,[15] and if Heine's letter of November 17, 1829, is correctly dated, as it seems to be, then he was still working at the Platen polemic the day before.[16] *Reisebilder III* appeared in December, and on that occasion Heine wrote to Friederike Robert that he had written the polemic against Platen "diesen Monath" (Hirth, *1*, 405). In fact, judging from a letter of Campe to Immermann of June 12, 1829, Heine was well along in *Reisebilder III* before he even saw Platen's *Romantischer Oedipus*;[17] later Heine said he had thought the matter over for three months before deciding what to do about Platen.[18] But we have evidence that the polemic belonged to the original conception of *Die Bäder von Lucca,* for, as early as September, Campe predicted to Immermann that the treatment of Platen would be a tough one.[19] As we shall see, Platen's presence may be felt in the book from beginning to end, and we shall be obliged to see him

* Heine did in fact do this in the French editions of 1834 and 1858. Except for the tulip references (see below, pp. 168–69), the specific allusions to Platen were removed or the name of Karl Wilhelm Ramler was substituted (E, *3*, 556, 562). The result bears out my contentions.

as a distinct foil to the poetic persona. Before turning to that problem, however, it may be appropriate to look at some of the other elements of the fictional narration in the work.

Die Bäder von Lucca shows a considerable degree of cohesion and narrative skill in its "fiction aspect." Indeed, it is a remarkable fact that, according to the memoirs of François Wille, in 1831 a Hamburg schoolteacher used this work in the classroom to demonstrate the skills of the true poet! [20] One of the skills displayed here is characterization. Gumpelino and Hyazinth-Hirsch are among the few rounded, independent characterizations to be found in Heine's works, conceived, as Manfred Windfuhr has pointed out, as parallel figures to Don Quixote and Sancho Panza.* We shall, for the usual theoretical reasons, take no notice of the fact that both figures are reportedly drawn from life; they will be discussed here exclusively as fictional elements. Although Heine was to come to rue the book altogether,[21] he was proud of his characterization of Hirsch, "die erste ausgeborene Gestalt, die ich jemals in Lebensgröße geschaffen habe" (Hirth, *1*, 411),[22] and Varnhagen, looking for a way to speak well of the book, called particular attention to the characterization of Hirsch and Gumpelino.[23]

Hirsch is both an object and a vehicle of satire. Heine's familiar strictures on Hamburg, that scene of his greatest disappointments, and its mercantile spirit are visible in Hirsch's single-minded attachment to monetary values, his basic indifference to culture, and his attention to the proprieties of his own position, which, though low and very petty-bourgeois, has certain rigid imperatives. He is, no doubt, somewhat ridiculous in his pride at having cut the corns of the mighty Rothschild. But his account of the *Kinderball* given by Rothschild, as Herman Salinger has demonstrated, is a remarkable satire on Rothschild's role in international relations.[24] Furthermore, the dryness and sobriety of Hirsch's character are

* Manfred Windfuhr. "Heines Fragment eines Schelmenromans *'Aus den Memoiren des Herren von Schnabelewopski,'" Heine-Jahrbuch 1967,* p. 25. Elster has further argued that these figures are a part of the defense against Platen and the attacks of Ignaz Döllinger in the Munich publication *Eos,* "zu zeigen, wie sehr er sich von ungebildeten oder halbgebildeten Männern jüdischer Herkunft unterschied" (E², *4,* 235).

qualities with a positive side in the context of the work. His suspicion of the cultural undertakings of Gumpelino's Grand Tour stands in refreshing contrast to the foggy dilettantism of that worthy; his judgments are not muddled by *Geltungsbedürfnis*; in fact, this integrity, which is developed not only in his own commentary but in the story he tells of his honesty, is the characteristic around which the figure is constructed and which lifts it into significance.

Hirsch has delivered to its rightful owner a lottery prize of 50,000 marks that came into his hands under conditions that would have made it easy for him to make off with it. This is the great event in Hirsch's life; he has been called, and he has proved himself a man. It is difficult to agree with Elster when, with Wilhelminian smugness, he dismisses Hirsch's deed as "selbstverständlich." [25] For Hirsch, and for Heine, it is not "selbstverständlich," but an act of significance, done in duty and uprightness against the nature of man, and it is the single great symbol of the quality of Hirsch's character in which his whole pride resides. The naive absurdity of his imagery, seen against the background of his blunt and limited rationality, stresses the importance the action has for him:

> "Wenn ich sterbe"—sprach Hyazinth, eine Thräne im Auge —"soll man mir diese Quittung mit ins Grab legen, und wenn ich einst dort oben, am Tage des Gerichts, Rechenschaft geben muß von meinen Thaten, dann werde ich mit dieser Quittung in der Hand vor den Stuhl der Allmacht treten, und wenn mein böser Engel die bösen Handlungen, die ich auf dieser Welt begangen habe, vorgelesen und mein guter Engel auch die Liste von meinen guten Handlungen ablesen will, dann sag' ich ruhig: Schweig!—ich will nur wissen, ist diese Quittung richtig? ist das die Handschrift von Christian Hinrich Klotz? Dann kommt ein ganz kleiner Engel herangeflogen und sagt, er kenne ganz genau Klötzchens Handschrift, und der erzählt zugleich die merkwürdige Geschichte von der Ehrlichkeit, die ich mal begangen habe. Der Schöpfer der Ewigkeit, aber, der Allwissende, der alles weiß, erinnert sich an diese Geschichte, und er lobt mich in Gegenwart von

> Sonne, Mond und Sternen und berechnet gleich im Kopf, daß wenn meine bösen Handlungen von 50,000 Mark Ehrlichkeit abgezogen werden, mir noch ein Saldo zu gut kommt, und er sagt dann: Hirsch! ich ernenne dich zum Engel erster Klasse, und du darfst Flügel tragen mit rot und weißen Federn." (E, *3*, 346)

Whereas Hirsch is mostly permitted to speak for himself without comment by the narrator, his master Gumpelino is subjected to the narrator's criticism and thus occupies a slightly different position. Gumpelino, though he is affably treated, lacks the thoroughgoing ingenuousness that distinguishes Hirsch. With his wealth, Gumpelino is in the process of acquiring culture—a fashionable kind of debased popular Romanticism. Its elements are verbalized nature-enthusiasm, the ostentatious practice of Catholicism, a habit of quoting sentimental poetry, and a mawkish amorousness misderived from Shakespeare. These features, it will be noted, are not entirely unrelated to some of the characteristics of Heine at the outset of the period of *Buch der Lieder*. The better part of the fourth chapter, into which the narrator manages to inject himself as a poet, is devoted to putting Gumpelino's fraudulent Romanticism into its proper perspective: the mindless vaporings of a middle-class Berlin lady about "die jrine Beeme" are put into the same class with Gumpelino's effusions over the Italian landscape and contrasted with the "Zerrissenheit" (E, *3*, 304), the discord at the bottom of being that the true poet senses and reproduces. Gumpelino tries to play, not very successfully, the part of the rich man who despises money:

> Was ist Geld? Geld ist rund und rollt weg, aber Bildung bleibt. Ja, Herr Doktor, wenn ich, was Gott verhüte, mein Geld verliere, so bin ich doch immer ein großer Kunstkenner, ein Kenner von Malerei, Musik und Poesie. (E, *3*, 303)

Gumpelino can afford this impracticality, especially as he is not likely to be called upon to prove his sincerity, just as he can afford to drug his brain with Catholicism; Hirsch cannot:

> Ich habe oft zu Herren Gumpel gesagt: "Ew. Ex. sind ein reicher Mann und können katholisch sein, soviel Sie wollen,

> und können sich den Verstand ganz katholisch einräuchern lassen, und können so dumm werden wie eine katholische Glock', und Sie haben doch zu essen; ich aber bin ein Geschäftsmann und muß meine sieben Sinne zusammenhalten, um was zu verdienen." Herr Gumpel meint freilich, es sei nötig für die Bildung, und wenn ich nicht katholisch würde, verstände ich nicht die Bilder, die zur Bildung gehören, nicht den Johann von Viehesel, den Corretschio, den Carratschio, den Carravatschio—aber ich habe immer gedacht, der Corretschio und Carratschio und Carravatschio können mir alle nichts helfen, wenn niemand mehr bei mir spielt, und ich komme dann in die Patschio. (E, *3*, 325–26)

At this point the contrasting portraits of Hirsch and Gumpelino converge toward some of Heine's most fundamental attitudes in the coming years.

There is an area where it seems to me that the figure of Gumpelino fails to maintain its unity, and that is in his function as "Romeo" to Lady Julia. As the fat, sentimental, middle-aged lover who finds joy in burying his long nose in the mighty bosom of the fifty-year-old ruin Signora Lätitia, he is a type, perhaps something like the figure of Cassandrino in the later Commedia dell' arte, and as such his love should not be returned by the young and lively Lady Julia; but it is: the honest Hirsch says so,[26] and the letter that arrives too late proves it. This awkwardness of characterization arises out of a mechanism of plot; the incongruity motivates the hilarious scene in which Gumpelino loses his last chance for a night with Lady Julia because Hirsch has talked him into taking a laxative, and this part of the tale eventually develops into the final stage of the attack on Platen. It is a failure of control, nonetheless, and illustrates Heine's basic lack of skill as a novelist; his strength lay in associating words and connecting ideas, not in describing the actions of living characters.

The narrator is, of course, also a character, and a very prominent one. The traditional fiction of the first-person narrator recording only what he sees and what is said to him is maintained with fair consistency; but another methodological problem arises when we attempt to interpret this figure, for Heine apparently confounds any effort to distinguish the fictional narrator from the author himself. Is it not stubborn and futile to insist upon this distinction when the first-person narrator is greeted on the first page as "Doktor des Himmels und der Erde" (E, *3*, 293)—that is, of civil and canon law—when he characterizes his own "Zerrissenheit" (E, *3*, 304), when he refers to his own poetic future and plugs his publisher Hoffmann und Campe,[27] when, for the sake of a bonmot, he gives his birthdate (not the correct one, to be sure, but one of those Heine supplied to the public),[28] when he advertises for *Die Stadt Lucca,*[29] and when, in the midst of all this, he identifies himself as "Johann Heinrich Heine, Doktor Juris"? (E, *3*, 305–06). We may call this, if we like, the penetration of the "essay aspect" into the fictional narrative, by saying that the real author has surrounded himself with a fictional milieu. But perhaps we should be bolder and stick with our theoretical position that the poet-persona is a fictional character, as, indeed, Bölsche, unique as always, was perfectly willing to do eighty years ago: "Das Ganze gruppiert sich um die Person des Erzählers, für den der Autor nicht einmal einen neuen Namen erfunden hat, sondern der einfach Doktor Heine heißt." [30] For one can, without difficulty, describe the figure of "Doktor Heine" in terms of the development of the fictive persona, and furthermore, as we shall come to see, the persona developed here stands in the sharpest contrast to the character of Platen as Heine is pleased to present it.

The presence of the narrator dominates *Die Bäder von Lucca.* At the beginning he is warmly greeted by Mathilde, who is to play a larger part in *Die Stadt Lucca,* as "Doktor des Himmels und der Erde" and as "Wahnsinnigster der Sterblichen" (E, *3*, 293), both to be understood as compliments. In the course of the dialogue with Lady Mathilde, the poet's amorous conquests in England are suggested with only slight obliqueness. He develops a posture of courageous suffering by comparing himself to Sisyphus, and in the digression on "Zerrissenheit," he gives an indication of his own poetic vision and, with only slight irony, slips into a comparison of himself to Byron. The pathos of the old poet, Bartolo, who twenty years earlier wrote renowned love poems and now, aged and forgotten, mechanically lives out his hopeless adoration of Signora Lätitia, is related to the narrator's own condition. Insofar as the narrator himself participates in the action of the story, the high point comes in Chapters 6 and 7, which describe his conquest of Signora Franscheska. His metier as poet is stressed when his high-hearted though ironic and ultimately patronizing description of her beauty is introduced by a call to the Muses for assistance. This conquest has three salient features. First of all, it is nearly effortless; his compliment and desire to kiss her foot arouse her instantly from her lethargy; she thanks Gumpelino for him "als sei ich ein Geschenk, das er ihr aus Artigkeit mitgebracht" (E, *3*, 314), and without much ado she promises him her favors in return for a modicum of patience: the narrator is sexually desirable! Secondly, it gives him an opportunity for a waggish spoof on the circumlocutions commonly used in conventional literature for erotic situations. He begins by describing her face and neck, then interrupts himself—"Ach! frommer Leser, ich komme zu weit, und außerdem habe ich bei dieser Inauguralschilderung noch kein Recht"—and in the same breath describes not only her breasts but also the manner in which he became acquainted with them: "von den zwei schweigenden Blumen zu sprechen, die wie weiße Poesie hervorleuchteten, wenn Signora die silbernen Halsknöpfe ihres schwarzseidnen Kleides enthäkelte" (E, *3*, 314). The narrator is clever, sexually successful, and a wit! Thirdly, the discourse on the mysteries of love in Chapter 8 gives him an opportunity to describe his own sensations during the Franscheska episode: the narrator is capable of expansive joy and healthy abandon! We shall anticipate only for a moment to remark that from the point of view of the whole work, poor, humorless, repressed, homoerotic Platen is here lurking in the background. The narrator is also capable of self-persiflage; Chapter 9 begins with the observation, "Es gibt nichts Langweiligeres auf dieser Erde als die Lektüre einer italienischen Reisebeschreibung" —which is true of some sections of *Reise von München nach Genua*—and he invites the reader to skip a few pages in order to finish more quickly, allowing us a glimpse at the same time of the labor of creation: "ach, ich wollt', ich könnt' es ebenso machen!" (E, *3*, 324). The portrait of the first-person narrator is thus clear: as a complex, troubled, but red-blooded Byronesque poet, he is not only superior to all those about him, but is instantly taken as a lover by the prettiest girl around. In a fictional world of the poet's own making, he creates an image of himself stressing features of superiority and sovereignty. He provides, moreover, as a hint of what is being done here, an allegorical representation or dramatization of the creative act—the puppet show Franscheska puts on with her feet to describe her unhappy love for Cecco: "indem sie ihre eigene Geschichte parodierte, ließ sie die beiden verliebten Füße voneinander Abschied nehmen, und es war ein rührend närrisches Schauspiel, wie sich beide mit den Spitzen küßten und die zärtlichsten Dinge sagten—und dabei weinte das tolle Mädchen ergötzlich kichernde Thränen, die aber dann und wann etwas unbewußt tiefer aus der Seele kamen, als die Rolle verlangte" (E, *3*, 315). By means of this parodistic presentation of the poet's creative process, reference is made to an aspect of the poet's situation not otherwise developed in *Die Bäder von Lucca,* except for such hints as the comparisons to Sisyphus and Byron: the poet's light-heartedness is an occasionally lifted mask for a deep hurt.

There is one more interesting feature of the narrator's manner: he has a tendency to break off the "essay aspect" rather abruptly and bring the reader forcibly back to the narrative. This is done in several ways. Chapter 4, containing the poet's meditation on "Zerrissenheit," ends with a glimpse of the narrator managing his material: "Genug davon; wir kommen zu einem besseren Gegenstande" (E, *3*, 305), and the narrative resumes. Another method is the sudden turn from the sublime to the ridiculous, a manner that is central to Heine's style and which he previously adverted to in *Das Buch Le Grand.* One version of this appears where Signora Lätitia sings an operatic aria in her finest soprano and, in the next breath, "mit der fettigsten Prosastimme" (E, *3*, 306), asks for the spittoon. Another is the scene where Signora Franscheska's presentation of her unhappy love is followed first by the joke about the poet's birthdate and then by the enormous nude Lätitia arising out of the bed-clothes. There is a further example at the end of Chapter 7, in which the poet's effusions about his love for Franscheska are brought to a sudden halt by the sobering, anti-poetic appearance of Hirsch. These satires thus have a tendency to appear whenever the narration comes too close to the poet's innermost concerns. On the whole, matters that tend to disturb the tone of comedy in the fictional part of the work, although they continually threaten to assert themselves, are kept under tight control. In this connection, Heine's rejection of a rather long passage published by Strodtmann in 1869 as an addition to Chapter 8 [31] is of some significance. Strodtmann's passage is a digression upon Heine's political situation and contains some ironic remarks about Prussia and Austria that may account for its suppression; but it is only remotely connected with the narration and carries the narrator of the present situation of the story into the present situation of the author. Nowhere in the ten narrative chapters of *Die Bäder von Lucca* is there so severe a confusion of narrative planes; thus the passage may have been suppressed for artistic as well as political reasons.

Die Bäder von Lucca employs a number of Heine's fundamental themes: love, money, culture, religion, and the poet and poetry. They are not only numerous and carefully interwoven, but are seen from a variety of vantage points, creating at times ambivalences that only the superior presence of the narrator can resolve. The structure of the thematic treatment is more often than not grounded in the contrast between Gumpelino and Hirsch. In the case of each of these five themes, the contrasting attitudes of Gumpelino and Hirsch provide the basis of development, but by no means exhaust the thematic treatment; the positive synthesis is usually provided by the narrator. Hirsch, for example, is unsympathetic to Gumpelino's amorous posturings and is shocked when Gumpelino claims he would prefer a night with Julia to winning the grand prize in the Hamburg lottery. Hirsch goes on in his dry way to compute that love has cost him twelve marks and thirteen shillings in his lifetime and that he managed to cure his single passion for "die dicke Gudel vom Dreckwall" (E, *3*, 331) by means of a laxative. For Hirsch, love is a disturbance of rationality that is to be kept to as minimal a role in life as possible. Gumpelino's love is an infatuation artificially intensified by Shakespearian verse. His self-induced intoxication with Shakespeare is so extreme that he postures not only as Romeo but also as Juliet (Platen is in the background again), and this absurdity brings him to grief, for Gumpelino would not have swallowed Hirsch's laxative had he not been lost in a fantasy of Juliet's poison scene. Well might the narrator ask, "Was ist die Liebe?" (E, *3*, 319). *His* love is a passion of the flesh, trouble-free and successful, in contrast to Gumpelino's blundering and Hirsch's repudiation.

There is, however, a hint of another, sadder dimension of love, not only in Franscheska's puppet show, where the parody is threatened by the appearance of a deeper, more genuine emotion, but also in the meeting with Mathilde at the beginning of the story, where the narrator senses the quality of Mathilde's past sufferings because they are related to his own: "sie finden immer ein gutes Echo in meiner eignen Brust. . . . Ach, Mylady, nur der verwandte Schmerz entlockt uns die Thräne, und jeder weint eigentlich für sich selbst" (E, *3*, 295). The narrator gives the problem still another facet when he himself introduces the explanation that love is a kind of electricity. This playing with rationalistic answers raises a serious question about the reality of human passions. It is prefigured in Chapter 4, where the professor, applying the critical method that was beginning to gain ground in the nineteenth century, gives a historical explanation of the Ariadne myth, and the narrator ironically outdoes him by suggesting that Ariadne's seduction by Bacchus indicates that she had become an alcoholic. The rationalistic explanation, which destroys love and beauty, is ridiculed, but it is also feared, and it injects itself into the narrator's own indecisive musings about the nature of love, as it had years before in the *Gespräch auf der Paderborner Heide*.

The contrast between Gumpelino and Hirsch on the subjects of money and culture has been touched upon above. In both cases Gumpelino's pretensions are confronted with Hirsch's sobriety. Both are attached to money, but Gumpelino pretends he is not; neither has a living relationship to art and nature, but Gumpelino deceives himself into a clumsy, second-hand imitation of it. As for the narrator, the touchstone is his own sensuality; he is inspired to an observation upon the relative merits of painting and sculpture and to a recollection of Canova's *Venus* by the living presence of the beautiful Franscheska. His cultural appreciation derives from his sensual experience, whereas Gumpelino proceeds in the opposite direction: his love for Julia is informed by the experience of late Romantic poetry and Shakespeare. The religious theme is closely connected to that of culture. The narrator treats Gumpelino's Catholicism as the pursuit of an expensive fashion: "Du mußt nämlich wissen, lieber Leser, daß der Markese . . . sich, wenn er in Rom ist, sogar einen Kapellan hält, aus demselben Grunde, weshalb er in England die besten Wettrenner und in Paris die schönste Tänzerin unterhielt" (E, *3*, 325). Gumpelino's devotion is closely involved with his artificially induced love passion, his wealth, and his posturing generally: "seine Nase schimmerte wehmütig wie ein verliebter Louisdor. 'O Jesus!'—seufzte er, als er sich in die Kissen des Sofas sinken ließ—'finden Sie nicht, Herr Doktor, daß ich heute abend sehr schwärmerisch aussehe? Ich bin sehr bewegt, mein Gemüt ist aufgelöst, ich ahne eine höhere Welt' " (E, *3*, 329); and he begins, as usual, to quote verse. Hirsch, meanwhile, has delivered his monologue, "episch breit," on the relative merits of the various religions, seen, to be sure, out of the limitations of his poor man's rationality. Catholicism is an opiate that dulls the senses. Protestantism does no harm, but does no good either, for in its austerity it is not even capable of performing a simple miracle for Hirsch by supplying him with winning numbers for the lottery. Judaism is "gar keine Religion, sondern ein Unglück" (E, *3*, 327); this statement is followed by a curious disquisition on the current state of Judaism in Germany. Hirsch, firm in his sense of superiority over the common man, declares himself for Reform Judaism, with its laxity in Law and minimal religious experience; but then he gives the famous description of the poor and unattractive Moses Lump enjoying the pleasures and gratifications of the Orthodox Sabbath, a theme to be taken up again years later in the poem *Prinzessin Sabbat* of 1851. Two things should be noted here. First of all, there is no resolution of the religious problem; no religion is satisfactory, and the tragic paradox of Judaism, which Heine, in *Die Stadt Lucca,* was to call a "Volkmumie" (E, *3*, 416), is left unresolved. Secondly, it is advisable to be hesitant in ascribing the views here presented to Heine or even to his narrative persona, particularly with regard to the declaration for Reform Judaism. These views are put into the mouth of Hirsch, the intelligent and upright but spiritually limited Hamburg bourgeois; the narrator does not comment on them, and since it is Hirsch's function, no less than Gumpelino's, to stand in contrast to the rich personality of the narrator, there is no justification for making an identification here. Rather, it must be said, the tension remains without resolution; the theme has been put in an exclusively negative context, and it is taken up again only in *Die Stadt Lucca,* where, with a highly ironic twist, the narrator is put in the position of having to defend the values of religion against the mordant sarcasm of Mathilde.

The theme of poetry is, of course, intimately connected with the execution of Platen, to which we shall turn presently. Some features of it, however, already have been touched upon and may be expanded here. Again the contrast between Gumpelino and Hirsch is sharply drawn. Gumpelino, indiscriminately quoting Matthisson and Shakespeare, is not interested in poetry as such; rather, he uses it as a stimulant for his emotions, acting out the parts of Romeo and Juliet to the point of absurdity. Hirsch, on the other hand, undertakes the study of poetry as one more painful task in the acquisition of culture and, encouraged by Gumpelino, finds himself obliged to master the artificial metrical forms of Platen's poetry: "Spondeus, Trochäus, Jambus, Antispaß, Anapäst, und die Pest" (E, *3,* 339). He reduces metrics to a problem which he sees from the point of view of his own obsessive uprightness; his task is to check the poems to see whether they fit the meter exactly, and he is worried as to whether "diese krummen und geraden Striche" (E, *3,* 343), which Platen, like Klopstock, placed before his odes in order to indicate the pattern, can be trusted, or whether the poet, like a dishonest bank clerk, might cheat. The narrator, of course, is far above all this. He is the poet who sees clearly into the "Zerrissenheit" of the world; far from deriving his inspiration from the poetry of others or laboring to fill out preconceived metrical arrangements, his verbal creativity flows from his own primary experience, as in the rhythms and images of his description of love in Chapter 7. So certain is he of his own mastery that he can permit himself an ironic expression of diffidence about the quality of his own work. This ease and control, too, stand in obvious contrast to the labored and strained manner of Platen, who could by no means permit himself such diffidence.

In the preceding discussion, it has been somewhat awkward to avoid any treatment of the victim of Heine's execution, since he is, I am about to argue, by direction and indirection one of the most prominent motifs in the work. The purpose of the foregoing has been to point out, with as little reference to Platen as possible, the extent to which *Die Bäder von Lucca* is otherwise *durchkomponiert* as a fictional narrative with individually drawn characters, including the narrator, and bound together by interwoven themes. Yet even here it has been necessary to note that the presence of Platen is felt by implication throughout the work. The narrator, in his attractiveness and in his mastery of his craft and his environment, establishes a stark contrast to the character of Platen as it is finally drawn, and the disaster that befalls Gumpelino while reciting Juliet's lines is surely part of the general satire upon Platen's homoeroticism. This satire appears in earnest in the eleventh and final chapter, where the "fiction aspect" gives way completely to the "essay aspect." But it is not an irrelevant item tacked on to the end of the fictional narrative; the Platen motif is composed into the work as thoroughly as any other and is an integral part of it.

Ignoring for our purposes two brief but cutting references to Platen in *Reise von München nach Genua*,[32] we can observe that the Platen motif develops gradually in five stages, and although Platen's name is not mentioned in the body of the text until Chapter 10, the work approaches the object of its satire by degrees from the very beginning. The first stage is found in the pair of malicious but well-chosen mottos that precede even the dedication to Immermann. The first of these is half a line from one of Platen's ghazels: "Ich bin wie Weib dem Manne—" (E, *3*, 290). It is clear from this very first line in *Die Bäder von Lucca* that Heine does not intend to make a fair fight of it, for he has altered the whole import of the line by suppressing the second half of it; the line reads in its entirety: "Ich bin wie Weib dem Mann, wie Mann dem Weibe dir!"[33] The second motto is a cheerful quotation from Mozart's *Figaro*: "Will der Herr Graf ein Tänzchen wagen, / So mag er's sagen, / Ich spiel' ihm auf" (E, *3*, 290).

The second stage, which is an interesting example of Heine's manner and has not, so far as I know, been elucidated by any of his interpreters except briefly by Mayerhofer, is the unexplained scene with the tulip in Chapter 2.[34] When Gumpelino attempts to present Lady Mathilde with a single, beautiful tulip, the high-tempered lady flies into a rage:

> "Morden! morden! wollen Sie mich morden? Fort, fort mit dem schrecklichen Anblick!" Dabei gebärdete sie sich, als wolle man sie umbringen, hielt sich die Hände vor die Augen, rannte unsinnig im Zimmer umher, verwünschte Gumpelinos Nase und Tulpe, klingelte, stampfte den Boden, schlug den Hund mit der Reitgerte, daß er laut aufbellte, and als John hereintrat, rief sie, wie Kean als König Richard:
>
> Ein Pferd! ein Pferd!
> Ein Königtum für ein Pferd!
>
> und stürmte, wie ein Wirbelwind, von dannen. (E, *3*, 297–98)

The narrator does not explain this remarkable uproar, but he understands it himself: "Ich aber kannte die Dame und ihre Idiosynkrasie weit besser, mich ergötzte dieses Schauspiel über alle Maßen" (E, *3*, 298). Now the tulip is by far the most important single image in Platen's poetry. Being a flower without a fragrance, a point Heine stresses when he takes up the jibe again in *Die Stadt Lucca*,[35] its beauty is merely visual without appealing to the "lower" senses; thus it is a symbol of the youth whom the poet contemplates with aesthetic affection unsullied by carnal lust.[36] This insistence upon purity, in contrast to the carnality of heterosexual love, is frequently encountered in the homosexual syndrome, and a passage from Platen's diary stresses it with complete clarity: "Ich glaubte, daß sich bei einem Gegenstande der Neigung meines eigenen Geschlechts treue Freundschaft und reine Liebe eng vereinen ließen, während bei Weibern immer mehr Begierde vermischt sei."[37] Only with this image of Platen's in mind is the outrage of the worldly Lady Mathilde comprehensible, for, assuming that all concerned are familiar with Platen's poetry, the presentation of a tulip to a desirable lady is both uncomplimentary to the lady and highly amusing to the initiated onlooker.

In Chapter 4, the narrator sets his modern and therefore appropriate and genuine "Zerrissenheit" against the Classicistic imitation of poets like Platen: "Einst war die Welt ganz, im Altertum und im Mittelalter, trotz der äußern Kämpfe gab's doch noch immer eine Welteinheit, und es gab ganze Dichter. Wir wollen diese Dichter ehren und uns an ihnen erfreuen; aber jede Nachahmung ihrer Ganzheit ist eine Lüge, eine Lüge, die jedes gesunde Auge durchschaut, und die dem Hohne dann nicht entgeht" (E, *3*, 304). This, too, however, looks ahead to the final attack upon Platen's homosexuality, in which Heine not only holds Platen up to scorn, but brings out into the open a feature of Greek mores that the German idealization of the Greeks usually had scrupulously avoided. Here, however, in his intentionally unfair manner, Heine takes as examples of ancient custom not the Greeks but the unspeakable Nero and the decadent Petronius.

The Platen theme does not appear again explicitly until Chapter 10. Here the satire that is to be carried on in essay form in Chapter 11 is begun in earnest. Platen is introduced as an object of Gumpelino's fraudulent cultural voracity. On the one hand his servant Hirsch is occupied with mastering Platen's complex meters; on the other, Gumpelino, who has been robbed of his night of love by Hirsch's laxative, receives consolation from Platen's indifference to women and *Knabenliebe;* the result is "Gleichgültigkeit gegen die Weiber" (E, *3*, 340). Here, as in the following chapter, a number of things begin to happen at once. There is an echo of lines from *Der Romantische Oedipus,*

> Wem Kraft des Gemüts, wem Tiefsinn fehlt, und die Kunst,
> die jegliches ordnet,
> Der wird niemals dem versammelten Volk vorführen die
> wahre Tragödie,[38]

in Gumpelino's fatuous remark, "Ein gebildetes Gemüt wird aber nur durch die gebildete Form angesprochen, diese können wir nur von den Griechen lernen und von neueren Dichtern, die griechisch streben, griechisch denken, griechisch fühlen und in solcher Weise ihre Gefühle an den Mann bringen" (E, *3*, 339); the latter idiom calls forth a predictable rejoinder from the narrator. Gumpelino has read the poems during his frequent journeys to the chamber pot in the night, which inspires a number of scatological associations. The theme of Platen's presumed homosexuality begins to be developed with a rich supply of ancillary sarcasms. It is interesting that at this point Hirsch's story of his great deed of honesty is introduced; the "Schwüle im Zimmer" (E, *3*, 338) is for the moment dispelled by the freshness of Hirsch's moral tale.

We will spare ourselves an analysis of the eleventh chapter and its hilarious obscenities, which are better enjoyed by the individual reader according to his own taste.[39] Although it is, for the most part, very funny and composed with skill, there was some justice in the ill temper of Karl Kraus when he wrote: "Wer über das Geschlechtsleben seines Gegners spottet, kann nicht zu polemischer Kraft sich erheben. Und wer die Armut seines Gegners verhöhnt, kann keinen bessern Witz machen, als den: der Ödipus von Platen wäre 'nicht so bissig geworden, wenn der Verfasser mehr zu beißen gehabt hätte.' "[40] Furthermore, when it came to Shakespeare's sonnets, Heine passed over the homoerotic problem with the barest hint,[41] for mention of it, in his view, would not have been appropriate to the praise of a poet. It is plain, therefore, that Heine whipped up all this outrage because of his fury at Platen, not because he found the literary exploitation of deviation fundamentally incompatible with poetry. One question, however, cannot fairly be avoided: what are we to make of this sudden and complete shift into the "essay aspect"? The Platen theme is an integral part of the fictional narrative; it is now lifted out of this context and separately treated. Another theme, however, also carries through, that of the genuine poet. The narrator (if we may continue so to call him) has a good deal to say in the eleventh chapter in support of the image of the genuine, sovereign poet. We are assured, for example, that Platen is a person of importance to the narrator, for he serves as material with which the satirist can earn his bread: "Bei solchem fühlbaren Mangel an ausgezeichneten Narren kann man mir nicht genug danken, wenn ich neue aufs Tapet bringe und allgemein brauchbar mache" (E, *3*, 347)—a reprise of the remarks on the value of fools in *Das Buch Le Grand*. He shows, in contrast to Platen, that he is well acquainted with his opponent's works by giving a history of them and satirizing an important characteristic of their versification, the significant confluence of accented syllables.* He describes himself as "ein wahrer Dichter, der die verschämte Süßigkeit und die geheimen Schauer der Poesie schon empfunden hat und von der Seligkeit dieser Empfindungen, wie ein glücklicher Page, der die verborgene Gunst einer Prinzessin genießt, gewiß nicht auf öffentlichem Markte prahlen wird" (E, *3*, 358), and he includes himself among "wir Götter" (E, *3*, 367). Like Rostand's Cyrano de Bergerac, he demonstrates his superiority by devising more imaginative insults against his own person than his opponent has managed to think of. The sardonic peroration ends with a laughing farewell: "Für etwaige Könige, die mir dafür noch extra eine Tabatiere schicken wollen, bemerke ich, daß die Buchhandlung 'Hoffmann und Campe in Hamburg' Order hat, dergleichen für mich in Empfang zu nehmen" (E, *3*, 368).

The structural unities in Heine's works cannot always be comprehended by the usual literary classifications. The shift in the narrative plane in Chapter 11 is undeniable; the narrator is now no longer a fictional character, but the public persona of the poet Heine. But all eleven chapters are bound together by thematic connections, and those features of the poet that appear in the "essay aspect" are present and functioning in the "fiction aspect." I would like to suggest, however, that the "essay aspect," the attack on Platen and the analysis of his work, is also a fiction in a sense. I believe this can be demonstrated by calling attention to a peculiarity of the eleventh chapter.

In the course of his discussion of Platen in Chapter 11, Heine has the following to say of Platen's metrics:

> Niemand in Deutschland ist gegen poetische Erzeugnisse billiger als ich, und ich gönne einem armen Menschen wie Platen sein Stückchen Ruhm, das er im Schweiße seines Angesichts so sauer erwirbt, gewiß herzlich gern. Keiner ist

* E, *3*, 351. Heine himself, of course, did this in the *Nordsee* poems. See Paul Remer, *Die freien Rhythmen in Heinrich Heines Nordseebildern. Ein Beitrag zur neuen deutschen Metrik* (Heidelberg, 1889), pp. 17–21.

> mehr geneigt als ich, seine Bestrebungen zu rühmen, seinen Fleiß und seine Belesenheit in der Poesie zu loben und seine silbenmäßigen Verdienste* anzuerkennen. Meine eignen Versuche befähigen mich, mehr als jeden andern, die metrischen Verdienste des Grafen zu würdigen. (E, *3,* 351)

The passage goes on to compare Platen's metrical virtuosity with that of a tightrope-walker and gradually turns into a complaint about the violence Platen does to language. The manner is intentionally condescending and patronizing; Heine graciously grants Platen a certain *Fallhöhe* before he cuts him down. Thus far there is no difficulty. But there is a passage in a letter to Immermann of April 25, 1830, which Elster found interesting enough to append in a footnote, although neither he nor anyone else seems to have pursued its implications: "aus Perfidie ließ ich sie [Platen's metrical achievements] gelten, der scheinbaren Gerechtigkeitsliebe wegen. Auch die Metrik hat ihre Ursprünglichkeiten, die nur aus wahrhaft poetischer Stimmung hervortreten, und die man nicht nachahmen kann" (E, *3,* 351).* [42] Heine maintained this view with some consistency. In *Über die französische Bühne* he stressed that significant metrical achievement does not consist primarily in displaying great prosodic difficulties overcome.[43] On other occasions, Heine made some comparisons that, from his own point of view, were less than flattering to Platen: in *Die Romantische Schule,* to Johann Dietrich Gries and August Wilhelm Schlegel [44] (Loewenthal noted that Heine left Voss, whom he admired for other reasons, out of this comparison[45]), and among the *Gedanken und Einfälle* to Freiligrath.[46] But these judgments are a little puzzling, for Platen did have genuine metrical and rhythmical gifts, and Heine, who was himself a prosodist of great skill, must have recognized this without difficulty. And so he did. In a letter to Immermann of February 24, 1825, Heine, who apparently had just become acquainted with Platen's poetry, certi-

* Erich Loewenthal explains this as a pejorative pun ("merita metrica" and "merita mediocria") in "Heines Stellung zum antiken Vers (Heine als Vorgänger Andreas Heuslers)," *Archiv für das Studium der neueren Sprachen und Literaturen, 145* (1923), 168.

* The point of the remark is to compliment Immermann's metrical "Vortrefflichkeiten" despite his technical weaknesses.

fied it as genuine "poesy," if relatively weak in wit and abundance,[47] and in a letter to Menzel in May 1828, before the whole storm broke, we read: "Lesen Sie doch so bald als möglich Cottas Grafen Platen, nemlich dessen eben erschienene Gedichte, er ist ein wahrer Dichter. Leider! leider, oder besser, schrecklich! schrecklich! das ganze Buch enthält nichts als Seufzen nach Pedrastie. Es hat mich daher bis zum fatalsten Mißbehagen angewidert (Hirth, *1*, 360).* In later years, Heine returned to an acknowledgment of Platen's talents. In an "Entwurf Heines zu einem Artikel von Alexandre Weill" of 1839, by means of which Heine planted a letter from Paris in a magazine under Weill's name, he wanted the public to believe that he had nothing but praise for Platen and had attacked him only for political reasons.[48] In a conversation with Kertbeny in 1847, Heine called Platen a poet of significance,[49] and in the same year he is said to have expressed to Müller von Königswinter his regrets at having attacked and underestimated a man "der ein Pfleger der edelsten Richtungen in der Poesie wurde" (Houben, p. 595).

What, then, was Heine's actual view of Platen's poetry? If we choose to ask ourselves this question, we find ourselves in the fix that occurs over and over again in Heine interpretation. Since Heine's famed "subjectivity" is assumed to mean that he always speaks in his own voice, there has been a tendency until rather recently to give the same propositional truth value to Heine's statements in his letters, his essays, and as persona in his fiction and poetry. This leads the researcher into impenetrable labyrinths of conflicts and contradictions; solutions must be found, the chronology weighed, changes of mind postulated, and reasons for them deduced. While the case at hand is a fairly simple one and doubtless open to a tolerable solution, we nevertheless find ourselves in a position of having to defend the statement of Heine's persona in a literary work against that of a commentary by Heine in his letter to Immermann.

* Hirth draws the diametrically wrong conclusion when he argues that the passage shows Heine had condemned Platen's poetry before the latter's attack (Hirth, *4*, 190); Heine's remark demonstrates quite the opposite. The outrage expressed in the letter may be addressed particularly to the fanaticism in matters of morals for which Menzel was notorious.

The question as to Heine's view of Platen's poetry cannot be satisfactorily answered, nor can we even be sure that Heine cared enough about it to have any serious opinion at all, a quite different thing from knowing it well enough to turn it against his enemy for the purposes of *Die Bäder von Lucca.* A question that defies an answer is likely to have been incorrectly put. In this case, the proper question is not, what is Heine's view of Platen's poetry? but: How does he develop the theme within the context of the work? Thus, the only operative words that can be identified in Heine's letter are "der scheinbaren Gerechtigkeitsliebe wegen." The left-handed praise of Platen's metrics belongs with the statement, "ich werde das Materielle, das sogenannt Persönliche, nur insoweit berühren, als sich geistige Erscheinungen dadurch erklären lassen" (E, *3*, 347–48), an out-and-out piece of hypocrisy. These statements serve to clear the deck, as it were, for the ruthless execution of Platen. It is this display of the destructive power of the true poet that is primary here, not the critique of Platen in any objective sense. The conclusion to be drawn is that even the "essay aspect" of *Die Bäder von Lucca* is more intimately connected with the structure of the whole work and is more valuable for an assessment of the work than for any attempt to characterize the man behind the fictive personality.

CHAPTER 7

Reprise and New Directions: *Neue Gedichte*

> Sei allem Abschied voran, als wäre er hinter
> dir, wie der Winter, der eben geht.
>
> —RILKE

Heine's *Neue Gedichte* achieved a good deal of popularity upon its appearance in 1844,[1] but the consensus among connoisseurs is that it is the least memorable of his four collections of poetry; Stuart Atkins has shown that although judgments on the book have been various, they have almost always tended to be pejorative in one way or other.[2] It is a very uneven performance, although Elster in his second edition remarked with some justice that it is far better than its reputation.[3] For one thing, the collection lacks a unified character; it neither exhibits the clear line of development of *Buch der Lieder* nor has it a stable core of attitude and atmosphere as the later collections do. Prawer may be correct when he asserts that Heine "sought to present the poems written between 1830 and 1844 in the same biographically meaningful sequence in which the *Buch der Lieder* had presented those of an earlier period," [4] but because of the turmoil in Heine's mind during the thirties and forties about the value and function of poetry, there is an effect of discontinuity between the various sections of the book. Heine used *Neue Gedichte* as a catchall for all sorts of poetic efforts, and in its final form, the third edition of 1852, the collection spanned nearly thirty years of his writing career; a few of the poems go back as far as the early 1820s, while the section *Zur Ollea,* of which Prawer has remarked that it "does not increase Heine's reputation as a poet" [5] and which will not much concern us here, consists mainly of cast-offs from *Romanzero.*[6] The book is a record of a profound development in Heine's career that has two major phases: the turn away from love poetry to verse of public and political relevance, and the return to a renewed poetic consciousness with greater maturity and deepened sensitivities. *Neue Gedichte* is like an obbligato to the great symphonic development from *Buch der Lieder* through *Atta Troll* and *Deutschland: Ein Wintermärchen* to *Romanzero.*

The history of the publication of *Neue Gedichte* is a story in itself. As early as 1838 Heine was ready to publish what he thought of then as a second volume of *Buch der Lieder,* but a censor in Darmstadt had refused to pass it. Campe had meanwhile turned over the editorship of the work to Karl Gutzkow, which seems a little strange because Gutzkow by that time was not very well disposed toward Heine, but for some reason Campe loved to see his authors embroiled with one another. On August 6, 1838, Gutzkow wrote Heine a stuffy letter in which he asserted that the German people would never tolerate such frivolous poems (although they had almost all been published before) and warned him that the book would ruin his already damaged reputation beyond repair; he advised Heine to refrain from publishing it at all.[7] Heine must have stared when he saw this letter. Gutzkow was a strange man, full of mutually destructive contradictions, but this was really a little too much. For here was the same Gutzkow who less than three years before had been obliged, unreasonably to be sure, to spend nearly three months in jail because of his "immoral" novel *Wally, die Zweiflerin,* an event that had played a prominent part in the government crackdown on Heine and Young Germany at the end of 1835. Heine was, of course, furious; this feud became one of the major rifts in the ranks of Young Germany,[8] and it boiled up again in 1840 when Heine's book on Börne appeared. How harsh Heine's attitude became appears in a vicious little verse on Gutzkow and his lady friend, probably written in 1842, which turned up only recently:

> Sie saßen in süßer Vereinigung
> Und liebten sich ganz ätherisch;
> Sie hatte ihre Reinigung,
> Er aber war venerisch.[9]

Given the normal tone of Heine's correspondence with Campe, one would have expected on this occasion a hysterical outburst.

But Heine, for once, was anxious not to provoke a destructive quarrel that would have taken place both in the ranks of Young Germany and in the house of Hoffmann und Campe,* and he managed a mood of icy calm. On August 23, 1838, he wrote Gutzkow a letter from Normandy that in style and manner is almost unique in his usually unedifying and ill-tempered correspondence. It is a masterpiece of dignity, self-assurance, and velvety contempt, and in it the poetic persona, in a sense, speaks for the poet. After pretending to thank Gutzkow for his good advice, he assumes a thoroughly elitist posture, asserting that such poems as his are not to be judged by the standards of the common crowd, but can be appreciated only by the few superior spirits. The question, Heine asserts, is one of the autonomy of art, and there follows a much-quoted self-definition: "Mein Wahlspruch bleibt: Kunst ist der Zweck der Kunst, wie Liebe der Zweck der Liebe, und gar das Leben selbst der Zweck des Lebens ist" (Hirth, 2, 278).† He concludes by thanking Gutzkow, with graceful vindictiveness, for calling his attention to the mote in his eye.

The attitude expressed in this famous letter, however, is but one pole of a dialectic, or, perhaps one ought to say, one horn of a dilemma, that informs *Neue Gedichte,* and interpreters should be careful about applying that "Wahlspruch" to Heine without serious qualification. For one thing, it seems likely that Gutzkow's letter did in fact touch a troublesome chord in Heine—that streak of "Nazarene" puritanism always lurking beneath the surface of his bravado. Heine could make very Victorian sounds when he wanted to. He condemned Friedrich Schlegel's *Lucinde* "wegen seiner unzüchtigen Nichtigkeit" (E, 5, 269), and could be as stuffy

* He made this clear in a letter to Campe of Aug. 18, 1838; Hirth, 2, 274–75. In subsequent letters to Campe on Sept. 18 and Sept. 30, 1838, and on Apr. 12, 1839, Heine ostentatiously sent greetings to Gutzkow (Hirth, 2, 282, 283, 310).

† A similar statement appeared some months earlier in *Über die französische Bühne* (E, 4, 525) and, before that, in *Die Romantische Schule* (E, 5, 250); on this occasion, however, it is applied to Goethe and criticized (E, 5, 252). The interesting thing is that part of the formulation appears verbatim in a letter of Goethe to Heinrich Meyer of February 8, 1796; it then reappears in Wienbarg's *Ästhetische Feldzüge.* See Paul Konrad Kurz, *Künstler Tribun Apostel. Heinrich Heines Auffassung vom Beruf des Dichters* (Munich, 1967), p. 178. Kurz sees the formulation as having passed to Heine by way of Wienbarg, but this presents chronological difficulties with respect to the occurrence in *Die Romantische Schule.*

as anyone about the immorality of French life.[10] Heine did not in fact press the publication of *Neue Gedichte.* On August 18 he wrote astonishingly to Campe that the book meant nothing to him, and on January 23, 1839, he wrote that he was willing to throw out all the poems that might cause offense; but in April 1839, the book was so brutally censored anyway that Heine finally let the whole project lie and did not take it up again until the end of 1843.[11] In the first edition he did remove the section *Diana,* which was not restored until the third edition.

More important, however, is the fact that there had been grave doubts in Heine's mind about the pure autonomy of art for some time. He was plagued by the concern that poetry, or "poesy," was simply not important and possibly even iniquitous, and that the writer's true task lay in subordinating his subjective autonomy to issues of more relevance to the general run of mankind. In February 1830, shortly before he began to write the poems of *Neuer Frühling,* he wrote to Varnhagen: "Mit der Poesie ist es also aus; hoffentlich aber werde ich deßhalb um so prosaisch länger leben" (Hirth, *1,* 423).[12] These concerns are worked out more explicitly in the preface to the second edition of *Reisebilder II* of 1831, where Heine first published *Neuer Frühling.* In this preface he makes a set of significant, if rather odd, associations. He makes no great claims for these poems, he says, for there is no lack of their like in Germany. In any case the old masters of the genre, particularly Ludwig Uhland, cannot be improved upon. This is a peculiar identification, because Uhland implies for Heine "diese frommen und ritterlichen Töne, diese Nachklänge des Mittelalters" (E, *3,* 521), but such echoes are faint in *Buch der Lieder* and, except for the now stylized persona of the knight, entirely absent from *Neuer Frühling.* It is clear from this confusion that Heine thought of his own love poetry as Romantic and for that reason subject to the same strictures he brings to bear against Romanticism: that it is religiously and politically reactionary. It is both surprising and significant that Heine should have believed this, for its very obtuseness indicates how bad a conscience he had about his lyric poetry, a genre, he asserts, that is being drowned out "im Lärmen der neuesten Freyheitskämpfe, im Getöse einer allgemein europäischen Völkerverbrüderung." How plain it seems to him that the sound of freedom and brotherhood should be noise and not poetry! As Lee B. Jennings has succinctly observed, for Heine "the fantasy world is worthwhile, but insubstantial; while the concrete, everyday world is substantial, but not worthwhile." [13]

Most of the poems of *Neuer Frühling* were commissioned by a composer, Albert Methfessel.[14] This is the only time this ever happened in Heine's career, and it has been held by some to be the reason why they fail to satisfy. But there is no inherent reason why this should be so. The source of the general dissatisfaction with *Neuer Frühling* lies elsewhere. For the reader who comes from *Buch der Lieder* and has learned to appreciate what Heine accomplished in that effort, it can be distinctly annoying to see him apparently revert to a stage in his poetic career that had exhausted its function and been overcome. *Neuer Frühling* seems to be effortlessly carried by the momentum of *Lyrisches Intermezzo* and *Die Heimkehr,* completely bypassing the more rugged landscape of *Die Nordsee;* and so the poems seem mannered and cynical, yielding to older forms of self-indulgence without the urgency and intensity that impel the poems of *Buch der Lieder.* Stuart Atkins has argued that in some respects the poems of *Neuer Frühling* are pre-Romantic—that they reflect the style of the eighteenth century and display the sovereign powers of the poet by reviving at will the modes of "Rococo" or Anacreontic verse.[15] Enlightening as this suggestion is with respect to the style of *Neuer Frühling* and the meaning of its prologue, *In Gemälde-Galerien,* it does not exactly encourage us, I think, to take *Neuer Frühling* as seriously as *Buch der Lieder.* Thus Prawer remarks: "All Heine's faults appear in *Neuer Frühling* in exaggerated profusion. The cycle exhibits everywhere his coquettish enjoyment of real or imagined sufferings coupled with vulgar insistence upon his nobility of soul." [16]

This judgment is understandable in every respect, particularly the last point. But it does not tell us very much about why the poems of *Neuer Frühling* are as they are, or what differentiates them from their counterparts in *Buch der Lieder.* For *Neuer Frühling* is not simply a reprise of the earlier manner, and if

Prawer was right in thinking that this is what Heine meant later in the *Schöpfungslieder,*[17] then Heine himself was wrong; there is a subtle but perceptible difference in most of these poems. Perhaps we can describe it roughly by saying that the poetic persona so laboriously constructed in *Buch der Lieder* has now become the narrator of the poems. The effect of this is a loss of intensity and of what American undergraduates like to call "sincerity," but a gain, not throughout the cycle but in a substantial number of places, of artistic mastery and distance. As a consequence, critics fixated on Goethean *Erlebnisdichtung* as the exemplary mode of lyric poetry will naturally find the poems, as Belart argued, *too good.*[18] *Neuer Frühling* is the ultimate stage, the final polishing-off, of the style of lyrical love poetry upon which much of Heine's traditional fame has rested; he was never again to write any more of it.

Before turning to some examples, a word about the title is in order. It is programmatic, but not entirely in the way one might expect, for the new spring, the reawakening, is thoroughly ambivalent in the cycle as a whole. These spring songs were written mostly in the glum fall and winter of 1830/31, and the cycle in its total impact is far from lighthearted; the new access of life and love is a source of torment as well as joy. The ambivalence of spring appears already in the oxymoron of the first poem of the cycle proper, in which the spring is perceived "mit freud'gem Schrecken" (E, *1,* 204); it echoes here and there in the cycle and comes to fullest expression in No. 38:

> Ernst ist der Frühling, seine Träume
> Sind traurig, jede Blume schaut
> Von Schmerz bewegt, es bebt geheime
> Wehmut im Nachtigallenlaut. (E, *1,* 219)

"April is the cruellest month" would well serve as a motto for *Neuer Frühling,* and tears are more appropriate than laughter to the love that arises in this spring; the conclusion is gloom and, even worse, annoyance and irritation.

The bad conscience of the poet is present in the cycle from the very beginning: the *Prolog* raises immediately the problem of relevance[19] in the image of the knight who wants to go out into the good fight but is restrained by amoretti and bound by garlands of flowers. A cycle of love poetry that begins with such an image cannot help but be in a dissonant key, for the pervasive dissatisfaction with self lies deeper than the problem of unrequited love; thus in principle the poet-persona of *Neuer Frühling* is more explicitly self-critical than that of *Buch der Lieder*. Prawer calls attention to oddities of diction in two of the poems: Number 11, where images of conspiracy reinforce the echo that the word "Verschwörung" must necessarily have released in the contemporary political context,[20] and No. 24, where the poet speaks of two hearts forming a Holy Alliance,[21] a willed incongruity of metaphor probably more striking in its time than it is now.[22] In these places the problem of relevance seems to be lurking in the very diction.

The love experience of *Neuer Frühling* is highly stylized and its object is vague. In fact, in No. 4, the identity of the object does not seem to matter:

> Ich lieb' eine Blume, doch weiß ich nicht welche,
> Das macht mir Schmerz. (E, *1*, 205)

This poem is an example of what is simultaneously irritating and interesting about *Neuer Frühling*. The "Schmerz" so laconically claimed in the second line almost inevitably rhymes with "Herz" in the fourth (one consequence of Heine and his imitators is that today not even a German schoolboy would dare rhyme those two words again). The sound of the nightingale is heard among the fragrant flowers, and the poet searches for a heart as beautiful as his own. The reader has a weary sense of déjà vu. The interesting thing is that the poet seems to have the same sense. There is no energy in this poem whatsoever; the rhythm is slow and falling; the metaphors simply lie there, making no pretense to be anything but as flat and worn-out as they are. The dimetrical first line, unusual for Heine, emphasizes distance from the potential beloved and a certain indifference as to who she might be. The poetic posture is set out and "shown" to the reader—Brecht's terminology seems unexpectedly appropriate here, because there is a distinct effect of alienation between the narrating poet and the narrated situation.

The next poem, *Gekommen ist der Maie,* which goes back in

its original form to 1822, is of a nature which particularly aroused Prawer's ire. "Mawkish and empty," he calls it, "a cento of folk-song reminiscences and reminiscences of images, words, and phrases from the *Buch der Lieder*." [23] He observes that Heine took great trouble with this poem, revising it considerably, but finds the effort to be of no avail and evidence that Heine was "forcing his imagination" in *Neuer Frühling*. Here I would humbly submit that Prawer has missed something; the revision is not without its effect. The final version is more controlled, more indifferent, and more stylized than the original. For example, in the manuscript the eleventh line reads: "Ich hör' ein süßes Klingen" (E, *1*, 537). Already in a published version of 1824 this has become: "Ich hör' ein fernes Klingen" (E, *1*, 537). The substitution of distance for sweetness, right within the limits of Romantic diction, is not trivial; it is part of a process, evident in a number of the variants, of substituting an elegiac, more resigned tone for one of naive directness and purity of feeling; this is what makes the poem appropriate to *Neuer Frühling*. In the final version, the line becomes: "Ich höre fernes Klingen" (E, *1*, 205). The effect is to regularize the meter exactly without even the trace of rhythmic coloration previously provided by the long diphthong of "ein" in unaccented position. The result is cool monotony. Heine made three tries at the third stanza. The problem is, quite literally, the posture of the persona. In the first attempt, he is sitting in the high green grass and falls asleep to dream.[24] In the second, his posture is left unclear and he weeps into the grass. The final version has neither the strength of sitting nor the pathos of weeping: "Ich liege krank im Gras" (E, *1*, 205). There are no pathetic claims made by the narrator on behalf of the persona; the narrated persona *is* pathetic; the narrator is *not*, necessarily. This is not to say, by a long way, that *Gekommen ist der Maie* is a good poem; but its genesis is instructive. This is the level, as Prawer himself well knows, to watch this poet really at work.

The following poem, No. 6, is by common consent the jewel of the collection. The first two lines,

> Leise zieht durch mein Gemüt
> Liebliches Geläute (E, *1*, 205),

with their gorgeous liquid alliteration, are a good example of what an inspired opening will do to make a poem famous forever; apart from Goethe and Eichendorff, hardly any poet was as skilled in extracting such sounds from the German language. But the whole poem continues to be superb. Although it contains not a single pure rhyme, the lattice of near-rhymes and near-assonances gives it a genuine musicality; Hammerich has observed that it is one of Heine's most outstanding accomplishments in trochaic rhythm.[25] It seems likely that the poem owes its inspiration to verses from *Des Knaben Wunderhorn*:

> Wenn du zu meim Schätzel kommst,
> Sag: ich ließ sie grüßen.[26]

But the messenger here, as in a number of Heine's poems, for example, *Lyrisches Intermezzo* 36, is the poem itself; it is a poem about the poem, and this feature not only throws its perfection into sharp relief, but also calls attention to the poem's maker.

Number 16 supplies a different variation on this poetic self-awareness, for it is not only a poem about the poems, but it is directed to the reader and makes substantial claims about the effectiveness of the poems:

> Wenn du gute Augen hast,
> Und du schaust in meine Lieder,
> Siehst du eine junge Schöne
> Drinnen wandeln auf und nieder. (E, *1*, 210)

The poem ends with the assertion that the reader will become as confused and love-struck as the poet. I submit that this poem is not easily imaginable anywhere in *Buch der Lieder*. It suggests that the life of the beloved is restricted to the poetic context; it bypasses the beloved altogether in favor of direct communication between poet and reader. The power of the beloved to wreak havoc with the emotions lies specifically in the poetic recreation. The poems of *Neuer Frühling* have the effect of causing the beloved to disappear, first by atomizing her into her metaphoric components and then by setting down these components in an observed distance.

The same is true of the experience of love. The supply of Romantic metaphor, which even in *Buch der Lieder* lacks real immediacy—Heine was early aware that it was the false coin of "poesy"—in *Neuer Frühling* is even more distantly treated. In No. 7 the nature metaphors are bound together in a pattern of love: the butterfly is in love with the rose, the sunbeam with the butterfly, and the rose with—the poet does not know. But this round robin is not, as in *Lyrisches Intermezzo* 39, a pattern of unrequited love in which the poet is the prime loser. Instead, the poet regards all the metaphors with indifferent good humor:

> Ich weiß nicht, in wen die Rose verliebt;
> Ich aber lieb' euch all:
> Rose, Schmetterling, Sonnentrahl,
> Abendstern und Nachtigall. (E, *1,* 206)

The metaphors have lost the power to represent urgent emotional concerns of the poet convincingly. An even more lighthearted version of this theme appears in the next poem, No. 8, in which the denizens of the forest appear as caricatures. The point is, however, that it is the poet who manages these metaphors, like the director of an orchestra, and ties them into the context of love as he sees fit:

> Nein, in meinem eignen Herzen
> Sitzt des Walds Kapellenmeister,
> Und ich fühl' wie er den Takt schlägt,
> Und ich glaube Amor heißt er. (E, *1,* 207)

The rhythm of the poetry is not inherent in the metaphorical landscape but is the property of the poet. Consequently it seems to me that Prawer is not quite correct when he says in connection with No. 20, *Die Rose duftet—doch ob sie empfindet,* that it is the "one poem . . . in which Heine unmistakably lifts the veil";[27] the poem, which, as Prawer rightly says, leaves "the voice in mid-air," [28] is closely connected with the revision of the function of Romantic metaphor that is observable in several places in *Neuer Frühling.* In this poem the pathetic fallacy is not entirely abandoned, but there is grave doubt whether the rose

empfindet
Das was sie duftet, ob die Nachtigall
Selbst fühlt, was sich durch unsre Seele windet. (E, *1*, 212)

Perhaps the rose and the nightingale are lying; yet, avers the poet, such lies may nevertheless be productive. Prawer connects this attitude with Ibsen's gloomy discussion of the *livsløgn*, the necessary life-lie, in *The Wild Duck*.[29] But the context is very different: Ibsen is concerned about the motivation of action and attitude in an ambiguous social and intellectual situation; Heine is engaged in a halfhearted and crumbling defense of poetry. The attitude of *Neuer Frühling* 20 has little vitality and not much survival potential.

Another poem, No. 35, shows that the problem remains full of dissonances. Here Heine is playing with the levels of fiction and reality; he is not publicly betraying his beloved, he asserts,

Wenn mein Mund ob deiner Schönheit
Von Metaphern überquellt.

Unter einem Wald von Blumen
Liegt, in still verborgner Hut,
Jenes glühende Geheimnis,
Jene tief geheime Glut. (E, *1*, 218)

By transposing his feelings into poetic metaphor, the poet deceives the world into believing that they are fiction: "sie nimmt's für Poesie." Walther Killy, in his rather harsh treatment of Heine, observes: "Die Kongruenz von poetischer und geschichtlich erlebter Wirklichkeit scheint nicht mehr zu gelten. Das Gedicht ist für den Hörer vorzüglich erdichtet, und nicht vorzüglich Wahrheit, poetische Wahrheit, die vorzubringen eben die Fähigkeit des dichterischen Bildes ausmachte." [30] Very well, but one is almost tempted to accuse Killy here of undialectical thinking, or at least of an application of critical method that does not pay sufficient attention to the larger poetic context. Seen in this context, the poem is regressive; it is as though the poet were suddenly trying to clutch the persona and, as it were, defictionalize him. Both perspectives are maintained simultaneously: that of the suffering poet and that of the poet of suffering. The poet is reverting to the attitude of *Lyrisches Intermezzo* 36:

> Aus meinen großen Schmerzen
> Mach' ich die kleinen Lieder. (E, *1,* 79)

But in *Neuer Frühling* 35 there is an awareness that the bond between reality and metaphor has been stretched to the breaking point. The metaphors are becoming autonomous, and Killy, I believe, fails to see that this is a necessary step in the development of the autonomy of the poet; the unsatisfactory metaphorical system must be disengaged from the poet's felt reality before it can be abandoned altogether.

Accompanying this process in *Neuer Frühling* is another revision of attitude: it is not merely unrequited love that is bitter, but love itself and the sense of its impermanence. Like the overriding metaphor of the spring, which blossoms and brings its promises only to fade away into the damp chill of autumn, so love is cruel and generates false expectations. Anticipating the theme of the first part of *Tannhäuser,* the poet himself tries to mobilize bitterness as an antidote to the access of love. In No. 12, which operates with oxymora like "süßes Elend," "bittre Lust," and "himmlisch quälend," this posture is still highly sentimental:

> Ach, ich sehne mich nach Thränen,
> Liebesthränen, schmerzenmild,
> Und ich fürchte, dieses Sehnen
> Wird am Ende noch erfüllt. (E, *1,* 208)

Perhaps the tone of the poem is due to the fact that it is a year or two earlier than most of those in *Neuer Frühling.* In No. 31, the feeling becomes more concrete with the opposition of images of winter to those of summer:

> Ach, ich will es dir, Geliebte,
> Gern bekennen, ach, ich möchte,
> Daß ein kalter Nordwind plötzlich
> Weißes Schneegestöber brächte. (E, *1,* 216)

This draws an acute observation from Prawer: "A longing for winter represents a longing for truth." [31] The truth is not only that the metaphorics of love have no real referent, but also that love has no lasting substance.

The latter part of *Neuer Frühling* is largely an effort to deal with the impermanence of love. Number 27 contains a lament using an image of winter:

> Ach! ich weiß wie sich verändern
> Diese allzuholden Träume,
> Wie mit kalten Schneegewändern
> Sich umhüllen Herz und Bäume. (E, *1*, 214)

In No. 30, the poet tries to gain control of the unhappy perception by means of a gesture to the beloved:

> Sag nicht, daß du mich liebst!
> Ich weiß, das Schönste auf Erden,
> Der Frühling und die Liebe,
> Es muß zu schanden werden. (E, *1*, 216)

In Nos. 33 and 34, the persona assumes postures of relative unconcern; the message of his flowers is plain and unsentimental:

> Treu sein sollst du mir am Tage
> Und mich lieben in den Nächten. (E, *1*, 217)

The poet mocks the twelve-page letter of farewell from the beloved, which he thinks is too long to be taken seriously. The set ends, however, on a note of autumnal deadness. Parting (No. 39) and the images of autumn (Nos. 41 and 42) combine to create a chilly, unpleasant atmosphere that is different from the final tones of *Lyrisches Intermezzo* and *Die Heimkehr*—the emotional temperature is much lower. In fact, No. 42 seems intentionally destructive of poetry itself; for the apparently metaphorically understood gloomy weather of autumn suddenly becomes itself the real subject of the poem; the poet's mundane irritation at the rain is expressed with a metrical monstrosity:

> Es seufzt der Wald, es dampft das kahle Feld,
> Nun kommt das Schlimmste noch, es regent. (E, *1*, 221)

The final poem (No. 44) descends to satire on Hamburg and ends, appropriately to Hamburg but inappropriately to the system of love-metaphor: "und dieses Wetter!" (E, *1*, 222).

In *Neuer Frühling* the poetry of unrequited love consumes and destroys itself. The persona is established as a poet in complete control of a style, but the judgment upon the style itself is merciless. Tones of despair and of the vanity of human emotion are struck that will recur strongly in *Romanzero.* The price for perfect poems like *Leise zieht durch mein Gemüt* is too high; it is the price of dishonesty. Heine was never to pay it again—at least not in this form.

The section called *Verschiedene* was the one that many of Heine's contemporaries found offensive. Most of the poems in the cycle are ungentlemanly and intensely coarse in sentiment. For the most part, "love" in these poems knows no nightingales, no chaste yearnings, and no sweet and pure maidens. The girls are treated with naked contempt; the situations are those of casual encounter and short-lived relationships; the atmosphere is one of carnal lust. However, the poems are not pornographic, although this point was missed for a long time.

Many foolish things have been said about the *Verschiedene,* and Gutzkow's complaints are far from the silliest.[32] The various cycles were presumed to correspond exactly to Heine's libertine experiences in Paris, and it was not only the character of these relationships that was regarded as reprehensible, but also their number.* Heine certainly had a series of liberating erotic experiences during his first years in Paris, although it may perhaps be doubted that he was quite as active as the poems suggest; in any case, the question is both difficult to answer and of little importance. What is plain, however, is that the cycles are not exact accounts of real experiences. The poems of the group in its various versions were shuffled and reshuffled so often—individual poems first in one cycle, then another, now newly added, now discarded altogether—that only with the help of a set of tables can one follow their comings and goings at all. We are dealing here, as usual, with fictional representation. This much has long been obvious; what has been less well understood is the true *Gehalt* of these poems. It was not in Paris that Heine began to write erotic verse in a more or less

* Thus the title of an article by one Lorenz Freigang entitled "Katharina, Heines elfte Geliebte seit 1832."[33]

cynical tone; scanning the poems contemporaneous with *Buch der Lieder* but not included in it, one finds several examples.[34] But in a poem of uncertain date, published in 1826 and entitled *Erinnerung,* a story is told of *niedere Minne,* followed by abandonment, regret, and guilt:

> Fort ist der alte Wahn, jedoch das Bildnis
> Des armen Kinds umschwebt mich, wo ich bin.
> Wo irrst du jetzt, in welcher kalten Wildnis?
> Dem Elend und dem Gram gab ich dich hin! (E, *2,* 15)

Behind the libertinism of Heine's erotic poetry this sobriety is almost always perceptible. This is particularly true of the *Verschiedene.* For taken as a whole, the cycles express not lust, but satiety, not liberated sensual abandon, but inevitable boredom. The theme is vanitas, vanitas, and the *Verschiedene* would serve as an excellent text for a homiletic on the insubstantiality of carnal pleasure.* Significantly enough, this does not seem to have been Heine's original intent. In the preface to *Salon I,* he asserts in reference to some of these poems, "daß all mein Wort und Lied aus einer großen, gottfreudigen Frühlingsidee emporblühte" (E, *4,* 13), a statement that is dubious indeed, not only when applied to Heine's poetic career up to that point, but also as a characterization of these, his most "liberated" poems.

The poem that was ultimately located as *Angelique* 1 was originally the prologue to the whole group. It is a defense of the turn to a different kind of poetry, and Heine diplomatically anticipates objections not to the content of these poems but to the abandonment of the style of *Buch der Lieder.* Against the imitation of that style he delivers an amusing warning that might well have been better heeded:

> Ich, der, als ich unbeglücket,
> So viel sang von meinem Kummer,
>
> Daß mir tausend arme Jungen

* Atkins, "The Evaluation of Heine's *Neue Gedichte,*" *Wächter und Hüter. Festschrift für Hermann J. Weigand,* ed. Curt von Faber du Faur, Konstantin Reichardt, and Heinz Bluhm (New Haven, 1957), p. 105, expands the significance of this "Baroque despair in a nineteenth-century secular-nihilistic form" to *Neue Gedichte* as a whole. I believe he is right in doing so.

Gar verzweifelt nachgedichtet,
Und das Leid, das ich besungen,
Noch viel Schlimmres angerichtet! (E, *1*, 231)

In this poem we still have choruses of nightingales, but they have a new song to sing, a song of ecstatic joy—*Wonne*.[35]

Seraphine, the first, longest, and most ambitious cycle of the *Verschiedene,* set out in its final version of 1834 to develop the program of the new poetry, and what happens in this cycle is symptomatic for the *Verschiedene* as a whole. The cycle begins with a recapitulation of Heine's poetry up to this point. The first two poems revive elements of *Buch der Lieder*: the dreamy forest and the tears of lover and beloved in No. 1, and the *Doppelgänger* of *Die Heimkehr* 20 in No. 2. The setting of the cycle is the seashore of *Die Nordsee* (that Heine was now taking his vacations at Boulogne and Dieppe has no discernible effect on the imagery), and the ruthless beasts of prey that made a brief appearance in *Die Nordsee* I, 9, reappear in *Seraphine* 3, watched, as Prawer says, "by an alert and rational mind." [36] The imagery reinforces the feelings of exile and loneliness that the poem expresses, and it is clear already that unrestrained joy is not to be the only topic of the cycle. Number 4 picks up a theme from *Neuer Frühling*: the sudden terror that the access of love can cause. The climax of the cycle comes in No. 7, Heine's most compact Saint-Simonian confession.

Much has been written about Heine's important Saint-Simonian phase in the 1830s.[37] The Saint-Simonian religion, or religious surrogate, played a major role in the thinking of the liberal German literary intelligentsia of the time, and Heine's selective interest in it is the foundation of *Die Romantische Schule* and *Zur Geschichte der Religion und Philosophie in Deutschland.* The topic is quite involved and cannot be pursued here in any detail, except to recall that Heine showed little interest in the social and political ramifications of the doctrine and tended to find the antics of Enfantin and his followers entertaining rather than impressive; in one of his aphorisms he remarked wittily that, in His incarnation as Enfantin, God had made the ultimate sacrifice: He had made Himself ridiculous.[38] Heine took from the movement features that met needs of his own, needs that antedated his Parisian experiences by some years, as the *Berg-Idylle* of *Die Harzreise* plainly shows. *Seraphine* 7 makes it quite clear what these features were. First of all—and this is both characteristic of the German response to Saint-Simonianism generally and of significance for Heine's later development—it is the religious implications of the doctrine that hold his interest. Deliberately he begins the poem by making parodistic reference to the rock on which the Church was founded and to the Johannine prophecy of the future third testament, to which he specifically refers in Book II of *Börne*.[39] This new testament is now at hand and will overcome the dualism of body and soul in a joyful synthesis. God participates in all things and thus also in lovemaking. The persona has found a religion that provides both integrity and liberation, and, presumably, a justification for the vigorous and urbane new poetry of the *Verschiedene.*

One may fairly ask, however, whether the confession of *Seraphine* 7 is really central to the group as a whole. Anyone who studies Heine's Saint-Simonian experience quickly discovers how fragile it was. His commitment appears at its strongest when it is accusatory, as in the two essays on the German tradition; the doctrine provides powerful weapons that can be turned against both political reaction and the restraints that religion, in Heine's view, unfairly imposes on human happiness. His commitment is not so strong when the problem is to generate a positive attitude. Heine was not a constructive thinker—he was far too much the perpetual victim for that. The Saint-Simonian commitment did not sustain him, and it did not sustain the *Verschiedene.* It did not even have sufficient momentum to carry through the *Seraphine* cycle. The theme of the impermanence of love intrudes promptly in No. 9, where it is not even lamented, but merely remarked upon to the girl. Number 10, *Das Fräulein stand am Meere,* is an expression of cool scorn for the girl and for the sentimentality of nature metaphor, but there is also an undertone of weariness at the way the sun and the world go around:

> Das ist ein altes Stück;
> Hier vorne geht sie unter
> Und kehrt von hinten zurück. (E, *1,* 229)

Numbers 11 and 12 are poems of accusation against the girl and her mistreatment of the poet. The ship with black sails in the opening line of No. 11 is traditionally a symbol of death and contrasts quite strikingly with the tone of the Saint-Simonian confession. Number 14 reverts to the irrelevance of nature and the metaphorical landscape, but here the hollow whistling of the wind and the meaningless movement of the waves is connected with the loss of love and friendship. It is difficult in this poem to interpret the image of the rune stone, which projects into the sea and on which the dreaming poet sits. Perhaps Heine thought of the runes as cryptic and impenetrable and used the symbol much in the way the Romantics used the motif of hieroglyphics.[40] In any case, the quietly dark tone of the poem expresses deep loneliness. In No. 15, the poet asks to be buried in the sea—the element of his most powerful poetic metaphor to date—although here he claims that the sea has had a cooling and calming effect on him.

Of the eight cycles of the *Verschiedene* proper (I include here *Katharina,* but not *Friedrike,* which is much earlier and has nothing to do with the complex), *Seraphine* is the only one that has any real claim to be taken seriously as poetry. The other poems of the group have some interesting features and several are highly amusing, but most of *Verschiedene* is rather minor verse. *Seraphine* does, however, establish the pattern to which all the cycles conform in one way or another: love and lust followed by disappointment, loss, and ennui. *Angelique* shows the pattern most clearly, and here the deterioration of the love relationship begins to set in almost at the very beginning. Number 2 laments that the girl's love has tamed the wildness that attracted her to the poet in the first place. Number 3 is an imperious demand for sexual submission:

> Diese braungestreifte Lüge,
> Streif sie ab; ich liebe dich.
> Laß dein weißes Herz mich küssen—
> Weißes Herz, verstehst du mich? (E, *1,* 232)

But in No. 4, a poem rhymed entirely in *-u-,* the vowel of kissing, as Barker Fairley has remarked,[41] the poet already seems to want to disappear out of the specific situation: he holds the girl's eyes shut when he kisses her; and in No. 5, he cannot bear to be reminded of Germany when he is in her arms, which means in this context, I believe, that memories of the lost love of *Buch der Lieder* continue to trouble him, although the allusion can as easily be interpreted as an access of distraction from his private pursuits by thoughts of political reality. After this the tone gets sour; Number 6 is a cynical observation on infidelity, and in No. 7 the poet has no time today for his "ideal"; she is to come back tomorrow afternoon. This poem is an outstanding example of what many Germans have liked least about Heine; upon the pleasures of love, when the poet succeeds in arousing them tomorrow, will follow the pleasures of eating. The third stanza frivolously and jarringly rhymes "kapabel" with "Robert-le-Diable," and the fourth stanza turns around to fracture French by rhyming "Scribe" with "Liebe" (E, *1*, 234). But the distaste Heine's critics have felt for such verse is no greater than the distaste the poet himself expresses for the whole situation. In No. 8, love has given way, with an accompanying loss of enthusiasm, to "friendship," and in No. 9 total boredom has set in; the carnival is over and the poet will remind the girl that she is dust by drawing the ashen cross on her forehead. Originally there were three poems in this group that Heine did not include in *Neue Gedichte*.[42] They are smooth and sovereign accounts of stylized seduction. It would seem unlikely that in 1844 Heine removed them because of their risqué content; rather, their removal and their replacement with the new Nos. 5 and 6 make the downward slide into satiety and boredom more precipitous. What might be called the Saint-Simonian aspect of the experience becomes even less enduring.

The remaining cycles need detain us only for a few observations. *Diana,* which was removed from the group after its appearance in *Salon I* and not restored until the third edition of *Neue Gedichte* in 1852, is the most trivial but also the gayest of the sets. This "mercenary mountain of flesh"[43] is not to be taken seriously on any terms; it is all a hyperbolic joke on her Herculean proportions. *Hortense* is more disconsolate in tone. It begins with a poem that was located in *Salon I* between this section and the preceding *Diana,* and it functions in a sense as a motto; in its original publication in *Der Freimüthige* it bore the title *Epilog,* but Heine was probably quick to see that as an epilogue it would not do, for it represents the attitude of the beginnings of the cycles but not of the ends. It is a statement of the new insouciance, contrasted with the seriousness of the poet's feelings about love in earlier days; he now realizes that kissing is "superfluous," something to be done with a light heart and no investment of faith.[44] But this attitude does not protect against disappointment, and it is quite interesting that in Nos. 4 and 5 pessimistic Biblical allusions make their appearance. In No. 4, Heine uses the image of the serpent in the Garden to describe how the girl was seduced into infidelity by the arguments of another woman:

> Dieses ist die Frucht des Lebens,
> Koste ihre Süßigkeit,
> Daß du nicht so ganz vergebens
> Lebtest deine Lebenszeit! (E, *1,* 238)

The tempting serpent is a Saint-Simonian! This becomes more explicit in the next poem, which turns sharply against the doctrine; now the poet is singing "new melodies," but the text is as old as Solomon: "das Weib ist bitter." The girl's infidelity has destroyed joy and causes the poet to remember more traditional attitudes:

> Also wahr ist jene Sage
> Von dem dunklen Sündenfluche,
> Den die Schlange dir bereitet,
> Wie es steht im alten Buche?

This poem is several years later than most of the *Verschiedene* and was added to *Hortense* only in 1844. By putting it in a cycle that begins with the older ex-*Epilog,* Heine shows clearly the development of his attitude and its direction.*

Clarisse begins with the most amusing poem of the set, a nicely compact account of the universal bachelor experience of a girl who cannot make up her mind either to submit or to refuse; it

* Elster (E^2, *1,* 490) dates the poem in 1835 because he believes it refers to a phase in Heine's relationship with Mathilde. This is fairly probable but not of particular interest to our present concerns.

ends with a witty prayer that God might dry her tears and illuminate her brain. In No. 2 the poet asserts that the girl can hold him only by mistreating him, clearly reminiscent of *Das Buch Le Grand*; the cycle ends with all feeling irretrievably dead and gone. In *Yolante und Marie* there is an initial attempt to make a separation between the persona's being as a poet and his life of sensual enjoyment; while the mother and daughter discuss literature, the poet ignores the conversation and enjoys his delicious dinner. A situation in which the persona considers at the same time sexual relations with a mother and daughter is admittedly somewhat unedifying (Heine's revisions of No. 3 for *Neue Gedichte* made the situation slightly less explicit[45]), although the poet mocks himself in No. 2 with the amusing image of the ass who cannot decide between two bundles of hay. But the ass reappears in No. 4 in a more sober context: the poet congratulates himself for his new courage and effectiveness in the erotic life, but the emptiness of the experience and the loss of youthful innocence troubles him:

> Doch, wenn ich den Sieg genieße,
> Fehlt das Beste mir dabei.
> Ist es die verschwundne, süße
> Blöde Jugend-Eselei? (E, *1*, 242)

The remaining cycles are of less interest. Emma is the only one of the *Verschiedene* proper who does not submit to the poet; it is a cycle of frustration, with the poet muttering about his own foolishness, and it comes to the familiar emotional dead end. The poems of *Katharina* are a good deal later: Numbers 3–5 and 8–9 appeared first in 1835, No. 1 in 1839, and Nos. 2, 6, and 7 in 1840. They indicate clearly that the lode has been worked out; they are more self-indulgently accusatory and less compact, and the group lacks a story. It has been suggested that the set served as a catchall for poems that did not fit in elsewhere.[46]

Before this group Heine placed *Der Tannhäuser* of 1836. It would be presumptuous to attempt to improve on Prawer's excellent, detailed interpretation of *Tannhäuser,*[47] which impresses me as just about the last possible word on that poem. But for our purposes it is necessary to touch upon at least two main problems: why Heine took the poem over from his essay on folklore, *Elemen-*

targeister, into the *Verschiedene,* and what we are to make of the jarring contrast of its third section. While it seems that the poem was motivated by Heine's troubled feelings with respect to Mathilde, his interest in the legend goes back at least as far as 1824, when he mentioned it in a letter to Christiani;[48] he touched upon it also in *Zur Geschichte der Religion und Philosophie in Deutschland.*[49] Elster, in his useful résumé of the history of the legend, remarks that "sie steht und fällt mit einer einseitigen dualistischen Lebensanschauung";[50] the medieval knight Tanhûsaere (ca. 1205–70) was reported to have abandoned love poetry and worldly pleasures for monkish asceticism. Thus the legend stands in clear contrast to the Saint-Simonian program announced at the beginning of the *Verschiedene.* This conflict is very stark in the poem.* The persona is cloyed with the pleasures of the senses and, in a phrase reminiscent of the longing for winter in *Neuer Frühling* 31, repines not for love but for its antidote: "Ich schmachte nach Bitternissen" (E, *1,* 245). But Tannhäuser cannot escape from Venus on such grounds, so he fabricates a perfectly specious attitude of jealousy. His torrid appeal to the Pope, however, is a despairing *contradictio in adjecto;* the very fervidness of his account of the pleasures of Venus evinces neither contrition nor any apparent possibility of cure; in fact, Tannhäuser, in the midst of this tirade, asserts flatly that the Pope has no power against the force of love:

> Das ist wie ein wilder Wasserfall,
> Du kannst seine Fluten nicht dämmen! (E, *1,* 248)

But Tannhäuser really does want release and he piteously begs the Pope for salvation. In the version of the legend that Heine originally quoted from *Des Knaben Wunderhorn,*[51] the Pope cynically says that Tannhäuser will be forgiven when a staff of dead wood blossoms. God intervenes, the staff blossoms, although too late to save Tannhäuser, and the moral chastisement at the end of the poem falls upon the Pope. In Heine's version, there is no contrition to be accepted; Tannhäuser is asking the Pope for

* Here, as in the case of the Flying Dutchman, it is Heine's poetic intelligence that mediates between the raw material of the legend and the intense sensuality of Richard Wagner's opera.

magic. The Pope has no magic, only the non-news for Tannhäuser that Venus is the worst of all devils and her torments are eternal. God stays out of the case, and the emotional dilemma of the *Verschiedene* is concentrated into a complete impasse. What to do?

Since there is no escape from the dilemma, Heine abolishes it; he shifts the narration into the realm of contemporary satire. In the third part of *Tannhäuser* we are given a foretaste of *Deutschland. Ein Wintermärchen.* Having heard the Pope confirm the hopelessness of his amorous entanglement, Tannhäuser turns about and races back to the arms of Venus. Gone is the longing for bitternesses; he tells her no more than that he had business with the Pope in Rome and that the Pope sends his greetings; the rest is satire on German political and literary conditions. Traditional critics have naturally always been appalled. Elster asserted that the third part fits the first two "wie die Faust aufs Auge." [52] Now it should be remembered, first of all, that in the preface to *Salon III* and in the *Elementargeister* Heine drops a number of broad hints about the kinds of things he would have been writing if he had not been muzzled by the censorship.[53] The Tannhäuser poem is presented there as the product of another, anonymous person.[54] Clearly it represents an effort to unleash, if possible, the energies of political and social satire trammelled up in Heine at this time. But in truth it is difficult to make a defense of the poem's structure that will stand up altogether. Sternberg does not help us when he traces the sharp contrast to the "für Heine so typische Dialektik zwischen Romantik und Rationalismus." [55] Andler suggests that in order to overcome the inertia of politics and literature in Germany, "il faut retourner chez Dame Vénus, revenir au dogme de la beauté et de la joie, de l'émancipation de la chair." [56] But this takes no notice of the problem of satiety and the longing for bitterness, nor does it account for the fact that strong sensual imagery is quite absent from the third part; instead, with what one suspects may be a comic note from Heine's life with Mathilde, Venus' excitement at Tannhäuser's return causes her nose to bleed. Venus with a nosebleed as a symbol of the Saint-Simonian doctrine!

In his preface to *Salon III,* Heine apologizes that the poem is not better than it is,[57] although as usual he does not go into detail about what dissatisfies him. For *Neue Gedichte* he wrote a new final stanza that gives the poem the appearance of a fragment, a doubtful solution that occurs again in the similar case of *Jehuda ben Halevy* in *Romanzero.* The whole procedure looks suspiciously like one of flight, and, uncomfortably enough, in two directions simultaneously. The flight from Venus was abortive, without having resolved at all the original clash with the Saint-Simonian doctrine that informs the cycles of *Verschiedene.* But Tannhäuser also flees through the landscape of Germany, over which he sprinkles his acid comments, in order finally to relax unconcernedly in his Venusberg. Laura Hofrichter observed succintly that "Tannhäuser speaks lyrically of the Venusberg when he is out in the world and satirically of the world when he is in the Venusberg." [58] The persona is homeless and does not have complete integrity. The problem is simply set out with all its unresolved dissonances. Heine at this stage does not know what to do about it.

The *Schöpfungslieder* that follow *Tannhäuser* are unexpected, and Elster complained that they fit badly into the *Verschiedene.*[59] Perhaps the best explanation of them is that, after the confusions of the cycles and the failure to sustain the attitude that originally impelled them, it is time for some aesthetic stock-taking. The result is an ironic presentation of the poet-persona that is not entirely reassuring. The group grew slowly, Nos. 1–4 appearing in *Salon I* in 1834, Nos. 5 and 6 in the first edition of *Neue Gedichte,* and No. 7 in the third edition; thus the group as a whole almost spans the period from *Neuer Frühling* to *Romanzero.* The most striking feature of these poems is the parallelism of the poet-persona with God the Creator. Yet there is no Romantic elevation of the poet to divine heights; instead, God is brought down to a level that is something less than majestic. Prawer interprets the amusing dialogue of the first two poems, in which Satan accuses God of self-imitation and God offers a defense, as an expression of self-criticism on Heine's part, evidence of a certain embarrassment at *Neuer Frühling.*[60] This view seems to me to be open to at least some doubt. If it is correct, then Heine is comparing the poems of *Buch der Lieder* with the sun, the ox, and the lion, as contrasted with the less impressive imitations, stars, calves and cats. This, I think, Heine would have been unlikely to do in 1834, when his feelings about *Buch der Lieder* were no happier than they were about *Neuer Frühling*. The element of defensiveness seems to me more prominent in the set. Number 2 protests against the criticism of those who, like Satan, can create nothing themselves; Number 3 tries to balance the values of what is important and significant with what is satisfying and enjoyable; and No. 4 stresses the intellectual labor that lies behind the creative process and is a defense against any suspicion of facileness. Number 5 is more troublesome; here there is self-irony, and perhaps even some bitterness, for the relationship of art and reality is perversely and intentionally set the wrong way around. God creates a world that is praised because it looks so much like the worn-out decor of nature metaphor:

> Wie die Bäume grün und glänzend!
> Ist nicht alles wie gemalt?
>
> Sind nicht weiß wie Alabaster
> Dort die Lämmchen auf der Flur?
> Ist sie nicht so schön vollendet
> Und natürlich die Natur? (E., *1*, 253)

What exactly troubles Heine here is not really clear, but there is no other poem in his career, I believe, in which the persona qua poet is treated with such contempt or Heine's own fundamental limitations so broadly hinted at. Number 6 serves as an antidote to this misery by claiming that the *Stoff* of reality acquires its value only through the form given it by the artist. Number 7 dates from the mattress-grave and is a strange poem indeed. In a striking anticipation of Thomas Mann, the creative urge is derived from sickness—in *Reise von München nach Genua* Heine had already observed that the sick are more elegant than the healthy[61]—and only the process of creation has a healing effect. While on the one hand this looks like a resolution of the problem of *Zerrissenheit* that Heine had talked about over twenty years before in *Die Bäder von Lucca*, the whole concept still has pessimistic overtones, especially insofar as the parallelism of the poet-persona with God is still being maintained.

The next group is a set of three poems of homesickness for Germany entitled *In der Fremde.* The first two are sentimental and slack, but the third is a compact masterpiece; it is one of those not infrequent poems of Heine that interpret themselves, so perfect are their rhythms and understated simplicity of diction:

> Ich hatte einst ein schönes Vaterland.
> Der Eichenbaum
> Wuchs dort so hoch, die Veilchen nickten sanft.
> Es war ein Traum.
>
> Das küßte mich auf deutsch und sprach auf deutsch
> (Man glaubt es kaum
> Wie gut es klang) das Wort: "Ich liebe dich!"
> Es war ein Traum. (E, *1,* 263)

Tragödie, the final group of *Verschiedene,* is a kind of experiment. In 1825 Heine found a *Volkslied* or an imitation of one[62] in the *Rheinische Flora,* which must have caught his attention because of the imagery of fading and withering applied to love:

> Es fiel ein Reif in der Frühlingsnacht,
> Er fiel auf die zarten Blaublümelein,
> Sie sind verwelket, verdorret. (E, *1,* 264)[63]

Heine scrapped the fourth stanza of the *Lied,* which is trivial, and built a frame around the remainder, two stanzas before and two following. The group was first published in 1829. There is nothing very impressive about these verses, but perhaps Heine hoped that they would do something to pull together the helter-skelter composition of the *Verschiedene.* The opening stanza, beginning with what, unexpectedly, seems to be a quotation from Donne, has muted tones of erotic emancipation:

> Entflieh mit mir und sei mein Weib,
> Und ruh an meinem Herzen aus. (E, *1,* 263)

The *Lied* tells of the ruin and death of the lovers; the final section shows another pair of lovers seated on the grave of the first pair. The elements of nature are so sad themselves that they cause the lovers to weep, although they do not know why. The ending is weak, but in a sense it is appropriate to the *Verschiedene,* which is the record of a failure. The persona could be strengthened and toughened, but could not be given lasting qualities of joy and erotic abandon. Suffering and sadness were ineradicable characteristics of Heine's muse.

Heine's ballads and romances are the most stable element in his total *œuvre*. It would be difficult, I think, to write a history of Heine's achievements in this genre that would show clear and progressive lines of development throughout his career. Certain trends are apparent; in the course of time these narrative and situational poems become more compact and terse, only to expand again in the last phase, and in that phase the dark tonality tends to be more consistent. But these are only trends; two of Heine's finest and most compact ballads, *Die Grenadiere* and *Belsatzar*, are quite early, while at all stages there are examples that are skillfully composed but otherwise rather lightweight. Although the pessimistic tone grows stronger with the years, *Romanzero* begins with two of Heine's gayest ballads. The ballad form seems to have been the least problematical for him, the one in which he was most comfortable. It permitted him to make use both of his talent for compression and of his urge to draw impressionistically his individual, central personae. Helene Herrmann has pointed out that they exploit Heine's impressionistic instincts while mediating between the epic and dramatic genres in which he could not achieve success; the ballads are "Höhepunktszenen eines ungeschriebenen Dramas. Es ist mehr Situation in ihnen als langsam sich entwickelndes Geschehen, mehr Geste als Handlung." [64]

The ballads and romances of *Neue Gedichte* are the product of several years: the first one first appeared in 1836; quite a number of them appeared in 1839–40, several in 1842 and 1844, while one, No. 19, goes back to about 1824. As Seeger has pointed out, only thirteen of these twenty-five poems are actually ballads in the usual sense.[65] The resulting section of *Neue Gedichte* has no discernible compositional order; a variety of themes occur and reoccur in the group. For our purposes, therefore, the poems are best organized according to the various representations of the persona.

First of all there is the persecuted lover. While the theme is hardly unexpected by this time, it is in the process of disappearing, in the sense that the representation of the persona as victim will eventually take on broader and more existential implications. There are signs of this development already in the *Romanzen* of *Neue Gedichte.* In the first poem of the group, *Ein Weib,* which is contemporaneous with *Tannhäuser,* the development is only barely in evidence. But the contrast is vivid between the woman whose laughter is not even stilled on the occasion of her lover's execution and the victim whose pleas for love and consolation in his last night go unheard; the emphasis of the poem is not exclusively upon the sufferings of the victim, and the amoral and completely unsentimental vitality of the woman seems to have some existential right to survival. The second poem, *Frühlingsfeier,* treats the matter in terms of the Adonis myth. The excursion into the realm of a legendary nature cult does not reduce the element of pathos in the portrait of the persona, but it does lend a more stylized and controlled form. While the irregular cadences of the first two stanzas, describing in uneven rhythms the destructive ecstasies of the maidens, culminate in heavy and jarring dactyls in line 9, the third stanza pictures the slaughtered youth in regularly alternating trochees, yielding a contrastingly calm lament. A variation on the theme occurs in No. 18, *Fortuna,* a rather weak poem that nevertheless is symptomatic of the shift in perspective that is taking place. Here the persona has bravely wooed in vain and is now dying; however, the object of his intentions is not a girl but Dame Fortune herself; the persona defeated in love is becoming the persona defeated by life and reality who is to become so prominent in the later poetry.

A second theme—the majesty of the poet-persona and the power of his song—is one that has variants at all stages of Heine's career. It is first introduced in No. 3, *Childe Harold,* a somber poem full of internal rhymes and assonances, which uses as a symbolic event the return of Byron's corpse to England. Byron's importance for Heine had long since receded into the background, and Byron is not characterized here in any way; he is simply the dead poet, and in this capacity alone is important enough to cause the waves and the nixies to lament the occasion. Other versions of the theme have more vitality. One is No. 10, *Ritter Olaf*—the knight and the poet are always interchangeable personae for Heine. Here the heroic pose is an attempt to extract a moral victory from defeat. Olaf, condemned to death for having seduced the king's daughter, squeezes the last drop of life out of his last day and gives expression to one of the most persistent, though ultimately unrealizable, yearnings of the persona:

> Laß mich leben, laß mich leben,
> Bis geleert der letzte Becher,
> Bis der letzte Tanz getanzt ist—
> Laß bis Mitternacht mich leben! (E, *1*, 274)

His peroration is a long blessing of the poetic nature metaphors and culminates in a blessing of the lilac bush under which the princess yielded to him. Thus a late appearance of Saint-Simonian affirmation is coupled with the pathos of death and defeat, making *Ritter Olaf* a significant poem of transition. The troubadour Bertrand de Born in No. 12, by contrast, suffers no defeats; the entire Plantagenet court yields submissively to the power of his song. It is important, it would seem, to the definition of the persona to show that this is at least possible. Number 14, *Ali Bei,* produces another variation that, as Prawer has pointed out, expresses an important wish-dream of the poet;[66] for here the persona, a Saracen transform of Ogier the Dane,[67] is hypnotized by his happy dreams of love into complete courage and total heroic effectiveness:

> Während er die Frankenköpfe
> Dutzendweis' heruntersäbelt,
> Lächelt er wie ein Verliebter,
> Ja, er lächelt sanft und zärtlich. (E, *1*, 278)

This contrasts, of course, with the prologue to *Neuer Frühling,* in which love, far from energizing the persona and releasing his courage, lames his effectiveness.

The power of song, finally, appears most clearly in No. 21, *Frau Mette,* a poem that tries to put the persona beyond good and evil. Peter corrupts Bender with the offer of his bet and corrupts Bender's wife with the power of his song; Frau Mette must die, which is apparently of no concern to Peter and, in a cynical twist at the end, it seems also to be of little concern to Bender, who equates the loss of his wife with that of his dogs. The significance of the situation is that the poet coldly masters the force of his song, which can bring ruin and heartbreak to another:

> Sein Lied ist stark als wie der Tod,
> Es lockt in Nacht und Verderben.
> Noch brennt mir im Herzen die tönende Glut;
> Ich weiß, jetzt muß ich sterben. (E, *1*, 283)

The effort for a posture of insouciance, which began in *Buch der Lieder* and the *Reisebilder,* continues in the ballads of *Neue Gedichte.* The bouncy rhythms of No. 16, *Die Unbekannte,* belie the claim that the poet is sick with yearning, and the discovery that the unknown girl's name is Laura releases an obvious association that combines resigned indifference with a proud literary self-identification:

> Laura heißt sie! Wie Petrarcha
> Kann ich jetzt platonisch schwelgen
> In dem Wohllaut dieses Namens—
> Weiter hat er's nie gebracht. (E, *1*, 280)

In No. 22, *Begegnung,* Heine tries to connect his interest in the elemental spirits of folklore to this manner. "The merman in the village world," asserts Prawer, "is in the position of a German in Paris, or a Jewish poet writing for a German audience";[68] he must maintain a disguise, keep his distance, and carry on his relationships in the second person plural. The penetration of the disguise by the nixie is an upsetting event and the merman must take polite but firm steps to restore his incognito. This interpretation is attractive, but there are aspects of the poem that seem to me to bear more exactly on the continuous experimentation with the fictional persona. The persona maintains a disguise right enough, that of a noble gentleman, but his true self is cold and wicked; his purpose is the seduction of the pretty girls. The nixie is also cold and scornful and thus belongs to the race of girls of whom the persona in the past has been the victim, but in this metamorphosis he has *become like her.* By this means he has managed to assume a quality of sovereign indifference that is not without its ironic aspect.

Such poems do not, however, set the tone of the group as a whole; much more pervasive is the theme of the loneliness and unreality of the poet and the related one of the doubtfulness of love. In No. 4, *Die Beschwörung,* the Franciscan monk has the spirits of the underworld bring forth the corpse of the most beautiful woman of antiquity—Helen, presumably—and bring it back to life. But there is no life; the dead beauty and the monk sit and look at one another in chill silence. A trace of *Schauerromantik* left over from Heine's earliest poetry has been translated into an image of fearful sadness and of the incongruence of life and love.[69] In No. 6, *Unstern,* the view of love is fouler; love is a star in a heap of filth, a dead mangy dog covered with garbage. The sounds of lust are the crowing of the cock and the grunting of the sow. This certainly is shocking language, and its hyperbolic "Nazarenism" puts the Saint-Simonian experiment into a most bitter and despairing perspective. The last stanza expresses a desire that the persona had remained with the purity of the abandoned system of poetic metaphor and could achieve a clean dying:

> O, fiel' ich doch in den Garten,
> Wo die Blumen meiner harrten,
> Wo ich mir oft gewünscht hab'
> Ein reinliches Sterben, ein duftiges Grab! (E, *1,* 271)

This is the blackest of Heine's poems before *Romanzero,* and its merciless acidity has the effect of dissolving some of the fabric of *Neue Gedichte.*

In two poems of exile, *Anno 1829* and *Anno 1839,* Heine abandons his fictional personae for a moment to write straight autobiography. The first recaptures his desperation in the period just before the July Revolution to get out of the stifling bourgeois atmosphere of Germany at any price. The second shows him in an emotional bind. Paris, which with true German prejudice he always persisted in seeing as superficial and frivolous, makes him homesick for Germany, but as soon as his thoughts turn thither, he cannot refrain from viewing it as the land of dullards and fools, and although at the moment he feels he would be happy to be among them again, one is permitted to doubt how long this sentiment would have survived. The exiled poet is truly and irreparably homeless. In No. 20, *Laß ab,* the persona is portrayed as a Jonah in regard to love. The girl addressed by the poem loves him as the day the night, the spring the winter, as life loves death —cheerless symbols for the persona. The girl, in turn, is fading away, and her soul is bleeding from love; she has assumed the previous role of the persona, but there is no gratification at her distress, as is occasionally attempted in *Buch der Lieder*; she is advised to abandon the poet and turn her love to the cheerful butterflies—how often in the later poetry the nature metaphors refer to a lost or unattainable happiness! The most striking feature of the poem is the utter collapse of the meter in the last line, which puts the word "Unglück" into such disharmonious relief that it is almost as though poetry itself were denied by it:

> Laß ab von mir, und liebe nur
> Die heiteren Schmetterlinge,
> Die da gaukeln im Sonnenlicht—
> Laß ab von mir und dem Unglück. (E, *1,* 282)

Appended to the ballads is the cycle *Unterwelt,* in which we find Heine in 1840 ruminating on his domestic situation. The parodistic treatment of the myth of Pluto and Proserpine is wickedly amusing, and Pluto's hyperbolic account of the hellish torments of marriage and his determination to drink "Punsch mit Lethe" (E, *1,* 289) to forget his wife are highly entertaining. But Ernst Feise, in his excellent metrical and rhythmical analysis of the group,[70] points out that its prominent position in this section of *Neue Gedichte* and its relative bulk suggest that there is more to it than just wry parody. The group is related to the ballads in that it "rounded out their common theme of tragic love and mismating." [71]

There are at least three important aspects of the group. First of all, it is not only Pluto who suffers in the marriage, but also Proserpine; she is grim and sour in this gloomy atmosphere filled with dull and grisly companions. If there is any one substantial gain in the characterization of the persona in *Neue Gedichte,* it is that he is not the only one in the world who is victimized. Secondly, there is a frontal attack on poetry in Part III, in which Heine plays a malicious trick with Schiller's ballad *Die Klage der Ceres.* The rhythm of Heine's introductory lines, as Feise has shown, speeds up the reading of Schiller's original "into a ridiculous jogging trot." * [72] The third feature is found in Part V, which as originally published was not a part of the group. It has always been assumed that this sad and quiet-spoken poem—"Zuweilen dünkt es mich, als trübe / Geheime Sehnsucht deinen Blick" (E, *1*, 289)—is addressed by Pluto to Proserpine, read by Heine to Mathilde,[73] in acknowledgment that the wife also had disadvantages from the marriage. I know of no evidence for this and I must say I find it improbable. I think it more likely that the poem is addressed *to* the persona by an unidentified and fictional speaker. Feise characterizes the poem as "softly resonant and emotionally harmonious, . . . of deep and tender seriousness." [74] Yes, indeed, and this is exactly the way Heine would like to have been talked to. The victimized posture, the secret longing in the facial expression, the sadness of lost youth and incurable heartbreak, are all features of the persona long familiar; they have nothing to do with anything we know about Heine's robust wife and are not really congruent with the waspish disagreeableness of Proserpine's attitude as it appears in Part II. Rather, it seems that a voice emerges out of the poetic context expressing the kind of sympathetic understanding for which the victimized persona longs; or perhaps it is just another *Doppelgänger* situation—the persona surveys and addresses himself. The point of the poem, in any case, lies in the refrain: "Verfehltes Leben, verfehlte Liebe!" (E, *1*, 289), and in the same phrases the other way around at the end of the second. Life and love stand in a mutual causative relationship to one another, and the failure of each determines the failure of the other. These words could very well serve as a motto to the *Romanzen* of *Neue Gedichte*. The "third testament"—Heine's version of the Saint-Simonian doctrine—is a dead letter.

In *Der Tannhäuser,* the poet, who can find no way whatever to extricate himself from the insoluble dilemma of his personal situ-

* Feise's detailed analysis of the contrast between these two rhythmical effects within the same metrical scheme, "Rhythm and Melody as a Parodistic Means in Heine's Unterwelt," *Studies in Honor of Hermann Collitz* (Baltimore, 1930), pp. 306–13, is a most valuable contribution to the study of Heine's poetics.

ation, turns abruptly to comment and satire on contemporary social and political conditions. Similarly, in *Neue Gedichte,* the irresolvable dissonances of the persona are simply abandoned for the entirely new poetry of the *Zeitgedichte.* Of course the shift was by no means as abrupt in the actual chronology of Heine's writing, but the contrast in the published volume does draw attention to the question of the congruence of Heine's political verse to his "poesy." This question is thorny and difficult, and to this day it has not received satisfactory treatment, because in the past it was not often considered worthy of attention and at present Heine's political writing is almost exclusively the property of Communist interpreters. I cannot pretend to solve the problem here, for the simple reason that it is too difficult and involved to be contained within the limits of this study, but perhaps a few observations on the *Zeitgedichte* and related poems of Heine's quasi-radical phase in the 1840s will contribute something to an eventual elucidation and evaluation of Heine's role as a political poet in a most depressing period of German history.

In retrospect, I think, it is to be regretted that Heine chose for these poems the title *Zeitgedichte,* a term that has lived on as a rubric for all of Heine's verse of this kind. Within the system of almost mystical idealism that has remained so difficult to shake out of the German intellectual consciousness, *Zeit* is a word with distinctly pejorative overtones. Time—which is to say, present time, contemporary reality, the flux of change and conflict—is opposed to eternity, a perspective from which the forms of the true and the beautiful are immutable and holy. Under such assumptions, poetry, if it is properly understood as a concentration of the most intense as well as the most cultivated human impulses, can deal only with eternal values. In such a value system, poetry classified as *Zeitgedichte* can be only of secondary importance, if not genuinely trivial. There is plenty of reason to suspect that Heine himself was not free of such an attitude. But the relevance of literature to the real life of real men right now is certainly not a trivial issue, and Fritz Strich has put his finger on the significant novelty of Heine's political poetry by pointing out that it has a *public* character.[75] Tannhäuser drops his preoccupation with his private emotions and turns his attention to the world around him.

In the 1830s and 1840s, political poetry blossomed everywhere, despite every effort Metternich's system could devise to squelch it. The drift toward the crisis of 1848 and the growing breach in the liberal camp between the patriotic nationalists and the radical democratic revolutionaries is well documented in the writings of Herwegh, Freiligrath, Dingelstedt, Anastasius Grün, Hoffman von Fallersleben, Georg Weerth, and a number of others. Heine tried hard to remain aloof from this company and yet at the same time to bring his own writing to bear on the political reality. The really crucial question in evaluating Heine's role in the situation is whether he was right in going about things in this way; we will confront it again when we look at *Börne* and the mock-epics of the 1840s. Heine's political verse has a quality that differentiates it from that of most of his contemporaries, and this quality is the paradoxical source of his superiority and his strength: it is that his aggressiveness is completely negative, ad hominem, and unpatriotic. There are no utopias argued for in Heine's writing; no idealized proletarians point the way to the future; there are no appeals to brotherhood, no pleas for a better world, or claims for a true, liberal Germany. Thus Heine does not lay himself open to the charges of political naïveté and simplistic faith in progress that have been made from all points of the political spectrum against so many of his liberal and radical contemporaries. Nor did he risk the fate of Hoffmann von Fallersleben, the beatnik poet of nineteenth-century Germany, whose *Deutschland, Deutschland über alles* (1841), in its time a powerful piece of liberal rhetoric that Heine's own publisher snapped up the minute he saw it,[76] now arouses feelings of distaste bordering on hatred among a very large number of people in the world. Heine attacks only, and he does it in as vicious and damaging a way as he can manage. Kings or not, Frederick William III, who promised a constitution and then broke his word, is a perjurer; Ludwig of Bavaria is a sentimental vulgarian,[77] and Frederick William IV a bombastic fool.[78] When stupidity and venality are allied with power, Heine's response is destructive. As was pointed out in a recent German dissertation, the principle of the Young Germans was *actio;* Heine's was *reactio.*[79] Related to this is Heine's self-appointed role as executioner; his political verse is another, undoubtedly more potent version of the word as weapon that was remarked upon in connection with the polemic against Platen in *Die Bäder von Lucca.*

Seven of the *Zeitgedichte* were first printed in the Paris *Vorwärts* and thus belong to the brief period during which Heine collaborated with Karl Marx. The extent of the influence of this relationship on Heine's writing in this period has never been assessed to everyone's satisfaction and, of course, in some parts of the world it raises rather emotional responses. The period of the personal relationship was not long; Marx came to Paris in 1843, where Heine met him, probably through Arnold Ruge, at the end of December,[80] and he was expelled in February 1845; since Heine was off on his second visit to Germany from the end of July to mid-October 1844, the direct personal contact covered only about eleven months. (It is interesting that this is just the period when Marx began to correspond with Friedrich Engels.) We have only three letters of Marx to Heine[81] and one from Heine, although there probably were more.* [82] In later years Marx kept tabs on Heine through the Communist League representative in Paris, Hermann Ewerbeck, through Friedrich Engels, who visited Heine occasionally, and through Heine's secretary Richard Reinhardt, who corresponded with the Communist League.† Marx himself visited Heine again when he was permitted to return to Paris in 1848 and 1849. In these years Marx showed enthusiasm for Heine's writing and with unwonted generosity forgave him his refusal to associate himself with the Communist movement; in the years around Heine's death Marx and Engels became harsher in their judgments.[83] In assessing the relationship, it should be remembered that at the time of their association Heine was forty-six years old and a famous man, whereas Marx was twenty-six and only four years past his doctorate; Marx was still battling in the

* In a letter to Freiligrath of Nov. 23, 1859, Marx indicates that he has at least two letters from Heine in his possession (Marx and Engels, *Werke,* ed. Institut für Marxismus-Leninismus bein ZK der SED [Berlin, 1956–67], *29,* 633).

† Richard Reinhardt's letters have not been published; even their location at present is unclear. Their publication would undoubtedly shed a great deal of light on the relationship between Marx and Heine and the context in which it occurred, and is consequently much to be desired. Both Hirth and Victor apparently saw the letters. See Hirth, "Heine und Marx," *Heinrich Heine. Bausteine zu einer Biographie* (Mainz, 1950), p. 128, and Victor, *Marx und Heine* (Berlin, 1953), p. 105.

Hegelian forests and had not yet penetrated to his theory of economic determinism, while Heine had been studying real political and social events in France for more than a decade.[84] So there is some reason to suspect that Heine may have influenced Marx rather than vice versa. Furthermore, their interests fitted together well. Marx needed Heine's prestige for his publications in Paris; "it would seem," wrote Ludwig Marcuse, "that Heine's role in the union consisted of allowing himself to be courted and used. In this function he was the first of a long line of renowned bourgeois writers." [85] Heine, for his part, needed an organ to proclaim his radicalism after the debacle of *Börne* in 1840 and the increased government pressure on his publisher in 1841. There is also the well-known, possibly legendary, anecdote about Heine saving the life of Marx's sick daughter, an event, if true, that Marx, with his deep devotion to his family, would not have been likely to forget.[86] But when all this is taken into account, there is still an unexplained residue. Neither Heine nor Marx was a good friend; both were quick to turn on old acquaintances at the slightest real or imagined offense, and the biographies of both are strewn with broken friendships. That these two choleric and unamiable geniuses managed to get along so well is an interesting feature of the history of both, and it makes one wish we knew more about the details of their relationship.

Friedrich Hirth, in his inimitable way, manages to cloud the issue by insisting, on the one hand, that Heine's poems in these years, including *Deutschland. Ein Wintermärchen,* are full of Communist ideas and definitely under the influence of Marx, and, on the other, that his association with Communism was religiously rather than politically motivated, that it was the atheism of the movement that attracted him, just as the pantheism of Saint-Simonianism had.[87] But there are no ideas, Communist or otherwise, to speak of at all in the *Zeitgedichte*; Hirth does not help us by equating revolutionary radicalism, which is an attitude, with Communism, which is a theory and a program. It is also obvious that Heine's interests at this time were not exclusively religious and nonpolitical; atheism, or rather, hostility to religion, was for him the lever that would permit change in society. Thus, in *Adam der Erste,* the second of the *Zeitgedichte,* it is argued that the Fall is evidence of God's mean-spiritedness and that man is well out of a Paradise which was incomplete because it contained forbidden trees. It is not atheism that is the primary theme here, but liberty, understood in terms that clearly hark back to the Sturm und Drang:

> Ich will mein volles Freiheitsrecht!
> Find' ich die g'ringste Beschränknis,
> Verwandelt sich mir das Paradies
> In Hölle und Gefängnis. (E, *1*, 302)

It is true that the only traces of a constructive program to be found in the *Zeitgedichte* are enthusiastic affirmations of material well-being that are left over from Heine's modifications of the Saint-Simonian system. This note is struck in the well-known first poem, *Doktrin,* which revives the persona of the drum major that had already been carried over from *Das Buch Le Grand* into *Börne*:

> Schlage die Trommel und fürchte dich nicht,
> Und küsse die Marketenderin!
> Das ist die ganze Wissenschaft,
> Das ist der Bücher tiefster Sinn. (E, *1*, 301)

The claim in the final stanza that this is the whole meaning of Hegel and that the persona has understood it because he is a good drum major helps a good deal to define Heine's attitude as a political poet. The drum major, we remember from *Das Buch Le Grand,* is an obvious poet-persona, who communicates only by means of his rhythms and meters. It is only he who can really understand Hegel; the poet circumvents the whole process of rigorous thinking and reduces Hegel's philosophy solely to its presumed implications of materialism; this and no more is the meaning of Heine's often quoted and highly overrated claim that he had revealed the "Schulgeheimnis" of Hegelian philosophy,[88] which there is no reason to believe he understood, as indeed he admitted in the *Geständnisse*.[89] But the persona of the drum major combines the mind and sensibilities of the poet with the courage of the soldier: he beats the drum and is not afraid. In this regard it is a little curious that the pathetic side of Le Grand—a version of the persona as victim—reappears in the portrait of the aged and decrepit drum major in No. 7 of the *Zeitgedichte*, a sardonically comic poem which stresses the humiliation of the Germans in Napoleonic times and urges piety on the part of the German boy for the old veteran of the occupation, who may be his father on his mother's side.[90] Apart from this interesting variant of the persona, this poem is a good example of the role insult plays in Heine's polemical manner. Heine must have been firmly convinced of two propositions: first, that the reactionary enemy was so utterly contemptible as to deserve any vileness heaped upon it regardless of justice or appositeness, and second, that it was possible to do damage to men and institutions by name-calling. Now it is true, as Helene Herrmann pointed out, that Heine was a caricaturist, and the standard of fairness cannot be applied to caricature.[91] But insofar as this verse has a public character in Strich's sense, it tends to be impolitic and makes no concessions to its audience. In a time when, rightly or wrongly, most liberals in Germany were coming to believe that the road to progress lay in the unification of the country under the leadership of Prussia, Heine surely did not accomplish anything tangible by calling Prussia, as he did in No. 16 of the *Zeitgedichte*, a monster fathered by a Sodomite.*

For these reasons Heine tends to be elusive as a poet of political commitment. To see the problem, Heine's polemics need only be compared with the lusty satires of Georg Weerth (1821–56),† who kept his own political position eminently and explicitly clear and simple at all points. Heine's anger and aggressiveness often seem to be absolute and lacking any real foundation, which inclines

* Heine's typically Rhenish suspicion of Prussian expansionism as a liberal cause is firmly expressed in the preface to *Französische Zustände* (E, 5, 15–16).

† Weerth's not uninteresting writings have a rare freshness and comedy, schooled in his reading of Heine but eventually quite independent in style and content. Weerth was the feuilletonist for the *Neue Rheinische Zeitung* under Marx's editorship, and he was undoubtedly one of the masters of the genre. After decades of having been ignored, he has recently come to the attention of literary scholarship. A *Gesamtausgabe* of his works, edited by Bruno Kaiser (Berlin, 1956–57), has appeared in East Germany. For an adequate and interesting introduction to his works, see Weerth, *Ausgewählte Werke,* ed. Kaiser (Frankfurt am Main, 1966), and *Fragment eines Romans,* ed. Kaiser and Siegfried Unseld, sammlung insel, vol. 8 (Frankfurt am Main, 1965).

one to agree with Börne's view that Heine's polemics were a wholly private undertaking. In fact, there is little difference in method and style between Heine's public and his private polemics. Hermann J. Weigand has acutely observed in connection with the violence of the struggle for Uncle Salomon's inheritance in 1845 that Heine "was incapable of any consistent plan or policy in his practical affairs, despite a shrewdness in regard to details which must arouse our astonishment. His machinations were of the subtlest order, each taken by itself, but taken all in all, as a whole, they fail to reveal any thread of consistent plan or purpose. The same conclusion has forced itself upon me in tracing out Heine's erratic political attitude." [92] We will look into this problem a little when we come to discuss *Börne,* but it is apparent in the *Zeitgedichte* that Heine's scorn has a tendency to lash out in all directions. That Frederick William IV was a dolt (which he was not) Heine insisted upon several times in scathing satires, for example, No. 17, *Der Kaiser von China,* and the poem called *Maultiertum* of *Zur Ollea,*[93] as well as *Der neue Alexander* of the *Nachlese*[94] and, of course, the notorious *Welsche Sage* (*Schloßlegende*),[95] which could not appear in Elster's first edition because its publication was forbidden in Imperial Germany.* But it is not only the king who is an ass; the people have long ears as well. The poem *Warnung* takes a pessimistic view of the effectiveness of protest:

> Fürsten haben lange Arme,
> Pfaffen haben lange Zungen,
> Und das Volk hat lange Ohren! (E, *1,* 302)

In the *Zeitgedichte* this poem is followed by one of 1832, *An einen ehemaligen Goetheaner* (Rudolf Christiani), where Heine, operating with a set of wild rhymes, turns the heat on Goethe:

* See E², *2,* 381; see also frd, "Schloßlegende und Sozialistengesetz," *Vorwärts,* no. 117 (March 4, 1920), p. [2], and idem, "Nochmals Schloßlegende und Sozialistengesetz," ibid., no. 131 (March 11, 1920), p. [2]. Even the East German edition of Hans Kaufmann, *Werke und Briefe* (Berlin, 1961–64), tucks the original allusions to the House of Hohenzollern away in the notes (*2,* 638) and prints as the basic version the one in which Italian references veil the point (*2,* 345–46); this is also the procedure of E², *2,* 293 and W, *3,* 370, 526. It is due to the choice of a manuscript version over a printed one, although this is not necessary, as the printed version is earlier.

> Hast du wirklich dich erhoben
> Aus dem müßig kalten Dunstkreis,
> Womit einst der kluge Kunstgreis
> Dich von Weimar aus umwoben? (E, *1*, 302–03)

Thus the polemical weaponry can be turned in any direction, and Heine as often as not turns it against his natural allies. He liked to make fun of his contemporaries in the liberal camp, like Georg Herwegh in No. 12 and Franz Dingelstedt in No. 6. Heine is usually defended, especially by Marxist interpreters, on the grounds that he sensed the shallowness and ultimate irrelevance of the bourgeois spokesmen of liberalism, and certainly he was remarkably aware of how fragile their commitment to liberty would turn out to be when the crisis finally came, as he prophesied in 1842 in *Verheißung:*

> Nicht mehr barfuß sollst du traben,
> Deutsche Freiheit, durch die Sümpfe,
> Endlich kommst du auf die Strümpfe,
> Und auch Stiefeln sollst du haben! . . .
>
> Werde nur nicht dreist und dreister!
> Setz nicht den Respekt beiseiten
> Vor den hohen Obrigkeiten
> Und dem Herren Bürgermeister! (E, *1*, 312)

Heine was certainly willing to set aside respect. But he was not happy in the company of the radicals; he was careful to include in the *Zeitgedichte* a poem written in 1843 for Hans Christian Andersen, *Lebensfahrt,*[96] which indicates that he is not at home with his new confederates. The poem divides the poet's life into two boat rides: the first began happily with good friends but was shipwrecked; and the second, with new companions, lacks the joy of the first, while the poet himself is heavy with the burden of exile. This is odd from a biographical point of view, for what that first happy voyage was and who the friends who went under with the boat might be quite defy explanation. What is apparent is that the account of the voyage with the radicals is packed with images of alienation and loneliness. Meanwhile, we search in vain among the *Zeitgedichte* for a binding definition of the true role of the political poet. Number 13, *Die Tendenz,* is a strange statement that illustrates Heine's ambiguous relationship to the rhetoric of liberalism. For a while, the verses give the impression that they are offering Heine's own recipe for a new sound in poetry:

> Girre nicht mehr wie ein Werther,
> Welcher nur für Lotten glüht—
> Was die Glocke hat geschlagen
> Sollst du deinem Volke sagen,
> Rede Dolche, rede Schwerter! (E, *1,* 311)

This is, in short, the program of *Die Romantische Schule.* As early as the *Englische Fragmente,* Heine expressed the wish that he could speak in catapults.[97] But here, in the next stanza, as the rhetorical cola become ever shorter and more breathless, it becomes plain that Heine is parodying the style, and the final lines bring an accusation of irrelevance against the political poets:

> Singe nur in dieser Richtung,
> Aber halte deine Dichtung
> Nur so allgemein als möglich. (E, *1,* 311)

In other words, the poets are criticized for not pursuing the style of direct insult and defamation that is characteristic of Heine. But it is doubtful whether in the long run Heine's style is really any less abstract.

If the poet, then, is not making common cause with the liberals and is only marking time with the radicals, what is he doing? Waiting, is the answer in No. 23:

> Weil ich so ganz vorzüglich blitze,
> Glaubt ihr, daß ich nicht donnern könnt'!
> Ihr irrt euch sehr, denn ich besitze
> Gleichfalls fürs Donnern ein Talent.
>
> Es wird sich grausenhaft bewähren,
> Wenn einst erscheint der rechte Tag;
> Dann sollt ihr meine Stimme hören,
> Das Donnerwort, den Wetterschlag.
>
> Gar manche Eiche wird zersplittern
> An jenem Tag der wilde Sturm,

Gar mancher Palast wird erzittern
Und stürzen mancher Kirchenturm! (E, *1*, 319)

Marxists will compliment Heine for sensing that Germany was not yet ripe for revolution. I doubt that the posture of this poem can be defended on these or any other grounds. There is no evidence in the *Zeitgedichte* that the poet will know how to recognize "der rechte Tag" when it comes, and the titanic persona whose voice on some unspecified day will split oaks and overthrow church towers reminds us rather too much of that rodomontade of Platen's about which Heine had such scornful things to say in *Die Bäder von Lucca.* One wants very much to say to him, *hic Rhodus, hic salta!* Nor is it surprising that the persona reverts to private considerations in the final poem, *Nachtgedanken.* The first lines of this poem,

Denk' ich an Deutschland in der Nacht,
Dann bin ich um den Schlaf gebracht, (E, *1*, 319)

have achieved some renown, and the nightmarish oppression at the end of the poem is effective, but the remainder, a series of jingles about homesickness for Mother, is, I am afraid, not moving, as Prawer argues,[98] but mawkish and trivial.* The *Zeitgedichte* do not manage to sustain a public character, and the poet-persona does not succeed in acquiring substance and weight as a public figure. There is too much compromise and too much substitution of private invective for genuine political radicalism. The superb and imperishable wit of Heine's verses flashes and blazes in a vacuum.

But Heine did succeed, somewhat paradoxically, in writing some effective political poems, and, indeed, among them what is probably the best one of all in its time, *Die schlesischen Weber* of

* Recently Werner Psaar, in a generally excellent article, "Zur Deutung Heinescher Gedichte im Deutschunterricht." *Heine-Jahrbuch 1967,* pp. 112–15, has made a hard try at interpreting this poem positively, in the course of which he argues that the repetitive rattle of the language and the ironically painful repression of homesickness is expressive of the fundamental condition of the poet in exile. I leave it to others to decide if his view is sounder than mine; for all the acuteness of his interpretation, I find it ultimately indecisive and possibly over-subtle.

1844.* This justly famous poem, with its evocation of the rhythms of the weaving machinery and its tough, tripartite curse against God, king, and fatherland (the motto on the white cross of the Prussian militia[99]), offers an appropriate occasion to raise the question of the evaluation of political poetry. The poem draws upon the strengths of Heine's manner, for it is entirely negative; it contains no hopes of utopia and its weavers have no beauties; they bare their teeth and have no emotion left but grim hatred. They do not plead for justice or appeal for sympathy; they make no claims for the value of their labor—they threaten. These features make *Die schlesischen Weber* a more powerful poem than those of Heine's contemporaries, for the most part, and, indeed, than most of Heine's, for the threats of the rebellious Silesian weavers are a good deal more convincing than those of the poet in Paris. It is necessary to point out, however, that the prophecy implied in the poem was false. The weavers were not weaving Germany's shroud; they were weaving, at tremendous cost to themselves in body and soul, part of the fabric of an industrial upsurge in Germany that was eventually to permit the nation to terrorize its neighbors three times in three-quarters of a century. Consequently the test of political truth, in the sense that the poet is taken at his own self-estimate as a prophet, will not serve for the evaluation of a political poem. The evaluation must be made, as Heine himself well knew, according to aesthetic standards. This problem will concern us in greater detail when we come to discuss the two mock-epics. Here I will pause only to remark that it is worth inquiring why the bulk of Heine's political verse is not better than it is. It seems, as far as *Neue Gedichte* is concerned, that Heine was not able to structure the persona in a way that would bridge the gap between "poesy" and politics.

The persona does not come to rest anywhere in *Neue Gedichte*; the total impression of the collection is one of dissonance and unresolved tensions. This is characteristic of Heine's writing gener-

* E, 2, 177–78. An excellent account of the background and history of the Weavers' Rebellion and some of the verse it generated will be found in Hans Schwab-Felisch's edition of Gerhart Hauptmann's *Die Weber,* Dichtung und Wirklichkeit, vol. 1 (Frankfurt am Main, 1959). A French song about the silk-weavers' rebellion in Lyons in 1831, which Heine might well have known, is printed in *Werke und Briefe,* ed. Kaufmann, *10,* 156.

ally in the 1830s and 1840s, as we shall soon see in greater detail. Love and poetry, love and sensuality, strength and pathos, poetry and politics, all continue to defy a synthesis in a single constructed personality. This is what accounts for the unevenness of *Neue Gedichte* but makes the work highly instructive about Heine's development toward the great achievements of his late years.

CHAPTER 8

The Elusive King: Heine and Louis-Philippe

> A king of beasts indeed. If aught but beasts,
> I had been still a happy king of men.
>
> —*Richard II,* v, 1

7

Heine's political journalism still stands in need of substantial research, for there are important aspects of it that are not at all clear. It would be worth knowing, more exactly than we do, what Heine's sources of information were and how he used them. That he was an avid reader of newspapers* and also of modern French history is plain, but it is not so plain whether these were his predominant sources of information. He was less susceptible to rumors picked up on the boulevards and in the salons than was Börne, but it is also true that Heine's attitudes regularly reflect the state of public opinion in Paris. The nature of his relationship to men of power, notably François Guizot and Adolphe Thiers,

* In this connection, the study of Margaret A. Clarke, *Heine et la Monarchie de Juillet* (Paris, 1927), which does not enjoy a very good reputation among Heine scholars, needs to be taken more seriously than it has been. It is true that the author tends to be bull-headed, vindictive, and sometimes confused. She has no sensitivity to the problem of Louis-Philippe as it formed itself in Heine's poetic consciousness. Her argument that Heine adapted his views to the supposed Austrian policies of the *Allgemeine Zeitung* (pp. 9–10, 213–32) and her broad hint that Heine was paid by Austrian agents (pp. 230–31) remain unproven and, I think, atrocious. This argument obliges her, among other contortions, to present Gentz as simultaneously an opponent and a servant of Austrian policy (pp. 226–27). On the other hand, she demonstrates beyond a doubt that much of the opinion and polemics of *Französische Zustände* were lifted directly and indiscriminately from opposition newspapers of both Right and Left. She argues convincingly that Heine lacked a sense of truthful reporting and, above all, a consistent center of political conviction. Scholarship with regard to *Französische Zustände* cannot remain within the confines of Heine's text and a few historical references while ignoring Clarke's book and the possibility of building on her approach.

remains rather obscure.* If we knew more about some of these things than we do, we should be in a better position to assess Heine's stature as a commentator on public affairs and the soundness of his understanding of the July Monarchy.

What the results of such an investigation might be I would not be prepared to say on the basis of the present state of research. Despite the fact that Heine's reportage is riddled with the most puzzling contradictions, as a total achievement it is remarkable on its own terms. The most striking feature of these writings, one that must be recognized if they are to be properly understood, is Heine's continually deepening sense of the disfranchised urban proletariat as a political force, which the *Juste-Milieu* steadfastly refused to acknowledge. This circumstance, naturally, gives Heine's political writing considerable popularity among the Communists, but, because of the peculiarities of the Marxist way of writing history, it will be unfortunate if the interpretation of this important part of Heine's career is totally abandoned in the West. Copiously annotated, philologically sound editions of *Französische Zustände* and *Lutezia,* which present the most complicated textual problems of any of Heine's works, are greatly needed; it is rather characteristic that in the ninth volume of Walzel's edition, which contains *Lutezia,* the effort to annotate was almost abandoned, and Kaufmann's East German edition is far from thorough in this regard. A good start in this direction has recently been made by Michael Mann's publication of some of the *Lutezia* articles in their original form, but the volume includes only those dealing with music and painting.† [1] Mann has pointed out that the complete variants are as yet nowhere to be found and that the original articles give a better picture of their time than the versions in *Lutezia.*[2]

* See the inconclusive results in Dresch's well-researched study, *Heine à Paris,* p. 55. Friedrich Hirth has made some contributions to the problem of Heine's French connections in *Heinrich Heine und seine französischen Freunde* (Mainz, 1949), but, as is always the case with Hirth, it is a great labor to separate fact and good judgment from wild speculation.

† In this respect the annotation to *Lutezia* in *Heines Werke,* ed. Hermann Friedemann, et al. (Berlin, Leipzig, Vienna, and Stuttgart, 1927), *15,* 287–312, has much to recommend it.

The characteristic brilliance and lucidity of Heine's expository writing combine with his flair for the pathetic and his unflagging awareness of political and social symptoms to make his reporting memorable. A good example is his account of the cholera that descended on Paris in the spring of 1832.* Disaster, of course, lends itself to highly colored reporting, and Heine's account exploits the morbid excitement of an urban catastrophe with sure skill; he was proud enough of this achievement to compare himself favorably with Thucydides and Boccaccio.[3] But Heine was not content with the meaninglessness inherent in disaster as such; his account captures those features of the situation that illuminate the perilous state of France in the first year of the July Monarchy. He points out how the wretched condition of the poor (France was still suffering from a severe depression that began in 1828) and the neglected sanitation of the city abetted the spread of the disease. In a grisly carnival scene that exactly anticipates Poe's *Masque of the Red Death,* Heine graphically symbolizes the deadly frivolity of high society at the approach of the epidemic.† He also understood very well a problem that has continued to plague the world up to the present time: in an inequitable society, the vested interests of the poor often desperately resist urgently necessary progressive measures. When the government tried to clean the garbage out of the city, an obvious enlightened measure in time of cholera, the chiffoniers, who lived by picking the garbage, revolted and had to be put down by armed force. It is possible that this event was a sort of *Bildungserlebnis* for Heine that may have had quite an influence on his attitudes toward the lower classes, for he responds to it in a tone of astonished comprehension:

> Es ist sonderbar, daß die Beweißtümer, die sie [the chiffoniers] in dieser Hinsicht vorbrachten, ganz dieselben sind, die auch unsere Krautjunker, Zunftherren, Gildemeister, Zehntenprediger, Fakultätsgenossen und sonstige Vorrechtsbeflis-

* E, 5, 90–105. By the recent discovery of the letters of Heine's cousin Karl, it has now been proved that Heine remained in Paris during the cholera to nurse him. See Fritz H. Eisner, "Verschollene Briefe an Heine: Ein neuer Fund," *Heine-Jahrbuch 1966,* p. 70.

† E, 5, 95–96. Clarke argues that this representation is taken directly from the legitimist press (pp. 113–14).

> sene vorzubringen pflegen, wenn die alten Mißbräuche, wovon sie Nutzen ziehen, der Kehricht des Mittelalters, endlich fortgeräumt werden sollen, damit durch den verjährten Moder und Dunst unser jetziges Leben nicht verpestet werde.*

He observes sardonically that in these circumstances the reactionary Carlists had found their natural allies among the garbage pickers. Heine's ire is aroused by the stupidity of the police in acquiescing to the superstitious notion that the epidemic was caused by poisoners, thus encouraging some disgusting killings in the street. But since the poisoners were supposed to be Carlists, Heine also draws the correct conclusion that the political power of the elder Bourbon line is to all intents and purposes dead. The absurdities of the archbishop, who pronounced the cholera a punishment of God upon France for having deposed Charles X, and of the Saint-Simonians, whose newspaper smugly asserted that a satisfactory moral state was sufficient protection against the calamity,[4] are also commented upon. Heine's achievement in his account of the cholera should not be underestimated; he has turned a report upon an accidental disaster into a set of penetrating perceptions about the state of Paris in 1832.[5]

The analysis of passages like this one, coupled with careful attention to the sources and the best reconstruction of actual events that can be made from this distance, would contribute a great deal to a comprehension of the total phenomenon of Heine. Such investigations are not within the scope of this book and will not be pursued here. It should be pointed out, however, that the lack of detailed studies on such matters makes conclusions drawn about Heine's middle years somewhat tentative and uncertain, and it is only fair to say that this applies also in some measure to what follows. What I should like to do is concentrate on a single aspect of Heine's writing on public affairs: his treatment of the citizen-king, Louis-Philippe. To separate this matter from its context—to discuss it without stressing equally Heine's account of the politicians who worked with the king and against him, the parties that plagued him, and the social situation that ultimately contributed to his downfall—is to distort it. Moreover, Margaret A. Clarke has

* E, *5*, 97. Clarke claims that Heine exaggerated this event (p. 116).

pointed out in connection with the *Französische Zustände* that Heine places the personality of Louis-Philippe at the center of all his judgments; she charges Heine with failing to see that the character of the king was of no importance, that the events of his time were conditioned by the *institution* of constitutional monarchy, regardless of who the king might be.* I am not enough of an historian to assess the soundness of this view. There seems to me, however, to be some clear justification for empathizing with Heine's perspective for the time being. Not only did Louis-Philippe appear to incarnate one of the purest examples of historical compromise the modern world has seen, but also for Heine, the citizen-king represented a potential solution to a set of conflicting inclinations: he was interested by "die Idee eines Bürgerkönigs," as he put it in 1831 in his introduction to *Kahldorf über den Adel,* "ohne Hofetikette, ohne Edelknechte, ohne Kurtisanen, ohne Kuppler, ohne diamantne Trinkgelder und sonstige Herrlichkeit" (E, 7, 291). Heine was highly susceptible to the appeal of authoritative individual power, as he demonstrated particularly in his fascinated discussion of absolutism in *Französische Zustände.*[6] He believed he had seen such power, in pristine form, in Napoleon, and he was anxious to believe also that the true poet possesses it; this is evident from the fact that the persona in Heine's works so frequently acquires the attributes of royalty; indeed, he describes himself in *Die Stadt Lucca,* with characteristic self-effacement, as emperor of the world.[7] He makes this attitude plain enough elsewhere. For all Heine's positive feelings toward the guillotine as a surgical tool in political renovation, he found it dreadful that the French had executed the head of state;[8] in his remarks on Delaroche in *Französische Maler,* he exhibits a great deal of sentimentality about the paintings of the murdered Edward V and the executed Charles I.[9] Heine hated the aristocracy with furious zeal, but the king is exempt from this condemnation. In the essay of 1822 on Poland, Heine asserts: "Nur vor dem Könige soll man sich beugen; bis auf dieses letztere Glaubensgesetz bekenne ich mich ganz zum nordamerikanischen Kathe-

* Clarke, pp. 166–70. As an example of her manner: "Ludwig Philipp—Ludwig Philipp—Heine ne se lasse pas de le nommer, et de se borner par là à une conception puèrile du monde politique" (p. 167).

chismus" (E, 7, 191). In the *Französische Zustände,* he wrote that the king must be liberated from the court and the nobility,[10] and in *Die Stadt Lucca* he presented himself as a monarchist.[11] Yet, as Alfred Fuhrmann has pointed out, there are difficult contradictions in Heine's political view of monarchy, which seems to differ in function only by its hereditary character from the presidency of a constitutional democracy.[12] But for Heine, one must add, the poetically envisioned majestic aura is the significant difference.

Yet how the exercise of such authority was to be kept consonant with the imperatives of liberty and revolution was a puzzle. From time to time Heine would fall back on a synthesis of the vox populi and absolutism that has strangely proto-Fascist undertones, as in *Shakspeares Mädchen und Frauen.** Again Heine sought the model in Napoleon, but he knew perfectly well that Napoleon's career would not bear close scrutiny from a libertarian point of view. Nothing Heine could see at the courts of Europe before 1830, with their feudal trappings, their reactionary policies, and their aristocracy standing between king and people, held out the slightest hope that he could associate himself with royalty in reality. Then, suddenly, Louis-Philippe appeared on the scene. Could he meet Heine's ideal of a king by the grace of the people, maintaining the symbolism of individualistic authority and yet protecting liberty and furthering the revolution? For the eighteen years of the citizen-king's reign, Heine vibrated with hope and disappointment, anger and defensiveness, and a considerable degree of monarchist sentimentality.

For a king in modern times, Louis-Philippe had a singularly eventful life. Most of the events in it, however, were dismaying and not infrequently terrifying. Yet he bore them. In retrospect, one of his outstanding characteristics seems to have been an inex-

* This remark may strike the reader as offensive and not credible. I therefore give the passage to let him judge for himself: "Demokratie und Königtum stehen sich nicht feindlich gegenüber, wie man fälschlich in unsern Tagen behauptet hat. Die beste Demokratie wird immer diejenige sein, wo ein Einziger als Inkarnation des Volkswillens an der Spitze des Staates steht, wie Gott an der Spitze der Weltregierung; unter jenem, dem inkarnierten Volkswillen, wie unter der Majestät Gottes, blüht die sicherste Menschengleichheit, die echteste Demokratie" (E, 5, 399). I shall return to this problem briefly towards the end of this chapter.

haustible supply of personal courage, not exclusively of the heroic variety, although this was given to him also, but a complete manly steadfastness that enabled him to bear almost every kind of misfortune that can come into a man's life: grief, exile, poverty, loneliness, boredom, enforced inactivity measured in years, mortal danger, calumny, hatred, and failure. That the man should have become rather stolid and unspectacular under these circumstances is hardly to be wondered at. But when he was called, he answered. He did what he thought was required of him as well as he knew how. Although he did not govern France with complete success, it is undoubtedly to his credit that he succeeded in governing that country at all in the circumstances under which he labored.

The elder Bourbon line had from the time of Louis XIV always jealously endeavored to keep the House of Orléans at a safe distance from the seat of power. At the time of the Revolution, the Orléans family found itself in a position of which the career of Louis-Philippe was the logical extension: caught between the Bourbon court, to which its relations were none too friendly, and the rebellious citizens, the House of Orléans opted, with varying degrees of enthusiasm, for the Revolution. Louis-Philippe's father, a not ungifted but morally indolent man who rather incongruously styled himself Philippe Égalité, weakly cast a vote that gave a majority for the execution of his cousin Louis XVI (on which occasion his son wrote him a harsh letter); the Revolution repaid him in the same coin two years later. His three sons, all teen-agers at the time of the Revolution, responded to it with a great deal more Romantic enthusiasm. For princes of the blood, they had been subjected to a remarkably solid and severe education at the hands of Madame de Genlis, who in turn was generally influenced by Rousseau. The result was that Louis-Philippe became a literate and well-read man who mastered four languages and knew quite a lot about a surprising variety of things. The most important and valuable thing he knew was that the Bourbons could not rule France endurably in his time.

As Duc de Chartres and a general officer at eighteen, Louis-Philippe served with genuine and recognized distinction in the campaigns of 1792, particularly at the historic cannonade of Valmy and the storming of Jemappes. On the latter occasion he conceived an implacable hatred of war that was never to leave him for the rest of his life and which lies at the root of one of the most touchy aspects of his reign and also of Heine's analysis of it. The events of 1793 obliged him to commence his long wanderings in exile, at the beginning of which he supported himself for a while as a schoolmaster in Switzerland, an occupation for which he seems to have been eminently suited. He tramped through Lapland at a time when that was an adventure of major proportions and through the American wilderness. He was received graciously for four days by George Washington, whom he greatly admired. His travels took him north to Canada and south to Cuba and, in 1800, to England. In order to forge a connection with the House of Habsburg, he married, most happily as it turned out, a Sicilian princess. But apart from this and a couple of brief and misguided forays into Spanish affairs, he did practically nothing to further his political fortunes. He converted himself into an English gentleman, cultivating his garden and both the merchant's instincts and the bourgeois domesticity for which he was to become so noted. The history of France ground on pretty much without him for thirty years. Napoleon came and went, and came again and went. Louis XVIII came and went; Louis-Philippe returned to Paris in 1814, fell into disgrace within a year, went back to England and again returned to Paris in 1817 to repair the family fortunes. Charles X came—and with him his egregious minister Polignac. Louis-Philippe's hour struck at last. The barricades went up in July 1830, the ubiquitous Lafayette, who had been attending revolutions for more than fifty years, proclaimed him "the best republic," and from the representatives of the bourgeoisie he accepted, somewhat uncertainly, first the Lieutenant-Generalcy of the Kingdom and then the crown as King of the French.

His prospects were poor. Paris was torn by violent factionalism, and there was no doubt that the powers of the Holy Alliance would take a dangerously dim view of the new king as an illegitimate usurper and a liberal threat. Louis-Philippe worked hard at his thankless task; he politicked in the streets with his famous umbrella, meek manners, and handshaking campaigns, while he juggled ministers and cajoled the Holy Alliance in order to stabilize the situation. If he constantly interfered in government policy, acting now as his own foreign minister, now as his own premier, it was perhaps not so much out of an abstract lust for absolutist power, of which he was interminably accused, but from the not totally unjustifiable opinion that he had better sense and more ability than most of the politicians at his disposal. He gave France good, if inequitable, prosperity, a measure of order, and eighteen years of peace. For his pains he was mercilessly calumnied and caricatured; forged documents were submitted to the public in evidence against him; reactionaries and radicals formed unscrupulous coalitions with each other to bring him down; and his spirits were depressed by eight attempted assassinations. There seems little doubt that he was completely devoted to liberty as he understood it: liberty of action and opinion for the taxpaying bourgeoisie, the *Juste-Milieu* who had the electoral franchise and upon whom Louis-Philippe and his supporters based the new order. Less than 100,000 people out of a population of more than thirty million had the right to vote in 1830, less than 200,000 after a change in the law in 1831, and only increased prosperity raised the figure to 241,000 by the end of the July Monarchy. Heine appreciated above all the freedom of the press and liberty of person under the regime, which, he pointed out in 1832, were still greater, even under a legal state of siege in France, than elsewhere on the Continent.[13] But he also observed acidly that when the Bastille fell, it contained only a handful of prisoners, while in July 1832, there were ten state prisons and six hundred political prisoners in Saint-Pélagie alone.[14] Principles of liberty had their limits in Louis-Philippe's France. It was clear that the *Juste-Milieu* intended to halt the Revolution with itself; parliamentary reform was debated on seventeen occasions between 1830 and 1847, but Louis-Philippe and Guizot became increasingly determined to block any extension of democracy. It should be noted, however, that at the outset of Louis-Philippe's reign the chief radical agitation was for the privilege of slaughtering political enemies and for the mobilization of France to carry a war of liberation into the rest of Europe. As to the first issue, Louis-Philippe had seen quite enough of that sort of thing in years past, and he determined to prevent it. The second issue not only collided with the king's hatred of war but also promised total disaster; France, in bad economic and financial shape and without allies for such an adventure, was in no condition to make war simultaneously against Austria, Prussia, Russia, and Holland. Louis-Philippe's pacific convictions, which may seem worthy of all admiration in our time, in his were a source of great unpopularity and seemed to be the perfect expression of the egotistical bourgeois order. All the critics could see was that France stood idly by while the Polish uprising was crushed, and that instead of seeking national gloire on the battlefield, Louis-Philippe demeaned the nation by coming to terms with the great powers through careful diplomacy.

But it is certainly possible to argue these matters in favor of Louis-Philippe; his fundamental failing lay elsewhere, in the pattern of his thinking, described by his biographer thus:

> Although as King of the French some of his more solid virtues seem perfectly well attuned to the outlook and ethos of the eighteen-forties, his character and thinking were indelibly moulded by what we tend to consider essentially eighteenth-century attitudes, so that the bourgeois monarch of July is not so much a new nineteenth-century political portent as the last of the enlightened despots. By education, by experience, by reading, he belonged to the civilization which Burke extolled and Paine despised, a civilization of the élite, aristocratic and intellectual, an élite from whom and by whom all reform and progress must flow, gradually, rationally and *de haut en bas*.* [15]

This mode of thinking made him unfit to cope with the forces at work in society below the level of the enfranchised bourgeoisie. The same biographer observes:

> In thinking in common with the aristocratic Whigs across the Channel that a steady volume of middle-class support and a little judicious and gradual reform would enable his government to contain the rising tide of working-class agitation, Louis-Philippe made an ultimately disastrous miscalculation.[16]

* Cf. Heine: "die Aufklärung, Toleranz und Philanthropie des 18. Jahrhunderts war bei ihm in Geist und Gemüt übergegangen" (E, 7, 379).

From this sketch it is easy to see why Louis-Philippe should have been an important personage for Heine. Courage, which the king possessed in obvious magnitude, was one of the virtues Heine admired most; and Louis-Philippe was free of the overbearing and Philistine pomposity Heine so hated in the aristocracy. The king was of royal blood, yet he had revolutionary credentials. Fundamentally, Heine had as little use for radical republicanism as did Louis-Philippe. But ultimately the king could not win the total allegiance of the poet, for the flawed reality did not coalesce into a majestic myth in the poetic imagination. Louis-Philippe was neither Napoleon nor Henri IV, neither a glorious conqueror nor a hero of the common people. He was, after all, only a brave, tenacious, and gifted old man undertaking an impossible task on inadequate assumptions. He was, however, in his bourgeois, unclassical way, tragic, and that had come to mean a lot to Heine by the time the July Monarchy had run its course.

It seems unlikely that before the July Revolution Heine was very much aware of the potential alternative to the Bourbon restoration represented by the Duc d'Orléans; in any case he does not mention it in his writings and letters. The theatrically symbolic event, when Charles X's hat fell off during his agitated and reactionary speech from the throne in 1830 and Orléans retrieved it for him, escaped Heine's notice. He does not mention Louis-Philippe at all until the spring of 1831, when, in the introduction to *Kahldorf über den Adel,* he compares the king to Hegel as the founder of an eclectic regime in which he himself is of little importance.[17] This is not a very sensible remark, and when Heine comes to speak of Hegel again in *Zur Geschichte der Religion und Philosophie in Deutschland,*[18] such parallels are no longer in evidence. Heine's prophetic political intuition at that time was not as impressive as the second book of *Börne* would have us believe; he needed to experience Paris and to see the king before he could write effectively on the subject. Heine appears to have seen Louis-Philippe for the first time in July 1831, on the first anniversary of the July Revolution. He describes the king's appearance in his account of the painting exhibition of 1831, the essay that gave the title to the four volumes of *Der Salon,* and it is not without significance that Heine proceeds to a description of the king from an experience of Ary Scheffer's portrait of him. For Louis-Philippe appears here as an allegory of himself and his situation. The king is half conqueror, half prisoner; the dethroned Emperor of Brazil "ritt symbolisch oder auch prophetisch an seiner Seite" (E, *4*, 30); his eyes gleam sweetly with joy and embarrassment. The scene becomes literature, and nothing is more characteristic of Heine's treatment of real persons and real events; his selection of detail and metaphor is such as to alienate the scene into a symbolic representation of itself. In one sense, this search for meaning among symptoms, an effort to co-ordinate real perceptions into an interpretation, is Heine's greatness as a reporter, yet it can also be his weakness, for little comes from Heine to us without passing through this process of artistic transformation. In this sense, Heine's treatment of real situations is analogous to the transformations the writing of his first period works upon his own self.

Heine's first long account of the king appears in his first article for the Augsburg *Allgemeine Zeitung,* dated December 28, 1831. A comparison of the attitude of this article with the remarks in *Französische Maler* suggests with some probability that Heine had originally honored Louis-Philippe with an investment of good will which had gone a little sour in the intervening six months, for the tone of the newspaper article is quite unfriendly. In view of the rapid deterioration of relations between Heine and Börne, Hirth's supposition that Heine's view of Louis-Philippe had been influenced by German republicans in Paris seems unlikely,[19] but there is no doubt that Heine was dissatisfied with the firm way the king was putting the brakes on the Revolution. The newspaper article, which Heine toned down a good deal before republishing it in *Französische Zustände,* rumbles with revolutionary undertones, particularly when he calls the current scandal in the Rohan family the Diamond Necklace Affair of the Orléans line.[20] Heine sees clearly that the situation of the poor is very bad and remarks acidly that the people who made the Revolution are being stamped back into the earth like the paving stones they employed.[21] The king, Heine is still willing to believe, means well, but has lost track of the sources of his power. Heine makes of Louis-Philippe's surely harmless though perhaps ill-advised project of building a private garden of his own at the Tuileries a symbol of building a barrier against the people[22] (in 1833 Heine comes back to this garden in his usual manner by calling attention to the symbolism of the statues: one of Spartacus, of all things for a king to put in his garden, and one of Theseus slaying the Minotaur[23]). These criticisms are not without force, but if one knows Heine well, one senses that something else is troubling him here as well. Heine did not know what to make of Louis-Philippe's carefully cultivated manner of bourgeois affability. On the one hand it seemed to encourage confidence; on the other, it seemed so unkingly, and Heine was instinctively concerned for the royal dignity, as we shall see. In this article Heine evades the problem by drawing the uncharitable conclusion that it is all dissimulation; he spreads the story that Louis-Philippe kept a dirty glove handy for shaking the hands of the folk[24]—something that would undoubtedly have occurred to Heine had he been king—and in the original article he takes a harsh tone when he calls the king "ein wahrer Jesuit der Bürgerlichkeit, ein Bürgerjesuit" (E, 5, 498).

A careful reading of this first article indicates that Heine had not yet succeeded in grasping the phenomenon of Louis-Philippe. His observations are stated with acuity, but they are mostly broad generalities and seem to reflect rumor and aspects of public opinion in Paris rather than an independent confrontation. The article, moreover, got Heine into a good bit of trouble, for it caused him to be dragged into the ferocious maelstrom of the Parisian press and put him briefly into an awkward situation.[25] At the beginning of the second article, dated January 19, 1832, Heine struck back at the press,[26] but the importance of the article is that in it the disparate elements of Heine's response to Louis-Philippe begin to crystallize. Heine sharply urges Louis-Philippe to remain a citizen-king and is characteristically piqued at his refusal to lead France into a general war of liberation in Europe.[27] He takes the republican view of the dismissal of Lafayette as commander of the National Guard,[28] although it is possible to see this event as a necessary act of self-defense by the king.[29] But he also takes the opportunity to dissociate himself bluntly from the republicans; in the final version of the statement he asserts: "Royalist aus angeborner Neigung, werde ich es in Frankreich aus Überzeugung" (E, 5, 37), and, introducing a theme that is basic to all his comments on this subject, he announces his distaste for the universal Spartan soup to which the egalitarians will reduce everyone's cuisine. Heine's tendency to see the continuation of the Revolution in terms of the puritan Terror of 1793 is no doubt understandable in view of the persistent Jacobinism of the republican cause, and by June 1832, he is ready to observe that despite all his admiration for republican virtues and ideas, he could not have stood to be guillotined every day and neither could anyone else.[30] Most of the rest of the article of January 19 deals, if one reads it carefully, with a problem of the mythic transforms of great personages. Heine identifies the current popular heroes of France as Napoleon and Lafayette.[31] But that this is a matter of their symbolic stature Heine makes quite clear in the admission that Napoleon is more attractive dead than alive, "was wenigstens mir das Liebste an Napoleon ist; denn lebte er noch, so müßte ich ihn ja bekämpfen helfen" (E, 5, 40). On the subject of Lafayette, Heine calmed down more slowly, but an occasional remark in later years indicates that Heine knew Lafayette was mortal.[32] But what, in this respect, was to be done with Louis-Philippe, who conquered no nations and released no new liberties?

By March of 1832 Heine apparently believed that Louis-Philippe had absolutist and restorative tendencies, and again he falls back on allegory:

> Was Ludwig Philipp betrifft, so spielt er noch immer seinen *Roi-citoyen* und trägt noch immer das dazu gehörige Bürgerkostüm; unter seinem bescheidenen Filzhute trägt er jedoch, wie männiglich weiß, eine ganz unmaßgebliche Krone von gewöhnlichem Zuschnitte, und in seinem Regenschirme verbirgt er das absoluteste Zepter. (E, 5, 79)

But he goes on in this article to try to understand the king's position; he accuses him of trying so hard to be on good terms with his enemies that he has lost the support of his friends, and, reflecting contemporary opinion, sees the king as a quondam hero of democracy who has turned out to be merely a trimmer and a miser.[33] Heine quite explicitly echoes the republican demand that the king put himself at the head of the Revolution,[34] which, of course, would mean war. The king, in Heine's view, is clearly not fulfilling the functions that belong to his raison d'être. But a different tone emerges when Heine speaks about the ubiquitous and notorious caricatures of Louis-Philippe's head as a pear. It is significant that Heine looked askance at this campaign, for he himself was not averse to mean caricature of physical features when writing about his enemies, and, to be sure, he helped keep this caricature in circulation by reporting on it so extensively. But his feelings about the royal dignity are sensitive to this form of lèse majesté. In this article, he writes soberly: "Ich will wahrlich den Unfug dieser Fratzenbilder nicht vertreten, am allerwenigsten wenn sie die Person des Fürsten selbst betreffen. Ihre unaufhörliche Menge ist aber eine Volksstimme und bedeutet etwas" (E, 5, 84). In his *Tagesbericht* of June 17, 1832, where he reports on the newest metamorphoses of the pear, he is more explicit: "Dem Gemüt eines Deutschen wird dergleichen auf die Länge lästig und widrig. Jene ewigen Spöttereien, gemalt und gedruckt, erregen vielmehr bei mir eine gewisse Sympathie für Ludwig Philipp. Er ist wahrhaft zu bedauern, jetzt mehr als je. Er ist gütig und milde von Natur" (E, 5, 183). This identification of himself as a German, by which Heine, as usual, implies a temperament in contrast to the frivolity of the French, is significant here, and the note of pity for the king, which Heine had sharply repudiated the preceding January,[35] is now established and will recur in future years. In 1834 Heine removed his own earlier comment on the shape of the king's head from the French edition of *Französische Maler*.[36]

The concern for royal dignity expresses itself in other ways as well. In his account of the king's sons, the Duc d'Orléans and the Duc de Nemours, Heine appears to be looking for evidence of aristocratic bearing and seems pleased when he finds it, as he does in the younger son: "Es sind nicht die anmaßenden Züge eines hannöverischen Krautjunkers, sondern eine gewisse Vornehmheit des Erscheinens und des Gehabens, wie sie nur unter dem gebildetsten hohen Adel gefunden wird" (E. 5, 89). Heine adds in a regretful tone that such features are disappearing or degenerating through mésalliances. In a curious passage in a report dated June 11, all three aspects of Heine's view converge: his sympathy, his resentment at what seem to be illiberal measures, and his disappointment that the king is not more kingly. He describes the king's sad, troubled, and mild appearance (it is a few days after the slaughter of the republican rebels in the Rue du Cloître-Saint-Merri), but he adds, with his characteristic suspicion of appearances: "Wahrlich, diesem Mann war es nicht anzusehen, daß er uns alle in Belagerungsstand erklärt hat" (E, 5, 177). But when the cry of "Vive le roi!" goes up, a mythic memory intervenes that shows how far Heine is from accepting Louis-Philippe *as a king:* "Ein bitteres Gefühl ergriff mich, wenn ich dachte, daß das Volk, welches jetzt den armen händedrückenden Ludwig Philipp umjubelt, dieselben Franzosen sind, die so oft den Napoleon Bonaparte vorbeireiten sahen mit seinem marmornen Cäsargesicht und seinen unbewegten Augen und 'unnahbaren' Händen" (E, 5, 177). Heine is offended by the king who cannot be identified with the poetic view of the royal persona, yet insists upon attempting to rule France. Heine once claimed that this attitude of his toward Louis-Philippe was shared by the Russian Czar.[37] It is ironic, but natural, that when Heine found himself among Carlists in Normandy, who were anxious to restore legitimate royalty and all its dignities, he became so disgusted with these reactionaries that he found Louis-Philippe and the *Juste-Milieu* most admirable indeed.[38] In October of 1832 in a letter to Ferdinand Hiller he flatly announced himself as "ein Anhänger von Ludwig Philipp" (Hirth, 2, 24).

The problem of the persona plays a more important role in Heine's confrontation with Louis-Philippe than has generally been recognized. But it is only one part of the situation in *Französische Zustände,* where Heine makes repeated efforts to understand the king as a political phenomenon. His discussions of the tricky constitutional question of the king's immunity[39] and of the king's difficult and shifting relationship to his council of ministers[40] indicate that Heine had a sense of where the issues lay and that he was doing his best to explain them to his German readers.* In June 1832, he captured the labile relationship between the people of Paris and their king by explaining lucidly

* Clarke, it should be noted, argues that Heine was often completely silent about vital issues, such as that of the decentralization of the provinces. See pp. 108–09.

that the king belonged to them, in terms of the true location of power, at least as much as they to him: "Man konnte deshalb ebenfalls sagen, das Volk habe den König die Revue passieren lassen, es habe Königsschau gehalten und habe bei dessen Manöver seine allerhöchste Zufriedenheit geäußert." * This mutual dependency is also partly responsible for Louis-Philippe's unkingly bearing; in 1840, Heine complained of the bourgeois miserliness of the Chamber in refusing a large allowance to the Duc de Nemours, observing that the by now relatively powerless king required outward magnificence to maintain his "moralisches Ansehen" (E, *6,* 146).[41] Moreover, Heine does not fix the king into a prearranged scheme and then simply run variations on it, as he was often inclined to do in his treatment of other public figures such as, for example, Wellington. Börne in his review of *Französische Zustände* complains that Heine presents Louis-Philippe, "als hätte er das kalte Fieber, an dem einen Tage für gut, an dem andern für schlecht, am dritten Tage wieder für gut, am vierten wieder für schlecht";[42] but, apart from the fact that the objection is overstated, it is not really fair, and Heine had already met it plausibly in a note added to the book, where he argues that his contradictory remarks on the person of the king are reflections of day to day events,[43] a feature of the articles that speaks as easily for as against their journalistic integrity. Heine adds at the end of this note that the attacks of the legitimists are generating in him a real inclination toward the king.

Heine's next extensive treatment of the king is in the *Nachtrag* to *Französische Maler* in *Salon I,* a passage that consists mostly of a memoir Heine says he wrote in July 1833, and that fairly vibrates with his tensely ambivalent responses. The key issue in this report is Louis-Philippe's plan to fortify the city of Paris; the ostensible purpose was to protect the city against invasion, but the people suspected the king of fortifying his own power against internal uprising. The instinct of the people must be correct, Heine argues: "Die Völker sind allwissend, alldurchschauend; das

* E, *5,* 178. The formulation was taken almost verbatim from the *Journal des Débats* of June 11, 1832 (Clarke, p. 200). But, as is often the case, Clarke makes too much of this; Heine's indicative "Man konnte . . . sagen" indicates that it *was* said elsewhere.

Auge des Volks ist das Auge Gottes" (E, *4*, 86). Yet only a few pages before, Heine described the model of an elephant on the Place de la Bastille as a symbol of "die bewußte Kraft und die gewaltige Vernunft des Volks" (E, *4*, 83). Similarly self-contradictory is Heine's analysis of the king's actions, for he seems at a loss to know how to set his values. On the one hand, he suspects the king of deceiving the people with a bourgeois pose and of secretly planning sinister coups; but on the other, he finds such behavior evidence of true royal strength, and he cannot repress his admiration for this sly dissimulation:

> Er ist vielleicht einer der geschicktesten, geistvollsten und mutigsten Menschen Frankreichs . . . Noch nie ist ein Fürst in seiner eignen Hauptstadt so sehr verhöhnt worden wie Ludwig Philipp. Aber er denkt wer zuletzt lacht, lacht am besten, ihr werdet die Birne nicht fressen, die Birne frißt euch . . . Es fehlt ihm wahrhaftig nicht an fürstlichem Selbstgefühl. (E, *4*, 85–86)

He goes so far as to equate Louis-Philippe with Napoleon as one of the two miracles that have saved monarchy in Europe.[44] The passage ends with one of Heine's familiar attacks on the republican cause. These ruminations are paradigmatic for Heine's view of the king during the next few years, torn restlessly between libertarian and authoritarian leanings, suspicion of the king's sincerity and admiration for his adroit instinct for the uses of power. In 1837, in his letters on the French theater, Heine's most thoroughgoing and revealing presentation of his fundamental attitude toward France, he expresses great dissatisfaction with the position of the constitutional monarch, who must jockey among the unpoetic forces of a bourgeois society:

> Hier müssen die Könige Comödie spielen, ein nichtssagendes Geschwätz mit noch weniger sagenden Gemeinplätzen beantworten, ihren Feinden huldreich lächeln, ihre Freunde aufopfern, immer indirekt handeln, und durch ewige Selbstverläugnung alle freien, großmüthigen und thatlustigen Regungen eines königlichen Heldensinns in ihrer Brust ertödten. (E, *4*, 626)

The dignity of royalty is divorced from the true honor that belongs to "dem Genie, der Schönheit, der Liebe und der Kraft" (E, *4,* 627). Here the mythic view of kingship, which troubled Heine all through his preoccupation with Louis-Philippe, is expressed in its plainest form. One would like to know why Heine cut this passage from the version published in *Salon IV.* He did leave, however, a veiled remark that expresses his acceptance of the general view of Louis-Philippe as a dissimulator; after describing the profession of a *chatouilleur,* who during the day is hired to weep at funerals and at night to laugh in the theater, Heine remarks: "Das ist entsetzlich! Ich möchte lieber König von Frankreich sein" (E, *4,* 540). Heine seems never to have doubted the wide-spread belief that Louis-Philippe was basically dishonest and insincere, although he sometimes regarded these characteristics as a necessity or perhaps as tarnished virtues. How they related to the royal dignity he was not sure, but one of his reports of the 1840s begins with an allusion to Schiller's Phillip II: "Der König hat geweint" (E, *6,* 233), and although he allows doubts about the king's sincerity to echo, he nevertheless is prepared to see him in a tragic light.

In 1838, in *Shakspeares Mädchen und Frauen,* we find another treatment of the king, and it is a strange one indeed, for here we find him seriously compared to Shakespeare's Henry IV. Heine quotes Richard II's sour comments on Bolingbroke's manner of winning the good will of the people (*Richard II,* I, 4) and then cites the rather unpleasantly Machiavellian advice Henry IV gives to his son on his deathbed (*Henry IV Part II,* IV, 5). Between these two quotations comes this remarkable passage:

> Ja, die Ähnlichkeit ist erschreckend. Ganz wie der ältere, entfaltete sich vor unsern Augen der heutige Bolingbroke, der nach dem Sturze seines königlichen Vetters den Thron bestieg, sich allmählich darauf befestigte: ein schlauer Held, ein kriechender Riese, ein Titan der Verstellung, entsetzlich, ja empörend ruhig, die Tatze in einem samtnen Handschuh und damit die öffentliche Meinung streichelnd, den Raub schon in weiter Ferne erspähend und nie darauf losspringend, bis er in sicherster Nähe . . . Möge er immer seine schnau-

> benden Feinde besiegen und dem Reiche den Frieden erhalten bis zu seiner Todesstunde. (E, 5, 428–29)

Apart from the question of the appositeness of the comparison, what in the world does the passage mean? It is an extended *contradictio in adjecto,* a stylistic feature of Heine's writing that undoubtedly deserves a separate study. Perhaps it is meant ironically, but it is very difficult to say for certain, for by this time Heine certainly had no sympathy for any of Louis-Philippe's enemies, and eventually he began to appreciate the virtues of keeping the peace more than he had in 1832. Perhaps the pessimistic Weltanschauung of Heine's last years was already in full development, and he was able to see the qualities of dissimulation ascribed to the king as positive values, for the other terms in this series of oxymora—hero, giant, titan, calm, the lion's paw, and the predatory leap—are attributes of the royal persona and remind one of nothing so much as of Heine's youthful view of Napoleon. But whatever one may make of this passage, it is a good example of how difficult it was for Heine to formulate his perceptions of reality in an unequivocal manner.

In Heine's newspaper articles of the 1840s, which he revised and republished in 1854 under the title *Lutezia,* Louis-Philippe naturally plays a prominent role once more, although the social movement is more in the foreground than the question of the monarchy as such.[45] Nonetheless, Heine originally wanted Louis-Philippe's name in the title of the book.[46] *Lutezia* is in one respect the most difficult of Heine's works to read, for it is like a palimpsest—the Heine of the 1840s is overlaid and obscured by the Heine of the 1850s. As one laboriously culls the variants out of Elster's back pages, one can easily become irritated at an undeniable lack of integrity in Heine's procedure. It is, of course, permissible for a man to change his opinions and revise his books accordingly. But the articles of *Lutezia* are keyed to specific dates and are thus historical documents with which, from our point of view, at least, Heine would have done better not to tamper. He made the matter worse by stating in his dedication to Pückler-Muskau that the revisions did not affect the original judgments.[47] On the other hand, with respect to Louis-Philippe, the general result of the revision is a moderation of the criticism of the king, making the kinder judgments somewhat more prominent, and since the July Monarchy had fallen six years before the publication of *Lutezia* and Louis-Philippe had died in 1850, we have some reason to believe that the apparent amelioration of Heine's opinion was genuine (we shall have occasion to return to this problem eventually).

Lutezia, like *Französische Zustände,* begins with an extended account of the king; on this occasion, however, the article, which is again not very complimentary to him, was not printed in the *Allgemeine Zeitung.* In the manuscript version of the article, Heine has harsh things to say about the bourgeois cast of the king's mind, which he finds exactly congruent with that of a tolerably well-educated and well-bred Parisian shopkeeper;[48] he also flays the king's foreign policy as disgraceful accommodation to the European oligarchy: "Mit allen Ketten, die ihm seine nordischen Eisengruben liefern, würde der Kaiser von Rußland dennoch die Franzosen nicht so gut binden, wie Ludwig Philipp es thut, durch sein schnödes, auf die schlechtesten, selbstsüchtigsten Interessen begründetes Regierungssystem!" (E, *7,* 633). The *Lutezia* version drops these observations, but still concentrates on the king's Jesuitical foxiness[49] and continues the perpetual topic of the king's humility before the powers of Europe[50] by translating his policy into the obsequious idiom of the bourgeoisie. Of course, says Heine, the king would never express himself in that fashion —according to the original manuscript, for reasons of tact;[51] in *Lutezia* because the king is "stolz und edel und klug" (E, *6,* 142). Contrasting passages like these show how valuable a republication of Heine's articles in their original form would be.

In the summer of 1840 it looked for a while as though Heine and the rest of the king's critics might get their war after all. England, by outmaneuvering France in the Middle East and secretly forming the Quadruple Alliance, made both France and the king very angry, and Louis-Philippe was briefly tempted to ride the tiger. But it was not long before his thorough pacifism prevailed and he addressed himself to the difficult problem of dampening the war fever in the country. In July Heine conceived a perfectly absurd confidence in France's ability to invade and conquer England, degenerate as the latter country was due to a century of peace,* and he seems still to have believed that the king's peaceful policies did not redound to the credit and glory of France. This time, he thought, the king might actually be propelled into war, and as a good example of what happens in the revision of *Lutezia,* he added at the end of the article a post hoc prophecy: "Herr Thiers versichert, daß er den aufbrausenden Unwillen des Königs manchmal nur mit Mühe besänftige. Oder ist solche Kriegslust nur eine Kriegslist des göttlichen Dulders Odysseus?" (E, *6,* 208). Heine's tendency to transform hindsight into second-sight reminds one of the case of the Helgoland letters in *Börne* (see Chapter 9, pp. 257–61). But it is of less importance than the employment in this revised version of the persona of Ulysses (it was originally located in the letter of August 25,[52] a month later, by which time Heine had realized that Louis-Philippe would not go to war). Although the adjective "göttlich" is missing in this passage, there is no doubt that the comparison is meant positively, for Heine asserts that the king is a hero who would fight as bravely as Ajax or Achilles if words no longer sufficed.[53] By September we find Heine admiring the king's courage in braving the fury of the nation at this blow to its honor,[54] and in the original version he expresses himself even more strongly: "Welche Hand muß das seyn, die es vermag, die empörten Volksleidenschaften zu zügeln, und die nicht zittert, selbst das Opfer zu werden!" (E, *6,* 591). The steady hand holding the reins recalls again attributes of the Napoleon persona,[55] and, indeed, at the end of October, Heine calls Louis-Philippe "der Napoleon des Friedens," to which startling opinion he added in *Lutezia* the words "lacht nicht" (E, *6,* 225).[56]

This positive attitude toward the king continues, on the whole, through 1841. In February Heine defends the patriotism of the king,[57] and in May, in an access of patriotic feelings of his own, Heine praises Louis-Philippe warmly for keeping the peace with Germany.[58] The month before, in an article dated April 29, Heine had taken a spirited position on a matter of lèse majesté: the editor of a newspaper, who had printed forged documents insulting to the king, was acquitted in the courts on the grounds of the king's

* E, *6,* 206–07. Since England had been at war as recently as 1815, it is hard to know what Heine meant by this.

immunity. Heine, in the course of his lament at the defenselessness of the king before slander and assassination, lets something interesting slip: he compares kings in this regard to great poets.[59] Now this is patent nonsense, for Heine certainly did not bear lies and slander "mit schweigender Langmut" (E, *6,* 268), and as for the inability to defend one's honor in a duel, Heine was to have that pleasure before the year was out. Since the comparison in this context is so inappropriate, the conclusion seems irresistible that the equation of poet-persona and king-persona lies consistently below the surface in most of these discussions.

In July 1842, shortly after an important election, freak accident struck Louis-Philippe a grievous blow: his son and heir to the throne, the Duc d'Orléans, who had been widely regarded, as crown princes tend to be, as a man of great promise, was killed by a fall from a carriage. Heine's latent sympathy with the sufferings of the king was naturally aroused;* and with respect to Orléans, whom Heine seems greatly to have admired, he quotes Schiller in a mood that anticipates the theme of his late poetry: "Doch das ist das Los des Schönen hier auf Erden" (E, *6,* 319)—by which he means that the event will be celebrated by bad verse and insincere sentimentality. In the *Lutezia* version Heine could not resist an addition that made it appear that he had foreseen the tragedy,[60] but more importantly, he sensed immediately that this event transcended the personal loss of the king and probably implied that the July Monarchy would now not be able to survive (not such an arcane prophecy, to be sure, for the king's grandson, now heir to the throne, was an infant of four, while Louis-Philippe himself was sixty-eight years old). "Dieser Todesfall," observed Heine quite correctly, "stellt alles Bestehende in Frage" (E, *6,* 317).

Article 25 of *Lutezia,* which deals extensively with Louis-Philippe and did not appear in the *Allgemeine Zeitung,* is dated November 6, 1840, but this cannot be correct. At the outset it adverts to Louis Blanc's *Histoire de dix ans,* which began to appear in 1841; and from the correspondence between Heine and the *Allgemeine Zeitung* it seems likely that the article was actually

* E, *6,* 318, 322. Alexandre Weill wrote Heine on September 14 that "Ihre weinerlichen Briefe über den Herzog von Orleans haben einen schlechten Eindruck in Deutschland gemacht" (Hirth, *5,* 361).

written in the fall of 1842.[61] How much revision it may have undergone for *Lutezia* is not known at this writing, which is unfortunate, for it is a major document of Heine's political attitude. It falls into three parts: a characterization of the socialist Louis Blanc, a refutation of Blanc's account of Louis-Philippe's dealings with Charles X immediately after the July Revolution, and an effort to sum up Louis-Philippe's character. The first part contains Heine's most sovereign repudiation of egalitarianism: "Es ist wahr, wir sind alle Brüder, aber ich bin der große Bruder, und ihr seid die kleinen Brüder, und mir gebührt eine bedeutendere Portion" (E, *6,* 230), and, in this mood concerning the persona, it is not inappropriate that he should turn to a definition of the king. Here Heine returns again to the comparison with Ulysses, giving ambivalent praise similar to that of the passage in *Shakspeares Mädchen und Frauen,* although on this occasion Heine asserts plainly that Louis-Philippe did not usurp the crown but had it forced upon him and that it certainly had been no blessing.[62] In a rather pessimistic tone, the putative dissimulations of the king are compared with the dishonesty of the people, who had intended to manipulate the king like a puppet; as an illustration, Heine tells the well-known story of how the passerby could get to see the king by paying the mob outside his palace to shout for him or sing the *Marseillaise*.[63]

This presentation is, on the whole, not very complimentary to the royal dignity. But in its strange, left-handed way, it is probably positively meant, for Heine was by now convinced, as he wrote in 1840 and again in 1843, that the king was the only guarantor of orderly calm.* [64] By this time Heine's eyes were on the gathering momentum of communism, and at the end of 1842 he observed that Louis-Philippe's security lay in the bourgeois fear of communism and the threat of a "redefinition" of property.[65] But Heine, despite his occasional willingness to describe the king as an eagle superior to all around him,[66] had little confidence that he would succeed in stemming the tide. In an article dated February 2, 1843, which did not appear in the *Allgemeine Zeitung,* Heine observes wearily that although the king is attempting to

* Cf. the article of Nov. 20, 1840, not printed in the *Allgemeine Zeitung,* where Heine expresses his fears of a republican regime most forcefully (E, 7, 356–59).

govern the country through the Chamber, the Chamber does not represent the country, and consequently, "so müssen wir doch bekennen . . . daß das ganze System keinen Schuß Pulver taugt" (E, *6*, 343).

From 1843 until the fall of the July Monarchy Heine has little to say about Louis-Philippe. Two undated aphorisms[67] must belong to around 1847, particularly the first, in which Heine urges the necessity of both deism and Louis-Philippe, and remarks pithily that God is the Louis-Philippe of Heaven. After the February Revolution, he wrote an elegiac account of the king that was not printed;[68] in it he stresses Louis-Philippe's virtues, accurately identifying them as those of the eighteenth century, and he certifies that the king lacked all aristocratic vices. His tone is strikingly different from the outburst of the proletarian sympathizer Georg Weerth, who exulted that France had "den niederträchtigsten aller gekrönten Schufte, samt seiner Clique, mit Stumpf und Stiel vernichtet."[69] Yet Heine knew that "Ludwig Philipp war für dieses Volk der einzig mögliche König, und sogar ihn haben sie, nach einem Versuch von 18 Jahren, nicht vertragen können" (E, *7*, 380). Heine's posture in this article is one of fatalistic acceptance of the republic, and the king has turned into a fairy-tale figure: "es war einmal ein König." For the remaining two-and-a-half years of Louis-Philippe's life in exile, Heine has nothing of significance to say about him; the king has receded into oblivion. In 1851, Heine adverts to him in passing in the *Nachwort zum "Romanzero,"* where he calls him the best monarch who ever wore the constitutional crown of thorns.[70] In the same year he wrote in a letter than Louis Napoleon, like Louis-Philippe, was a miracle for France,[71] a rather dubious remark, not only because it was made just a few months before the *Coup d'État,* which naturally elicited from Heine at least one bitterly satirical poem[72] and probably several,[73] but also because it was written to the editor of the *Allgemeine Zeitung,* who may have been expected to quote it to Heine's benefit.

The last time Heine speaks of Louis-Philippe is in the so-called "Waterloo fragment," written in connection with the *Geständnisse* in 1853/54 but not published in Heine's lifetime. Again Heine lists the king's familiar virtues, and the compliments he bestows on him are simple and straightforward: "Ludwig Philipp war ein großer und edler König." "Er war ein Mensch" (E, *6,* 539). But, argues Heine, who is working here toward a paean of praise to Napoleon III, Louis-Philippe was not the representative of the whole people: "er war nicht nationalen Ursprungs, er war nicht der Erwählte des Volks, sondern einer kleinen Koterie von Geldmenschen, die ihn auf den vakanten Thron gesetzt, weil er ihnen die beste Garantie ihrer Besitzthümer dünkte." It is sadly necessary to say that Heine here comes close to a mystique that is not unrelated to certain features of Fascist ideology, and it will not do to interpret this cut at the monied bourgeoisie of the *Juste-Milieu* as a socialist view. This is clear from the rest of the fragment, in which Heine sees Napoleon reincarnated in his newly-crowned nephew as the true ruler and elect of the people—the people understood as a single, organic being with a single will. The "Waterloo fragment" puts Heine's whole critique of Louis-Philippe's supposed absolutist and aristocratic urges in a most doubtful light, for certainly Louis Napoleon possessed these qualities in a much more fundamental form. Louis-Philippe's failing was that he did not match the glorious ideal of the monarchical persona, which, it turns out after all these years, is still informed by the Napoleon myth. In contradiction to some of his imagery in previous years, Heine finds that Louis-Philippe's success lay in his mediocrity—"weil er kein Adler war" (E, *6,* 540). Heine knew perfectly well that Louis-Philippe was not a mediocre man, but he was a *symbol* of mediocrity, of compromise and inglorious muddling-through. This the ruler must not be; better, Heine says in criticism of the Provisional Government of 1848, to have shed much blood and done something great for the people.[74] The firm relationship between Heine's political reactions and the myth-making quality of his poetic imagination is ultimately evident in the case of his final judgment upon Louis-Philippe.

In all the preceding discussion, the principle has been to take Heine's observations on Louis-Philippe at face value and try to interpret them without reference to external considerations that might have influenced them. This is a difficult matter upon which I am not prepared to give a firm opinion. It is not always easy to tell whether Heine is expressing independent attitudes or whether some momentary motive has inspired a certain utterance. His repeated avowals of allegiance to the monarchist principle are often obviously directed to the authorities in Germany in order to mollify them and inspire them to lift their proscriptions.[75] Hirth, with his tendency to energetic speculation, has introduced much confusion into this problem; he insists, for example, that Heine's account of life at the Castle of Eu[76] proves that he must have been on social terms with the royal family and that this accounts for Heine's enthusiasm for the crown prince,[77] but despite Hirth's customary insistence that he has provided an "unumstößlicher Beweis," [78] the text in question does not prove this remarkable claim at all.* Heine himself provided problems in this regard. In the "Retrospektive Aufklärung," which he added to *Lutezia* in 1854 in order to defend himself on the notorious subject of his French government pension, he claims that Louis-Philippe had taken the censor of the *Allgemeine Zeitung* into the *Legion d'honneur* and that the gentleman so honored saw to it that any critical remark on Louis-Philippe's policies was deleted.[79] Now, whether this is true or not—and it is true that some of Heine's most pointed treatments of the king were not printed in the *Allgemeine Zeitung* and true also that after the publication of *Französische Zustände* the French Ministry of the Interior put Heine under surveillance[80]—it distorts the situation; many of Heine's critical remarks did appear in the newspaper, and the revisions of *Lutezia,* which were made in part, at least, from the original drafts,[81] are not noteworthy for a more negative view of Louis-Philippe; indeed, it is rather the contrary. And, at the very last, Heine leaves us with his usual neat contradiction. To an objection of Campe's about the role played by Louis-Philippe in *Lutezia,* Heine responds blithely that the king is "bloß Staffage" and that the real hero of the book is "die sociale Bewegung" (Hirth, *3,* 410). But to François Guizot he writes on March 6, 1855, that in the epoch described in *Lutezia,* the world will see nothing but three personages: "Louis-Philippe, Mr. Thiers et Mr. Guizot" (Hirth, *3,* 602–03).[82] We are left, as usual, to make what we can out of what Heine actually wrote.

* Dresch, who has carefully studied Heine's French connections, doubts Hirth's conclusion (*Heine à Paris,* p. 57).

Seen from the perspective of Heine's poetic imagination, his long-range view of Louis-Philippe falls into two components: he is the better man who is defeated, a precursor of all the broken victims of the late poetry; but he is also a king who does not coalesce with the royal persona, for he is too mundane, too unheroic, and too bourgeois, and so the poet can neither identify with him nor assume him onto the poet's own elevated level. Since the king did not yield the stuff of myth, he remained a mere political phenomenon. Had this not been so, it is very likely that Heine would not have been able to comprehend the political forces operating in the reign of Louis-Philippe as acutely as he did.

CHAPTER 9

Poet Versus Tribune: *Börne*

> When to the mob you make a speech
> My boy Hobbie O,
> How do you keep without their reach
> The watch within your fobby O?
>
> But never mind such petty things,
> My boy Hobbie O;
> God save the people—damn all Kings,
> So let us crown the Mobby O!
>
> —BYRON

At the beginning of 1831 Ludwig Börne presented Julius Campe with a proposition that in retrospect fairly takes one's breath away. Börne wanted to publish a political journal from Paris in collaboration with Heine, or, failing that, a political correspondence between the two writers to be published quarterly.[1] One can easily imagine what an exhibition of wit and rhetorical fireworks such a project by these two extraordinarily gifted polemicists would have turned out to be. Of course, the chances that any of the German governments would have permitted the importation of such dynamite into their sleepy kingdoms were exactly nil. But Börne was not a practical man, and such considerations troubled him little. What did trouble him very much was that Heine, as Börne gradually came to realize, wanted nothing whatever to do with the project. It was not that Heine had anything against political journalism; on several occasions during his Paris years he tried to set journalistic projects in motion.[2] It was Börne he objected to, and in the book version of *Französische Zustände* Heine publicly stressed that he had nothing to do with the radical party.[3] At first Börne was puzzled by this, then saddened, then frustrated, and finally infuriated. The decay of the relationship proceeded quickly. By the fall of 1831, Börne knew that Heine was not interested in cooperating with him; by May of the following year Heine had reached the point of referring to Börne as a madman.[4] The resulting animosity smouldered under the surface of the life of the German community in Paris until Börne's death in 1837 and did much damage to the solidarity of the opposition cause. The issue burst into flame in 1840 when Heine published one of his best written and worst conceived books, *Ludwig Börne. Eine Denkschrift,* which, through a blunder of Campe's, appeared with the disastrous though wholly accurate title of *Heinrich Heine über Ludwig Börne.*[5] Börne's friend Jeanette Wohl counterattacked by publishing a maliciously selective collection of Börne's private animadversions on Heine,[6] suppressing, among other things, Börne's plan for the common journalistic enterprise.[7] Gutzkow added a scathing attack on Heine to his biography of Börne,[8] and the fat was in the fire for good.

Heine's attack on Börne was impolitic, for Börne's standing, even among those who were not his allies, was still very high; his absolute integrity and total devotion to his principles had earned him respect and admiration everywhere. By the summer of 1841, when the whole affair culminated in Heine's duel with Salomon Strauss, Heine's public reputation had reached a nadir from which, it seemed for a while, it would never recover. The attacks on him drove him to the most radical defense mechanisms, such as his ludicrous remark to Campe in September 1840: "an dem goldnen Harnisch den ich trage prallen alle diese Pfeile ab" (Hirth, 2, 370). But with the virtual disappearance of the German radical republican movement, the emotional force of the conflict was lessened, and today, it would seem, Heine has emerged the blemished victor, as he has in the case of the polemic against Platen. Heine's admirers have always found reason to speak well of *Börne.* Elster struck the tone that is found everywhere on this side of the issue:

> Börne war das beschränkte, ingrimmig-charaktervolle Haupt der deutschen Jakobinerpartei, während Heine auf die Länge mit dieser nichts zu schaffen haben wollte. Bei seiner großen satirischen Begabung konnte er weder die Mängel der dort verfochtenen Grundsätze, noch die Unfähigkeit ihrer Ver-

> treter übersehen; und so zog er sich aus diesen Kreisen zurück. (E, 7, 3)

The Marxists, who have the convenient trick of stamping Börne as a "petty-bourgeois radical," defend Heine on the grounds that he had a superior insight into the true nature of society and realized that Börne's purely political solutions could not generate revolution. There are no wholehearted devotees of Börne anymore; even his admirers, like Barthélemy Ott[9] and Ludwig Marcuse,[10] have a way of yielding ultimately to the force of Heine's arguments, and the same is true, by and large, of the most recent East German biography of Börne.[11] Laura Hofrichter goes out of her way to praise Heine's book: "it proved to be for him the most significant of all his books and a work of decisive importance . . . every image is harmoniously and profoundly related to the larger context of his view of the world." [12] One can observe, however, that the various defenses of Heine proceed from differing premises and that the whole matter has a chameleon-like aspect that is intimately related to the character of the book itself. Liberal critics are pleased by Heine's repudiation of Jacobinism and his moderate political posture. Marxists find that he recognized Börne's Jacobinism as historically obsolete and admire Heine's revolutionary political posture. Champions of the autonomy of art are enthusiastic about Heine's insistence upon poetic integrity at the expense of political relevance. *Börne* is clearly a more complex work than one would gather from many of the things that have been written about it. The major difficulty in understanding the book is that Heine's argument seems to proceed simultaneously from two different attitudes, one political and democratic, the other aesthetic and aristocratic. It is a conflict of personae, which is of central importance to the whole phenomenon of Heine, and this conflict admits of no easy resolutions, for, as we shall see, some aspects of *Börne* are utterly weird.[13]

In assessing Heine's book, it is useful not to lose sight of its subject, and perhaps Börne deserves to be seen in a more positive light than the aftermath of Heine's book has permitted. Börne came to his radicalism slowly; he was driven to it by events and experience. Born Löb Baruch in 1786 in the wretched Frankfurt ghetto, he developed first into a patriotic German with a strong dislike of Napoleon, a stance that remained consistent throughout his career. Even though the reaction of 1815, when Frankfurt restored the Jewish disabilities that the Napoleonic occupation had abolished, cost Börne his career in the civil service, he continued to believe in the possibility of reform from above until 1819, the year of the Carlsbad Decrees.[14] When he came to Paris after the July Revolution, he was a constitutional monarchist who, like Heine, invested considerable hope in Louis-Philippe; but the economic depression at the time of the Revolution, the removal of Lafayette from his position of influence, and the insight that the grand bourgeoisie and not the people had won control of the nation eroded his faith. By the fall of 1832 he had washed his hands of his allegiance to the July Monarchy and assumed the radical democratic position he was to maintain henceforth.[15]

In some respects, it is rather easy to make fun of Börne. Because of his consuming hope for revolution, or, rather, for the continuation of the revolution already begun, and because he underestimated how much indignity people will tolerate from political authority, he developed an embarrassing gullibility and susceptibility to rumor; it is piteous to watch him predict the revolution day by day and then struggle for a new optimistic interpretation when events chronically fail to meet his expectations. His persistent devotion to religious faith and to the tenets of bourgeois morality made him look rather odd to some, and, indeed, resulted in the only moment in his career when his position, briefly, appeared ambiguous. Because of his moralistic attitude, he remained friendly with Wolfgang Menzel after Menzel had turned into a reactionary huckster of virtue, and he was sympathetic to Menzel's attack on Gutzkow's *Wally, die Zweiflerin* in 1835, although he refused to join the witch-hunt.[16] Börne was not named in the proscription of Heine and the Young Germans that followed upon that uproar. It was not long, however, before Börne explosively cleared up any misunderstanding with his last great essay, *Menzel, der Franzosenfresser*. His bitter attacks on Goethe have not won the approval of posterity, and his proto-Leninist views on the subordination of art to revolutionary politics can be distressing when one views their consequences, although it is not true, as critics sometimes assert and Heine appeared to believe, that Börne lacked all sensitivity to literary values. It was a confession of faith in the value of poetic literature, after all, that supplied the motto for Heine's *Harzreise*. Börne greatly admired Lessing and especially Jean Paul, who influenced his style and on whom he wrote a famous eulogy in 1825, and he was able to appreciate the stature of Kleist and Grillparzer at a time when few others did.[17] Nor did Börne fail to recognize Goethe's greatness, as did Menzel; on the contrary, he was offended that so mighty a genius should ignore the cause of the people.[18] It was, as Bock says, not a polemic against an equal, but an accusation born of disappointed hope and love transformed into hate.[19] Marcuse made a substantial contribution to a judicious assessment of the conflict when he argued that Heine was a far more formidable opponent of Börne than the "läppische Streitschrift" would indicate, because Heine confronted Börne's untragic, eighteenth-century "Aufgeklärtheit" with the skeptical pessimism of the nineteenth century.[20]

It should not be forgotten, however, that no German, whether liberal, socialist, or communist, has ever mastered the rhetoric of liberty like Ludwig Börne; in fact, he invented it. The American he resembles most is William Lloyd Garrison. Like Garrison, Börne was often wrong about events or misjudged an issue. Like Garrison, he was distressingly, annoyingly, immovably single-minded; "Ich hatte eine Richtung des Geistes, *eine*," [21] he wrote justly of himself in 1828. Like Garrison, he argued for things that today we would not be without, insofar as we have yet managed to realize them, and like Garrison, he deserves the respect and gratitude of posterity above all else. Peter Demetz has compared his language to a rapier,[22] and often that is what it was; at other times it was like a mousetrap or like poisoned honey. In the course of his career it became increasingly like a sledgehammer. In his attack on Menzel of 1836 there is an example of this that is interesting because it is in defense of constitutional monarchy. As a republican Börne was opposed to this system, but he was so outraged at Menzel's hypocrisy in playing off constitutional monarchy against his republicanism that he showed what he could do in terms of solidarity against the common enemy:

> Gehört es zum Wesen der konstitutionellen Monarchie, daß die Volksvertreter das Budget anerkennen müssen, daß sie nicht sprechen dürfen, worüber sie wollen, daß sie ihre Reden nicht bekannt machen, die Protokolle ihrer Sitzungen nicht drucken lassen dürfen? Gehört die Zensur zum Wesen der konstitutionellen Monarchie? . . . Gehören die heimlichen Gerichte zum Wesen der konstitutionellen Monarchie? [23]

On and on the passage roars in more than two dozen anaphoric questions: is it in the nature of constitutional monarchy that princes buy judges, the accused are imprisoned for years without trial, schoolboys go to jail, the names of the accused and their crimes are kept secret, mothers and sisters are punished for attempting to obtain the release of their loved ones, the police confiscates mail, a four year old is obliged to testify against his mother?—this is Börne as he lives and breathes, scandalized, apart from all distinctions of political ideology, at the *obvious* intolerableness of conditions in Germany. This moralistic simplicity was Börne's weakness, but it was also his strength, and it informed a style the influence of which was vast. It supplied the energy for Ludolf Wienbarg's *Ästhetische Feldzüge* of 1834, which first put the slogan of Young Germany into circulation, and for Friedrich Engels' early critical writings.[24] When Heine claims in *Börne* that he was always uninfluenced by and critical of Börne's style,[25] he is simply not telling the truth. He always speaks admiringly of Börne in his letters up to 1830: in 1825 he expressed great admiration for Börne's wit and its serious foundation;[26] he dedicated a copy of *Reisebilder I* to him;[27] and the style of such polemics as the *Vorrede zu den Französischen Zuständen* shows that Heine, too, was in a tradition of which Börne was the source.[28] Börne, for his part, also admired Heine at the outset; he received Heine most cordially in Frankfurt in 1827, and even before Börne had made his acquaintance, he had recommended Heine as an editor to the publisher Vieweg.[29] Heine admits himself that Börne made several attempts in Paris to restore the relationship.* [30]

* A few months before his death, Börne seems to have employed Heine's uncle Henry for this purpose; see Hirth, *6*, 260.

There is no point in trying to assess what measure of blame Börne may have borne for the unhappy situation. But since he did behave rather strangely, it is worth making some effort to understand his feelings. It is likely that Heine's refusal to participate in what was, from Börne's point of view, the common cause hurt him more than any other event in his life. For Börne, unlike Heine, was not ordinarily a vindictive man, and there is no parallel anywhere else in his life for the subterranean campaign of slander which he began to conduct against Heine, and which approached the proportions of an obsession. Although Börne kept the worst of it out of print, Heine could not help becoming aware of it. Börne was talkative, and there is evidence that he expressed his bitterness in conversations that, in the gossipy German community of Paris, could not help but come to Heine's ears.[31] Heine's sharp attacks on Börne in his letters begin before Börne had published any part of his critique of Heine,[32] and, in a letter to J. H. Detmold of July 29, 1837, Heine hints that he knew of the slanders Börne had left as a legacy to Jeanette Wohl.[33] These letters make strange reading and do not redound to Börne's credit. Börne asked Jeanette Wohl to accumulate every petty slander of Heine that he put into his letters, and it seems likely that he planned to use this material in a book against Heine (and Campe) sometime in the future.[34] By her selective editing, Jeanette Wohl made these remarks seem even more childish and ill-willed than they were in fact. With the honesty that Börne could not abandon even when it made him appear absurd, he admitted that he was making an effort to collect every shred of gossip about Heine he could manage to hear, and he grouched about everything from Heine's impiety and aestheticism to his desire to make people laugh.[35] In keeping with the insistence upon the superiority of the persona in *Börne,* Heine attributes Börne's behavior to jealousy, first of all ascribing it to his inhibited love life and then reviving the image of the drum major from *Das Buch Le Grand* to establish the persona as more colorful, more daring, and more attractive in every respect.[36] This seems pretentious, but it is apparent that Heine was not far from the truth; in an unpublished passage in a letter to Jeanette Wohl, Börne admits that he envies Heine's ability to stay youthful, and in another he remarks that he is slandering Heine—he uses the word himself—because Heine is more attractive to women than he.[37] Although Börne may well be making an effort at a joke here, it is plain that he regarded himself as in the grip of a not very creditable passion. But there is some reason to think that the jealousy may have been mutual. In *Börne,* Heine makes the odd claim that his secret ambition was never to be a poet, but rather a great public orator.[38] This passage, which includes Heine's famous remark that after the people had shaken his hand he would wash it,[39] immediately reverts to satire, so that its actual propositional value, like so much in *Börne,* is unclear. But it is quite possible that, in his heart, Heine envied Börne his prestige, his political dependability, and his honest character.

Heine's defense mechanisms in the matter of his own character were peculiar, to say the least. The account in *Börne* makes it appear that Heine confronted Börne with an affected cynicism and egotism that, on the one hand, was a way of making fun of Börne, and, on the other, a method of distracting attention away from the real contrast in character. That Börne was both misled and greatly nettled by this procedure is clear from his comments to Jeanette Wohl.* It is curious that *Börne* as a whole has this paradoxical quality of putting Heine's self-image in an unflattering light; the book is such a tissue of sophistry and mendacity that one feels again that Heine as a person has eluded our grasp and a very strangely organized persona has been put in his place. This feature of *Börne* has never been very clearly seen, and it is worth demonstrating at some length, not only to show that the work is really of very little value as a source book on Börne, but also to point out that it is a far more ambiguous self-definition than many students of Heine have wanted to comprehend.

All, of course, have agreed that Heine's attack on Frau Wohl is beneath contempt. There has been a tendency, however, to ignore this feature of the book as a regrettable lapse of taste. But the matter is not so easily disposed of. For one thing, the passages are quite characteristic of Heine's style of ad hominem polemic: they are both grossly unfair and irrelevantly insulting. By con-

* See especially Houben, p. 214. Heine confessed this custom in credible terms to Meyerbeer in a letter of Apr. 6, 1835 (Hirth, *2,* 77).

centrating upon Jeanette Wohl's putative ugliness, Heine as always takes the position that the content of an attack is less important than its capacity to injure an enemy. The pose of moral outrage at Börne's supposed ménage à trois would be reprehensible even if it were not hypocritical. This emergence of sexual puritanism is related to some features of the polemic against Platen, and indeed Heine gives us a reprise of that performance by accusing his Swabian enemy Gustav Pfizer of homosexuality.[40] The overt purpose of this line of attack is to catch Börne in a pincer: either his relationship is platonic, in which case he is contemptible because of his inhibited sexuality, a topic raised earlier in the book,[41] or it is not platonic, in which case Börne is contemptible for tolerating Jeanette's marriage to Salomon Strauss and the latter's position as a voluntary cuckold. Beyond this, it seems to mirror in a grotesque way Börne's own strictness in matters of morality and to establish the persona on equal terms with Börne as a man of principle: Heine takes this opportunity to defend himself against an attack on his private morals that had appeared the year before.[42] Moreover, Heine possibly did not even believe that the insinuations he had made were true, even though he repeated them in a furious letter to Campe after Frau Wohl's book appeared.[43] He confessed he was in the wrong in a letter to Alexandre Weill before the duel with Strauss,[44] and four years later he blandly repudiated the slander.[45] His excuse that he was merely misinformed seems unlikely in view of the extent of his information otherwise. This question of the truth value of *Börne* deserves more attention.

Gutzkow, in his attack on Heine in the introduction to his biography of Börne, expressed doubt as to the genuineness of the conversations, or rather monologues, that Heine put into Börne's mouth.[46] Strodtmann agreed with him,[47] and there is plenty of reason that we should also. There is, for example, a striking passage in which Börne conducts Heine about the Jewish community of Frankfurt and, inspired by the Hanukah lights, makes some comments about Jewish history.[48] Walzel comments on this passage that Heine was actually in Frankfurt at that time.[49] He certainly was not. Heine's visit to Börne in 1827 took place around November 15, judging from the dedication of a copy of *Buch der Lieder* he presented to Jeanette Wohl;[50] by about November 28 he was in Munich, from where he reported to Varnhagen about his visit to Börne.[51] In 1827 Hanukah began on the evening of December 13. The conversation described in *Börne,* therefore, never took place. It is not nit-picking to point this out; the supposed conversations with Börne play a major role in the book, and in order to approach an understanding of this work, we shall eventually have to inquire as to their meaning, especially if there is substantial doubt about their genuineness. Other purely factual discrepancies are easily noted. For example, Heine tells us that when his father took him to Frankfurt in 1815, he pointed out Börne as the man "welcher gegen die Komödianten schreibt" (E, 7, 15), but Heine's father cannot possibly have said this, because Börne did not begin writing his sardonic theater reviews until 1818. It seems odd, too, that when Heine sets the stage for his reaction to the news of Börne's death, he gives the time as an autumn evening, whereas Börne died in February.[52] That points of such basic simplicity should be so completely out of kilter makes one wonder about the relative roles of imagination and memory in the composition of *Börne.*

A more substantial problem is that of Book 2, the so-called letters from Helgoland. It is very doubtful that any major part of them was written, as they were purported to have been, on the island of Helgoland in the summer of 1830, and it really is high time that this persistent fiction, which has led to considerable confusion about the development and consistency of Heine's thinking, be recognized as a fiction once and for all. Book II seems to have been written at the instigation of Heinrich Laube, who failed to understand the anatomy of Heine's problem with Börne and was appalled by the lack of a positive position on Heine's part to contrast with the harsh critique; he urged Heine to erect a "mountain" in the book so that the attack on Börne would appear as a reflex of a consistent attitude.* [53] The result, which greatly disappointed Laube, was the letters from Helgoland. Laube gives the impression that Heine labored a considerable time on the "mountain," and, although he was usually a slow writer, it does not seem as though it should have taken him long to edit eight

* Laube's various accounts over the years of this event are not entirely consistent.

letters already in existence. In the first place, these letters are not letters but carefully composed essays; in style and tone they are unlike Heine's genuine letters, and they have practically no point of contact with the correspondence preserved from Heine's Helgoland vacation in 1830. To Campe, incidentally, Heine does not call them letters at all, but refers to Book 2 as an integral part of his memoirs "welche die Enthusiasmusperiode von 1830 schildert" (Hirth, *2,* 332–33). Nevertheless, Hirth has included a version of the first Helgoland letter in his edition of Heine's correspondence.[54] It is supposed to have been addressed to Friedrich Steinmann, who published the version in a book on Heine in 1857. Steinmann is the worst possible guarantor for the genuineness of a letter; he was a notorious forger and literary confidence man who tried for years to maintain the public fiction of an intimacy with Heine.[55] There is no reason to believe that Heine had any connection with Steinmann at all after 1825,[56] despite the efforts of Hirth and E. M. Butler to argue the genuineness of the letter.* The dates Heine gives to the individual letters in *Börne* are clearly haphazard. If the Steinmann letter is at all genuine, Heine shifted the date from July 6 to July 1;[57] the second letter, dated July 8, begins: "Da gestern Sonntag war" (E, *7,* 45), but July 7, 1830, was a Wednesday.

Much in the Helgoland letters points to the end of the 1830s rather than the beginning. There is the reference in the first letter to Heine's interest in the folklore of elemental spirits,[58] which occupied him around 1835. The second letter contains a description of himself as a "heimlicher Hellene" (E, *7,* 46), which, as Butler points out, would be by far the first occurrence of this term if the letter dates from 1830.[59] In this connection, Butler goes on to point out that in 1834 Heine still maintained the

* Hirth, *4,* 241 argues that Steinmann did not begin his forgeries until 1861, which is not proven and improbable. F. Eisner in his corrections to Hirth's edition takes the position that the letter cannot be to Steinmann (Hirth, *6,* 380). E. M. Butler, "Heine and the Saint-Simonians." pp. 68–85, makes a tolerably good case that Steinmann's version could be genuinely earlier than that of *Börne,* but she herself exposes so many anachronisms in the letters generally that it is hard to understand why she clings to the belief that there must be a genuine core. It is, in fact, remarkable that apart from two fleeting references (Hirth, *1,* 459, 461), Heine is completely silent about the July Revolution in his unchallenged preserved correspondence from Helgoland.

Saint-Simonian notion that Judaism is more sensual than Christianity,[60] whereas in the fourth Helgoland letter, as elsewhere in *Börne,* both Judaism and Christianity are subsumed under "spiritualism" or "Nazarenism." [61] Butler also calls attention to the remarks about the "schwäbische Gelbveiglein" (E, *7,* 48), which could only have occurred after Heine's quarrel with the Swabian poets in 1837.[62] Also in the second letter there is a specific reference to the Johannine prophecy of the third testament,[63] a reflection of Heine's Saint-Simonian interests that is related to *Seraphine* 7, first published in 1834. In the following letter there is a bitter remark about Wolfgang Menzel,[64] whom Heine savages in a long digression later in the book,[65] but in 1830 Heine was by no means as furious with Menzel as he was after the events of 1835; in December 1830 he wrote Menzel a letter complaining about criticisms of himself and Immermann,[66] but he was still clearly trying to maintain tolerable relations with the "Pope of literature" (who shortly after this letter wrote an admiring review of *Reisebilder IV* [67]). In his account of the exhibition of painting in Paris in 1831 he quoted Menzel approvingly;[68] and he wrote him a friendly note in 1832.[69] Even in *Die Romantische Schule*[70] his criticism of Menzel is quite moderate in tone; the storm had not yet broken.*

On the other hand, the letters from Helgoland as a group give a definite impression of carefully organized literary composition. They construct a controlled contrast between the depression and pessimism of the persona—who is ready to give up his political and philosophical interests altogether for art and, of all things, "Naturbetrachtung" (E, *7,* 55)—and the carefully prepared outburst of joy at the news of the July Revolution. The account of the joyous moment itself has all the earmarks of emotion recollected in tranquillity and is hardly in the style of a letter at all. The feelings of the poet-persona respond with sympathetic sensitivity to the events of the world; in fact, the poet anticipates events because his metaphorical thinking is completely in phase with nature. When the Revolution that bears the promise of

* The first indication of hatred of Menzel appears in a letter to Heinrich Laube of Sept. 27, 1835 (Hirth, *2,* 100). Nearly two years before, Laube had warned Heine that his view of Menzel was too sanguine (Hirth, *5,* 151).

emancipation from material suffering has already taken place but the news has not yet reached Helgoland, the sea smells like cake and the poet apprehends that something extraordinary has taken place.* But the poet's enthusiasm is quickly tempered by the even more acute premonition that something will go wrong with the Revolution; he remarks ironically that the people went home after making their Revolution without asking any benefits for themselves, and he grows anxious at the remark of an East Prussian official that the poor will have no benefit from the Revolution unless the law of inheritance is abolished. These prophetic remarks about the ultimate failure of the Revolution, discussed further in the postscript to Book 2, are the result of hindsight; their purpose is to establish for the persona a quality of uncanniness. Nor does the outburst of revolutionary fervor—"Ich bin der Sohn der Revolution und greife wieder zu den gefeiten Waffen" (E, *7*, 59) —have any parallel in Heine's responses at the time; it is part of the defensive structuring of the persona against Börne's reproach. The poet is as revolutionary as Börne, but much wiser and more sensitive. This is the "mountain" that Laube urged on Heine, and Butler is more or less right when she remarks of Laube's disappointment that "he missed the point, and that Heine had done what he had promised to do," [71] although Heine admitted to Campe that he had not included positive ideas of his own to counterbalance the polemic.[72] It is possible that Heine did have some written material from Helgoland that supplied a basis for Book 2, or, as a letter from Varnhagen to his sister makes probable,[73] that he wrote some political commentary on the July Revolution after he had returned to Hamburg from his vacation.[74] But there can be little doubt that he proceeded as he had intended to do in 1826, when he was considering the inclusion of his *Briefe aus Berlin* in 1822 in *Reisebilder II*: "dies ist bloß eine Form, um mit besserer Bequemlichkeit alles zu sagen, was ich

* Cf. here to Varnhagen, Nov. 19, 1830 (Hirth, *1*, 464), where Heine gives a somewhat different account: here there is no mention of depression; he claims rather that in anticipation of the Revolution he was in high spirits all year up to the end of July. Hirth makes a good point when he observes that Heine's anticipation of coming events was undoubtedly nourished by reading the Parisian newspapers that pushed the Polignac crisis to a head, as well as the *Allgemeine Zeitung*, to which Thiers was a contributor (Hirth, *4*, 245–46).

will, ich schreibe die Briefe eigentlich jetzt und benutze dazu einen Theil des äußern Gerüstes der Briefe, die ich wirklich im Jahre 1822 im 'Westfälischen Anzeiger' drucken ließ" (Hirth, *1*, 294)[75]

Heine has provided us with another philological puzzle in *Börne* that sheds some doubt on the veracity of his reportage. The problem is that Börne often seems to speak with Heine's voice. Two striking examples of this are found in Book 1. Heine has Börne say that he was able to love Napoleon only until the coup d'état of 18 Brumaire, a statement that Heine makes on his own behalf in almost exactly the same words in Chapter 29 of *Reise von München nach Genua*;[76] the same idea recurs in *Französische Zustände*.[77] Now it is possible that Börne said some such thing during the conversations in Frankfurt and that Heine simply appropriated it as his own thought (Holzhausen is of the opinion that Börne on this occasion had a decisive influence on Heine's thinking about Napoleon[78]). It is also possible that the phrase is Heine's. Close on its heels follow the ironic remarks on the effect of property upon one's political opinions: Börne discovers that his new fragile porcelain tea service makes him less willing to risk flight into exile.[79] This passage was originally written for *Die Bäder von Lucca*;[80] there the tea service was to have been Heine's, and the remark is followed by some observations on the Rothschilds similar to those put in Börne's mouth in the later book.[81] Thus Heine either appropriated ideas of Börne for his own, or attributed his own ideas to Börne; in either case there is an interesting mutual interaction of the two personalities that are supposed to stand here in such striking contrast. This is also true of the unmistakable intrusion of Heine's style upon the remarks attributed to Börne. Just a few examples:

on the Middle Ages—

> Es ist wahr, viel gläubige Herrlichkeit blühte einst in den alten Mauern, und sie waren späterhin eine fromme Reliquie des Mittelalters, gar poetisch anzuschauen des Nachts im Mondschein" (E, 7, 69)

on the Jews—

> "Widerwärtiger war mir noch der Anblick von schmutzigen

> Bartjuden, die aus ihren polnischen Kloaken kamen, von der Bekehrungsgesellschaft in Berlin für den Himmel angeworben wurden und in ihrem mundfaulen Dialekte das Christentum predigten und so entsetzlich dabei stanken. Es wäre jedenfalls wünschenswert, wenn man dergleichen polnisches Läusevolk nicht mit gewöhnlichem Wasser sondern mit Eau de Cologne taufen ließe. (E, 7, 37)

on the King of Bavaria—

> Ja, . . . der König von Bayern, dieser kleine Tyrannos und schlechte Poet . . . sollte niederknien vor dem Bilde der Musen und Abbitte thun wegen seiner schlechten Verse, wegen beleidigter Majestät der Poesie! (E, 7, 76–77)

No one familiar with the styles of Börne and Heine can entertain much doubt as to whose remarks these are. When Heine has Börne urge the distrust of reason,[82] or make a connection between sickness and creativity,[83] he is made to take positions familiar from Heine's poetic self-understanding. In another place, where Heine is making fun of Börne's unaesthetic entourage, he has Börne himself do much the same thing and pick on one unfortunate character particularly.[84] This scene is quite unlike what we otherwise know of Börne, who was a fiercely witty, but also kind and courteous man, and besides it is not supported by Börne's own account of this meeting with Heine.[85] But it does have the interesting effect of obscuring the distinction between Börne and himself that Heine is presumably trying to make.*

All these considerations enable us not only to dispose of *Börne* as a reliable account of the man and his relations with Heine, but also to draw some conclusions about the true nature of this work.

* It is also noteworthy that some of the things Heine reports Börne as having said to him are found in the latter's writings. Examples are the story of the dog Medor (E, 7, 60, 65–66), told by Börne in the *Briefe aus Paris* (Börne, *Gesammelte Schriften, 8,* 208–10), and the comical story of the watch stolen from Börne at the Hambach festival (E, 7, 90–91), which Börne tells on himself in *Menzel, der Franzosenfresser* (*Gesammelte Schriften, 6,* 312). One cannot prove that Börne did not discuss these things with Heine, or, in the first instance, that Heine did not have the story from the newspapers in 1830 as he claims; it is evident throughout *Börne,* however, that Heine read his writings with attention, and it seems to me at least probable that these conversations were manufactured from Börne's works.

First of all, the Börne of *Börne* is a fictional construct, although the contruct may relate to the real Börne much as the poet-persona relates to the real Heine. Secondly, this construct is confronted with that of the poet-persona, which Heine is desperately trying to pull together. It is not unfair to say that the effort to do so is damaged by the dishonesty of the undertaking; the result is far from satisfactory. The persona achieves no convincing harmony, and the challenge posed by Börne is not convincingly met. Heine is attempting to establish for the persona the privileges of poetic autonomy and a claim of true revolutionary commitment and political integrity, a personality balanced properly between the senses and the spirit in contrast to Börne's "Nazarenism." A look at some of the details of the book will show how problematical the effort was. For it turned out that it was not as easy for Heine to distinguish himself successfully from Börne as he may have thought.

Towards the end of Book 1, Heine asserts that Börne was mistaken in thinking that he had found in Heine a like-minded person and that even in Frankfurt they had agreed only in politics; otherwise they were contrasting natures.[86] But the interaction of style and attitudes we have just noted qualifies the assertion considerably. The content of Börne's conversations as Heine reports them only rarely seems at variance with Heine's own view of the political and social situation (as distinct from the difference in attitude toward tactics and solutions), and the frequent rawness of language is by no means foreign to Heine's own style in such matters. Heine lets Börne ramble on in these polemics, but on four occasions[87] Heine cuts him off abruptly with the suggestion that his further remarks were too seditious to be printed. This is a trick, of course, but one is entitled to wonder why, if his purpose was to display the worst side of Börne's Jacobinism, Heine appears to protect him against the wrath of the establishment. It seems, weirdly enough, that Heine is using Börne as a mouthpiece: since, on the one hand, Heine had been under accusation of political moderation ever since the *Französische Zustände* and, on the other, his troubles with the censorship had been greatly exacerbated since 1835, he appears to have taken his critique of Börne as an opportunity to get into print a great deal of otherwise unprintable polemic, a trick he had used years before in the *Briefe aus Berlin*.[88] The tactic was successful, for the censor, apparently of the opinion that anything in an attack on a radical was printable, passed the book without a single objection.[89] But it contributes to the confusions within the book itself. The best part of *Börne* in which to study this problem is the passage on Friedrich von Raumer in Book 3. This little game begins with a monologue in which Börne is made to slash away at the Prussian historian. Then Heine intervenes to say that he does not want the reader to believe that he agrees with Börne in his judgment, and then continues that he regards Raumer as dirty, but not as stupid. In this style of polemic, in which slanderous epithets are interchangeable and their truth value is irrelevant, this is a distinction without a difference. Heine makes sport of the fact that Raumer, like Börne, had also published a correspondence from Paris and was seriously regarded as a competitor of Börne; but then he turns around to compare the Börne of the *Briefe aus Paris* to a policeman who has lost his mind and turned infantile, and goes on to say that Börne was less insane in his conversations—which, be it noted, Heine has now been recounting for some time—than in that book.[90] This kind of wobble is evident all through *Börne*. What masquerades as considered and balanced judgment is in fact a continuous equivocation. Another example is the juxtaposition of the hilarious spoof of the Hambach Festival in Book 3 with the remarks upon the progressive features of that event at the beginning of Book 4. This gives Heine an opportunity to fall into some political rhetoric of his own and also to turn on a much more vulnerable target than Börne, the German nationalists. But in this attitude he is certainly in agreement with Börne, and, sure enough, Heine himself suddenly assumes a Jacobin posture: he observes that the only solution to the nationalists is the guillotine and expresses the opinion that "in Revolutionszeiten bleibt uns nur die Wahl zwischen Töten und Sterben" (E, 7, 97). This will not do, however, for Heine seems to have missed the point of Börne's objection to him altogether: he asserts that despite his differences of opinion he had always made common cause with the German radicals against the common enemy; but this is exactly what he did not do, and it was his failure to do it that infuriated Börne.

Heine tries to concentrate the attack on Börne around the contrasting pairs of "sensualism" and "spiritualism," or "Hellenism" and "Nazarenism." By this means he combines in his analysis psychological, moral, aesthetic, and political aspects, and at the same time tries to ground the persona in a unified principle. In this connection it should be remembered that whenever Heine speaks of radical revolution, he is thinking primarily of the Terror of 1793, and the classic radical type for him is Robespierre; it is because of this persistent model in his mind that he supposed the Communist revolution of the future would be ascetic, puritan, and destructive of art and the pleasures of the senses.[91] Now Börne basically thought of revolution in much the same way, and his manuscript studies on history, first published only a few years ago, show how much he admired Robespierre.[92] It is this really substantial difference between Heine and Börne around which the dichotomy of "Hellene" and "Nazarene" is constructed; Heine not unreasonably compares Börne to Robespierre and quite convincingly expresses the opinion that the moralistic terrorism of both derived from their repressed evil urges.* This comparison permits Heine to shift the confrontation onto aesthetic ground without altogether losing track of the political issues. Thus Heine takes a stand with Goethe against Börne, although a few years earlier, in *Die Romantische Schule,* Heine was closer to the Young German view that Goethe's presumed aesthetic indifference to real events was now obsolete.† From this base Heine unashamedly builds up the persona as a great poet; he reports, with double-edged irony, that Börne himself found Heine's visit in 1827 a greater honor than Goethe's would have been;[93] he defines the persona as a "gekröntes Dichterhaupt" (E, 7, 38) and establishes as the poet par excellence Shakespeare because he was simultaneously Jew and Greek, that is, "Nazarene" and "Hellene" (E, 7, 53).

If, despite the elegance of this dialectic, *Börne* is nevertheless

* E, 7, 99. It is a remarkable sidelight on the mutual interaction of the two personalities that Börne once wrote of Heine that in a time of revolution he would be capable of the bloodiest atrocities. See Houben, p. 212.

† Neither man, of course, understood the nuances of Goethe's position at all. Helge Hultberg has pointed out that as early as 1786, Goethe wrote that the age of beauty was over and that the present requires attention to stern realities ("Heines Bewertung der Kunst," *Heine-Jahrbuch 1967,* p. 81).

an unclear and enigmatic book, it is partly because Heine overestimated Börne's "Nazarenism" and underestimated his own. In his younger days, at any rate, Börne was quite ready to argue the rights of material pleasures and even proclaimed the third testament; like all German intellectuals, Börne felt envy and admiration for the supposedly free and whole-souled Greeks.[94] Heine, on the other hand, is not without his ambiguities in these matters. One need only read his reaction to the Catholic procession in Lucca, where he compares his own inner weaknesses and wounds to those of the monks,[95] to realize that his attitude toward sensualism and spiritualism was never able to come to rest. In a letter of 1846 to Varnhagen about Lassalle, Heine identifies *himself* with the age of "Entsagung und Bescheidenheit" and yearning for Romantic insubstantials, while Lassalle is described in the healthier, "sensualist" terms that in earlier years Heine used to describe the persona.[96] In *Börne,* Heine makes an effort to define for the persona a moral balance that is qualitatively different from the one-sided obsession with virtue of the "Nazarene" temperament, as he had already done in *Zur Geschichte der Religion und Philosophie in Deutschland.*[97] In the attack on Jeanette Wohl, the appeal to "Sittlichkeit," as we have seen, misfires outrageously. The theme appears elsewhere, however, in a context that is to have a considerable echo in Heine's later years. The third of the Helgoland letters begins with an outburst of praise of the Bible that, as Sternberg noted years ago, is completely "unhellenisch." [98] It is this persistent attachment to the Bible that makes it difficult for Heine to reject the Judaic tradition completely. In this context, however, he attempts to separate the Bible from the issue of "Nazarenism" by arguing for a morality that will survive church and state, and, indeed, he propounds an unexpectedly absolutist and nonrelative view of morality, denying that morality is derivable from mores:

> Aber wahre Sittlichkeit ist, wie von Dogma und Legislation, so auch von den Sitten eines Volks unabhängig. Letztere sind Erzeugnisse des Klimas, der Geschichte, und aus solchen Faktoren entstanden Legislation und Dogmatik. Es gibt daher eine indische, eine chinesische, eine christliche Sitte,

> aber es gibt nur eine einzige, nämlich eine menschliche Sittlichkeit. (E, 7, 49)

There are few places where the fundamental idealism of Heine's mode of thinking comes through more clearly than here, and few where he seems less like the herald of the later nineteenth century he is often taken to be. Nor does Heine seem to have any use for the convenient solution of regarding the Bible aesthetically; he insists that there is no trace of art in the Bible: it is pure spirit, the word of God.[99] This judgment is significant because it is so wrong. If Heine, with his poetic sensibilities, had had the slightest inclination to do so, he would have had no difficulty in discovering in the Bible the fine organization of poetry, the rhetoric of prophecy, and the frequent artfulness of prose narration. It was not only his theory that prevented him from doing so; it was always the "spiritual" aspect of the Bible that commanded his attention and his admiration. The result in *Börne* is that Heine simultaneously attempts to construct the "Hellene" persona as a dialectical contrast to the "Nazarene" Börne and the poetic persona as a synthesis of the two positions.

Thus the gap between world view and poetic existence is not completely bridged,[100] and this disharmony conditions also the awkwardness of the persona's political posture. Heine is at great pains in *Börne* to appear as a revolutionary. He announces that he has progressed so far beyond the radicals that they no longer can see him and consequently believe he has fallen behind, although immediately following this assertion he refuses to define the differences that distinguish him from them.[101] In another place, he says that he refused to discuss political principles with Börne and that "höhere Sorgen und die Treue, die ich meinem Denken und Wollen schuldig bin" (E, 7, 104–5) forced him to break with Börne. He could not give Börne a helping hand because Börne's cause was sure to fail, while Heine was bearing the gods of the future.[102] Marxist apologists of Heine like to advert to these self-estimates without considering that assertion is not demonstration. Heine saw clearly, as did Börne, that the July Revolution had brought the great mass of the people little immediate benefit—in his preface to *Deutschland. Ein Wintermärchen* he observes that bourgeois liberties are perfectly desirable, but do little to satisfy the hunger of the masses—and the peroration to Book 2 sounds as much like Börne as anything Heine ever wrote. But Heine was more intelligent than Börne, and in addition, he had a somewhat sounder grasp of political realities. He was closer to Marxist theory in his understanding of the complexities of revolution and its timing, and in a passage on the radical Polish exiles he points out irrefutably that uproar in the streets is not the same thing as revolution.[105] Because of his anti-Philistine instincts and the hatred of plutocracy that his experiences with his Uncle Salomon had engraved on his spleen, Heine had no illusions about bourgeois liberalism and political moderation.* His scornful story of the liberals at the Hambach festival refusing to proclaim the Revolution because they feared they were not competent to speak in the name of the German people[106] prefigured the events of 1848. Heine shares with Marxists a vast disgust at Börne's deism and his late interest in Lamennais' Catholic socialism, and it was Heine who in this connection coined the phrase criticizing religion as "geistiges Opium" (E, 7, 116).

Marxists have every right to appreciate such attitudes. They may also argue wth some plausibility that Heine's insights into the structure of society were superior to Börne's and that Börne was trying to bind him to an obsolete Jacobinism.[107] They may take comfort from Heine's remark of 1844 to Gustav Kolb on Börne: "Nur ist der jetzige Communismus doch eine weit respektablere und imposantere Erscheinung als der damalige schale nachgeäffte Jakobinismus" (Hirth, 2, 554). But they have no right to claim, as Gerard Ras, for example, has done, that Heine's opposition to Börne derived from socialist thinking and that his apparent repudiation of democracy is only a distinction between natural inequality and the inequality that results from capitalism.[108] The text of *Börne* will simply not bear such an interpretation. Heine's objections to the United States, for example, are not motivated by political disagreement with liberal social struc-

* For some observations on Heine's political pessimism with respect to the intellectual ballast of the liberals at this time, see L. L. Hammerich, *Heinrich Heine: Deutschland. Ein Wintermärchen* (2d ed. Copenhagen, 1946), p. 47.

ture or even exclusively by the issue of slavery, about which he makes some very sharp remarks, but derive from the belief that American democracy means the tyranny of the mob and the equality of boors.[109] He is offended by the impertinence of a shoemaker's apprentice who dares to say at one of the radical meetings that all men are equal,* and his description of the common people as a many-headed rat-king with tails grown together is plain enough.[110] These objections do not derive from ideological opposition to "petty-bourgeois radicalism," as some Marxists would have it, but from intellectual elitism and aesthetic fastidiousness. (It is true that the behavior of the republicans and their press throughout the July Monarchy did not inspire confidence, and Heine tended to measure Börne by the yardstick of extreme radical excess.) In any case, the important thing is not that Heine had these opinions—this is well enough known—but that they are so prominently presented in *Börne*. For these opinions are precisely the substance of the charge brought against Heine by Börne, and so it is completely unclear whether Heine means that Börne's objections to him were unfounded, or whether he accepts Börne's analysis in general terms and defends only his right to be as Börne said he was.

Heine does not make matters any clearer by constructing Book 5 around a long quote from Börne's *Briefe aus Paris* that criticizes Heine in extenso. That he does this out of "coldest impartiality," as he claims elsewhere about his portrait of Börne,[111] is absurd in the context of this book. Nor can he have meant to make Börne look ridiculous, for Heine must have known, in that elusive innermost heart of his, that this critique contained a substantial portion of truth and fair judgment; of all Börne's observations on Heine, this one is the most subtle and accurate. Börne's point is that Heine is interested in political matters only insofar as they are artistically exploitable, and he gives enough pertinent

* E, 7, 79–80. One is reminded here strongly of Heine's account of his meeting with the radical Wilhelm Weitling in the *Geständnisse* (E, 6, 44), where he is not only horrified by Weitling's habit of rubbing the spots where the manacles had chafed his legs in prison, but offended that the proletarian does not remove his hat while speaking to the poet.

examples from the *Französische Zustände* to support this. Here, too, is Börne's best characterization of Heine's situation in these years:

> Uns andern miserablen Menschen hat die Natur zum Glücke nur Einen Rücken gegeben, so daß wir die Schläge des Schicksals nur von Einer Seite fürchten; der arme Heine aber hat zwei Rücken, er fürchtet die Schläge der Aristokraten und die Schläge der Demokraten, und um beiden auszuweichen, muß er zugleich vorwärts und rückwärts gehen. (E, 7, 139)

The inclusion of this passage from Börne without any substantial effort at refutation is the ultimate stage of a process in *Börne* that repeatedly erases the lines of demarcation between the fictionalized figure of Börne and the persona of the poet.

Book 5, the context in which the passage is set, is concerned with a definition of the poet-persona. It begins with some remarks on conditions in France and Germany in 1799 that the censor had struck out of *Zur Geschichte der Religion und Philosophie in Deutschland*;[112] they are illustrative of Heine's method of poeticized representation of political history. These are followed by a posture of gloomy homesickness with some atrocious nonsense about the good fortune of those imprisoned in their homeland as compared to the sufferings of the exile; the most fortunate, says Heine in anticipation of the moods of his last years, are the dead.[113] The sensitive poet has the gift of being able to feel all these things; there is a melancholy harp in his heart; he is plagued by almost nihilistic visions and dreams of helplessness and ineffectuality, and bemoans his enforced inactivity.[114] In the midst of this lament, Heine switches back momentarily to the subject of Börne; he speaks of the value of the constant presence of his own person in his account for helping the reader to a true judgment, a remark that under the circumstances has a rather wry effect. He asserts that the "aristocrats" knew that his moderation was much more dangerous than the agitation of the radicals, although he gives no reason why this should be so, and indeed the reports by Metternich's police spies do not give this impression.[115] Heine blames the radicals for weakening his effectiveness by insisting upon solidarity with them, and he claims that Börne did him a favor by attacking him and making the difference apparent.

Heine then turns to the question of the poet and his character. He will not define a poet, but defines character as integrity.[116] The true poet's character, however, is not evident from his writing, because he masters language with objective willfulness. This is a most important statement, one of the most revealing confessions in all of Heine's writing, and, as Krüger has pointed out, it reflects a theory of truth and objectivity grounded in the creativity of original genius.[117] The fact that one is a poet is prima facie evidence of inner integrity. So, with a peaceful soul, Heine magnanimously offers his hand, unsullied by the touch of the people or bribery, to Börne in the grave.[118] Heine's insistence upon the integrity and autonomy of the artist and his refusal to allow the true artist to be subordinated to party or ideology have been much admired by those who believe that the maintenance of these values is urgent to the preservation of art and the liberty of the human spirit, and it is true that Börne was not one of those who believed this, or, at least, he did not believe it very strongly. Heine had already defended this position in *Über die französische Bühne* with exemplary clarity: "ich bin für die Autonomie der Kunst; weder der Religion noch der Politik soll sie als Magd dienen, sie ist sich selber Zweck, wie die Welt selbst" (E, *4*, 525). It has not always been noticed, however, that this attitude, admirable though it may be, does not meet Börne's objections squarely. Börne complains that Heine has carried his aesthetic objectivity into the political arena, like a boy chasing butterflies on the battlefield.[119] His point, in essence, is that Heine's aesthetic system of values is irrelevant to and destructive of his posture as "ein braver Soldat im Befreiungskriege der Menschheit" (E, *3*, 281). Heine does not succeed in amalgamating these two features of the persona because deep down he agreed with Börne and could not get over the basic feeling that poet and political activist are incompatible. "Was habe ich mit Börne zu schaffen," he is reported to have said to Ferdinand Hiller; "ich bin ein Dichter!" (Houben, p. 209).*

* He did want to believe that the poet is more than the activist and includes the latter. Of Gutzkow he once remarked, "Er hat Heine nachahmen wollen, aber es fehlte ihm an aller Poesie, und er brachte es nur bis zur Nachahmung Börnes" (E, *7*, 422).

His claims in *Börne* that he is the true revolutionary stand as assertions without proof; his reference to "Willkür" in his discussion of the poet's character, on the other hand, reinforces the impression that we are witnessing the arbitrary rearrangement of reality according to artistic principles and the construction of a fictive persona. The effect of this is to throw the long quotation from Börne into high relief. It is as though Börne himself and his opinion were being absorbed into the total presentation of the persona.

Heine does not attempt to follow up the quotation with a refutation, but only asserts his faith in his own uprightness. He seems exhausted by the whole situation; thus far, he says, his career has been great, but now he is tiring. Yet he chooses as an image for himself the unshakeable Obelisk of Luxor,* a gift to a king of France located on a square named for another king of France. And then Heine quite clearly argues the incompatibility of democratic revolution and poesy that has plagued the book from the very beginning: for beauty and genius are also a kind of royalty, and no poet is possible without a faith in authority. This passage helps us to understand the meaning of the myth of the chained Messiah recounted at the end of Book 4. The time for the Messiah has not yet come, impatient as he may be; the world is not yet ready for its salvation. But the symbol of the revolution to come is not one of democracy or socialism, but of absolute authority—the Messiah will be "der rettende König der Welt" (E, 7, 125).[120]

Heine is not well served by an overestimation of his stature as a political force or as a herald of the future. His recognition of the claims of the growing urban proletariat need not be interpreted as a proto-socialist attitude, for he shared it with some very reactionary Romantics, such as Franz von Baader;[121] it is grounded in similar elitist resentment at the ugly power of capitalist parvenus (for whom Uncle Salomon and, later, Cousin Karl are the fateful prototypes), and it is equally devoid of any desire to see the common people take for themselves a genuine, freely exercised political franchise proportionate to their numbers. Nor, I believe, should we be too quick to justify Heine at Börne's expense;

* E, 7, 142. It is entertaining that in the following year he described the Obelisk as *wobbly* and thus used it as a symbol for the French government (E, *6*, 284).

Heine's view that the artist is compromised by association with the unwashed and the oppressed, or that the existence of art is dependent upon the maintenance of some form of elitist authority, would not find much of a hearing in the artistic community of any part of the world today. The political history of the modern world has shown that the forces of freedom must maintain some solidarity or, as Brecht neatly pointed out in the fourth scene of *Furcht und Elend des dritten Reiches,* the oppressors will create unity in bondage. With the cause of freedom so beleaguered in Germany in the 1830s and 1840s, Heine would have done well to keep the peace with Börne and lend his prestige to the effort to create some measure of cohesion among the radicals; Börne knew better than Heine that in times of political stress, as he put it, one must attack one's enemies and praise one's friends, no matter what they do.[122] Heine need not have abandoned his independence or compromised his artistic integrity; and with his intelligence and articulateness he might have contributed something to sharpening the thinking of the radicals that he found so inadequate.* By writing a mendacious and vindictive book against the dead Börne, Heine did no one, least of all himself, any good.

As a document in Heine's literary career, however, *Börne* is of central importance; it reveals the difficulties he had in harmonizing politics and "poesy" successfully, and it has the effect of atomizing rather than synthesizing the persona. Ludwig Marcuse has written that Heine's "Antipathie gegen Börne war die Antipathie gegen den Heine in ihm, den er nicht überwinden konnte und nicht überwinden wollte—und nicht liebte: in Börne bekämpfte Heine—den Nazarener Heine."[123] Thus the Börne of *Börne* is actually a fraction of the Heinean persona. Only by looking at it in this way is it possible to make some sense out of this very strange performance.

* There is some evidence that Heine did participate to an extent in the publishing ventures of the radicals, although these are rumors passed on by police spies about the substance of which we do not as yet know a great deal. See particularly Glossy, *Literarische Geheimberichte aus dem Vormärz* (Separatdruck aus dem *Jahrbuch der Grillparzer-Gesellschaft,* Jahrgang 21–23) (Vienna, 1912), Part 1, pp. xli, 10, 18, 24–25, and Hans-Joachim Schoeps, "Ein unbekannter Agentenbericht über Heinrich Heine," *Heine-Jahrbuch 1967,* pp. 67–80.

CHAPTER 10

Hunting Bears and Trapping Wolves: *Atta Troll* and *Deutschland*

> Ich träume mit aufgemachten Augen,
> und die Augen sehen.
>
> —ATTRIBUTED TO HEINE

Atta Troll. Ein Sommernachtstraum and *Deutschland. Ein Wintermärchen* are Heine's most ambitious attempts to solve the problem of politically relevant literature. They are also Heine's most ambitious poems, both running to over two thousand lines. They are thus distinctly major works in Heine's own career and also in the literary situation of Germany at this time, when the vexed question of the proper relationship between public affairs and literature demanded some sort of answer. The two poems are also of considerable significance for the present state of Heine's reputation. In a sense, the front of the Cold War runs right between them. They crystallize a dichotomy in Heine's attitude that has remained intact throughout the whole history of the problem of politically engaged literature.

That the two poems are closely related to one another is immediately obvious. The Shakespearean subtitles, *Midsummer Night's Dream* and *Winter's Tale,* indicate a polar contrast. Both works were ultimately composed in twenty-seven "capita," Heine's mock-epic designation for his sections, and both have, in rough terms, the form of "versifizirte Reisebilder" (Hirth, 2, 502) that Heine used to describe *Deutschland.* In view of this, it is surprising that in the critical literature the works are rarely treated primarily in relation to one another. It would seem desirable to do so, not only because of implied contrasts and formal similarities, but also for reasons of chronology. *Atta Troll* is a little difficult to date exactly. In his preface Heine stated that he began it in the late fall of 1841,[1] which Elster disputed[2] because Heine does not mention the work until a letter to Cotta of October 17, 1842;[3] Elster found it unlikely that Heine should leave so important a work lying about for a year. Jonas Fränkel, however, defended Heine's date in the Walzel edition,[4] which apparently caused Elster in his second edition to moderate his opinion somewhat, although he still stuck by it.[5] Heine's memory about the dating of his own works tended to be unreliable, but there is good reason to suspect that at least the conception of this one occurred when he said it did. First of all, its setting is inspired by Heine's vacation in the Pyrenees, the land of the *Song of Roland*, in the summer of 1841, on which occasion he used the image of the Wild Hunt in a letter.[6] Secondly, as Heine himself indicates in his preface, the work is obviously related to the aftermath of *Börne:* the defense and the consolidation of the persona as an autonomous, independent poet is the underlying formative principle of the work. But, even for Heine, the poem was very slow to develop. Not until 1843 was Heine able to publish a first version of it, and it was 1846 before the finished product was ready to be printed. A number of distractions had intervened in the meantime, among them the family feud over Uncle Salomon's inheritance, the two visits home, and the first dangerous stages in the deterioration of Heine's health. Another was *Deutschland,* which, in contrast to *Atta Troll,* was written rather quickly: the first twenty capita seem to have been composed in about six weeks at the beginning of 1844,[7] and the whole poem was ready to go to press by April.[8] Thus, from a chronological point of view, the work on *Atta Troll* surrounds that on *Deutschland,* so that, in a sense, the one phenomenon includes the other.

This fact is important because it bears directly upon our interpretation of these two contrasting poems and upon the difficult question of which of the two more nearly corresponds to Heine's own self-understanding and whether it is possible to extract a synthesis from them. In the Communist world, this question presents no difficulties; there, *Deutschland* has by far the greatest prestige of all of Heine's works. It is a central text in the education of East German schoolchildren,* and, indeed, it has been elevated

* It is recommended that 30–40% of the time spent on Heine be devoted to

to the stature of a classic of German literature. Taking Heine at his word that *Deutschland* would have "den bleibenden Werth einer klassischen Dichtung" (Hirth, *2*, 506), the outstanding Heine scholar of the DDR writes of the work that Heine created "eines der großartigsten politischen Gedichte . . . die die deutsche, ja die Weltliteratur kennt." [9] Western critics are naturally more temperate, but among the best of them *Deutschland* is also held in high esteem. Nevertheless, it seems to me that, despite the obvious excellences of *Deutschland, Atta Troll* is much the superior poem, and that this superiority is significant for our understanding of Heine's development as a poet. Because this opinion runs rather counter to the consensus, and since Heine is such a notorious touchstone for the political and social morality of those who comment upon him, I feel obliged to say that I am much more sympathetic to the general political stance of *Deutschland* than to that of *Atta Troll;* indeed, the political premises of *Atta Troll* border on nonsense. My judgment of the artistic values of the two poems is, however, the reverse. Therefore I hereby forbid any Communist commentator to describe what follows as bourgeois aestheticism, West German revanchism, or a defense of NATO.

Heine first called up the image of the dancing bear fifteen years before *Atta Troll* in *Nordsee III,* where he used it to satirize the ill-breeding of the Hanoverian nobility.[10] It is not known, I believe, whether Heine ever actually saw a dancing bear, but one suspects, at any rate, that some news story or the like may have been the original inspiration, for the passage in *Nordsee III* shows that the core of his animal fable was intact even then. It is natural enough that the comic incongruity of the dancing bear should have occurred to him again when the occasion arose to satirize what Heine regarded as the clumsy posturings of the political poets. Possibly it was recalled to him in 1840, when a number of French writers, including Heine's acquaintances Balzac, George

Deutschland. See Fritz Mende, *Heinrich Heine im Literaturunterricht* (Berlin, 1962), pp. 43–44. The East German Heine monument was designed with reliefs of which one-quarter are scenes from *Deutschland.* See Waldemar Grzimek, "Gedanken zu meinem Heine-Denkmal," *Bildende Kunst* (1956), pp. 310–14.

Sand, Musset, and Jules Janin, wrote a composite set of animal fables in which a captive bear is forced to dance but escapes, and a giraffe accuses men of falsely appropriating the hides of animals.[11] The trouble is, however, that the satire is full of irrelevancies to its object. A most capable reviewer, quoted at length by Elster,[12] pointed out at the time that the character of *Atta Troll* is incompatible with anything in reality: he is simultaneously the artist who subordinates aesthetics to political agitation, a doctrinaire communist, and an enthusiast of deism. One cannot satirize with a single symbol Georg Herwegh, Vater Jahn, Ludwig Börne, Hans Ferdinand Massmann, and Louis Blanc. Legras, observing that the categories represented by Atta Troll are mutually exclusive, commented: "La satire, en s'appuyant sur une base trop large, perd de sa force," [13] but nevertheless he is right only in a limited sense. For although Atta Troll represents nothing really existing in political reality, he is a conglomerate of Heine's antipathies. Because of this, the lines are much more clearly drawn than they are in *Börne,* and although Börne's deism (Caput 8) and his uneasiness at laughter (Caput 7) have contributed to the portrait, there is no danger of a confusion of personae such as occurs in the earlier book. Atta Troll *is* the opponent Heine means, whether he exists or not. "Phantastisch zwecklos. . . ."

For there is another confusion about this matter of contemporary poetry that cannot help but be very noticeable in *Atta Troll.* In the preface the political poets are characterized unforgettably "als Marketenderinnen der Freiheit oder als Wäscherinnen der christlich-germanischen Nationalität" (E, 2, 352) who plunge fearlessly into an ocean of generalities. The poet who must bear the brunt of the satire is Ferdinand Freiligrath (1810–76), whose lines about the Moorish prince stepping out of his white tent like the dark moon out of the light clouds supplied the motto for the poem. Heine found this metaphor horrendous (although as an optical illusion it can occur in nature), and his exploitation of it throughout *Atta Troll* is really very funny. (Perhaps he had meanwhile forgotten his own image of the black stars in *Florentinische Nächte.*[14]) Freiligrath was distinctly a minor poet, but among his contemporaries in the oppositional camp he was in some ways the most attractive character. He had begun as a defender of poetic autonomy against the more radical claims of Georg Herwegh, and his first book of poems, which included *Der Mohrenfürst,* had earned him a medal and pension from Frederick William IV; but when it became apparent that the king was not going to honor his father's promise of a constitution, Freiligrath threw up the pension and went to England, where he remained loyal to the radical exiles for a long time. Eventually, however, the pressures put on him by Marx were too great, and again he firmly insisted on his right to independence as a writer. As Peter Demetz has said, Freiligrath "in his own way anticipated and solved one of the central problems confronting the modern intellectual." * The point here is that the lines Heine found so hilarious antedate Freiligrath's career as a radical political poet. They belong to his early style of exotic poetry, which, with its overheated metaphors and outlandish rhymes, made him rather notorious; it is an imitation of a French style that followed in the wake of Napoleon's Egyptian campaign and the development of France's influence in the Near East.[15] In his preface, Heine handsomely takes note of Freiligrath's shift of position and tenders one of the very few gracious apologies of his career.[16] There is the rub, however, for the whole presumed polemic against the "Marketenderinnen der Freiheit" is vitiated by the inappropriateness of the early Freiligrath as an object of satire and also by Heine's disclaimer.

The preface to *Atta Troll* is a very carefully prepared defense. With easy contempt, Heine disposes of the Börne uproar and makes rough sport of the issue of talent versus character; he describes himself as a representative of the inalienable rights of the spirit. Yet the problem of "poesy" still troubles him. He speaks most humbly about the aesthetic value of his poem and insists that he does not mean to attack the great ideas of humanity: it is only that—and here Heine gives the game away—the great ideas are clearest and greatest in the mind of the poet.[17] This is the fundamentally undemocratic intellectual elitism that breaks

* Peter Demetz, *Marx, Engels, and the Poets* (Chicago and London, 1967), p. 101. Demetz does not call attention to the fact that after 1871 Freiligrath exhibited a regrettable susceptibility to the hurrah-patriotism of that period. See René Taube's contribution to the symposium on Realism in *Monatshefte, 59* (1967), 123.

through whenever Heine is being most himself, and it is the posture of the poet-persona in *Atta Troll.* It is given unambiguous expression in the poet's rejoinder to the philippic delivered by the bear against the rights arrogated by man:

> Ja, ich bin ein Mensch, bin besser
> Als die andern Säugetiere;
> Die Intressen der Geburt
> Werd' ich nimmermehr verleugnen.
>
> Und im Kampf mit andern Bestien
> Werd' ich immer treulich kämpfen
> Für die Menschheit, für die heil'gen
> Angebornen Menschenrechte. (E, 2, 366)

The vague sense of double entendre developed in this passage is due to the slight alienation effect achieved by the convention of the animal fable. But it is characteristic of the animal fable as a genre from Aesop to George Orwell that the animals are allegorical representations of human types, and Heine himself says in the preface to the French edition that the fable is merely a pretext for literary, political, and social allusions.[18] "Menschenrechte" must therefore be translated in this context to rights of *Aristokraten des Geistes.* But the ironic ambiguity that makes Heine so maddeningly elusive never quite comes to rest. The following three stanzas, which open Caput 7, defy definitive interpretation because Heine is cheating with language:

> Doch es ist vielleicht ersprießlich
> Für den Menschen, der den höhern
> Viehstand bildet, daß er wisse,
> Was da unten räsonniert wird.
>
> Ja, da unten in den düstern
> Jammersphären der Gesellschaft,
> In den niedern Tierweltschichten,
> Brütet Elend, Stolz und Groll.
>
> Was naturgeschichtlich immer
> Also auch gewohnheitsrechtlich,
> Seit Jahrtausenden bestanden,
> Wird negiert mit frecher Schnauze. (E, 2, 366)

Heine's vocabulary choices here quite simply cancel one another out. The pejorative word "Viehstand" is slightly alienated from Atta Troll's perspective as an animal and expresses universal contempt for the human race. *Räsonnieren* belongs to the vocabulary of the oppressors and denotes the impertinence of independent opinion in the lower ranks. The line about the "Elend, Stolz und Groll" of the poor and oppressed seems to demand some sympathy with them, and the third stanza is expressed in the language of the historical school of law that Heine continually fought as a tool of reaction. Out of context the lines could perhaps be taken as an ironic imitation by the narrator of the attitude of the reactionaries, but in context it is plain that he is in fact of the opinion that Atta Troll has a "fresh trap." No clear political posture can be read out of these lines because Heine had none. He was permanently caught between the imperatives of the age and his artistic elitism.

But these problems do not materially damage *Atta Troll* as a poem; in fact, the work is by far Heine's most successful attempt to make a virtue out of vacillation. The intent of *Atta Troll,* if one may be forgiven the critical concept, is to overwhelm all objections from all sides with a display of poetic power, and in this Heine is eminently successful. The fundamental greatness of the poem is probably to be found in its rhythm and meter. The unrhymed trochaic tetrameters are Heine's second most important verse form, after his numerous variations on the folk song or ballad stanza, and it is here enriched by a simple but immensely effective rhythmical element, the occasional substitution of a spondee for a trochee at the end of a line. Normally the spondee is made by a compound of two monosyllables bearing equal stress.[19] Although less than ten percent of the lines in *Atta Troll* have this ending, these are sufficient to give the poem its characteristic sound, a kind of ironic solemnity, constantly putting the brakes on the rising trochaic rhythm and perfectly suited to the mock-heroic atmosphere. "Die schweren Trochaën," Heine wrote to Immermann in 1830, "machen sich überhaupt im komischen Pathos sehr gut." [20] The verse form is both bound and flexible; it is light and even, but variable enough to allow Heine to display his rhythmic virtuosity. The poem was clearly composed with great care, and the manuscript shows Heine at his most meticulous.*

The poem falls roughly into two parts: the account of Atta Troll in Capita 1–11, and the description of the hunt in the remainder. But the poet-narrator makes his presence felt from the outset. At the beginning, the scene is set in a Romantic mode by comparing the Pyrenean setting to a "Traumbild" (E, 2, 355). The self-conscious Romanticizing of *Atta Troll* is one of the most prominent features of the work, and although the Romantic aspect, as is usual with Heine, remains restricted to nature metaphor and a substantial admixture of Gothic, the work shows emphatically how inextricable Romanticism and "poesy" were in Heine's mind. Insistently the poet announces at the beginning of Caput 4 that the landscape of the *Song of Roland* causes the vanished symbol of Romanticism to bloom in his heart:

> Ronceval, du edles Thal!
> Wenn ich deinen Namen höre,
> Bebt und duftet mir im Herzen
> Die verschollne blaue Blume! (E, 2, 360)

In a famous phrase of the peroration in Caput 27, the poem is called "das letzte / Freie Waldlied der Romantik" (E, 2, 422), and both in the preface and in a letter to Varnhagen of January 3, 1846,[21] Heine portrays himself, with very audible tones of regret, as the last Romantic, obliged by necessity to turn to the soberer demands of the modern world. Whether Heine was a Romantic at all is an awkward question and one that is probably not answerable in that form. But it is clear that in his thinking if not in his practice, "poesy" meant something dangerously close to insubstantial prettiness, elevated into significance only by the formal virtuosity of the sovereign artist. This accounts for the insistent disclaimer that opens Caput 3:

> Traum der Sommernacht! Phantastisch
> Zwecklos ist mein Lied. Ja, zwecklos

* By describing the manuscript of five stanzas of Caput I, Manfred Windfuhr has been able to show how carefully Heine balanced his lines and matched the images and gestures to the political allusions, in "Zu einer kritischen Gesamtausgabe von Heines Werken," *Heine-Jahrbuch 1962*, pp. 73–77.

Wie die Liebe, wie das Leben,
Wie der Schöpfer samt der Schöpfung! (E, *2*, 359)

The variants to this passage are even more emphatic; the first version in the *Zeitung für die elegante Welt* abjured all political and social relevance with the imperative line: "Wittert nicht darin Tendenzen" (E, *2*, 526), while a manuscript variant goes even farther and tries to separate poetry and prose into two worlds that do not impinge on one another:

Sucht darin nicht die Vertretung
Hoher Vaterlandsintressen;
Diese wollen wir befördern,
Aber nur in guter Prosa.

Ja, in guter Prosa wollen
Wir das Joch der Knechtschaft brechen—
Doch in Versen, doch im Liede
Blüht uns längst die höchste Freiheit.

Hier im Reich der Poesie,
Hier bedarf es keiner Kämpfe,
Lasst uns hier den Thyrsus schwingen
Und das Haupt mit Rosen kränzen! (E, *2*, 526)

Now it is self-evident that this program does not very exactly define the *Gehalt* of *Atta Troll;* there is plenty of *Tendenz,* the realm of fable is not and cannot be divorced from the world it allegorizes, and the explicitness of the political and literary satire causes the poem to mediate between the two worlds in a way that Heine does not seem to believe possible when describing his program. This mediation is concentrated in the persona, who, more than the bear, is actually the subject of the poem.

The narrator makes his presence felt at the end of Capita 1 and 2 as he watches the dancing bear with his Juliette.* Prawer has pointed out, incidentally, that Heine carefully constructed the

* For some unknown reason, this is what Caroline Jaubert called Heine's wife (Houben, p. 662); Meissner in one place calls her Julie (quoted Hirth, *6*, 63). The passage, incidentally, reveals Heine's characteristic German view of Frenchwomen as superficial, without *Gemüt,* and subject to unnatural sentiment. Cf. Henri Lichtenberger, *Heinrich Heine als Denker* (Dresden, 1905), p. 286.

persona in a way that would leave him sovereign and free from the debilitations that were actually plaguing Heine at this time; the manuscript of Caput 2 shows that he briefly yielded to the temptation to present the persona as a sick poet, but then crossed out the lines and changed the phrase to a "good German poet." [22] The logic of *Atta Troll* requires that the poet-narrator be able to react fully to stimuli and arrange things as he chooses. In Caput 3 his Pegasus carries him into the realm of fable, where the magic spring expands his perceptions so that he can see and hear the bear.[23] Throughout the work we see the poet managing his material: in his address to the reader in Caput 8,[24] in the promise of a second epic to describe the career of Atta Troll's son,[25] and in the final stanza of Caput 17, where he announces what he is about to relate.[26] In Caput 4, which adverts to the setting of the *Song of Roland,* the narrator enriches the scene with historical memories that arise in his own poetic imagination.[27] Even though the first part of the poem is about the bear, the poet's presence is constantly felt, so that the switch of scene to his hunting expedition in Caput 11 is less abrupt than it otherwise might be.

It is noteworthy that the narrator takes hardly any part in the bear hunt itself; most of the time he occupies himself with dreams and visions that round out the poetic persona; even though in Caput 14 the poet identifies himself as a bear hunter of Germany,[28] the hunting itself is done by Laskaro. This figure and his witch-mother Uraka present a real problem of interpretation. It has been suggested that the taciturn and possibly ghostly Laskaro represents reactionary government power, and his mother Uraka "Nazarene" Catholicism.[29] This would mean that reactionary power destroys the egalitarian radical with weapons made from religion. But the effect of this would be to martyr Atta Troll, which cannot be what Heine intended to do; thus the interpretation strikes one as over-subtle.* It seems more likely that Laskaro and Uraka have wandered into *Atta Troll* from the casting department of *Schauerromantik,* and thus it might not be too unfair

* Adolf Paul is, however, probably correct in his suggestion that the Cagots, the pariahs of the land, are symbols of the Jews ("Heinrich Heines 'Atta Troll,'" *Zeitschrift für deutsche Philologie, 56* [1931], 268) because of the narrator's fraternal gesture toward them (E, 2, 386).

to call them the most shallow aspect of the work. Laskaro's ghastly pallor and the indication that he might be a demon[30] suggest badly imitated Hoffmann. Laskaro is rehumanized, however, in Caput 25, when he displays unwonted pleasure at the honor accorded him as a bear slayer.[31] Similarly, the question of whether Uraka is a witch is left open in Caput 17, where the old conflict of Romanticism and rationality is left as unresolved as ever;* the passage does imply, however, that Uraka is supposed to belong to the world of "poesy." The two figures have a function in the development of the gloomy tone that echoes several times before the vision of the Wild Hunt. In Caput 13, as Laskaro sits gloomily by, the poet, melancholy and joyless, wonders whether he is not dead himself.[32] Laskaro seems here to be a projection of the darker side of the persona, which is perhaps also the satirical side, for, while Laskaro is the bear hunter, the slayer of absurdity, the poet calls himself the bear hunter in Caput 14. The task of the satirist is inimical to the liberated gaiety for which the persona strives. The passage in Caput 13 is immediately followed by a defense of sensualism in the scene of the girls rowing the boat.[33] In Caput 15 there is a sharp darkening of the imagery; Laskaro and the poet are presented as death accompanied by madness, and the landscape contains crippled trees with bloody roots.[34] While Laskaro kills a vulture in Caput 16, the poet carries on a conversation with the snow; the snow longs for the warmth and cheerfulness of the valley below, but the poet warns that the snow would be more likely to be sullied in a filthy puddle; the lonely misery of the heights is a prerequisite for purity.[35]

One senses a rather pointed concern in *Atta Troll* with the proper function of poetic imagery and scene. Here in the genuine outdoors the nature metaphors undergo a sobering transformation into banality. Caput 16 begins with the observation that from a distance the snow appears to gleam majestically in gold and purple, but upon closer inspection it turns out to be just plain snow.[36] The beginning of Caput 21 remarks ironically upon the unheroic sufferings of the narrator in the rainy weather of the mountains, which is more real but less poetic than the dangers faced by the

* E, 2, 389. Uraka is the name of a witch in a tale by Karl Musäus that Heine might have known. See *Heines Werke,* ed. Ewald A. Boucke (Berlin, 1928–30), *3*, 95.

Argonauts.[37] Elsewhere, however, Heine tries to maintain the total *ambiance* of artistic imagery. The setting in which the village children dance and play in Caput 14 explicitly suggests a painting:

> Aus dem sonn'gen Goldgrund lachen
> Violette Bergeshöhen,
> Und am Abhang klebt ein Dörfchen,
> Wie ein keckes Vogelnest. (E, *2*, 383)

In the confrontation of the poet with the children, as Prawer has pointed out in his excellent interpretation of this section, "a genuine delight in the poetry and innocence of childhood coexists with awareness, at once sorrowful and amused, of adult disillusion." [38] The fragile innocence of the children generates pure sound in the refrain of their song: "Girofflino, Girofflette!"; the introduction of these sounds, which have no denotative referent, are a recrudescence of the persistently Romantic element in Heine's aesthetics, to which he gave expression years before in *Die Bäder von Lucca,* where he spoke of "tiefe Naturlaute, wie wir sie im Volksliede, bei Kindern und anderen Dichtern finden" (E, *3*, 352.)* On the other hand, in the actual midsummer night's dream that climaxes the poem, Heine's ironic diction somewhat modifies the purely poetic quality of the vision of the Wild Hunt: we get "Spektakel"; "zum Beispiel"; Ogier the Dane in his green armor described as "ein großer Wetterfrosch"; Diana, who "Einst den Aktäon verhirschte"; and a sardonic first-person observation on the nature of women that intrudes upon the descriptive flow.[39] It seems that the bad conscience about "poesy" is still grumbling even in this eminently poetic scene.

The three phantom women of the Wild Hunt, Philipp Veit observes, "dramatize a crucial phase in Heine's development as a poet, and set pace and pattern for a reorientation already in progress." [40] The passage exhibits a compression that is extraordinary even for Heine. Out of his lean stock of philosophical and cultural ideas he takes the dichotomy of "Hellenism" and "Nazarenism," here made very much more subtle than ever before, and the notion, first argued in *Zur Geschichte der Religion und Philoso-*

* Prawer's translation of this passage, where he construes "and *some* poets" (*TS*, p. 87), slightly obscures the genuinely Romantic equation of children and poets.

phie in Deutschland,[41] that in Christian Europe the ancient gods and spirits were not abolished but demonized; from his own past he extracts his total experience with women, love, and sensuality; and through his poetic imagination he transforms these materials into a vision by means of which the allegiances of the persona are defined. In the process the clash and struggle that are evident whenever Heine directly confronts the elements of tradition which nourish his poetic consciousness are assumed into the vision of the persona, which thereby acquires a substantial degree of integration; thus the Wild Hunt of *Atta Troll* is a vital stage in the biography of the persona equal in importance to and following logically upon the stages in the *Nordsee* poems and *Das Buch Le Grand.* It is very felicitous of Veit to call the three wild huntresses imperfect muses; they are muses, in that they symbolize elements of Heine's poetic inspiration, and their imperfections are part of the dynamics of his restless spirit. Heine's permanently ambiguous relationship to the aesthetic heritages of Classical antiquity, Romanticism, and the Bible, what Veit calls the "strange combination of physical beauty and moral degeneracy," [42] and the rugged dualism of sensualism and spiritualism all are located in the consciousness of the persona and related to one another.

Upon Diana Heine performs an act of revenge. Heine accused Börne of being like a child, "welches, ohne den glühenden Sinn einer griechischen Statue zu ahnen, nur die marmornen Formen betastet und über Kälte klagt" (E, 7, 18). But the marmorean coldness of the Greek tradition troubled Heine, too. On the one hand, it impelled him to sense the Dionysian aspect of ancient Greece more clearly than was customary in his time—this is one of the aspects of Heine that connects him to Nietzsche—and to stress this aspect in *Die Götter im Exil, Die Göttin Diana,* and in the frequent appearance of the ecstatic and destructive Bacchae that appear also at the head of the Wild Hunt. On the other, Heine's trammelled sensuality generates images of the stone-cold, dead beloved, an example of which is the marble statue of *Florentinische Nächte.*[43] The unmerciful chastity of Diana is a Nazarene dissonance in the Hellenist myth, and the poet punishes the archetype of the recalcitrant beloved with terrible justice by trapping her forever in the same dilemma that tormented him:

Hochgeschürzte Tunika,
Brust und Hüfte halb bedeckend.
Fackellicht und Mondschein spielten
Lüstern um die weißen Glieder.

Auch das Antlitz weiß wie Marmor,
Und wie Marmor kalt. Entsetzlich
War die Starrheit und die Blässe
Dieser strengen edlen Züge.

Doch in ihrem schwarzen Auge
Loderte ein grauenhaftes
Und unheimlich süßes Feuer,
Seelenblendend und verzehrend. (E, *2*, 394–95)*

The metaphors of sensuality have lost the affirmative connotations of the early 1830s; they are hellish.

No revenge is taken on the Celtic fairy who bounces out of the world of Romanticism. She is purely gay and beautiful or, perhaps one should say, pretty, and totally lovable; her Romantic attractiveness, as Veit says, is "as patent as her lack of complexity and reality." [44] But Abunde is in exile on her legendary island of Avalun, the land of "poesy," as Heine remarks in the *Elementargeister,*[45] and the attitude of the persona toward her is hopelessly elegiac. The route of escape from Nazarenism into Romantic poesy is a blind alley; the poet is lonely in a world from which the Fay Abunde has been expelled. Therefore the poet confesses his love to Herodias, the symbol of the exoticism of the Orient and of Jewish sensuality (the retreat from the attitude in *Börne* is evident here), and the combination of eroticism and total cruelty.†

* A similar transformation is worked on the Biblical Susanna in the *Nachwort zum "Romanzero"* (E, *1*, 488–89).

† Hirth proposed (Hirth, *I*, xxxiii–xxxiv) that Herodias was meant to personify Cécile Furtado, who married Heine's cousin Karl. This is connected with Hirth's wildly improbable theory that Heine was Cécile's lover, abandoned her for Mathilde, and thus caused a hatred that was one of the causes of the inheritance struggle (Hirth, *5*, 282–83). E. M. Butler, who, despite her Anglo-Saxon hardheadedness, is highly susceptible to any Don Juan legend that can be imposed on Heine, cheerfully extrapolated that Diana must be Amalie, and Abunde, Mathilde, in *Heinrich Heine: A Biography* (London, 1956), p. 190. Veit spends the bulk of his article ("Heine's Imperfect Muses in *Atta Troll:* Biographical Romance or Literary Sym-

The poet remythologizes the Biblical story of the death of John the Baptist and at the same time intentionally obliterates its transcendental and prophetic intent. The Baptist, the central person of the New Testament account, interests the poet not at all; instead, he would like to free Herodias from the interaction of erotic obsession and Nazarenism:

> Ja, ich liebe dich! Ich merk' es
> An dem Zittern meiner Seele.
> Liebe mich und sei mein Liebchen,
> Schönes Weib, Herodias!
>
> Liebe mich und sei mein Liebchen!
> Schleudre fort den blut'gen Dummkopf
> Samt der Schüssel, und genieße
> Schmackhaft bessere Gerichte.
>
> Bin so recht der rechte Ritter,
> Den du brauchst—Mich kümmert's wenig,
> Daß du tot und gar verdammt bist—
> Habe keine Vorurteile—. (E, *2*, 401)

Veit is right to warn against seeing the confession to Herodias as the embodiment of religious heritage instead of as the "blending of a secularized Jewish culture with a similarly adulterated Hellenism of [Heine's] own coinage." [46] The poetic persona is engaged in an effort to disentangle erotic sensuality from Nazarene obsession, by means, as it were, of the very force of poetic exorcism. But a subterranean pressure is perceptible here, nonetheless; the Hebrew language rings loudly in the form of the name of the Holy City, "Jeruscholayim" (E, *2*, 400, 401), and the choice of the cruel and sensual Jewess over the Greek goddess and the Romantic fairy is not without significance for the direction Heine's poetic vision is to take in the ultimate stage of its development. For the present, however, Heine is engaged in combining a revalued transform of the religious posture with features of the persona drawn from the

bolism," *Germanic Review, 39* [1964], 262–73) demolishing this nonsense; it is a good illustration of the unfortunate state of Heine studies that Veit, who was concerned with supplying a really excellent interpretation of the Wild Hunt, found himself obliged to expend so much argument in laying these self-generating arguments to rest.

past: Caput 20 ends in a combination of sensual joy and melancholy: the poet sits by day at the gates of Jerusalem bewailing the dead Herodias while those who pass by believe he is lamenting the fall of the Temple and the city. The last echo of this complex is transferred in Caput 21 into the context of *Schauerromantik:* the poet's ghastly companion Laskaro lies in the lap of his mother, and the scene turns into a grotesque Pietà.[47]

In the remainder of *Atta Troll* there is a progressive withdrawal from the inner poetic world of the Wild Hunt. The death of the dancing bear, premonitory for the inevitable demise of the clumsiness and confusion he represents, is in turn prefigured by the dream of bears dancing with ghosts in Caput 21. While Laskaro goes off on the hunt again in Caput 22, the satire is turned upon another band of the narrator's enemies, the Swabian poets; in an amusing twist on the story of Beauty and the Beast, the Swabian who has been changed into a pug-dog can only be released if a pure maiden reads the poems of Gustav Pfizer on New Year's Eve without falling asleep.[48] Originally Heine had attached to this scene another long caput extending the satire to German conditions generally, along with a number of quite private allusions,[49] but in the final version of the poem Heine resisted this tendency to allow his long poems to overflow their banks and removed the section. At the beginning of Caput 23, the poet leaves the world of *Schauerromantik* and turns explicitly to rationality:

> Aus dem Spuk der Hexenwirtschaft
> Steigen wir ins Thal herunter;
> Unsre Füße fassen wieder
> Boden in dem Positiven.
>
> Fort, Gespenster! Nachtgesichte!
> Luftgebilde! Fieberträume!
> Wir beschäft'gen uns vernünftig
> Wieder mit dem Atta Troll. (E, 2, 410–11)

The final peroration of Atta Troll follows, and in Caput 25 his death and transfiguration; his epitaph reverses the charge made against Heine with respect to talent and character and is composed in the participial verse style of King Ludwig of Bavaria:

Atta Troll, Tendenzbär; sittlich
Religiös; als Gatte brünstig;
Durch Verführtsein von dem Zeitgeist,
Waldursprünglich Sanskülotte;

Sehr schlecht tanzend, doch Gesinnung
Tragend in der zott'gen Hochbrust;
Manchmal auch gestunken habend;
Kein Talent, doch ein Charakter! (E, 2, 415)[50]

Like much in *Atta Troll,* this is amusing without making much political sense, for how does King Ludwig come to be memorializing a Jacobin artist? Caput 25 returns to the brighter, bourgeois world of the poet and his Juliette, who in the meantime have acquired Atta Troll's pelt as a rug. Caput 26 describes the infidelity of Mumma and introduces us personally to Freiligrath's Moorish prince. At the end of the poem the urbane outward surface of the persona closes over the poetic depths without in any way repudiating them.

Caput 27 is an epistle to Varnhagen von Ense. It is not an integral part of the poem but rather an epilogue; the voice speaking out of it is that of the preface rather than of the narrating persona. It begins with a far from humble self-comparison to Ariosto, and then raises the question of the relationship of the poem to Romanticism and "poesy." Heine asserts that the tones of the poem are in a sense a literary atavism, punctuated with the familiar tinkling of the bells on his fool's cap:

Klang das nicht wie Jugendträume,
Die ich träumte mit Chamisso
Und Brentano und Fouqué
In den blauen Mondscheinnächten?

Ist das nicht das fromme Läuten
Der verlornen Waldkapelle?
Klingelt schalkhaft nicht dazwischen
Die bekannte Schellenkappe? (E, 2, 421)

The answer to the question is, of course, no, but it is doubtful that Heine himself was very clear about this, so closely connected in his mind were the materials of Romanticism with poetry itself; he does, however, confess to the obtrusion of "modern" elements:

> Nur daß oft moderne Triller
> Gaukeln durch den alten Grundton. (E, 2, 421)

The next stanza remarks acutely that despite the bravado of the tone there are some signs of fearful hesitation in it. The advent of the "Völkerfrühling"—by which Heine means revolution in the cause of liberty—will destroy the poem, but Heine himself has no ears for the new sounds and the new songs:

> Andre Zeiten, andre Vögel!
> Andre Vögel, andre Lieder!
> Sie gefielen mir vielleicht,
> Wenn ich andre Ohren hätte! (E, 2, 422)

The stanza, which in this form belongs to the final version of 1846, reads as though Heine were by then convinced that it was not his gift to correlate poetry to the new social and political situation.

Almost exactly midway between the conception of *Atta Troll* and the formulation of its final confession falls the composition of *Deutschland. Ein Wintermärchen.* In a letter to Campe of February 20, 1844, Heine makes propaganda for the poem in no uncertain terms. The public, he says, "wird mich in meiner wahren Gestalt sehen," and the content will be politically superior to that of the political verse that is part of the object of satire in *Atta Troll;* the versified *Reisebilder* "werden eine höhere Politik athmen als die bekannten politischen Stänkerreime" (Hirth, 2, 502). By April 17 he is hopeful that the poem will kill off "Tendenzpoesie" (Hirth, 2, 506). It is not long, however, before Heine, quite characteristically, begins to speak rather differently about it. In a letter to Campe of December 19, Heine makes his customary disclaimer that the work is unfinished and imperfect,[51] and as early as June 10 he had written to Meyerbeer that the poem was "politisch und schlecht" (Hirth, 2, 521). Now Meyerbeer was a wealthy man, and Heine may have feared that the radical poem would offend him, but nevertheless we find ourselves in our usual position of not knowing with any certainty what Heine's opinion was and thus obliged to fall back upon our own judgment.

Older critics have rejected *Deutschland* in ways that do not really meet the problem. H. G. Atkins wrote that the two poems were not to be mentioned in the same breath: reading *Deutschland* after *Atta Troll* "is to experience a plunge from the realms of serene humour and airy romantic phantasy to the level of ruthless and rather vulgar polemics"; [52] and Andler found that "le danger que recèle cette formule d'art . . . c'est que la réflexion tend peu à peu à évaporer le lyrisme." [53] But Atkins is accepting Heine's own suspicions about the nature of poetry, which are not necessarily binding, and Andler's comment is irrelevant because there is no sense in which *Deutschland* can be judged according to the criteria of lyricism: the poem is prosaic and rhetorical; its melody is spoken and not sung. *Deutschland* is written in Heine's familiar dactylic-trochaic ballad verse in a four-line stanza rhymed *xaxa,* the lines alternating four and three feet (according to traditional German metric theory, the second and fourth lines also have four beats, three filled measures and a pause). This verse form lacks the suppleness of the unrhymed trochees of *Atta Troll* and in a poem of over two thousand lines threatens to rattle monotonously over long stretches. Heine attempted to meet this difficulty while tailoring the form to its content by writing some of the most rugged verse of his career; his choppy, prosaic rhythms strain against the bonds of the meter and occasionally escape them altogether. The effect is a sound that is aggressively nonliterary,[54] and so one cannot criticize the poem by arguing that it is not lyrical. It is fair to observe with Hammerich, however, that language and style of *Deutschland* are not outstanding relative to Heine's other achievements.[55]

But the major problem of *Deutschland* lies not in its diction and verse form but in its composition as a whole. It is, of course, of no importance that Heine reverses the stages of his journey home and describes them as a journey *to* Hamburg.* But the *Reisebild* form imposes restrictions on the ordering of the material that Heine

* Even this is not done quite correctly; see L. L. Hammerich, *Heinrich Heine: Deutschland. Ein Wintermärchen* (2nd ed. Copenhagen, 1946), p. 58.

was not quite able to master. It is striking that in his letter to Campe of February 20, 1844, he speaks of "ein Cyklus von 20 Gedichten" (Hirth, 2, 502), and it is true that the various sections of the poem (although not always individual capita) are tacked together with little relationship to one another, so that the effect is to atomize the whole poem in a way that is not true of *Atta Troll*. The work is strung like a clothesline from a series of high points—the confrontation with Germany and the crossing of the Rhine, the definition of the poet's role during his tour through Cologne, the exchange with Barbarossa in the Kyffhäuser, and the final conversation with the goddess of Hamburg—and what Heine must supply in order to maintain the continuum of the journey is often slack or forced. After a very good beginning the intensity of the poem drops off in Capita 8, 9, and especially 10, the dull chapter about food, a pretty girl, and the character of the Westphalians. Caput 18, describing the poet's nocturnal anxiety in Minden, is not very memorable, and Caput 19 seems to miss some good opportunities: it begins in Bückeburg, the seat of Heine's paternal ancestors, but the description is chiefly of mud, and it concludes in Hanover, where the satire on King Ernest Augustus loses itself in stock observations and makes no references to the king's political significance—his outrageous abrogation of the Hanoverian constitution of 1837. The description of Hamburg, the account of the great fire of 1842, and the reprise of Heine's youthful satire upon the city's bourgeoisie in Capita 22 and 23 are almost a total loss. One observes in Caput 22 how hard Heine tries to extract some political significance out of the Hamburg fire by claiming that the Prussians tried to exploit the disaster by sending troops, which makes for a few clever lines but does not happen to be true.* The hyperbolic praise of Julius Campe in 23 is fun and amusing, but what of it? The very conception of *Deutschland* obliges Heine to give the persona a public character, so that the intrusion of private interests and reminiscences is very problematical and becomes increasingly so toward the end of the

* The Prussians sent army engineers to help with the explosives necessary to contain the fire. Christian VIII of Denmark did try to send troops, but was prevented. See Hammerich, *Heinrich Heine. Deutschland,* p. 108.

poem: Hamburg, with all of its memories and associations in Heine's mind, arouses in him the desire to pursue a private quarrel.

It is true in general that Heine has difficulty stabilizing the persona in *Deutschland.* In *Atta Troll* the persona is a whole creation living within the confines of the poetic imagination; in *Deutschland* the effort is made to isolate the political commitment of the persona—which was certainly not its strongest feature in *Atta Troll*—and put it into a competitive position in the realm of activist literature. There are actually two related but separate programs in *Deutschland.* The first, which appears at the beginning of the poem, is a late version of Heine's Saint-Simonianism. In contrast to "das alte Entsagungslied, / Das Eieapopeia vom Himmel," the poet offers "Ein neues Lied, ein besseres Lied" (E, 2, 431–32), and the new freedom is symbolized in terms of sexual love:

> Die Jungfer Europa ist verlobt
> Mit dem schönen Geniusse
> Der Freiheit, sie liegen einander im Arm,
> Sie schwelgen im ersten Kusse.
>
> Und fehlt der Pfaffensegen dabei,
> Die Ehe wird gültig nicht minder—
> Es lebe Bräutigam und Braut,
> Und ihre zukünftigen Kinder!
>
> Ein Hochzeitkarmen ist mein Lied,
> Das bessere, das neue! (E, 2, 432–3)

This theme continues in the conversation with the Rhine in Caput 5; the river, who longs for the lighthearted, singing and dancing French, must be told that they no longer have these qualities and are turning into Philistine philosophers just like the Germans.[56] Caput 6, however, is more closely related to the political verse Heine was writing just around this time, and it exhibits the two outstanding qualities of that verse: it is totally negative and destructive, and it is impelled by the belief that the word is a weapon—a theme picked up in the final peroration in Caput 27, where the poet-persona, identified as the son of Aristophanes, warns the kings of the poet's power to pronounce inescapable damnation. The famous scene of the lictor who follows the poet about and will in the future wreak practical destruction on the objects of the poet's damnation shows both features of the persona as political poet quite clearly. Hammerich has pointed out that the poet has not seen the lictor for a number of years[57]—that is, he has not given expression to such revolutionary ideas for some time. In the following caput the lictor becomes the angel of death in the strange dream in which the poet requires of his companion, by way of illustration of this relationship, the destruction of the Three Kings of Orient whose remains were believed to be preserved in the Cologne Cathedral. What is remarkable about this dream is that the poet marks the doorposts of those upon whom he pronounces doom with blood that gushes from his own heart, and at the end, when the Three Kings are hacked to pieces by the lictor, streams of blood pour from the poet's breast. The only possible interpretation of this scene is that put on it by Prawer: "the dreamer is involved, in the most intimate way, with the very things he has pledged himself to destroy." [58]

Here, and sporadically throughout the poem, the revolutionary commitment of the persona is subjected to a kind of subliminal qualification. The double entendre in Caput 12—"Ich bin ein Wolf und werde stets / Auch heulen mit den Wölfen"—has frequently been noted (E, 2, 456)[59] and indeed the whole passage has a false ring. The poet is clearly playacting when he gets up on his soapbox, as it were, and engages in the rhetorical demagoguery that elsewhere has so often drawn his scorn; the posture ("Positur," Heine calls it) is that of an after-dinner speaker at a radical conclave and combines imbecile platitudes with ironically pejorative diction:

> Mitwölfe! Ich bin glücklich, heut'
> In eurer Mitte zu weilen,
> Wo so viel' edle Gemüter mir
> Mit Liebe entgegenheulen. (E, 2, 455)

This is the oratory of Atta Troll. Moreover, considering the state of Heine's relations with the radicals at that time, the thanks he gives for the trust they have put in him can only be pure irony. It is, to be sure, a tactic; when Heine was angry and frightened at the ban Prussia placed on Campe's publishing house in 1841, he asserted that he would make common cause with the "demagogues"; at the same time he stressed his distaste for them.[60] In *Atta Troll* this sort of alliance shows up as a maneuver only. It appears that the poet is less joining the wolves than attempting to trap them; he means to mollify them by pretending to be on their side, and, trusting in the dullness of their perceptions, to maintain his independence through veiled scorn.*

The great scene with Barbarossa also ends on a somewhat ambiguous note. Heine was often at his very best when manipulating the materials of folklore, and the scene is justly famous. The preparation for it reaches poetic intensity briefly at the beginning of Caput 14 with its exploitations of the folk song refrain, "Sonne, du klagende Flamme," but the section ends in irony, for the song, like the legend of Barbarossa, belongs to superstition and old wives' tales. In Caput 15 Barbarossa is demythologized into a bumbling old man who speaks in a flood of old saws justifying inaction, and in 16 the poet demeans the emperor further by addressing him with the familiar *du* and using him as an example in a cheerful account of the function of the guillotine. At the end of this caput the poet comes to the conclusion that the emperor is no longer needed and should sleep in his mountain forever, but he changes his mind again in Caput 17. The reason is that the restoration of the real medieval empire with all its injustices and terrors would be preferable to the phoniness of present-day Germany with its hybrid institutions (the symbol of which is Frederick William IV—compare the similar motifs in the poem *Der neue Alexander*[61]). The attitude is understandable in view of the persistent anachronisms of nineteenth-century Germany, but one senses in it also an undertone of Heine's desire for clear hierarchical distinctions in the affairs of men.

In the conversation with his mother in Caput 20, which is constructed like the dialogue in a fairy tale or folk song, the poet evades questions about his political feelings and refuses to admit to any party commitment. Caput 23, at the outset of the conver-

* In a letter to Dumas père in 1855, he remarked that the wolves who had beleaguered him at times in the forest had never frightened him (to Alexandre Dumas, Feb. 8, 1855; Hirth, *3*, 591).

sation with Hammonia, presents a most interesting state of affairs. In the manuscript, the poet on returning to Hamburg misses the streetgirls he used to know; Hammonia recites their names and tells him that they have passed away with the old times, and she connects their disappearance with liberal progress:

> Die Reste der Vergangenheit
> Verwittern und verschwinden,
> Du wirst jetzt auf der Schwiegerstraß'
> Ein neues Deutschland finden. (E, 2, 547)

The poet confesses that he has a certain sentimental attachment to the old:

> Ja, ich gesteh', es hängt mein Herz
> Ein bißchen an dem alten
> Deutschland noch immer, ich denke noch gern
> An die schönen verlornen Gestalten.

This passage, then, qualifies the poet's political commitment. In the published version, however, Heine made a substantial and important revision; here the *Saint-Simonian* program is subjected to doubt. The vanished girls no longer represent the passing of an old world, but now symbolize the ancient theme of the transitoriness of all earthly things:

> Du findest die holden Blumen nicht mehr,
> Die das junge Herz vergöttert;
> Hier blühten sie—jetzt sind sie verwelkt
> Und der Sturm hat sie entblättert.
>
> Verwelkt, entblättert, zertreten sogar
> Von rohen Schicksalsfüßen—
> Mein Freund, das ist auf Erden das Los
> Von allem Schönen und Süßen! (E, 2, 482)

This passage is a bridge between the developing pessimism of the *Verschiedene* and poems of *Romanzero* such as *Pomare*. Thus, *both* programs of *Deutschland* fail to stand firmly throughout the poem.

The conversation with Hammonia gets off to a limping start; Caput 24 vacillates between the old dislike of Hamburg and the poet's need that its goddess should treat him as an important personage. The poet is lost in homesick reveries, including references to Uncle Salomon and the Calvary of his youthful love; ludicrously he asserts that, unlike the patriotic poets, he modestly hides his wound from the public.[62] The climax of the dialogue is the vision of the future of Germany seen in Hammonia's chamber pot, one of Heine's most tantalizing and elusive passages. The poet claims that he made a promise to Hammonia to keep to himself what he saw, and so he only drops hints that are very unclear. Kaufmann claims that the stink and filth of the chamber pot represent the future of "Altdeutschland," [63] but this interpretation is ideologically motivated and is not supported very well by the text, especially when one looks at the variants.[64] The passages in the variants are difficult to understand, for it seems on the one hand that the stink comes from the recrudescence of reaction and religion, and on the other from the slaughter of the scoundrels in the inevitable revolution:

> Es roch nach Blut, Tabak und Schnaps
> Und nach gehenkten Schuften—
> Wer übelriechend im Leben war,
> Wie mußt' er im Tode duften! (E, 7, 630)

Tobacco, as will be remembered from the passage in *Börne* explaining why Heine could not take part in radical meetings,* [65] is for him always an unpleasant attribute of the atmosphere of radical politics. A stanza Heine kept in the text, referring to Saint-Just's mot that revolutions are not made with musk and rose water,[66] supports the interpretation that the vile vision refers to the Revolution as a whole. By cutting the passage, however—Heine left dashes to show where the cuts were made[67]—the meaning is obscured even further than it is in the variants, and we are left with what looks like a muddled political equivocation.

Moreover, it is striking and perhaps even somewhat frightening that this equivocation should be connected with the most stupendously disgusting posture of the poet-persona to be found anywhere in Heine's writing. One is tempted to say that only a psy-

* See also Gutzkow's graphic account of Heine's unease at such meetings, Houben, pp. 220–21.

chiatrist could offer a satisfactory interpretation of the poet, who from beginning to end wrestles with images of his own dignity, with his head in a chamber pot. How even a doctrinaire Marxist can live easily with this scene is hard to understand. Against the background of the aesthetic idealism that Heine uneasily inherited from his German tradition, it is possible to say that this posture is symbolic for the poet, who, in spite of his divine calling, is forced by hateful circumstance to descend to the satirical treatment of a foul reality. Perhaps Schiller would have understood the scene in this sense, given the unlikely possibility that he could have stomached it at all. Even taken in such terms, however, the scene belies any effort to define the poet of *Deutschland* as the true Heine; the contrast to the laboriously generated self-image is too stark and obvious. Beyond this, one can only speculate, but the proximity of what looks very much like an attack of anal infantilism to the scenes describing the poet's reunion with his mother makes one ponder; it is as though the effort to run with the wolves has so overstrained the poet's self-conception that it has resulted in a brief outbreak of insane regression.

One cannot claim, in view of all this, that *Deutschland. Ein Wintermärchen* holds together as a whole; its composition is forced and awkward, and the fictionalized persona is placed in an uncomfortable role that is not convincingly sustained if one looks at the poem closely. This is not to say that the poem lacks greatness in detail; it is, after all, a work of Heine, a central fact once amusingly stressed by Alfred Döblin.[68] It is full of memorable passages: the poet crossing the border with his contraband in his head;[69] the erect Prussian soldier who looks as though he has swallowed the stick he was beaten with;[70] the whole treatment in Caput 4 of the Cologne Cathedral and the project to complete it (a good example of the advantages of Heine's destructive negativism for rhetorical effect, although it is both entertaining and characteristic that Heine himself was involved in a minor way in fund raising for the Cathedral project[71]); the ruminations in Caput 11 on what the state of Germany would be if Varus had won the battle of the Teutoburg Forest. The centerpiece of the poem, the scene with Frederick Barbarossa, is very skillfully managed. But as a total artistic achievement, *Deutschland* has grave weaknesses and, furthermore, if there is such a thing as a category of truth that can be applied to a work of art, in terms of the attitude of the persona *Deutschland* has less of it than *Atta Troll.* Yet, though the Communists may overestimate the value of the poem, it does not seem to me that the East Germans are wrong to give it a prominent place in teaching literature; there is little enough in German literature in the nineteenth century that calls things by their right names.

CHAPTER 11

The Elusive Novel: *Der Rabbi von Bacherach*, *Schnabelewopski*, and *Florentinische Nächte*

> What I most need to do is to record experiences, not in the order in which they took place—for that is history—but in the order in which they first became significant for me.
> —LAWRENCE DURRELL, *Justine*

Heine's lack of complete success with traditional literary forms other than poetry, the mock-epic, and, we should add, the essay, has often been remarked upon. This fact in and of itself is not remarkable; Hebbel, after all, wrote no novels, Thomas Mann wrote no poetry worth mentioning, and Rilke wrote no memorable plays. It attracts our attention only because of the repeated frustrations Heine met in trying to write in genres to which he does not seem to have come naturally; he shared with Goethe and most of the major German writers of the nineteenth century a desire to excel in every branch of literature. But Heine's formal genius was *sui generis;* everything he touched quickly took on original and characteristic shapes, and when he tried to adapt himself to the familiar conventions of dramatic and narrative genres he almost always ran into trouble.

It is customary to ascribe these failures to that convenient abstraction, subjectivity. But the problem becomes more differentiated the closer one looks at it. With some plausibility, although, I believe, not a great deal of exactness, the issue of subjectivity may be raised in connection with Heine's plays. It is less compelling an argument with respect to Heine's efforts with the novel and the *Novelle,* for a severely subjective point of view need by no means be incompatible with prose art. Furthermore, many of the determining factors in Heine's three disappointments in these efforts are rather different from one another. In *Der Rabbi von Bacherach,* he set himself a most ambitious task that, frankly, was beyond his powers. *Schnabelewopski* is a case of an experiment gone awry. The weaknesses of *Florentinische Nächte* are to a considerable extent conditioned by external circumstances. In all three cases, however, there are failures in controlling the fictive persona.

Interpretations of *Der Rabbi von Bacherach* are often dependent upon the credence given to Heine's assertion that the bulk of the work was destroyed by the fire in his mother's house in 1833. Here one encounters the usual problems in operating with information Heine himself supplies. There is reasonable doubt that there ever was much more to the work than the fragment we now possess. Heine's own progress reports are persistently vague. On June 25, 1824, he wrote to Moser that one-third was written;[1] four months later he spoke of some editorial work, but still remarked that "kaum ⅓ davon geschrieben ist" (Hirth, *I,* 183). In March of the following year, he wrote to Ludwig Robert that he had written little and that the *Rabbi* was "noch nicht zur Hälfte fertig" (Hirth, *I,* 196). For the next eleven months he asked Moser repeatedly for information, but spoke always of the work on the *Rabbi* as something to be done, never as something completed;[2] in April, 1825, he said that it lay on his soul like a hundredweight.[3] Over a year later Heine talked to Leopold Zunz about including the *Rabbi* in *Reisebilder II,* "und zwar sehr beschnitten" (Hirth, *I,* 263), which at least suggests that there may have been no more of it extant then than there was after the fire. Only at the time of the publication in 1840 does Heine allege, in two letters to Campe[4] and in the note appended to the fragment,[5] the loss of the remainder. Of the situation in general, Erich Loewenthal observed: "Daß Heine diese Handschrift der Anfangskapitel und seine sonstigen Vorarbeiten für den 'Rabbi' nach Paris mitgenommen, die Fortsetzung dagegen mit anderen Papieren bei seiner Mutter gelassen haben soll, wo sie dann durch Feuer zugrundegegangen sei, ist völlig unglaubhaft." [6] The first two chapters of the manuscript are in a secretary's hand, revised by Heine, and the third in Heine's own hand,[7] indicating that the latter may have been written at the time of publication in 1840. Studies of the manuscript by Hirth[8] and, more recently and more thoroughly, by Franz Finke,[9] make it highly probable, if not completely certain, that the dating of the composition corresponds to the dates of the manuscripts.[10] The abrupt shift in style supports these assumptions.

Interpretations of the *Rabbi* have usually followed the theory developed by Lion Feuchtwanger in 1907.[11] Feuchtwanger identifies two separate plans. The first is motivated by Heine's contact, beginning in the fall of 1822, with the "Verein für Kultur und Wissenschaft der Juden" in Berlin and is to be an ethnic description in the manner of Sir Walter Scott contrasting Jewish life with its hostile environment. This plan envisions a passionate polemic against the Christian world and its centuries of persecution of the Jews. The immense epic plan is eclipsed, however, by Heine's more immediate anguish in the face of his forthcoming baptism; in the second plan the focus is shifted from the historic Jewish situation to the conflict between the traditional Jewish world and the modern emancipated Jew. The work is to become the arena where Heine wrestles for justification of his apostasy. It can be pointed out in passing that the medieval setting is no longer suitable for the second plan; a clearly modern issue has been introduced. Indeed, in the second plan, the contrast between Hellenism and Nazarenism is to be worked out for the first time, and Heine's representative in the work, Don Isaak Arbarbanel, is to displace Rabbi Abraham as the hero.

The theory is plausible and deserving of respect, but, aside from general methodological considerations, it is open to three main objections. First of all, it is doubtful whether one should stress Heine's torment preceding the conversion. Heine (and his family) must have been aware from the beginning of his legal studies that licensing would probably entail an official conversion to Christianity. Although this step was made more difficult and embarrassing by the revival of Heine's sense of Jewishness through his work in the "Verein," as his troubled comments in a famous letter to Moser of 1823 indicate,* at no time did he waver from his original intention to obtain a law degree. Heine's discouragement was much deeper after the conversion, when he was subjected to attack from both Christians and Jews, and there is no sound evidence that any work on the *Rabbi* was done after the conversion.† Secondly, as Feuchtwanger himself admits, "die Darstellung dieses zweiten Plans wird dadurch erschwert, daß von seiner Ausführung nichts erhalten ist, daß wir hier im wesentlichen auf ganz allgemeine Andeutungen in Heines Briefen angewiesen sind." [12] The reconstruction is purely hypothetical. An analysis of the third chapter does not help here, because there is no reason to believe that it necessarily reflects part of the original of 1824/25. Third, and most important, the theory, even if accepted, does not adequately explain why the work could not be finished. The assumption that the author's basic concerns shifted in the course of the work does not dispose of the problem. We shall see later that Heine was quite capable of coping with such conflicting attitudes if cast in a form he could manage. Only by examining the fragment itself, quite apart from biographical considerations, can we determine why "das arme, flügellahme Werk" [13] resisted completion.

The plot of the *Rabbi* is easily retold. The fragment begins with a general description of the situation of the medieval Jews in the Rhineland and introduces Rabbi Abraham and his household on the night of the Passover feast. Two strangers come to the feast, and the Rabbi extends to them traditional hospitality. In the course of the dinner, however, he is horrified to discover that the strangers have smuggled in the body of a child in order to fabricate a charge of ritual murder. During a hand-washing ceremony, the Rabbi and his wife Sara flee from Bacherach up the Rhine and Main to Frankfurt. In the second chapter they wander through the crowds of the Frankfurt fair to the ghetto, where they are admitted after some difficulty. They attend the holiday services in

* "Wie Du denken kannst,—kommt hier die Taufe zur Sprache. Keiner von meiner Familie ist dagegen, außer ich. . . . Ich werde noch aus Aerger katholisch und hänge mich auf" (to Moser, Sept. 27, 1823; Hirth, *I*, 107–08).

† Heine was baptized on June 28, 1825. The letters following show no progress on the *Rabbi*, except possibly for the cryptic remark to Moser on July 1 that the contrast between Heine and Goethe will be found in the work (Hirth, *I*, 217).

the synagogue, which are seen from the perspective of the women's gallery. The satirical presentation is interrupted by a fainting fit of Sara, who has heard the Rabbi recite the prayer for the dead for those left behind in Bacherach. The third chapter opens with Sara's recovery and the end of the service, whereupon the Rabbi encounters an old friend from his student days in Spain, Don Isaak Abarbanel, the nephew of a famous sage of Spanish Jewry but himself an apostate. The fragment ends as Abraham, Sara, and Don Isaak sit down to the holiday meal. At the close is appended a note asserting that the rest of the novel has been lost "ohne Verschulden des Autors" (E, *4,* 488).

Very little that Heine wrote lacks the touch of his genius, and the *Rabbi* is no exception; there is much in it to be praised. In the opening four paragraphs, Heine narrows the perspective step by step from a large historical canvas to a portrait of a single individual. In the first paragraph he describes the Rhine setting of Bacherach (*recte* Bacharach), calling attention in the final sentence to the Jewish community there. The second paragraph recites the history of medieval persecutions in this area, with particular attention to the accusation of well-poisoning during the Plague and the charge of ritual murder arising out of the "martyrdom" of St. Werner; the final sentence carries us up to the present time of the story. The third paragraph introduces us to Rabbi Abraham, his strange marriage, and his studies in Spain; the last sentence fixes the present time more exactly as the night of the first Passover *seder.* The fourth paragraph gives a general description of the Passover feast; the action proper can now get under way. With the greatest economy Heine has mastered a difficult setting and situation, the details of which are likely to be unfamiliar to non-Jewish readers,* and has presented them in such a way as to make the disaster that follows perfectly comprehensible. Nor does Heine's art fail elsewhere. The description of the *seder* itself, with its richness of detail, is famous in its own right, and Rabbi Abraham's

* The fact that Heine is mistaken in some details of the ritual, including the calendar date of the first *seder* (E, *4,* 453 and n. 1), is of no importance here. For a general discussion of inaccuracies in Heine's Jewish materials, including those of the *Rabbi,* see Israel Tabak, *Judaic Lore in Heine. The Heritage of a Poet* (Baltimore, Md., 1948), pp. 83–92.

eerie, forced gaiety after discovering the body under the table is a successful evocation of genuine horror. The scene in the Frankfurt ghetto exhibits some of Heine's most skillful caricature, and the presentation of the atmosphere in the women's gallery of the synagogue is maliciously apt. We shall not be able to account for the failure of the novel by claiming a dearth of descriptive power or of creative imagination.

It will be more fruitful to ask whether or not there are formal structural difficulties that cripple the forward movement of the novel. To do this we must establish the structural pattern implicit in the fragment as we have it, and thus turn our attention not primarily to *Gehalt,* which involves us in speculative considerations, but to *Gestalt,* taken in a broad sense, where the necessary materials are before us. Here we can identify four separate epic tensions that demand resolution. The first is the conflict between the threatened Jewish people and their Christian environment, the second the guilt Rabbi Abraham incurs by abandoning his family and congregation to the pogrom, the third the apparent paradox of the high ideals and aspirations of Israel compared with the shabby and ridiculous bearing of Israel in the ghetto, and the fourth the conflict of type between Rabbi Abraham and Don Isaak Abarbanel. These are the limits of discourse in what Heine is known to have written. By examining the potentialities and difficulties inherent in them, we will discover what possibilities remained for completing the novel.

With respect to the first conflict, Feuchtwanger is of the opinion that a real basis for plot does not exist because "es findet in dem Werk eigentlich kein Kampf statt, sondern nur eine ständige Niederlage." [14] Be that as it may, it is apparent that Heine drops the task of developing the conflict almost as soon as he takes it up. The point where this happens can be precisely identified. The conflict is between the Jewish world and the Christian world. The Jewish world is concentrated and individualized in Rabbi Abraham and his entourage. The Christian world, the great amorphous antagonist that breaks in suddenly upon the Jewish world from without, is concentrated and symbolized in the two strangers who, masquerading as fellow Jews, smuggle the body of the child under the table in order to set up the charge of ritual murder. In contrast, however, to his detailed development of the protagonist, Heine does nothing to characterize the representatives of the Christian world; they function only as a mechanism to move the plot forward. It may be, as Feuchtwanger suggested, that Heine's purpose was "den Judenhaß als etwas nicht auf Individuen Zurückzuführendes, sondern als etwas Typisches, in seiner dunklen Gestaltlosigkeit zwiefach Schaudervolles und zwiefach schwer zu Bekämpfendes erscheinen zu lassen," [15] but the conflict cannot be effectively treated in this fashion. As soon as the true mission of the two strangers is made clear—it is not explained until the flight of Rabbi Abraham and Sara is in progress—all sorts of questions begin to plague the reader. What did the two men look like? How did they behave during the *seder* ritual? It is extremely uncommon for non-Jews to be familiar with the *seder,* because according to Biblical law the uncircumcised may not be invited to participate (Exod. 12:48). Thus it would have been difficult for Gentiles to masquerade as Jews on this occasion. (To be sure, Heine may not have known this; his knowledge of Jewish law was spotty.) Were the two men, then, possibly apostate Jews? * Such a possibility, though contributing to the horror of the situation, would lead somewhat away from the theme of the conflict. Is the mission of the two men official, a scheme devised by Church and state, or is it a spontaneous action? To what extent is the force they represent monolithically and violently anti-Semitic? The answers to these questions or any form of characterization of the strangers would have identified the outside force that exerts pressure on the Jews. As it is we have a clearly delineated protagonist, but no comprehensible antagonist. By failing to do this at the critical moment, Heine permits the whole thrust of his magnificent exposition, with its progressive concentration, to be dissipated to the vanishing point. The Christian world can no longer be the enemy of the Jews and cannot represent one side of a conflict. It is reduced to a mindlessly hostile environment. Although the theme is revived again in Chapter 2 in the person of the cheerfully cold-

* Heine's cousin Hermann Schiff believed this, as he argued in *Heinrich Heine und der Neuisraelitismus. Briefe an Adolf Strodtmann* (Hamburg and Leipzig, 1866), p. 16. Schiff, however, was a confused man and his judgments are not worth much. See below, Appendix 2, pp. 452–53.

blooded drummer who guards the gates of the Frankfurt ghetto, the connection with the opening presentation can no longer be made because the continuity of development has been broken; by reducing the two strangers to a mere function of plot, the reader's attention is allowed to drift away from this concern.

The second tension, which is established by Rabbi Abraham's abandonment of his household, presents real difficulties. Every interpreter is baffled and uneasy at Heine's offhand treatment of this sinister act. For the reader it is another exercise in frustration. Here Rabbi Abraham, entrusted with the care of his flock, gives them no warning when disaster strikes, but sneaks away with his wife. Although he tells her that only he is in danger and that the others will merely be plundered, he recites for them on the next day the prayer for the dead, showing that he knew they would be killed. Thus Rabbi Abraham is not only a coward but a liar. So much we are willing to accept—an author has, after all, the right to draw his characters as he pleases—but we expect this action to take some toll of torment upon the Rabbi. There is no sign of it. On the morning afterward he is "heiter lächelnd" (E, *4*, 463); following the service, where he has said the prayer for those left to their fate, he meets his wife "mit heiterem Antlitz" (E, *4*, 482), and throughout Chapter 3 he banters cheerfully with Don Isaak. The situation as it stands is both improbable and intolerable. There are only two possible solutions to the problem; either the question of the Rabbi's guilt is entirely bypassed because it inconveniently arises out of the mechanism that motivates his flight, or the reaction to the guilty act is delayed and postponed to bear fruit later, while the Rabbi's cheerfulness represents only a repression of torment. If we assume the first, then the question of the failure of the *Rabbi* is adequately answered; if Heine cannot motivate the elements of plot any better than this, the whole undertaking is doomed. The second possibility cannot be discussed without becoming hopelessly involved in speculation about the subsequent development of the novel. But two difficulties present themselves at once. If it is assumed that the novel was to progress through scenes of flight and misery, then from an aesthetic point of view this flight is already sufficiently motivated by the curse of the Rabbi's father-in-law, "Sieben Jahr sollt ihr betteln gehn!" (E, *4*, 461). Moreover, the calm cheerfulness that the Rabbi exhibits bears no resemblance to the nervous hilarity that was a transparent mask for his terror at the *seder* table. Heine would have had to cope with this problem somehow if he meant to complete the novel.

The third structural tension is the contradiction between the high mission of Israel and its unfortunate reality. Here Heine set himself a difficult task. To combine this dialectic with the first conflict, that of the Jewish people with its environment, demands great skill, because it means defining as the collective hero of an epic struggle a people almost totally lacking in conventional heroic qualities. Today of course we know that this can be done, but in terms of the techniques available to the novel in the early nineteenth century, Heine would have had to produce a creative breakthrough of large proportions. That the problem is in some sense explicit in the fragment is shown by the fact that it is Rabbi Abraham who makes the pithy observation, "Sieh, schöne Sara . . . wie schlecht geschützt ist Israel! Falsche Freunde hüten seine Thore von außen, und drinnen sind seine Hüter Narrheit und Furcht!" (E, *4*, 474). Any solution of the problem on the basis of the fragment, however, is made difficult because no real sense of the greatness of Israel is communicated in it. The descriptions of the *seder* and the synagogue service, vivid as they are, are more a reflection of an aesthetic interest in the ritual and of Romantic fascination with the exotic than of symbolization of inner values. Thus there is no sufficient counterweight against the satiric presentation of what is ridiculous in Israel, so that the position of the protagonist is eroded. Although the Rabbi's calm dignity is put in striking contrast to the characteristics of Jäkel the fool, Nasenstern, and Rindskopf, his own force is weakened by the guilt he bears. Heine's fundamental anti-clericalism and the strong satirical elitism of his aristocratic mind made it impossible for him to sustain for very long a sympathetic account of pious folkways. Lasher-Schlitt is perfectly right to say that "with the second chapter Heine's subconscious antagonism comes to the fore." [16]

The fourth antithesis, that between Rabbi Abraham and Don

Isaak, belongs exclusively to the third chapter. There is scarcely a hint of it in the earlier part, except for the rumor, immediately denied,

> daß Rabbi Abraham auf der hohen Schule zu Toledo zwar emsig genug das Studium des göttlichen Gesetzes getrieben, aber auch christliche Gebräuche nachgeahmt und freigeistige Denkungsart eingesogen habe, gleich jenen spanischen Juden, die damals auf einer außerordentlichen Höhe der Bildung standen. (E, *4*, 452).

This suggests that the Rabbi may have had to overcome difficulties in a confrontation with the urbane world of Spanish Jewry. Of such an inner conflict no trace remains in the third chapter; the contrast is externalized in the persons of the Rabbi and the newly introduced character. This is one point at which it is impossible to ignore the probable genesis of the fragment. The third chapter of 1840 is so different in style and theme from the preceding chapters that it is clear Heine no longer was willing to carry through the implications of his original structure. The *Rabbi,* published in the same year as *Börne,* is similarly concerned with the theme of "Hellenism" versus "Nazarenism." The third chapter presents this theme without regard for the unresolved tensions remaining from the first two, and yet it is clear that the earlier interests cannot be entirely displaced by this one without destroying the structure of the whole. The new conflict further undermines the position of the protagonist vis-à-vis the hostile environment, makes it even more difficult to develop the traditional values of Judaism, and turns the Rabbi's guilt into a blind motif.

If it is agreed that the *Rabbi* is doomed partly by the overambitious nature of its conception, it is worth pointing up another aspect of the fragment that contributes to the difficulty of the undertaking. The work is clearly an attempt at a Romantic novel with Jewish materials. This synthesis is apparent in a number of places in Heine's work,[17] and it is not only particularly prominent in the *Rabbi,* but particularly unsuccessful. The Romantic aspect of the fragment is apparent in many details: the attention to Spanish and Jewish-Oriental exotica, the moonlit Rhine landscape of the flight with its reference to the hoard of the Nibelungs, the mysterious mute boatman who gazes on Sara with unexplained significance, the folktales of the Teufelskädrich and the Wispertal remembered by Sara from her childhood, the tournament staged by Kaiser Max in Frankfurt, to name only the most obvious. The effort at synthesis is evident, but not without incongruities. The Romantic landscape belongs to Christian Europe; the Jews of the fifteenth century do not live in it.* *Rheinromantik* comports badly with the cramped, urbanized culture of the medieval ghetto, isolated as it is from the land and nature. Moreover, elementary verisimilitude obliges Heine to emphasize the wall that separates Jewish life from the ethos around it. Thus Sara's father chides her aunt for filling the girl's head with the folktales of the Rhine region,[18] and as Sara marvels at the luxurious wonders of the Frankfurt fair, Rabbi Abraham must continually warn her, "Mach die Augen zu, schöne Sara" (E, *4,* 464, 466, 467). The attempted synthesis is at its most maladroit where Rabbi Abraham throws his last possession, a silver basin, into the Rhine as an offering of appeasement to the Almighty.[19] This bit of primitive magic, though Romantically appealing, has no place in the mainstream of Jewish thought, which does not include sacrifice to appease an irrationally angry God, and thus it jars badly with Rabbi Abraham's symbolic character and the tenor of Jewish ritual elsewhere in the fragment.

The foregoing considerations show a widening breach between *Gehalt* and *Gestalt,* and to some extent between *Gehalt* and *Stoff.* Heine's sense of form was acute, and it cannot be expected that he would continue to suffer indefinitely over a work in which the formal elements are from the very beginning in such disarray. It is probably out of a sense of this failure of form that Heine remarked to Moser, quite early in the course of his work on the *Rabbi*: "Bei dieser Gelegenheit merkte ich auch daß mir das Talent des Erzählens ganz fehlt; vielleicht thue ich mir auch Unrecht es ist bloß die Sprödigkeit des Stoffes" (Hirth, *1,* 172).

* Neither did Heine, as Jules Legras pointed out in *Henri Heine Poète,* pp. xi–xii. It should be remembered that the landscape around Düsseldorf is not "Rhineland" in the Romantic sense. It is flat and uninspiring, and consequently Heine's exploitation of the landscape of the Rhine is more likely to be a reflection of an impression from literature rather than from actual sensory experience.

In this regard it is pertinent to ask what future the thematic conflicts of the *Rabbi* were to have in Heine's later work. The first two do not play an important part subsequently. Never again did Heine attempt an epic presentation of the struggle between the Jews and the Christian world. Nor does the type of guilt that the Rabbi acquires have an analogue in the later work; tragic situations founded in guilt, whether in a Jewish setting or not, are not a feature of Heine's writing. The contrast between the real and the ideal in Israel, however, finds classic expression in Heine's late poem, *Prinzessin Sabbat,* where the shabby, absurd Jew is transformed into a prince in his own domain on the Sabbath day. Here Heine succeeds in doing what he could not do in the more ambitious form of the *Rabbi*: he communicates a sense of the spiritual force of Israel that transforms and transcends the dismal external reality. But from the point of view of inner form the chief difference between the novel and the poem is the character of the narrator or speaker. In the *Rabbi* this feature is by no means consistent. The first chapter presents a narrator who is a passionate partisan of the Jews; the illusion of dry objectivity in the exposition is merely a device to allow the terrible facts to imply the accusation. In the second chapter the character of the narrator already begins to change; satire and irony start to prevail, and the descriptions of Rindskopf praying and of the holiday service in the synagogue fasten almost exclusively on external detail. The narrator is no longer completely a Jewish partisan, but begins to exhibit the features of an informed observer who describes the visible characteristics of curious customs. In the poem no such confusion is present. The speaker is outside the contrast, not involved in it, and he can operate with incongruous metaphors and allusions. The speaker views from the perspective of European culture and treats his subject with balanced irony: both the Jew as "Hund mit hündischen Gedanken" and, on the Sabbath, as "Mensch mit menschlichen Gefühlen" (E, *1*, 433) have equal truth. Moreover, the poem is written in Heine's brilliant last style, with its fine mastery of diction and rhythm. The speaker is clearly a poet displaying his virtuosity; there is no question of art hiding art. The narrative attitude in the poem is thus clearer than in the *Rabbi,* but also more remote from the Jewish *Stoff*.

It can be said further that the dialectic between Rabbi Abraham, the traditional pious Jew, and Don Isaak, the worldly, chivalrous apostate, is to some extent resolved in the figure of Jehuda ben Halevy in the four-part poem of that name. For although Jehuda is strictly pious, he is portrayed in the poem also as a Spanish gentleman who composes devotional poetry in the manner of Provençal love poems. But these thematic considerations are absorbed into another one more central to the impact of the poem: that of the sovereign, ironic poet. It is here that the characteristic description of the poet-persona in Heine's work occurs:

> Doch zumeist erkannt' ich ihn
> An dem rätselhaften Lächeln
> Jener schön gereimten Lippen,
> Die man nur bei Dichtern findet. . . .
>
> Unverantwortlicher König
> Des Gedankenreiches ist er. (E, *1,* 438, 443)

The poem itself gives expression to the sovereignty of the poet over his material by proceeding from the narrative of which Jehuda is the subject to an ironic discussion of the *Stoff* between the poet and his wife. In both poems Heine has succeeded in mastering, and thus subordinating, the Jewish materials by means of poetically adequate forms (see below, Chapter 13, pp. 389–95). In the more ambitiously conceived *Der Rabbi von Bacherach,* no such victory was possible.

No work of Heine's falls to pieces in its conception so thoroughly and so promptly as *Aus den Memoiren des Herren von Schnabelewopski.* The second of Heine's novel fragments, written, in part at least, in 1833,* collapses within the space of a page and a half; the original impulse could be maintained no longer than

* In conception it is probably earlier. See Manfred Windfuhr, "Heines Fragment eines Schelmenromans '*Aus den Memoiren des Herren von Schnabelewopski,*'" *Heine-Jahrbuch 1967,* p. 22, where Heine's remark in a letter to Friedrich Merckel of Aug. 24, 1832 (Hirth, 2, 231), "Ein Roman ist mir mißglückt," is definitely referred to *Schnabelewopski.* Walter Wadepuhl, "Heines Verhältnis zu Goethe," *Goethe. Neue Folge des Jahrbuchs der Goethe-Gesellschaft, 18* (1956), 125, argues that all except the first three chapters were written between 1827 and 1829.

that, and for this reason the work makes a rather unclear impression upon a first reading. Consequently the reputation of *Schnabelewopski* has rested primarily upon the two compact jewels it contains: Heine's version of the legend of the Flying Dutchman, and the story of Simson, the pathetic champion of God whom God fails to defend. But the fragment as a whole sheds some light on the situation of Heine as an artist at this time.

What the work seems to promise at the beginning is something new in terms of narrative perspective and a new kind of persona. It seems as though an effort were being made to divorce the persona further from the author by making a caricature of him and putting him into a distinctly comic setting. For this purpose Heine chose a Polish milieu; despite his conventional liberal sympathy with the disastrous Polish Revolution of 1830/31 and its bitter conclusion, and either despite or because of his trip to Poland in 1822, Heine was enough of a German to share the conventional contempt for the Poles that produced such vile consequences in our own century. By means of this not particularly elegant trick it is possible to devalue the narrator-persona, with his funny name,* his shabby surroundings, and his birth on April Fools' Day. The indications are for a comic first-person novel in which the persona is to be fictionalized to a greater degree than heretofore. Manfred Windfuhr has argued persuasively that Heine was attempting to realize a genuine *picaro* novel and accounts in this way for its episodic character and low style.[20] But the effort apparently ran up against the particular limits of Heine's genius. On the second page Heine introduces a description of Schnabelewopski's father that is clearly an account of his own, as is proved by a comparison with the passage about Heine's father in the *Memoiren*.[21] The effort to objectify the persona has begun to fail at this point, because the loving characterization of the narrator's father leads away from caricature. The result is an irreparable rift in the inner structure of the work that dooms it to failure as a novel.

The reason for this failure is probably more specific than Heine's characteristic incapacity to construct a work *à longue*

* Windfuhr suggests conscious or unconscious analogy to Christian Reuter's *Schelmuffsky* ("Heines Fragment cines Schelmenromans," p. 26).

haleine in a conventional genre. The work is symptomatic of the churning about of a set of attitudes in Heine's mind that were just at this time apparently coming to a temporary rest in *Die Romantische Schule* and *Zur Geschichte der Religion und Philosophie in Deutschland.* Walter Höllerer has observed that the work seems to limp along with one foot on an elevated plane and the other on the level of factual reality.[22] The comic persona is not appropriate to the severe tension between "poesy" and reality that underlies *Schnabelewopski;* he cannot operate unambiguously on either plane, nor can he mediate successfully between them. The result is that the attempted persona is abandoned and is not replaced with one sufficiently integrated to serve as a focus for the heterogeneous elements of the work as does, for example, the narrator of *Das Buch Le Grand.* The conclusion to be drawn is that Heine's artistic self-understanding was not well integrated at this time, and that the relative balance observable at the end of *Buch der Lieder* and in *Das Buch Le Grand* was out of kilter once more.

This problem has at least three closely interrelated aspects, that is, three facets of the conflict between imagination and reality, which are central to the whole phenomenon of Heine. One is discussed in the preface to *Salon I,* the book in which *Schnabelewopski* appeared. It is one of Heine's many attempts to define his political position, and it vibrates with the unresolved tension between the artistic calling and the revolutionary urge in the face of the real situation, although in the story told of the confrontation with the Swabian emigrants Heine tries to maintain the posture of the artistic persona by concentrating upon his own reactions and gestures.[23] A second aspect was noted in the interesting review by Wolfgang Menzel that Elster quoted in his introduction to *Salon I.*[24] Menzel had not yet begun the brutal attack upon Heine and Young Germany that was to derail him from his liberal course, and his critique reflects the new aesthetic concerns of the 1830s. In *Schnabelewopski* he sees a movement toward "objectivity," that is, toward a kind of *Sittengemälde,* a poetic description of manners and morals that is closely bound to the real experience of life—what, in Menzel's version of it, was later to develop into the so-called Poetic Realism. Here Menzel has captured an important element of *Schnabelewopski,* and he sees also that Heine was not able to realize it consistently and fully. Menzel turns Heine's own concept of the *Kunstperiode,* which Heine used in *Die Romantische Schule* to characterize the age of Goethe, against Heine himself, and accuses him of being unable to break out of it, as evidenced by the failure to abandon subjectivity and self-presentation. Here, seen from a somewhat different angle, is a problem that we must recognize as acute in *Schnabelewopski.* The third aspect, which in Heine's mind is closely bound up with the other two, is the religious one: on the one hand, there is a considerable amount of Saint-Simonian propaganda, on the other, the ambiguous story of Simson with which the work ends.

The movement away from an objective comic narrator to the familiar persona more closely bound to the author himself is complete by the end of the first chapter, which returns to a realm related to that of *Buch der Lieder.* The dream of the boat ride with Panna Jadwiga in Chapter 2 connects the themes of love and death in a scene whose elegiac post-Romantic tone reminds one of a painting by Arnold Böcklin. A sense of weariness and loss accompanies all the retrospection in *Schnabelewopski.* Heine has not yet been able to abandon completely the love-complex of his youth, but at thirty-five the contemplation of it begins to make him feel old. "Ich war damals jung und thöricht," says the narrator; "Jetzt bin ich alt und thöricht" (E, *4,* 104). This weariness is not well integrated with the role of the narrator in the work, which, after the comic Polish persona is dropped, is that of a cheerful student.

The next two chapters, it is believed, are the *Briefe über Hamburg* about which Heine wrote to Moser on December 15, 1825,[25] and which were originally intended for *Reisebilder II.*[26] That these chapters belong to that earlier stage in Heine's career seems likely because the satirical description of Hamburg which they contain is closely related stylistically to the description of Göttingen in *Die Harzreise,* particularly with regard to the enumeration of heterogeneous sights. For all its cleverness it is thus a regression and does not contribute much to the structural integration of the work. Only the theme of food, which undergoes innumerable variations in *Schnabelewopski* and is related to a central and more serious concern, connects the two chapters with what follows. It is clear, nevertheless, that the chapters were revised for *Schnabelewopski.* The allusion to Lafayette's championship of Louis-Philippe as "the best republic" (E, *4,* 98) could not, of course, have been written before 1830. More importantly, there are new tones that do not belong to the Heine of the 1820s: the distinctly non-Romantic description of the girls Heloise and Minka. The portraits are earthy and sensual with a lewd undertone, and the girls are not idealized either in body or soul. The stupidity of the one, "wie ein trüber Wolkenflor über einer prangenden Frühlingslandschaft" (E, *4,* 100) and the freckles of the other are important modifications that tend away from the pure, unreal, verbally constructed female figures of the early period and toward a blunt and rather sour realism. This sour tone continues in the contrasting description of the bourgeois "Anstandsdamen" with their pastimes of slander, and in the sardonic account of the temple of virtue that was supposed to have been erected in Hamburg.

In Chapter 4 there is a further development more closely related to the later rather than to the early Heine. The technique of *Das Buch Le Grand,* in which Düsseldorf is seen again after a passage of time, unpleasantly transformed, is here applied to Hamburg. The pale, hollow people look like numbers; one girl has died, and the other is an alcoholic. The bad end to which these loose girls come, the account of which is related to the poem *Pomare* of *Romanzero,* contrasts quite noticeably with the Saint-Simonian attitude that otherwise pervades *Schnabelewopski* and is early evidence that Heine's "sensualism" was not unaccompanied by puritan inhibitions. The end of the chapter is also related to Heine's late attitudes: it is a farewell to the pathetic fallacy so dear to the Romantics. The stars are not loving, sympathetic beings, but illusions and lies in a dark blue void. The curious way this is expressed indicates feelings of despair and offense that Romantic *Naturphilosophie* did not fulfill its promise.

The following chapter is entirely devoted to the poem of *Herr Vonved* that Heine took over nearly verbatim, although with extensive cuts and some changes, from Wilhelm Grimm's *Altdänische Heldenlieder* of 1811.[27] Vonved has the status of a persona in the context of Heine's works. His story begins and ends in the realm of poetry, as he plays his golden harp. In between, however, he is obliged to go out into the world, put his questions to it, and fight. The borrowed poem is one of the versions of Heine's self-understanding as a poet in a political age, and it reflects the tensions apparent in the preface to *Salon I*. Vonved cannot accept the service offered him by the king—that is, a function in the outer world, in public life—and upon his return home he hacks his mother, who sent him out in the first place, into five thousand pieces. This is beyond question the most pessimistic appraisal of his political mission to be found anywhere in Heine's works before 1848, and it sheds some light on the tergiversations of the 1840s. There is, however, another aspect of *Herr Vonved* that Heine must have noticed. The riddles and the answers given to them by the second shepherd (Heine is mistaken when he indicates that the first shepherd solves the riddles[28]) exhibit an only partly assimilated mixture of pagan and Christian elements that is characteristic of late Old Norse literature of this kind. This ambiguous feature of the poem corresponds to the tensions apparent later in the story of Simson.

The remainder of *Schnabelewopski* is made up of the two sections for which it is best remembered: the legend of the Flying Dutchman, introduced in Chapter 6 and worked out in Chapter 7, and the story of Simson, with its setting in Chapter 8 and its development in Chapters 9–14. The legend of the Flying Dutchman is introduced by a set of variations on the motif of the sea. First the motif is fit together with what has gone before: the contrast between the gaiety of youth and the storms that come after, and the return home as a wreck. The contrast corresponds both to that of the two Hamburg chapters and to the career of Vonved. The meaning of the second variation is unclear:

> Aber es gibt auch Menschen, die nicht mit gewöhnlichen Schiffen verglichen werden dürfen, sondern mit Dampfschiffen. Diese tragen ein dunkles Feuer in der Brust, und sie fahren gegen Wind und Wetter—ihre Rauchflagge flattert wie der schwarze Federbusch des nächtlichen Reuters, ihre Zackenräder sind wie kolossale Pfundsporen, womit sie das Meer in die Wellenrippen stacheln, und das widerspenstisch

> schäumende Element muß ihrem Willen gehorchen wie ein Roß—aber sehr oft platzt der Kessel, und der innere Brand verzehrt uns. (E, *4,* 114)

Obviously the steamer, a notably modern image, is a symbol for the strong-willed activist. It is uncertain, however, whether it is also a symbol for the persona; the "uns" at the end of the passage is ambiguous and problematic. The whole paragraph seems to reflect an unsteadiness in the conception of the persona. The third variation is related in an interesting way to the theme of *Nordsee* I, 10, *Seegespenst.* In that poem the poet was almost lured to his destruction by the vision of the sunken city in the sea; here he can hear the nixies singing, but he cannot see the city below; the distance is greater, the danger is less, but the poetic echo is still present. The chapter ends, finally, with a vision of the legendary Flying Dutchman.

Heine did not, of course, invent the legend, which dates from the sixteenth century. He adverted to it as early as 1826 in *Die Nordsee III.*[29] But it is fairly well established that his version of the Dutchman's salvation is original; the play in Amsterdam of which the narrator speaks is evidently a fiction, and Heine's solution has no precedent anywhere in the Flying Dutchman literature.[30] It is well known that Heine's version inspired Wagner's opera, which follows Heine's account quite closely, although in later years, after Wagner had become irritated with Heine in particular and Jews in general, he tried to belittle Heine's achievement. The Flying Dutchman is a type of the Wandering Jew figure, and is loosely related both to the wandering student narrator and to Herr Vonved. The Dutchman's original crime, like that of the Wandering Jew, is religious irreverence; he is forced to bear the consequences of a vain oath. The door to salvation that is left open is meant to be only a torment of Tantalus; the Devil, stupid as he is, as the narrator remarks with bitter sarcasm, does not believe in female faithfulness.[31] The Dutchman is empty and miserable, and has no relationship to either life or death because he lacks love. He must sail forever because he does not have the anchor of hope—a symbol the narrator applies to his own condition at the beginning of Chapter 6. Heine's resolution of the Dutchman's dilemma has a characteristic false bottom. The Dutchman's last wife performs the ultimate sacrificial act of loyalty: to seal her oath of "true unto death" she plunges into the sea, and so the Dutchman, too, can be released into death. The implication is that female faithfulness will not bear the test of time, that even so heroic a woman can escape temptation only by destroying herself. (It would be interesting to know if Lessing's *Emilia Galotti* crossed Heine's mind at this point.) Thus the sardonic "moral" with which Heine ends the tale: even at best men can only hope to perish through women.[32]

The story of despair and salvation through self-sacrifice is constructed as a frame for an erotic interlude in the theater in Amsterdam. The contrast is meant to be that of spiritualism and sensualism; the laughter of the real-life girl breaks in at the sound of the words "treu bis in den Tod" (E, *4,* 118) from the stage; her laughter comes not from Hell but "vom Paradiese"—that is, from the theater balcony. The limited but genuine pleasure of an amatory experience is contrasted with the rigorous absolutism of the legend. This is part of the Saint-Simonian plea, although the narrative manner goes back to a model antedating Heine's interest in Saint-Simonianism: the story of the seduction of Franscheska in *Die Bäder von Lucca,* which is quite plainly revealed amidst the insistence that it is not to be revealed. However, there are some other elements in this anecdote that reduce the sharpness of the contrast. For one thing, the girl is described as a female counterpart to the poetic persona; her smile is poisoned by the apple from the Tree of Knowledge, and her lips have that sardonic curl familiar from the *Bergidylle* of *Die Harzreise* and also from any number of contemporary descriptions of Heine's own appearance. She has the cold, pale exterior related to the marble-statue motif that occurs in Heine's poetry from time to time and is particularly prominent in *Florentinische Nächte.* Furthermore, she is described as a bit of a nymphomaniac, "eine holländische Messaline" (E, *4,* 119). Thus coupled with the contrasting picture of sensual freedom and the fiction of the persona's erotic attractiveness is a hint of moralistic devaluation that always lurks behind Heine's "sensualism."

In Chapter 8 there is another effort to bind up the themes that are lying about in such troublesome profusion. The almost grotesque variations on the subject of food are gathered together in a dream into the symbol of the weeping willow, which seems like a rather unconvincing attempt to absorb the theme of death into that of sensualism. The pleasures of the senses are combined more amusingly by means of the figure of the "Wirtin zur roten Kuh," to whom the narrator makes love in order to extort good meals for himself and his companions. It is consonant with the aesthetic principles of the work that she is no ideal beauty, but a short, fat woman. It is remarkable how the apparently frivolous gastronomic theme is here worked into a more serious context; on the one hand, it is connected through the "Wirtin zur roten Kuh" with the theme of eros; on the other, it is placed in opposition to the spiritualist antithesis. For, as is remarked at the beginning of Chapter 9, when the roast was bad, the students discussed the existence of God, and this, in turn, leads to the pathetic end of Simson.

It has been thought that Simson was meant as a caricature of Ludwig Börne. This supposition was first made publicly, as far as I have been able to discover, in 1838 by Eduard Kolloff in Gutzkow's *Jahrbuch der Literatur*[33] (the same publication in which Heine's censored *Schwabenspiegel* appeared); in 1840, during the uproar over Heine's book on Börne, Jeanette Wohl reiterated the assertion in her counterattack,[34] and Elster quoted it also from a review in the *Zeitung für die elegante Welt,* where it is indicated that this was Börne's own understanding.[35] One can see why this connection should have been made; Simson, like Börne, comes from Frankfurt; like Börne, he is not physically strong; and Börne had distinct religious inclinations that Heine found offensive. It is therefore possible that there was a typological connection in Heine's mind.* But it should be regarded as no more than that for the simple reason that the figure of Simson has no political referent; the treatment of the spiritualist type is kept ex-

* Strodtmann doubted it (*Heine's Leben,* 2, 109–110). Helmut Ernst Ruhrig, in "Heinrich Heine. Beiträge zur Bestimmung seines ironischen Humors" (diss. Freiburg im Breisgau, 1953), pp. 181–82, suggested that he may have been a representation of Ludwig Markus; Helene Herrmann (*Heines Werke,* ed. Hermann Friedemann, et al [2d ed. Berlin, Leipzig, Vienna, and Stuttgart, 1927], *6,* 19) also thought so.

clusively in the religious realm. In any case, what is of interest about the figure of Simson is not any similarity it might have to Börne, but the ambiguous dialectic it incarnates.

The dialogue of the students is a dramatization of the dialogue in German philosophy as Heine understood it: Vanpitter's Hegelian pantheism is confronted with Driksen's Fichtean ontological abstractions. What is important in the scene is not these characterizations, however, but Simson's hopeless championship of God, and God's failure to help him. So Simson is erected into a symbol of the Jews, maintaining his faith despite God's apparent indifference—a problem with which the theology of the Diaspora has always had to cope and which has become agonizingly acute since Auschwitz. The narrator's guess that God is embarrassed by the Jews because they remind Him of His barbarian origins is witty and not without a certain degree of Nietzschean acuity, but it is hardly adequate. Perhaps one should remember that the narrator is a born Christian.

Chapter 10 becomes lost in comic anecdotes, the relevance of which I have not been able to discover; perhaps another interpreter will be able to make some sense out of Professor van der Pissen's secret playacting.* The next two chapters, however, interrupt the course of Simson's story with some rather interesting, if not totally integrated, considerations. Chapter 11 begins with one of Heine's most important aesthetic discourses: the characterization of Jan Steen. Heine's aesthetic perceptivity was not visual like Goethe's, but almost exclusively verbal. Yet it is a curious fact that his poetics are often most clearly expressed in connection with painting, as is evident from the remarkable essay that gave *Der Salon* its title, *Französische Maler* (1831). The technique of painting interested Heine less than the content, which he tended to see in a quite realistic way as a captured form of dramatic action. In the witty paintings of Jan Steen, Heine responded to the combination of sensual realism with earthy

* Windfuhr suggests: "Schon das untheologische Verhalten des Theologieprofessors deutete auf die innere Widersprüchlichkeit der zur Schau getragenen Religiosität" ("Heines Fragment eines Schelmenromans," p. 33). This is reasonable, but strikes me as a little abstract for a scene described in such grotesque and, one would think, symbolic detail.

gaiety, and thus his account of Steen serves as a kind of wistful programmatic description of an aesthetic purpose that is implied but not really achieved in *Schnabelewopski*; it was very likely this passage that touched off the observations of Wolfgang Menzel noted above. Steen is seen here from a Saint-Simonian perspective; he is a herald of the religion of joy, and in his paintings the Holy Spirit is revealed in light and laughter. But Heine was mistaken if he thought his own talents could be turned completely in this direction; his soul was much too hag-ridden. Thus the artistic Dutch gaiety of Steen is immediately contrasted with an unaesthetic and gloomy Dutch reality: the sadly comic account of the narrator's landlord and landlady, one of those passages in Heine's works where the whimsical grotesquerie inherited from Jean Paul is given a distinctly dark tonality. These folk are not only excruciatingly bad musicians and ugly, but, worse than that, Anabaptists. In his dreams the landlord consorts with figures of the Bible, and his repressed sexuality particularly calls forth visions of Biblical women; he becomes a "heiliger Roué" (E, *4*, 131). The ensuing complications with the landlady's jealousy set off the chain of events that leads to Simson's death.

But Chapter 12 brings another interruption, a rumination upon dreams and death. The curious thesis is argued that dreams are an indication of a soul out of balance, a split between senses and soul; the men of Classical antiquity, it is incredibly claimed, did not dream; dreaming began with the Jews and the Christians. These considerations form an uneasy synthesis with the implied Saint-Simonian attitude; the chapter in fact presents an unresolved dialectic. The traditional German assumption about the psychic harmony of Classical antiquity is confronted with the Saint-Simonian charge against Judeo-Christian asceticism. But the lure of the dream world, which, as is made clear at the beginning of the chapter, is related to death and is sweet, and the stylized dream that follows combines a reprise of motifs from *Buch der Lieder* with an effort at Saint-Simonian argument. The persona is once again at the feet of the beloved Jadwiga. The poems flutter down to the world of nixies below—the threatening Romantic world of Chapter 6 and of the poem *Seegespenst*—and the nixies comment on the inability of mortal lovers to communicate, the theme of *Die Heimkehr* 33. The failure to achieve happiness appears the more melancholy to the immortal nixies because of the shadow of death and transitoriness under which men must live; there is so little time for joy. Nowhere else in Heine's works is there so intense and compact an effort to combine the motifs of the love poetry with themes of the Saint-Simonian religion. Yet it all leads nowhere. When the narrator tries to move Jadwiga with these considerations, she turns to marble, and two tears are the only sign of life remaining. The negative result of this remarkable passage, it seems to me, would have to be taken into prime consideration for any overall understanding of Heine's middle years.

After this dream sequence the scene switches to the comic side of the issue; the landlady hauls Schnabelewopski out of bed to witness her husband dreaming of the beautiful Queen Vashti from the Book of Esther. The result of this nocturnal event is that the "Wirtin zur roten Kuh" becomes jealous of the landlady, the food becomes very bad, the religious discussion very heated, and the duel ensues in which Simson acquires his mortal wound. While the ideational connection is cleverly managed, the story itself is not completely convincing, for Simson's mystical parable of the soul in the light of God and his adversion to Paley's Proof hardly seem sufficiently insulting to motivate the duel. The important point, however, was to establish Simson as the brave but powerless champion of God whom God abandons. His is a martyrdom to no purpose.

The grim comedy continues at the beginning of Chapter 14, with Schnabelewopski's merciless tirade against the "Wirtin zur roten Kuh" for not having sent the soup—such small sensual deprivations lead to such great and pointless spiritual tragedies. But the matter is not allowed to rest there. The final note is to be one of ambiguity, due, it is fair to say, to Heine's indomitable love of the Bible. Through the whole layer of fiction one seems to hear Heine's own voice in Simson's words:

> Das ist ein liebes Buch. Meine Vorfahren haben es in der ganzen Welt mit sich herumgetragen und gar viel Kummer und Unglück und Schimpf und Haß dafür erduldet oder

> sich gar dafür totschlagen lassen. Jedes Blatt darin hat Thränen und Blut gekostet, es ist das aufgeschriebene Vaterland der Kinder Gotts, es ist das heilige Erbe Jehovahs. (E, *4*, 138)

This is the sort of high rhetoric Heine himself used about the Bible in the latter part of his life and it does not characterize Simson satirically. Most of the remainder of Chapter 14 is given over to the story of Samson and Delilah taken verbatim from the sixteenth chapter of Judges. It is possible that Heine had a satirical purpose in quoting this passage at such length, for of all the heroes of the Bible Samson is by far the most doltish. The imbecilic way in which he allows himself to fall into Delilah's trap is told with that terse, unobtrusive humor that occasionally sparkles in the Old Testament. But his personal qualities are of no importance; he is a Nazirite, one sworn to God, and becomes God's instrument for destroying the Philistines. Simson is sworn to God also, but he is not God's instrument for anything. He plays his part in what seems to be an empty universe under a silent heaven. And his fate is trivial. In his delirious identification with Samson brought on by the Bible reading, Simson lays hold of the bedposts with the cry, "Es sterbe meine Seele mit den Philistern" (E, *4*, 142), but the bedposts do not budge and only Simson dies; the Philistines live on, and God does not permit Himself to be vindicated.

Aus den Memoiren des Herren von Schnabelewopski is not a success, and it is hard to conceive how the fragment might have been continued. The narrative perspective is confused, not only because the original conception of the persona is abandoned, but also because of a lack of unity between the narrator's function as observer and his lapses into self-reflection. It does show some signs of movement in new directions, both in the abortive effort to objectify a comic persona at the beginning and, as Ruhrig has pointed out,[36] in that finally Simson rather than the narrator is the hero. But the heterogeneous elements of the work get out of control; the narrator is not able to bind them together in a compositional unity such as he achieved in *Das Buch Le Grand.* The centripetal force generated by Heine's associative technique has not been tamed here, and the objections that have always been brought to bear against Heine's composition are valid in this case. This is not to say that there is no effort at composition visible in the work; on the contrary, the attempt to bind together the various dialectical themes—poetry and reality, love and death, sensualism and spiritualism—is painfully evident. The unsuccessful result indicates that the state of Heine's mind in the early 1830s was by no means as stable as a work such as *Die Romantische Schule* might suggest.

The third of Heine's efforts to write a traditional prose work, the *Florentinische Nächte,* is not a novel but a series of *Novellen* related within a frame, and it turned out to be, as a whole, one of the least impressive of Heine's works. It was published at a time when events were threatening to strangle his writing altogether. Although *Florentinische Nächte* was begun before the storm of December 1835 broke, the first two volumes of *Der Salon* had been banned, and during the course of 1835 Heine exhibited a great desire to write something that would contain nothing at which the authorities could take offense. In August, when he had developed some hopes that his life would become a little more peaceful, he promised Campe an amusing book that would offend no censor in the world,[37] and on December 4, less than a week before the roof was to fall in, he spoke of *Salon III* as a popular book "für alle Classen berechnet" (Hirth, *2,* 108). The Federal Decree of December 10, 1835, which threatened all the works of Heine, along with those of Gutzkow, Laube, Mundt, and Wienbarg, with nationwide suppression, made this effort urgent if Heine was to survive as a writer at all. Never in his life did he need the foxiness, loyalty, and courage of Julius Campe as badly as he did at this moment, and although Heine, with characteristic maladroitness, took the occasion to annoy Campe by publishing the *Florentinische Nächte* in the Stuttgart *Morgenblatt* without informing him,[38] writer and publisher together eventually worked out a test of the effectiveness of the decree by producing a book as absolutely harmless as Heine could manage; for a time they even considered entitling it *Das Stille Buch* or *Märchen* in order to stress its innocuous character.[39]

The whole case of the decree of 1835 is a particularly wretched chapter in the wretched history of literary censorship. To put any writer into this kind of situation is to emasculate him—which is precisely what the authorities wanted—and for a writer like Heine it was a disaster. In May 1836 he wrote to August Lewald that the *Florentinische Nächte* proved that he could live from writing *Novellen* if he had to, but he admitted that his heart was not in it.[40] Months later, in September, he was still having trouble filling up the twenty signatures necessary to free *Salon III* from the routine censorship.[41] According to Heine, he was having no trouble writing, but he was having a good deal of trouble avoiding what later he was to call "Erschießliches" (E, *1*, 412); in one of his more heartbreaking laments to Campe, he wrote on September 1, 1836: "was hilft mir schreiben, wenn mir's nicht gedruckt [wird]" (Hirth, *2*, 140). Heine's claim to have written more than he could print was substantiated by Wadepuhl, who published part of a suppressed section of the *Florentinische Nächte* that included a vision of the execution of the Pazzi conspirators against the Medici in 1478.[42] According to Wadepuhl, this touched off a set of observations on Prussian politics, which Heine naturally had to cross out, causing him to lose interest in the (rather slack) remainder.[43] In this situation, the quality of *Florentinische Nächte,* a potboiler born of necessity, suffered accordingly. If it is not Heine's worst piece of writing—over long stretches it is stylistically immaculate—it certainly has a claim to being the dullest, at least at the outset. To begin with, it is desperately padded. Along with other nonessentials, it contains a reprise of Heine's views on England that he had set down eight years before in the *Englische Fragmente* and a long characterization of the atmosphere of Paris, both of which come as close as Heine ever can to being not only boring but stupid. Secondly, it panders to "alle Classen" with an attempt at genteel pornography, a kind of writing for which Heine was not suited. On two occasions female limbs peek at us through translucent garments;[44] three times the moribund Maria urges the narrator to get on to the sexy part of the story of Mademoiselle Laurence;[45] the tale itself tries hard to be lewd and, in the concluding remarks about the narrator's warm friendship with the cuckold,[46] cynical. But Heine was not good at this sort of thing: both the *Verschiedene* and *Der Doktor Faust,* not to mention his acid remark about Clauren's popular "Taschenbordellchen" in *Das Buch Le Grand,*[47] prove sufficiently that Heine had a moralist's distaste for coquettish prurience. Consequently the sensual gorgeousness that properly belongs to the conventions of erotic phantasy is lacking; the seduction of the narrator—who is, characteristically, quite passive—takes place not in a harem-like setting but among desolate furnishings of worn-out magnificence. Even more distracting is the perversity of the narrator's libido, bordering on necrophilia. This is a feature of the third and most ruinous weakness of the work: the totally regressive treatment of the persona.

Before turning to that matter, it might be mentioned parenthetically that there was once an effort to show that the *Florentinische Nächte* is not, as it appears to be, a total capitulation to the forces of political reaction, but rather a subtle allegory by means of which Heine attempted to mask an attack upon the current political constellation. In an article in 1895, a W. Rudow argued a series of entertaining identifications: Maximilian is Heine, the doctor with his medicinal potion is the German Diet, the shabby ancestral palace without doors and windows is Germany after the foreign occupation, the white marble statue in the green park is poesy, the dead girl Very is Romanticism (Rudow, for some reason, connects her with the fact that Heine once met Bettina von Arnim in Potsdam), and Mademoiselle Laurence is the Revolution.[48] That this interpretation is a lot of hilarious nonsense will, I think, appear self-evident; I mention it only because no one, to my knowledge, has ever taken any note of it, and because it might be worthwhile for someone to look more closely at the strangulated elements of *Florentinische Nächte* to see to what extent Heine's fundamental concerns maintain themselves under these circumstances.

What is most distressing about the work is that Heine's effort to develop the fictional persona seems to have been torpedoed by the reactionary counterattack, and the result is that he is driven back upon the most hopeless self-indulgence. It is instructive that this should happen under these circumstances, for it indicates that the law of Heine's artistic development was intimately connected both with the inner imagination and the external world. In the *Florentinische Nächte* the identity of author and persona is nearly complete; we know from fragments of the manuscript that Heine originally intended to call Maximilian "Signor Enriko" (W, *6,* 506), and this fits together with the impression that the work is a reprise of the *Italien* pieces of the *Reisebilder.* Furthermore, it is easier to make exact biographical connections in this work than is usual in Heine's prose narratives. The date Maximilian gives for his journey to England corresponds to that of Heine's, and the chronology of his arrival in Paris is off by only one year. The name-dropping description of Paris society corresponds closely to what we know of Heine's connections there; this is particularly true of the longish account of Bellini,[49] which is confirmed in the memoirs of Caroline Jaubert[50] and which includes what is evidently a description of Heine's friend Princess Belgioioso.[51] In the spring of 1829, Heine, like Maximilian, was in Potsdam, where, as his letters show, he was plagued by loneliness and depression, and years before that he spoke of being in love with a statue on the terrace of Sans Souci.[52] Since Heine's original Paganini experience goes back to 1830,[53] and few of the events recounted refer to a period later than 1831, one wonders whether some materials that first belonged to the memoirs may not have been worked in here.

The precious self-indulgence of Maximilian's posture is also related to the pre-Paris years: the soft voice coming out of the wounded heart[54] belongs to the atmosphere of *Buch der Lieder;* the love for the Madonna[55] is a very old memory indeed;[56] the love for the dead child Very seems to be related to the dead Veronika of *Das Buch Le Grand* and possibly to the dead Maria of *Reise von München nach Genua* (see above, Chapter 5, pp. 133–35); indeed, Maximilian's passionate, self-consuming love, divorced from its object and existing only in the imagination, belongs to earlier days—and earlier reading, for the ruined palace and the marble statue in the garden are rather obviously taken from Eichendorff's *Marmorbild,* a scene Heine revived again in the *Elementargeister.*[57] Here, to be sure, the perverse eroticism of the scene is more pronounced than was customary in Heine's younger days: the narrator speaks of "schwüle Scheu" (E, *4,* 325), and he kisses the statue passionately with a feeling of "knabenhafte Lüsternheit" (E, *4*, 327); the relationship between love and death is also more explicit, not only in the "beseligende Kälte" of the statue, but also in Maximilian's desire to possess a death mask of Maria after she has died.[58] Maximilian's true love for a dream figure of the imagination, transparent and ethereal,[59] takes us back to the very outset of Heine's poetic career. The trouble is that this exercise in memory is lacking in irony and recalls not only past events but generates anew attitudes and weaknesses that in the meantime had been overcome. Apparently this is due to the censorship, which prevented the development of any effective counterweight to this atavistic sentimentality.

To what extent the story of Madame Laurence may also reflect a real experience is not known and is of no importance. The grotesque group of street musicians is described in such impressive detail that they may be a visual memory, although it seems that Heine took the name of the dwarf Türlütü from Béranger.[60] This section is the only part of *Florentinische Nächte* that points ahead rather than backward in Heine's career. Mademoiselle Laurence is a symbol of the protest against Classical and social dancing in favor of passionate, Dionysian improvisation that ten years later was to generate Heine's ballet scenarios.* The nasty and grotesque deaths of both the dwarf who crows like a cock and the dog who can spell Wellington's name are the closest Heine comes in the work to realistic description combined with social and political comment. But, apart from its erotic aspects, the story develops into an exercise in *Schauerromantik.* At first Maximilian cannot extract any meaning from Mademoiselle Laurence's dance, suggesting that it might be pure expressiveness,[61] but later its pantomimic meaning is made explicit when Mademoiselle Laurence describes her childhood, which includes having been born to a mother believed dead and already buried, a familiar convention of the Gothic thriller. In the end, Mademoiselle Laurence is completely absorbed into the imagination of

* An interesting comparison to the art of Isadora Duncan is made by Max Niehaus, *Himmel Hölle und Trikot. Heinrich Heine und das Ballett* (Munich, 1959), p. 26.

the narrator-persona, as she joins in *his* dream of her weird entourage.[62]

In the midst of this labored work is the passage on Paganini. It will be useful, first of all, to point out what it is not. Although Heine seems to have made Paganini's acquaintance briefly in 1830,[63] the passage gives us no information about Paganini himself; it operates exclusively with his well-known public bearing and the legends that had assiduously been built up around him.[64] While Walter Silz may be overstressing the point when he argues that "Heine might have written his description of Paganini without ever hearing him play," [65] there is no specific music as such described in the passage; it is a translation of the effect of music upon the hearer into theatrical visions.[66] Although Heine wrote much and well about musical events, he does not himself seem to have been musical in the pure sense; he knew little about music technically, and he neither danced nor played an instrument. The composer Ferdinand Hiller, who was well acquainted with Heine, attested that he understood nothing about music either practically or theoretically.[67] Music for Heine has either social relevance (e.g., music as a substitute for political freedom in Italy[68]) or it generates literary images.[69] The narrator of *Florentinische Nächte* speaks of "mein musikalisches zweites Gesicht, meine Begabnis, bei jedem Tone, den ich erklingen höre, auch die adäquate Klangfigur zu sehen" (E, *4*, 342). What is meant by this, however, as Walzel [70] and Silz[71] have argued, is not the phenomenon called synaesthesia, the generation of one subjective sensory impression by a different sensory stimulus; the experience of Paganini is, as Silz has put it, "simply revery induced and accompanied by music." [72] The music itself is only subliminally heard—Maria says of Maximilian that he goes to the opera to see rather than to hear[73]—and it serves as a system of impulses for the poetic imagination. Other examples of this are the early poem, *An eine Sängerin,*[74] the vision of Sara in the synagogue in *Der Rabbi von Bacherach,*[75] and, to some extent, the evocation of the Revolution and of Napoleon's career by the drum major in Chapter 7 of *Das Buch Le Grand.* Moreover, as Michael Mann has pointed out, the "second sight" is not achieved without the help of previously acquired information.[76] This is not to say that the experience of music is an indifferent one; in his fine and detailed stylistic analysis of the Paganini passage, Steven Scher has shown how the violinist's spectacular virtuosity generates a similar virtuosity in color combinations and dynamic motion in space.[77] But the final product is divorced from music as such and is purely poetic in the narrow sense. In attempting an interpretation, concentration upon the musical aspects of the Paganini passage would lead away from a critical understanding of it.

For Paganini is a persona of the poet in a far more artistic sense than the regressed narrator Maximilian. The violinist is presented as a wizard of demonic creativity, and it is undoubtedly because of the legend constructed around him that Heine chose him for this purpose rather than, for example, Liszt, whom Heine elsewhere describes as calling forth a vision the description of which corresponds almost verbatim to one of those in the Paganini passage.[78] In the four visions, Paganini stands at the center of a creative act of the poetic imagination and thus corresponds in many respects to Heine's richly organized construct of the autonomous poet. In the first vision, his playing creates a "farbiges Schattenspiel," a little drama with himself as "Hauptperson" (E, *4*, 343). The gawky violinist is transformed, as Heine transformed himself in the writing of his earlier period, into an elegant and handsome young man who acts out with the girl a dialogue of courtly gallantry and a crime of passion, corresponding to the Paganini legend. The girl is totally a creation of the artist; she springs into being as he begins to play, and although she goes through the motions of singing, she does not in fact do so; her voice, like his, is in the violin. The parallel with the exclusively contextual existence of the beloved in *Buch der Lieder* is obvious. Gradually the vision becomes autonomous in the sense that at the end Paganini is no longer seen as playing the violin but is totally occupied with the beating of his rival and the murder of the beloved; the artist as technical performer vanishes into his creation.

In the second vision, again following the legend, the Devil becomes visible and helps Paganini play. Heine always bears in mind that the Devil is a fallen angel, filled with terrifying and bottomless despair because he has been expelled from God's kingdom.[79] The music generates the scene of the Last Judgment as it is prophesied in Joel 3:12. The violinist himself appears to wear a costume divided into yellow and red; Scher takes note of the fact that these colors remind one of a fool's costume, but interprets them in context as representing the fires of Hell;[80] yet surely they are both: the artist as *Narr,* so ubiquitous in Heine's works, and as a despairing, demonically tormented creator. So intense does this vision become that it no longer can be sustained; with the breaking of a string, a symbol of overstrained tension, the scene vanishes.

The third vision presents the artist as a monk, combining a demonic destructiveness with an ascetic bearing. Here his powers are even greater; he commands the elements and releases the spirits that Solomon had imprisoned and sunk in the sea; out of the underlying levels of the artistic consciousness emerge frightening images reminiscent of Bosch. Art has cosmic, elemental referents, but they are not soothing. The scene terrifies the narrator, who closes his ears and eyes to it, causing it to evaporate. At this point it is clear that the narrator's sensibilities are contrasted with the perceptions of the ordinary man, symbolized throughout by the pedestrian comments of the bourgeois fur-dealer in the audience and at the end of this scene pointed up by the delighted applause of the audience, obviously completely unreceptive to the frightening character of Paganini's art; only the virtuosity is perceived, not the majestic torment.

In the final vision, the artist creates a vast space of monumental beauty in the imagination. It is first restricted to the limits of the stage as seen by the observer, but then expands into cosmic dimensions.[81] Paganini is transformed into a God ruling his creation, and his universe revolves around him, vibrating with the music of the spheres. A victory chorus of a thousand bards celebrates him; it is an apotheosis of the autonomous and completely sovereign poet-creator. The intensity of his experience is comparable only to the ecstasy of love.[82] All of Heine's borrowed metaphors of "poesy" are gathered into this climax, including Romantic "Waldhorntöne im Mondschein" (E, *4,* 348) and the harmonies of Greek beauty. It all ends, as each of the visions has, with the voice of the Philistine, this time of Maria's physician, who reduces Maximilian's ecstasies to the level of alcoholic intoxication.

Quite obviously, the Paganini passage in *Florentinische Nächte* is a substantial contribution to Heine's aesthetics. What little it has to do with Niccolò Paganini and his music is of minor importance. As Lee B. Jennings has observed, the episode shows Heine's "tendency to identify art and artistic insight with the untrammeled wandering of the imagination." [83] Heine takes the occasion to project into Paganini a version of the poet-persona that is as intense and sharply delineated as it is to be found anywhere before the late poetry. Both the sovereign creativity of the poet and the godless terror of his imagination are condensed into visions of great compactness. The Paganini passage compensates us to a considerable extent for the weak and puerile narrator-persona and the indifferent content of the rest of *Florentinische Nächte.*

CHAPTER 12

The Masked Dancemaster: *Die Göttin Diana* and *Faust*

> And Babylon . . . wild beasts of the desert shall lie there; and their houses shall be full of doleful creatures; and owls shall dwell there, and satyrs shall dance there.
>
> —ISAIAH 13:19–21.

S. S. Prawer has identified one of the significant image clusters in Heine's poetry as the "Masked Dancer" [1]—a most characteristic version of the Persona, combining the elusive fiction (Heine did not dance) with a fascination for this form of sensual expression. Given the prominence of this image and Heine's interest in dance generally, as well as the great popularity of the ballet in Heine's Paris, it is not astonishing that he should have tried his hand at constructing ballet scenarios. Yet it seems to have come about more or less by accident; Heine wrote the scenarios at the suggestion of Benjamin Lumley, the director of Her Majesty's Theatre in London, who was impressed by the success of Adolphe Adam's *Giselle* (1841), the motif of which had been taken from Heine's *Elementargeister.** At the same time, Heine's reading pointed in a similar direction; there had been presentations of *Faust* in dance pantomime in the seventeenth century, and shortly before Lumley made his offer, one was published in volume 5 of J. Scheible's *Das Kloster,* a work Heine owned and used for his studies in folk-

* E, *4,* 391–92. See Gerhard Weiss, "Die Entstehung von Heines 'Doktor Faust.' Ein Beispiel deutsch-englisch-französischer Freundschaft," *Heine-Jahrbuch 1966,* pp. 41–57. *Giselle* has maintained an important place in the international ballet repertoire; it has been danced by almost every famous dancer up to modern times. See Max Niehaus, *Himmel Hölle und Trikot. Heinrich Heine und das Ballett* (Munich, 1959), pp. 33–45.

lore.[2] The resulting two works have been rather neglected in Heine research, yet they are of considerable interest because they are fundamentally unlike anything else he wrote and suggest that his gifts were at least potentially broader than is usually believed. For they are just about the only works of Heine in which the fiction is very nearly pure and the poetic persona as a fictive projection of Heinrich Heine absent. They succeed where his youthful dramas failed in creating self-enclosed wholes operating exclusively with literary materials, and the skill with which they are composed, as Enders has pointed out, suggests that Heine did in fact possess a certain degree of dramatic ability.[3] This is true despite the fact that the works are no more than sketches that describe the effects Heine envisioned from the point of view of the spectator and make no effort to meet technical problems or go into details of choreography.

It is doubtful that Heine knew any more about the ballet than what could be learned by a regular Parisian theatergoer, although in Florence in 1828 he spoke of studying the ballet among the fine arts.[4] It is immediately obvious that the scenarios were unproduceable in his time, and that Heine did not understand this, or pretended not to, is a little strange. A really extraordinary power of raw erotic sensuality is absolutely central to both works, and it is an iron certainty that Queen Victoria would have been "not amused" by them. Heine says in his introductory remarks to *Faust* that it was never produced because the appearance of Jenny Lind monopolized the attention of the public, which seems to have been true, and because of the machinations of the ballet master, which may or may not have been true.[5] It is undoubtedly true that the technical effects required by the scenarios were quite impossible; Heine seems to have envisioned them as mechanical, but in fact they could only be achieved at all only with skilled use of the lighting console of a modern, well-equipped theater. Lumley himself in later years pointed this out convincingly:

> Upon examination it [*Faust*] was found, unfortunately, impracticable in respect of its "situations" and scenic effects for stage purposes. True, it was the work of a poet; but of a poet unacquainted with the necessities of stage representation, espe-

> cially in England—of a man of powerful imagination, who presupposed that a public would see the effects as *he* saw them, and feel with *his* feelings. In short, the execution of the ballet was an impossibility. In spite of the expenses already lavished on this work of a poet by the manager, it was found necessary to lay the ballet aside.[6]

Heinrich Laube tried in 1849 to have *Faust* produced in Vienna or Berlin, but was turned down on technical grounds.[7] Although Heine did not realize it, both with respect to content and technical requirements, he was writing for the theater of the twentieth century, and so the scenarios are Heine's most remarkable anticipation of the art of the future. After having inspired ballet versions in Prague in 1926 and Sydney, Australia, in 1941,* [8] Heine's *Faust* became in 1948 Werner Egk's most interesting ballet *Abraxas*.[9] For his part, despite his disappointment, Heine had reason to be satisfied with Lumley, for the 6,000 francs Lumley paid for *Faust* made it by far the most spectacular literary business deal of Heine's career.[10]

The modernity of Heine's scenarios is due in part to his dislike of the classical ballet in principle. He stresses this in an article on dance fashions written for the *Allgemeine Zeitung* and dated February 7, 1842.[11] Here he argues that of all the arts, only the dance was not absolved into the liturgy of the Church and that in consequence it was regarded as an attribute of the Devil. The classical ballet has disciplined and Christianized the essentially pagan art of the dance to such an extent that Heine compares it with the ascetic spiritualism of classical French tragedy and of Jansenism[12] (how Heine would reconcile this argument with his usual view of the frivolity and sensual superficiality of the French character he does not say). Social dancing, he finds, is not dance at all but merely indifferent walking through a set of prescribed steps.[13] Popular dancing Heine claims to like better, but here his fundamental ambivalence whenever he is confronted with lower-class phenomena asserts itself. He remarks sardonically upon the state of liberty in a nation where the police supervises dance halls to watch for any sign of the cancan, but, on the other hand, the tone in which he

* Niehaus also says that Heine's *Faust* inspired Gounod's opera in 1859.

describes the popular dances vacillates between fascination and dismay.[14] Heine feels that these dances express not only sensual lust but a complete scorn of all values, and he compares the scene in a Parisian dance hall to the Witches' Sabbath.[15] How much he was interested in the potential of the dance as a medium of liberated expression is evident, however, from the second part of *Florentinische Nächte*.[16]

This account of Heine's attitude toward the dance sheds a good deal of light on the two ballets, particularly on *Faust.* Heine forces into prominence in both ballets the aggressively sensual, Dionysian aspect of the dance that European fashion and convention had tried to legislate out of the art form. However, in these years Heine is well past the stage in which he regarded sensual emancipation as the infallible source of salvation, so that this aspect is only one element of a dialectic, a subtle one in *Die Göttin Diana* and a more obvious and grim one in *Faust.* But, apart from this aspect of the ballets, there is another important feature: the works operate exclusively with materials drawn from cultural tradition. This is more significant than it might seem at once. At the root of the whole agony of dealing with Heine critically is the fact that so very few of his works are purely *literary;* either they are located in a no-man's-land between "poesy" and personal, self-defining statement, or they mediate, with great strain and urgency, between fiction and the contemporary public situation. The ballets do not belong to either of these categories; although they are motivated by a set of intellectual ideas that are peculiarly Heine's and appear elsewhere in his work, they remain entirely within the objective aesthetic realm.

Die Göttin Diana is the smaller and the less important of the two scenarios; however, it is given a certain amount of resonance by the essay entitled *Die Götter im Exil* that Heine published along with it in the *Vermischte Schriften* in 1854. We do not know when this essay was written; it appeared first in French translation in 1853, but it would surprise no one if it were to turn out that, in conception, at least, it were several years older than that. It belongs in general to Heine's extensive writings on Germany and in particular to his researches in folklore. These interests, which Heine pursued with remarkable diligence, are perhaps a symptom of exile. Overwhelmingly the emphasis is on the German and Germanic traditions; except for the allusions to the *Song of Roland* in *Atta Troll* and an occasional reference elsewhere, the French, Provençal, and Celtic traditions play a minor role; even the King Arthur cycle is referred to only rarely and fleetingly. Heine's famous tale of the "Willis" in *Elementargeister,*[17] which inspired the ballet *Giselle,* is his only excursion into Slavic materials. It is not unreasonable to suppose that, psychologically, these studies are part of Heine's effort to maintain himself as a German poet against the obstacles imposed by exile in a foreign land and a foreign language.

Heine synthesized these interests with another of his obligations as a German poet: the need to come to terms with ancient Greece. Like all Germans, Heine had to believe that Greece was a lost paradise of aesthetic calm and cheerful natural religion. Like Schiller and Hölderlin, he knew that the paradise was lost forever, but unlike them and such post-Romantics as Platen, he was utterly uninterested in any efforts at classicistic revival. Gone is gone. He was more interested in giving some account of where it had gone, and this problem he solved with his well-known view that spiritualist Christianity had transformed the ancient deities and nature spirits into demons as part of the process of condemning human joy and sensuality as evil. Consequently, Heine had for his time an unusual appreciation of the Dionysian element of the Greek tradition and this, in turn, led him to the dance. But although this Dionysian element charged Heine's art with a great deal of energy, it was not a totally liberating factor, at least not in a positive sense. In *Die Götter im Exil* Heine describes the effect of representations of Bacchic festivals as "ästhetisches Grüseln" (E, *6,* 83), and their total lack of restraint affects him as ambiguously as the popular dancing he described in his newspaper article. Moreover, the Dionysian element is strongly tempered by the elegiac tone of Heine's stories of the gods in exil, and the essay towards the end begins to develop a theme that is pervasive in his later poetry. The battered glory of Jupiter, who is exiled to his lonely island in the frozen north and weeps bitter tears at the account of his ruined temple, is a symbol of irretrievably decayed greatness, and at the end of the essay Heine derives his sour moral: "An jeder Größe auf dieser Erde nagen die heimlichen Ratten" (E, *6,* 98).

Die Göttin Diana of 1846 locates a resolution of all these problems in the poetic realm. The principle of its structure is the alternation of disillusion and hope.* In the first "tableau" the knight breaks through Diana's reserve, and the event is celebrated by a Bacchic festival in which Apollo and the Muses also participate. In the second, the knight in his castle is suffering from gloom and boredom, from which he is released by the invasion of Diana and her following, and he is invited to the Venusberg. But in the third he is killed by Eckart, the champion of "Nazarenism" who guards the entrance of the Venusberg and prevents the tempted from entering. In the final tableau, Venus is unable to revive him, for her power is less than that of death, but Apollo manages to waken him briefly into life, and Bacchus arouses him completely into joyful existence. The sketch ends with a "Glorie der Verklärung" (E, *6,* 110), and everyone lives happily forever after . . . but not quite. For the only inhabitants of the Venusberg are figments of the poetic imagination and ghosts of deceased notables. Their existence is literary only; they continue to survive in the land of "poesy." Thus it would seem that only in the realm of art is the soul liberated, joyful, and at rest.

Heine himself was aware that *Die Göttin Diana* is a fleeting sketch only.[18] Moreover, it is a rather odd kind of fantasy to build around Diana. In *Atta Troll,* it is true, Heine had already relieved Diana of her attribute of chastity, but in its place he put an unhealthy, insatiable sensuality that still recalls Diana's original character by contrast. In the ballet neither the presence nor absence of this attribute is felt at all to speak of. She is no more than the divine huntress and a symbol of ideal Greek beauty, so that in the ballet she represents less than her total implications as a mythological figure; the work, as a consequence, is weak at the center. Nor is it clear, to me at least, just what is happening

* Here as elsewhere in this chapter, I owe valuable insights to an unpublished paper on the ballet scenarios written by a former student, Robert Stiefel, currently at Harvard.

when in the third tableau the knight wanders through a Romantic landscape, and the elemental spirits tempt and obstruct him; Mücke may not have been far wrong when he suggested that these foreign elements have been forced into the ballet in order to develop more spectacle on the stage.[19] The undines try to seduce the knight into the water, and the salamanders, after forcing a crown and scepter upon him, nearly burn him up; he is saved only by the appearance of Diana. It would seem that Heine is dividing the realm of "poesy" into Romantic and Classical components, in which the first is dangerous and to be shunned, while the second offers protection and salvation. But the Venusberg, where the knight is ultimately revived, is not a Classical locale, despite the presence of Venus, Diana, Apollo, and Bacchus; it is the place of exile of these deities *within* the Romantic landscape; even its decor is not Classical, but of the Renaissance.[20] Here Heine seems to be trying to do too much with too little.

Other aspects of *Die Göttin Diana* point to *Faust*. The Dionysian intrusion in the second tableau contrasts sharply with the rude gravity of medieval Germany; the positive evaluation is clearly awarded to the Dionysian element in the pas-de-deux in which "griechisch heidnische Götterlust" dances a duel "mit der germanisch spiritualistischen Haustugend" (E, *6,* 106). But the dance of Venus and Tannhäuser in the final tableau illustrates that a critique of pure sensuality is never far from Heine's mind: they are united "durch eine unverwüstliche Liebe, die aber keineswegs auf wechselseitiger Achtung beruht" (E, *6,* 109). We are reminded of the poem *Der Tannhäuser,* in which it is clear that such "Liebe" is not always even "unverwüstlich," and in *Faust* we are to be shown drastically that it is not.

When Goethe created his *Faust,* he was competing with a roughhewn popular tale, a puppet play, and Christopher Marlowe. Those who have subsequently attempted a *Faust* have been competing with Goethe, and that is another matter altogether. Of all of them, only Thomas Mann has stayed in the race, and there are some who would dispute that. Heine's David-and-Goliath act in this regard is not without an element of farce, although it should be remembered that the task, if task in any serious sense it was, looked a little easier to him than it does to us because he was competing only with Goethe's first part; like most others in his time, he had no appreciation, except for the Helena episode, of the monumental greatness of *Faust II*—"jenen lendenlahmen zweiten Teil" (E, *6*, 496),[21] as he called it with almost comical obtuseness. In measuring his work against Goethe's, Heine asserts that within the much more restrictive limitations of the ballet form, his work has certain advantages over Goethe's because it better captures the true spirit of the legend.[22] One is somewhat reminded here of Shaw's argument in the *Preface to Three Plays for Puritans* that his *Caesar and Cleopatra* is better than Shakespeare's; the self-assertiveness is genuine, but its gross hyperbole reveals the roguishness that underlies it all. This quality pervades what little we know of Heine's plans to write a *Faust* in the 1820s. He speaks vaguely of it in several letters,[23] but we know no more about its progress than about that of the contemporaneous *Der Rabbi von Bacherach.* In Eduard Wedekind's interesting conversations with Heine in 1824 there are details aplenty,[24] but they are of a nature, as even the sometimes rather humorless Elster noted,[25] to suggest that Heine was pulling Wedekind's leg. Maximilian Heine's famous tale of Heine's visit to Goethe in 1824, in which he is said to have told the forbidding old man that he was writing a *Faust,*[26] looks like another of Heine's canards—it is hard to believe that even he could have been that impudent—but undoubtedly all this is an element of Heine's insistent need to believe in his own greatness. In any case, there is no reason to think that the earlier plan had anything to do with the *Faust* Heine eventually wrote, which definitely belongs, in form and content, to the 1840s. As usual, we do not know exactly what Heine thought of his work; when advertising it, he praised it highly, as was his wont,[27] but in a letter to Georg Weerth he spoke of it with indifference[28]—and after having traced the history of the subject, he yields gracefully and foxily to Goethe: "Abraham zeugte den Isaak, Isaak zeugte den Jakob, Jakob aber zeugte den Juda, in dessen Händen das Scepter ewig bleiben wird" (E, *6*, 478).

The only part of Goethe's *Faust* that Heine discusses in his commentary with any detail and enthusiasm is the Helena act of

Part II, but Heine's own Helena scene is not the most striking feature of his scenario. Instead, it seems that the part of Goethe's *Faust* that impressed him most was the Witches' Sabbath of Part I, for its demonic and violent sensuality colors Heine's whole work with varying degrees of intensity. Although Heine does not seem to have known the *Paralipomena* to Goethe's Witches' Sabbath, which contain obscenities and allusions too strong to have been published at that time, there is evidence that both Goethe and Heine worked independently from some of the same folkloric sources.[29] The result is that Heine's *Faust* tends to the grotesque in an almost surrealistic manner, and the elements of his poetic vision are stylized and related to one another in a way that transcends literal interpretation. The whole ballet is pervaded with a sense of threat and terror that is lacking in Goethe; where the dance patterns are described as even and harmonious, they are tense and scornfully ungenuine and always subject to dissolution by the onslaught of frantic movement. Goethe's Mephisto is a Machiavellian gentleman who is more absurd than terrifying; Goethe's universe is, in the last analysis, benign. Heine's female demon is thoroughly terrifying and, indeed, invincible; there is no God in Heine's universe and no active force of good; only evil and ineluctable damnation. Heine is quite correct that this is closer to the original impact of the Faust legend (although, of course, in the original the divine law is felt by implication), and it is of no little significance that he was concerned to restore it against what he not unreasonably identifies as Goethe's eighteenth-century rationalism.[30] But the ballet is not merely the reconstruction of a period piece; many of Heine's attitudes were absorbed into it, and its unrelieved pessimism definitely belongs to the nineteenth century.

Only in the first act do we have any outstanding impression that Faust is one of Heine's projected personae. The characterization of Faust as "eine Mischung von Unbeholfenheit und Mut" (E, *6*, 481) would not be a bad description of Heine's bearing, especially in his younger days. The violence of Faust's jealousy when the Duchess first rejects him in favor of a handsome and insipid ape and the effort he must expend to learn gracefulness also relate vaguely to the development of the persona in the years before Paris. But Faust exists so completely within the context Heine has made for him that it is not productive to pursue such parallels. Similarly, Heine's transformation of Mephistopheles into a woman is not to be interpreted exclusively as an expression of his grudge against women, appropriate as this metamorphosis may be to Heine's own experience and attitude. Heine took from the tradition the view that the human animal is the most terrifying form the Devil can assume,[31] and the metamorphosis of the Devil into a woman is only a further ironic extension of this bitter pessimism. Nor was Heine the first to suggest this extension, as Walzel has pointed out.[32] That Faust's seducer should be a woman is determined in part by the logic of the ballet genre, since this permits the necessary duets. It is of greater importance to remember that there is nothing real about Mephistophela's femininity; she, like all the other demons and spirits of the ballet, can appear in any number of shapes, so that there is nothing essential about her womanly form. It is assumed only for the purpose of creating illusions of sensuality in order to delude and destroy Faust. The emptiness of erotic sensuality, the fact that it is an assumed façade, is the most important single feature of *Faust*; it roundly disposes of any effort to present Heine as an unambiguous champion of materialist emancipation. The "Nazarenism" of the work is not ascribable merely to the tradition Heine is attempting to recover, for it lay within his power, as it did within Goethe's, to make of the Faust legend whatever he chose.

Not until the fourth act, however, does the hopelessness and, indeed, absurdity of Faust's desires become manifest. In the first act the sensuality encouraged by Mephistophela is developed within the spiritualist realm, and this may appear to account for its unhealthiness. Mephistophela herself is a product of medieval Christian Europe. Her dancing when she first appears is precious and courtly. Just as the medieval imagination saw corporeal beauty as a mask for the evil lurking within, so here the demons are effortlessly transformed into pretty danseuses. But Faust himself does not transcend this world of fakery and delusion. Whereas Goethe's Faust always maintains an ironic dignity and independence in his dealings with Mephistopheles, Heine's Faust is Mephistophela's fool. Although he can see with his very eyes that sensual beauty is conjured at will out of vileness, he is nevertheless totally susceptible to it. The perspective from which Faust's erotic arousal and jealousy are presented is extraordinarily mean. The Duchess rejects him in favor of an insipid fop metamorphosed from an ape, and Faust learns to dance in order to become more like him. When he has achieved this, he is able to capture the attention of the Duchess. Metaphistophela is literally making a monkey out of him.

From this beginning, Faust is conducted through a variety of illusions and never succeeds in penetrating to any substantial reality. In the second act, Faust is permitted to make the acquaintance of the Duchess and arrange an assignation at the Witches' Sabbath. In order to entertain the court he is requested to produce King David dancing before the Ark. He does not, however, succeed in doing so; instead he conjures up a vision as it might have existed in the popular medieval mind: David looks like a playing card king, and his bodyguard is made up of Polish Jews in caftans and fur hats. This travesty shows that Faust has not penetrated at all into the world of the Biblical past and has no power to bring it to life; what he offers the Duke is as threadbare an illusion as that which Mephistophela offers Faust. In the third act, Faust appears to have an opportunity to learn this. The stage setting Heine envisioned for the Witches' Sabbath, with the goat, directly in the middle, with a candle between his horns, is highly picturesque. Heine is careful to explain that even in the midst of all this bizarre corruption artistic beauty must be maintained. The effect, whether Heine was fully aware of it or not, is to prevent beauty from being put into dialectical opposition to the nightmarish evil and illusory sensuality of this scene, revealing once more the tormented ambiguity of Heine's aesthetics. The eroticism aroused in Faust is finally exposed and destroyed in this act. His passionate dance with the Duchess is parodied by the dance of Mephistophela with her Spanish knight, which is "nur der buhlerische Ausdruck der Galanterie, der zärtlichen Lüge, der sich selbst persiflierenden Lüsternheit" (E, *6*, 488). This does not imply, however, that Faust's own passion is any more enduring, for no sooner has he satisfied his sexual desire for the Duchess than he is filled with satiated disgust, which is reflected in turn by the cosmic ennui of Satan. The attitude of the *Verschiedene* is here sharply contracted into a grim suspicion of pure sensuality that has no trace of frivolity.

At this point Faust comes to believe that there is an escape open to him, and his thoughts turn to Classical Greece: "Er empfindet eine unendliche Sehnsucht nach dem Reinschönen, Gestalten der Homerischen Frühlingswelt!" (E, *6,* 489). In view of the outcome of this, Heine's exclamation point may be ironic. For the moment, however, Faust perceives that the evil of the Witches' Sabbath is only an inverted version of Christian asceticism—and so it is, for the last act overwhelms the despair of the rejected Duchess with the parodistic religiosity of the Black Mass—and thus Faust comes to hope, as have many German intellectuals, that Classical antiquity will provide a refuge from the abrasive dilemmas of modern Europe. Mephistophela, who knows better, is quite willing to conduct him to Arcadia.

Heine's setting for Act IV is a transposition of German literary metaphor for Greece into stage decoration. The sea is emerald and the sky turquoise; the sun shines on an ideal landscape of pines and laurels; fabulous plants grow in marble vases.[33] As Heine makes quite clear in his commentary, we are not presented here with any Greece of reality, but "das Hellenentum selbst, welches plötzlich im Herzen Deutschlands emportaucht, wie beschworen durch Zaubersprüche" (E, *6,* 505). Heine sets down the clichés of German Graecophilia with blasé ease: "Heiterkeit"; "klassische Ruhe"; "Anblick des Urschönen" (E, *6,* 490). Yet he is German enough to be serious about it; for a moment this milieu really does seem to present an alternative to Romantic spiritualism and modern homelessness of the spirit: "Nichts erinnert an ein neblichtes Jenseits, an mystische Wollust- und Angstschauer, an überirdische Ekstase eines Geistes, der sich von der Körperlichkeit emanzipiert; hier ist alles reale plastische Seligkeit ohne retrospektive Wehmut, ohne ahnende leere Sehnsucht" (E, *6,* 490). Here eroticism is calmed into harmony with natural religion; a cheerful festival is being celebrated before the temple of Aphrodite.

Faust and Mephistophela burst upon this scene, apparently liberated from the medieval nightmare out of which they have fled; Faust takes his ease with Helena. Walzel has argued that even Mephistophela is affected by the experience of pure Greek beauty,[34] but Enders is probably closer to the spirit of the work as a whole when he counters that Mephistophela only accommodates herself to the circumstances out of evil intention.[35] It is significant, first of all, that Faust never dances a duet with Helena, and secondly, that it is Mephistophela with her Bacchic dance who introduces a Dionysian element into this otherwise Apollonian scene; even in the Greek landscape she is the symbol of unbridled sensuality. Faust's idyll with Helena is quite brief; the Duchess comes storming out of her medieval Hell and in her frustrated passion destroys the landscape. The symbols of antiquity cannot withstand this onslaught; the scene falls into ruin and Helena turns into a fleshless corpse. The Greece into which Faust has attempted to flee is an insubstantial fantasy that crumbles before the Duchess' magic. Christian Europe has destroyed Classical Greece, and no amount of repudiation of the former can bring the latter back to life; Faust may kill the Duchess, but the Greek island sinks below the sea. Mephistophela conducts Faust away as she has conducted him there. Here Heine really seems to have absorbed something of Hegel's historical dialectic, although in a most pessimistic way.

The fifth act is a little more difficult to understand than the rest of *Faust*. Whether it is primarily inspired by the logic of the work itself or whether it may be to some extent a fragment of a confession is all but impossible to judge. By locating Faust in the eminently bourgeois surroundings of sixteenth-century Holland and by suggesting that there Faust comes closest to achieving true happiness, Heine seems to be giving some expression to the outsider's characteristic longing for bourgeois normality. For the first time, Faust loves, and he seems to be potentially domesticated and at peace with himself: "Der Doktor hat endlich im bescheiden süßen Stillleben das Hausglück gefunden, welches die Seele befriedigt. Vergessen sind die Zweifel und die schwärmerischen Schmerzgenüsse des Hochmutgeistes, und er strahlt vor innerer Beseligung wie der vergoldete Hahn eines Kirchturms" (E, *6*, 493). The language ends up being ironic, but not devastatingly so. But it is doubtful whether this scene has any more real substance than the other delusions that Mephistophela has conjured up for Faust. This setting, like all the others, is artistically conditioned; the scene clearly reminds us of the cheerful and realistic Dutch painting of the period, for which Heine had a weakness. In order to enter into this world, Faust must humble himself and, indeed, divest himself of his identity; he must attempt to become not-Faust. This is not possible, for Faust is Faust, and he is damned; as in the Faust legend, he is not to be permitted to make his peace with normality by marrying. When Mephistophela presents the reckoning for the wages of sin, she drives Faust into the final indignity: he attempts to flee "in den Schoß der Kirche" (E, *6*, 494), a phrasing that alludes to the conversions of the Romantics that Heine found so detestable. Faust's attempt to make a bargain with erotic sensuality has caused him to lose his soul irretrievably.

Faust, brief and sketchy though it may be, is an interesting work. Although Heine rides his intellectual hobbyhorses in it, it contains nothing prescriptive; nothing can save Faust, and Heine's formulae for the emancipation of European society fade away; only the definition of the problem remains. At the same time, the scenario is informed by Heine's permanent worry about the relatedness of beauty and delusion. Mephistophela places Faust in a series of literary and artistic settings; nowhere does he achieve any contact with reality. He bears the guilt for this himself because of his preoccupation with his own liberation. He is totally susceptible to the products of the imagination, and as a result he is quite literally a damned fool. Nowhere else does Heine so thoroughly cut the ties of a fictional character to the factual reality of his own experience and to the details of the mundane world. Thus released, Faust goes straight to Hell.

CHAPTER 13

The Poet Prostrate: *Romanzero*

The earth is given into the hand of the wicked;
He covers the faces of its judges—
If it is not He, who then is it?

—JOB 9:24

Drum soll der Sänger mit dem König gehen,
Sie beide wohnen auf der Menschheit Höhen.

—SCHILLER

Laura Hofrichter has pointed out cleverly that no one ever thinks of Heine as anything but a young man.[1] But he was fifty-three when *Romanzero* was published and nearly sixty when he died. His late poetry is the work of a mature artist, and, indeed, it is difficult to imagine what Heine's reputation would be today if he had died, as he easily might have, before 1850. Contemporary interpreters of Heine usually like to believe that only in relatively recent times have we come to appreciate the late poetry, but this is true mainly of his popular and international reputation, borne as it was by thousands of musical settings of poems from *Buch der Lieder* and *Neuer Frühling*. *Romanzero* was a substantial success when it was published, and in 1890, Elster, whose aesthetic judgment was rarely original, wrote calmly of "unvergleichliche Gedichte." [2] The weight given to the total phenomenon of Heine by this work is vastly increased by the conditions under which it was written. Even Heine's worst enemies have rarely been able to suppress pity at the unspeakable agony in which he passed his last years, and most observers have remarked with amazed admiration that his mind remained so clear, courageous, and creative during the years when his body was wracked with pain and his mind distracted by drugs. It is not true, as is sometimes alleged, that Heine bore his terrible affliction in patient silence; he did prevent his mother from knowing how desperate his case was, but otherwise he complained bitterly and long in all directions and with every right; yet he continued to survive and expand as a poet under conditions that would have reduced other men to stasis or suicide. This strength of Heine's while lying interminably in the very jaws of death seems to me to demand some sort of explanation. Schiller also had remained intensely productive while his body literally disintegrated from under him, but he had always survived on a tremendous energy of will. As we follow Heine up to the mid-1840s, we find little in his character that would enable one to predict the superhuman stoutness of spirit of his later years. It is perhaps neither overly harsh nor unjust to Heine's reputation to suggest that in a certain sense the pain-wracked paralysis of his last years met a psychological need, for he certainly showed a strong masochistic streak from the very outset. The sufferings of his youth and young manhood are to a considerable extent self-generated, and they arouse irritation in Heine himself as well as in his readers. It is hard to forgive Campe for his deafness to Heine's complaints up to 1851, but he had experienced the man's laments for nearly a quarter of a century and had simply got out of the habit of taking them seriously. Only after a visit at firsthand did Campe realize that the sufferings of Heine's last years were spectacularly real. With them came a relative calm and a less endangered self-satisfaction. His tendency to self-pity now had an objective justification, which is the best interpretation of a typical remark in a letter of 1850 to L. Wertheim: "Mein Zustand ist so tragisch, daß ich selber anfange, Mitleiden mit mir zu haben, was bisher der alte Uebermuth noch nicht erlaubte" (Hirth, *3*, 199). Hans Kaufmann has remarked that now Heine needed no longer to play the "sterbende Fechter," for that is what he had become in reality.[3]

The transformation—it is more than a readjustment and less than a metamorphosis—that accompanied Heine's illness is closely bound up with his famous acknowledgment of God. This fascinating topic has been much remarked upon and has been closely analyzed by Hermann J. Weigand [4] and by William Rose;[5] yet, like Heine himself, it tends to be elusive. It should be remembered, first of all, that Heine had always professed a vague theism; even in his most aggressively anticlerical work, *Die Stadt Lucca,* he acknowledges "die Herrlichkeit Gottes" (E, *3,* 417) and in *Zur Geschichte der Religion und Philosphie in Deutschland,* he hangs on tightly and explicitly to a belief in the existence of God and refuses to admit even a discussion of the subject.[6] The "return" is not as abrupt as it sometimes is made out to be. We cannot pursue its progress here in depth, for an understanding of it requires the analysis of a considerable number of scattered and by no means consistent remarks. Nor is it necessary to labor its obvious features: that Heine's religious return was completely undogmatic and noninstitutional; that it was lacking in reverence and ordinary humility, qualities for which Heine could never find any use; that it was not a mystical *Erleuchtung* or an experience of grace but a decision of the mind, maintained with full rationality and not without connections to a spiritualist substratum evident in Heine's career from start to finish; that it was frankly and avowedly a capitulation to the disaster that had befallen his physical being; and, above all, that it took place exclusively in the only realm in which Heine was able to subsist, the literary imagination. Even in the 1830s, his objection to atheistic doctrines was that they are antipoetic.[7] Consequently the experienced student of Heine will not give unhesitating credence to his claims that he burned a large number of manuscripts that contained matters disrespectful to God, although the sheer number of these references to such an act does not allow us to reject the possibility out of hand.[8] Furthermore, his position does not come to rest in any easily definable form. In some places he seems to have discovered a new "spiritual dignity of morality," [9] as in the *Geständnisse,* where he announces that "Gutsein ist besser denn Schönheit" (E, *6,* 60); elsewhere, as in the late poem *Bimini,* there is an attempt to reconcile the dialectic of morality and beauty;[10] but in his long poem *Für die Mouche* at the very end of his life the dissonances between sensualism and spiritualism sound again. Nor did the admonition of Leviticus 19:18, to love one's neighbor as one's self, make much impression on Heine; enemies are enemies, a point he reiterated in the poem *Vermächtnis* in *Romanzero,* in the remark in his posthumous papers that he would be ready to forgive his enemies once he could see them hanging from a tree outside his door,[11] and in the violent poem *Stoßseufzer:*

> Nicht zum Lieben, nein, zum Hassen
> Sollt ihr uns den Herrgott lassen,
> Weil man sonst nicht fluchen könnt'—
> Himmel-Herrgott-Sakrament! (E, *2,* 167)

It is of some interest not only that the total collapse of Heine's health and his fully conscious acknowledgment of God coincide, but also that both occur in the revolutionary year of 1848. "Auf dem Totenbette sind so viele Freidenker bekehrt worden" (E, *4,* 288), he had remarked with prideful scorn in the 1830s, but in 1849 he found himself obliged to describe to the public his illness and his new religious views in the same breath.[12] Similarly, Heine found it appropriate to relate his theism to his views of the Revolution of 1848. In July, Heine wrote to Campe: "das ist Universalanarchie, Weltkuddelmuddel, sichtbar gewordener Gotteswahnsinn! Der Alte muß eingesperrt werden, wenn das so fort geht.—Das haben die Atheisten verschuldet, die ihn toll geärgert" (Hirth, *3,* 151). A key to Heine's repudiation of atheism lies in his artistic elitism; in the *Geständnisse* he makes it quite clear that now that atheism is the property of the revolutionary masses, it holds terrors for him that it did not have when it was merely among the ideas of progressive intellectuals:

> ich sah nämlich, daß der Atheismus ein mehr oder minder geheimes Bündnis geschlossen mit dem schauderhaft nacktesten, ganz feigenblattlosen, kommunen Kommunismus. . . . Mich beklemmt . . . die geheime Angst des Künstlers und des Gelehrten, die wir unsre ganze moderne Zivilisation, die mühselige Errungenschaft so vieler Jahrhunderte, die Frucht der edelsten Arbeiten unsrer Vorgänger, durch den Sieg des Kommunismus bedroht sehen. (E, *6,* 42)

After 1848, Heine found himself in a world in which he could no longer actively participate due to his health, whereas his analysis of the political situation, particularly his convictions about the inevitability of Communist revolution, alienated him from the progressive attitude he had so stridently tried to maintain in the early 1840s. The turn inward to the sources of the poetic imagination and the conscious effort to posit a God reigning in the poetic realm as a partner of the autonomous creator are thus aspects of the same event. Another part of the experience is the stark confrontation with death. Heine exhibits a paradoxical combination of self-destructiveness and traces of a death-wish with an elemental love of life and devotion to his own existence. Thus in the epilogue to *Romanzero* he turns to the topic of immortality. It seems that Fichte's son, with whom Heine had become acquainted in Paris, had aroused in him an interest in Swedenborg,[13] and Heine appears to have taken Swedenborg's visions of the world beyond with some seriousness, although his description of them is not without its satirical purpose.

Heine's refusal to keep a straight face or a solemn tone when discussing his religious "regression," as he put it,[14] has made it difficult for many people to believe that any substantial transformation took place. His remarks about immortality, which he compares to the soup bone thrown in the package free by the butcher,[15] are a good example. Another is his remark: "Ja, wie mit der Kreatur, habe ich auch mit dem Schöpfer Frieden gemacht" (E, *1*, 485), for it follows directly and intentionally upon a display of how he had made his peace with the "Kreatur," a more than usually insulting treatment of his old whipping boy, Hans Ferdinand Massmann. Some of this irrepressible flippancy is due to Heine's lurking embarrassment at the whole matter, his great desire not to be misunderstood as a pious convert to established religion, and a need to maintain a continuity in style and attitude that is part of the struggle for the unity of the persona. His familiar elusiveness, naturally, also plays a part; Ferdinand Hiller observed: "ich weiß nicht, was er glaubt—aber wenn ich auch glaube, daß er es weiß, so glaube ich doch nicht, daß er so leicht hierüber irgend jemanden ganz reinen Wein einschenkt." [16] Yet the tone of sincerity is often not only absent, but also deliberately avoided. Heine's God is so obviously created and manipulated by the poet for his own ends, that the question of whether the whole complex transcends poetic fiction is a fair one, especially in view of the renewed stress Heine puts upon his dignity as a poet above all else in the *Geständnisse*. Weigand, in studying this crucial stage in Heine's development, came to "the unqualified conclusion that theoretical issues of any kind whatever did not touch the core of his personality. To put it briefly and in the form of an ethical thesis: Heine lacked intellectual integrity of the highest order." [17] Weigand argues that all of Heine's attitudes are grounded exclusively in his narcissistic self-regard. Thus he explains the special quality of Heine's late writing not as a pose but as a spontaneous attitude growing out of a readjustment of the self-enamoured poet to the new situation:

> a mood of grave, tranquil, sometimes somber seriousness instinctively began to replace in Heine's heart the lighthearted laughter of his former days, as becoming to his altered status. Sallies of wit, choice conceits, bizarre anachronisms, flashes of fantastic humor adorn his language as of old—but now they occur as quaint arabesques traced against a background of solemn gravity. The poetry of the *Romanzero,* and the last poems, is that of a sage whose dying body is transfigured with a spiritual beauty.[18]

"Religion," remarked E. M. Butler, "if it did not console Heine, always exhilarated him greatly." [19] The justice of these views must be admitted, but they are perhaps susceptible to some revision. First of all, one may fairly ask whether Heine's laughter of former days is genuinely lighthearted; we have had occasion to call attention to somber undertones in a great many places. Secondly, although one does get a feeling that, beginning with *Romanzero,* the persona has become more closely merged with Heine himself, we nevertheless continue to cope with him primarily at the level of a self-created poetic fiction and so must continue to be cautious with psychological assumptions about the elusive poet.

Apart from this, one can approach the specifically religious problem from another direction altogether. Weigand found it impossible to reconcile the pervasive pessimism of Heine's final attitude with his religious rebirth.[20] This strikes me, however, as a judgment from a Christian perspective, whereas Heine's wrangling with God, his refusal to accept the moral order of the universe as he experienced it, is the most substantial emergence of specifically Jewish religious attitude to be found anywhere in his career: for Heine was of the seed of Job, and like Job in Heine's interpretation of that book, a suffering man must weep and cry out his desperation and doubt if he is to have any hope of ease.[21] To Laube he wrote in 1850: "Ich liege zusammengekrümmt, Tag und Nacht in Schmerzen, und wenn ich auch an einen Gott glaube, so glaube ich doch manchmal nicht an einen guten Gott. Die Hand dieses großen Thierquälers liegt schwer auf mir" (Hirth, *3*, 232). Caroline Jaubert reported that after Heine received a letter from his mother thanking God for preserving his health, he cried out that God accepted this with no pangs of conscience.[22] This is the attitude of Sholom Aleichem's Tevye the Dairyman, with a characteristic Heinesque shift into arrogance and irreverence: an acknowledgment of God's power coupled with reservations about His justice and mercy. Heine's religious experience is not a Christian one primarily of grace and an outpouring of God's love (here Weigand's claim that Heine created his God out of a desire to be loved seems to me misleading[23]), but one of being forced to taste the grapes of wrath. Heine wrote to his brother Max in 1849:

> Unsere Väter waren wackere Leute: sie demüthigten sich vor Gott und waren deßhalb so störrig und trotzig den Menschen, den irdischen Mächten, gegenüber; ich dagegen, ich bot dem Himmel frech die Stirne und war demüthig und kriechend vor den Menschen—und deßwegen liege ich jetzt am Boden wie ein zertretener Wurm. Ruhm und Ehre dem Gott in der Höhe! (Hirth, *3*, 180).

Perhaps this aspect of Heine's confrontation with God can be understood better from the perspective of a more modern despair profounder than anything Heine's age could have imagined. Some years ago a document was published that was described as having been written by an Orthodox Hasidic Jew in the last hours of his life while the Germans were destroying the Warsaw Ghetto in April 1943. German aircraft had killed his wife and infant children on the road, and as artillery pounded the Ghetto into dust, he wrote his final reckoning with God, in which he reaffirmed his own faith in the face of God's refusal to honor it. A few quotations from this testament may be pertinent here:

> I bow my head before Your greatness, but will not kiss the lash with which You strike me. . . . Do not put the rope under too much strain, lest, alas, it may snap. The test to which You have put us is so severe, so unbearably severe, that You should—You must—forgive those members of Your people who, in their misery, have turned from You. . . . I cannot extol You for the deeds that You tolerate. I bless You and extol You, however, for the very fact of Your existence, for Your awesome mightiness. . . . I die peacefully, but not complacently; persecuted, but not enslaved; embittered but not cynical; a believer, but not a supplicant; a lover of God, but no blind amen-sayer of His. . . . And these are my last words to You, my wrathful God: nothing will avail You in the least. You have done everything to make me renounce You, to make me lose my faith in You, but I die exactly as I have lived, crying: Eternally praised be the God of the dead, the God of vengeance, of truth and of law, Who will soon show His face to the world again and shake its foundations with His almighty voice. Hear, O Israel. . . .[24]

Neither by upbringing nor by temperament did Heine have access to faith of this quality. In depth of religious sentiment the two cases are incommensurable. But there are points of contact in the acknowledgment of God and His power as an act of defiant will even though He does not appear to keep His part of the Covenant, in the appeal for a show of divine vengeance at last, and in the recognition that although one appeals to God for help because it is His due, God does not help—He reigns. For Heine, God is an omnipotent projection of the poetic persona, a humorist of unmerciful grimness Whose actions are real enough but not exempt from criticism:

> Ja, die Lauge der Verhöhnung, die der Meister über mich herabgeußt, ist entsetzlich, und schauerlich grausam ist sein Spaß. Demütig bekenne ich seine Überlegenheit, und ich

> beuge mich vor ihm im Staube. Aber wenn es mir auch an solcher höchsten Schöpfungskraft fehlt, so blitzt doch in meinem Geiste die ewige Vernunft, und ich darf sogar den Spaß Gottes vor ihr Forum ziehen und einer ehrfurchtsvollen Kritik unterwerfen. Und da wage ich nun zunächst die unterthänigste Andeutung auszusprechen, es wolle mich bedünken, als zöge sich jener grausame Spaß, womit der Meister den armen Schüler heimsucht, etwas zu sehr in die Länge; er dauert schon über sechs Jahre, was nachgerade langweilig wird. (E, *6*, 73)

Heine's religious turnabout is intimately connected with the pessimism and blasphemy of his late writing. Undoubtedly it has aspects that ring truer to us today than they did to the age of David Friedrich Strauss and Feuerbach.

Neither the blasphemy nor the pessimism is entirely new. In 1823, when Heine was quite interested in his Jewish heritage, he wrote a passage to Moser that anticipates his later style in these matters:

> Es ist sehr unartig von unserem Herrgott, daß er mich jetzt mit diesen Schmerzen plagt; ja, es ist sogar unpolitisch von dem alten Herrn, da er weiß, daß ich so viel für ihn thun möchte. Oder ist der alte Freiherr von Sinai und Alleinherrscher Judäas ebenfalls aufgeklärt worden und hat seine Nazionalität abgelegt und giebt seine Ansprüche und seine Anhänger auf, zum Besten einiger vagen, kosmopolitischen Ideen? Ich fürchte, der alte Herr hat den Kopf verloren, und mit Recht mag ihm le petit juif d'Amsterdam [Spinoza] ins Ohr sagen: entre nous Monsieur, vous n'existez pas. (Hirth, *1*, 90)

The theme of the victory of the worse man also has its antecedents, for example, in the section on Wellington, the victor over Napoleon, in the *Englische Fragmente,*[25] and in a very early jingle addressed to Steinmann, which Elster has dated in the fall of 1820;[26] it begins:

> Die Schlechten siegen, untergehn die Wackern,
> Statt Myrten lobt man nur die dürren Pappeln. (E, *2*, 64)

The consolidation of this theme seems to absorb the persona in his various metamorphoses more thoroughly into the fabric of the poetry than Heine had ever done before. The poetic intelligence of *Romanzero* is rarely overtly or aggressively on display; instead it ranges about in the sources of poetic inspiration with subdued bitterness, abstracting the concerns of the persona and giving them, for the most part, a loosely balladesque form. An outstanding feature of the performance is the abandonment of lyrical compression; with few exceptions, the poems of *Romanzero* are rambling and in places even diffuse; the rhythms vary between deliberate prosiness and adroitly manipulated versification. Elster found this apparent laxness overdone,[27] but Prawer has shown how deliberately it was worked into the poems and how necessary it is to their total effect.[28] The presence of the poet manipulating his language is constantly felt by implication. This is appropriate enough, for the poet-persona and his fate remain throughout the central concern of the work.

It is rather striking that a collection of poetry so filled with defeat and barely escaped indignity should begin with two of the most amusing poems Heine ever wrote. *Rhampsenit* and *Der weiße Elefant* are most remarkable displays of the wit and humor Heine was able to retain on his deathbed. Their gaiety, however, is of a particular kind: sardonic in one case, satirical in the other, and in both relevant to the atmosphere of *Romanzero*. *Rhampsenit* is an entertaining anecdote that Heine found in Herodotus.[29] Its character as a kind of joke Heine stresses first of all by his little trick with the dates—not only is the king aware that the time is B.C., but the chronology of the two years given is the wrong way around—and secondly by the laughter that peals in the poem: forms of the verb *lachen* occur no fewer than eight times in the first thirty-two lines. But perhaps there is too much laughter, too much hilarity at the princess' loss of her virginity to a thief and a stranger, and too much comedy in the king's solution to the raids on the treasury—the only way he can prevent them is to make the thief heir to the throne, which does not alter notably the quality of government. *Der weiße Elefant,* by contrast, is a piece of literary satire, a spoof of the hyperbolic, exotic poetry of Victor Hugo and Gautier.[30] It is one of Heine's longest orientalizing poems: seventeen of the forty-four stanzas describe the magnificence of the Siamese court. The satire reflects also on Heine's lyrical sentimentality of earlier days, for the literary allusions attached to the love-struck elephant are most absurd:

> Sehnsucht verzehrt ihn seit jener Stund'
> Und er, der vormals so froh und gesund,
> Er ist ein vierfüßiger Werther geworden,
> Und träumt von einer Lotte im Norden.
>
> Geheimnisvolle Sympathie!
> Er sah sie nie und denkt an sie.
> Er trampelt oft im Mondschein umher
> Und seufzet: wenn ich ein Vöglein wär'! (E, *1*, 335)

But there may be an undertone of bitterness in the description of the monstrous carnality of the beautiful white countess in Paris; Elster speculated that "die vielgefeierte, allzu stattliche Frau mit der blendend weißen Haut erschien dem totgeweihten Dichter wie ein herausfordernder Gruß des quellenden Lebens." [31] If so, however, the elegiac feelings of betrayed sensuality are not obtrusive; the narrator's attitude of high good humor is maintained throughout.

But after this the tones darken rather rapidly. The shift into the more direct treatment of the theme is mediated by *Schelm von Bergen,* which in construction is one of Heine's finest ballads. The patterning of vowels and rhythms and the composition of the poem show Heine's total mastery of what for him was a most grateful form.[32] The thrice-repeated question and evasion in the middle of the poem, an ancient folktale pattern, is skillfully applied to build the dramatic tension. The climax of the tenth stanza is heightened by the enjambement in the first line, which causes the rhythm to pick up in speed, and the following dead pause in the third line:

> Das ist der Scharfrichter von Bergen! so schreit
> Entsetzt die Menge im Saale
> Und weichet scheusam—die Herzogin
> Stürzet fort zu ihrem Gemahle. (E, *1*, 337)

In the middle of the next stanza, the verbs shift suddenly into the imperfect—the action, up to this point breathless and tense, now recedes into calm historical narrative. There is nothing evidently tragic about this ballad if we compare it with earlier examples like *Ritter Olaf*; the tragedy is avoided. It is also distinctly non-heroic, a predominant, if not exclusive, characteristic of the poems of *Romanzero*; it sets the minor key that particularly characterizes the *Historien*. The executioner, properly the pariah of society, who, however, like Heine himself, can merge with good society so long as "his real nature and calling" remain unknown,[33] tries to maintain his aloofness; but he is unmasked by the irresponsible curiosity and coquetterie of the Duchess: there is almost, but not quite, a disastrous collision of eros and death. The tragedy is avoided by the Duke, who elevates the executioner to the nobility, thereby not only retroactively restoring the honor of the Duchess, but also removing Schelm by fiat from his realm of death. Schelm is thereby denatured; he becomes nothing more than a historical name and the ancestor of a noble line of which nothing more can be said but that now it lies in stone coffins. Death has the victory after all, but in the meantime the characteristic poignancy of romance has been blunted. One is tempted to see in *Schelm von Bergen* an end point of the ballad tradition as a serious poetic undertaking.

Walküren goes a step farther; it is antiheroic. The song of the victory of the worse man is sung by the Valkyries, that is, by immortals, who are in some sense associated with the moral order of the world; in Germanic mythology it was they who chose who was to die on the battlefield. Their attitude is one of total moral indifference:

> Fürsten hadern, Völker streiten,
> Jeder will die Macht erbeuten;
> Herrschaft ist das höchste Gut,
> Höchste Tugend ist der Mut. (E, *1*, 338)

But the apparent virtue is really a matter of justification by success. The victor over the better man receives the unqualified adulation of the powerful and of the mob, and he himself relaxes into a posture of dignified calm that perfectly masks his true character. *Walküren* is, in a subtle sense, a political poem, although it has nothing to do with ideology. It is a pessimistic commentary on the characteristics of power and its amorality, and the symbol of the Valkyries intimates God's complicity in this distasteful order of things.

There is a return to the pathos of the fallen hero in *Schlachtfeld bei Hastings,* although the poem has little to do with King Harold himself, except to note that his death signals the defeat of the better cause and that the Saxons are about to be subjected to oppression by vulgar Norman parvenus. Instead, the pathos of the situation, expressed by the lamenting monks, is shifted to a level of individual tragedy. The spiritualist monks cannot find Harold's body, for they are not properly related to the king-persona; to find the king, the abbot must acknowledge the sensualist realm and remember the mistress whom the king loved and abandoned:

> Er hat sie geliebt, geküßt und geherzt,
> Und endlich verlassen, vergessen.
> Die Zeit verfließt; wohl sechzehn Jahr'
> Verflossen unterdessen. (E, *1*, 340)

But, as Gebhard has pointed out, time has not passed for Edith; her destiny has stood still since her abandonment by the king.[34] Unerringly she leads the monks through the grimly described field of corpses to find the king, and the confrontation of love and death is as stark as Heine ever formulated it, for Edith identifies the blood-drenched corpse by the scars of bygone ecstasy:

> Auf seiner Schulter erblickt sie auch—
> Und sie bedeckt sie mit Küssen—
> Drei kleine Narben, Denkmäler der Lust,
> Die sie einest hinein gebissen. (E, *1*, 342)

At the end of the poem her grief is absorbed into the piety of the requiem; the understated tone of the final stanza is an acknowledgment of the law of loss.

Karl I. and *Maria Antoinette* are contrasting treatments of the royal dignity that reflect Heine's ambivalence about it. On the one hand, king-persona and poet-persona are related to each other in Heine's aristocratic perspective; on the other, the reality of aristocracy is shabby and does not correspond to the ideal; the ambivalence is complicated by Heine's whole view of "poesy" as doomed by the necessity of mundane revolution. The tragic aspect of this ambivalence is captured in *Karl I.,* which is so finely organized that Hofrichter has called it "perhaps the most perfect of the Heine poems." [35] The rhythms and diction of lullabies and children's songs are interspersed and interrupted with harder and more prosaic lines expressing the revolutionary threat of the new age.[36] The tableau is totally stylized and unrealistic: King Charles sits at the cradle of the proletarian child who one day will behead him. He is already lost in his own mind, for he knows that with the vanishing of naive popular faith his own fate is sealed as well. His posture is without bitterness, but the Romantic substratum of "poesy" is so closely woven together with his attitude and situation that the poem transcends its historical referent and becomes a symbolic treatment of Heine's elegiac belief that beauty must necessarily vanish as the hierarchical old order is destroyed. *Maria Antoinette,* on the other hand, is a rough satire of absolutist anachronisms and may be directed obliquely at the recently dissolved court of Louis-Philippe. The beheaded ghosts of the pre-revolutionary French court wander through their trivial doings just as they had in life, as brainless as ever. The *pointe* lies in the last stanza, which reverses the usual end of ghost stories:

> Wohl durch die verhängten Fenster wirft
> Die Sonne neugierige Blicke,
> Doch wie sie gewahrt den alten Spuk,
> Prallt sie erschrocken zurücke. (E, *1,* 345)

Ordinarily the appearance of the sun causes ghosts to vanish; these, however, are persistent, and are not so easily driven away. It is the sun, here undoubtedly a symbol of rationality and the new age, that recoils from them.

Pomare is one of the memorable poems of *Romanzero,* and in it are concentrated several themes that hark back to the years of the *Verschiedene,* of *Florentinische Nächte,* of the Wild Hunt in *Atta*

Troll, and of the ballet scenarios, and are then connected with the tragic darkness of Heine's late vision. The poem begins with a ringing homage to this queen of the demimonde, and the second part describes the excitement of her dancing with Dionysian rhythms that continually pick up speed so that toward the end the words begin to rush frantically over one another. Once more the poet recollects his fascination with the cruel sensuality of his Herodias-figure, and her dangerousness is even more stressed than it was in *Atta Troll*: "Ihr Auge sprüht wie Blitze des Todes" (E, *1,* 346). The third part, however, abandons the bouncing trochees for rhymed iambic couplets of almost sepulchral calm. This part expresses a social observation of a kind Heine does not frequently make but did touch upon in Chapter 4 of *Schnabelowopski*; and he took it up again in his letters on the French theater[37]—the demimondaine, dancer and whore, will come to a bad and unappetizing end. If Heine sounds a bit the Victorian gentleman here, it is for a number of good reasons. At the time of the *Verschiedene* he had already discovered that "sensualism" understood as the pursuit of superficial carnal pleasure could have for him no lasting value; furthermore, he could not help observing, in the context of nineteenth-century society, how a life lived outside the restraints of bourgeois morality was likely to end in the most wretched misery. But this experience is deepened and complicated by his now urgent sense of the transitoriness of beauty and joy. There is true poetry and gorgeous exultation in Pomare's dance, as there is in that of the Duchess in *Faust,* but it ends, as all things must, in death—not a Wagnerian *Tod und Verklärung,* but grubby and sour decay. All this is rather easy to understand; the sentimental escape of the fourth part is less so. Death has come more gently to Pomare than her way of life implied; she dies comforted in her mother's arms and thus relieved of the trashy world around her. Here, it seems to me, Heine has loosened his grip slightly on the discipline that is otherwise characteristic of the *Historien* and has permitted himself a self-indulgence. Perhaps it came of his longing for his own mother and for a death more comfortable than the one he was now facing; certainly it was an effort to supply some retrospective justification for the life of the cocotte by alluding, with carefully altered sense, to Luke 7:47: "Therefore I tell you, her sins, which are many, are forgiven, for she loved much":

> Wie die Mutter, so der Vater
> Hat Barmherzigkeit geübt,
> Und ich glaube, dieses that er,
> Weil auch du so viel geliebt. (E, *1*, 348)

But this kindly intervention of God is not consistent with His ordering of the world as it otherwise appears in Heine's late poetry, and thus it introduces a foreign element into *Romanzero*.

Thus far Heine has skirted around the problem of the poet-persona as such. In *Der Apollogott* he plunges directly into it, with shocking, nerve-wracking results. *Der Apollogott* is one of Heine's greatest poems, although it is not altogether easy to understand and is so destructive of aesthetic idealism in import and so mean and violent in procedure that the reader is more likely at first to take offense than sense the pain and the wounded but surviving pride to which it gives expression. Certainly the poem seems upon first reading to be totally negative and destructive. It appears so to Walther Killy, whose interpretations of Heine poems are, on the whole, characteristic of contemporary West German critical attitudes outside the small fraternity of connoisseurs and are illustrative of an inability to accord Heine ungrudging respect as a poet because Heine's concern so often seems to be the dismantling of a fine and great tradition. Thus Killy writes of this poem: "So endet in der Mitte des Jahrhunderts, das Goethes und Hölderlins Gebrauch der griechischen Mythologie, Görres' und Creuzers Mythologeme an seinem Anfang sah, Apollo in der Gosse. Der Glaube nicht nur an die ehrwürdigen Erscheinungen, auch der an die Kunst ist dahin." [38] Prawer has countered this with a careful rebuttal in which he points out that Killy "has not seen the complexity of the structure of this poem and its shifting angles of vision." [39] There are three perspectives in *Der Apollogott*: that of the nun, that of the persona, and that of the Jewish peddler; they add up, not to a repudiation of poetry, but to a complex and troubled view about its substance and its relation to reality. In the first part of the poem, the nun, apparently secure in her cloister built on a rock, is nevertheless overwhelmed with love when she hears the beautiful song of the handsome poet; the sensualist impact of poetry has totally destroyed her spiritualist discipline. The setting is quite clearly the Lorelei situation in reverse, and the diction is carefully chosen to echo the lyricism of that period:

> Da fährt ein Schifflein, märchenhaft
> Vom Abendrot beglänzet. (E, *1*, 349)

This binding of the first part to Heine's poetic past is obviously significant. Moreover, it has been shown that there are substantial echoes of Eichendorff in these lines,[40] and Heine was not the man to despise that Romantic magician.* Nothing that happens in the rest of the poem negates the reality of the aesthetic experience that so affects the nun. But she makes a mistake; she tries to penetrate through the poetic illusion to a reality that the illusion does not necessarily reflect. The nun is the prophetic percursor of all of Heine's biographical interpreters; the illusion created by the persona is a trap for her, as Heine's poetic fictions became traps for his critics.

The song of the persona in the second part is remarkably complex. It has some of the features of *Bänkelgesang,* particularly in the opening lines:

> Ich bin der Gott der Musika,
> Verehrt in allen Landen,

and it ends with the cadence of a popular song:

> Doch ist mein Herz in Grācia,
> In Grācia geblieben. (E, *1*, 349, 350)

The character of Apollo is nothing more than a persona of the persona; he is not Apollo at all, but a modern poet from Paris,

* Admittedly this is a bit of speculation. It is extraordinary that Heine referred to Eichendorff so rarely; only twice, in fact. In *Die Romantische Schule,* at a time when no separate volume of Eichendorff's poetry had yet appeared, Heine briefly compared his poems to the best of Uhland's: "Der Unterschied besteht vielleicht nur in der grüneren Waldesfrische und der kristallhafteren Wahrheit der Eichendorffschen Gedichte" (E, *5*, 350). The other occasion is a fleeting reference to *Das Marmorbild* in *Elementargeister* (E, *4*, 427). But echoes of Eichendorff are not infrequent in Heine, and it would be surprising indeed if he had not recognized Eichendorff's amazing, almost instinctual genius.

and his home is not Parnassus, but "Mont-Parnaß." All this indicates corruption of the ancient ideal. But the section becomes distinctly more lyrical in its middle stanzas and the self-characterization as poet acquires more conviction. He has sipped of the inspiring waters of Castalia, and he stresses particularly the ease with which he creates beautiful song:

> Ich sang—und wie von selbst beinah'
> Die Leier klang, berauschend. (E, *1*, 350)

He displays his virtuosity, incidentally, in the song itself by rhyming all the first and third lines of the eight stanzas on the same final vowel, *-a*, no easy trick in the rhyme-poor German language. The poet impersonating Apollo is long since in exile from ancient Greece, but it is true, as he claims, that in a sense his heart has remained there. The poet-persona takes a nervous stance on a shaky middle ground. He is truly a poet, although the purity of the poetic tradition is corrupted in the modern world. He is in exile, but his spirit remains close to the wellspring of Castalia. It is he, after all, who has moved the soul of the nun. Pages of Thomas Mann about the illusion and reality of the modern artist are compressed into these thirty-two lines.

The nun is the victim of a confusion. She goes in search, not of the poet, but of Apollo himself. When one considers Heine's theory about the demonization of the ancient gods by the Christian Church, one sees that this doomed quest is not without its vengeful ironies. Thus the confrontation in the third part altogether misses the reality of the poet, who sails on down the river, out of reach of the nun forever. She achieves only the humiliation of hearing her love-struck questions parodied in the Yiddish cadences of the Jewish peddler and suffers the drastic disillusion of learning that her beloved Phoebus is in "reality" the apostate cantor Faibisch. This peddler is a harsh and vulgar caricature of a poor, grasping, and pompously ignorant Jew that in most contexts would be regarded as anti-Semitic. He certainly gives an undignified account of the poet's background and his way of life. But it is first of all perverse of Killy to claim that Heine has located Apollo in the gutter, for the point is that the poet is *not* Apollo. Furthermore, the peddler's petty-bourgeois reprobation of the poet's tacky Bohemianism does not touch upon the effect of his song in the first part. The vulgarity of the peddler's account, ending demonstratively with the nasty word *Sau,* is chargeable to him and not to the reality of the poet. That Heine allows the poem to end on this note is consistent with the atmosphere of *Romanzero,* for the peddler speaks with the voice of the shabby and insensitive world that surrounds the poet. The nun and the peddler meet one another in a common failure to comprehend the poet and his created fiction. The poet has his own concerns, which escape their understanding. Nowhere else in Heine's poetry is his sense of the poet's situation compressed into so small a space.

Four of the *Historien* turn to matters of politics and power. The first of them, *Zwei Ritter,* pours scorn upon the exiled Polish freedom-fighters. This poem, which expresses characteristic prejudices against the Poles, makes a rather unpleasant impression, as Prawer has pointed out, especially in the light of subsequent history.[41] The explanation for this attitude is found in *Börne,* where Heine discusses the German enthusiasm for the refugees from the crushed Polish uprising of 1831 and remarks, not very attractively although probably correctly, that if the Germans had had the refugees on their hands for any length of time, their enthusiasm would have cooled rapidly.[42] It all seems a little cheap—the funny and insulting names given to the Poles, as in *Schnabelewopski,* and the lines made almost unpronounceable with consonant clusters in order to parody the Polish language.[43] But we must accept the fact that it is all genuine Heine. He was not interested in revolutionaries if they were not well washed, and in the course of time he had acquired a deep suspicion of heroism, which is, after all, one of the themes of *Romanzero.* Furthermore, it is significant that the Poles of *Zwei Ritter* are noblemen, and Heine found offensive the contrast between their aristocratic station and the depravity of their impoverished lives and souls.* Heine knew no charity in matters like these.

Das goldne Kalb is a far more impressive performance, although there is no absolute certainty as to what it is actually about. The

* Contemporary Polish observers defend Heine on ideological grounds. See Anna Milska, "Heine über Polen," *Sinn und Form, 8* (1956), 66–77, and Maria Kofta, "Heinrich Heine und die polnische Frage," *Weimarer Beiträge,* 6 (1960), 506–31.

Golden Calf has long been a symbol for the corrupting influence of money, and there is a temptation to see the poem as another of Heine's attacks on financial power, here coupled with a satire on the greed of the Church. Such an interpretation cannot be dismissed, and perhaps Heine did have such matters in mind, but if so, something more elemental and poetic crept into the poem to compete with the satirical intent. For *Das goldne Kalb* is another of Heine's presentations of Dionysiac dance and its dubious fascination. The instruments, the sounds, and the movements of the poem all bear directly on this theme. Aaron, whose responsibility as high priest it was to prevent this sensualist outburst, is himself intoxicated by the dance and seduced from his office:

> Und er selbst, der Glaubenswächter,
> Tanzt im Hohenpriesterrock,
> Wie ein Bock—. (E, *1*, 356)

The *Bock* is of course the symbol of insatiable carnal lust, the form assumed by Satan in the Witches' Sabbath of Heine's *Faust*. The Biblical situation, it will be remembered, has nothing to do with the evil of money; it is a particularly tense moment in the struggle between the Mosaic ethic and the seductive and sensual nature religions of the other Semitic peoples (Exodus 32). Heine read his Bible carefully, especially in these years, and it seems possible that the poem connects the original sense of the drama of the Golden Calf episode with his own continuing dialectic between spiritualism and sensualism.

With what attention Heine studied the Bible is apparent in the next poem, *König David*. The colorful and magnificently narrated epic of David in the Bible ends on a most unpleasant note: Joab, who has served his king and with ruthless energy and reliable intelligence has helped him consolidate his power, is consigned to death by the senile David on his deathbed (I Kings 2:5–6). From that whole glorious career Heine singles out the moment when the exercise of power has become most corrupt and—unlike the case of Bathsheba and Uriah, where David's crime at least had the motive of passion—arbitrary and almost meaningless.* The

* It is possible that David's deathbed scene is a reflection of a conspiracy of

whole performance is unworthy of a king, and Heine underscores this by having him speak in a flippant and unserious conversational tone, achieved as usual by the use of French phrases. The great king suddenly becomes an evil king and with a casual word wipes out the life of the better man. The poem *König Richard,* immediately following, seems therefore to be an effort to rehabilitate the royal persona. Prawer has pointed out that it is both exhilarated and stylized;[44] the king is free and full of cheerful energy, but the tone is kept within the confines of a popular narrative poem; there is no probing beneath the external appearance of the persona. Heine is not in a mood to concentrate on a genre portrait with positive implications.

Of the six concluding poems of the *Historien,* three are, in very different senses, love poems. The first of them, *Der Asra,* is most conventionally so. The slave who dies of love, hero of an Arab legend that Heine found in Stendhal,[45] reminds us of the personae of earlier days, although the style here is incomparably disciplined and cool, in accord with the generally elegiac tone of *Romanzero.* Hammerich has remarked upon the great refinement of its poetic resources—"mit der Vollkommenheit der einfachen Wortstellung, mit Wiederholung und Abwandlung, mit Alliteration und Vokalspiel, mit dem Wechsel der Akzente der Haupt- und Nebenhebungen. Die Reimlosigkeit ist wohltuend; der Reim würde Überladung bedeuten."[46] Despite all these virtues, *Der Asra* is little more than a very fine set piece, a skilled poem that lends itself to recitation, but without the depths and contours that make the bigger pieces of *Romanzero* more interesting.

One of these is *Der Mohrenkönig,* in which Heine takes up again the theme of the Christianization of Moorish Spain that had fascinated him in earlier days. From Washington Irving's *Conquest of Granada,* translated into German in 1829, Heine took the figure of the defeated King Boabdil and was evidently struck particularly by the words of consolation offered the king by his vezir: "Consider, sire, that the most signal misfortunes

---

Nathan and Solomon to assure the succession to the latter. See B. Davie Napier, *From Faith to Faith* (New York, 1955), p. 146. Heine's sensitivity to the critique of royal power implied in this part of the Bible shows how acutely he read and understood it.

often render men as renowned as the most prosperous achievements, provided they sustain them with magnanimity." [47] Characteristically, Heine puts these words into the mouth not of an advisor but of a gentle and loving concubine to counter the harsh accusation of unmanliness made by Boabdil's mother. The effect of the whole poem is to build a bridge from defeat to poetry by way of love. Boabdil's state of gloomy defeat on his retreat is symbolized by the absence of music:

> Keine Zymbel, keine Pauke,
> Kein Gesangeslaut ertönte;
> Nur des Maultiers Silberglöckchen
> Wimmern schmerzlich in der Stille. (E, *1*, 360)

But the concubine tries to convince the defeated persona that his dignity resides in the issue of fame:

> "Boabdil el Chico," sprach sie,
> "Tröste dich, mein Heißgeliebter,
> Aus dem Abgrund deines Elends
> Blüht hervor ein schöner Lorbeer." (E, *1*, 361)

The laurel mentioned here begins the transposition into the realm of poetry and song that is completed in the last stanza:

> Nimmer wird sein Ruhm verhallen,
> Ehe nicht die letzte Saite
> Schnarrend losspringt von der letzten
> Andalusischen Guitarre. (E, *1*, 362)

This poem is a good example of how self-sufficient the poetic persona has become in *Romanzero*. The lines of consolation reflect what Heine often seemed to believe about his own position:

> Nicht allein der Triumphator,
> Nicht allein der sieggekrönte
> Günstling jener blinden Göttin,
> Auch der blut'ge Sohn des Unglücks,
>
> Auch der heldenmüt'ge Kämpfer,
> Der dem ungeheuren Schicksal
> Unterlag, wird ewig leben
> In der Menschen Angedenken. (E, *1*, 361–62)

But the persona has been totally objectified into the figure of King Boabdil. Seeger has justly observed: "Im glühenden Bekenntnis aber wird . . . einem persönlichen Glauben, nicht des Dichters Dr. Heinrich Heine, sondern der poetischen Gestalt des Erzählers unmittelbare Aussage gestattet." [48]

The interrelationship of love and poetry is taken up from a different perspective in *Geoffroy Rudèl und Melisande von Tripoli.* There is an insubstantiality to this poem that modifies the conviction expressed in *Der Mohrenkönig,* as though Heine's old doubts about "poesy" had reasserted themselves. The situation is one of Classic romance: the troubadour, consumed with love for a lady he has never seen, dies of exhaustion at the moment when he finally succeeds in meeting her. Thus the unreality of the beloved and the relationship of love and death, familiar themes in Heine's love poetry, appear again. But Heine gets over the actual narrative elements of this romance rather quickly; the figures of Geoffroy and Melisande are completely alienated into a context of art. They live in the tapestries of Blaye, or rather, as ghosts detached from them. They are not demonic spooks, however; they are gentle shades acting out a dialogue of "posthume Galanterie," (E, *1*, 363), an exchange of well-bred poetic compliment. Geoffroy asserts that only in love is there truth,[49] but this is perhaps to be doubted; as in *Buch der Lieder,* the beloved inspires poetic metaphors that remain in a realm of ideal abstraction. Unlike the persistent imbecilities of Marie-Antoinette's court, these ghosts do vanish with the first light of morning, back into their tapestry, the realm of art in which they survive. As gentle and pretty as this poem is, one wonders whether it is not in total effect more pessimistic than *Der Mohrenkönig.*

A curious fate befell *Der Dichter Firdusi* in this century: it was praised in no uncertain terms by Börries Freiherr von Münchhausen in his *Meisterballaden.*[50] Münchhausen, his ballads, and his nationalist and aristocratic enthusiasms are rather forgotten today, although he died only a little over twenty years ago. In his essay on *Der Dichter Firdusi* he turns a professional's eye on the poem and is filled with wonder at the technical accomplishment. Heine may have been a Jew, but "wer vor solchen Versen nicht tief den Pallasch senkt, der ist entweder ein verblendeter Rassenhasser oder ein hoffnungslos unkünstlerischer Mensch!"[51] Münchhausen is obviously thrilled at his own tolerance and admiration of a Jew, even though Heine "nahm seine Helden nicht deutsch-ernsthaft genug,"[52] and complete admiration is, of course, impossible: "ich bin eben Deutscher, und restlos genießen kann man nur gleichwüchsige Kunst." * This essay is a genuine document of conservative German intellectual history and would repay analysis of style and content by anyone interested in the structure of the elitist artistic mind in the pre-Nazi days. Werner Psaar has recently put Münchhausen's interpretation into a historical perspective: "was Münchhausen daran als wertvoll und meisterhaft hervorhob, hat für uns seine Geltung verloren. [The meaning of the ballad] ergibt sich aus dem thematichen Zusammenhang des Zyklus, sie ist Teilstück eines Ganzen."[53] Psaar is right, to be sure, although the purely technical aspects to which Münchhausen calls attention are still worth studying.

Goethe refers to the story of Firdusi and the Shah fleetingly in the notes to the *West-Östlicher Divan*.[54] But he does not dwell on it; the problem that interested Heine, the dignity of the poet and his revenge on a king who fails adequately to recognize it, would not have interested Goethe much; as in *Tasso,* he would have been more likely to concentrate on the problems of the inner constitution and equilibrium of the poet himself. This, in turn, does not interest Heine at this point; † there is nothing questionable about Firdusi or his attitude. It is the king only who is at fault for failing to be kingly, that is, an adequate partner for the

* Börries Freiherr von Münchhausen, "Der Dichter Firdusi," *Meisterballaden* (2d ed. Stuttgart, 1958), p. 66. Münchhausen continued this role into the Nazi period. In 1936 a suggestion was made that new poems be written to the music of Heine *Lieder,* a typically embarrassed Nazi response to Heine's place in German culture. Münchhausen submitted a memorandum opposing this silliness, and certainly he deserves credit for standing by artistic principles when they were threatened by barbarism. But he added to his remarks a strong and ignoble disclaimer: "Ich nenne Heinrich Heine einen Schweinehund." The case is self-explanatory. See Josef Wulf, *Literatur und Dichtung im Dritten Reich. Eine Dokumentation* (Gütersloh, 1963), p. 410.

† Heine also ignores the important motif in his source that Firdusi was a heretic, as well as the fact that he wrote a lampoon on the Shah. See Hella Gebhard, "Interpretationen der 'Historien' aus Heines 'Romanzero' " (diss. Erlangen, 1956), pp. 97–98.

poet. The poet may chastise the king when he does not meet the standards common to them both: one is reminded of Heine's wondering remark in the preface to *Französische Zustände* about Frederick William III's failure to honor his promise of a constitution: "Oder ist das Wort eines Königs nicht so heilig wie ein Eid?" (E, *5*, 21). But the hard fact is that power and the goods of the earth remain with the king, and if he has not the wit to share them properly with the poet, the poet can do nothing but gather up his dignity and die demonstratively in exile. In his last years Heine expands to cosmic proportions the implications of this losing conflict of the poet with his powerful and callous adversary, and it is just about the whole scope of his sense of tragedy. Few of Heine's poems, however, achieve the definition of the issues with such eminently poetic means as this one. His choice of the Persian Firdusi permits him to revive the Romantic accoutrements of "poesy" that belong to this complex: roses, nightingales, legends, and magic; the poet has preserved the ancient Romantic atmosphere of Zoroastrianism despite the "spiritualism" of the Koran.[55] When he receives the silver instead of the expected gold and distributes it scornfully among the servants, the lyrical rhythms suddenly turn hard and prosaic. When the poet himself speaks in the second part, the form shifts into the tough rhymed trochees of Heine's satirical verse. The easygoing, lax, rhymed couplets of the third part characterize the Shah's luxurious inattention, although the diction becomes harder in tone and the meter more regular as the great and irrelevant heap of elegant gifts is ordered; toward the end of the poem, which concludes with Firdusi's funeral procession, the tone is darkened by an increasing use of masculine verse endings.[56] The case of the poet and the defense of his injured dignity can be presented only in the poetic realm; there is not even a pretense that the Shah is moved by Firdusi's death.

Nächtliche Fahrt is by far the most difficult of Heine's poems to interpret. He must have held it in some regard, for he submitted it as a text for a competition in song composition.[57] At that time Heine offered an exegesis of the poem in the recognition that it is "nicht ganz verständlich" (Hirth, *3*, 274).[58] These remarks shed only a limited amount of light on *Nächtliche Fahrt*, as Hella Gebhard has pointed out, without herself being able to give a convincing interpretation.[59] Heine explains that the beautiful woman in the boat has been murdered from motives that are not certain, and he calls attention to the impact of the rhyme, which is a shrill, screaming *-ei* throughout; he suggests that the murder was an act of "Schwärmerey" (Hirth, *3*, 275) by a moral rigorist or a small-time savior who is not himself certain of the justification or rationality of the motive. The peace at the end of the poem expresses the indifference of nature, which takes no notice of human suffering. It seems evident from this explanation, the tone of which is quite serious and anxious to be helpful, that Heine was puzzled by his own poem. His explanation does not help us to understand why there are *three* people in the boat: the narrator, the beautiful woman, and a third person neither identified in the poem nor mentioned in Heine's own interpretation. Nor does Heine call attention to the fact that there is a mysterious interaction of dream and non-dream in the event as it is recounted. At first it seems that the "liberation" of the beautiful woman into death may take place in a dream:

> Bin ich im Fieber? Ist das ein Spuk
> Der nächtlichen Phantasei?
> Äfft mich ein Traum? Es träumet mir
> Grausame Narretei. (E, *1*, 370)

But the boat in fact returns in the clear light of day with only two passengers. In the letter Heine distances himself completely from the persona in the poem and indicates that the murder is an act of cruel and insane zealousness. But the voice of the persona has a familiar ring and fits exactly into the pattern of the unjustly suffering personae of *Romanzero*:

> Mir träumt,
> Daß ich ein Heiland sei,
> Und daß ich trüge das große Kreuz
> Geduldig und getreu. (E, *1*, 370)

That beauty is threatened by shame, sin, and suffering is a firm conviction of Heine's in his latter years, and that the poet frees beauty from this threat is part of the logic of Heine's attitude toward the relationship of "poesy" and reality. In the combined feelings of love and hate toward the woman, which cause the narrator to kill her with a breaking heart, a familiar substratum of Heine's psychological makeup seems to have risen to the surface.

The last two stanzas but one, containing the desperate appeal to God, are an enigma of the first order. In his letter Heine suggests that the cry of fear in the penultimate stanza *might* have been uttered by the drowning woman. But this is all but impossible to believe, unless she is supposed to be echoing exactly the terror of the murderer, for it is clear that in the third-last stanza the latter is the speaker: the first line, "O Narretei, grausamer Traum" (E, *I*, 371) is a variation of the first line of the seventh stanza, "Grausame Narretei! Mir träumt" (E, *I*, 370). Where the shift of speakers takes place, if there is one, is uncertain, for the last line of the third-last stanza, "O Gott! o steh mir bei!" (E, *I*, 371), echoes in the first line of the next stanza: "O steh mir bei, barmherziger Gott!" Most remarkable is that the appeal is now made to two traditional Hebrew names of God.* Ought Classical beauty, "Dianens Konterfei" (E, *I*, 370), speak "spiritualist" Hebrew at the instant of death?

Prawer, who uncharacteristically avoids interpreting this poem, sees it as a particularly concentrated expression of the shadows and dreams of the morphinist.[60] But one wonders about this. The effect of drugs on Heine's mind in his latter years is, I think, sometimes overestimated. The visions and dreams of his late poetry are not conspicuously hallucinatory and metarational; they are as literary as his earliest *Traumbilder,* lucid images that refer to themes which are part of a long continuity in his poetic career. The breakdown of the effort at rational control over the conflicting and familiar elements of Heine's poetic consciousness

* From the time of the Vulgate, *Shaddei* has been understood to refer to God in his character of the Almighty, but a comparison of passages where it occurs indicates that it may refer to God's attributes as a dispenser of benefits and reconciler of strife. See *The Pentateuch and Haftorahs,* ed. J. H. Hertz (London, 1956), pp. 57–58, 568. It seems improbable that Heine could have known this, yet there is the line, "Barmherziger Gott Schaddey!" (E, *I*, 371). We should probably be on surer ground if we suspect an ironic juxtaposition of mercy with God's terrifying omnipotence.

is atypical here. The earliest substantial attempt at an interpretation of the poem with which I am acquainted is that of Georg Plotke in 1913. He stresses the symbolic meaning of the destruction of the Classical, southern "Marmorbild" and the return to some of the Jewish-oriented imagery of *Der Rabbi von Bacherach*.[61] This does not explain very much, however, for it makes some rather simplistic assumptions about the development of Heine's poetic consciousness, and it is not sensitive to the terror in the poem common to persona and victim. Herman Salinger tries to operate with Jungian archetypes to interpret the poem in a way that I must say I find methodologically unconvincing.[62] Hans Kaufmann has suggested, not implausibly, that the theme of the poem is the murder of beauty and that the silent person in the boat is Charon.[63] Such an interpretation would help us to connect the poem to Heine's ambivalent attitude toward beauty and its relation to death. But it does not rest altogether comfortably, for it seems too facile for the eminent oddity of the poem's details. The poem remains unexplored ground, and would be deserving of a longer interpretative discourse than space permits here. In view of its careful organization, however, it seems evident that its lack of clarity is willed, while at the same time the unresolved thematic turmoil in Heine's mind freely produces images that are not forced into a rational order. *Nächtliche Fahrt* is thus closest to the breakthrough to a more modern kind of pure poetry toward which some of Heine's late work is today often believed to tend.[64]

The *Historien* end with a long, cruel poem of barbaric pessimism, *Vitzliputzli*.* The *Präludium* to the poem is a kind of versified theoretical discourse on the poetic setting. America before its Europeanization is presented as a non-Romantic land of poesy, an obvious and relatively rare attempt, except for the related poem *Bimini*, to establish a kind of nature imagery distinct from Romantic conventions—although Heine's use of imagery in the remainder of the poem shows that he was not really able to achieve this. Related to this problem is an uncharacteristic bit of

* In his first edition, Elster obscured the fact that the *Präludium* is not a separate poem but the prologue to *Vitzliputzli*; this was corrected by Fränkel (W, *3*, 58) and by Elster in his second edition (E², *2*, 57).

Rousseauism, where Heine's irony presents Montezuma as a noble savage:

> Dieser unzivilisierte,
> Abergläubisch blinde Heide
> Glaubte noch an Treu' und Ehre
> Und an Heiligkeit des Gastrechts. (E, *I*, 375)

The prelude gives an account of the poet's own sensual perceptivity, followed by a rousing claim on life and vitality:

> Leben kocht in meinen Adern,
> Bin des Lebens treuster Sohn. (E, *I*, 373)

The prelude ends in political satire; it is, like the main body of the poem, and that in turn like many other poems of *Romanzero,* about everything Heine could think of.[65] In *Vitzliputzli* Heine's restless dialectics are even more in evidence than usual. The first part of the poem proper opens with a severe critique of Cortez as a piratical conquerer rather than a true hero like Columbus or particularly Moses, who expanded the world for the rest of mankind. The conquistadores, dreaming of the comforts of church bells and cuisine at home, are thoroughly unheroic and are motivated only by crass materialism; their flight is hindered by the weight of the gold they have looted, and the loss of twelve horses receives prominent mention in the report of the day's disaster. The narrator's description of the Spaniards watching the slaughter of their comrades as "Armes Publikum am See" (E, *I*, 383) suggests a deliberate withholding of sympathy. Yet Heine was addicted to pathetic gesture, despite his disclaimer in *Jetzt wohin,*[66] and the ruffian is restored to sympathy for a brief moment when the death of his son moves him to tears. As at the end of *Schlachtfeld von Hastings,* the bloody disaster that has befallen the Spaniards is soothed and dissolved in a liturgical chorus.[67]

From here, however, the poem proceeds with harsh tones of negative religious relativism. Vitzliputzli's priest scornfully observes that the Christians absurdly sacrifice and eat their God in their ceremonies instead of properly sacrificing humans to Him. Prawer's castigation of this passage as "obtuseness in things of the spirit"[68] seems to me inappropriate, for it is part of the self-characterization of the pagan priest, who is certainly not presented in a noble or attractive way. Both Vitzliputzli and his priest are grotesque and, seen close-up, inspire no awe:

> Dort auf seinem Thronaltar
> Sitzt der große Vitzliputzli,
> Mexikos blutdürst'ger Kriegsgott.
> Ist ein böses Ungetüm.
>
> Doch sein Äußeres ist so putzig,
> So verschnörkelt und so kindisch,
> Daß er trotz des innern Grausens
> Dennoch unsre Lachlust kitzelt—. (E, *1*, 380)

There is to be no glorification of the mindless cruelties of pagan religion—in his address to the god, the priest even offers to sacrifice his own grandchildren. Vitzliputzli is anyway in an advanced state of decay; the forces of history, symbolized by the banner of the Virgin carried by the conquistadores, are about to do him in. Yet, although his glory is doomed, his evil is immortal, and he will live on in Christian Europe as one of Heine's metamorphosed gods, tempting and torturing. Despite the positive elements of the poetic imagination developed in the prelude, the poem as a whole is arranged so that no cultural values remain intact. Cortez and his Spaniards are contemptible, Vitzliputzli and his priest are contemptible. All are subject to the unappetizing and unbeautiful doom that Heine in his last years saw hovering over all existence.

The second part of *Romanzero,* the *Lamentationen,* is not aptly titled, for the reader is unfairly invited to make a comparison with Jeremiah. The Biblical prophet's tightly composed poems (in Hebrew they are alphabetical acrostics) bore into a single woeful theme, the destruction of the city of Jerusalem; Heine's *Lamentationen* are scattered in theme, are by no means all laments, and include some quite lightweight pieces, which Heine added, with a bad conscience, to fill up space in the volume after Campe had decided to publish *Faust* separately.[69] Thus *Romanzero* is a little weak at the center. The satirical poems against Herwegh and Dingelstedt (*Der Ex-Lebendige* and *Der Ex-Nachtwächter*) seem flat in these surroundings. A reprise of the attack upon Platen and his disciples (*Plateniden*) seems hardly to have been necessary, since in 1851 Platen had been dead for sixteen years. *Mythologie, In Mathildens Stammbuch, K.-Jammer,* and *Zum Hausfrieden* are so thoroughly trivial that one prefers to forget about them altogether. The love poems, particularly *Altes Lied, Solidität,* and *Alte Rose,* also seem out of place. The first is not uninteresting, as it bears upon the theme of the dead beloved, but it was written in 1824 and is thoroughly out of harmony with the late poetry; the light mocking tone of the other two would have been more appropriate to *Neue Gedichte.* Once these poems have been subtracted from *Lamentationen,* the remainder can be seen as of considerable importance.

The first of them, *Waldeinsamkeit,* is a long poem written in easy, loose rhythms and presents a biography of the poetic persona. If one were obliged to point to a single poem that would best elucidate the stage of development of the persona as Heine saw it at this time, *Waldeinsamkeit* would not be a bad choice—it is a fairly thorough summing-up and consequently a key poem in *Romanzero.* At the same time we must remember that this is a projection that contains elements of fiction and is not totally reliable as a guide to Heine's actual history as a poet, particularly as it is colored by the equation of poetry with Romantic "poesy" with which Heine more obscured than elucidated the essence of his imagination: it is an intellectual and literary construct superimposed upon a more complex and less easily defined situation. For it is undeniable that Heine was never as comfortably located in the Romantic landscape as the elegiac retrospection of this poem would indicate. It is not a world that he describes, but a system of imagery, literary inspirations, and emotional allegiances: the Romantic forest and popular legend, "tödliches Glück" (E, *1,* 391) and the Dionysian dance. All this has passed away somehow, although the loss is rather misleadingly described as something that was done *to* the poet rather than something embedded in the logic of his development:

O schöne Zeit! wo voller Geigen
Der Himmel hing, wo Elfenreigen
Und Nixentanz und Koboldscherz
Umgaukelt mein märchentrunkenes Herz!

O schöne Zeit! wo sich zu grünen
Triumphespforten zu wölben schienen
Die Bäume des Waldes—ich ging einher,
Bekränzt, als ob ich der Sieger wär'!

Die schöne Zeit, sie ist verschlendert,
Und alles hat sich seitdem verändert,
Und ach! mir ist der Kranz geraubt,
Den ich getragen auf meinem Haupt. (E, *1*, 394)

In place of the "schöne Zeit" has appeared a world of masked creatures under a desolated heaven; the elves have disappeared and the poet himself appears to the nixie as a ghost. Killy stresses, apropos of this, the problem of the loss of an objective world, which he sees as central to Heine's late experience.[70] But surely this realm of highly selective Romantic images is not to be identified as a world; this was never the case from the very beginning of Heine's career.

Waldeinsamkeit is followed by another large poem, *Spanische Atriden,* which might as easily have been placed among the *Historien.* The bitter cruelty of the tale itself is accented by the easygoing, courtly manner in which it is recounted and the festive atmosphere. The first-person persona in this case is only a nonparticipating listener through whom the story is communicated. But the persona is mirrored in Don Fredrego, who is another version of the defeated paragon, handsome and erotically attractive, and the imagery used in describing him relates him to the race of poets:

Das war eben jene Sorte,
Die geliebt wird von den Feen,
Und ein märchenhaft Geheimnis
Sprach aus allen diesen Zügen.

He is, in fact, another version of Heine's old friend, the drum major, with a new dignity:

Seines Hauptes Helmbusch wehte
Frei galant, jedoch des Mantels
Strenges Calatrava-Kreuz
Scheuchte jeden Buhlgedanken. (E, *1*, 397)

It is not politics, love-entanglements, or guilt of any kind that brings Don Fredrego to his doom, but pure, elementary envy of the superior man; Don Pedro simply cannot forgive Don Fredrego for his fame. If this is a tragic vision, it is so in a mode remotely related to that of Hebbel.

An die Jungen and *Jetzt wohin?* are expressions of political concerns transformed into private attitudes. The first of these is presumed to have been addressed to the young Ferdinand Lassalle;[71] it was first printed at a time when Lassalle's youthful revolutionary élan had made a great impression on Heine.[72] The most interesting feature of the poem is not, however, its atypical heroic zealousness, but the revision of the third stanza made for *Romanzero*. Originally it read as follows:

Wir sind die Erben. Wir schlagen in Scherben
Die Becher, woraus wir getrunken schon!
Und müssen wir sterben, zuletzt wir erwerben
Den schönen Triumphtod in Babylon. (E, *1*, 556)

The inheritors smash their own tradition and earn as an ultimate reward a heroic death. The version of *Romanzero* changes the sense altogether:

Wir wagen, wir werben! besteigen als Erben
Des alten Darius Bett und Thron.
O süßes Verderben! o blühendes Sterben!
Berauschter Triumphtod zu Babylon! (E, *1*, 410)

First of all, the revolutionary relevance of the poem has all but vanished; what in the first poem is symbolic of a political situation with intimations of progress and the overcoming of a tradition becomes a historical parable of uncertain referent. The meaning of the word *Erben* has been changed: in the first version it refers to the inheritance we have absorbed but now are to overcome; in the second, the inheritance is something gained by succeeding to the glory of the old king. Death, in the first version a fateful misfortune transformed by heroism into a triumph, is in the second instantly bound up with the succession to the king's bed and throne and seems indeed to be the intoxicating goal of all this bravery. We are witnessing the depolitization of Heine's thinking and the emptying of action of all positive significance. Aesthetic pessimism and the fascination of death have gained the day over heroic commitment and acceptance of its risks.

Jetzt wohin? is undated, but it echoes almost verbatim the passage in the first Helgoland letter of *Börne* where Heine mulls and rejects the alternatives to his exile.[73] Circa 1840 would therefore be a good guess for the conception of the poem, if we accept that the bulk of the Helgoland letters were probably written then rather than in 1830, and consider that it must have been conceived after Heine's sojourn in France had begun to seem permanent, but before his total paralysis, for the poem clearly supposes freedom of movement. In its final form, however, it must be later than that, as the second stanza shows:

> Zwar beendigt ist der Krieg,
> Doch die Kriegsgerichte blieben,
> Und es heißt, du habest einst
> Viel Erschießliches geschrieben. (E, *1*, 412)

In 1842 there was a brief relaxation of the pressures of censorship with the removal of the ban on Campe, but the heat was on again by 1844, and not until 1848 did Heine enjoy a relative freedom from these outrages (although not for long, for they were perpetrated on *Romanzero* itself in 1851[74]). The sense of the stanza seems to demand a date after 1848. The poem as a whole, with its lament for missed destiny in the last two stanzas, is sad, although it does not arouse complete sympathy; neither Heine's familiar and frantic prejudices against England nor his characterization of America as a "Freiheitsstall, / Der bewohnt von Gleichheitsflegeln" (E, *1*, 412) is particularly attractive. It is a poem, however, from which the fictional persona is virtually absent; as in the late poetry generally, we have a more audible impression of Heine's genuine voice, so that this poem seems among the closest to Heine's actual emotional state, although only in his more reflective moods.

Certainly the most memorable part of the *Lamentationen* is the end, with its twenty short poems entitled *Lazarus*. Of them E. M. Butler has written: "So personal as to be in many cases autobiographical and anecdotal, they yet convey the impression of impersonal forces seeking for utterance through the mouth of a poet intent on his private history." [75] We might wish to substitute "poetic" for "private" history, but Butler has indeed captured here the compelling fascination of these verses. They express an overwhelming sense of loss and unfulfilled existence, but they vibrate with a tension that reveals an undimmed, vital allegiance to life. It is in this sense that the prostrate poet could say in the prelude to *Vitzliputzli:* "Leben kocht in meinen Adern, / Bin des Lebens treuster Sohn" (E, *1*, 373). Prawer has shown how appropriate this persona is, with its reference both to the Lazarus of Luke 16:19–21, the beggar covered with sores, prostrated among dogs, and dependent upon the crumbs of the rich, and to the other Lazarus of John 12 who was believed dead and yet rose again.[76] These are religious poems, in the sense that they measure the individual experience against the order of creation and wrangle with God about the incongruities. The very word of the Bible (Luke 19:26) appears at the beginning, transformed into a sardonic commentary on a mismanaged world:

> Hat man viel, so wird man bald
> Noch viel mehr dazu bekommen.
> Wer nur wenig hat, dem wird
> Auch das wenige genommen.
>
> Wenn du aber gar nichts hast,
> Ach, so lasse dich begraben—
> Denn ein Recht zum Leben, Lump,
> Haben nur die etwas haben. (E, *1*, 415)

Number 3, *Auferstehung,* takes as its source the Last Judgment as it is described in Matthew 25, but the flippant and summary tone suggests plainly that profundity cannot be expected of divine justice:

> Das Böcklein zur Linken, zur Rechten das Schaf,
> Geschieden sind sie schnelle;

Der Himmel dem Schäfchen fromm und brav,
Dem geilen Bock die Hölle! (E, *1*, 417)

But the note of humility and confession in No. 2, *Rückschau,* is fairly new to the persona in this form: the trivialization of the past pleasures of the poet and the present feelings of a damaged soul seeking rest have never been expressed in this quiet way before, although Heine cannot avoid ending the poem on a sour note, with an expectation for the future that cannot have given him much pleasure:

Lebt wohl! Dort oben, ihr christlichen Brüder,
Ja, das versteht sich, dort sehn wir uns wieder. (E, *1*, 416)

It is interesting in connection with this tone that the memory of a sort of guilt, acquired long ago in childhood, reasserts itself in No. 6, *Erinnerung.* In *Das Buch Le Grand,* the story is told of the boy who had drowned because Heine had suggested he attempt to save a drowning cat.[77] Now Heine remembers this event again, but it is not so much his own guilt as the absurdity of the universe that is stressed in the continual refrain, "Doch die Katze, die Katz' ist gerettet" (E, *1*, 418–19). The opportunity to express a now characteristic longing for death is also not missed:

Seit langen Jahren, wie oft, o Kleiner,
Mit Neid und Wehmut gedenk' ich deiner. (E, *1*, 419)

Number 8, *Fromme Warnung,* and No. 9, *Der Abgekühlte,* express in different and tentative ways the poet's longing for peace and comfort, whether in Heaven or on earth, although it is the same kind of comfort in both cases. *Fromme Warnung* describes with intentionally childish naïveté the reception at the gates of Heaven for the good, tired soul:

Kehr ein, hier findest du Ruhe,
Und weiche Pantoffeln und schöne Musik. (E, *1*, 420)

Der Abgekühlte is a plea for one more blonde, gentle, and unpassionate love before the poet dies—a prayer that was to be most unexpectedly realized at the very end of Heine's life. For the moment, however, it is Heine's wife Mathilde who plays an important role in this context. Thus No. 12, *Gedächtnisfeier,* in which the poet ruefully considers the expected unceremoniousness of his funeral—no mass will be sung and no *kaddish* recited—grasps on to his sentiments toward Mathilde in order to gain control over his lachrymose feelings; he comforts himself with the thought of her affliction at his death, but this is not really the main function Mathilde serves here; rather, the key lies in the double entendre "Leider wohn' ich viel zu hoch" (E, *1*, 423); the poet's love and concern for his cherished but inferior and unthreatening wife help him to regain a pose of sovereignty and mild persiflage. As No. 15, *An die Engel,* shows, Mathilde really offers the poet an opportunity of sidestepping slightly the fear, or rather, dislike, of death, "der böse Thanatos" (E, *1*, 425), for she provides him an opportunity for turning his attention away from himself; the prayer which he offers for her protection, builds up to an expression of some urgency.

Number 16, *Im Oktober 1849,* the longest poem of *Lazarus,* turns to politics as a prime example of the wretched way the world runs. It is, as Prawer has observed, "the most powerful political poem of *Romanzero.*" [78] In May 1848, Frederick William IV had refused to accept the imperial crown from the Frankfurt Parliament, and the events of the summer proved that the hope of a liberal constitutional government for a united Germany was lost. The poem describes a sense of terror underlying the peaceful Biedermeier surface—from time to time the pseudo-Romantic landscape is disturbed by a shot, perhaps the execution of a friend, perhaps, in one of Heine's most brilliantly sardonic observations that says much about the nature of nineteenth-century Germany, a firecracker celebrating Goethe's one-hundredth birthday. As the poem turns to the Hungarian uprising that had been crushed in August 1849, the response to politics becomes more explicitly poetic. The relationship of artist to politics is concentrated in a contrast between the narrator and Franz Liszt, who is described as having done nothing to help his country. Whether the contrast here is either stark enough or just enough to bear the interpretation Heine wishes to put on it is a fair question, which is again involved with Heine's tendency to transport political matters into the realm of poetic pathos. The Hungarian disaster, in turn, calls forth a recollection of the catastrophe at the end of the *Nibelungenlied,* an apposite example, for Heine, of the defeat of the better man:

> Es ist dasselbe Schicksal auch—
> Wie stolz und frei die Fahnen fliegen,
> Es muß der Held, nach altem Brauch,
> Den tierisch rohen Mächten unterliegen. (E, *I*, 427)

The bestial powers in the present case are the Austrian ox and the Russian bear, decent beasts, at any rate, compared to the wolves, swine, and common dogs with which "wir"—presumably the Germans—must now contend. The poor poet suffers at their offensiveness:

> Das heult und bellt und grunzt—ich kann
> Ertragen kaum den Duft der Sieger.
> Doch still, Poet, das greift dich an—
> Du bist so krank und schweigen wäre klüger. (E, *I*, 427)

The political experience of the failure of the Revolution of 1848 is poetically united with the rule that the better man shall suffer defeat.

The last three poems of *Lazarus* approach the doomed persona from three different angles. In No. 18, *Sie erlischt,* one of Heine's most moving poems anywhere, the life of the poet is a play now over and the public has gone home, leaving only the rubbish and the rats of the desolate theater behind. The sound effects of the second half of the poem are so dissonant, like the image of the snapping violin string, as to be almost painful to the ear: the harshness of the first line, "Doch horch! ein schollernd schnöder Klang"; the last flicker of the poet's dying soul, "Die letzte Lampe ächzt und zischt"; and finally, the long, demonstrative impure rhyme, like a miserable groan "Öle . . . Seele" (E, *I*, 429). Number 19, *Vermächtnis,* a testament that wills all the poet's pains to his enemies and ends with the curse that their names should be blotted out, is part of the attitude of unforgiving obduracy that Heine assumed after his religious turnabout. The poem is in any case milder and less obscene than a similar one in the *Nachlaß, Testament,*[79] which Elster has dated at the beginning of the 1840s.[80] In number 20, *Enfant perdu,* the persona resumes the familiar posture of a brave and mortally wounded fighter for freedom; the better man has been brought down by a "schlechter Gauch," and the poem, the group, and the *Lamentationen* all end, characteristically and appropriately, with a familiar shift from insistent heroics to sentimentality:

> Ein Posten ist vakant!—Die Wunden klaffen—
> Der eine fällt, die andern rücken nach—
> Doch fall' ich unbesiegt, und meine Waffen
> Sind nicht gebrochen—nur mein Herze brach. (E, *1*, 430)

The three long poems of the *Hebräische Melodien* are quite different from one another and not easily brought under a common heading. What is not to be found in them is a consistent affirmation of the Jewish heritage. They seem to me to be substantially less religious than many other poems of *Romanzero*, particularly the *Lazarus* group, even though they deal with specifically Jewish materials. Nowhere in the three poems is there the direct confrontation with God that is characteristic of Heine's religious revival at its most convincing. He is dealing here with *a* religion, and in religion, as in politics, Heine could work up no allegiance to a form that had been defined by anyone other than himself. In addition, religion in Heine's mind was an irrational illusion, supportable only when it was related to the illusions generated by the autonomous poetic imagination. The three poems reflect this problem in three different ways.

Prinzessin Sabbat is Heine's most thorough treatment of Jewish ritual since *Der Rabbi von Bacherach*. The sense of appreciation of the Sabbath experience in the poem is genuine and its presentation is congruent with traditional Jewish feeling about it. But it is observed from the outside, not from within. The "prince's" everyday reality as a dog is no less real than his metamorphosis on the Sabbath, perhaps more so. One is reminded here of Heine's account of the drunken beggar in *Über die französische Bühne:*

> der die scharfsinnige Bemerkung gemacht hatte, daß, solange er nüchtern blieb, seine Wohnung nur eine erbärmliche Hütte, sein Weib in Lumpen gehüllt und sein Kind krank und hungrig war, daß aber, sobald er einige Gläser Brannt-

> wein getrunken, dieses ganze Elend sich plötzlich änderte, seine Hütte sich in einen Palast verwandelte, sein Weib wie eine geputzte Prinzessin aussah und sein Kind wie die wohlgenährteste Gesundheit ihn anlachte. (E, *4*, 517).

The perspective of *Prinzessin Sabbat* is somewhat different, for it is "Hexenspruch" (E, *1*, 433) that has turned Israel into a dog; nevertheless, the curse has worked:

> Hund mit hündischen Gedanken,
> Kötert er die ganze Woche
> Durch des Lebens Kot und Kehricht,
> Gassenbuben zum Gespötte. (E, *1*, 433)

In his latter years Heine was obsessed with the relative priorities of a trashy, repulsive reality and the beauties of imaginary illusion; there is no sufficient poetic faith to allow the latter to veil the former entirely from view. Consequently a satirical and, to some extent, unsympathetic tone prevails in the poem. The Queen of Sheba is trivialized by Heine's standard practice of introducing modern social referents and French vocabulary when he wants to undermine dignity and profundity:

> Schöner war
> Nicht die Königin von Saba,
> Salomonis Busenfreundin,
>
> Die, ein Blaustrumpf Äthiopiens,
> Durch Esprit brillieren wollte,
> Und mit ihren klugen Rätseln
> Auf die Länge fatigant ward. (E, *1*, 435)

There is a similar effort to prevent the liturgical experience from rising to awesome dimensions. The vain coquetry of the cantor is stressed, and the expansive joy of the *L'cho dodi* is flattened out by calling it "dieses hübsche Hochzeitkarmen" (E, *1*, 435). Princess Sabbath herself is reduced to the size of a harmless, very bourgeois Jewish wife, whose chief blessing for the "prince" is the Sabbath cuisine. The experience cannot rise above this level because of the irreparable vulgarity of the "prince" and his low cultural status; compared with the Sabbath meal,

Ist nur eitel Teufelsdreck
Das Ambrosia der falschen
Heidengötter Griechenlands,
Die verkappte Teufel waren. (E, *1*, 436)

Yet the poetic space in which all this is described is not cramped. Contributing to this effect is the virtuoso performance of the poet himself—the familiar sovereignty over the unrhymed trochaic form, stressed by the ease with which he can transform a piece of Hebrew liturgy into German verse:

Sei gegrüßt, geliebte Halle
Meines königlichen Vaters!
Zelte Jakobs, eure heil'gen
Eingangspfosten küßt mein Mund! (E, *1*, 434)

The Sabbath experience, too, is poeticized in that it is permeated with delicate sensual pleasures; the pleasures, moreover, are at their most delicate when they are on the point of vanishing. The spicy aromas of the *havdalah* ceremony are an elegiac farewell to the Sabbath, and the final image, the extinguished candle flame, has an undertone of death imagery. The weekly interlude of pleasure that sustains the "prince" is only transitory and quite possibly grounded in an illusion. It is undoubtedly correct that the ultimate sense of the poem, as Elster has suggested, is "das Doppelleben in zwei Welten, insbesondere die tragische Spaltung der Persönlichkeit des Künstlers," [81] but it is of equal significance that Heine refuses to allow this tragic conflict to be carried out on a high and dignified plane.

Jehuda ben Halevy is a more ambitious poem and is more explicitly concentrated on the poetic persona. It is identified as a fragment, but Elster doubted that any essential part of the total conception was missing;[82] Heine had a tendency to use the word "fragment" when he was uncertain that he had achieved inner cohesion and aesthetic unity in a work, and such doubts are not out of place in connection with this long, rambling discourse in verse. Again we do not want to overestimate the specifically Jewish import of the poem; even the incorrect name he gives to his hero shows his estrangement from the tradition ("ha-Levi" is not a patronymic but a designation that the poet was a Levite; Jehuda's patronymic was "ben Samuel"). Nevertheless, the treatment of the persona suggests a kind of experimentation with a potential alternative, for Jehuda does combine the character of the true poet with a complete religious allegiance. He is thus both related and contrasted to the poet in whose imagination he lives, the narrator of the poem. It is no wonder that the narrator recognizes Jehuda as a poet, for his features have been familiar since *Die Harzreise*:

> Ich erkannt' ihn an der bleichen
> Und gedankenstolzen Stirne,
> An der Augen süßer Starrheit—
> Sahn mich an so schmerzlich forschend—
>
> Doch zumeist erkannt' ich ihn
> An dem rätselhaften Lächeln
> Jener schön gereimten Lippen,
> Die man nur bei Dichtern findet. (E, *1,* 438)

The sense of fraternity, one might say, inspires the poet-narrator to probe somewhat into the sources of inspiration of a religious poet. Heine extrapolates from his own experience of the Bible in his account of Jehuda's training in Torah and Talmud. Once the distinction is drawn between *halacha,* the statutes of the Law, and *haggada,* the homiletic and illustrative supplement to the purely legal discourse, it is inevitable that the source of poetic inspiration must be located in the latter, which Heine describes with a long simile, extended over seven stanzas, of the garden of Semiramis. *Halacha* is rather flippantly disposed of as trivial disputation; for example,

> Über das fatale Ei,
> Das ein Huhn gelegt am Festtag,
>
> Oder über eine Frage
> Gleicher Importanz. . . . (E, *1,* 441)

The legendary materials of *haggada* expand the imagination and determine the workings of the poetic mind, here as explicitly defined as Heine knows how to do it:

Und des Knaben edles Herze
Ward ergriffen von der wilden,
Abenteuerlichen Süße,
Von der wundersamen Schmerzlust

Und den fabelhaften Schauern
Jener seligen Geheimwelt,
Jener großen Offenbarung,
Die wir nennen Poesie.

Auch die Kunst der Poesie,
Heitres Wissen, holdes Können,
Welches wir die Dichtkunst heißen,
That sich auf dem Sinn des Knaben. (E, *1*, 442)

By this impetus the poet-persona is gradually elevated beyond the specific confines of religious faith; because he has a poet's soul, he has direct access to divine grace and cannot sin, "Nicht in Versen, noch in Prosa" (E, *1*, 443). He is beyond the people and responsible to God only:

Unverantwortlicher König
Des Gedankenreiches ist er. (E, *1*, 443)

The identification of the poet-narrator with the persona so described comes in the last lines of the first part:

Wie im Leben kann das Volk
Töten *uns,* doch niemals richten. (E, *1*, 443)[83]

In the second part of the poem, the experiment is carried a considerable step farther; the narrator abandons Jehuda for the moment and identifies himself with the immortal Jewish spirit. With his unerring sense for the parts of the Bible most upsetting to the complacent mind, Heine weaves the moving and terrifying 137th Psalm into his verse. Part of the Psalm had already been quoted at the beginning of the first part, where the lines are attributed to Jehuda:

Lechzend klebe mir die Zunge
An dem Gaumen, und es welke

Meine rechte Hand, vergäß' ich
Jemals dein, Jerusalem. (E, *1*, 437–38)*

In the second part, the famous opening lines of the Psalm are associated with the narrator himself:

Bei den Wassern Babels saßen
Wir und weinten, unsre Harfen
Lehnten an den Trauerweiden—
Kennst du noch das alte Lied? (E, *1*, 443)

The narrator's emotions, however, are not primarily those of religious lament, but of rage at the sufferings of his people, and he bursts out with the bloodthirsty lines at the end of the Psalm that are so discomfiting to conventional Jewish apologists:

Heil dem Manne, dessen Hand
Deine junge Brut ergreifet
Und zerschmettert an der Felswand. (E, *1*, 444)

But this excursion into poetry inspired by religious allegiance is a blind alley for the narrator, for it leads him away from Jehuda's fundamental quality of faith. The narrator disposes of the digression as "Mein westöstlich dunkler Spleen" (E, *1*, 444) and takes a more sanguine attitude toward poetry. The shift in perspective is sharper than may appear on the surface and emphasizes differences rather than congruities between the narrator-persona and Jehuda. The narrator's assumption of Jewish allegiance has led him to polemical engagement, whereas Jehuda's inner essence is that of a troubadour who substitutes the city of Jerusalem for the conventional beloved—his counterpart is not the angry Psalmist but a secular poet of whom we have already heard, Geoffroy Rudèl.[84] Nevertheless, Jehuda's zeal and ultimately his pilgrimage are motivated by the same catastrophe that generates the anger of the 137th Psalm. He hears of the Wandering Jew (a figure Heine refers to several times[85]) who sings a song of the ruined city, with echoes from the first chapter of Lamentations. Like Rudèl, Jehuda dies at the feet of his beloved.

* These lines are related to a different version originally written for *Atta Troll* but then discarded. See Prawer, *TS*, pp. 68–69.

Jehuda ben Halevy presents no substantial difficulties of interpretation thus far. The third part, however, begins to puzzle the reader with its demonstrative compositional looseness. The story of Darius' casket is a vast digression that seems out of proportion to its apparent intent, which is to set up a comparison between Jehuda and Homer. Nor is one easily satisfied with the explanation that Heine's mind, undisciplined by his shadowy existence in the sickroom, is simply wandering, for the digression is compounded by a second one so remote from the subject that it can only be intentional: the whole history of the pearls that were originally in the casket is a blind alley that ends with, of all things, Baroness Rothschild. Only then, after fifty-six lines about the pearls, does the narrator come to the casket, the *tertium comparationis* between Homer's fame and that deserved by Jehuda. The function of this long passage seems to redirect attention back to the narrating poet, within whose imagination, it must be remembered, Jehuda dwells. It is he who is the "unverantwortlicher König des Gedankenreiches," and he may range over his poetic landscape as he sees fit, creating legends out of history and images out of artistic objects. The poet reminds his reader who the creator of all this actually is: with an echo from *Atta Troll*—"Andre Zeiten, andre Vögel" (E, *I*, 452)—he contrasts his previous affinity to the Greeks to his present broken condition, and goes on immediately to express his desire to own a manuscript of the *Jewish* poet and preserve it in the casket that once contained a manuscript of Homer. The changed priorities of sensualism and spiritualism are maintained within the poetic realm, while, in the meantime, the pearls, symbol of worldly wealth, have gone irretrievably out into the decidedly unpoetic world of the Rothschilds. This accomplished, the narration returns to the pathos of Jehuda's death, to which Heine has added, by his own invention, it seems,[86] a final apotheosis: the Saracen who kills Jehuda is an angel in disguise, and the poet's assumption into Heaven is celebrated by the "himmlische Sürprise" (E, *I*, 456) of hearing his own songs sung by choirs of angels. A self-enamored wish-dream, undoubtedly, but comic enough to suggest that the poet does not take it seriously and that Jehuda's senseless death in the ruins of his beloved Jerusalem is the more probable poet's destiny.

Now one would certainly think that the poem should end here. That it does not is a problem not unrelated to the problem of the third part of *Tannhäuser*. After the poem has carefully delimited the world of the imagination in which the poetic experiment takes place, the fourth part brings the problem of the poet's fate to another, more mundane level. For the poet has a wife. We who have been wondering about the propriety of the digression on Darius' casket find our doubts expressed by this unpoetic creature, by a voice from the practical world. This is a joke on the reader, but behind it lurks the fear of the bankruptcy of poesy in the modern age. The wife's complaint incorporates the insistent claims of a pedestrian and paltry reality, against which the poet tries to play off the exotic aesthetic richness of the Sephardic golden age. Even in such a context, however, the stupidity of fate may run the poet to the ground. The poet is a *Schlemihl*—a man without luck despite his right to a special relationship with God. This is the only point in the poem where it can be said with assurance that Heine momentarily allowed the thread of his composition to run loose, for the digression on the Berlin criminologist Julius Eduard Hitzig really is of no functional value. This is not true, however, of the connection of the *Schlemihl* legend to the story of Phinehas in the Bible, where Heine once again exhibits his instinct for picking out of the Bible a passage that makes one wince. Phinehas, who, according to Numbers 25: 7–8, killed the man who brought the plague on Israel by taking in a Midianite woman, in Heine's version has missed the culprit and instead killed the original *Schlemihl,* an innocent bystander. Heine no doubt noticed that God's reward for the fanatic Phinehas is to make him the ancestor of all the high priests (Numbers 25:12–13), and similarly all poets, the perpetual victims, are descended from Schlemihl. It is their fate to be struck, in perfect innocence, by the spear of a Nazarene fanatic, and of this the case of the Sephardic poet Gabirol is given as an example. The poet does not die unavenged—the intervention of God and prince brings the murderer to justice—but too late to save the poor poet, as in the case of Firdusi. Heine has allowed the original theme of the poem—the possibilities of religious allegiance for a poet—to disappear; our attention is redirected to the situation of the poet in the modern world, which leaves only the prospect of shabby defeat.

Jonas Fränkel speculated that *Disputation,* the final poem of *Hebräische Melodien,* was written "aus dem Bedürfnis, sich von der tiefen Herzensanteilnahme, die dem Dichter die Arbeit an 'Prinzessin Sabbath' und 'Jehuda ben Halevy' abgenötigt hatte, durch ein Satyrspiel zu befreien." [87] Perhaps so, but one may say with equal probability that it is an attempt to expose the vulgarity of zealous religious faith where it is not ennobled by the poetic imagination. The effect of these trochees is to deny any dignity to anything that is asserted by either of these dogmatic disputants:

> Er erzählt: wie Gott der Herr
> Ward zu Bethlehem geboren
> Von der Jungfrau, welche niemals
> Ihre Jungferschaft verloren;
>
> Wie der Herr der Welt gelegen
> In der Krippe, und ein Kühlein
> Und ein Öchslein bei ihm stunden,
> Schier andächtig, zwei Rindviehlein. (E, *1,* 468)

Not even the sentimental naïveté of religious *Kitsch* survives this acid bath.

The public disputations that were occasionally arranged between Jews and Christians in the Middle Ages were, as Heine probably knew from his studies, no laughing matter for the Jews;[88] they were a particularly sinister trap. He has made the whole complex more harmless by setting his dispute in the time of the Spanish King Pedro, who was well-disposed toward the Jews and probably did not organize such events.[89] In order to balance the disputants evenly and engage in some rather bad jokes, such as the description of the Rabbi's supporters gleefully sharpening their circumcision knives, Heine ignores the fact that the Jews historically have had no urge to proselytize. It is sad that Heine in this mood calls up for his more recent readers infinitely hateful memories of anti-Semitic pornography, but such things are an integral part of his general attitudes and reflect in a gloomy way the nature of the Jewish crisis of his time. It is true that at first the contrast in the poem seems to be prejudiced in favor of the Jewish side, and no doubt this is the result of a combination of some of Heine's latent sympathies in the matter and what he had read about the character of such events in actual fact. The monk looks more the benighted and evil fool:

> Der Gardian der Franziskaner
> Bricht hervor mit frommem Grimme;
> Polternd roh und widrig greinend
> Ist abwechselnd seine Stimme. (E, *1*, 467)

He loses himself totally in hysterical rodomontade and Baroque heaps of slanderous epithet, against which the doctrine of Christian love is set in absurd juxtaposition, and his presentation ends with a swinishly hedonistic vision of the joys of Heaven.

Against this imbecility, the rabbi appears more dignified—although the adjective "wasserscheu" (E, *1*, 471) suggests that he is not only averse to baptism but also dirty—and, above all, he is more ironic. But he, too, only pounds out dogmatic assertions, and he, too, has a primitively materialistic vision of Heaven—he counters the priest's presentation with a promise of the future feast on Leviathan. The rabbi does have a more tough-minded view of God than the priest:

> Unser Gott ist stark. In Händen
> Trägt er Sonne, Mond, Gestirne;
> Throne brechen, Völker schwinden,
> Wenn er runzelt seine Stirne.
>
> Und er ist ein großer Gott.
> David singt: Ermessen ließe
> Sich die Größe nicht, die Erde
> Sei der Schemel seiner Füße.* (E, *1*, 472–73)

But his dignity entirely breaks down when his devotion to a minor work of the word is insulted. The rabbi turns out to be an idolator; his allegiance is to his "Tausves-Jontof" (E, *1*, 475), a book of popular commentary on the Law, rather than to basic

* Heine may well be quoting from memory, for the reference is not to the Psalms but to Isaiah 66:1 (noted in W, *3*, 499 and E[2], *2*, 363).,

things of the spirit. It is all very boring, this dispute; the wearied king turns to his beautiful French queen—the aesthetic and sensual principle—and her only reaction is that both disputants stink.

The seventh poem of the *Lazarus* group, *Unvollkommenheit,* pretends to comment upon the banality that nothing beautiful is without blemish. But the verses are nastier and more brutally vengeful than that. They are, if one may say so, a spray of filth upon a great variety of things held more or less in awe or respect:

Der Marmorsteiß
Der Venus von Canova ist zu glatte,
Wie Maßmanns Nase viel zu ärschig platte. (E, *1,* 419)

Romanzero ends with the verb *stinken.* Few, it is safe to say, have ever loved Heine the more for it. But this is the voice of one of the nineteenth century's greatest poets, fifty-three years old, broken in body but at the height of his creative powers; it must be taken seriously. It is the expression of an investment in an aesthetically oriented idealism gone bankrupt. The resignation of Schiller, the despair of Hölderlin, the incredible chaos of Kleist, and the mean anger of Heine are related to one another, and are symptoms of a cultural phenomenon of the gravest significance.

CHAPTER 14

Reintegration: The Last Poetry

> Wie der Wind zu Herbsteszeit
> Mordend hinsaust in den Wäldern,
> Weht mir die Vergangenheit
> Von des Glückes Stoppelfeldern.
>
> —LENAU

It may be partly the fault of Ernst Elster that the poetry of Heine's very last years has only slowly come to receive concentrated attention, for the great editor quite inexplicably broke up Heine's last collection of poems, *Gedichte—1853 und 1854,* and scattered them in the *Nachlaß* volume. In his second edition, Elster admitted that this was a blunder[1] and, following the practice of Jonas Fränkel in the Walzel edition,[2] restored the integrity of the group.[3] But the second edition was never finished, and since the first has remained standard to the present day, there has been a lack of awareness that Heine's main published collections of poetry number four rather than three. Even in the second edition, Elster insisted upon presenting *Gedichte—1853 und 1854* as part of the *Nachlese zum "Romanzero"* and treating these poems, along with those of the *Nachlaß,* as a second volume of *Romanzero.*[4] By so doing he helped to blur some interesting distinctions, for these poems are not merely a continuation of *Romanzero,* any more than the *Neue Gedichte* are properly a second volume of *Buch der Lieder.* The last poems suggest, rather, that Heine as a poet underwent some rather substantial changes in the years after 1850/51.

The fundamental differences between *Romanzero* and the last poetry are, it seems to me, three, of which two are rather obvious, while the third is a little more difficult to define. There is, first of all, an almost complete disappearance of ballads and romances; all that is left is a handful of sardonic fables with even more sardonic morals tacked on and the ambitious but abandoned fragment

Bimini, which may in any case be roughly contemporaneous with *Vitzliputzli*. The effect of this is that the various surrogate personae drawn from the realms of history and literature vanish. Secondly, there is a notable recrudescence of two earlier complexes: the pathos of unrequited love from the 1820s,* and the bitter quarrel over Salomon Heine's inheritance from the 1840s; thus the quality of reminiscence grows strong at the end. These differences bear on the more general character of the late poetry, which can perhaps best be described by saying that the poetic persona has become closely integrated with the poet himself. It is at the edge of the grave that we hear Heine's voice most clearly. The fading of the fictional posture is due, it seems to me, to a kind of weary resignation that is not exactly contrite or humble, but is *unambitious* in the sense that the need for assertive definition of the poet-persona and his power and dignity has yielded to the grim and defeating realities of suffering, loss, and imminent death. If one observes the long curve from *Buch der Lieder* to the last poetry, one may fairly speculate that what prevented Heine from proceeding on the road of direct and genuine sincerity rather than fictional self-realization in the realm of the poetic imagination was a sense of the indignity and unbeauty of his own being. Over a hundred years ago Matthew Arnold sensed this undercurrent: "Goethe says that he [Heine] was deficient in *love;* to me his weakness seems to be not so much a deficiency in love as a deficiency in self-respect, in true dignity of character." [5] But now, in the "mattress-grave," the indignity and unbeauty are too patent to be ignored; these qualities have, moreover, been accounted for by the theme of the defeat of the better man and, in the latter years, have been credited to the existential logic of the world. They may therefore be freely admitted and, indeed, stressed and reiterated. This has the effect, among others, that Heine feels free to fall back upon attitudes that he had previously striven to overcome or to accommodate to the ideal posture. Whether these attitudes are defensible

* The complex, of course, never disappeared completely. In a poem published in 1836 entitled *An Jenny,* Heine reiterated the whole fiction again (E, 2, 29); the "facts" in this poem, which Heine described as a formal experiment in working dates into poetry (to Laube, Nov. 23, 1835; Hirth, 2, 104–05), are, as usual, completely changed from the real situation. See E², *1,* 501.

or appropriate no longer matters. Among the haunting beauties and terrible laments of the last poetry is a new kind of truth.

Many of the poems of the *Nachlaß* that are properly considered with *Gedichte—1853 und 1854* have not as yet been exactly dated; a number of them go back to the period of *Romanzero* or even to the years before that. But, regardless of the dates of genesis, it is reasonable to accept a substantial number of these poems, along with *Gedichte—1853 und 1854,* as belonging to a larger book of collected poetry that Heine would undoubtedly have put together had he lived longer. A good example is the powerful unrhymed poem *Morphine.* Heine had originally included this poem in *Romanzero* but on second thought demanded its removal.[6] He gives no reason for this, but it is quite clearly more closely related to the tone of the later collection than to *Romanzero,* where the poet's present condition is more intimated than directly confronted. (Perhaps this is a fair reply to Prawer's surprise that Heine did not include it in *Romanzero.*[7]) Here the vision of the brothers Sleep and Death is not located in an imaginary poetic space but is perceived by the poet on his own sickbed. The vision is adjusted exactly to his situation: Sleep wears a wreath of poppies, for only opium provides the poet with any relief.* The final lines, echoing Ecclesiastes 4:2–3 and Sophocles' *Oedipus at Colonus,* ll. 1224–26, state the theme that is most particular to the last poetry:

> Gut ist der Schlaf, der Tod ist besser—freilich
> Das beste wäre, nie geboren sein. (E, 2, 102)

This same statement appears in very similar language in the last two lines of the first poem of *Gedichte—1853 und 1854, Ruhelechzend:*

> Der Tod ist gut, doch besser wär's,
> Die Mutter hätt' uns nie geboren. (E, 2, 103)

Ruhelechzend, in turn, is constructed in a way that is paradigmatic for the late poetry. The first three stanzas contain so much

* Heine used the image of the poppy wreath some years before he was obliged to take opiates. See E, *4,* 521. The history of the two brothers Sleep and Death from Lessing to Heine is recounted by Henry Hatfield, *Aesthetic Paganism in German Literature* (Cambridge, Mass., 1964), pp. 24–32.

humble and naive simplicity and sententiousness that at first they seem as though they could be by a poet other than Heine, although even here the language is levelled down to where the irony becomes audible:

> Auch danke hübsch dem lieben Gott,
> Wenn Zähren deine Wangen netzen. (E, 2, 102)

But the words "Schelm" and "Tölpel" already herald a more resentful tone, and the poem goes on to complain of the sound of piano playing, which greatly tormented Heine in his sickroom, and to make a swipe at Meyerbeer, the recurrent whipping boy of the last poetry. To proceed from these little annoyances to a classically pessimistic view of the undesirability of all life may seem incongruous and disproportionate, but this kind of juxtaposition is characteristic of many of the poems of this period. The perpetual abrasion of minor irritations in a vastly agonizing and despairing situation is undoubtedly a real experience; what is interesting for our purposes, however, is that there is no effort to make the prostrate persona in the least measure heroic, even by contrast. This is a substantial part of the new truth in the late poetry.

Gedichte—1853 und 1854 and a number of the poems of the *Nachlaß* contain a tense dialectic between a bitter repudiation of life and a vital lust for it. This is a major conflict in Heine that was doubtless always present to a greater or lesser degree but in these mortal circumstances has risen starkly to the surface. One version of this is found in the second poem of the collection, *Im Mai*, which the blossoming springtime, the metaphorical inheritance of Romanticism that Heine never abandoned, is experienced with furious resentment:

> O schöne Welt, du bist abscheulich! (E, 2, 103)

More consistent with the poet's present relationship to life would be the horrors of Hell, which he describes in a series of grating acoustical images. A poem that was published a year after Heine's death recites a litany that is reminiscent of the theme of transitoriness in German poetry of the seventeenth century:

> Ganz entsetzlich ungesund
> Ist die Erde, und zu Grund,

Ja, zu Grund muß alles gehn,
Was hienieden groß und schön. (E, 2, 87–88)

The poem goes on to describe young women torn away by early death and the "genius" breaking his lyre in disgust; the stars, not wishing to be drawn into this misery, maintain a mild aloofness. *Im Mai,* however, is a personal accusation against those who have betrayed the poet and are thus responsible for his present condition:

Die Freunde, die ich geküßt und geliebt,
Die haben das Schlimmste an mir verübt. (E, 2, 103)

Whether this is in any way a rational view of Heine's wretched situation is, of course, beside the point; the point is that he felt these resentments very strongly indeed, and into the verses they go, without qualms as to whether the bald expression of them redounds to the dignity of the persona.

In the *Nachwort zum "Romanzero,"* it will be remembered, Heine expressed some interest in Swedenborgian notions of immortality.[8] He continued to think about this matter vaguely, although in fact it offered him scant consolation. For one thing, he could not help associating an afterlife with the view of Heaven traditional in the popular imagination, a rather paltry and dull promise that in Heine's mind took on decidedly bourgeois aspects; for another, the perpetual continuation of the self he had suffered with these fifty years was undoubtedly a sobering prospect. The third poem of the collection, *Leib und Seele,* deals in an unexpected way with the immortality of the soul; it is a kind of experiment in searching for consolation that falls just short of succeeding. In the first part of the poem, the poet's soul addresses his body in a mood strongly reminiscent of the days when Heine was vociferously arguing the parity of the flesh and the spirit:

Du warst ja stets mein zweites Ich,
Das liebevoll umschlungen mich . . . (E, 2, 90)

The soul fears that "ganz ohne Körper, ganz abstrakt" (E, 2, 91), eternal life will be a leaden bore, and begs to accompany body into death and oblivion. The body, however, encourages the soul on its way, arguing that it was only the wick of the lamp and must burn down, while the pure spirit will gleam in glory:

> Ich bin nur Plunder,
> Materie nur, wie morscher Zunder
> Zusammensinkend, und ich werde,
> Was ich gewesen, eitel Erde. (E, *2*, 91)

But the best the body can suggest is the hope that Heaven is more amusing than the soul expects. It is a left-handed consolation toying with a weak hope with little faith and an underlying suspicion of God's universe. Again one has the feeling that when Heine mulled such matters this is exactly the way they stood. This topic is taken up again in No. 10, *Himmelfahrt*,[9] but is dealt with in a more satirical vein; the poem, uncharacteristically for this collection, makes use of a clearly distinct persona, that of a deceased and very ordinary Prussian philosopher. The poem is amusing, but the objects of its satire are familiar and need not detain us here; its relevance to the context lies in the bourgeois stuffiness of St. Peter, who behaves as though he were the doorman of a wealthy banker with second-rate tastes and Philistine prejudices.

A set of brief and quite brittle animal fables turn up in the late poetry. It is a question whether these fables, some of them with grimly sardonic "morals" tacked on the end, have any objective referent. Herman Salinger has undertaken an elaborate biographical interpretation of *Rote Pantoffeln,* No. 4 in the collection,[10] based on the fact that Heine first found Mathilde in a shoe shop; thus the red slippers are Mathilde, the cat who owns the shop is Mathilde's aunt, and the mouse who gets her head bitten off for her greed is Heine himself.* Apart from its fundamental insensitivity, this interpretation suffers from the dislike of Mathilde that Heine fortunately did not share with his later interpreters. In the late poetry, Heine's wife plays a much more delicate role, to which we shall return presently; for the moment

* Herman Salinger, "Heine's 'Rote Pantoffeln': Wit and Autobiography," *Monatshefte, 33* (1941), 213–16. In view of the dubiousness of this interpretation, Salinger would have done well not to throw stones at critics of the stature of Prawer and E. M. Butler for ignoring it, especially as he did so in the wild Jungian excursion he undertook to interpret *Nächtliche Fahrt*: "Helping Heinrich Heine Explain his Archetypal 'Night Journey' Poem," *Literature and Psychology, 13* (1963), 35, n. 1.

it is sufficient to point out that if Salinger's interpretation were accepted, it would be hard to understand the next poem, *Babylonische Sorgen,*[11] which gives powerful expression to Heine's agonizing concern for the welfare of his wife after his death (for reasons connected with his general view of women, he preferred to underestimate his wife's indestructible robustness). There seems no need to press the interpretation of these fables so hard, for they were written with a child in mind, Campe's son; at least two of them, *Der tugendhafte Hund*[12] and *Pferd und Esel,*[13] were sent to the boy, although apparently two-and-a-half years after they were composed.[14] To Campe Heine explained that he wrote them to ease the nervous hypertension brought on by his suffering.[15] It is true that they have their grim side: the frivolous mouse loses her head; the virtuous dog joins in the undisciplined hooliganism of the other dogs (undoubtedly a political allegory), and the ass lasts forever while the noble horse has been technologically unemployed by the railroad. These are all consistent with Heine's view of life and the world at this time, but they do not require exact coordination with specific referents. A somewhat different case is that of No. 9 in the collection, *Die Libelle,*[16] which, as we know by comparison to an older version,[17] was considerably expanded to bring out the lament of the exiled and prostrate poet; this poem, however, belongs more properly to a different complex that will be touched upon below.

Just as the dying poet repudiated life while lusting for it, so he despaired of the way of the world without abandoning outraged protest. Thus it comes about that Heine, whose cousins in the French branch of the family were engaged in the slave trade,[18] made a mordant contribution to the anti-slavery literature of the time: No. 6 is the collection, *Das Sklavenschiff.*[19] This is an example of Heine's polemical verse at its very best: it is bitter and accusatory by implication, yet allows the bourgeois brutality to define itself by concentrating exclusively on the idiom of the trader and his equally callous ship's doctor. This is the sort of poem over which Heine's Marxist admirers rejoice, and with good reason, for there is no doubt that Heine accurately recorded the bourgeois mentality at its very worst. Anyone who doubts that this nauseating combination of calm respectability, degenerate sentimentality, naked self-interest, and utter human insensitivity plays a substantial and ultimately catastrophic role in the development of German (if not to say, European) society need only read the memoirs of the commander of Auschwitz, Rudolf Höss,[20] to return to Heine with renewed respect. In this regard Heine's mordant satire shares a point of contact with the searing ironies of Georg Büchner. A good example is the poem *Jammerthal,* in which the health official comments on the death by starvation and freezing of two paupers in tones that even today are sometimes audible in such matters:

> Die strenge Wittrung, erklärte er,
> Mit Magenleere vereinigt,
> Hat beider Ableben verursacht, sie hat
> Zum mindestens solches beschleunigt.
>
> Wenn Fröste eintreten, setzt' er hinzu,
> Sei höchst notwendig Verwahrung
> Durch wollene Decken; er empfahl
> Gleichfalls gesunde Nahrung. (E, 2, 124)

The slave trader's final prayer in *Das Sklavenschiff* is an unconscious declaration of the hypocrisy of bourgeois piety:

> Um Christi willen verschone, O Herr,
> Das Leben der schwarzen Sünder!
> Erzürnten sie dich, so weißt du ja,
> Sie sind so dumm wie die Rinder.
>
> Verschone ihr Leben um Christi willn,
> Der für uns alle gestorben!
> Denn bleiben mir nicht dreihundert Stück,
> So ist mein Geschäft verdorben. (E, 2, 121)

Prawer has pointed out that the social protest of these poems is linked to the flaws in the world order with which Heine was continually confronting God.[21] They also have some interesting connections to Heine's poetic practice as such. Quite overwhelming is his use of the old themes of music and the dance in *Das Sklavenschiff*; the demonic and amoral quality of these arts, which Heine had always stressed, has now shifted completely into the perverse, as the slaves are forced and whipped into the pleasures of the dance in order to improve the health of this commodity. The contrast is stark—a bitter and extended oxymoron—yet it is clearly not totally irrelevant to Heine's view of dance and music generally. Gleefully he points to a remark of Lorenzo in *The Merchant of Venice* (V, 1):

> Trau keiner Bestie, die nicht liebt
> Musik! sagt Albions großer Dichter. (E, 2, 121)

To see that this is not merely the perversion of harmless aphorism, we must turn to Heine's view of Lorenzo as he set it out in *Shakspeares Mädchen und Frauen* some fifteen years before:

> Was gar den Lorenzo betrifft, so ist er der Mitschuldige eines der infamsten Hausdiebstahle, und nach dem preußischen Landrecht würde er zu fünfzehn Jahre Zuchthaus verurteilt und gebrandmarkt und an den Pranger gestellt werden; obgleich er nicht bloß für gestohlene Dukaten und Juwelen, sondern auch für Naturschönheiten, Landschaften im Mondlicht und für Musik sehr empfänglich ist. (E, 5, 451)

It is quite convenient for us that Heine should also have mentioned these Romantic tropes in this context. For Romantic imagery, the weak reed on which Heine tried all his life to balance a concept of "poesy," is finally revealed in the last poetry as all but devoid of conviction and truth. The second part of *Das Sklavenschiff* begins with a seascape entirely couched in Heine's most persistent mode of imagery:

> Hoch aus dem blauen Himmelszelt
> Viel tausend Sterne schauen,
> Sehnsüchtig glänzend, groß und klug,
> Wie Augen von schönen Frauen.
>
> Sie blicken hinunter in das Meer,
> Das weithin überzogen
> Mit phosphorstrahlendem Purpurduft;
> Wollüstig girren die Wogen. (E, 2, 119–20)

This is the setting Heine chooses for the grisly dance on the slave ship. Related to this ultimate devaluation of the imagery of purity and natural harmony is Heine's treatment of the annual outdoor stroll of the orphans in No. 16 of the collection, *Erinnerung an Hammonia*.[22] The refrain of "O, die hübschen Waisenkinder!", the self-satisfied sentimentality of the citizens, and the picnic, set up as a tableau to touch the heart of the onlooker, all carefully avoid the feelings and true condition of these orphans, or the quality of their lives during the rest of the year, and the whole scene generates, in the last two stanzas, an awareness of the poor and suffering the world over. The decay of sentiment and the imagery that accompanies this bitterness is an old story with Heine, and in the last poetry it is tied closely into personal experience.

A key to the whole history of this decay is in the poem that follows *Das Sklavenschiff*, the notorious *Affrontenburg*. Here, as elsewhere in the last poetry, Heine's violent resentment against the real or imagined distreatment he suffered at the hands of his uncle's family is sharply revived; *Affrontenburg* is a particularly satanic form of the revenge Heine tried to take against the members of his family, for, like the censors of the 1830s, they were too obtuse to notice that the bitterness was directed against them.[23] Heine's grotesquely unedifying, if not to say irrational, attitude toward the whole matter of Uncle Salomon's inheritance may, of course, be regarded from a psychological point of view, as it was by Weigand in a careful analysis of the whole affair a few decades ago.[24] It is quite correct, as Weigand observes, that Heine absorbed the affair into his late poetry by "building up the legend, finally, that made him the guileless hero slain by family treachery. This legend, first sketched out in his letters . . . and rounded out subsequently by poems calculated for posthumous revenge, must in its later stages be regarded rather as an expression of the will to survive as a person, than as conscious make-believe." [25] In the terms of this study, the whole complex becomes an element of justification for the poetic persona. But there are more penetrating truths in *Affrontenburg* than such an analysis alone would suggest. Let us consider the following account of the garden of Uncle Salomon's mansion:

> Des Gartens Rosen waren schön,
> Und lieblich lockten ihre Düfte;

Doch früh hinwelkend starben sie
An einem sonderbaren Gifte.

Zu Tod ist auch erkrankt seitdem
Die Nachtigall, der edle Sprosser,
Der jenen Rosen sang sein Lied;—
Ich glaub', vom selben Gift genoß er.

Vermaledeiter Garten! Ja,
Es war, als ob ein Fluch drauf laste;
Manchmal am hellen, lichten Tag
Mich dort Gespensterfurcht erfaßte. (E, *2*, 106–07)

This language leaves little to be desired in confessional clarity. The roses, obviously, are Amalie, or Amalie and Therese, or Heine's love for them; the singing nightingale is the poet himself. Thus the Romantic images are tied closely to the doomed hopes of unrequited love, and they are destroyed by a peculiar poison. Now this poison may be understood to refer to the slander of third persons who damaged Heine's relations to his uncle and his cousins, a recurring theme in the construction he insisted on putting on these relations and one that is introduced here in the preceding stanzas. But one will remember the image of the poisoned songs from *Lyrisches Intermezzo* 51,[26] and here the poison is an integral part of the situation; the garden seems cursed and the poet is plagued by the fear of spooks in broad daylight. This passage taken in isolation seems to me a pretty fair account of what actually must have happened in Heine's youth: the love experience is intertwined with Romantic motifs that carry no substantial conviction, and there is a darkness within the poet himself that is at least partly responsible for the way his affairs turned out. That he was a victim of his own obsessions as well as of the indifference and / or wickedness of the family is plainly admitted in the last stanza:

Mit Neid sah ich die Schiffe ziehn
Vorüber nach beglückten Landen—
Doch mich hielt das verdammte Schloß
Gefesselt in verfluchten Banden. (E, *2*, 107)

These insights do not prevent Heine from laying the blame for his present miseries upon others, as we shall see in *Zum Lazarus.* This is the way he chooses to feel, just as he knows also that something went sadly wrong with his *poetic* history. The last poetry requires us to confront the whole man, clay and all.

The group *Zum Lazarus,* for all its similarities of form, is less like the *Lazarus* group of *Romanzero* than might appear at first glance. The poems are a good deal less religious in the sense I tried to elaborate in the preceding chapter. It is true that the religious connection is established in the first and last poems of this set by specific adversions to God. The first poem is most congruent with the tone of *Romanzero,* for in it the poet puts harsh questions to God about the justice of the moral order—questions that sound blasphemous yet, characteristically, have their specific counterparts in the Bible: e.g., Jeremiah 12:1; Job 21:7; the 73d Psalm. These immortal agonies of doubt Heine compresses into one of his toughest and most effective stanzas:

> Woran liegt die Schuld? Ist etwa
> Unser Herr nicht ganz allmächtig?
> Oder treibt er selbst den Unfug?
> Ach, das wäre niederträchtig. (E, 2, 92)

At the end, as Felix Stössinger[27] and Werner Kraft[28] have pointed out, Heine deliberately avoids a rhyme:

> Also fragen wir beständig,
> Bis man uns mit einer Handvoll
> Erde endlich stopft die Mäuler—
> Aber ist das eine Antwort? (E, 2, 92)

The German idiom *es reimt sich nicht* means "it does not accord," and Kraft has perceptively argued that "Handvoll / Antwort" is a semirhyme (actually a near assonance) suggesting that Heine *wanted* the universe to "rhyme," but it did not.[29] All this fits the religious complex of *Romanzero* very well.

But the last poem of the group, a prayer to let the poet live and remain with his wife,[30] shows the shift of emphasis in the last poems away from generalized religious lament and the products of the creative imagination to the details of the poet's situation and feelings. Thus, though it has the form of a prayer, it is not a religious poem in the sense that the first one is. It is part of a set of ruminations on the poet's own present feelings that develops from poem to poem in the group, and these in turn have a number of counterparts in the collection and among the poems of the *Nachlaß*. After the first poem has called attention to the dubiously ordered universe within which the poet suffers, the second turns to a declaration of the poet's total powerlessness; this stands in sharp and probably intended contrast to the poet-persona of the middle years with his illusions of power and destructiveness. The dark woman who turns the poet's hair gray and sucks the marrow out of his spine is a composite of the vampire and witch figures of Heine's earliest poetry and the "Frau Unglück" of the motto to *Lamentationen*,[31] an interesting and rather ominous image from a psychological point of view. The poet knows now that his anathemas are of no avail and that he can only capitulate:

> Ohnmächtige Flüche! Dein schlimmster Fluch
> Wird keine Fliege töten.
> Ertrage die Schickung, und versuch
> Gelinde zu flennen, zu beten. (E, 2, 92)

The pejorative word "flennen" indicates the poet's contempt for his own situation and the new, enforced modesty of his desires, a theme that recurs, as we shall see, in a different form in the final poem. In the third poem we hear something about the state of the poet's imagination. This is perhaps Heine's most moving lament; in successive stanzas he describes the terrible slowness of passing time while he himself does not move at all, the hopeless darkness of the sickroom and the knowledge that he will exchange it only for the grave, and the suspicion that he is in fact dead while figures of fantasy cavort in his brain. At the end of the poem he describes his effort to write down these nightly visions in the morning. This account is consistent with what we know of Heine's practice in his last years; the interesting thing about the persona is the apparent passivity of the creative act: the poet's gestures of sovereignty over his materials and creations are a thing of the past.

The next poems, rather unexpectedly, revive memories of the poet's long lost love. Elster argues that the sixth, seventh, and eighth poems refer to Therese, who in the summer of 1853 visited

Heine and then wrote him a tender letter of sympathy for his condition.[32] William Rose, despite his thorough skepticism on the subject of Therese, is not able to dismiss this connection,[33] and indeed it is probably the strongest evidence that Heine had once been in love with Amalie's sister. The two poems preceding these are memories, one of a missed opportunity for love now regretted, the other of a girl long dead; neither of these have any clear counterpart in earlier poems. The second of them is striking because it is an act of contrition: the poet accuses himself of insensitivity to the beloved's suffering and death; now he wants from her an odd kind of forgiveness, an embrace to sweeten his last hour. This poem is not very easy to understand, but it is an example of the way memories and pathetic desires rise to the surface in the last poetry without being subjected to an effort of sovereign control. The first of the "Therese" poems, the sixth of *Zum Lazarus,* is peculiar for another reason. It is a distinct reprise of the mode of *Buch der Lieder,* describing the cool and unsentimental beloved who does not react to the Romantic landscape that inspires the poet's metaphors, and ending with a pointed rhyme that accuses the girl of heartlessness:

> Als wie ein Mädchenbild gemalt von Netscher;
> Ein Herzchen im Korsett wie'n kleiner Gletscher. (E, 2, 95)

The odd thing is that it is a very bad poem; the rhythms are clumsy and the slackness and lack of energy comport strangely with the poet's claims of devotion to elevated things of the spirit:

> Begeisterung für jene hohen Dinge,
> Die zwar Verstand und Prosa achten gringe,
> Für die jedoch die Edlen, Schönen, Guten
> Auf dieser Erde schwärmen, leiden, bluten. (E, 2, 94)

One would like to speculate that the substandard quality of this poem was intentional—that it is another aspect of the retrospective dismantlement of the illusions that in earlier years informed the creation of the persona. The next poem is a commentary on the poet's experience of unrequited love from the perspective of his newly-admitted truths. It says in essence that the beloved is guilty of no wrongdoing and did nothing to encourage or arouse the poet's passion; *nevertheless,* she is the cause of the poet's ruin. The autonomy of the love experience, which is evident in *Buch der Lieder* only after interpretation, has now risen to the surface of the poet's own consciousness, and he confronts it with a curious acceptance. He flatly refuses to draw any consequences from the insight or to refrain from blame and resentment, for only his own wretchedness is of any importance to him:

> Nur Eins bleibt im Gedächtnis mir,
> Das ist: ich bin zu Grund gerichtet. (E, 2, 95)

The irrelevant connection of the poet's present sufferings to the long past experience of unrequited love is a persistent theme in *Gedichte—1853 und 1854.* The poet does not bother to ask whether these feelings are fair or reasonable, although *Zum Lazarus* 6 indicates that he knows they are not; he simply records them. The theme is part of the expansion of the fable *Die Libelle,* which exploits the image of the insect flying into the flame:

> O wehe dem Käfer, welchem verbrannt
> Die Flügel sind! Im fremden Land
> Muß er wie ein Wurm am Boden kriechen,
> Mit feuchten Insekten, die häßlich riechen. (E, 2, 149)[34]

Here the poet's exile and his wretched company are the direct consequence of the beloved's perfidy. Number 13 of the collection, *Die Launen der Verliebten,* revives in a grotesque way the old delusion of the beloved who missed the love she really wanted and ends in misery. The bug makes his proposal to the fly, who refuses coquettishly, claiming that she is far above the bug's station and referring to her enthusiasm for "ideals." She then absurdly goes off to boast of her conquest and prepare her wedding; just how elevated her sensibilities are appears when she has herself anointed with perfumes,

> Damit ich gar nicht stinken thu',
> Wenn ich in des Bräut'gams Armen ruh'. (E, 2, 152)

The refused bridegroom does not, of course, appear at the wedding; he sulks seven years on a garbage heap until his beloved rots. In contrast to the beginning of *Romanzero,* Heine made few attempts at humor in his last poetry, and from *Die Launen der Verliebten* it is easy to see why. The light and capricious tone is sadly modified by the underlying impulses of the poem—revenge on the vulgar and stupid beloved, and the derivation of the poet's misery from unrequited love. Heine tries a more sober tack in No. 11, *Die Wahlverlobten*. This poem proceeds with grueling, if somewhat paranoid, logic. It is probably addressed, as Elster suggested, to no woman in particular but to "das Weib . . . das in Heines Träumen lebte und, kaum begrüßt, wieder verschwand." [35] She is the one whom fate meant to be united with the poet, but since this did not happen, they are both doomed to perish. An echo of the poet's earlier arrogance appears in his claims of the benefits he would have conferred upon the otherwise insignificant beloved:

> Ich hätt' dich aus dem Pflanzentume
> Erlöst, emporgeküßt, o Blume,
> Empor zu mir, zum höchsten Leben—
> Ich hätt' dir eine Seel' gegeben. (E, 2, 45)

The bitterness of parting is total, and there will be no reunion after death; beauty turns to dust. Then, quite unexpectedly, the poet flings his immortality into the beloved's teeth:

> Viel anders ist es mit Poeten;
> Die kann der Tod nicht gänzlich töten.
> Uns trifft nicht weltliche Vernichtung,
> Wir leben fort im Land der Dichtung,
> In Avalun, dem Feenreiche—
> Leb wohl auf ewig, schöne Leiche! (E, 2, 45)

This is just about the last gasp of the poet-persona's self-regard. Its purpose is revenge against the one who withheld her love and thus doomed the poet to destruction. It is surely disconcerting to see Heine expend so much poetic energy upon an interpretation of his fate that seems to bear so little relation to reality. Yet perhaps there is a bleak truth in all this at a deeper level, for indeed the lack of love in Heine's life and in his soul is intimately involved with his fundamental unhappiness.

The figure of woman is raised to terrifying mythological proportions in the ninth poem of *Zum Lazarus,* which picks up the image of the sphinx that Heine had used in the preface to the third edition of *Buch der Lieder* in 1839.[36] Here Heine makes a complete equation of sphinx and woman:

> Die Gestalt der wahren Sphinx
> Weicht nicht ab von der des Weibes;
> Faselei ist jener Zusatz
> Des betatzten Löwenleibes. (E, 2, 96)

The riddle of woman-Sphinx is "todesdunkel," and it is well that women do not know the answer to their own riddle, for if they were to utter it, the world would fall to pieces. What exactly these verses may mean is anybody's guess. One can only speculate that they are a generalization from the bitter experiences that have been recalled in the poems preceding: if women were as aware of their mysterious and destructive power as is the poet, the world, or at least human life, would come to an end. This is a version of the terrifying aspect of women that recurs intermittently throughout Heine's poetic career. Theatening women appear in more traditional form in the next poem, which stresses the witch-like ugliness of the three Fates. The poet begs the third of the Fates, the one with the shears, to cut the evil thread of his life.[37]

This poem leads us back to the theme of life against death. Heine undoubtedly did not want to die, otherwise he would have died much sooner than he did. But his agonies and the gloom of his outlook naturally made him long for release. Thus, in the next and final poem of *Zum Lazarus,* the poet splits the difference, as it were, between the death-wish and the lust for exuberant life—he utters a prayer for a minimally tolerable existence. This is the poem in which the poet pleads to be allowed to live on with his wife. Heine returns repeatedly to this matter in the late poetry, and it seems to me perverse to deny, as observers so often do,[38] that Heine's exasperation with his wife and his characteristic lack of respect for her—such as appears, for example, in a wry passage in *Die Romantische Schule*[39]—were tempered with a genuine and permanent love; certainly he felt an almost clutching attachment to her as his one real link with life. The moods, of course, shift violently. In *Celimene,*[40] Heine borrows the vain beloved from Molière's *Misanthrope* (an appropriate enough allusion) and growls that another man would have long since killed her for her deviltries; she is his purgatory, and death will free him from her "bad arms"—a very strange locution. Yet he borrows two lines from Molière almost verbatim to give a statement of the case that has some ironic justification:

> Wisse, Weib, daß ich dich liebe,
> Um zu büßen meine Sünden. (E, 2, 41)[41]

But in the poem Elster placed next in his first edition, the poet laments the inevitable separation from "Mein Weib, du engelsüße Person" (E, 2, 41) and compares the separation of man and wife to that of body and soul; here Mathilde's function as a symbol of living reality is quite clear. In the following poem, the poet weeps at the flowers his wife has brought him because they remind him of past pleasures,[42] and in a third, he describes himself as the shepherd appointed to shield his lamb and who now, in the face of death, must consign this task to God.[43] It is true that the pathos of this poem is directed more toward the person of the poet than toward his wife, but the tone of the poem is gentle and, for Heine, uncommonly sentimental. To be sure, the Mathilde of his poems is one more created figure, as, indeed, Mathilde herself seems to have been for him; he is once reported to have described himself as her Pygmalion.[44]

The poet's love of life is also subject to a number of moods and variations. In the last poem of *Zum Lazarus* he asks God "only" for health and money:

> Gesundheit nur und Geldzulage
> Verlang' ich, Herr! O laß mich froh
> Hinleben noch viel schöne Tage
> Bei meiner Frau im *statu quo!* (E, 2, 98)

This sad reduction of the persona to a longing for the simplest bourgeois comforts appears also in the *Epilog* to the collection,[45] where he alludes to Achilles' famous remark in Canto 11 of the *Odyssey* that he would rather be the serf of a landless man than the ruler of all the underworld; this allusion recurs in an otherwise undistinguished and disingenuous poem, *Der Scheidende,* in which the poet gives ironic stress to the modesty of his desire:

> Der kleinste lebendige Philister
> Zu Stukkert am Neckar, viel glücklicher ist er,
> Als ich, der Pelide, der tote Held,
> Der Schattenfürst in der Unterwelt. (E, 2, 110)

In a rare sonnet, the hatred of death is expressed with terrible urgency:

> Der Hand entsinkt das Saitenspiel. In Scherben
> Zerbricht das Glas, das ich so fröhlich eben
> An meine übermüt' gen Lippen preßte.
>
> O Gott! wie häßlich bitter ist das Sterben!
> O Gott! wie süß und traulich läßt sich leben
> In diesem traulich süßen Erdenneste! (E, 2, 89)

If, as has been suggested, this poem goes back as far as 1846,[46] that would explain why the poet-persona remains so prominent here, for it is the glorious past of song and poetry that is elegiacally mourned. Later this quasi-heroic element slips out of the picture. But Heine does not forget that his death is the death of a poet. In the poem that in Elster's first edition is incorrectly titled *Miserere,*[47] it is regarded as astonishing of God that He should create a gay poet and then subject him to an interminable martyrdom for which, he says, he has no talent:

> Ob deiner Inkonsequenz, o Herr,
> Erlaube, daß ich staune:
> Du schufest den fröhlichsten Dichter, und raubst
> Ihm jetzt seine gute Laune . . .
>
> O Miserere! Verloren geht
> Der beste der Humoristen! (E, 2, 90)*

But finally, despite Heine's protestations that in his present circumstances he asks little of life, he hates the triviality of accommodation to life as it is ordinarily lived. Number 15 of the collection, *Guter Rat,*[48] is a cynical account of the opportunism and

* See Prawer's excellent analysis of the combination of persiflage and grim seriousness in this poem, *TS,* pp. 236–38.

dissimulation that wins success here below and in the kingdom of Heaven above. Heine's demands on life tend to be absolute after all; it is only under the pressure of his agonized suffering that he offers tentative compromises that in any case will not be accepted.

The remaining poems of *Gedichte—1853 und 1854* need not detain us very long; they are polemical verses that are not among Heine's best. The satires on Wagner are ignorant and thus of little importance, and the broadside against Jakob Venedey in *Kobes I.*[49] is totally out of proportion to the importance of the man and the magnitude of his trespass against Heine. The only one of these poems that is of particular interest is *Die Audienz,* a brisk satire on the abortive confrontation between Georg Herwegh and Frederick William IV, which touches upon the poet's relationship to political power. Heine makes fun of Herwegh, whom he once called the "iron lark" (E, 2, 169), for trying to act out the plea of Schiller's Marquis Posa:

> "Erbitte dir eine Gnade," sprach
> Der König. Da kniete nieder
> Der Schwabe und rief: "O geben Sie, Sire,
> Dem Volke die Freiheit wieder!
>
> "Der Mensch ist frei, es hat die Natur
> Ihn nicht geboren zum Knechte—
> O geben Sie, Sire, dem deutschen Volk
> Zurück seine Menschenrechte!" (E, 2, 209)

The irrelevance to present politics of literary reminiscences from the period of idealism is total; entrenched reactionary power is not to be moved by such means. The king dismisses the thought as "Ein schöner Traum," advises the poet to wise up ("werde gescheiter"), and presents him with two gendarmes to accompany him over the border.[50] Heine's last commentary on the relationship of literature and politics is a snort of scornful amusement.

There are two other poems of the *Nachlaß,* however, that demand our attention briefly. One of them is the long narrative poem *Bimini,* which, judging from the last stanzas we have, is apparently a fragment. In the course of his excellent and detailed analysis of this poem, Prawer observes that "Don Juan Ponce de Leon is the last important *persona* of Heine's poetry." [51] It is also Heine's last attempt to generate, under the inspiration of his historical reading,[52] a poetic landscape of beauty and wonder. The result is a little incoherent, for the undertaking runs up against the dark pessimism that is now a permanent feature of Heine's treatment of the persona or his setting. In the long and rather rambling prologue, Heine is clearly trying to create a poetic *ambiance* in contrast to, but as full of wonder as, that of Romanticism, the "blaue Blume, / Die verschollen jetzt" (E, 2, 125). Thus he tries to exploit the advent of the modern world for poetic purposes in terms of the "Buch der Schönheit"—the New World—and the "Buch der Wahrheit"—human invention, especially that of printing.[53] But the modern world, with its new "Weltkrankheiten" (E, 2, 126), does not sustain such an effort; the sensual spices that are a part of the exotic metaphor in the description yield in importance and desirability to crass gold.[54] In keeping with Heine's practice in the last poetry, the legend of Bimini arouses in him memories of past images that are now ruined in the general decay of his life:

> Bimini! bei deines Namens
> Holdem Klang, in meiner Brust
> Bebt das Herz, und die verstorbnen
> Jugendträume, sie erwachen.
>
> Auf den Häuptern welke Kränze,
> Schauen sie mich an wehmütig;
> Tote Nachtigallen flöten,
> Schluchzen zärtlich, wie verblutend. (E, 2, 129)

This is why the persona of the decrepit Ponce de Leon and his effort to evade death are appropriate to Heine's last period. But it is all futile. The wreaths will not flourish again, nor the dead nightingales revive; Ponce de Leon will not find the Fountain of Youth, and the ship that the poet carpenters out of trochees, imagination, wit, metaphor, and hyperbole, solid as he may claim it to be,[55] will not reach its goal. The task of extracting some measure of poetic dignity from the situation and longings of Ponce de Leon is not going to be easy.

The poem proper begins with a long, sad prayer to the Virgin about the lost glories of youth and the ravages of old age. In the course of it, Ponce de Leon offers to give up the prerogatives of fame and honor, and suffer any indignity of station, a proposal heightened by his traditional Spanish austere pride:

> Nehmt mir Reichtum, Ruhm und Würden,
> Nennt mich nicht mehr Excellenza,
> Nennt mich lieber Junger Maulaff',
> Junger Gimpel, Bengel, Rotznas'! (E, 2, 136)

In the next stanza, he freely confesses his vanity; that, too, is of no importance one way or another in comparison with the desire to regain youth:

> Hochgebenedeite Jungfrau,
> Hab Erbarmen mit dem Thoren,
> Der sich schamhaft heimlich abzehrt,
> Und verbirgt sein eitles Elend! (E, 2, 136)

What we are witnessing here is the collapse of the laboriously constructed persona in the face of death. None of the things that have sustained Ponce de Leon in the years of his flourishing have any relevance any more. The persona is being transformed into the pathetic reality of the poet. At the end of this soliloquy, Ponce de Leon's self-control forsakes him completely, and he gives way to a paroxysm of weeping:

> Als Don Juan Ponce de Leon
> Vor sich hinsprach solcherlei,
> Plötzlich in die beiden Hände
> Drückte er sein Antlitz schmerzhaft.
>
> Und er schluchzte und er weinte
> So gewaltig und so stürmisch,
> Daß die hellen Thränengüsse
> Troffen durch die magern Finger. (E, 2, 137)

This is the end of the dignity described at the beginning of the first part:

> Dieser Mensch ist alt, doch spanisch
> Kerzensteif ist seine Haltung.

Halb seemännisch, halb soldatisch
Ist sein wunderlicher Anzug. (E, 2, 131)

Ponce de Leon will die; there is no escaping it. Whatever happens in the remainder of the poem, therefore, is by way of retardation. The detour, however, will be taken through the realm of poetry, which holds out hopes that have no counterpart in reality but do have some justification within the boundaries of the poetic imagination. In the second part, Ponce de Leon is rocked to sleep with a song from the world of legend; the magic promise of Bimini is held out to the dozing knight. One is given reason to believe, however, that the Fountain of Youth exists only as a metaphor for poetry; the lines "Aus dem teuren Wunderborn / Fließt das Wasser der Verjüngung" (E, 2, 139) recall Heine's treatment of the brothers Schlegel in *Die Romantische Schule,* where he agrees, with some sarcasm, that Romantic poesy is "der Trank der Verjüngung" (E, 5, 234). In the third part, Ponce de Leon's attempt to redeem the promise of poetry in the real world not only galvanizes him into action but inspires the whole population with enthusiasm. The aged knight is not alone in his desire to cheat death; the possibility is universally welcomed. Immediately, however, Heine's tone slips into satire; the poetic vision is vulgarized and cheapened when it is introduced into the mundane world and becomes a practical inspiration. Ponce de Leon makes himself rather ridiculous by dressing in the colorful trappings of youth in anticipation of the magic discovery. The fantastically tricked out ship that sets off on the futile voyage is named, with heavy irony, *Speranza.* Yet the poet remains ambiguous about the validity of poetic truth. He asserts that Ponce de Leon was no fool, for the legend was a guarantee of truth:

Juan Ponce de Leon wahrlich
War kein Thor, kein Faselante,
Als er unternahm die Irrfahrt
Nach der Insel Bimini.

Ob der Existenz der Insel
Hegt' er niemals einen Zweifel—
Seiner alten Kaka Singsang
War ihm Bürgschaft und Gewähr. (E, 2, 145–46)

But the truth of the real world is, after all, ineluctable and of a different sort from that of poetry; the healing water at the end of the voyage is the river of death and oblivion:

> Lethe heißt das gute Wasser!
> Trink daraus, und du vergißt
> All dein Leiden—ja, vergessen
> Wirst du, was du je gelitten—
>
> Gutes Wasser! gutes Land!
> Wer dort angelangt, verläßt es
> Nimmermehr—denn dieses Land
> Ist das wahre Bimini. (E, 2, 146)

The boundary of death can be neither transcended nor dissolved in poetic substance; it must be confronted and accepted with good grace or ill. In the face of death the postures of the persona become wholly irrelevant—but perhaps this is not entirely so of the autonomous poetic imagination.

It seemed, as Heine's semi-existence dragged on through the 1850s, that he would die as he lived, without lasting pleasure or comfort, without drums or trumpets, without external dignity. Heine's life is not the stuff of which romance is made. But God had a surprise for His humorist after all; having let the poet live undramatically and sometimes not very attractively for more than fifty years, He wrote an unexpected and most charming scene into the last act. The appearance from nowhere in the final months of Heine's life of the girl who called herself Camille Selden has often been described in touching detail. No magician could have conjured up anything, short of the unachievable "Gesundheit nur und Geldzulage," that could have eased the pain of Heine's dying more effectively than this clever girl, who served as a lightning rod for the poet's trammelled-up passions and as the audience for a final appearance of the persona. The poems Heine wrote for her are a kind of final farewell gesture to posterity and a brief but appropriate coda to his whole poetic career.

The utter desolation of Heine's last years seems ever so slightly less forlorn in these poems, where the poet has someone to whom his lament may be directly addressed. An example is the leaden sense of time that afflicted him in the sickroom. In two poems that Elster originally attached to *Zum Lazarus,* the poet expresses the hellish eternity, the snail's pace of time that seemed to stretch his suffering out into infinity.[56] But "Die Mouche" gave Heine something to wait for, and her visits broke time up into manageable units by permitting the poet the luxury of hope. Thus the poem *Laß mich mit glühnden Zangen kneipen,*[57] an outburst of perfectly believable impatience when "Die Mouche" did not come when she was expected and the poet suffered hours of futile waiting, is despite, or perhaps because of, its hyperboles and its reproachful grumpiness, less utterly despairing than the verses born of unrelieved and agonized loneliness. Heine's passion for "Die Mouche" also resurrected his humorous sense of the incongruous; the nearly sixty-year-old poet joked with her in the most gallant fashion that his paralyzed condition prevented the sexual fulfillment of their love:

> Die Lotusblume erschließet
> Ihr Kelchlein im Mondenlicht,
> Doch statt des befruchtenden Lebens
> Empfängt sie nur ein Gedicht. (E, 2, 51)

Perhaps only when the sexual act was totally impossible could Heine treat it so plainly and yet so decorously. "Ich bin nur noch ein Geist," he wrote to the girl, "was vielleicht Ihnen, aber nicht mir sonderlich zusagt" (Hirth, *3,* 617). The whole situation aroused wry but real laughter in the poet:

> Worte! Worte! keine Thaten!
> Niemals Fleisch, geliebte Puppe,
> Immer Geist und keinen Braten,
> Keine Knödel in der Suppe! (E, 2, 51)

To hear such tones again is a relief after all the gloom of the late poetry.

The most important of the poems written for "Die Mouche" is a long one that, according to Alfred Meissner,[58] was Heine's last, written two or three weeks before his death. It is a remarkable summation of the restless dialectics of Heine's poetic imagination.* Here, as usual, an excellent interpretation of the poem, which takes into account its probable genesis as it appears in the manuscript, is offered by Prawer,[59] so that I will restrict myself to the most necessary observations. The poet is now dead, lying in his coffin with "leidend sanften Mienen" (E², *2*, 277), and associated with his ruin is the general wreckage of the imagery out of his poetic tradition; it is unfortunate that in the nineteenth century it was not seen fit to print the stanza that makes this point with unappetizing but graphic bluntness:

> Auch manches Frauenbild von Stein liegt hier,
> Umkrautumwuchert in dem hohen Grase;
> Die Zeit, die schlimmste Syphilis, hat ihr
> Geraubt ein Stück der edlen Nymphennase. (E², *2*, 277)

Carved onto the sarcophagus itself is a large variety of images, arranged primarily according to the old and still restless dialectic of "Hellene" and "Nazarene," but within the terms of this dialectic the images grouped together are often in conflict with each other: Balaam's ass, the proving of Abraham, and the drunken Lot are grouped together; the chaste Diana is described, as in *Atta Troll,* leading her Wild Hunt, while Hercules sits in women's clothes and spins; and the stanza describing Israel at Sinai and Jesus disputing in the temple rhymes "Ochsen" with "Orthodoxen" (E², *2*, 278). This technique of presenting images as a kind of incarnated oxymora is unquestionably deliberate and is, I believe, the simple key to understanding the poem. The fastening upon a poetic image does not cause Heine's chaotic sensibilities to come to rest, even briefly, as it does, for example, in the case of poets like Conrad Ferdinand Meyer and Rilke. In this sense Heine falls short of being a "symbolist" poet of the sort that developed in the course of the nineteenth century. His mind, in perpetual turmoil, speeds along the surface of the heritage and

* *Für die Mouche* is the most inadequately transmitted of Heine's poems. The best text seems to be in Erich Loewenthal, *Der lyrische Nachlaß von H. Heine* (Hamburg, 1925), pp. 329–34. A thorough description of the manuscript at Harvard is given by Stuart Atkins, "The First Draft of Heine's 'Für die Mouche,'" *Harvard Library Bulletin, 13* (1959), 415–43. For convenience I will follow here the fairly good text in E², *2*, 277–81. A usable text is also in *Werke und Briefe,* ed. Hans Kaufmann (Berlin, 1961–64), *2*, 445–50.

snatches at elements that suggest not fixed points or deep truths, but incongruities. The shrill uproar of *Für die Mouche* reflects this aspect of Heine's poetic practice from beginning to end and so this last poem is a fitting, if dismaying, conclusion to the whole affair. Insofar as the aesthetically oriented temperament seeks salvation in the poetic realm, Heine died unshriven.

Before the ultimate consequence of this interpretation of the heritage and the world is drawn, however, the course of the poem is interrupted by a vision within the vision—the dream of the passionflower. Prawer has pointed out that the manuscript shows this was an afterthought.* But the fact strikes me as of minor importance, because if the poem is so organized, as it seems clearly to be, in order to draw the sum of Heine's whole poetical existence, then the poet's overwhelmingly disastrous experience of love must be integrated into it. Upon reflection, it is a little surprising that Heine did not exploit the image of the passionflower more than he did. Before *Für die Mouche,* it appears only in *Die Romantische Schule,* where Heine's treatment of it completely divorces it from his own poetic practice and applies it as a symbol of "Nazarene" Romanticism in which Heine wants to appear to have no part; consequently it is called "jene sonderbare mißfarbige Blume" (E, 5, 217). Yet he nevertheless gives himself away when he speaks of its appearance as symbolic of the sweet pleasures of pain that he here ascribes to Christianity, "dessen schauerlichster Reiz eben in der Wollust des Schmerzes besteht." In his last poem, such, it is fair to say, specious distinctions have fallen by the wayside. For here is the logical extension of his quasi-Romantic flower imagery: the flower that, in turn, contains the images of instruments of torture, is the perfect symbol for his indestructibly perverse view of the object of his love. Prawer finds the logic that transforms the passionflower into a woman strange,[60] but surely this is all but inevitable. From the days of

* Prawer, *TS,* pp. 259–60. Camille Selden describes the whole scene, including the appearance of the passionflower, as a genuine dream, in *Les derniers jours de Henri Heine* (Paris, 1884), pp. 81–83 (included, in German translation, in Houben, pp. 951–52). Perhaps Heine recounted a dream to her in this way. But the images of the poem are much too well-ordered and lucidly detailed to be genuine dream material; although a dream, or series of them, might well have supplied the inspiration, the poem is definitely a conscious creation.

the *Traumbilder,* beauty always contained a sinister component for Heine, especially the beauty of women. The experience of this vision turns out to be beyond poetry; in a stanza missing in the first publications of the poem, an eloquent silence expresses the depth of love:

> Und wie beredsam dieses Schweigen ist!
> Man sagt sich alles ohne Metaphoren,
> Ganz ohne Feigenblatt, ganz ohne List
> Des Silbenfalls, des Wohllauts der Rhetoren. (E², 2, 280)

Prawer, referring to Walther Killy, adverts in connection with this stanza to Heine's presumed sense of the inadequacy of words to experience and reality.[61] One may ask whether this contemporary issue is really appropriate to Heine, the most glib of poets. Heine's perspective in these matters is rather different; for it is not his practice to capture reality with poetry, but to create an independent poetic reality. The difficulty for him is that, although his investment in this undertaking is profound, such truth as the created poetic realm contains threatens to be evanescent and illusory. These stanzas in *Für die Mouche* are, on the one hand, a rhetorical device to stress the profundity of this fleeting experience of love; on the other hand, they imply the poet's dilemma, for, after all, the vision of this woman is a poetic creation and derives from the poetic vision of the passionflower; yet, to complicate the matter further, the confrontation eludes the poetic realm, and, insofar as it is *wesentlich,* repudiates it. Silence is death for the poet, and it is the silence of death toward which he now turns, away from foolish reality:

> O Tod! mit deiner Grabesstille, du,
> Nur du kannst uns die beste Wollust geben;
> Den Krampf der Leidenschaft, Lust ohne Ruh',
> Gibt uns für Glück das albern rohe Leben! (E², 2, 280)

But death is not to come peacefully; the dialectical chaos in the poet's mind will accompany him to the very end—the squabble between the claims of the flesh and the spirit rises to a deafening clatter, ending in the cacophonous hee-hawing of Balaam's ass, which, it will be remembered from the Bible, was the vehicle of God's word.

The paradoxical fascination of Heine's late poetry is that it is a great synthesis of disparate elements and unresolved contradictions. Its unity lies in the poetic realm only, for there are no harmonies and no solutions; there are only futile hopes and indelicate resentments, incurable agonies and frustrated lusts, reverence unachieved and hatred unappeased, yearning for life and contempt for reality, faith in the transcendent veracity of the poetic imagination and distrust of poetry. The laboriously constructed poetic persona vanishes into oblivion before the poet himself consummates his endless dying. Only the shattered and flawed poet remains, his pride in shreds and his memories devoid of consolation. But one catastrophe was spared Heine. He did not live, as some other poets have, to see his gift desert him. The brittle voice trembled but did not break, and the incomparable verse flowed on and on until almost the last flicker of life had left his ravaged body.

APPENDIX 1

The Communist Image: Hans Kaufmann

> . . . so muß ich vor allem sagen, daß die materialistische Methode in ihr Gegenteil umschlägt, wenn sie nicht als Leitfaden beim historischen Studium behandelt wird, sondern als fertige Schlablone, wonach man sich die historischen Tatsachen zurechtschneidet.
>
> —FRIEDRICH ENGELS

The memorials to Heine in the city of his birth are as follows:[1] a section of busy avenue on the edge of the *Altstadt* called Heinrich-Heine-Allee—on it is located the handsome new Düsseldorf *Oper;* a plaque on the house located on the site of Heine's birthplace, attached, to be sure, at the second-floor level so that only the well-informed visitor is likely to see it; a Heine corner, including a bust, in the restaurant "Im Goldenen Kessel" across the street, whose owner had the wit to hide the bust during the Nazi years; another bust in the foyer of the *Ratshaus,* which is not accessible to the interested visitor making casual inquiries; the Heine-Archiv in the dilapidated *Landes- und Stadtbibliothek,* now the nerve center of Heine scholarship in the Western world, where devoted and capable scholars are preparing the critical edition.* Here also is published the *Heine-Jahrbuch,* a most

* In 1957 it was proposed that a museum be erected for this great collection, but thus far nothing has come of it. See Erich Carlssohn, "Erinnerung an bedeutende Sammler (VIII). 'Heinrich Heine—Sammlung Meyer,' Düsseldorf," *Börsenblatt für den deutschen Buchhandel* (Frankfurt Edition), 3 (1957), 578–81. In the contemporary West German academic atmosphere, the plan to publish a critical edition was developed with some difficulty; it was originally hoped that the edition could be ready for the anniversary year of 1956, but a whole set of characteristic inflexibilities prevented this. For a mordant résumé of the background, see Petra Kipphoff, "Heinrich Heine und keine Folgen," *Die Zeit* (Sept. 4, 1959), p. 9.

valuable compendium of scholarly progress. It is noteworthy, however, that in the first six years of its existence (1962–1967), only one West German university professor contributed to it[2] (in keeping with the traditional solidarity of the profession, there have been none from Austrian or Swiss professors). And finally, there is at long last a monument to Heine in Düsseldorf. It was donated by the art society of the city in 1953 and is located on a rise in the *Hofgarten* where Heine, as a thirteen-year-old boy, saw Napoleon with his own eyes. It is a life-size, armless nude by the French sculptor Aristide Maillol, entitled *Harmonie.* The best that can be said of it is that it is pretty; in an age when sculpture is one of the genuinely flourishing arts, it seems a pity to dedicate to Heine a smooth-surfaced garden decoration symbolic of harmony. For, despite all the fine-sounding speeches at the statue's unveiling on Heine's role as a model for French-German friendship,[3] harmony is the last quality that comes to mind when thinking of his stormy career and even more chaotic posthumous history, and surely the conflict and toughness of contemporary sculpture would have been more appropriate. This little monument seems to me to reflect the situation in West Germany today: there is much good will and desire to make restitution, but these are sometimes relativized by half-measures and persistent atavisms that undermine the confidence of the foreign observer. It has been remarked fairly of the statue that it represents "künstliche Um- und Auswege, . . . die eigentlich Sackgassen sind." [4]

On balance, it would be unfair to say, as critics in Communist countries regularly do, that Heine is totally neglected or *verschwiegen* in West Germany, but it is true that interest does not seem entirely proportional to Heine's importance, that he has not been unquestionably restored to the canon, and that, apart from the admirable operation in Düsseldorf, Heine scholarship in West Germany is recovering rather slowly. In the atmosphere of liberation immediately following the end of the war in Europe, there was an instantaneous revival of interest in Heine. From 1945 to 1948, sixty-five editions of varying completeness appeared in Germany and Switzerland. After 1948, this flood of material ebbed considerably.[5] By 1965 there had been eighteen dissertations writen on Heine in the Federal Republic, as contrasted with four in the DDR,[6] but Heine is still treated rather rarely in the lectures and seminars in the universities.[7] Some of this difficulty is due, naturally, to the radical break in the tradition that took place in the Nazi period; in 1956, at any rate, it was discovered in a poll of Bavarian schoolchildren that few knew who Heine was, most of those recalled only that he was a Jew, and no copies of Heine were to be found in the school libraries;[8] in that same year it was possible to find a graduate of a humanistic Gymnasium who had never heard of Heine.[9] Occasionally more sobering events occur. In 1938 an article appeared in the Nazified version of the venerable *Euphorion,* renamed *Dichtung und Volkstum,* comparing Heine unfavorably to Joseph Görres on the grounds that Heine, the alien, could never penetrate to the essence of Rhineland man;[10] this exercise in *völkisch* obscurantism, somewhat relieved of its anti-Semitic excesses, was reprinted in 1951 in the newspaper that stands closest to the Christian Democratic Party.[11]

Made perhaps hypercritical by such events, the observer begins to notice other symptoms, of which one example may suffice. For several years the publishing house of Rowohlt has been putting out a series called *Monographien in Selbstzeugnissen und Bilddokumenten,* critical biographies of major authors that may be used with profit by teachers and students alike. For the Heine volume, however, Rowohlt apparently could not find an author, and so the text is a somewhat revised version of a book published by Ludwig Marcuse in 1932.[12] It is called a biography, but in fact it is a series of thoughtful but rather anecdotal essays centered on successive stages in Heine's life. It is not a scholarly product, by contrast to other volumes in the series, and it is certainly not free from objections. It is, as one might expect, quite dated; Sol Liptzin has said of it accurately that it has "less value as a statement of facts than as a collection of insights and intuitive flashes and as a seismograph of the German state of mind during the dying days of the Weimar Republic." [13] It seems significant that Rowohlt had to go back twenty-eight years to find a biographical text on Heine. In fact, apart from printed dissertations, collections of papers, books written in other countries, and two volumes by the elderly Friedrich Hirth, not a single scholarly book-length study of Heine had appeared in West Germany by mid-1968.

In East Germany the atmosphere is quite different, for reasons that are readily apparent. Communism always shows considerable interest in national cultural traditions, and nowhere does this practice encounter more difficulties than in the history of German literature, where, for better or worse, most of the major figures have been in some degree conservative, anti-progressive, anti-industrial, suspicious of democracy, and, above all, resolutely and programmatically disinterested in the realities of politics and society as a broad whole. The German Communists, who nevertheless wish to display themselves as the legitimate inheritors of an undeniably great tradition, find themselves obliged, on the one hand, to reinterpret wrenchingly those figures without whom the tradition is unthinkable, chief among whom is, of course, Goethe,[14] and, on the other, to shower a great deal of attention on those who depart somewhat from the conservative pattern, such as the younger Schiller, Büchner, and the Young Germans, but most particularly Heine, who, though less suitable for these purposes than Büchner, has the advantage of a productive career nearly twenty times as long. The prominent position Heine occupies in the cultural politics and educational policy of East Germany is quite understandable. Heine was, after all, a perceptive critic of bourgeois society and particularly of the July Monarchy; he was, like Engels after him, shocked by the character of England's exploitative industrial society; he placed himself in opposition and sometimes in radical opposition; he was on warm terms with Marx and shared with him a disdain for radical utopians; indeed, he regarded himself, because of *Lutezia,* as responsible for the progress of the Communist movement;[15] he had a healthy respect for the role played by money in the structure and fate of nations, society, and individual lives. There is more to Heine than all that, but in these matters he is outstanding among the important writers of his time.

However natural this affinity may seem, it is, on the other hand, difficult for us in the West to approach East German scholarship without prejudice. Since we know that in Communist

Germany everything published must be in accord with the ruling principles of the state,* and since it is notorious also that those principles are such that their beneficiaries must be literally walled in to keep them from running away, it is difficult to approach East German publications with a tolerant mind. Events in the DDR, with its persistent Stalinist petrifacts and its resistance to the gradual gentling and humanizing process that seems to be going on elsewhere in Communist Europe, make it no easier from year to year to overcome this repugnance. The prejudice is supported by some logical considerations. The dictation of the general results of scholarly studies in a totalitarian state, especially in the humanities, lames the whole thinking process by obliging it to work backwards. The results of scholarship must support a system so weak on its own merits that it requires the assistance of repression and physical force to keep it in operation. Thus one's trust in intellectual integrity is undermined in two ways; the critic's free intelligence, which is his most important quality in meeting the free imagination of the artist, is fettered by extraneous and irrelevant principle, and his argument is sophistically debilitated by the imposed need to make the worse cause appear the better. One can never be sure of the intellectual integrity of a Communist scholar† because options are not open to him. Thus one suspects in the official Communist critic primarily the party hack, the modern counterpart to the Nazi professor, and the Communist is in a poor position to prove otherwise. It follows that the study of Communist criticism is often a subdivision of Kremlinology; that is to say, it is read not for the main im-

* Constitutionally there has been no censorship in the DDR. But orthodoxy is maintained in other ways, such as state control over paper allocations. See Hans Peter Anderle, "DDR. Der Zensurapparat im Kopf," *Die Grenzen literarischer Freiheit*, ed. Dieter E. Zimmer (Hamburg, 1966), pp. 150–58. The new constitution of 1968 makes fewer pretenses of civil rights than its predecessor.

† I fear that I may be suspected of fighting the Cold War by using this terminology. The scholars in question would prefer, I am sure, to be described as Marxists or perhaps as Socialists. But there are Marxist scholars in the West whose work often looks quite different from that of those under the Communist system (and in some cases has *become* different since they have fled it), and to define what goes on in the DDR, especially in the intellectual realm, as Socialism is not very appealing. For purposes of clarity, therefore, it seems best to identify scholars working in East Germany as "Communist."

pact of the argument, but to discover within its sharply circumscribed universe of discourse the subtle nuances and accents that suggest a greater or lesser liberalization of mind, indicating in turn possible changes in the party line.

The prejudice has its logical elements, but it is not less a prejudice for all that. Communist behavior makes it fairly easy for us in the West to develop illusions about our absolute moral superiority and to transfer them to our intellectual positions, and the tensions of the world situation do not help us to keep a balanced perspective. But it is certainly wrong to argue, as one critic did several years ago, that scholarship from East Germany should simply be ignored.[16] There is a real if sometimes rather naive élan in the best Communist critical work, leading to a cohesiveness and seriousness worthy of respectful confrontation. The primary difficulty is not political but methodological; Marxist criticism derives from what seems to us a devaluation of the autonomy of great literature in favor of its subordination to the large social context presumed to bring it forth. To the Marxists, our "modernistic" methods of textual interpretation and hermeneutic aesthetics, which imply some recognition of the uniqueness of the great artist and the transcendent qualities of art, appear to avoid intentionally the effect of sociological and political considerations upon the intellectual consciousness. This opposition is now polarized to extremes, but some critics in the West, and even a few in the East (although not, apparently, to any notable extent in East Germany), are becoming slowly aware that it contains the potential of a fruitful critical dialogue if one day it can be carried on with integrity in a civilized manner. It becomes increasingly likely that, barring some terrible political catastrophe, this is the direction that criticism in both East and West will take in the relatively near future.

To return from this digression to Heine in East Germany: interpretations tend to fall roughly into three categories: the naive and kindly, the viciously partisan, and the seriously ideological. An example of the first is a little book published in 1952 by Werner Ilberg with the title *Unser Heine*. The work is a popular presentation, not a scholarly one; here and there it is weak philologically, and Ilberg seems to know little about Heine that cannot be culled from the notes to the standard editions. Like many books of this kind, purportedly addressed to a proletarian audience not privileged with a humanistic education, it reads on the whole as though it were written for children. (An extreme example of this phenomenon is the glossary of terms in one of Walther Victor's books, which with sinister ludicrousness defines "existentialists" as "Modephilosophen neofaschistischer Prägung." [17]) It is amusing that in the same mood Ilberg praises Heine's legère treatment of philosophical issues as the virtue of easily comprehensible lucidity.[18] The homely title of the book in fact suggests its purpose, which is to make a connection between the indestructible popular appeal of Heine despite establishment attitudes and his relevance, from a Communist point of view, as a representative of the German (and French) "progressive" forces of his time. Ilberg's interpretations are mostly superficial and biased, but not always foolish: in certain matters, Ilberg sees more clearly than some leading observers, as for example in his useful point that the role played by anti-Semitism (as we understand it today) in the opposition to Heine was far subordinate to predominantly political matters.[19] In other interpretations he is less sound: for example, his argument that *Der Rabbi von Bacherach* was not finished for psychological reasons, since it breaks off at the point where the renegade appears,[20] is simply wrong, and his humorless interpretation of the libertinism of the *Verschiedene* as a protest against the bourgeois *Kaufehe* is a characteristic phenomenon of Communist puritanism.[21] Significant about the book and a point in its favor is that it does not seem to be intentionally dishonest or misleading. Heine presents certain difficulties for the Communist hagiographer: the unpleasantness of many of his personal relations, the dubious quality of some of his political positions, his unconcealed arrogance and scorn toward the lower classes, and, above all, the ambivalent and indeed terrified comments about Communism in his later years. For the official Communist interpreter, the temptation must be strong either to suppress these things (I shall come back to this point later on), or to explain them "dialectically," a method for showing that an embarrassing fact is really all right because it had to be that way. How troublesome these matters are can be seen from Fritz Mende's most interesting recommendations on the teaching of Heine in East German schools, where detailed advice is given for explaining and refuting Heine's fears of Communism.* Ilberg does not suppress the problematic features of Heine, and his solutions, while less sophisticated than those of the idealogues, are sometimes less absurd. He makes an interesting and perhaps partially correct argument that Heine, especially in his younger years, really *wanted* to be a libertine in morals and a cynic in politics, but that the compelling force of his poet's vision of the truth and the urge to express it regardless of consequences simply did not permit this.[22] He points out reasonably that many of Heine's more unseemly personal relations, such as those with Meyerbeer, were determined by "Konkurrenz" in the art world,[23] and, far from suppressing Heine's dark thoughts about Communism, Ilberg quotes at length the strongest expressions of them,[24] while pointing out correctly that Heine had confused Communism with historical memories of the Terror of 1793.[25] But another comment on this matter is rather less comforting: "Dieser Furcht lag die Mißkonzeption einer individuellen Freiheit zugrunde, die er sich nur in der Gesellschaft, wie sie bestand, vorstellen konnte." [26] While we understand what Ilberg is talking about, "die Mißkonzeption einer individuellen Freiheit" seems a rather significant solecism at this point. But considering that this book antedates Stalin's death, what is of interest is not so much its specific content as the relative mildness of its tone, by which I do not mean objectivity—that is naturally absent—but the naive kindliness I mentioned before. In summing up, Ilberg says, "In Heine schlug die Menschheit zum erstenmal die Augen auf, ehe sie in Marx und Engels zum Bewußtsein erwachte," [27] a

* Fritz Mende, *Heinrich Heine im Literaturunterricht* (Berlin, 1962), p. 56. East Germans naturally take umbrage at suggestions that they falsify the image of Heine. A defense of the treatment of Heine in the schools was mounted by Siegfried Seifert in "Der unbewältigte Heine," *Neue deutsche Literatur, 13* (1965), p. 177: "Ausdrücklich verlangt der Lehrplan, Heines 'Widersprüchlichkeit in seiner Beurteilung des Kommunismus' an Hand des Vorwortes zur französischen Ausgabe der 'Lutezia' gründlich zu klären. Also keine Spur der . . . Propagierung eines 'Sozialisten' Heine, sondern das historisch fundierte Abwägen der Heineschen Position." This is fair as far as it goes, but if Seifert's article is an example, the "fundiertes Abwägen" is not in good shape.

remark that strikes me as more notable for boyish exuberance than hard-line propaganda. On the whole, Ilberg's book is harmless, no worse and perhaps a little better than the general run of indifferent books on Heine that appear everywhere and at any time. Furthermore, it is never certain to what extent the qualities of writing in an East German work are determined by the requirements of the regime. Even the wily Hans Mayer, in his present incarnation in West Germany a subtle and highly literate critic, once wrote in the East a short article on Heine that exhibits the same kind of willed naïveté that characterizes Ilberg.[28]

In sharp contrast to this style is a representative of a different genre, Gerhard Schmitz's *Über die ökonomischen Anschauungen in Heines Werken* (1960), a harsh and foolish book. Even the title arouses suspicion, for although Heine was very intelligent and perceptive about such things as the influence of bankers on the July Monarchy, and like many other observers in Europe he could see the increasing consolidation and consciousness of misery among the urban poor, he did not have economic views in the strict sense. At the very beginning Schmitz admits that Heine had little interest in economics;[29] no matter, the book has other purposes. In quick succession Schmitz produces an obligatory attack on Georg Lukács,* a completely unsupported and implausible argument that Heine was well acquainted with Hegel's theory of property, and a programmatic statement that the purpose of the book, in accordance with the program of the SED, is to turn Heine's satire against the *Bundesrepublik*.[30] This insistence upon the practical uses of Heine in the present is a frequent feature of East German writing about him. Schoolchildren are to be encouraged to acquire Heine's polemic manner in order to mature

* The reader may object that I have not included Georg Lukács in this essay. The reasons are that I wanted to concentrate on the situation in East Germany (where Lukács is no longer in favor, although most contemporary Marxist scholars are indebted to him), and to avoid going too deeply either into the history and theory of Marxist criticism, which would involve us with, among others, Franz Mehring, or into the variations in Lukács' own career. For a review of Lukács treatment of Heine in regard to theories of realism, see Richard Brinkmann, *Wirklichkeit und Illusion* (2d ed. Tübingen, 1966), pp. 64–68; cf. also Peter Demetz, *Marx, Engels,* and the Poets (Chicago and London, 1967), pp. 199–227.

into progressive and patriotic personalities,[31] and the teacher is to point out that a work like the *Harzreise* will be particularly appreciated by peoples like the Japanese, who are defending themselves against "die fremden Einflüsse eines volksfremden Okkupanten." * The bulk of Schmitz's book consists of adducing parallel passages from Heine and Marx/Engels, most of which are nothing more than similar comments upon obvious phenomena in public and social life. Where Heine deviates from the official line, it is explained that he was twenty years older than Marx and Engels and thus could not, by the laws of the historical dialectic, be "scientific" [32]—a quaint though far from uncommon argument; nevertheless, Heine was able to satirize the bourgeoisie in terms that are compared to a quotation from Stalin (in 1960!).[33] There can be little doubt that Marx, with his classical training in literature and admiration for Heine, would have regarded such arguments with contempt. Over long stretches Heine disappears from view altogether while Schmitz quotes from Marx and Engels; the presentation is interspersed with violent attacks on critics who see Heine's so-called revolutionary qualities in a more balanced perspective and with such digressions as a comparison between the nineteenth-century squabble over the Heine monument and "revanchism" in the *Bundesrepublik,*[34] not to mention a parallel between Heine's description of the misery of English industrial workers in the 1820s and the sufferings of the working class in today's West Germany.[35] It is clear that the fundamental integrity of Ilberg's book is not to be found here. Schmitz flatly denies Heine's dismay at Communism,[36] and towards the end presents the proposition that it was only the victory of the Red Army that made Heine's texts again available to their only proper public, the class-conscious proletariat,[37] a view not suprisingly shared by the *Great Soviet Encyclopedia,* which also pointed out that Stalin once quoted Heine in a speech.†

* Fritz Mende, *Heinrich Heine im Literaturunterricht,* p. 119. Observe the jargon inherited from the Nazis. But is it remotely possible that this is a hidden irony directed at a foreign occupation closer to home?

† L. J. Reinhard, *Heinrich Heine* (Berlin, 1956), p. 14. This is a translation of the passage in the *Bolshaya Sovetskaya Entsiklopedia,* 2d ed. *10* (1952), 332. In the shorter article of the later *Malaya Sovyetskaya Entsiklopedia,* 3d ed. 2 (1958), 898–99, there is no mention of Stalin.

It would be a thankless and pointless task to confront individually the absurdities of this hack. Again, the main issue is not the content of the book, which is beneath serious consideration, but, as in the case of Ilberg's work, the tone. The book is written in that cliché-ridden party jargon in which words acquire a life of their own and all effort to make them in some sense congruent with recalcitrant reality is abandoned. Schmitz's method is in fact indistinguishable from the procedure whereby a rightist critic would attempt to establish a connection between Heine and Communist doctrine in order to defame him. In this sense, style, intent, and quality of argumentation, reminds one forcibly of the worst excesses of Nazi writing on cultural topics. I am far from sharing the view that Communism and Fascism are similar versions of the totalitarian phenomenon, but it is not infrequent that the language of East German publications calls up echoes that are very unpleasant indeed.*

If the whole character of East German Heine criticism were exhausted in such writers as Ilberg and Schmitz, it would not be necessary to take any notice of it from the point of view of literary scholarship—such books are political phenomena and are of genuine interest only to the student of contemporary Communism. But Marxist literary theory has a long and significant history, and its most intelligent and gifted practitioners cannot be disposed of so easily. Such a person is Hans Kaufmann, the most important Heine scholar in East Germany, who has performed a great

* Other examples of Schmitz's type of study may be briefly noted. All the studies of Walther Victor come under this heading, including the above-mentioned *Marx und Heine* as well as *Heine. Ein Lesebuch für unsere Zeit* (Weimar, 1963). In the former Victor amazingly describes Julius Campe as a "reactionary publisher" (p. 52); he excoriates Friedrich Hirth for wanting to make of Heine "eine Heldengestalt des Kosmopolitanismus" (p. 72), cosmopolitanism being one of the more recent mortal sins in the Communist demonology. Victor demonstrated his literary sensitivity more than thirty years ago by writing a perfectly ludicrous pot-boiler about Heine's wife, *Mathilde. Ein Leben um Heinrich Heine* (Leipzig and Vienna, 1931). Even writers of some accomplishment can fall into this unhappy pattern; cf. Stephan Hermlin, "Über Heine," *Begegnungen 1954–1959* (Berlin, 1960), pp. 233–48, where it is argued that Heine's aspirations have now become social reality in the DDR and that at the turn of the century his reputation was only established among the proletariat. A more recent example is Ulrich Geisler, "Die sozialen Anschauungen des revolutionären Demokraten Heinrich Heine," *Wissenschaftliche Zeitschrift der Karl-Marx-Universität Leipzig, 14* (1965), 7–15.

service by providing us with the first extensively annotated edition of Heine's complete works in several decades.[38] This is not a newly edited or critical edition;[39] it is based on published texts and pulls together some materials scattered here and there in individual studies over the years, a useful achievement in itself; it is clearly a stopgap that will be obsolete when the new critical edition appears in Düsseldorf, but since that will take some time, the Kaufmann edition is highly welcome and now has been republished in West Germany, provided, not unsurprisingly, with a new commentary.[40] The edition has a few weaknesses, for the annotation by Gotthard Erler is not free of errors.[41] But we would have reason to be grateful for this edition even if it had a great many more sins than it appears to have, for it is provided with a thorough index, an indispensable tool for studying Heine because of his tendency to free association; Elster's standard critical edition has no index, and the index volume to Walzel's edition, published separately in 1920, has become something of a bookseller's rarity. It is unfortunate that the paperback republication of Kaufmann's edition in West Germany does not include the index.

The commentaries on individual works are almost completely unpolemical, perhaps with an eye to West German publication; they restrict themselves to factual information and a selection of the more substantial variant readings. Erler refrains, with good judgment that might well be imitated elsewhere, from offhand capsule interpretations. Instead, the interpretative commentary is presented at length in an ambitious 160-page essay by Kaufman that appears as a *Nachwort* in volume 10. Here we are clearly at a different intellectual level from that of Ilberg or Schmitz. The essay is written with calm lucidity and avoids condescension to a presumed proletarian audience; here, too, there is more than one Western scholar who could imitate the sober and clear style with profit. Kaufmann is an expert on Heine and knows what he is talking about; only rarely does an argument occur that is weak on philological grounds, and then usually the point is at least disputable.* He wastes no time recounting Heine's biography

* I have only located one error in Kaufmann's essay; he dates Jeanette Wohl's pamphlet against Heine in the year 1839, before *Börne* (*Werke und Briefe,* ed. Kaufmann, *10,* 66), whereas it appeared in 1840 as a reaction to *Börne.*

or giving a chronology of his works; the apparent assumption that these basic facts are known suggests something about the position Heine occupies in East German education. Instead, Kaufmann's essay is an approach to Heine's life, personality, works, and context, as a total phenomenon. Out of his considerable knowledge and his ideological assurance he argues compellingly and cogently; here and in his other writings Kaufmann makes the best case for a Communist interpretation of Heine that can well be imagined, and it is only fair that if Communist interpretation is to be confronted, it should be confronted as it appears at Kaufmann's level, not at that of Ilberg or Schmitz. I will not attempt here to refute Kaufmann's presentation; it is grounded in some fundamental assumptions about the nature of literature and its relationship to society that I do not share, and to reach into the roots of that disagreement would be an involved matter. Rather, I would prefer to call attention to a few aspects of Kaufmann's presentation that seem to me to be of symptomatic interest.

The essay begins unpromisingly enough with a polemic against the attitudes of "bourgeois philologists." [42] What is annoying here is not so much the jargon, which is inevitable in studies of this provenance, but the mendacious dogma that scholarly attitudes in the West are as monolithic as they are obliged to be in the East, along with the refusal to differentiate and the unwillingness to debate in detail with Western scholars. After Kaufmann gets this polemic out of the way, however, and covers some predictable methodological ground by arguing that all views toward Heine will be determined by the political and historical standpoint of the observer, he launches into an argument extending over some thirty pages that is so subtly developed that a Western reader might easily miss its import, as I nearly did, although I dare say it would be clear enough to the East German reader. In attempting to locate Heine historically, Kaufmann suggests that for the Classical period which Heine superseded, bourgeois society with its humanistic underpinnings was still an unrealized ideal, whereas in Heine's time it was beginning to be a reality, especially in France. Heine's value was in showing that the exploitative society is not eternal and can be overcome. But, unlike a genuinely proletarian writer such as Georg Weerth, Heine could not take the next step and see the proletariat as the *only* revolutionary force confronting the old society. In an argument derived directly from Marx, Kaufmann asserts that in Heine's situation an artistic product functioned as a saleable commodity, subject to the laws governing economic transactions at that stage of society, which impede the free unfolding of the poet's talent and his advanced sociological insight.[43] The argument is conventional and not without flaws; for example, Kaufmann steadily confuses the presumed *Poesiefeindlichkeit* of capitalism, which is in reality the object of the old Sturm-und-Drang attack on Philistinism (by no means dead in the East, where the official doctrine encourages petty-bourgeois tastes), with the repressive measures of restoration Germany, which was if anything stubbornly pre-industrial.[44] But the point of this argument taken as a whole is actually something different. We are in fact back to the problem of Heine's inconsistencies and the dubious aspects of his private and public character, problems East German schoolteachers are strenuously advised to avoid.[45] Because these problems are explicable in an orthodox way, "Wir brauchen daher das Zitatenduell um Politik und Poesie bei Heine nicht zu fürchten, noch viel weniger aber die größtmögliche Popularisierung des Gesamtwerks mit all seinen Widersprüchen." [46] The operative word here is "fürchten"; the argument is directed against a potential objection from within Communist orthodoxy to publishing the more embarrassing part of the *œuvre*. This clearly defensive theme echoes here and there in Kaufmann's essay; it appears most explicitly towards the end in a comment on Heine's late poem *Die Wanderratten*: "Nur ein gänzlich humorloser Doktrinär wird sich entrüsten über ein Gedicht, das das Proletariat mit Ratten vergleicht, aber dabei allen Verteidigern der Ausbeutergesellschaft eine prächtige Lektion erteilt." * I am sure Kaufmann is aware that there was a time in the history of Communism when one could be shot for less than approving a comparison of the proletariat to rats, and for his safety I hope he

* *Werke und Briefe,* ed. Kaufmann, *10,* p. 149. A recent study of the poem in the East, Karl-Heinz Hahn, "Die Wanderratten," *Aus der Werkstatt deutscher Dichter* (Halle, 1963), pp. 57–70, is less inclined to be generous; instead, Hahn interprets the poem as a *Rollengedicht* satirizing the bourgeois attitude. This is very dubious.

knows there are no built-in assurances in the system that such a time could not come again.

Kaufmann's brave efforts to resolve some of these embarrassments in an orthodox way often lead him onto shaky ground. He tries to account for Heine's often reiterated opposition to equality with an argument from Marx that equality in the liberal sense means equality only as a producer of commodities,[47] which has little or nothing to do with what Heine meant. Kaufmann's view that Heine's attitude toward Louis-Philippe is a combination of democratic ideals and Romantic reminiscences of the *Volkskaisertum*[48] is promising without being directly on the point. Kaufmann, like Ilberg and most Communist critics, is at his weakest when it comes to Heine's love lyrics and his erotic themes; there is something in the neo-puritanism of Communism that makes it difficult to believe that these things are what they purport to be. That Heine's differentiation between "spiritualism" and "sensualism," or "Nazarenism" and "Hellenism," is fundamentally sexual and psychological, seems obvious to the Western reader, but not so to the Marxist ideologue, who feels obliged to see this eroticism as symbolic of something else. Kaufmann goes so far as to argue that the failure of Heine's youthful dramas lies in an inability to motivate unhappy love by social concerns,[49] and the effort to see in the neuroses of the early love lyrics a social referent comes close to complete nonsense; he talks of Heine's "inner biography" in terms of the failure to gain acceptance in the grand bourgeoisie, symbolized by the beloved Amalie.* Here, as often in this essay and in those of other Marxist critics, a potentially useful insight is spoiled by the need to argue rearwards from the ideology. Things get twisted around the wrong way; Kaufmann points out that Heine seems to have gotten along more easily with girls "aus dem Volke,"[50] but somehow fails to see that

* Even in the West an outstanding Marxist critic like Theodor W. Adorno feels obliged to make such constructions; in "Die Wunde Heine," *Noten zur Literatur, I*, p. 151, he argues that Heine's theme of unrequited love is a simile of his "Heimatlosigkeit"; why it cannot mean simply what it says, namely, unrequited love, I am unable to understand. The persistence of bourgeois morality in sexual matters is a prominent atavism of contemporary Communism; Mende, *Heinrich Heine im Literaturunterricht*, p. 35, carefully advises teachers to steer pupils away from this aspect of Heine.

this does not derive from proletarian sympathies but rather from Heine's neurotic need to feel superior to and unchallenged by his beloved. Again, in respect to the girls of the *Verschiedene,* Kaufmann is on his way to a meaningful interpretation when he doubts that these poems necessarily reflect real events, but he jumps the track again when he takes the fiction not as an element of Heine's poetic persona, but as a form of aggression against bourgeois morality.[51]

But, on the other hand—and I want to stress this point, because it seems to me to involve an endemic weakness in current Western criticism—it is possible to learn from a scholar like Kaufmann. This is true in general terms, for much of what he says about the social tensions of Heine's situation is beyond refutation, and a great deal of the rest is potentially productive. I can conceive of an enlightening study of these matters by a student in the West who is not obsessed by Marxist preoccupations but is willing to learn from Marxist scholarship. It is true also in detail. In Kaufmann's case, this is sometimes so because his practice stands in refreshing contrast to his principles. He is quite simply mistaken when he says, in polemical opposition to the critical techniques of the West, that "über ihn [Heine] wird uns die mikroskopische Methode nichts lehren" [52]—there are few things more necessary in Heine scholarship than a close and respectful reading of the texts—and in any case, Kaufmann's view is not universally held in East Germany. Several years before Kaufmann's edition, Joachim Müller, argued for work-oriented interpretation and, in a qualified way, he pursued it.[53] Indeed, some of Kaufmann's own insights serve to refute the polemical dogma. Just an example or two: of the *Reisebilder* in general he writes, "Dieser Anschein von Willkür ist zu einem guten Teil poetische Fiktion, eine besondere Erzählhaltung, die dem Dichter erlaubt, ohne sich endgültig festzulegen, gleichsam auf Widerruf, neue Arten erzählerischer Darstellung zu erproben." [54] The word "Erzählhaltung" betrays principles of criticism developed in the West, and the argument, which implies detailed analysis, is, as I hope has been demonstrated in my own study, an urgent presupposition for understanding Heine. Or again, in wrestling with the familiar problem of subjectivity in Heine's works, Kaufmann argues that where Heine cannot see a progressive force, he represents it in his own voice, but where there is something his revolutionary feelings can identify with, as in *Die schlesischen Weber* or *Das Sklavenschiff,* he falls back on cool, objective presentation.[55] This idea may not be entirely correct in the terms in which it is presented, but it could easily serve as the starting point for a particularly fruitful investigation.

For all the acuity and careful thought in Kaufmann's essay, it does attempt to capture the essentials of a literary career of more than a third of a century in a relatively short space and thus must remain largely within general perspectives. To round out this sketchy survey, therefore, a word about the impression Kaufmann makes in concentrated interpretation of a particular work is in order. Kaufmann published a version of his doctoral dissertation of 1955 under the title *Politisches Gedicht und klassische Dichtung. Heinrich Heine. Deutschland. Ein Wintermärchen* (Berlin, 1959).[56] I find it interesting that the beginnings of a promising career, if Kaufmann manages to stay out of trouble with the watchdogs,* lie not in vague meanderings in the ideological realm, but in the careful interpretation of an individual work. A book of 219 pages on a poem that in Kaufmann's own edition takes up eighty-one pages, if it is at all intelligent, cannot help containing some penetrating analysis. This study has failings and virtues similar to those I tried to point out in the *Nachwort* to his edition; one or two outstanding features demonstrate how important the study is to anyone seriously concerned with Heine and his relevance to affairs in his world. Kaufmann argues first of all that Heine saw himself as a tribune of the people, in contrast to the radicals and liberals whose tendentious poetry seemed to him too much compromised by idealist notions. But since there was no consciously revolutionary proletariat in Germany, "Lyrische Selbstdarstellung des Dichters als Antagonist der deutschen Misere, offenes Aussprechen seiner Überzeugung von der

* It is by no means certain. One of his outstanding predecessors, Wolfgang Harich, has already been silenced and his edition of 1951 has been removed from sale because he became involved in the dispute about the Hungarian Revolution of 1956 and was put on trial. See Eberhard Galley, "Heine und sein Werk in Deutschland nach 1945. Eine kritische Übersicht," *Düsseldorfer Jahrbuch 50* (1960), p. 153.

kommenden besseren Zeit, das war der angemessene künstlerische Ausdruck der eigentümlichen deutschen Situation." [57] This judgment seems to me characteristic of Kaufmann: from the larger perspective it has value, but it does avoid the inner tensions and uncertainties within this revolutionary posture that cannot escape the alert reader. The curious thing is that Kaufmann avoids the problem with exactly the same procedure of which he accuses the "bourgeois philologists": he flees into stylistic analysis, making good the promise of the title that he will define the quality of the work in contrast to the conventions of "klassische Dichtung." What he has to say about style is well worth considering—for instance, his discussion of the confrontation between the parodistic treatment of traditional Romantic elements and Heine's own characteristic loose narrative; or, his comments on the ruggedness of the verse, the effect of which is that "dem Volke der Respekt vor dem Gegner genommen wird." [58]

But it is not long before he gets into difficulties. After a detailed argument to show that *Deutschland* presents an outstandingly "progressive" standpoint in the Marxist sense, he is obliged to admit that "Es bleibt ja ein auffallender Widerspruch, daß im 'Wintermärchen,' wo jede Zeile die Interessen des Volkes verteidigt und verkündet, keine realen Repräsentanten der unteren Schichten vorkommen." [59] Instead of finding the solution to this problem in the independence of the autonomous poet who refuses to be co-opted by the partisans Kaufmann is ultimately obliged to find refuge in the balanced view of dialectical tolerance:

> Angetrieben von einem glühenden Haß gegen die ganze Ausbeutergesellschaft, geleitet von einer tiefen historisch-dialektischen Einsicht und einer intellektuellen Redlichkeit, die ihm nicht gestatten vor unbequemen Konsequenzen die Augen zu verschließen, blickt er über die Grenzen des bürgerlichen Denkens weit hinaus in die sozialistische Zukunft, kann aber dennoch die Bindungen an die Denk- und Empfindensweise der Vergangenheit nicht abschütteln.[60]

One cannot help thinking that all the intelligence that this comment and indeed most of Kaufmann's writing exhibit come to greater fruition if it were not bound by the limitations of an orthodoxy ultimately defined by apparatchiks indifferent to culture.

There are ironies aplenty in the history of Heine's present status in his own culture. At twenty-three he wrote the prophetic lines: "dort wo man Bücher / Verbrennt, verbrennt man auch am Ende Menschen" (E, 2, 259), yet it was in the city of his birth where in 1965 the police found it appropriate to issue a permit for a book burning, on which occasion many of the same books were burned as in 1933. There was no freedom that concerned Heine more than freedom of speech and expression, yet it is in the DDR, where what little freedom of expression that can be extorted from Communist conventions of government seems to be in retreat, if anything, that Heine is represented as a cultural hero. And the East Germans too, of course, have their Heine monument, in Ludwigsfelde near Berlin. It is a seated figure, part proletarian street singer, part village idiot. It bears no resemblance to Heine that I can detect.[61]

APPENDIX 2

The Jewish Image: Max Brod

> Es ist wie ein Wunder! Tausendmale habe ich es erfahren und doch bleibt es mir ewig neu. Die einen werfen mir vor, daß ich ein Jude sei; die andern verzeihen mir es; der dritte lobt mich gar dafür; aber Alle denken doch daran. Sie sind wie gebannt in diesem magischen Judenkreise, es kann keiner hinaus.
>
> —BÖRNE

The topic I should like to touch upon in the next few pages is a difficult one for two reasons of a very different order. In the first place, it is obviously not decent to sit in the house of the bereaved and coolly weigh the virtues and failings of the deceased. This sense of indecency becomes an acute feeling of gross coarseness whenever one touches upon any aspect of the modern history of the Jews in Germany, so vast is the house of the bereaved and so ineffable the catastrophe that befell it. The great German Jewry, which at the beginning of the 1930s numbered some half a million souls, is no more, and before many decades, as things now appear, even its memory will be preserved only in books and documents. The remnant in Germany today shows little promise for the future; the median age is high, the birth rate very low, and relations between Jews and other Germans, despite any number of demonstrative acts of reconciliation, remain nervous with the gory heritage. Meanwhile, the world has by and large absorbed the knowledge of Auschwitz and everything the place implies without appreciable effect, for all that one might expect that politics and human affairs would forever after be carried on in the somber and cautionary shadow of those memories. One seems in a way to contribute to this sinister return to normalcy when one raises some doubts about the use Jewish interpreters have made of a phenomenon in some ways so symptomatic of the Jewish fate as Heinrich Heine and his reputation. Nevertheless, it seems to me desirable to approach the problem, not only because it is an instructive segment of German-Jewish intellectual history, but also because Heine is rightly and understandably of importance to the Jews and ought therefore to be regarded with as clear an eye as possible. It is curious that the German-speaking Jews, with all their achievements in the arts and sciences, in politics and other practical affairs, with all the intellectual and cultural momentum that burst forth with the emancipation, did not produce a literary figure of international standing in the three-quarters of a century between Heine and the generation of Kafka and Hermann Broch. I would not care to venture an opinion as to why this is so; the answer probably lies in a combination of a variety of sociological factors, the direction German literature took after the 1840s, and accident—Heines and Kafkas do not turn up in every decade. It is therefore inevitable and reasonable that Jews should care about Heine a great deal. It is rather less reasonable to attempt to isolate him from the context of German literature and define him as a Jewish writer.

This brings us to the second difficulty, which is apparent particularly to an American accustomed, at least in theory, to a pluralistic society. As one surveys contemporary American literature, the Jewish names come to mind without effort: Roth, Malamud, Mailer, Bellow, Ginsberg, Shapiro, Friedman, Heller, and so on. The Jewishness of these men is, in varying degrees, an important element of their perspective and their art, but no rational person, I should think, would question that they are American writers. Who but an American could have written the novels of Saul Bellow or the poetry of Allen Ginsberg? Similarly, one is inclined to think, who but a German could have written *Buch der Lieder,* or *Die Romantische Schule,* or *Deutschland. Ein Wintermärchen,* or *Lutezia*? But the European mind, preoccupied with the chimera of national identity, has often in the past tended to see Heine differently. Golo Mann, in a recent controversial address to a Jewish congress, tried to assert that the German Jews were Germans in the same sense that American Jews are Americans.[1] He gives some evidence for this, but the situations are not really comparable in this way, for the formulation leaves out of consideration the ferocious pressures exerted by large sections of the Gentile majority. The fortunes of Heine's reputation tended to correspond to the development of nationalist ideology in Germany even more closely than to the growth of the related phenomenon of anti-Semitism.[2]

I do not wish to go into this matter at any length, for it is not really accessible to the literary critic. The history of Heine's reputation in Germany is, in many of its aspects, a wretched affair, appropriately symbolized by the farce that for years surrounded the non-issue of the various Heine monuments. When one looks into the matter, one discovers without difficulty that the rejection of Heine is grounded in the assumption that German and Jew are totally incommensurable and that in the arts there can be no community between them because the Jew is uncreative and unpoetic by nature and immune to the mystique of the cohesive nation. Thus Wagner, in a very left-handed compliment:

> Zur Zeit, da Goethe und Schiller bei uns dichteten, wissen wir allerdings von keinem dichtenden Juden: zu der Zeit aber, wo das Dichten bei uns zur Lüge wurde, unserem gänzlich unpoetischen Lebenselement alles Mögliche, nur kein wahrer Dichter entsprießen wollte, da war es das Amt eines sehr begabten dichterischen Juden, diese Lüge, diese bodenlose Nüchternheit und jesuitische Heuchelei unsrer immer noch poetisch sich gebaren wollenden Dichterei mit hinreißendem Spotte aufzudecken.[3]

By the 1890s, the distinctly anti-Semitic element becomes raucously audible, as in the sarcasm of a commentator writing under the pseudonym of J. Staarstecher: "Heine wurde als Sohn jüdischer Eltern zu einer Zeit geboren, wo die Juden nicht, wie heute, Herren der Welt, sondern eine unterdrückte Rasse waren." * The

* J. Staarstecher [pseud.], *Heinrich Heine der Antisemit und Nihilist. Bausteine zum Heine Denkmal aus Heine's sämmtlichen Werken* (Cologne, 1893), p. 5. In the *Heine Bibliographie* of Gottfried Wilhelm and Eberhard Galley, 2 (Weimar, 1960), 25, this writer is identified as Heinrich Keiter, who two years before had written a book critical of Heine from a Roman Catholic standpoint, but much more moderate in tone: *Heinrich Heine. Sein Leben, sein Charakter, seine Werke* (Cologne,

furious and obsessive attacks on Heine by the literary historian Adolf Bartels became practically legendary.* In this regard, as in others, it should be remembered that anti-Semitism was a general European phenomenon and certainly not a German specialty. In 1921 a breathtakingly stupid book appeared in France in which it is argued that the Russian Revolution is an example of what happens if Jews are permitted rights of citizenship,[4] and the author observes that Heine demonstrated his unfitness to be either a German or a Frenchman by being in favor of human rights against the claims of the collective.[5] Here the Fascist link between anti-Semitism and nationalist totalitarianism has been forged. By the Nazi era this unholy combination of ideas was firmly ensconced in the upper reaches of the intellectual world. In 1937 Hermann Pongs, who still enjoys a reputation as a literary scholar in some quarters in Germany today, published a comparison of *Die schlesischen Weber* with a genuine weavers' song used by Gerhart Hauptmann in his drama *Die Weber,* in the course of which, among other fascinating conclusions, Pongs observes that Heine uses the first person plural in this poem, while the folk song does not; this shows that Heine was an outsider with no possible connection to the event, whereas the folk song evinces an "unbewußte Gruppenexistenz." [6] The Nazis themselves had no need of such subtleties. Perhaps the fairest statement of the case appeared in 1935 in *Das Schwarze Korps,* where the German Academy in Munich is excoriated for proposing to publish a volume of Heine in a series of German poets; the article is written with that combination of insouciant terrorism and boyish enthusiasm (or perhaps, as Meno Spann has suggested, taking off from Heine's characterization of Vater Jahn, "idealistic loutish-

1891). If this identification is correct, as it appears to be, it would indicate, as Dr. Galley suggested to me, that even in 1893 a Catholic apologist did not want to be widely known as a raving anti-Semite.

* Bartels' interminable writings on this subject are too numerous to list here. They are catalogued in Wilhelm and Galley, *Heine Bibliographie, 2,* 1, 7, 25, 29, 30, 31, 50, 99, 102, 129, 135, 199, 200, 201, 224, 227, 240. Yet even in this extreme case, racism is not entirely the fundamental motivation. Werner Ilberg, in *Unser Heine* (Berlin, 1952), p. 101, has pointed out that Bartels spoke well of the Jewish-born writer Berthold Auerbach because he wrote *Dorf-* and *Heimatsnovellen* in a tone pleasing to the reactionary temperament. Even here nationalism is, in a sense, at least, the basic issue.

ness"[7]) so characteristic of the *SS* in its earlier phases. It asserts with refreshing bluntness that Heine was indeed a good writer, but: *"Entscheidend ist ausschließlich, daß dieser Mann Jude war und daher nicht in den Raum unserer deutschen Literatur gehört."* * All this is well known and the examples could be multiplied ad infinitum; my purpose in calling attention to some of them is to give a frame of reference for certain Jewish interpretations of Heine. For the sad truth is that the German Jews often found themselves forced, in one way or another, to accept the disastrous logic of these nationalist and racist distinctions.

I have taken Max Brod as my central example, not out of disrespect, but for the opposite reason. Apart from his own considerable achievements, he will always be remembered as the friend and encourager of Kafka and the executor who preserved Kafka's unpublished works for posterity. His biography of Heine, first published in 1934,[8] although by no means a scholarly study, has many valuable insights and sensitive observations, and it is besides a pleasurable book to read because of its humaneness. But when Brod gets on the subject of Heine's Jewishness, some quite strange things begin to happen. From his strictly Zionist point of view, Brod claims that Heine's achievements are "of marginal importance" for German art and culture[9] and that we are "here dealing with a Jewish spirit working in an alien material."[10] Thus far the point is perhaps defensible, in a more moderate version, insofar as Heine's Jewishness did make him something of an outsider in his society and affected his perspective. But Brod forces the point to extremes; he goes on to say: "As yet little or no attempt has been made to place Heine's work in the Jewish literary line to which it organically belongs,"[11] whereby, incidentally, he is pursuing a task proposed by Oskar Walzel, who argued for a "scientific" study of the "tribal" element in Heine by examining Jewish literature before him.[12] Who are the repre-

* M. B., "Was denkt die deutsche Akademie von Heinrich Heine," *Das Schwarze Korps* (Oct. 31, 1935), p. 2. Emphasis in the original. The *Deutsche Akademie* took the hint and blacked out Heine's name in the prospectus; see Jonas Fränkel, *Heinrich Heine. Ein Vortrag* (Biel, 1960). As late as 1936 there were still complaints that there was too much mention of Heine in schoolbooks on literature. See Josef Wulf, *Literatur und Dichtung im Dritten Reich. Eine Dokumentation* (Gütersloh, 1963), p. 409.

sentatives of this Jewish literature in Brod's account? They include a thirteenth-century Provençal satirist, a Roman contemporary of Dante, an obscure eighteenth-century epigrammist named Ephraim Kuh whom Heine never mentions, and, finally, a medieval Jewish poet in Germany, Süsskind von Trimberg, twelve of whose religious *Sprüche* turn up in the Manesse Manuscript.[13] One wonders: what possesses an intelligent man of wide literary experience to make such outlandish comparisons? How can one conceivably bend Heine to suit them? We shall see, however, that Brod is part of a long tradition of adapting Heine to whatever Jewish position happens to be held by the commentator in question.

This was not noticeably true, it might be mentioned, during Heine's lifetime. In 1834, to be sure, Heine was included in a collection of sketches of outstanding Jewish personalities, an event that seems to have annoyed him enormously;[14] one observer believed that it was done out of malice.[15] But Heine certainly was sharply attacked by prominent members of the Jewish community such as the tireless champion of emancipation in Hamburg, Gabriel Riesser.* Sol Liptzin, from his own moderate Zionist standpoint, observes that Riesser did not regard the Jews as a people but as a religious fellowship;[16] his objection to Heine was to his apostasy and his apparently atheistic views. This tradition has never died out completely; in Tel Aviv some years ago a street could not be named after Heine because of a city ordinance forbidding the naming of streets after renegades.[17] How wise such a policy may be is certainly a question. Anti-Semitic detractors of Heine have occasionally found it appropriate to fall back on Riesser's attack to show that even from a Jewish point of view Heine was despicable.[18] During the phase of the *Denkmalstreit* that took place in Mainz, it was noted with glee that Orthodox and Reform Jews, including the rabbi of the city, had signed the protest against the monument.[19] Such an attitude

* See Georg J. Plotke, *Heinrich Heine als Dichter des Judentums* (Dresden, 1913), pp. 65–67. Riesser apparently wanted to challenge Heine to a duel during the Salomon Strauss affair in 1841. See to Jakob Venedey, Aug. 19, 1841; to Alexandre Weill, same date; to Campe, Aug. 23; to Venedey, Aug. 24; to Weill, Aug. 26; to Campe, Sept. 1; Hirth, 2, 400–08.

is perhaps understandable for tactical as well as religious reasons, but in retrospect it is not without its disturbing aspect.

On the boundary between Jewish repudiation and Jewish appropriation of Heine stands a book by his cousin Hermann Schiff, in the form of letters to Adolf Strodtmann.[20] In it he claims that Heine was a Reform Jew in every respect.[21] Schiff was an author of rather vulgar humoresques on Jewish life, the most important of which was *Schief-Levinche und Mariandel seine Kalle* (1848), which Heine plugged (unenthusiastically) in his letters as a favor to Schiff.[22] Schiff's letters on Heine, like his novel, are so confused and weirdly expressed that his fundamental sanity is open to serious question, and his opinion on Heine as a Reform Jew is not worth a great deal. Schiff does have a good many things to say about Heine's religious upbringing. He claims that Heine never learned Hebrew or his prayers, did not make his bar mitzvah, never went into the synagogue, and never wore the *arba kanfos,* the prescribed fringed garment.[23] Like almost everything about Heine's boyhood, these matters remain a little unclear. Israel Tabak's valuable study, *Judaic Lore in Heine* (1948), makes it evident that Heine cannot have been anywhere near as estranged from his religious tradition as Schiff makes out. But Rabbi Tabak's book must be regarded with caution, for he, in turn, forces the issue more than it will bear. The several hundred allusions to the Bible that Tabak so assiduously collected do not prove his point, for it has always been fundamental that German writers are *bibelfest,* and Heine, after all, responds exclusively to that inexhaustible wellspring of the German language, Martin Luther's translation. In addition, Tabak adduces parallel passages from the Talmud in unconvincing numbers.[24] I find it a little difficult to believe in so thorough an immersion in Jewish tradition on the part of a man who did not know the calendar date of Passover;[25] who nearly put the anniversary of the fall of the Temple on the tenth day of Ab when the Hebrew name of the fast, *Tisha b'Av,* means literally "the ninth of Ab";[26] and who apparently thought that a medieval rabbi could be acquainted with the flavor of turtle.[27] In any case, the Jewish claims on Heine in the past generally have not rested upon the closeness to the tradition that Rabbi Tabak argues for him, but upon his distinct Jewish nationality.

Two years after Schiff's book, Gustav Karpeles took exactly the opposite view; he argued that Heine would have remained a loyal Jew if it had *not* been for the Reform, which, as Karpeles rightly realized, Heine regarded with scorn.[28] Israel, Karpeles claims, has a right to claim Heine as its poet.[29] To see how baldly Karpeles reads into Heine views that are determined by the atmosphere of his own time, one need only look farther on in the pamphlet to find the following astonishing passage: "Die Zeit der Zerrissenheit und Zerfahrenheit ist in Deutschland vorüber. Mächtig und gigantisch soll der Riesendom deutscher Einheit ein lautes Zeugniß der Zukunft geben: es giebt keinen Weltschmerz mehr!" [30] How strange is this Imperialist rodomontade from the pen of one of Heine's most active Jewish admirers! But we shall eventually see more of this problem of Jewish identification with nationalist Germany as it touches upon the assessment of Heine.*

Around the turn of the century, acceptance of the definition of Heine as a non-German poet proceeded apace. In a pamphlet friendly to Heine written in 1896, we find the following conclusion: "Und so muß man wohl oder übel dem Xanthippus beipflichten, wenn er, obgleich im vorwurfsvollen Tone, behauptet: 'Heine ist eben durch und durch Jude, kein echter Deutscher.' "[31] One stares at this calm acceptance. "Xanthippus" was the pen name of a violent anti-Semite named Franz Sandvoss, who in 1888 wrote a vicious little book entitled *Was dünket euch um Heine? Ein Bekenntnis.* One would think that to associate one's self in any way whatever with such views would be felt to be not

* Karpeles reflects a fairly common point of view in Imperial Germany. Georg Mücke begins his study, *Heinrich Heines Beziehungen zum deutschen Mittelalter* (Berlin, 1908), p. 1, by claiming that Heine was incapable of sensing the "still forces" under the reactionary surface that were leading to the glories of 1870. Today, I think, we will prefer to take Heine. Goeo Mann has given a number of examples of extreme German nationalism among Jews, from Ernst Lissauer's *Haßgesänge gegen England,* distributed by the High Command to feed the feverishness of World War I, to Bruno Frank's love of Prussia ("Zur Geschichte der deutschen Juden," *Neue Rundschau,* 77 [1966], pp. 564–66). These examples may not prove Mann's thesis altogether, but they do demonstrate the sanguinary futility of rabid nationalism.

only critically indefensible but morally offensive. But the acceptance of Heine as a Jewish poet was becoming a commonplace; perfectly irrelevant comparisons, such as between *Leise zieht durch mein Gemüt* and the Song of Songs, are offered as self-evident.[32]

Shortly before the first World War, two substantial efforts were made to think more seriously about these matters. The first was a book by Max Bienenstock, *Das jüdische Element in Heines Werken. Ein kritisch-ästhetischer Beitrag zur Heine-Frage* (1910). We are here entering the age of *Geistesgeschichte*: Bienenstock begins by asserting that poetic talent is a result of the poet's times, and proceeds to argue that everything in Heine is a superstructure built upon a Jewish foundation.[33] Bienenstock is certainly not wrong in seeing Heine as a typical figure of a period of transition,[34] and there is some sense to his claim that Heine's case was paradigmatic for the process of Jewish emancipation.[35] But he cannot distinguish between literature and autobiography, and he reads Jewish elements into Heine's writing in an undisciplined way. He argues that *Lyrisches Intermezzo* is permeated with Jewish elements, particularly from the Song of Songs,[36] and interprets the famous *Ein Fichtenbaum steht einsam* as an expression of Jewish homesickness for the warm climate of the Holy Land.* He claims that Heine's experiment with Catholic mysticism, *Die Wahlfahrt nach Kevlaar,* is "eben ein Ausfluss seines Judentums,"[37] and that Heine wrote poems about the sea because the unruly element corresponded to his inner Jewish disquiet.[38] Tabak is right to dismiss these arguments as forced and circuitous.[39]

The second full-length study, Georg J. Plotke's *Heinrich Heine als Dichter des Judentums* (1913), is not altogether an improvement, although in matters of detail Plotke occasionally displays more critical sensitivity than Bienenstock, particularly in his treatment of *Der Rabbi von Bacherach*.[40] But, as in the case of Brod,

* M. Bienenstock, *Das jüdische Element in Heines Werken. Ein kritisch-ästhetischer Beitrag zur Heine-Frage* (Leipzig, 1910), p. 114. This interpretation is not original with Bienenstock; he refers to similar arguments in Felix Melchior, *Heinrich Heines Verhältnis zu Lord Byron* (Berlin, 1903), p. 88; and Alexander Pache, *Naturgefühl und Natursymbolik bei Heinrich Heine* (Leipzig, 1904), p. 160. This support does not make the interpretation any more convincing.

Plotke's arguments are frequently muddled by Zionist presuppositions. His treatment of the "Verein für Kultur und Wissenschaft der Juden," to which Heine attached himself in Berlin, as a proto-Zionist organization is defensible,[41] but Plotke is not convincing when he argues that in this organization Heine soon came *"zu jüdisch-nationalem Bewußtsein."* * Plotke, too, interprets *Ein Fichtenbaum steht einsam* as "die ursprünglichste zionistische Heimwehstimmung seiner Seele." [42] He argues also that Heine became a Reform Jew, but unlike Schiff, he does not see this as a lifelong phenomenon, but something that appeared in his last will and testament of 1848.[43] Tabak, although he runs roughshod over the chronology, is right to reject this view;[44] it obliges one to expand the concept of Reform Judaism to the vague theism of Heine's last years. These judgments, however, are not as troubling in retrospect as others in Plotke's book that come dangerously close to accepting racist distinctions. Of Heine's treatment of nature he says, "Für Heine spricht die bloße Natur nicht; er muß sie beleben mit Visionen und Spukerscheinungen, die sein erregter *Intellekt* hineinhetzt, mit Symbolen, die sich stets und ausschließlich auf seinen Zustand beziehen. Er ist und bleibt in seiner Lyrik echter jüdischer Spiritualist." [45] Now it is true that Heine was a creature of the city and had little direct and genuine response to nature. But to connect this characteristic to a particularly Jewish cast of mind is to run parallel to anti-Semitic prejudices. One cannot argue that Heine is influenced by Biblical poetry, which is full of nature imagery of the most precise and poignant kind, and then assert that his own estrangement from nature is a Jewish trait; this is a serious confusion of racial heritage with sociological circumstances.† Plotke also

* Plotke, *Heine als Dichter des Judentums,* p. 24; emphasis in the original. On this subject Louis Untermeyer, in *Heinrich Heine. Paradox and Poet. The Life* (New York, 1937), p. 93, showed finer judgment: "It was wholeness that Heine wanted at twenty-five. He could bear the 'dark inheritance,' but not maladjustment; it was the sense of division which gripped him with secret terror."

† Heinz Politzer in "Heinrich Heine," *Neue Rundschau, 59* (1948), 16–17, goes even farther by asserting that the limitations on imagery are characteristic of Jews because they lacked the childlike vision that comes with native mastery of language. That Heine did not master German is certainly an unexpected bit of news. One might, with more justice, detect tones in Politzer's language at this point that are dangerously close to the German reactionary tradition.

touches on the old critical saw that the quality of Heine's imagery is "oriental." [46] To assert this is simply to ignore fashions in poetry in Heine's time; are we to claim Jewish elements in the orientalizing poetry of Goethe, Platen, Rückert, or Freiligrath? This is another example of the almost unconscious acceptance of a racist argument. Toward the end of his book, Plotke argues that Heine was endangered by a lack of tradition.* Plotke has confused sociological considerations with the poetic inheritance. Heine was, if anything, overburdened by tradition; he was so hexed by the Romantic mode that he could not achieve, except in hints and undertones, a breakthrough to a new sound in poetry. Furthermore, as has been pointed out in a recent dissertation, he certainly did have an intellectual tradition: that of the Enlightenment.[47]

Plotke's book did not please all segments of the Jewish community. A sharp review reproached him that the attribution of Zionist concepts to Heine is frivolous, that the poet's posture was that of an assimilationist, his "theism" only the expression of a longing that grew out of his sufferings, and that Plotke had endeavored unreasonably to make of Heine a partisan champion.[48] These points are not badly taken, but the editorship of the journal in which the review appeared, the organ of the *Centralverein deutscher Staatsbürger jüdischen Glaubens,* dissociated itself in principle from the reviewer's remarks. This journal and its successor, the *C. V.-Zeitung,* are publications that arouse in today's observer a set of most uncomfortable feelings. It is obvious beyond any doubt that those associated with this effort to present the Jews as loyal citizens of Germany and to stress the Jewish contribution to German life and culture were men of intelligence and sincerity. The movement is an urgent response to heavy nationalist and racist pressures; in 1880, a quarter of a million Germans signed a petition urging the government to restrict the civil rights of Jews.[49] But in the light of subsequent events, the under-

* Plotke, *Heine als Dichter des Judentums,* pp. 99–100. Theodor W. Adorno has secularized this argument in his neo-Marxist treatment of Heine, "Die Wunde Heine," *Noten zur Literatur, I* (Frankfurt am Main, 1958), p. 148–49. The argument has its counterparts in the East. See Martin Greiner, *Zwischen Biedermeier und Bourgeoisie. Ein Kapitel deutscher Literatur geschichte imzeichen Heinrich Heines* (Leipzig, 1954), p. 123.

taking of the *Centralverein* appears quixotic, to some extent humiliating and self-lacerating, and possibly almost disgraceful. Gerschom Scholem, in a harsh review of this aspect of German-Jewish history before a Jewish congress in Brussels in 1966, has nothing but scorn for the Jewish effort to appear as German nationalists. "Die Liebesaffäre der Juden mit den Deutschen," writes Scholem, "blieb, aufs Große gesehen, einseitig, unerwidert";[50] and he touches on a sore point when he asserts: "Das unendliche Verlangen, nach Hause zu kommen, verwandelte sich bald in die ekstatische Illusion, zu Hause zu sein." [51] Scholem's presentation is colored by dogmatic Zionism under the surface, but he does point up the futility of the whole endeavor when he observes that German liberals expected not that the Jews should integrate themselves into the nation as Jews, but that in their process of assimilation they should totally abandon their religious and communal identity.[52] Thus Jews and even Germans of good will were working at irreconcilable cross-purposes, for the Continental mystique of nationhood apparently left an American or even English solution out of the question.

A look at the special issue of the *C. V.-Zeitung* of August 5, 1927, will tend, I fear, to support the justice of Scholem's critique. This issue is devoted to setting forth the Jewish contribution to German culture. In, unfortunately, perfectly atrocious German, the introduction speaks of "das Hohelied unerschütterlicher Heimats-, Kulturzugehörigkeit der deutschen Juden, die in deutsche Kultur hineingeboren sind und, unbeschadet ihrer Treue zu Glauben und Abstammung, Höchstes und Letztes für diese Kultur einsetzen und verarbeiten, nicht, weil 'das Gesetz es befahl,'—weil Herz und Gefühl es so heischen." [53] None other than Süsskind von Trimberg turns up in the columns of this issue,[54] and one begins to understand a little of the background of Max Brod's strange associations. But, unlike Brod, these German-Jewish nationalists have little use for Heine. Robert Neumann, a clever essayist and parodist who has since grown into something of a Malcolm Muggeridge of German letters, launches an attack on Heine that shows great similarities to the earlier attitude of Karl Kraus.[55] "Für den reifen und vernünftigen Leser," he writes, "sei er Jud oder Christ, sind heute neuneinhalb Zehntel jenes berühmten 'Buch der Lieder' von einer schlechtweg nicht mehr erträglichen Abgeschmacktheit"; Heine is a "Lyriker aus dem Handgelenk"; his poems are "Gefühls-Ersatz" and "höchst spießbürgerliche Herz-Schmerz-Poesie." [56] Perhaps such attitudes are understandable in the literary atmosphere of the time.* But they are not the most disturbing aspect of Neumann's article. What bothers him is that Heine is an embarrassment to the Jewish effort to identify with Germany: "Denn die Tadler wie die Verteidiger *reden vom Dichter—und meinen den Juden.*" [57] So it is inconvenient of "unseren wohlmeinenden jüdischen Freunden" [58] to praise Heine. That the judgment on Heine should be separated from generalized attitudes toward Jewishness is certainly desirable, but that he should be thrown overboard to lighten the load of German-Jewish nationalism is unbearable. Heine's reputation, as usual, is here caught in the mill of problems and conflicts that have nearly nothing to do with him.†

The proof of this is that there is absolutely nothing stable about the manner in which the reputation is manipulated. What, for example, is a Jew outside of Germany to do after the first World War, when Allied hysteria had established that German was the language of the Hun? He must move to the opposite pole of the *C. V.-Zeitung* and separate Heine from his German context in a positive sense. An article of 1925 in the *Contemporary Review* undertakes this solution with ignorant bluster. The bad name of the German language makes it impossible to regard Heine as a German poet; with a hilarious non sequitur, the author goes on to remark that the medieval German Minnesinger were "coarse" compared to the French and Provençal troubadours. No, Heine cannot have been a German poet; he was a secret, true Jew—like Disraeli.[59]

* What Neumann was worth as a critic of Heine he demonstrated two years later in Tucholsky's and Ossietzky's admirable *Weltbühne, 25* (1929), 602, where he wrote: "Heines Lyrik ist in extremem Maße undicht. Ökonomie des Wortes ist ihr fremd." The judgment is impossible when expressed in so sweeping a way.

† One will note here that the Jewish German nationalists passed up an opportunity to exploit Heine's curious equation of the spirit of Judaism with that of Germany in *Shakspeares Mädchen und Frauen* in E, *5*, 455–56; cf. the variant to the essay on Ludwig Markus printed by Walter Wadepuhl, *Heine-Studien* (Weimar, 1956), p. 149, and also E, *6*, 62 and E, *7*, 406. Perhaps they thought the public would not take a very sympathetic view of it.

Such arguments have only curiosity value on their own merits, but they are symptomatic of attitudes that sometimes lurk beneath the surface of more substantial treatments of Heine. An example is Louis Untermeyer's 1937 biography, a book that is well worth studying, particularly because the author, himself a poet of some reputation and a remarkably successful translator of Heine, is often able to describe the subtle characteristics of his poetry in a quite convincing way. On the whole, the claims Untermeyer makes about Heine's Jewishness are restrained and usually discussable. He does, however, revive Plotke's thesis about Heine's "oriental" imagery and in the process proceeds to a rather serious misrepresentation of the *Hebräische Melodien*: "Background, diction, and emotion are characteristically Jewish in the voluptuous use and celebration of the senses, in the hot colors and sharp flavors. . . . No Hebrew poet has ever been more unreasonably confident, more hand-in-hand with God." [60] By way of refutation of this I recommend a careful reading of the *Hebräische Melodien* followed by a look into the standard Jewish prayer book. Untermeyer also presents an example of the way in which admirers of Heine perennially shift the stress of interpretation to conform with prevailing intellectual values. Because of his social concerns, Heine was a "Jewish Jew"—in Thorstein Veblen's excellent phrase, "a disturber of the intellectual peace" —like Isaiah, he bent his efforts to balance nationalism and universalism.[61] Such assertions are not so much wrong as undemonstrable; they draw attention away from the complicated and tumultuous character of Heine's social and political utterances. Untermeyer ends his biography with a not uninteresting poem representing Heine in the last hour of his life, full of cleverly introduced echoes of Heine's own words. At the moment of death, Untermeyer's Heine begins to recite, as tradition requires of the dying, the most fundamental prayer of Judaism, *Sh'ma Yisroel*.[62] The rhetorical trick is effective but unfair; even as a poetic truth, as a symbol of an underlying Jewish allegiance in Heine, it will not stand; it is false to the state of Heine's mind as he approached death.

That the Jewish attitude toward Heine would deepen in intensity after 1945 was predictable for obvious and heartbreaking reasons. One of those who contributed to the reassessment was the venerable Fritz Strich, who delivered a most interesting lecture on Goethe and Heine before a Jewish audience in 1947. For Strich the tragic aspect of Heine was that he was a Jewish poet "dessen Gestalt von europäischem Geist geformt war." [63] I confess that I do not understand this argument, unless it is supposed to imply that the essences of Jew and European are dialectical poles. If this is what Strich means, then I do not believe him. I suspect a failure to make a clear distinction between external and internal determinants. Whatever alienates Heine in any sense from his European context is determined by the situation of a Jew in society in his particular moment of time. Even to suggest that there might be some kind of congenital inevitability in the matter is both misleading and dangerous. Some such presupposition seems to generate Strich's argument that Heine's attitude toward Goethe is not an expression of a conflict between two ages, "sondern auch eine Auflehnung jüdischen Geistes gegen etwas, das ihm von Natur und Tradition nicht gemäß ist." * This assertion is illogical in view of the substantial agreement on the matter of Goethe, for example, between Heine and a non-Jewish Young German like Ludolf Wienbarg. To raise the issue of the priestly and prophetic tradition in this context and to mention that prophetic literature in the Bible is not literature for its own sake[64] leads away from the point; such arguments operate with categories too large and diffuse to help in an understanding of Heine's particularity.

Although Strich seems to me to share some of the failings of Jewish interpretation of Heine, his contribution to the discussion is nevertheless important and highly intelligent. Not all Jewish commentators were able to maintain as much clarity of mind on the subject of Heine after the catastrophe. This is understandable,

* Fritz Strich, "Goethe und Heine. Ein der Jüdischen Vereinigung Zürich 1947 gehaltener Vortrag zur Feier von Heines 150. Gebrutstag," *Der Dichter und die Zeit* (Bern, 1947), pp. 207–08. Also involved in this rather complex argument is Strich's turn away from Romanticism toward an allegiance to Classical antiquity as a result of experiences of the 1930s and the 1940s, a shift he describes in the preface to the republication of his famous *Deutsche Klassik und Romantik oder Vollendung und Unendlichkeit* (5th ed. Bern and Munich, 1962), pp. 9–17.

but it is also depressing. In 1948, Hannah Arendt published an essay in which she argued that Heine was the first Jew "für den Freiheit mehr bedeutete als die 'Befreiung aus dem Haus der Knechtschaft,'" and concludes that this is why Heine's poems are so free from bitterness.[65] The first judgment makes one blink when one recalls Ludwig Börne, and the second is so outlandish that it defies understanding. Miss Arendt goes on to say that Heine was the first Jew to be Jewish and German at the same time,[66] which disposes, among others, of Moses Mendelssohn, and she submits that the Jewish allusions make his art "volkstümlich," [67] a remark that may have Adolf Bartels spinning in his grave but otherwise begs several questions. The whole performance is unworthy of Miss Arendt's intellectual stature and is explicable only on the assumption that the horror of the Jewish catastrophe has here interdicted the course of common sense. In 1944 Miss Arendt had already claimed that Heine is a poet of the Jewish people with an affinity for the proletariat,[68] an argument that was sharply criticized by Hugo Bieber.[69]

Two studies by Felix Stössinger, one on Heine's mythopoeic treatment of his gods and the other the introduction to his collection of Heine texts, have attracted a good deal of attention among Heine specialists. Stössinger's rhapsodic rhetoric is indeed impressive, and he has a number of interesting observations to make, for example, the important point that Heine was the first partisan of Jewish self-defense.[70] With regard to the often debated problem of the relative importance of Heine's Jewishness and his Rhenish background, Stössinger tries to strike a balance: "Er ist nicht derselbe Rheinländer wie die Deutschen, aber auch nicht derselbe Jude, wie es die nichtrheinischen Juden sind." [71] But Stössinger's florid writing often misdirects the reader's attention away from the doubtfulness of some of his judgments. Sometimes one detects traces of a theory of congenital determination, as in this remark: "Als Jude gehört Heine zu der älteren Schicht der Baal und Astarte, und er hat den Sieg des Gesetzes über das Reich der Instinkte dem Vatergott nie ganz vergeben" [72]—Heine as a pre-Mosaic Canaanite pagan is the most radical representation of the "oriental" yet offered. Stössinger also has an inflated but rather simplistic view of Heine's "return":

> Heine brauchte zu seinem Judentume nicht zurückzukehren, weil er es nie verlassen hatte. Aber in der Matratzengruft kehrte er nicht zu dem zurück, was er war, sondern dort hinauf, wo er nicht gewesen war: zum Wesen. Er wurde nicht wieder Jude, wie man einen abgelegten Paß zurücknimmt, sondern wurde jesajanisch Jude, und das heißt Knecht Gottes, Hiob.[73]

He argues that Heine's sufferings were not the reason for his "return," but a sign of divine election.[74] Stössinger is fascinated by what he interprets as Heine's process of internalizing myth and rather strangely compares him with James Joyce in this regard;[75] yet he himself mythologizes Heine by putting him in a variety of mythical contexts, some of which are Jewish and all of which are vaguely defined. The elusive poet is hard enough to grasp without setting him at an even greater distance from our understanding.

Stössinger also has his share in the process of interpreting Heine according to prevailing intellectual values. He argues that socially conscious ballad and lyric poetry begins with Heine, although he modifies this uncertain statement with the qualifier "sozusagen,"[76] and, in harmony with the internationalism of contemporary European thought, he observes: "durch Heine wurde Frankophilie seit 1918 ein untrügliches Signum der Europafähigkeit und Franzosenhaß zum Pränazismus."[77] This is a strong statement, though probably not unjust, and since it deals with Heine's reputation rather than with Heine himself, it does not run the usual risks of oversimplification.* But other commentators show how elastic the view of Heine continues to be. In the anniversary year of 1956, in an article that tried to make Heine conform to prevailing European ideals while expressing contempt for his lyric poetry, it was argued that Heine must be seen as a supranational Jewish writer—an excellent example of the way fashion dictates judgment in the study of Heine.[78] This author offers also the interesting argument that to

* Cf. Alfred Schellenberg, *Heinrich Heines französische Prosawerke* (Berlin, 1921), p. 80, where, out of the spirit of that time, it is argued that reconciliation between France and Germany is inherently impossible, and that Heine's life was lived in vain.

regard Heine as a German writer severely detracts from the quantity of Jewish intellectual achievement.[79] In the same year, we get an article from a Zionist point of view claiming Heine as a Jewish nationalist.[80] Apparently only a scholar who is genuinely and unchallengeably expert on Heine can resist the need to make this kind of use of him; Jonas Fränkel, also in the anniversary year, writing on Heine as a Jew in a Jewish newspaper in Switzerland, stressed carefully that Heine is a German poet,[81] and there are few men in the world who know Heine's poetry as well as he.

The question of the role Heine's Jewishness plays in his writing and personality is a difficult and subtle one; the issue as to whether he is a Jewish writer to the exclusion of being a German writer does not seem to me subtle at all. There have been, of course, modern Jewish writers, although they are all much younger than Heine: outstanding ones in Yiddish like Mendele Mocher Sforim, Sholom Aleichem, and I. L. Peretz, in modern Hebrew like Achad Ha-am and Bialik. That they may have been Russian, Polish, or whatever by citizenship is of less importance (of course they are *European* writers, but that is another matter). The language in which they write is a major consideration here, but not necessarily the exclusive criterion. André Schwarz-Bart's inimitable and almost incredible novel of 1959, *Le dernier des Justes,* probably demands to be thought of as a Jewish book rather than as a French novel. The primary distinction is a matter of the internal perspective of the writing from within or without the Jewish community—whether it is suffused with Jewish concerns or relativizes them from without. Heine's poetic persona is located in a wide Western tradition, including, of course, the Bible and some aspects of Jewish tradition, but also Classical antiquity, popular legend, and, above all, the German literary tradition of the two or three generations preceding him, which almost exclusively supplies the literary impulses of his poetic consciousness. Moreover, there are in his cast of mind German elements so fundamental that he never subjects them to analysis: among them his fascination with Luther and his belief in the importance of philosophical ideas, his tendency, insofar as he was a thinker, to subsume the elements of reality under comprehensive and dichotomous abstractions, his imperturbable convictions about the shallowness and inartistic superficiality of the French, some quite characteristically German, almost mystical notions about the German language,[82] and his continuing sense of discomfort and foreignness in France, along with many other details. These aspects are not relativized by elements that he may have inherited from the Jewish and possibly to some extent Yiddish milieu of his youth: certain cadences in his language, a propensity toward hyperbolic simile, and his ironic wit;* these do not make of Heine a poet writing in a medium alien to him.

A brief comparison with Sholom Aleichem, who is sometimes inaccurately thought of as the Yiddish Heine, will illustrate this. Like Heine, Sholom Aleichem was full of wit and irony and possessed an unerring sense for the incongruous and the absurd that generate satire; like Heine much of the time, he was gifted with an extraordinary suppleness of language within a very restricted diction. But the differences are more telling. In Sholom Aleichem's stories, the Gentile world is a shadowy, vaguely inimical setting inside of which Jewish life is carried on as independently as the world outside will allow; in Heine, except briefly in *Der Rabbi von Bacherach,* one gets no sense, either in a personal or communal way, of a Jewish existence incapsulated from the age in which Heine himself lived, and consequently to draft him as a Jewish nationalist in any sense totally obscures his role. Moreover, his wit and satire are aggressive and damaging—seldom more so than when turned on the Jews themselves—demanding change of behavior and situations that fill him with intolerant scorn and anger; Heine was a radical of, to be sure, a most singular and individual kind. Sholom Aleichem was not a radical; he tended rather to be an elegist, with a subdued but very evident sense that the world and ethos he described in his stories was crumbling. His irony is more even-handed and tolerant, mutatis mutandis more like Thomas Mann's than Heine's. His satire and his humor, unlike Heine's, are filled with pity for the shabby wretchedness and implacable frustrations of the hope-

* See Erich Eckertz, *Heine und sein Witz* (Berlin, 1908), esp. p. 51; a careful criticism of the tendency to regard Heine's irony as a Jewish trait is given by Helmut Ernst Ruhrig, "Heinrich Heine. Beiträge zur Bestimmung seines ironischen Humors" (diss. Freiburg im Breisgau, 1953), pp. 3–11.

lessly impoverished Jews he describes. It embraces the Jewish community about which and for which he wrote. Heine is nowhere close to being a Jewish writer in this sense.*

Sol Liptzin quotes a letter by Arthur Schnitzler in which it is said that as long as poets continue to write in German they must call themselves German poets.[83] It is not a matter of irrelevant terminology, for if Heine is important, then it is important to try to understand him in intrinsic terms. To make willful use of Heine for all sorts of ulterior purposes is to squander a treasure one does not possess in the first place because one does not know what it is. In general terms, moreover, it is of the utmost importance to be careful about accepting in any form the nationalist and racist obsessions of the nineteenth century, even with reversed values, for the earth of Europe reeks with the inevitable results. Above all we must not believe that Heine was a Jewish alien just because an illiberal society so insisted. It does not diminish the honor of the Jewish people to recognize that Heine (and Max Brod, too, for that matter) was a German writer.

* Heine, too, expressed pity and understanding for the state of the Jews in Poland (E, 7, 194–95), but in a manner that clearly showed his revulsion and disgust.

Notes

CHAPTER 1

1. Friedrich Steinmann, *H. Heine. Denkwürdigkeiten und Erlebnisse aus meinem Zusammenleben mit ihm* (Prague and Leipzig, 1857), p. 10.

2. Notes to Heine's poems in *Agrippa* (June 25, 1824), and *Rheinische Flora* (Jan. 20, 1825); cited by Walter Wadepuhl, "Heines Geburtsjahr," *PMLA, 61* (1946). 127.

3. Adolf Strodtmann, *H. Heine's Leben und Werke* (2d ed. Berlin, 1873). *1,* 677.

4. Hermann Hüffer, "Heine auf dem Lyzeum und Gymnasium zu Düsseldorf," *Heinrich Heine. Gesammelte Aufsätze,* ed. Ernst Elster (Berlin, 1906), pp. 267–70.

5. Ernst Elster, "War Heine französischer Bürger?" *Deutsche Rundschau, 112* (1902), 224–25.

6. Ernst Elster, "Zu Heines Biographie," *Vierteljahrschrift für Litteraturgeschichte, 4* (1891), 473–74.

7. Philipp F. Veit, "Die Rätsel um Heines Geburt," *Heine-Jahrbuch 1962,* pp. 20–22.

8. Hermann Hüffer, "Wann ist Heine geboren?" *Heinrich Heine. Gesammelte Aufsätze,* ed. Ernst Elster (Berlin, 1906), p. 247.

9. W. T., "Die Taufe des deutschen Aristophanes," *Die Gartenlaube* (1877), p. 20. Friedrich Hirth, in *Heinrich Heine. Bausteine zu einer Biographie* (Mainz, 1950), p. 24, identifies the author as "Superintendent W. Felgenhäger in Heiligenstadt," but the initials in the article are clearly "W. T."

10. Hirth, *4,* 194.

11. Jan. 15, 1835; Hirth, 2, 69.

12. Philarète Chasles, *Etudes sur l'Allemagne au XIXe siècle,* 2 (Paris, 1861). 273–77.

13. E, *6,* 32.

14. Maria Embden-Heine, Principessa della Rocca, *Erinnerungen an Heinrich Heine* (Hamburg, 1881), p. 1.

15. Maximilian Heine, *Erinnerungen an Heinrich Heine und seine Familie* (Berlin, 1868), p. 7.

16. Saint-René Taillandier repeated this communication in "Poètes Contemporains de l'Allemagne," *Revue des deux mondes, Nouvelle période, 14* (1852), 9.

17. Wadepuhl, "Heines Geburtsjahr," pp. 140–41.

18. Veit, "Die Rätsel," p. 25, n. 29.

19. Hirth, *1,* 203.

20. Wadepuhl, "Heines Geburtsjahr," pp. 140–41.

21. See Gordon A. Craig, *The Politics of the Prussian Army 1640–1945* (2d ed. New York, 1964), p. 69.

22. Wadepuhl, "Heines Geburtsjahr," pp. 126–56.

23. Hirth, "Das Geburtsjahr," *Heinrich Heine. Bausteine,* pp. 16–24.

24. Veit, "Die Rätsel," p. 13.

25. See, for example, Louis Untermeyer, *Heinrich Heine: Paradox and Poet: The Life* (New York, 1937), pp. 6–7.
26. E, *3*, 407; cf. W, *5*, 488–89.
27. Houben, p. 121.
28. E. M. Butler, *The Saint-Simonian Religion in Germany* (Cambridge, England, 1926), pp. 103, 127.
29. Joseph Dresch, *Heine à Paris (1831–1856) d'après sa correspondance et les témoinages de ses contemporains* (Paris, 1956), p. 12.
30. Hirth, *5*, 268–69.
31. Houben, pp. 63, 236–37, 847.
32. Houben, p. 784.
33. E, *6*, 46.
34. Benedetto Croce, *Poesia e non poesia* (Bari, 1923), p. 173.
35. W, *1*, xx.
36. Norbert Fuerst, *The Victorian Age of German Literature* (University Park, Pa., and London, 1966), p. 99.
37. Karl Glossy, *Literarische Geheimberichte aus dem Vormärz* (Separatabdruck aus dem *Jahrbuch der Grillparzer-Gesellschaft*, Vols. *21–23*) (Vienna, 1912), *1*, xcv.
38. Fuerst, pp. 78, 80, 99.
39. R[obert Bulwer-] Lytton, "Heinrich Heine's Last Poems and Thoughts," *The Fortnightly Review*, n.s. *39* (Jan.-June 1870), 259–60.
40. Fuerst, p. 84.
41. Laura Hofrichter, *Heinrich Heine* (Oxford, 1963), pp. 20–21.
42. William Rose, *The Early Love Poetry of Heinrich Heine: An Inquiry into Poetic Inspiration* (Oxford, 1962).
43. Houben, p. 762.
44. Rose, *The Early Love Poetry*, p. 17.
45. Hirth, *1*, 327.
46. Rose, *The Early Love Poetry*, pp. 81, 82.
47. E, *2*, 36.
48. E, *3*, 157–58.
49. E, *2*, 11.
50. To Salomon Heine, Sept. 15, 1828; Hirth, *1*, 373.
51. Houben, p. 50.
52. E, *1*, 21, 38–39, 41, 513.
53. To Moser, May, 1823; Hirth, *1*, 77.
54. Cf. here Maria Anna Bernhard, *Welterlebnis und gestaltete Wirklichkeit in Heinrich Heines Prosaschriften* (Stuttgart, 1961), p. 86, and the finely nuanced discussion by Helmut Ernst Ruhrig, "Heinrich Heine. Beiträge zur Bestimmung seines ironischen Humors" (diss. Freiburg im Breisgau, 1953), pp. 75–77.
55. Wilhelm Bölsche, *Heinrich Heine. Versuch einer ästhetisch-kritischen Analyse seiner Werke und seiner Weltanschauung* (Leipzig, 1888), p. 41.
56. Strodtmann, *Heine's Leben* 3d ed., *1*, 203.
57. Karl Schulte-Kemminghausen, "Tagebuchaufzeichnungen des westfälischen Freiherrn Ludwig von Diepenbrock-Grüter über Heinrich Heine," *Festschrift für Jost Trier*, ed. Benno von Wiese and Karl Heinz Borck (Meisenheim, 1954), p. 296.
58. "François Willes Erinnerungen an Heinrich Heine," ed. Eberhard Galley, *Heine-Jahrbuch 1967*, p. 9.
59. Charles Andler, *La Poésie de Heine* ([Paris], 1948), pp. 32, 147.

60. Bölsche, *Heinrich Heine,* pp. 11–12.

61. Lion Feuchtwanger, "Die Masken Heinrich Heines. Zur 70. Wiederkehr seines Todestages," *Frankfurter Nachrichten,* no. 48 (February 17, 1926).

62. Walter A. Berendsohn, "Heines 'Buch der Lieder.' Struktur und Stilstudie," *Heine-Jahrbuch 1962,* p. 27.

63. An important attack has been mounted recently in E. D. Hirsch's study, *Validity in Interpretation* (New Haven and London, 1967).

64. Jules Legras, *Henri Heine Poète* (Paris, 1897), pp. 55–56.

65. For a brief discussion of some of the possibilities, see Ernest K. Bramsted, *Aristocracy and the Middle-Classes in Germany: Social Types in German Literature 1830–1900,* (2d ed. Chicago and London), pp. 1–12.

CHAPTER 2

1. Berendsohn, "Heines 'Buch der Lieder,'" *Heine-Jahrbuch 1962,* p. 26.

2. S. S. Prawer, *Heine: Buch der Lieder* (London, 1960), p. 9.

3. Friedrich Sieburg, "Beschwörung und Mitteilung. Zur Lyrik Heinrich Heines," *Jahresring, 3* (1956/57), 70–71.

4. Theodor W. Adorno, "Die Wunde Heine," *Noten zur Literatur, 1* (Frankfurt am Main, 1958), 144.

5. Michael Hamburger, "Heinrich Heine," *Reason and Energy* (London, 1957), p. 152.

6. Prawer, *Heine: Buch der Lieder,* p. 9.

7. Prawer, *TS,* p. 283. A number of similarities in phrase and content are pointed out by Georg Mücke, *Heinrich Heines Beziehungen zum deutschen Mittelalter* (Berlin, 1908), pp. 29–32.

8. See Marie Luise Gansberg, *Der Prosa-Wortschatz des deutschen Realismus unter besonderer Berücksichtigung des vorausgehenden Sprachwandels 1835–1855* (Bonn, 1964), pp. 63–64.

9. See a refined version of this objection by Heinz Seeger, "Der Erzähler in Heines Balladen und Romanzen: Zur Deutung und Kritik seiner Dichtung" (diss. Bonn, 1953), p. 17.

10. Hofrichter, p. 11.

11. Paul Beyer, *Der junge Heine. Eine Entstehungsgeschichte seiner Denkweise und Dichtung* (Berlin, 1911), p. 47.

12. Cf. in this connection Ilse Weidekampf, *Traum und Wirklichkeit in der Romantik und bei Heine* (Leipzig, 1932).

13. Barker Fairley, *Heinrich Heine: An Interpretation* (Oxford, 1954), pp. 1–23.

14. Christoph Siegrist, "Heines Traumbilder," *Heine-Jahrbuch 1965,* p. 21; the essay provides good interpretations of the first and last of the *Traumbilder.*

15. E, *1,* 500. In his second edition (E^2, *1,* 433), Elster doubted this. The poem was published in May 1821.

16. *Goethes Werke,* ed. Erich Trunz, et al. (Hamburger Ausgabe), *1* (Hamburg, 1948), 282.

17. See E, *1,* 501.

18. Beyer, p. 97.

19. Beyer, pp. 55–58.

20. Paul Holzhausen, *Heinrich Heine und Napoleon I.* (Frankfurt am Main, 1903), p. 263, n. 266, believed with Elster in his first edition (E, *1,* 39, n. 1) that

1819 is right for *Die Grenadiere.* Beyer, *Der junge Heine,* pp. 115, 121, believed 1820, and Elster followed him in his second edition (E^2, *1,* 437). Similarly for *Belsatzar* (Beyer, p. 115; E^2, *1,* 440).

21. Cf. the interpretation by Ernst Simon, "Heine und die Romantik," *Brücken. Gesammelte Aufsätze* (Heidelberg, 1965), pp. 149–54.

22. Prawer, *TS,* p. 6.

23. E. M. Butler, *Heinrich Heine, A Biography* (London, 1956), p. 29. Cf. also the enthusiastic judgment of Kurt Weinberg, *Henri Heine. "Romantique défroqué." Héraut du symbolisme français* (New Haven and Paris, 1954), pp. 120–21.

24. For a poet's judgment on this, see Untermeyer, *Heinrich Heine,* p. 82.

25. Strodtmann, *Heine's Leben,* p. 83.

26. Hirth, *1,* 27–28.

27. Helene Herrmann, *Studien zu Heines Romanzero* (Berlin, 1906), pp. 33–34.

28. Urs Belart, *Gehalt und Aufbau von Heinrich Heines Gedichtsammlungen* (Bern, 1925), p. 45. Another effort at ordering the poems was made by Helen Meredith Mustard, *The Lyric Cycle in German Literature* (New York, 1946), pp. 94–102. See also Rose, *The Early Love Poetry,* pp. 33–34.

29. E, *2,* 301–02.

30. E, *1,* 68–69.

31. E, *1* [Introduction], 60–61.

32. Bölsche, as usual, is an exception. See *Heinrich Heine,* p. 79.

33. *Du sollst mich liebend umschließen,* E, 2, 9.

34. This view was reiterated recently by Meno Spann, *Heine* (London, 1966), p. 78.

35. Andler, *La Poésie de Heine,* p. 52.

36. Rose, *The Early Love Poetry,* p. 34.

37. Prawer, *Heine: Buch der Lieder,* p. 17; see also Max Seelig, *Die dichterische Sprache in Heines "Buch der Lieder"* (Halle, 1891), p. 46.

38. See with regard to this problem Jürgen Brummack, "Heines Entwicklung zum satirischen Dichter," *Deutsche Vierteljahrsschrift, 41* (1967), 114.

39. Houben, pp. 33–34.

40. E, *1,* 521.

41. Edward Dahlberg, *New York Review of Books* (Sept. 30, 1965), p. 4.

42. Cf. Prawer, *Heine: Buch der Lieder,* pp. 18–19.

43. Rose, *The Early Love Poetry,* p. 36. See Seelig for statistics.

44. To Steinmann, Apr. 10, 1823; Hirth, *1,* 67.

45. Oskar Walzel, *Gehalt und Gestalt im Kunstwerk des Dichters* (2d ed. Darmstadt, 1957), p. 41.

46. E, *1* [Introduction], 67.

47. Belart, pp. 60–61.

48. Legras, *Henri Heine Poète,* p. 51. Mustard, pp. 102–07, also makes an effort to group the poems, but she agrees that there is little visible narrative order.

49. Andler, p. 91.

50. Artur Weckmüller, *Heines Stil* (Breslau, 1934), p. 83, calls attention to the changes Silcher made in Heine's text in order to smooth out the rhythm.

51. Karl Kraus, *Heine und die Folgen* (Munich, 1910), p. 23.

52. Andler, p. 77.

53. Erich Kästner, *Kästner für Erwachsene,* ed. Rudolf Walter Leonhardt (Frankfurt am Main, 1966), p. 78.

54. Among numerous studies, see particularly Mücke, *Heines Beziehungen,* pp. 94–96; Allen Wilson Porterfield, "Graf von Loeben and the Legend of the Lorelei," *Modern Philology, 13,* no. 6 (Oct. 1915), 65–92; Rotraud Ehrenzeller-Favre, *Loreley. Entstehung und Wandlung einer Sage* (Flensburg, 1948); and Willy Krogmann, "Lorelei. Geburt einer Sage," *Rheinische-westfälische Zeitschrift für Volkskunde, 3* (1956), 170–96.

55. J. J. A. A. Frantzen, "Zu Heine's Loreley," *Neophilologus, 3* (1918), 131–34.

56. *Clemens Brentanos Werke,* ed. Friedhelm Kemp, 2 (Munich and Darmstadt, 1963), 427.

57. Joseph von Eichendorff, *Werke,* ed. Wolfdietrich Rasch (2d ed. Munich, 1959), p. 304.

58. Quoted by Ehrenzeller-Favre, p. 121.

59. Some poems from this group seem to have been lost. See to Christiani, Mar. 7, 1824; Hirth, *1,* 151.

60. Prawer, *TS,* p. 5.

61. Hirth, *1,* 6.

62. E, *2,* 335.

63. Cf. *Der Hals ist mir trocken* (E, *2,* 98) as well as the function of the lictor in the sixth caput of *Deutschland. Ein Wintermärchen* (E, *2,* 443–45).

64. Prawer, *Heine: Buch der Lieder,* p. 37.

65. Ibid., pp. 41–42.

66. Ibid., p. 41.

67. The other two are *Blamier mich nicht, mein schönes Kind* (E, *2,* 10) and *Schöne, wirtschaftliche Dame* (E, *2,* 13).

68. Hirth, *1,* 180.

69. See Wilhelm Ochsenbein, *Die Aufnahme Lord Byrons in Deutschland und sein Einfluß auf den jungen Heine* (Bern, 1905), pp. 182–88.

70. Ibid., pp. 175–82.

71. Hirth, *1,* 119.

72. See E, *1,* 491.

73. Hirth, *1,* 119.

74. Hirth, *1,* 122.

75. See E^2, *1,* 463.

76. For the background of this poem, see J. Nassen, "Heinrich Heine und die sogenannte katholisierende Richtung seines Jünglingsalters," *Literarische Beilage der Kölner Volkszeitung, 44* (1904), 123–24. Cf. Legras, pp. 58–62, and William Rose's discussion of *Die Weihe* (E, *2,* 111–12) in *Heinrich Heine: Two Studies of his Thought and Feeling: Heine's Political and Social Attitude; Heine's Jewish Feeling* (Oxford, 1956), pp. 99–100.

77. E, *1,* 527–8.

78. Bölsche, *Heinrich Heine,* p. 58.

79. Hans-Udo Dück, "Heinrich Heine: Die Wallfahrt nach Kevlaar," *Wege zum Gedicht,* ed. Rupert Hirschenauer and Albrecht Weber (Munich and Zurich, 1963), *2,* 270–77.

80. E, *1,* 529.

81. Prawer, *Heine: Buch der Lieder,* p. 29

82. On the rhythms, see Legras, pp. 157–68. An early attempt to discuss Heine's prosody is Paul Remer, *Die freien Rhythmen in Heines Nordseebildern. Ein Beitrag zur neuen deutschen Metrik* (Heidelberg, 1889).

83. E, *2,* 70–71.

84. E², *1,* 264.

85. Cf. Edgar C. Cumings, "Parallel Passages in Heine's Poetry and Prose," *Germanic Review, 14* (1939) , 285.

86. Aug. 4, 1826; Hirth, *1,* 276.

87. E, *2,* 91–92.

88. Heine had some trouble ordering this part of the section. See Marianne Thalmann, "Heinrich Heine, 'Die Nordsee,' eine Lesartenstudie," *Zeitschrift für deutsche Philologie, 52* (1927), 156–57.

89. E, *1,* 191–93.

90. Ludwig Marcuse, *Heine: A Life Between Love and Hate* (New York, 1933), p. 71.

CHAPTER 3

1. Harry Maync, *Eduard Mörike. Sein Leben und Dichten* (Stuttgart and Berlin, 1902), pp. 104–05.

2. Emil Ermatinger, *Gottfried Kellers Leben* (8th ed. Zurich, 1950), p. 239.

3. Hegel, *Vorlesungen über die Ästhetik, 3, Sämtliche Werke,* ed. Hermann Glockner, *14* (Stuttgart, 1928), esp. p. 479.

4. George Eliot, "German Wit: Heinrich Heine," *Essays and Leaves from a Note-Book,* ed. Charles Lee Lewes (New York, 1884), p. 80.

5. Adolf Strodtmann, *H. Heine's Leben und Werke* (3d ed. Hamburg, 1884), *2,* 266.

6. To Moser, June 18, 1823; Jan. 9, 1824; to Rudolf Christiani, May 24, 1824; Hirth, *1,* 90, 135, 169.

7. To Johann Vesque von Püttlingen, June 22, 1851; Hirth, *3,* 287.

8. To Laube, Jan. 25, 1850; Hirth, *3,* 196.

9. To Friedrich Steinmann and Johann Baptist Rousseau, Oct. 29, 1820; Hirth, *1,* 15.

10. To Steinmann, Feb. 4, 1821; to Immermann, Apr. 10, 1823; to Fouqué, June 10, 1823; Hirth, *1,* 23–24, 70–71, 81.

11. To Immermann, Apr. 10, 1823; to Eduard von Schenk, Apr. 2, 1828 (Hirth, *1,* 68, 355); E, *3,* 375–76 (1830); E, *7,* 325 (1838); note to a translation in the *Revue de Paris* of 1840 (Hirth, *5,* 289; there incorrectly dated 1848); to Laube, Feb. 7, 1850; to Campe, Oct. 1, 1851 (Hirth, *3,* 198, 317); E, *2,* 522 (1851).

12. Houben, pp. 573–74.

13. Weckmüller, *Heines Stil,* pp. 3–5.

14. Kurt Sternberg, *Heinrich Heines geistige Gestalt und Welt* (Berlin, 1929), pp. 27–30.

15. Heinrich Mutzenbecher, *Heine und das Drama* (Hamburg, 1914), p. 26.

16. E, *4,* 523.

17. Seeger, "Der Erzähler in Heines Balladen und Romanzen" (diss. Bonn, 1953), p. 50.

18. See to Ferdinand Dümmler, Jan. 5, 1823; Hirth, *1,* 52–53.

19. Bölsche, *Heinrich Heine,* p. 131.

20. E, *2,* 261, 262.

21. E, *2,* 262, 306.

22. E, *2,* 275–77.

23. E, *2,* 276.
24. E², *3,* 253.
25. Untermeyer, *Heinrich Heine,* p. 90.
26. Strodtmann, *Heine's Leben, 1,* 258.
27. E, *2,* 66, 67.
28. E, *2,* 323.
29. See Peter Demetz, *Marx, Engels, and the Poets* (Chicago and London, 1967), p. 149.
30. Ochsenbein, *Die Aufnahme Lord Byrons in Deutschland,* pp. 211–12.
31. E, *7,* 167.
32. Hirth, *1,* 35.
33. E, *3,* 128.
34. See Mutzenbecher, p. 48.
35. Houben, p. 574.

CHAPTER 4

1. Erich Loewenthal, *Studien zu Heines "Reisebildern"* (Berlin and Leipzig, 1922), p. 1
2. Gansberg, *Der Prosa-Wortschatz,* pp. 63–64
3. May 26, 1825; Hirth, *1,* 211–12.
4. Maria Anna Bernhard, *Welterlebnis und gestaltete Wirklichkeit in Heinrich Heines Prosaschriften* (Stuttgart, 1961), p. 82.
5. E, *3,* 14.
6. Wilhelm Bölsche, *Heinrich Heine,* p. 165.
7. See Richard M. Meyer, "Nicht mehr als sechs Schüsseln: 2. Göttinger Würste," *Euphorion, 8* (1901), 706–09; C. B. Ibershoff, "Concerning a Passage in Heine's *Harzreise,*" *Philological Quarterly, 4,* (1925), 239–40; Ibershoff, "Heine's *Harzreise* Once More," ibid., *5* (1926), 54–55; Ibershoff, "Lichtenberg's 'Wuerste, Bibliothek,' " ibid., pp. 282–83.
8. E, *3,* 29–30.
9. E, *3,* 303–05.
10. E, *1,* 151–57.
11. E², *3,* 461–62.
12. E, *3,* 25–26.
13. E, *3,* 39.
14. Hofrichter, *Heinrich Heine,* p. 42.
15. E², *3,* 379–84. Heine salvaged a passage about quotations for *Das Buch Le Grand.*

CHAPTER 5

1. It has been given an exemplary stylistic interpretation by Peter Bürger, "Der Essay bei Heinrich Heine" (diss. Munich, 1959), pp. 114–16.
2. For references on the history of the word, see W, *4,* 525–26.
3. See Ernst Feise, "Form and Meaning of Heine's Essay 'Die Nordsee,' " *Monatshefte, 34* (1942), 223–34.
4. E², *4,* 52.
5. To Friedrich Merckel, Oct. 6, 1826; to Moses Moser, Oct. 14, 1826; to Merckel,

Dec. 16, 1826; to Joseph Lehmann, Dec. 16, 1826; to Merckel, Jan. 10, 1827; to Moser, June 9, 1827; Hirth, *1*, 282, 287, 301, 303, 306, 315–16.

6. E.g., E, *4*, 43; E, *5*, 253; E, *7*, 134, 413.
7. E, *3*, 86.
8. Léon Polak, "Heinrich Heines *Buch Legrand*," *Neophilologus*, 7 (1921/22), 260.
9. E, *1*, [Introduction], 80.
10. E[2], *1*, 54*.
11. E, *3*, 86.
12. E, *1* [Introduction], 80.
13. E[2], *4*, 57.
14. E[2], *4*, 519. Cf. Hirth, *6*, 86 and Rose, *The Early Love Poetry*, p. 65. Some of these problems were cleared up once and for all by Hermann J. Weigand, "The Double Love-Tragedy in Heine's *Buch Le Grand:* a Literary Myth," *Germanic Review*, *13* (1938), 121–26
15. E, *1* [Introduction], 81
16. Karl Hessel, "Heines 'Buch Legrand,'" *Vierteljahrschrift für Litteraturgeschichte*, *5* (1892), p. 553.
17. See Hirth, *5*, 79.
18. Hirth, *1*, 196, 198, 231. Cf. E, *3*, 192–93
19. Hirth, *1*, 233.
20. Hessel, p. 553.
21. Ibid., p. 550.
22. E, *3*, 102.
23. To Moser, Oct. 14, 1826; Hirth, *1*, 286–87; cf. to Varnhagen, Oct. 24, 1826; Hirth, *1*, 293.
24. See Walter Wadepuhl, "Heines Memoiren," *Heine-Studien* (Weimar, 1956), p. 155.
25. See Hessel, p. 555.
26. E, *3*, 139–40.
27. E, *3*, 150.
28. E, *3*, 169.
29. E, *3*, 175.
30. E, *3*, 132.
31. E, *7*, 372.
32. Cf. *Die Braut von Messina*, l. 2838.
33. Quoted E, *7*, 541.
34. E, *1*, 239.
35. In Chapters 14, 15, 20, 21, 25 and 34 (E, *3*, 242, 244, 252–53, 264–65, 287).
36. E, *3*, 242.
37. E, *1*, 418.
38. E, *3*, 146.
39. Holzhausen, *Heine und Napoleon I.*, p. 51.
40. See Hirth, "Wie Heinrich Heine las," *Heinrich Heine. Bausteine*, pp. 94–100.
41. Holzhausen, pp. 65–66.
42. Ibid., pp. 56–67.
43. See Hüffer, *Heinrich Heine. Gesammelte Aufsätze*, p. 94. The uncertain allusion appears also in a poem, *Wir wollen jetzt Frieden machen* (E, *2*, 11).
44. Holzhausen, pp. 116–19.

45. E, *3*, 160.

46. Hirth, *1*, 233.

47. Erich Loewenthal, *Studien zu Heines "Reisebildern,"* pp. 54–59.

48. The image recurs in a passage in a letter to Friederike Robert of Dec. 1829 (Hirth, *1*, 405).

CHAPTER 6

1. To Moser, Oct. 14, 1826; to Varnhagen, Oct. 24, 1826; Hirth, *1*, 287, 294. Varnhagen was highly amused; see his remarks, years later, in his diary, quoted Hirth, *4*, 142.

2. See E², *4*, 237–38.

3. Rudolf Schlösser, *August Graf v. Platen*, *2* (Munich, 1913), 116–18.

4. Quoted E, *3*, 201.

5. Horst Krüger, "Die freie Kunst als ästhetisches Prinzip bei Heinrich Heine" (diss. Würzburg, 1949), p. 136, n. 60.

6. August Graf von Platen-Hallermünde, *Sämtliche Werke in 12 Bänden*, ed. Max Koch and Erich Petzet (Leipzig, 1910), *4*, 227.

7. E, *5*, 244–45.

8. E, *2*, 443–48.

9. See E², *1*, 502 and cf. E, *7*, 59.

10. Hirth, *4*, 224.

11. See Helmut Gruber, "The Political-Ethical Mission of German Expressionism," *German Quarterly*, *40* (1967), 186–203.

12. C. P. Snow, "On Stalin's Triumph, on Stalin's Madness," *Esquire*, *68*, no. 5 (May 1967), p. 116.

13. Martin Greiner, *Zwischen Biedermeier und Bourgeoisie. Ein Kapitel deutscher Literaturgeschichte im Zeichen Heinrich Heines* (Leipzig, 1954), p. 109.

14. H. G. Atkins, *Heine* (London and New York, 1929), p. 108.

15. See Hirth, *4*, 216.

16. Hirth, *1*, 400; the letter is dated by the Hamburg premiere of Immermann's *Trauerspiel in Tirol* on the preceding day (Hirth, *4*, 217).

17. Hirth, *4*, 211.

18. To Immermann, Feb. 3, 1830; Hirth, *1*, 419.

19. Hirth, *4*, 216 and Houben, pp. 150–51.

20. "François Willes Erinnerungen" ed. Galley, *Heine-Jahrbuch 1967*, p. 4.

21. See Houben, p. 142.

22. Heine wrote similarly to Immermann, Dec. 26, 1829, Hirth, *1*, 406.

23. E, *3*, 207.

24. Herman Salinger, "The Riddle of the 'Kinderball' in Heine's 'Bäder von Lucca,'" *Monatshefte*, *34* (1942), 145–52.

25. E, *1*, [Introduction], 84.

26. E, *3*, 330.

27. E, *3*, 307.

28. E, *3*, 316.

29. E, *3*, 324.

30. Bölsche, *Heinrich Heine*, p. 183.

31. E, *3*, 558–62.

32. E, *3*, 215, 220.

33. E, *3,* 290.

34. Alfred Mayerhofer, *Heinrich Heines Literaturkritik* (Munich, 1929), pp. 64, 121, 133. E[2], *4,* 556, in a note on *Die Stadt Lucca,* hints at the connection without really grasping it.

35. E, *3,* 410–11. Cf. *Lazarus* 7 in *Romanzero,* E, *1,* 419.

36. See my discussion of this matter in "Platen's Tulip Image," *Monatshefte, 52* (1960), 293–301.

37. Quoted by Max Kaufmann, *Heines Charakter und die moderne Seele* (Zurich, 1902), p. 94.

38. Platen, *Sämtliche Werke,* ed. Koch and Petzet, *10,* 101.

39. A brief analysis will be found in Erich Eckertz, *Heine und sein Witz* (Berlin, 1908), pp. 190–91.

40. Kraus, *Heine und die Folgen,* p. 34. Kraus quotes from E, *3,* 363.

41. E, *5,* 381.

42. Also Hirth, *1,* 449–50.

43. E, *4,* 632.

44. E, *5,* 272.

45. Erich Loewenthal, "Heines Stellung zum antiken Vers (Heine als Vorgänger Andreas Heuslers)," *Archiv für das Studium der neueren Sprachen und Literaturen, 145* (1923), 168.

46. E, *7,* 424.

47. Hirth, *1,* 194.

48. Hirth, *6,* 274–75; cf. Hirth, *4,* 236.

49. Houben, p. 531.

CHAPTER 7

1. E, *1,* 200.

2. Stuart Atkins, "The Evaluation of Heine's *Neue Gedichte,*" *Wächter und Hüter. Festschrift für Hermann J. Weigand,* ed. Curt von Faber du Faur, Konstantin Reichardt, and Heinz Bluhm (New Haven, 1957), pp. 99–107.

3. E[2], *1,* 267.

4. Prawer, *TS,* p. 13.

5. Ibid., p. 224.

6. See to Campe, Oct. 21, 1851; Hirth, *3,* 326. For a clear account of the development of *Neue Gedichte,* see Prawer, *TS,* pp. 91–92.

7. Full text of Gutzkow's letter in *Heinrich Heines Briefwechsel,* ed. Friedrich Hirth (Munich, 1914–20), *2,* 237–41.

8. For a review of the relations of Heine and Gutzkow, see Eberhard Galley, "Heine im literarischen Streit mit Gutzkow," *Heine-Jahrbuch 1966,* pp. 3–40.

9. F. H. Eisner, "Echtes, Unechtes und Zweifelhaftes in Heines Werken," *Heine-Jahrbuch 1962,* p. 59.

10. E, *4,* 506–07. On this topic, cf. Horst Krüger, "Die freie Kunst," p. 94.

11. Hirth, *2,* 274, 289, 307, 497.

12. Cf. the previous letter to Varnhagen of Feb. 4; Hirth, *1,* 420.

13. Lee Byron Jennings, *The Ludicrous Demon: Aspects of the Grotesque in German Post-Romantic Prose* (Berkeley and Los Angeles, 1963), p. 48. For a careful examination of this problem, see Helge Hultberg, "Heines Bewertung der Kunst," *Heine-Jahrbuch 1967,* pp. 81–89.

14. See to Varnhagen, Nov. 30, 1830; Hirth, *1,* 468.

15. Atkins, "The Evaluation of Heine's *Neue Gedichte*," pp. 103–05. He is here following a suggestion made by Helene Herrmann in *Heines Werke*, ed. Hermann Friedemann, et al. (Berlin, 1927), *1*, 26, 28–29. The rococo aspect of *Neuer Frühling* was also noted by Ewald A. Boucke in his edition of Heine's *Werke* (Berlin, 1928–30), *1*, 305.
16. Prawer, *TS*, pp. 15–16.
17. Ibid., pp. 37–38.
18. Belart, *Gehalt und Aufbau*, p. 75.
19. Cf. Prawer, *TS*, p. 21.
20. E, *1*, 208.
21. E, *1*, 213.
22. Prawer, *TS*, p. 21.
23. Prawer, *TS*, p. 17.
24. E, *1*, 537.
25. Louis L. Hammerich, "Trochäen bei Heinrich Heine, Zugleich ein Beitrag zum Werdegang eines alten Germanisten," *Formenwandel. Festschrift zum 65. Geburtstag von Paul Böckmann*, ed. Walter Müller-Seidel and Wolfgang Preisendanz (Hamburg, 1964), p. 400.
26. *Des Knaben Wunderhorn*, ed. Willi A. Koch (Darmstadt, 1963), p. 157. Cf. E^2, *1*, 482.
27. Prawer, *TS*, p. 17.
28. Ibid., p. 18.
29. Ibid., p. 17.
30. Walther Killy, "Mein Pferd für'n gutes Bild," *Wandlungen des lyrischen Bildes* (3d ed. Göttingen, 1961), p. 102.
31. Prawer, *TS*, p. 15.
32. See a collection of outraged commentaries in J. Nassen, "Zu Heinrich Heines Salon IV und seinem Gedichtzyklus 'Katharina,' " *Euphorion*, *10* (1903), 624–26.
33. *Leipziger Universitätszeitung*, 2d semester, nos. 8, 9 (July 13, 20, 1889).
34. E.g., E, *2*, 9–10 and E, *2*, 12–13.
35. Cf. Prawer, *TS*, pp. 26–27.
36. Ibid., p. 33.
37. Butler, *The Saint-Simonian Religion*; Wingolf Scherer, "Heinrich Heine und der Saint-Simonismus" (diss. Bonn, 1950); George G. Iggers, "Heine and the Saint-Simonians: A Re-examination," *Comparative Literature*, *10* (1958), 289–308. A review of Heine's statements on the subject will be found in Alfred Fuhrmann, *Recht und Staat bei Heinrich Heine* (Bonn, 1960), pp. 64–68.
38. E, *7*, 408.
39. E, *7*, 50.
40. See Lieselotte Dieckmann, "The Metaphor of Hieroglyphics in German Romanticism," *Comparative Literature*, *7* (1955), pp. 306–12. Heine may have known that the word "rune" is cognate with *raunen*, which means "to whisper mysteriously" and has magical overtones.
41. Barker Fairley, *Heinrich Heine: Selected Poems* (Oxford, 1965), p. 232.
42. In Elster's *Nachlese*, *1*, 43, 44, 45 (E, *2*, 22–23).
43. Prawer, *TS*, p. 28.
44. E, *1*, 236.
45. See E, *1*, 542.

46. Friedrich Stamm, "Die Liebeszyklen in Heines 'Neuen Gedichten,'" *Euphorion, 23* (1921), 90.
47. Prawer, *TS*, 35–46.
48. Hirth, *1*, 147.
49. E, *4*, 173–74.
50. Ernst Elster, *Tannhäuser in Geschichte, Sage, und Dichtung* (Bromberg, 1908), p. 2.
51. E, *4*, 429–32.
52. Elster, *Tannhäuser*, p. 15.
53. E, *4*, 305–08, 421.
54. E, *4*, 433.
55. Sternberg, *Heinrich Heines geistige Gestalt*, p. 188.
56. Andler, *La Poésie de Heine*, p. 124.
57. E, *4*, 305.
58. Hofrichter, *Heinrich Heine*, p. 85.
59. E², *1*, 493.
60. Prawer, *TS*, pp. 37–38.
61. E, *3*, 270.
62. See Fairley, *Heinrich Heine: Selected Poems*, p. 233.
63. This is Heine's version, which differs slightly from the original, for which see E, *1*, 492–93.
64. *Heines Werke*, ed. Friedemann, et al., *1*, 32.
65. Seeger, "Der Erzähler in Heines Balladen und Romanzen," p. 112.
66. Prawer, *TS*, pp. 50–51.
67. Heine adverts to this legend in *Über die französische Bühne* (E, *4*, 542).
68. Prawer, *TS*, p. 59.
69. See also Prawer, *TS*, pp. 49–50.
70. Ernst Feise, "Heine's 'Unterwelt,'" *Germanic Review, 31* (1956), 276–78. The metrical scheme Feise gives for Part II is not quite correct.
71. Ibid., p. 277.
72. Ibid., p. 276.
73. E.g., E², *1*, 496; Feise, "Heine's 'Unterwelt,'" p. 278.
74. Feise, "Heine's 'Unterwelt,'" p. 278.
75. Fritz Strich, "Heinrich Heine und die Überwindung der Romantik," *Kunst und Leben* (Bern and Munich, 1960), p. 133.
76. For a lively account of this event, see Carl Brinitzer, *Das streitbare Leben des Verlegers Julius Campe* (Hamburg, 1962), pp. 201–07.
77. *Lobgesänge auf König Ludwig* (E, *2*, 169–73).
78. *Der neue Alexander* (E, *3*, 173–75).
79. Krüger, "Die freie Kunst," p. 97.
80. Walther Victor, *Marx und Heine* (Berlin, 1953), p. 33.
81. Karl Marx and Friedrich Engels, *Werke*, ed. Institut für Marxismus-Leninismus beim ZK der SED (Berlin, 1956–67), *27*, 434, 435, 441.
82. See also Hirth, *2*, 541–43.
83. See Demetz, *Marx, Engels*, pp. 78–82.
84. See Wolfgang Harich, "Heinrich Heine und das Schulgeheimnis der deutschen Philosophie," *Zur Geschichte der Religion und Philosophie in Deutschland*, ed. Harich, sammlung insel, *17* (Frankfurt am Main, 1965), 29–30.

85. Ludwig Marcuse, "Heine and Marx: A History and a Legend," *Germanic Review, 30* (1955), 114.

86. Houben, p. 451. Marcuse ("Heine and Marx," p. 122, n. 6), doubts the veracity of this report.

87. Hirth, "Heine und Marx," *Heinrich Heine. Bausteine,* pp. 117–18, 121. See the critique of Hirth's procedure by Bernhard, *Welterlebnis,* p. 58.

88. E, *4,* 147.

89. E, *6,* 46.

90. E, *1,* 305–06.

91. *Heines Werke,* ed. Friedemann, et al., *1,* 38.

92. Hermann J. Weigand, "Heine's Family Feud—The Culmination of his Struggle for Economic Security," *Journal of English and Germanic Philology, 21* (1922), 95.

93. E, *1,* 313–14, 290.

94. E, *2,* 173–75.

95. E^2, *2,* 293.

96. E, *1,* 308

97. E, *3,* 503.

98. Prawer, *TS,* p. 101.

99. Marcuse, "Heine and Marx," p. 119.

CHAPTER 8

1. Heinrich Heine, *Zeitungsberichte über Musik und Malerei,* ed. Michael Mann (Frankfurt am Main, 1964).

2. Ibid., p. 19.

3. E, *5,* 94–95.

4. E, *5,* 103. The text by Michel Chevalier from the *Globe* is given by Butler, *The Saint-Simonian Religion,* p. 98.

5. Cf. the stylistic analysis of this passage by Bernhard, *Welterlebnis,* pp. 100–01. See also Werner Rahmelow, "Zu den Anfängen des feuilletonistischen Stiles (Untersuchungen an Heine)" (diss. Freiburg im Breisgau, 1936), pp. 57–62.

6. E, *5,* 112–15.

7. E, *3,* 385.

8. E, *3,* 499.

9. E, *4,* 59, 67.

10. E, *5,* 149; cf. E, *5,* 111.

11. E, *3,* 417.

12. Fuhrmann, *Recht und Staat,* pp. 184–85.

13. E, *5,* 176.

14. E, *5,* 186.

15. T. E. B. Howarth, *Citizen-King: The Life of Louis Philippe King of the French* (London, 1961), p. 103.

16. Ibid., p. 164.

17. E, *7,* 281–82.

18. E, *4,* 287.

19. Hirth, *5,* 23. Clarke's references to opposition newspapers seem more to the point.

20. E, *5,* 498–99.

21. E, *5*, 29–30.
22. E, *5*, 32–33.
23. E, *4*, 81–82.
24. E, *5*, 29
25. See to Baron Cotta, Jan. 20, 1832; Hirth, *2*, 11, and the account of the whole uproar in the press and the courts in Hirth, *5*, 23–39.
26. E, *5*, 34.
27. E, *5*, 34–35.
28. E, *5*, 36.
29. See Howarth, pp. 188–89.
30. E, *5*, 133–34; cf. E, *5*, 511.
31. E, *5*, 39.
32. See E, *7*, 65–66; E, *6*, 373.
33. E, *5*, 81–83.
34. E, *5*, 84–85.
35. E, *5*, 32.
36. E, *4*, 30–31; cf. E, *4*, 572.
37. E, *7*, 440–41
38. E, *5*, 203.
39. E, *5*, 115.
40. E, *5*, 124.
41. In an article dated Feb. 4, not printed in the *Allgemeine Zeitung*, Heine took a more ironic view of the affair (E, *7*, 351–53).
42. Quoted by Heine in *Börne* (E, *7*, 136).
43. E, *5*, 155.
44. E, *4*, 89.
45. See Bernhard, *Welterlebnis*, p. 79.
46. To Campe, Aug. 12, 1852; Hirth, *3*, 401. Campe apparently vetoed this suggestion; see to Campe, Aug. 24, 1852; Hirth, *3*, 410.
47. E, *6*, 132. See Michael Mann, "Heine-Handschriften als Quellenmaterial zu einem biographischen Revisionsbericht," *Heine-Jahrbuch 1963*, pp. 85–101, for a discussion of the revision. For Heine's version of the principles of his revision, see to Campe, Aug. 12, 1852, and Apr. 18, 1854; Hirth, *3*, 399, 503.
48. E, *7*, 632.
49. E, *6*, 139.
50. E, *6*, 141–42.
51. E, *7*, 633.
52. E, *6*, 588.
53. E, *6*, 588–89.
54. E, *6*, 223.
55. Cf. E, *3*, 159.
56. Cf. E, *6*, 591.
57. E, *6*, 252.
58. E, *6*, 603.
59. E, *6*, 268.
60. E, *6*, 317; cf. E, *6*, 610.
61. See Hirth, *5*, 359.
62. E, *6*, 231–32.
63. E, *6*, 232–33.

64. E, *6,* 226, 369.
65. E, *6,* 332–33.
66. E, *7,* 642.
67. E, *7,* 402, 438.
68. E, *7,* 379–80
69. Weerth to his mother, Mar. 11, 1848, *Ausgewählte Werke,* ed. Bruno Kaiser (Frankfurt am Main, 1966), p. xiii.
70. E, *1,* 486.
71. To Gustav Kolb, Apr. 21, 1851; Hirth, *3,* 281.
72. *König Langohr I.,* E, *2,* 192–95.
73. See E^2, *2,* 384–85.
74. E, *6,* 540.
75. Most notably to Varnhagen, Feb. 13, 1838; Hirth, *2,* 237–38.
76. E, *5,* 201–04.
77. Hirth, *2,* xii–xiii.
78. Hirth, *2,* xiii.
79. E, *6,* 387.
80. Glossy, *Literarische Geheimberichte,* Part 3, p. 25.
81. See to Campe, Aug. 12, 1852; Hirth, *3,* 399.
82. Heine wrote similarly to Thiers, Apr. 14, 1855; Hirth, *3,* 606.

CHAPTER 9

1. See Hirth, "Heine und Börne," *Heinrich Heine. Bausteine,* pp. 30–31, 40.
2. To Cotta, June 10, 1835; to Varnhagen, Feb. 12, Feb. 13, 1838; to August Lewald, Mar. 1, Mar. 6, 1838; to Meyerbeer, Mar. 24, 1838; to Campe, Mar. 30, 1838; Hirth, *2,* 86–88, 236–45, 253, 256. See also Alfred Schellenberg, *Heinrich Heines französische Prosawerke* (Berlin, 1921), pp. 37–38.
3. E, *5,* 153–54.
4. To Varnhagen, mid-May 1832; Hirth, *2,* 21.
5. See to Campe, July 24, 1840; Hirth, *2,* 358–59.
6. Jeanette Wohl, ed., *Ludwig Börne's Urtheil über H. Heine. Ungedruckte Stellen aus den Pariser Briefen. Als Anhang: Stimmen über H. Heine's letztes Buch, aus Zeitblättern* (Frankfurt am Main, 1840). See Hirth, "Heine und Börne," *Bausteine,* pp. 32–36.
7. See Houben, p. 195.
8. Karl Gutzkow, *Börne's Leben* (Hamburg, 1840).
9. Barthélemy Ott, *La Querelle de Heine et de Börne. Contribution à l'étude des idées politiques et sociales en Allemagne de 1830 à 1840* (Lyon [1936]).
10. Ludwig Marcuse, *Revolutionär und Patriot. Das Leben Ludwig Börnes* (Berlin, 1929).
11. Helmut Bock, *Ludwig Börne. Vom Gettojuden zum Nationalschriftsteller* (Berlin, 1962).
12. Hofrichter, *Heinrich Heine,* p. 101.
13. The only interpreter who has seen the matter at all clearly in these terms, to my knowledge, is Kurt Sternberg; see *Heinrich Heines geistige Gestalt,* pp. 207–08.
14. Marcuse, *Revolutionär und Patriot,* pp. 80–84.
15. See the documentation of this change in the eighty-second *Brief aus Paris,*

dated November 21, 1832, *Ludwig Börne's Gesammelte Schriften* (Rybnik, 1884), *10,* 19–23.

16. See Marcuse, *Revolutionär und Patriot,* pp. 284–91

17. See Bock, *Ludwig Börne,* pp. 127–29.

18. See Demetz, *Marx, Engels,* p. 161.

19. Bock, *Ludwig Börne,* p. 331.

20. Marcuse, *Revolutionär und Patriot,* p. 300.

21. Börne, *Gesammelte Schriften, 1,* 6.

22. Demetz, *Marx, Engels,* p. 17.

23. Börne, *Gesammelte Schriften, 6,* 259–60.

24. Demetz, *Marx, Engels,* pp. 16–23.

25. E, *7,* 18.

26. To Moser, July 1, 1825; Hirth, *1,* 217.

27. Hirth, *1,* 262.

28. For Börne's influence on Heine's early prose, see Erich Eckertz, "Heine und Börne," *Euphorion, 13* (1906), 167–37; Eckertz, *Heine und sein Witz* (Berlin, 1908), pp. 86–94; Holzhausen, *Heinrich Heine und Napoleon I.,* pp. 135–42, 165–66; Paul Santkin, *Ludwig Börnes Einfluß auf Heinrich Heine* (Betzdorf, 1913). On Heine's gradual emancipation from the breathless short sentences of Börne's style, see Weckmüller, *Heines Stil,* pp. 10–13.

29. Ludwig Geiger, "Börne als Protektor Heines. Mit einem ungedruckten Briefe Börnes," *Frankfurter Zeitung* (Dec. 14, 1913).

30. E, *7,* 105.

31. Gerard Ras, *Börne und Heine als politische Schriftsteller* (The Hague 1926), p. 69.

32. To Varnhagen, May 1832; July 16, 1833; Hirth, *2,* 21, 43. See W, *8,* 549.

33. Hirth, *2,* 202.

34. Hirth, "Heine und Börne," *Bausteine,* pp. 27–28.

35. *Ludwig Börne's Urtheil,* pp. 11, 7, 17.

36. E, *7,* 25–26, 99.

37. Hirth, "Heine und Börne," pp. 28, 29.

38. E, *7,* 80.

39. E, *7,* 81.

40. E, *7,* 114.

41. E, *7,* 38–39.

42. E, *7,* 102; see Walzel's note, W, *8,* 617.

43. To Campe, July 7, 1841; Hirth, *2,* 391.

44. To Weill, Aug. 19, 1841; Hirth, *2,* 403.

45. To L. Wertheim, Dec. 22, 1845; Hirth, *3,* 33–34.

46. Gutzkow, *Börne's Leben,* pp. xxi–xxv.

47. Strodtmann, *Heine's Leben, 2,* 276.

48. E, *7,* 32.

49. W, *8,* 610.

50. Hirth, *1,* 332.

51. Hirth, *1,* 332–34.

52. E, *7,* 106.

53. Houben, pp. 344–45, 350, 353.

54. Hirth, *1,* 455–56.

55. See Walter Wadepuhl, "Steinmanns Heinefälschungen," *Heine-Studien* (Weimar, 1956), pp. 39–46.

56. This according to Heine's claim to Laube, Jan. 24, 1843; Hirth, 2, 451–52.

57. Hirth, *1*, 455; E, 7, 42.

58. E, 7, 42.

59. Butler, "Heine and the Saint-Simonians: The Date of the Letters from Heligoland," *Modern Language Review, 18* (1923), p. 74.

60. Ibid., p. 75; cf. E, *4*, 192, 583–84.

61. E, 7, 53.

62. Butler, "Heine and the Saint-Simonians," p. 74.

63. E, 7, 50.

64. E, 7, 53.

65. E, 7, 109–14.

66. Hirth, *1*, 469–70.

67. Hirth, *4*, 250.

68. E, *4*, 43.

69. Hirth, 2, 16.

70. E, *5*, 242–43, 255–56.

71. Butler, "Heine and the Saint-Simonians," p. 73.

72. To Campe, Apr. 18, 1840; Hirth, 2, 346–47

73. Hirth, *4*, 243.

74. Whether this is as certain as Hirth claims (Hirth, *4*, 247) is open to question.

75. It is noteworthy that in a sharp review of the book, Karl Goedeke stated flatly the opinion that the Helgoland letters had been written after Börne's death (reprinted Hirth, *5*, 313).

76. E, *3*, 273–74.

77. E, *5*, 39.

78. Holzhausen, p. 142.

79. E, 7, 21–22.

80. E, *3*, 560–61.

81. E, 7, 32–33; see in this connection Hirth, "Heine und Börne," p. 38.

82. E, 7, 26.

83. E, 7, 27.

84. E, 7, 73–75.

85. See Houben, 198–99

86. E, 7, 39.

87. E, 7, 22, 29–30, 32, 77.

88. See E, 7, 185–86.

89. See Hirth, *5*, 293–94.

90. E, 7, 72–73.

91. See the remarks on this subject in *Französische Zustände* (E, *5*, 37–38) and the much quoted and misquoted passage from the French preface to *Lutezia* (E, *6*, 572); a similar remark occurs in the text of *Lutezia* (E, *6*, 239).

92. Bock, *Ludwig Börne*, pp. 353–54.

93. E, 7, 25.

94. For pertinent quotations, see W, *8*, 608–09.

95. E, *3*, 393.

96. To Varnhagen, Jan. 3, 1846; Hirth, *3*, 36–37.

97. E, *4*, 185, 208.

98. Sternberg, p. 199
99. E, *7*, 52.
100. Cf. on this point Krüger, "Die freie Kunst," p. 24.
101. E, *7*, 97. Two years before *Börne,* in *Der Schwabenspiegel* (E, *7*, 334), Heine tried to argue that his tactical shifts were due to the complications of the cause of freedom, but as usual he remains vague about specific issues.
102. E, *7*, 41.
103. E, *2*, 429.
104. E, *7*, 66.
105. E, *7*, 86.
106. E, *7*, 88–89.
107. E.g., Bock, *Ludwig Börne,* pp. 346, 348.
108. Ras, pp. 120–21.
109. E, *7*, 44–45.
110. E, *7*, 105–06.
111. E, *7*, 106.
112. E, *7*, 126–27; verbatim E, *4*, 279–81.
113. E, *7*, 128–29.
114. E, *7*, 129–31.
115. E, *7*, 132. See, for example, Glossy, *Literarische Geheimberichte,* Part 1, pp. 173, 312.
116. E, *7*, 133–34
117. Krüger, "Die freie Kunst," pp. 37, 53.
118. E, *7*, 135.
119. E, *7*, 137.
120. This interpretation seems to me preferable to that proposed by H. G. Reissner, "Heinrich Heine's Tale of the 'Captive Messiah,'" *Der Friede. Idee und Verwirklichung. The Search for Peace. Festgabe für Adolf Leschnitzer* (Heidelberg, 1961), pp. 327–40.
121. See Paul Gottfried, "Catholic Romanticism in Munich 1826–1834" (diss. Yale, 1967), pp. 220–33.
122. Marcuse, *Revolutionär und Patriot,* p. 170.
123. Ibid., pp. 299–300.

CHAPTER 10

1. E, *2*, 351.
2. E, *2*, 347, n. 1.
3. Hirth, *2*, 435–36.
4. W, *2*, 411.
5. E², *3*, 13.
6. To Kolb, July 3, 1841; Hirth, *2*, 390–91. Heine's studies of the Roland material go back a number of years before that. See Mücke, *Heinrich Heines Beziehungen,* pp. 54–55.
7. To Campe, Feb. 20, 1844; Hirth, *2*, 502.
8. To Campe, Apr. 17, 1844; Hirth, *2*, 506.
9. Hans Kaufmann, *Politisches Gedicht und klassische Dichtung. Heinrich Heine. Deutschland. Ein Wintermärchen* (Berlin, 1959), p. 64. See also Georg Lukács, "Heine und die ideologische Vorbereitung der achtundvierziger Revolution," *Aufbau, 12* (1956), 103–18.

10. E, *3,* 110.
11. L. Reynaud, "La source française d''Atta Troll,'" *Revue germanique, 10* (1914), 145–59.
12. E, *2,* 349–50.
13. Legras, *Henri Heine Poète,* p. 265.
14. E, *4,* 346.
15. A detailed criticism of Freiligrath's exotic manner was found in Heine's posthumous papers (E, *7,* 423–25).
16. E, *2,* 353–54. He also praised Freiligrath again in 1855 in the preface to the second edition of *De la France* (E, *4,* 570).
17. E, *2,* 352–53
18. E, *2,* 524
19. On this important feature of Heine's rhythm, cf. L. L. Hammerich, *National og fremmed. Om den rytmiske teknik hos Heine og Platen* (Copenhagen, 1918).
20. E, *7,* 262; Hirth, *1* 434.
21. Hirth, *3,* 35–37
22. Prawer, *TS,* p. 65.
23. E, *2,* 360.
24. E, *2,* 370.
25. E, *2,* 375.
26. E, *2,* 391.
27. E, *2,* 360–61.
28. E, *2,* 384.
29. Adolf Paul, "Heinrich Heines 'Atta Troll'—eine literarisch-politische Satire," *Zeitschrift für deutsche Philologie, 56* (1931), 268.
30. E, *2,* 385, 388.
31. E, *2,* 417.
32. E, *2,* 382.
33. E, *2,* 382–83.
34. E, *2,* 385.
35. E, *2,* 387–88; cf, Prawer, *TS,* p. 81.
36. E, *2,* 387.
37. E, *2,* 402.
38. Prawer, *TS,* p. 85.
39. E, *2,* 391, 392, 395, 396.
40. Philipp F. Veit, "Heine's Imperfect Muses in *Atta Troll:* Biographical Romance or Literary Symbolism," *Germanic Review, 39* (1964), 273.
41. E, *4,* 174.
42. Veit, "Heine's Imperfect Muses," p. 275.
43. E, *4,* 325–27. See below, Chapter 11, p. 329.
44. Veit, "Heine's Imperfect Muses," p. 275.
45. E, *4,* 388. Cf. the poem *Die Wahlverlobten* (E, *2,* 44–45).
46. Veit, "Heine's Imperfect Muses," p. 278.
47. E, *2,* 403.
48. E, *2,* 406–10.
49. E, *2,* 532–36.
50. For another reference to this style of King Ludwig's, see E, *6,* 258.
51. Hirth, *2,* 560.
52. H. G. Atkins, *Heine,* p. 176.

53. Andler, *La Poésie de Heine* p. 144.
54. Cf. Prawer, *TS*, p. 121.
55. L. L. Hammerich, *Heinrich Heine: Deutschland. Ein Wintermärchen* (2d ed. Copenhagen, 1946), p. 61.
56. E, *2*, 440–42.
57. Hammerich, *Heinrich Heine. Deutschland*, p. 80.
58. Prawer, *TS*, p. 126.
59. See especially ibid., pp. 123–24.
60. To Campe, Feb. 28, 1842; Hirth, *2*, 419.
61. E, *2*, 173–75.
62. E, *2*, 485.
63. Kaufmann, *Politisches Gedicht*, pp. 152–53, 156.
64. The variants in question are not in the apparatus to vol. *2* of Elster's first edition. They will be found in E, *7*, 629–30, more carefully organized in E², *3*, 426–28, and in W, *2*, 368–69.
65. E, *7*, 80–81.
66. E, *2*, 490.
67. See the effort to reconstruct the passage, E², *3*, 427.
68. Alfred Döblin, "Einleitung zu Heines 'Deutschland' und 'Atta Troll,'" *Aufsätze zur Literatur* (Olten and Freiburg im Breisgau, 1963), p. 279.
69. E, *2*, 433–4.
70. E, *2*, 435.
71. See Eberhard Galley, "Heine und der Kölner Dom," *Deutsche Vierteljahrsschrift*, *32* (1958), 99–110.

CHAPTER 11

1. Hirth, *1*, 172.
2. To Moser, Apr. 1, July 1, July 22, ca. Oct. 7, Dec. 14, 1825; Jan. 9, Feb. 14, 1826; Hirth, *1*, 201, 215, 218–19, 228, 244, 250, 252.
3. To Moser, Apr. 1, 1825; Hirth, *1*, 201.
4. To Campe, July 17 or 18, 1840; Hirth, *2*, 355, 357–58.
5. E, *4*, 488.
6. Heine, *Der Rabbi von Bacherach*, ed. Erich Loewenthal (Berlin, 1937), p. 100. See also Adolf Strodtmann, *Heine's Leben*, *1*, 391, n. 309, and M. Bienenstock, *Das jüdische Element in Heines Werken. Ein kritische-asthetischer Beitrag zur Heine-Frage* (Leipzig, 1910), p. 198.
7. Strodtmann, *Heine's Leben*, *1*, 391, n. 309; Loewenthal, *Der Rabbi*, p. 101. Cf. Hirth, *4*, 89.
8. Hirth, "Wie Heinrich Heine las," *Heinrich Heine. Bausteine*, p. 96.
9. Franz Finke, "Zur Datierung des 'Rabbi von Bacherach,'" *Heine-Jahrbuch 1965*, pp. 26–32.
10. One problem is that the manuscript of the second chapter is not a draft but a fair copy (Finke, "Zur Datierung," p. 27). Finke has shown (p. 30) that the translation of the Passover song *Chad gadya* in Chapter 2 (E, *4*, 472) is taken from a *Haggada* published in 1839. Thus it is possible that even the second chapter in its present form dates from 1840.
11. Lion Feuchtwanger, *Heinrich Heines Fragment: "Der Rabbi von Bacherach." Eine kritische Studie* (Munich, 1907). His conclusions are generally followed by the

most recent interpretation of the work, Dorothy Lasher-Schlitt, "Heine's Unresolved Conflict and *Der Rabbi von Bacherach*," *Germanic Review*, 27 (1952), 173–87. I should say that the account of the dynamics of the work given by Helene Herrmann in *Heines Werke*, ed. Hermann Friedemann, *6*, 9–12, is more independent of Feuchtwanger and much closer to my own analysis, which was worked out before I had studied Herrmann's.

12. Feuchtwanger, *Heines Fragment*, p. 88.

13. Ibid., p. 115.

14. Ibid., p. 107.

15. Ibid., p. 104, n. 288. This formulation seems somewhat alien to Heines's thinking.

16. Lasher-Schlitt, p. 181.

17. One of the most admirable features of Israel Tabak's *Judaic Lore in Heine: The Heritage of a Poet* (Baltimore, Md., 1948) is his study of Heine's Romantic treatment of Jewish subjects (pp. 167–86). See also Tabak's "Jewish 'Volkstum' and Romanticism in Heine," *Monatshefte*, *33* (1941), 289–307.

18. E, *4*, 460.

19. E, *4*, 458.

20. Manfred Windfuhr, "Heines Fragment eines Schelmenromans *'Aus den Memoiren des Herren von Schnabelewopski'*" *Heine-Jahrbuch 1967*, pp. 21–37.

21. E, 7, 489.

22. Walter Höllerer, *Zwischen Klassik und Moderne* (Stuttgart, 1958), p. 68.

23. Cf. the interpretation by Bürger, "Der Essay bei Heinrich Heine," p. 58.

24. E, *4*, 10–12.

25. Hirth, *1*, 244.

26. See E, *3*, 83; Wadepuhl, "Heines Memoiren," *Heine-Studien*, p. 156; Houben, p. 155.

27. For the missing stanzas, see E, *4*, 5–9.

28. E, *4*, 109.

29. E, *3*, 101.

30. See Loewenthal, Heine, *Der Rabbi*, pp. 148–58; Mücke, *Heinrich Heines Beziehungen*, pp. 101–03; Claude Owen, "Heinrich Heines Kenntnisse der Weltliteratur ohne Berücksichtigung der deutschen Literatur" (M.A. Thesis, University of Alberta, 1961), pp. 195–96.

31. E, *4*, 116.

32. E, *4*, 120.

33. H. H. Houben, *Jungdeutscher Sturm und Drang* (Leipzig, 1911), p. 170.

34. Jeannette Wohl, ed., *Ludwig Börne's Urtheil über H. Heine* (Frankfurt am Main, 1840), p. 74.

35. E, 7, 8.

36. Helmut Ernst Ruhrig, "Heinrich Heine. Beiträge zur Bestimmung seines ironischen Humors," (diss. Freiburg im Breisgau, 1953), p. 194.

37. Hirth, *2*, 91.

38. See Wadepuhl, "Eine unveröffentlichte Episode aus Heines 'Florentinischen Nächten,'" *Heine-Studien*, pp. 109–10. Heine did so because Campe would not try to publish the book without submitting it to censorship. See to Campe, Mar. 8, Mar. 14, Mar. 22, 1836; to Baron Johann Georg Cotta, Mar. 28, Mar. 29, 1836; Hirth, *2*, 119–26.

39. To Campe, Mar. 8, 1836; Hirth, *2*, 119.

40. Hirth, *2,* 134
41. Hirth, *2,* 140.
42. Wadepuhl, "Eine unveröffentlichte Episode," pp. 111–13.
43. Ibid., pp. 110–11.
44. E, *4,* 324, 331.
45. E, *4,* 361, 369, 376.
46. E, *4,* 378.
47. E, *3,* 182. Cf. a similar remark on Clauren in *Gedanken und Einfälle* (E, *7,* 416).
48. W. Rudow, "Ein noch nicht erklärtes Werk Heines," *Internationale Litteraturberichte, 2* (1895), 346–47.
49. E, *4,* 335–39.
50. See Houben, pp. 252–55.
51. See Hirth, *5,* 111–12.
52. To Ernst Christian August Keller, Apr. 27, 1822; Hirth *1,* 39.
53. See Houben, pp. 154–55.
54. E, *4,* 350.
55. E, *4,* 328.
56. See to Sethe, Oct. 27, 1816; Hirth, *1,* 9.
57. E, *4,* 423–24; cf. W, *6,* 549.
58. E, *4,* 348.
59. E, *4,* 331.
60. See Holzhausen, *Heinrich Heine und Napoleon I.,* p. 184. The grotesque aspect of this section is well analyzed by Jennings, *The Ludicrous Demon,* pp. 36–42.
61. E, *4,* 358.
62. E, *4,* 377.
63. See Houben, p. 154.
64. For Heine's sources, see W. *6,* 551. See also Friedrich Hirth, *Johann Peter Lyser. Der Dichter, Maler, Musiker* (Munich and Leipzig, 1911), p. 75–76.
65. Walter Silz, "Heine's Synaesthesia," *PMLA, 57* (1942), 477.
66. See Steven Paul Scher, *Verbal Music: Literary Evocation of Music in Works by Wackenroder, Tieck, Hoffmann, Heine, and Thomas Mann* (New Haven, 1968), pp. 85–86.
67. Houben, pp. 209–210. Börne made a similar observation (Houben, pp. 213–14).
68. E, *3,* 250–52.
69. See Otto G. Graf, "Heine and the Muse of Music," *Germanic Review, 25* (1950), 198–209.
70. W, *6,* 552.
71. Silz, "Heine's Synaesthesia," pp. 473–77.
72. Ibid., p. 477.
73. E, *4,* 332.
74. E, *1,* 51–52.
75. E, *4,* 476–77.
76. Heine, *Zeitungsberichte über Musik und Malerei,* ed. Michael Mann, p. 13.
77. Scher, pp. 93–95.
78. Cf. E, *4,* 559 with E, *4,* 345.
79. Cf. *Faust,* E, *6,* 488, and *Englische Fragmente,* E, *3,* 458.

80. Scher, p. 91.
81. Ibid., p. 94.
82. E, *4*, 348.
83. Jennings, *The Ludicrous Demon*, p. 46.

CHAPTER 12

1. Prawer, *TS*, pp. 149–58. See also Fairley's discussion of dance motifs, *Heinrich Heine: An Interpretation*, pp. 34–46.
2. See Mücke, *Heinrich Heines Beziehungen*, p. 107, and Eberhard Galley, "Heinrich Heines Privatbibliothek," *Heine-Jahrbuch 1962*, pp. 100, 105.
3. See Carl Enders, "Heinrich Heines Faustdichtungen. Der Tanz als Deutungs- und Gestaltungsmittel seelischer Erlebnisse," *Zeitschrift für deutsche Philologie*, *74* (1955), 375.
4. To Baron Cotta, Nov. 11, 1828; Hirth, *1*, 378.
5. E, *6*, 473.
6. Benjamin Lumley, *Reminiscences of the Opera* (London, 1864), p. 199.
7. Niehaus, *Himmel Hölle und Trikot. Heinrich Heine und das Ballett* (Munich, 1959), pp. 53–54.
8. Ibid., pp. 55–57.
9. Werner Egk, *Abraxas. Ein Faustballett. Textbuch* (Mainz, 1950). See also Enders, pp. 381–92.
10. For an account of this transaction, see Gerhard Weiss, "Die Entstehung von Heines 'Doktor Faust,'" *Heine Jahrbuch 1966*, pp. 41–57. Cf. also Heinz Moenkemeyer, "Die deutschen Erstdrucke von Heines 'Doktor Faust,'" *Heine-Jahrbuch 1966*, pp. 58–67.
11. *Lutezia* text E, *6*, 294–300; original article in Heine, *Zeitungsberichte*, ed. Michael Mann, pp. 130–36.
12. E, *6*, 296.
13. E, *6*, 297.
14. E, *6*, 298–99.
15. E, *6*, 299–300.
16. E, *4*, 357. See above, Chapter 11, pp. 330–31.
17. E, *4*, 391–92.
18. E, *6*, 101.
19. Mücke, *Heinrich Heines Beziehungen*, p. 150.
20. E, *6*, 109.
21. Cf. to Friedrich Merckel, Sept. 11, 1827, and to Rudolf Christiani, Sept. 19, 1827; Hirth, *1*, 322, 323.
22. E, *6*, 495–96.
23. To Moser, Oct. 25, 1824, Apr. 1, 1825; to Varnhagen, May 14, 1826; to Friedrich Merckel, July 28, 1826; Hirth, *1*, 185, 202, 261, 273–74.
24. Houben, pp. 74–75.
25. E, *6*, 469.
26. Maximilian Heine, *Erinnerungen an Heinrich Heine*, p. 123.
27. To Campe, June 20, 1847; to Johann Vesque von Püttlingen, June 22, 1851; Hirth, *3*, 116–17, 287–88.
28. To Weerth, Nov. 5, 1851; Hirth, *3*, 335.

29. See Roderich Warkentin, "Gemeinsamkeit der Quellen für Goethes Paralipomena zur Walpurgisnacht und Heines Faust," *Zeitschrift für vergleichende Litteraturgeschichte,* n.s. 11 (1897), 30–35.

30. E, *6,* 496.

31. E, *6,* 504.

32. Oskar Walzel, *Heines Tanzpoem Der Doktor Faust* (Weimar, 1917), pp. 11–12.

33. E, *6,* 489–90.

34. Walzel, *Heines Tanzpoem,* p. 36.

35. Enders, p. 374.

CHAPTER 13

1. Hofrichter, *Heinrich Heine,* p. xi.

2. E, *1,* 323.

3. Hans Kaufmann, "Heines Schönheitsbegriff und die Revolution von 1848," *Weimarer Beiträge, 6* (1960), 276.

4. Hermann J. Weigand, "Heine's Return to God," *Modern Philology, 18* (1920/21), 309–42.

5. Rose, *Heinrich Heine. Two Studies,* pp. 94–156.

6. E, *4,* 256–57.

7. E, *4,* 276.

8. *Geständnisse,* E, *6,* 51; to Laube, Feb. 7, 1850; to Campe, June 1, 1850; Hirth, *3,* 198, 216–17; Houben, p. 669; *Nachwort zum "Romanzero,"* E, *1,* 485; last will and testament, E, *7,* 522.

9. Weigand, "Heine's Return to God," p. 316.

10. E, *2,* 126.

11. E, *7,* 400.

12. E, *7,* 537.

13. E, *1,* 488–89; cf. to Immanuel Hermann Fichte, Oct. 6, 1851; Hirth, *3,* 318.

14. E, *1,* 487.

15. E, *1,* 486.

16. Houben, p. 784

17. Weigand, "Heine's Return to God," p. 329.

18. Ibid., p. 337.

19. Butler, *Heinrich Heine,* p. 228.

20. Weigand, "Heine's Return to God," p. 324.

21. E, *6,* 126.

22. Houben, p. 596.

23. Weigand, "Heine's Return to God," p. 313.

24. Zvi Kolitz, "Yossel Rakover's Appeal to God," *The Tiger Beneath the Skin* (New York, 1947), pp. 91–95. I am indebted to Rabbi Richard J. Israel of Yale for this reference.

25. E, *3,* 490–94

26. E², *1,* 205

27. E², *2,* 14.

28. Prawer, *TS,* p. 211.

29. The source is given in full in E, *1,* 478–80.

30. For echoes of Gautier, see Legras, *Henri Heine Poète,* p. 352.

31. E², *2,* 9.

32. See Hella Gebhard, "Interpretation der 'Historien' aus Heines 'Romanzero,'" (diss. Erlangen, 1956), p. 25.
33. Prawer, *TS,* p. 156.
34. Gebhard, p. 33.
35. Hofrichter, *Heinrich Heine,* p. 131.
36. For an analysis, see Gebhard, p. 39.
37. E, *4,* 504.
38. Killy, "Mein Pferd für'n gutes Bild," p. 113.
39. Prawer, *TS,* p. 165.
40. Gebhard, p. 49.
41. Prawer, *TS,* p. 171.
42. E, *7,* 83–84.
43. See Gebhard, p. 61.
44. Prawer, *TS,* p. 202.
45. The source is quoted in E, *7,* 624–25.
46. Hammerich, "Trochäen bei Heinrich Heine," p. 405.
47. Quoted E^2, *2,* 353.
48. Seeger, "Der Erzähler in Heines Balladen und Romanzen," p. 66.
49. E, *1,* 364.
50. Börries Freiherr von Münchhausen, "Der Dichter Firdusi," *Meisterballaden* (2d ed. Stuttgart, 1958), pp. 55–66; the essay originally appeared in *Das Literarische Echo,* *22* (1919/20), cols. 15–21, and then in the first edition of *Meisterballaden* (Berlin and Leipzig, 1923), pp. 59–72.
51. Ibid., p. 58.
52. Ibid., p. 65.
53. Werner Psaar, "Zur Deutung Heinescher Gedichte im Deutschunterricht. Probleme und Versuche," *Heine-Jahrbuch 1967,* p. 118.
54. *Goethes Werke,* ed. Erich Trunz, et al., 2 (Hamburg, 1949), 153.
55. E, *1,* 365.
56. See Gebhard, p. 100.
57. See to Michael Schloss, Feb. 15, 1851; Hirth, *3,* 271–72, and the note on the letter, Hirth, *6,* 106–07.
58. The pertinent passage is supplied also in E, *1,* 493.
59. Gebhard, pp. 102–05.
60. Prawer, *TS,* p. 221.
61. Georg J. Plotke, *Heinrich Heine als Dichter des Judentums* (Dresden, 1913), p. 82.
62. Herman Salinger, "Helping Heinrich Heine Explain his Archetypal 'Night Journey' Poem," *Literature and Psychology, 13* (1963), 30–36.
63. Hans Kaufmann, "Heines Schönheitsbegriff," *Weimarer Beiträge, 6* (1960), 274–75.
64. See, for example, Kurt Weinberg, *Henri Heine. "Romantique défroqué." Héraut du symbolisme français* (New Haven and Paris, 1954).
65. For a discussion of themes and elements, see Hermann, *Studien zu Heines Romanzero,* pp. 14–27
66. E, *1,* 412
67. Cf. Gebhard, p. 111.
68. Prawer, *TS,* 146–47.
69. To Campe, Sept. 20, 1851; Hirth, *3,* 309.

70. Killy, "Mein Pferd für'n gutes Bild," p. 102.
71. W, *3,* 480; E^2, *2,* 358.
72. See to Varnhagen, Jan. 3, 1846; Hirth, *3,* 36–37.
73. E, *7,* 43.
74. See H. H. Houben, *Verbotene Literatur von der klassischen Zeit bis zur Gegenwart* (Berlin, 1924–28), *1,* 393–94, 414, 424–26.
75. Butler, *Heinrich Heine,* p. 225.
76. Prawer, *TS,* 179–81.
77. E, *3,* 144.
78. Prawer, *TS,* p. 173.
79. E, *2,* 220–22.
80. E^2, *1,* 416.
81. E^2, *2,* 360.
82. E^2, *2,* 363.
83. My italics.
84. E, *1,* 448.
85. Cf. to Moser, July 28, 1826; Hirth, *1,* 285; E, *3,* 416; E, *6,* 513.
86. See E^2, *2,* 362.
87. W, *3,* 497.
88. See W, *3,* 497 for some of the historical background.
89. See Bienenstock, *Das jüdische Element in Heines Werken,* p. 173.

CHAPTER 14

1. E^2, *1,* 9*.
2. W, *3,* 209–66.
3. E^2, *2,* 187–235.
4. E^2, *2,* 181.
5. Matthew Arnold, *Heinrich Heine* (Reprint from the *Cornhill Magazine,* Aug. 1863) (Philadelphia, 1863), pp. 50–51.
6. To Campe, Sept. 10, 1851; Hirth, *3,* 306.
7. Prawer, *TS,* p. 225.
8. E, *1,* 488–89.
9. E, *2,* 217–20.
10. E, *2,* 147–48.
11. E, *2,* 43–44.
12. E, *2,* 154–56.
13. E, *2,* 156–58.
14. See to Campe, Aug. 12, 1852; Hirth, *3,* 405, and the evidence of a missing letter of Feb. 8, 1855; Hirth, *6,* 326; cf. E^2, *2,* 372.
15. Hirth, *3,* 405.
16. E, *2,* 148–50.
17. E, *2,* 150–51.
18. See Hirth, *5,* 89.
19. E, *2,* 117–21; he had already touched upon this topic bitterly in *Reise von München nach Genua* (E, *3,* 235).
20. Rudolf Höss, *Kommandant in Auschwitz. Autobiographische Aufzeichnungen* (Stuttgart, 1958).
21. Prawer, *TS,* pp. 244–45.

22. E, *2*, 215–17.
23. Cf. the observations by Butler, *Heinrich Heine,* p. 238, and Prawer, *TS,* p. 253.
24. Weigand, "Heine's Family Feud," pp. 70–106. Weigand's judgments against Heine should probably be revised somewhat in the light of the letters of Karl Heine that have recently turned up. See Fritz H. Eisner, "Verschollene Briefe an Heine. Ein neuer Fund," *Heine-Jahrbuch 1966,* pp. 68–89.
25. Weigand, "Heine's Family Feud," p. 105.
26. E, *1*, 85.
27. Heine, *Mein wertvollstes Vermächtnis, Religion, Leben, Dichtung,* ed. Felix Stössinger (Zurich, 1950), pp. 627–28.
28. Werner Kraft, "Heine und die Hiobsfrage," *Augenblicke der Dichtung. Kritische Betrachtungen* (Munich, 1964), p. 42. See also Walter Weiss, *Enttäuschter Pantheismus. Zur Weltgestaltung der Dichtung in der Restaurationszeit* (Dornbirn, 1962), p. 180.
29. Kraft, "Heine und die Hiobsfrage," p. 42.
30. E, *2*, 97–98.
31. E, *1*, 390.
32. E^2, *2*, 366–67.
33. Rose, *The Early Love Poetry,* p. 76.
34. This theme recurs in *Die Lehre* (E, *2*, 112–13).
35. E^2 *2*, 369; the poem is too early, as Fränkel pointed out *contra* Strodtmann, to be addressed to Camille Selden (W, *3*, 508).
36. E, *1*, 8–9.
37. E, *2*, 97.
38. Strodtmann, in this respect, as in many others, is a refreshing exception. See *Heine's Leben, 2*, 235–42.
39. E, *5*, 346.
40. E, *2*, 41.
41. Cf. E^2, *2*, 378.
42. E, *2*, 42.
43. E, *2*, 42–43.
44. Houben, p. 400.
45. E, *2*, 110.
46. Cf. E^2, *2*, 380.
47. E, *2*, 89. As to the provenance of the title, see W, *3*, 533.
48. E, *2*, 186–87.
49. E, *2*, 210–15.
50. E, *2*, 210.
51. Prawer, *TS,* p. 272.
52. For a discussion of the historical background, see W, *3*, 513–14.
53. E. *2*, 126.
54. E, *2*, 127–28
55. E, *2*, 130.
56. E, *2*, 101.
57. E, *2*, 50–51.
58. Alfred Meissner, *Heinrich Heine. Erinnerungen* (2d ed. New York, 1856), p. 249.
59. Prawer, *TS,* pp. 259–62.

60. Prawer, *TS*, p. 260.
61. Ibid., p. 261.

APPENDIX 1

1. For an account of the traces of Heine in Düsseldorf, see Gerhart Söhn, *Heinrich Heine in seiner Vaterstadt Düsseldorf* (Düsseldorf, 1966).

2. Hans-Joachim Schoeps, "Ein unbekannter Agentenbericht über Heinrich Heine," *Heine-Jahrbuch 1967*, pp. 67–80. Manfred Windfuhr, a collaborator and frequent contributor, has since become a professor.

3. For the remarks of the French ambassador, André François-Ponçet, on the occasion, see "Weihereden auf Heinrich Heine," *Das Tor, 19* (1953), 110–13; see also Fritz Strich, "Heinrich Heine und sein Denkmal in Düsseldorf. Eine Deutung," *Das Tor, 19* (1953), 126–30.

4. H. H. Biermann-Ratjen, *'Festrede—Heine nach 100 Jahren,' Gedenkfeier aus Anlaß des 100. Todestages von Heinrich Heine* (Hamburg, 1956), not paginated.

5. Eberhard Galley, "Heine und sein Werk in Deutschland nach 1945. Eine kritische Übersicht," *Düsselodorfer Jahrbuch, 50* (1960), 151–52.

6. Galley, "Vor Heine wird nicht gewarnt," *Die Welt der Literatur* (May 27, 1965), pp. 261–62.

7. Wilhelm Höck, "Deutsche Dichter im Wandel des Urteils. Eine Aufsatzreihe (VI). Heinrich Heine," *Der junge Buchhandel* (1964), no. 12 (Beilage zum Beiblatt no. 97, Dec. 4, 1964), p. 189.

8. hwb, "Gewerkschaftler Heinrich Heine, Traurige Ergebnisse einer Schülerumfrage," *Die Welt* (Feb. 16, 1956), p. 4.

9. Pierre Abraham, "Pourquoi Heine?" *Europe, 34*, nos. 125/26 (May/June, 1956), 3–11.

10. G. H. Theunissen, "Vom Wesen des rheinischen Journalisten. Ein Versuch über Görres und Heine," *Dichtung und Volkstum, 39* (1938), 51–60

11. Theunissen, "Wesen des Journalismus. Versuch über Görres und Heine," *Rheinischer Merkur* (Oct. 19, 1951), p. 7.

12. Ludwig Marcuse, *Heinrich Heine in Selbstzeugnissen und Bilddokumenten*, Rowohlts Monographien, no. 41 (Hamburg, 1960). The original title was *Heinrich Heine. Ein Leben zwischen Gestern und Morgen* (Berlin, 1932). A revised English translation appeared as *Heine. A Life Between Love and Hate* (New York, 1933).

13. Sol Liptzin, *The English Legend of Heinrich Heine* (New York, 1954), p. 159.

14. See Demetz, *Marx, Engels*, pp. 159–69.

15. E, *6*, 572.

16. H. S. Reiss, "The Study of Heine: Retrospect and Prospect," *German Quarterly, 32* (1959), 3–10.

17. Victor, *Marx und Heine*, p. 151.

18. Werner Ilberg, *Unser Heine. Eine kritische Würdigung* (Berlin, 1952), p. 90.

19. Ibid., p. 101.

20. Ibid., pp. 48–49.

21. Ibid., p. 106.

22. Ibid., p. 54.

23. Ibid., p. 75.

24. Ibid., pp. 85–86, 129–30, 165–66.

25. Ibid., p. 145.

26. Ibid., p. 144.
27. Ibid., p. 167.
28. Hans Mayer, "Anmerkungen zu einem Gedicht von Heinrich Heine," *Sinn und Form, 3,* no. 4 (1951), 177–84.
29. Gerhard Schmitz, *Über die ökonomischen Anschauungen in Heines Werken* (Weimar, 1960), p. 6.
30. Ibid., pp. 6–10.
31. Fritz Mende, *Heinrich Heine im Literaturunterricht* (Berlin, 1962), pp. 42–43.
32. Schmitz, p. 34.
33. Ibid., p. 38.
34. Ibid., p. 55.
35. Ibid., pp. 66–67.
36. Ibid., pp. 84–99.
37. Ibid., p. 109.
38. Heine, *Werke und Briefe,* ed. Hans Kaufmann (Berlin, 1961–64).
39. See Galley, "Heine und zweimal Deutschland," *Die Welt der Literatur* (May 14, 1964), p. 163, and "Vor Heine wird nicht gewarnt," ibid. (May 27, 1965), pp. 261–62.
40. Heine, *Sämtliche Werke,* ed. Hans Kaufmann, Kindler Taschenbücher nos. 1007–28 (Munich, 1964).
41. See Galley, "Vor Heine wird nicht gewarnt," and Christoph Trilse, "Heine-Ausgabe kritisch betrachtet," *Der Morgen* (Berlin, Apr. 10, 1965), p. 4.
42. Heine, *Werke und Briefe,* ed. Kaufmann, *10,* 7.
43. Ibid., p. 20.
44. Ibid., p. 18.
45. Mende, *Heinrich Heine im Literaturunterricht,* p. 74
46. Heine, *Werke und Briefe,* ed. Kaufmann, *10,* 34.
47. Ibid., p. 37.
48. Ibid., p. 39.
49. Ibid., pp. 93–94.
50. Ibid., p. 109.
51. Ibid., pp. 122–23.
52. Ibid., p. 7.
53. Joachim Müller, "Heines Nordseegedichte. Eine Sprach- und Stilanalyse des ersten Teils," *Wissenschaftliche Zeitschrift der Friedrich-Schiller-Universität Jena. Gesellschafts- und Sprachwissenschaftliche Reihe, 6* (1956/57), 191. Cf. Müller, "Romanze und Ballade. Die Frage ihrer Strukturen, an zwei Gedichten von Heinrich Heine dargelegt," ibid., 7 (1957/58), 377–85; reprinted in *Germanisch-romanische Monatsschrift, 40* (1959), 140–56.
54. Heine, *Werke und Briefe,* ed. Kaufmann, *10,* 98.
55. Ibid., pp. 139–40.
56. Critiques of this study have been made by Galley, "Heine und sein Werk," pp. 158–61, and S. S. Prawer in *German Life and Letters,* n.s. 13 (1959), 76–77.
57. Kaufmann, *Politisches Gedicht und klassische Dichtung,* p. 77.
58. Ibid., p. 116.
59. Ibid., p. 169.
60. Ibid., p. 193.
61. A description and photographs of the monument are given in an article by

the sculptor, Waldemar Grzimek: "Gedanken zu meinem Heine-Denkmal," pp. 310–14.

APPENDIX 2

1. Golo Mann, "Zur Geschichte der deutschen Juden," *Neue Rundschau, 77* (1966), 563.

2. For a valuable review of Heine's place in the historiography of literature, see Harry Slochower, "Attitudes Towards Heine in German Literary Criticism," *Jewish Social Studies, 3* (1941), 355–74.

3. Richard Wagner, *Das Judenthum in der Musik* (Leipzig, 1869), pp. 31–32.

4. Robert Launay, *Figures Juives* (Paris, 1921), p. 8.

5. Ibid., p. 112.

6. Hermann Pongs, "Neue Aufgaben der Literaturwissenschaft II. 1. Masse," *Dichtung und Volkstum, 38* (1937), 275.

7. Spann, *Heine,* p. 56

8. I shall refer here to the most recent English edition, Max Brod, *Heinrich Heine: The Artist in Revolt* (New York, 1957).

9. Ibid., p. 218.

10. Ibid., p. 220.

11. Ibid., p. 222.

12. W, *1,* xxxii–xxxviii.

13. Brod, pp. 222–27.

14. See Hirth, *5,* 121–22; Houben, pp. 259, 279–80.

15. Houben, p. 279.

16. Solomon Liptzin, *Germany's Stepchildren* (New York, 1944), pp. 90–91.

17. Harry Steinhauer, "Heinrich Heine," *Antioch Review, 16* (1956/57), 445.

18. Ludwig Müller von Hausen, "Heinrich Heine bei jüdischer Beleuchtung," *Deutsche Tageszeitung* (Berlin, May 5, 1910).

19. Hans R. Fischer, "Will das Judenthum das Heine-Denkmal?" *Die Gegenwart* (Berlin, Aug. 4, 1906), pp. 76–77.

20. Hermann Schiff, *Heinrich Heine und der Neuisraelitismus. Briefe an Adolf Strodtmann* (Hamburg and Leipzig, 1866).

21. Ibid., p. 9.

22. To Baroness Rothschild, May 14, 1851; to Betty Heine and Charlotte Embden, July 9, 1851; Hirth, *3,* 284, 288–89.

23. Schiff, pp. 11, 12, 47.

24. For a critique of some of the weaknesses in Tabak's argument, see Hugo Bieber, "Recent Literature on Heine's Attitude toward Judaism," *Historia Judaica, 10* (1948), 182.

25. E, *4,* 453.

26. To Campe, Sept. 7, 1851; Hirth, *3,* 303.

27. E, *1,* 473.

28. Gustav Karpeles, *Heinrich Heine und das Judenthum* (Breslau, 1868), p. 14.

29. Ibid., p. 18.

30. Ibid., p. 24.

31. Max Jungmann, *Heinrich Heine als Nationaljude. Eine kritische Synthese* (Berlin, 1896), p. 48.

32. J. Chotzner, "The Influence of Hebrew Literature on Heinrich Heine," *Hebrew Humour and Other Essays* (London, 1905), p. 169.
33. Bienenstock, *Das jüdische Element,* pp. 1–2.
34. Ibid., p. 78.
35. Ibid., p. 3.
36. Ibid., pp. 105–19.
37. Ibid., p. 137.
38. Ibid., p. 140.
39. Tabak, *Judaic Lore in Heine,* p. 3.
40. Plotke, *Heine als Dichter,* pp. 37–38.
41. Ibid., p. 23.
42. Ibid., p. 45
43. Ibid., p. 92.
44. Tabak, pp. 4–5.
45. Plotke, p. 75.
46. Ibid., p. 76.
47. Bernhard, *Welterlebnis,* pp. 20–23.
48. Alfred Goldschmidt (review of Plotke), *Im neuen Reich. Zeitschrift des Centralvereins deutscher Staatsbürger jüdischen Glaubens, 19* (1913), 500–03.
49. Bismarck adroitly managed to quash the issue. See Liptzin, *Germany's Stepchildren,* p. 97.
50. Gerschom Scholem, "Juden und Deutsche," *Neue Rundschau,* 77 (1966), 558.
51. Ibid., p. 554.
52. Ibid., p. 551.
53. *C. V.-Zeitung. Organ des Central-Vereins deutscher Staatsbürger jüdischen Glaubens, 6,* nos. 31/32 (Aug. 5, 1927), p. 433.
54. Ibid., pp. 454–55.
55. Kraus, *Heine und die Folgen.*
56. *C. V.-Zeitung,* p. 456.
57. Ibid., p. 456; emphasis in the original.
58. Ibid.
59. Samuel Gordon, "Heine, the German and the Jew," *Contemporary Review, 127* (1925), 230–31, 234.
60. Untermeyer, *Heinrich Heine,* pp. 337–38.
61. Ibid., pp. 292–93.
62. Ibid., p. 384.
63. Fritz Strich, "Goethe und Heine. Ein der Jüdischen Vereinigung Zürich 1947 gehaltener Vortrag zur Feier von Heines 150. Geburtstag," *Der Dichter und die Zeit* (Bern, 1947), p. 194.
64. Strich, "Goethe und Heine," pp. 208–09.
65. Hannah Arendt, "Heinrich Heine: Schlemihl und Traumweltherrscher," *Sechs Essays* (Heidelberg, 1948), p. 88.
66. Ibid., p. 89.
67. Ibid., p. 90.
68. Arendt, "The Jew as Pariah: A Hidden Tradition," *Jewish Social Studies, 6* (1944), 99–122.
69. Hugo Bieber, "Recent literature on Heine's Attitude toward Judaism," *Historia Judaica, 10* (1948), pp. 178–79.
70. Heine, *Mein wertvollstes Vermächtnis,* ed. Felix Stössinger, p. lxxxix.

71. Ibid., p. xv.
72. Ibid., p. xvii.
73. Ibid., p. lxxxv.
74. Ibid., pp. lxxxv–lxxxvi.
75. Stössinger, "Heines Götter," *Neue Schweizer Rundschau,* n.s. *18* (1950/51), 418.
76. Heine, *Mein wertvollstes Vermächtnis,* ed. Stössinger, p. xciii.
77. Ibid., p. xcviii.
78. Ernst Alker, "Heine-Probleme. Randnotizen," *Orbis Litterarum, 11* (1956), 140–42, 144–45.
79. Ibid., p. 144.
80. Alfred Werner, "Heinrich Heine. Jewish Nationalist," *Judaism, 5* (1956), 76–84.
81. Jonas Fränkel, "Heine, der Jude," *Israelitisches Wochenblatt für die Schweiz* (Feb. 17, 1956, special printing), not paginated.
82. See especially E, *4,* 226.
83. Liptzin, *Germany's Stepchildren,* p. 137

Bibliography

Heine's Works

Buch der Lieder, nebst einer Nachlese nach den ersten Drucken oder Handschriften, ed. Ernst Elster, Deutsche Litteraturdenkmale des 18. und 19. Jahrhunderts, *27,* Heilbronn, 1887.

Sämtliche Werke, ed. Ernst Elster, 7 vols. Leipzig and Vienna, [1887–90].

Sämtliche, Werke, ed. Oskar Walzel, Jonas Fränkel, Ludwig Krähe, Albert Leitzmann, and Julius Petersen, 10 vols. Leipzig, 1910–15. Index Volume, Leipzig, 1920.

Werke, ed. Ernst Elster, 4 vols. (incomplete), Leipzig, [1924].

Werke, ed. Hermann Friedemann, Helene Herrmann, Erwin Kalischer, Raimund Pissin, and Veit Valentin, 2d ed. 15 vols. in 5 vols. Berlin, Leipzig, Vienna, and Stuttgart, [1927].

Werke, ed. Ewald A. Boucke, 12 vols. in 6 vols. Berlin, [1928–30].

Werke and Briefe, ed. Hans Kaufmann, 10 vols. Berlin, 1961–64.

Letters

Heine-Briefe, ed. Hans Daffis, 2 vols. Berlin, 1906–07.

Heine-Reliquien. Neue Briefe und Aufsätze Heinrich Heines, ed. Maximilian Freiherr von Heine-Geldern and Gustav Karpelcs, Berlin, 1911.

Briefwechsel, ed. Friedrich Hirth, 3 vols. Munich, 1914–20.

Briefe, ed. Friedrich Hirth [and Claire Hartgenbusch], 6 vols. Mainz, 1950–51.

Conversations

Gespräche mit Heine, ed. H. H. Houben, Frankfurt am Main, 1926.

Secondary Literature

Abraham, Pierre, "Pourquoi Heine?" *Europe, 34,* nos. 125/6 (May–June 1956), 3–11.

Adolf, Helen, "A Mid-Century Duel: Gottfried Keller and Heine," *Germanic Review, 28* (1953), 180–89.

Adorno, Theodor W., "Die Wunde Heine," in Adorno, *Noten zur Literatur, 1* (Frankfurt am Main, 1958), 144–53.

Alker, Ernst, "Heine-Probleme. Randnotizen," *Orbis Litterarum, 11* (1956), 138–49.

Allen, Philip Schuyler, "Studies in Popular Poetry. III: Heine and the 'Schnaderhüpfel,'" *The Decennial Publications of the University of Chicago: Investigations Representing the Departments,* 1st ser., *8* (Chicago, 1903), 144–55.

Anderle, Hans Peter, "DDR. Der Zensurapparat im Kopf," *Die Grenzen literarischer Freiheit,* ed. Dieter E. Zimmer (Hamburg, 1966), pp. 150–58.

Andler, Charles, *La Poésie de Heine,* [Paris], 1948.

Arendt, Hannah, "Heinrich Heine: Schlemihl und Traumweltdeuter," in Arendt, *Sechs Essays* (Heidelberg, 1948), pp. 84–91.

———, "The Jew as Pariah: A Hidden Tradition," *Jewish Social Studies, 6* (1944), 99–122.

Arnold, Matthew, *Heinrich Heine,* Reprint from the *Cornhill Magazine,* Aug. 1863, Philadelphia, 1863.

Arnsberg, Paul, "Heinrich Heine als linksintellektuelles 'Anti'-Symbol. Ein Bildersturm in vorigen Jahrhundert," *Tribüne, 2* (1963), 643–57.

Asbach, J., "Neue Beiträge zu einer Heine-Biographie," *Allgemeine Zeitung,* Beilage, no. 112 (May 16, 1900), pp. 4–6; no. 132 (June 11, 1900), pp. 4–5.

Atkins, H. G., *Heine,* London and New York, 1929.

Atkins, Stuart, "The Evaluation of Heine's *Neue Gedichte,*" *Wächter und Hüter. Festschrift für Hermann J. Weigand,* ed. Curt von Faber du Faur, Konstantin Reichardt, and Heinz Bluhm (New Haven, 1957), pp. 99–107.

———, "The First Draft of Heine's 'Für die Mouche,'" *Harvard Library Bulletin, 13* (1959), 415–43.

———, "The Unpublished Passages of Heine's Letter to Charlotte Embden, July 11, 1844," *Modern Language Notes, 76* (1961), 824–26.

Ayrault, Roger, "Le Symbolisme du décor dans le *Lyrisches Intermezzo,*" *Etudes Germaniques, 11* (1956), 105–13.

b, hw., "Gewerkschaftler Heinrich Heine. Traurige Ergebnisse einer Schülerumfrage," *Die Welt* (Feb. 16, 1956), p. 4.

B., M., "Was denkt die deutsche Akademie von Heinrich Heine?" *Das Schwarze Korps* (Oct. 31, 1935), p. 2.

Babler, Otto F., "Ein Heine-Gedicht als georgisches Volkslied," *Heine-Jahrbuch 1965,* pp. 64–67.

Bacon, Grace Mabel, *The Personal and Literary Relations of Heinrich Heine to Karl Immermann,* Ann Arbor, Mich., 1910.

Baer, Lydia, "Anklänge an Homer (nach Voß) in der *Nordsee* Heinrich Heines," *Journal of English and Germanic Philology, 29,* (1930), 1–17.

Baerlein, Henry, *Heine the Strange Guest,* London [1928].

Barto, P. S., "Sources of Heine's *Seegespenst,*" *Modern Language Notes, 32* (1917), 482–85.

Beissner, Friedrich, "Lesbare Varianten. Die Entstehung einiger Verse in Heines 'Atta Troll,'" *Festschrift Josef Quint,* ed. Hugo Moser, Rudolf Schützeichel, and Karl Stackmann (Bonn, 1964), pp. 15–23.

Belart, Urs, *Gehalt und Aufbau von Heinrich Heines Gedichtsammlungen,* Sprache und Dichtung. Forschungen zur Sprach- und Literaturwissenschaft, *38,* Bern, 1925.

Berendsohn, Walter A., "Heines 'Buch der Lieder.' Struktur- und Stilstudie," *Heine-Jahrbuch 1962,* pp. 26–38.

Bernhard, Maria Anna, *Welterlebnis und gestaltete Wirklichkeit in Heinrich Heines Prosaschriften,* Stuttgart, 1961.

Betz, Louis P., *Heine in Frankreich. Eine litterarhistorische Untersuchung,* Zurich, 1894.

Bianquis, Geneviève, "Heine et George Sand," *Etudes Germaniques, 11* (1956), 114–21.

———, *Henri Heine l'homme et l'œuvre,* Paris, 1948.

Bieber, Hugo, ed., *Heinrich Heine: A Biographical Anthology,* trans. Moses Hadas, Philadelphia, Pa., 1956.

———, "Recent Literature on Heine's Attitude Toward Judaism," *Historia Judaica, 10* (1948), 175–83.

Bienenstock, M., *Das jüdische Element in Heines Werken. Ein kritisch-ästhetischer Beitrag zur Heine-Frage,* Leipzig, 1910.

Biermann-Ratjen, H. H., *'Festrede—Heine nach 100 Jahren,' Gedenkfeier aus Anlaß des 100. Todestages von Heinrich Heine,* Hamburg, 1956.

Bock, Helmut, *Ludwig Börne. Vom Gettojuden zum Nationalschriftsteller,* Berlin, 1962.

———, "Die ökonomisch-politischen Auffassungen Heinrich Heines in den Briefen an die Augsburger Allgemeine Zeitung von 1840–1843," *Zeitschrift für Geschichtswissenschaft, 5* (1957), 826–35.

Bölsche, Wilhelm, "Heine im Abendrot seines Jahrhunderts," *Xenien,* (1908) no. 1, pp. 29–45.

———, *Heinrich Heine. Versuch einer ästhetisch-kritischen Analyse seiner Werke und seiner Weltanschauung,* Leipzig, 1888.

Börne, Ludwig, *Gesammelte Schriften,* Rybnik, 1884.

———, *Ludwig Börne's Urtheil über H. Heine. Ungedruckte Stellen aus den Pariser Briefen. Als Anhang: Stimmen über H. Heine's letztes Buch, aus Zeitblättern* [ed. Jeanette Strauss-Wohl], Frankfurt am Main, 1840.

Boucke, Ewald, "Heine im Dienste der 'Idee,' " *Euphorion, 16* (1909), 116–31, 434–60.

Bousquet, Jacques, *Les Thèmes du rêve dans la littérature romantique (France, Angleterre, Allemagne). Essai sur la naissance et l'évolution des images,* Paris, 1964.

Bramsted, Ernest K., *Aristocracy and the Middle-Classes in Germany: Social Types in German Literature (1830–1900)*, 2d ed. Chicago, Ill., 1964.

Brandes, Georg, *Ludwig Börne und Heinrich Heine. Zwei litterarische Charakterbilder,* Leipzig, 1896.

———, *Main Currents in Nineteenth Century Literature,* vol. 6: *Young Germany,* London and Paris, 1906.

Braun, Wilhelm Alfred, *Types of Weltschmerz in German Poetry,* New York, 1905.

Brauweiler, Ernst, *Heines Prosa. Beiträge zu ihrer Wesensbestimmung,* Bonner Forschungen, *9,* Berlin, 1915.

Brecht, Walther, "Heine, Platen, Immermann. (Aus einer Darstellung des 19. Jahrhunderts)," *Germanistische Forschungen. Festschrift anlässlich des 60semestrigen Stiftungsfestes des Wiener Akademischen Germanistenvereins* (Vienna, 1925), pp. 177–201.

Brinitzer, Carl, *Das streitbare Leben des Verlegers Julius Campe,* Hamburg, 1962.

Brod, Max, *Heinrich Heine: The Artist in Revolt,* New York, 1957.

Brokerhoff, Karl Heinz, "Zu Heinrich Heines Ironie," *Heine-Jahrbuch 1964,* pp. 37–55.

Brummack, Jürgen, "Heines Entwicklung zum satirischen Dichter," *Deutsche Vierteljahrsschrift, 41* (1967), 98–116.

Bürger, Peter, "Der Essay bei Heinrich Heine," diss. Munich, 1959.

Bulwer-Lytton. See Lytton.

Burkhard, Arthur, "Presenting the Rivals, Uhland and Heine," *German Quarterly,* 4 (1931), 56–80.

Butler, E. M., "Fragments of a Great Confession," *University of Toronto Quarterly, 25* (1955/56), 109–20.

———, "Heine and the Saint-Simonians: The Date of the Letters from Heligoland," *Modern Language Review, 18* (1923), 68–85.

———, "Heine in England and Matthew Arnold," *German Life and Letters,* n.s. *9* (1955/56), 157–65.

———, *Heinrich Heine: A Biography,* London, 1956.

———, *The Saint-Simonian Religion in Germany,* Cambridge, England, 1926.

———, *The Tyranny of Greece over Germany,* Cambridge, England, 1935.

Carlssohn, Erich, "Erinnerung an bedeutende Sammler (VIII). 'Heinrich Heine—Sammlung Meyer,' Düsseldorf," *Börsenblatt für den deutschen Buchhandel,* Frankfurt edition, *3* (1957), 578–81.

Chasles, Philarète, *Etudes sur l'Allemagne au XIXe siècle,* Paris, 1861.

Chiles, James Alburn, "Ueber den Gebrauch des Beiwortes in Heines Gedichten," *Journal of English and Germanic Philology, 7* (1902), no. 3, 1–60; no. 4, 1–53.

Chotzner, J., "The Influence of Hebrew Literature on Heinrich Heine," in Chotzner, *Hebrew Humour and Other Essays* (London, 1905), pp. 165–73.

Christmann, Helmut, "Heinrich Heine: Belsazar," *Wege zum Gedicht,* ed. Rupert Hirschenauer and Albrecht Weber (Munich and Zurich, 1963), *2,* 261–66.

Clarke, Margaret A., *Heine et la Monarchie de Juillet,* Paris, 1927.

C[olden], W[olfgang], "Heinerich, uns graut vor Dir. Zur Geschichte des Düsseldorfer Heine-Denkmals," *Heute und Morgen, 1* (1951), 73–75, 101–04, 132–34.

Colditz, Carl, "Über den Denunzianten," *Modern Language Quarterly, 6* (1945), 131–46.

Croce, Benedetto, *Poesia e non poesia,* Bari, 1923.

Cumings, Edgar C., "Echoes in Heine's *Gedanken und Einfälle,*" *Germanic Review, 13* (1938), 48–55.

———, "Parallel Passages in Heine's Poetry and Prose," *Germanic Review, 14* (1939), 284–90.

d, fr, "Nochmals Schloßlegende und Sozialistengesetz," *Vorwärts,* no. 131 (Mar. 11, 1920), p. [2].

———, "Schloßlegende und Sozialistengesetz," *Vorwärts,* no. 117 (Mar. 4, 1920), p. [2].

Demetz, Peter, "Ezra Pound's German Studies," *Germanic Review, 31* (1956), 279–82.

———, *Marx, Engels, and the Poets,* Chicago and London, 1967.

Dietze, Walter, *Junges Deutschland und deutsche Klassik,* Berlin, 1957.

Döblin, Alfred, "Einleitung zu Heines 'Deutschland' und 'Atta Troll,' " in Döblin, *Aufsätze zur Literatur* (Olten and Freiburg im Breisgau, 1963), pp. 273–80.

Dresch, Joseph, *Heine à Paris (1831–1856) d'après sa correspondence et les témoinages de ses contemporains,* Paris, 1956.

———, "Heine et la révolution de 1848," *Etudes Germaniques, 4* (1949), 39–47.

Dück, Hans-Udo, "Heinrich Heine: Die Wallfahrt nach Kevlaar," *Wege zum Gedicht,* ed. Rupert Hirschenauer and Albrecht Weber (Munich and Zurich, 1963), *2,* 270–77.

Ebert, Max, *Der Stil der Heineschen Jugendprosa,* Berlin, 1903.

Eckertz, Erich, "Heine und Börne," *Euphorion, 13* (1906), 136–37.

———, *Heine und sein Witz,* Literarhistorische Forschungen, *36,* Berlin, 1908.

Edschmid, Kasimir, *Heinrich Heine,* Reprint from *Jahrbuch 1955 der Deutschen Akademie,* Berlin, 1956.

Egk, Werner, *Abraxas. Ein Faustballett. Textbuch,* Mainz, 1950.

Ehrenzeller-Favre, Rotraud, *Loreley. Entstehung und Wandlung einer Sage,* Flensburg, 1948.

Eisner, F. H., "Echtes, Unechtes und Zweifelhaftes in Heines Werken," *Heine-Jahrbuch 1962,* pp. 50–69.

———, "Heine's Letters: A New Edition," *German Life and Letters,* n.s. *9* (1955/56), 220–25.

———, "Verschollene Briefe an Heine. Ein neuer Fund," *Heine-Jahrbuch 1966,* pp. 68–89.

Eliot, George, "German Wit: Heinrich Heine," in Eliot, *Essays and Leaves from a Note-Book,* ed. Charles Lee Lewes (New York, 1884), pp. 79–144.

Elster Ernst, "Heinrich Heine's erstes Gedicht," *Deutsche Dichtung, 25* (1898/99), 7–9, 80.

———, "H. Heine und H. Laube. Mit sechsundvierzig bisher ungedruckten Briefen Laubes an Heine," *Deutsche Rundschau, 133* (1907), 210–32, 394–412; *134* (1908), 77–90; *135* (1908), 91–116, 232–59; *136* (1908), 233–51, 441–55.

———, *Tannhäuser in Geschichte, Sage, und Dichtung,* Bromberg, 1908.

———, "Das Vorbild der freien Rhythmen Heinrich Heines," *Euphorion, 25* (1924), 63–86.

———, "War Heine französischer Bürger?" *Deutsche Rundschau, 112* (1902), 222–30.

———, "Zu Heines Biographie," *Vierteljahrschrift für Litteraturgeschichte, 4* (1891), 465–508.

Embden-Heine, Maria, Principessa della Rocca, *Erinnerungen an Heinrich Heine,* Hamburg, 1881.

Enders, Carl, "Heinrich Heines Faustdichtungen. Der Tanz als

Deutungs- und Gestaltungsmittel seelischer Erlebnisse," *Zeitschrift für deutsche Philologie, 74* (1955), 364–92.
frd. See d, fr.
Fairley, Barker, "Heine, Goethe, and the *Divan,*" *German Life and Letters,* n.s. *9* (1955/56), 166–70.
———, *Heinrich Heine: An Interpretation,* Oxford, 1954.
———, ed., *Heinrich Heine: Selected Poems,* Oxford, 1965.
Feise, Ernst, "Form and Meaning of Heine's Essay 'Die Nordsee,'" *Monatshefte, 34* (1942), 223–34.
———, "Goethes 'Kriegserklärung,' Heine und die Schnadahüpfel," *Modern Language Notes, 61* (1946), 325–30.
———, "Heine's Poem 'Ein Fräulein stand am Meere,'" *Modern Language Notes, 70* (1955), 350–51.
———, "Heine's 'Unterwelt,'" *Germanic Review, 31* (1956), 276–78.
———, "Heinrich Heine, Political Poet and Publicist," *Monatshefte, 40* (1948), 211–20.
———, "Rhythm and Melody as a Parodistic Means in Heine's Unterwelt," *Studies in Honor of Hermann Collitz* (Baltimore, Md., 1930), pp. 306–13.
———, "Some Notes on Translating Heine," *German Life and Letters,* n.s. *9* (1955/56), 189–91.
———, "Typen Heinischer Ballade," *Monatshefte, 34* (1942), 153–56.
Feuchtwanger, Lion, *Heinrich Heines Fragment: "Der Rabbi von Bacherach." Eine kritische Studie,* Munich, 1907.
———, "Die Masken Heinrich Heines. Zur 70. Wiederkehr seines Todestages," *Frankfurter Nachrichten,* no. 48, Feb. 17, 1926.
Finke, Franz, "Heine-Bibliographie 1954/59, *Heine-Jahrbuch 1964,* pp. 80–94.
———, "Heinrich Heine als Lyriker des Übergangs," *Heine-Jahrbuch 1963,* pp. 33–42.
———, "Zur Datierung des 'Rabbi von Bacherach,'" *Heine-Jahrbuch 1965,* pp. 26–32.
Fischer, Hans R., "Will das Judenthum das Heine-Denkmal?" *Die Gegenwart* (Berlin, Aug. 4, 1906), pp. 76–77.
Fischer, Max, *Heinrich Heine. Der deutsche Jude,* 2d ed. Stuttgart and Berlin, 1916.
Fleischmann, Jakob, "Heine und die Hegelsche Philosophie," *Deutsche Universitätszeitung, 14* (1959), 418–26.
Fränkel, Jonas, "Heine, der Jude," *Israelitisches Wochenblatt für die Schweiz,* special printing, Feb. 17, 1956.
———, *Heinrich Heine. Ein Vortrag,* Biel, 1960.

———, [Review of Friedrich Hirth, *Heinrich Heine. Bausteine zu einer Biographie,* Mainz, 1950, and Hirth, *Heinrich Heine und seine französischen Freunde,* Mainz, 1949], *Deutsche Literaturzeitung, 75* (1954), 82–90.

———, "Studien zu Heines Gedichten," *Euphorion, 19* (1912), 645–52, 774–80.

Frantzen, J. J. A. A., "Zu Heine's Loreley," *Neophilologus, 3* (1918), 131–34.

Franzos, Karl Emil, *Heines Geburtstag,* Berlin, 1900.

Fuerst, Norbert, *The Victorian Age of German Literature,* University Park, Pa. and London, 1966.

Fuhrmann, Alfred, *Recht und Staat bei Heinrich Heine,* Bonn, 1960.

Funder, Walther, *Zur Heine-Zensur im Kampf gegen den Liberalismus,* Hamburg [1932].

Galley, Eberhard, "Die Düsseldorfer Heine-Sammlung," *Weimarer Beiträge, 2* (1957), 278–82.

———, "Heine im literarischen Streit mit Gutzkow," *Heine-Jahrbuch 1966,* pp. 3–40.

———, "Heine und der Kölner Dom," *Deutsche Vierteljahrsschrift, 32* (1958), 94–110.

———, "Heine und sein Werk in Deutschland nach 1945. Eine kritische Übersicht," *Düsseldorfer Jahrbuch, 50* (1960), 151–62.

———, "Heine und zweimal Deutschland," *Die Welt der Literatur* (May 14, 1964), p. 163.

———, *Heinrich Heine,* Sammlung Metzler, vol. M30, Stuttgart, 1963.

———, *Heinrich Heine. Aus der Werkstatt des Dichters. Faksimiles nach Handschriften zu Heines 100. Todestag am 17. Februar 1956,* Düsseldorf, 1956.

———, "Heinrich Heines Privatbibliothek," *Heine-Jahrbuch 1962,* pp. 96–116.

———, "Heines 'Briefe über Deutschland' und die 'Geständisse.' Eine Textgeschichte an Hand der Manuskripte des Heine-Archivs," *Heine-Jahrbuch 1963,* pp. 60–83.

———, "Der 'Neunte Artikel' von Heines Werk 'Zur Geschichte der neueren schönen Literatur in Deutschland," *Heine-Jahrbuch 1964,* pp. 17–56.

———, *Der religiöse Liberalismus in der deutschen Literatur von 1830 bis 1850,* Rostock, 1934.

———, "Vor Heine wird nicht gewarnt," *Die Welt der Literatur* (May 27, 1965), pp. 261–62.

Gansberg, Marie Luise, *Der Prosa-Wortschatz des deutschen Realismus unter besonderer Berücksichtigung des vorausgehenden Sprachwandels 1835–1855,* Bonn, 1964.

Gebhard, Hella, "Interpretation der 'Historien' aus Heines 'Romanzero,' " diss. Erlangen, 1956.

Geiger, Ludwig, "Börne als Protektor Heines. Mit einem ungedruckten Briefe Börnes," *Frankfurter Zeitung,* Dec. 14, 1913.

———, *Das junge Deutschland und die preußische Censur,* Berlin, 1900.

———, "Zur Geschichte der Heineschen Schriften. Aus den Akten des Hamburger Archivs," *Euphorion, 8* (1901), 337–40.

Geis, Robert, "Heinrich Heine. Die jüdische Bestimmung eines deutschen Dichters," *Frankfurter Hefte, 11* (1956), 277–80.

Geisler, Ulrich, "Die sozialen Anschauungen des revolutionären Demokraten Heinrich Heine," *Wissenschaftliche Zeitschrift der Karl-Marx-Universität Leipzig, 14* (1965), 7–15.

Glossy, Karl, *Literarische Geheimberichte aus dem Vormärz* (Separatabdruck aus dem *Jahrbuch der Grillparzer-Gesellschaft,* Jahrgang *21–23*), Vienna, 1912.

Goldschmidt, Alfred, [Review of Georg J. Plotke, *Heinrich Heine als Dichter des Judentums,* Dresden, 1913], *Im neuen Reich. Zeitschrift des Centralvereins deutscher Staatsbürger jüdischen Glaubens, 19* (1913), 500–03.

Gordon, Samuel, "Heine, the German and the Jew," *Contemporary Review, 127* (1925), 230–236.

Graf, Otto G., "Heine and the Muse of Music," *Germanic Review, 25* (1950), 198–209.

Graupe, Walter, "Der Treibjagd der preußischen Junker auf Heinrich Heine im Jahre 1844," *Der Deutschunterricht, 9* (1956), 731–33.

Greenwood, M., "Heinrich Heine," *Saturday Review of Literature, 4* (1927/28), 1029–31.

Greiner, Martin, *Zwischen Biedermeier und Bourgeoisie. Ein Kapitel deutscher Literaturgeschichte im Zeichen Heinrich Heines,* Leipzig, 1954.

Grzimek, Waldemar, "Gedanken zu meinem Heine-Denkmal," *Bildende Kunst* (1956), pp. 310–14.

hwb. See b, hw.

Haber, Tom B., "Heine and Housman," *Journal of English and Germanic Philology, 43* (1944), 326–32.

Hahn, Karl-Heinz, "Die Wanderratten," in Hahn, *Aus der Werkstatt deutscher Dichter* (Halle, 1963), pp. 57–70.

Hamburger, Michael, "Heinrich Heine," in Hamburger, *Reason and Energy* (London, 1957), pp. 147–75.
Hammerich, Louis L., "Heinrich Heine als politischer Dichter," *Orbis Litterarum, 11* (1956), 125–37.
———, *Heinrich Heine. Deutschland. Ein Wintermärchen,* 2d ed. Copenhagen, 1956.
———, *Heinrich Heine som politisk digter. Tale ved mindehøjtideligheden på Københavns Universitet 17. Februar 1956,* Tønder, 1957.
———, *National og fremmed. Om den rytmiske teknik hos Heine og Platen,* Copenhagen, 1918.
———, "Trochäen bei Heinrich Heine. Zugleich ein Beitrag zum Werdegang eines alten Germanisten," *Formenwandel. Festschrift zum 65. Geburtstag von Paul Böckmann,* ed. Walter Müller-Seidel and Wolfgang Preisendanz (Hamburg, 1964), pp. 393–409.
Harich, Wolfgang, "Heinrich Heine und das Schulgeheimnis der deutschen Philosophie," in Heine, *Zur Geschichte der Religion und Philosophie in Deutschland,* ed. Harich, sammlung insel, *17* (Frankfurt am Main, 1965), 7–48.
Harsing, Erich, *Wolfgang Menzel und das Junge Deutschland,* Düsseldorf, 1909.
Hatfield, Henry, *Aesthetic Paganism in German Literature,* Cambridge, Mass., 1964.
Hayens, Kenneth C., "Heine's Love of Country," *Journal of English and Germanic Philology, 30* (1931), 74–79.
Hegemann, Daniel V. B., "Heine's Indebtedness to Walter von der Vogelweide," *Monatshefte, 42* (1950), 331–40.
Heim, Harro, "Freiligrath über Heine. Eine Anekdote," *Heine-Jahrbuch 1965,* pp. 48–50.
Heine, Maximilian, *Erinnerungen an Heinrich Heine und seine Familie,* Berlin, 1868.
Hermlin, Stephan, "Über Heine," in Hermlin, *Begegnungen 1954–1959* (Berlin, 1960), pp. 233–48.
Herrmann, Helene, *Studien zu Heines Romanzero,* Berlin, 1906.
Hess, John A., "Heine as a Prophet of Modern Europe," *Kentucky Foreign Language Quarterly, 6* (1959), 103–10.
———, "Heine's Return to Religion: Two Catholic Factors," *Kentucky Foreign Language Quarterly, 5* (1958), 88–94.
Hessel, Karl, "Heines 'Buch Legrand,' " *Vierteljahrschrift für Litteraturgeschichte, 5* (1892), 546–72.
Hirth, Friedrich, *Heinrich Heine. Bausteine zu einer Biographie,* Mainz, 1950.

———, *Heinrich Heine und seine französischen Freunde,* Mainz, 1949.

———, *Johann Peter Lyser. Der Dichter, Maler, Musiker,* Munich and Leipzig, 1911.

———. "La pension d'Henri Heine," *Mercure de France, 234* (Feb./Mar. 1932), 732–39.

Höck, Wilhelm, "Deutsche Dichter im Wandel des Urteils, Eine Aufsatzreihe (VI). Heinrich Heine," *Der junge Buchhandel,* no. 12, Beilage zum Beiblatt no. 97 (Dec. 4, 1964), pp. 186–92.

Höllerer, Walter, *Zwischen Klassik und Moderne,* Stuttgart, 1958.

Hofrichter, Laura, *Heinrich Heine,* Oxford, 1963.

Holzhausen, Paul, *Heinrich Heine und Napoleon I.,* Frankfurt am Main, 1903.

Hoppe, Gerhard, *Das Meer in der deutschen Dichtung von Friedrich L. Graf zu Stolberg bis Heinrich Heine,* Marburg, 1929.

Houben, H. H., *Verbotene Literatur von der klassischen Zeit bis zur Gegenwart,* Berlin, 1924–28.

Howarth, T. E. B., *Citizen-King: The Life of Louis Philippe King of the French,* London, 1961.

Hüffer, Hermann, *Heinrich Heine. Gesammelte Aufsätze,* ed. Ernst Elster, Berlin, 1906.

Hultberg, Helge, "Heines Bewertung der Kunst," *Heine-Jahrbuch 1967,* pp. 81–89.

Ibershoff, C. B., "Concerning a Passage in Heine's *Harzreise,*" *Philological Quarterly, 4* (1925), 239–40.

———, "Heine's *Harzreise* Once More," *Philological Quarterly, 5* (1926), 54–55.

———, "Lichtenberg's 'Wuerste, Bibliothek,'" *Philological Quarterly, 5* (1926), 282–83.

———, "Vitzliputzli," *Modern Language Notes, 28* (1913), 211–12.

Iggers, George G., "Heine and the Saint-Simonians: A Re-examination," *Comparative Literature, 10* (1958), 289–308.

Ilberg, Werner, *Unser Heine. Eine kritische Würdigung,* Berlin, 1952.

Inoue, Shozo, *Der Dichter Heine im fernen Osten. Sonderdruck aus dem Gedächtnisnummer zum 10-jährigen Jubiläum,* Tokyo, 1960.

Jaspersen, Ursula, "Heinrich Heine, 'Abenddämmerung,'" *Die deutsche Lyrik. Form und Geschichte,* ed. Benno von Wiese (Düsseldorf, 1964), *2,* 134–43.

———, "Heinrich Heine. 'Das Fräulein stand am Meere,'" *Die deutsche Lyrik. Form und Geschichte,* ed. Benno von Wiese (Düsseldorf, 1964), *2,* 144–49.

———, "Heinrich Heine. 'Ich weiß nicht, was soll es bedeuten . . . .'"

Die deutsche Lyrik. Form und Geschichte, ed. Benno von Wiese (Düsseldorf, 1964), *2,* 128–33.

Jennings, Lee B., "The Dance of Life and Death in Heine and Immermann," *German Life and Letters,* n.s. 18 (1965), 130–35.

———, *The Ludicrous Demon: Aspects of the Grotesque in German Post-Romantic Prose,* University of California Publications in Modern Philology, *71,* Berkeley and Los Angeles, Calif., 1963.

Jung, Gustav, "Der Erotiker Heinrich Heine," *Zeitschrift für Sexualwissenschaft, 11* (1924), 113–28.

Jungmann, Max, *Heinrich Heine als Nationaljude. Eine kritische Synthese,* Berlin, 1896.

Karpeles, Gustav, "Ein Gedicht von Heinrich Heine," in Karpeles, *Unter Palmen* (Berlin, 1871), pp. 95–101.

———, *Heinrich Heine und das Judenthum,* Breslau, 1868.

Kaufmann, David, *Aus Heines Ahnensaal,* Breslau, 1896.

Kaufmann, Hans, "Heines Schönheitsbegriff und die Revolution von 1848," *Weimarer Beiträge, 6* (1960), 266–77.

———, *Politisches Gedicht und klassische Dichtung. Heinrich Heine. Deutschland. Ein Wintermärchen,* Berlin, 1959.

———, "Zum 'Empfindungsgedicht' bei Heine," *Sinn und Form, 15* (1963), 914–35.

———, "Zur Entwicklung der Weltanschauung Heinrich Heines in den Jahren 1840–1844," *Wissenschaftliche Zeitschrift der Humboldt-Universität zu Berlin. Gesellschafts- und Sprachwissenschaftliche Reihe, 6* (1956/57), 59–70.

Kaufmann, Max, *Heines Charakter und die moderne Seele,* Zurich, 1902.

———, *Heinrich Heine contra Graf August von Platen und die Homo-Erotik, Leipzig,* [1907].

———, *Heinrich Heines Liebestragödien. Litterarhistorische Studie,* Zurich and Leipzig, 1897.

[Keiter, Heinrich], J. Staarstecher (pseud.), *Heinrich Heine der Antisemit und Nihilist. Bausteine zum Heine Denkmal aus Heine's sämmtlichen Werken,* Cologne, 1893.

———, *Heinrich Heine. Sein Leben, sein Charakter, seine Werke,* Cologne, 1891.

Kesten, Hermann, "Deutschland, Ein Wintermärchen," in Kesten, *Der Geist der Unruhe* (Cologne and Berlin, 1959), pp. 62–78.

———, "Heinrich Heine. Der Witz im Exil," in Kesten, *Lauter Literaten* (Vienna, Munich, and Basel, 1963), pp. 279–91.

Killy, Walther, "An der Schwelle. Über Heinrich Heine," *Tribüne, 1* (1962), 192–97.

———, "Mein Pferd für'n gutes Bild," in Killy, *Wandlungen des lyrischen Bildes,* 3d ed. Kleine Vandenhoek-Reihe, *22–23* (Göttingen, 1961), 94–115.

Kipphoff, Petra, "Heinrich Heine und keine Folgen," *Die Zeit* (Sept. 4, 1959), p. 9.

Kloss, Waldemar, "Herodias the Wild Huntress in the Legend of the Middle Ages," *Modern Language Notes, 23* (1908), 82–85, 100–02.

Koch, Hans-Gerhard, "Heinrich Heine und die Religion. Eine Auseinandersetzung mit dem marxistischen Heine-Bild," *Zeitwende. Die neue Furche, 32* (1961), 742–53.

Kofta, Maria, "Heinrich Heine und die polnische Frage," *Weimarer Beiträge, 6* (1960), 506–31.

Kohn, Hans, "Heinrich Heine—Poet and Patriot," in Kohn, *The Mind of Germany* (New York, 1960), pp. 99–127.

Kolar, Renate, "Die Stellung der 'Revue des deux mondes' zu den deutschen Dichtern der Romantik," diss. Vienna, 1960.

Kraft, Werner, "Ein Lied von Heine," in Kraft, *Augenblicke der Dichtung. Kritische Betrachtungen* (Munich, 1964), pp. 125–29.

———, "Heine und die Hiobsfrage," in Kraft, *Augenblicke der Dichtung. Kritische Betrachtungen* (Munich, 1964), pp. 41–45.

Kraus, Karl, *Heine und die Folgen,* Munich, 1910.

Krauss, Wilhelmine, *Das Doppelgängermotiv in der Romantik. Studien zum romantischen Idealismus,* Germanische Studien, *99,* Berlin, 1930.

Krinitz, Elise. See Selden, Camille.

Krogmann, Willy, "Lorelei: Geburt einer Sage," *Rheinisch-westfälische Zeitschrift für Volkskunde, 3* (1956), 170–96.

Krüger, Horst, "Die freie Kunst als ästhetisches Prinzip bei Heinrich Heine," diss. Würzburg, 1949.

Krummacher, Hans-Henrik, *Das 'Als ob' in der Lyrik,* Kölner Germanistische Studien, *1,* Cologne and Graz, 1965.

Kubacki, W., "Heinrich Heine und Polen," *Heine-Jahrbuch 1966,* pp. 90–106.

Kühn, Heinz, "Überlegungen zu einer Feierstunde für Heinrich Heine im Februar 1956," *Der Deutschunterricht, 9* (1956), 7–10.

Kurz, Paul Konrad, *Künstler Tribun Apostel. Heinrich Heines Auffassung vom Beruf des Dichters,* Munich, 1967.

Lachmanski, Hugo, "Eine neue Heine-Büste im Deutschen Dichtergarten in Cleveland," *C. V.-Zeitung, 11* (1932), 80.

Landsberg, Abraham, "Last Traces of Heinrich Heine in Hamburg," *Year Book of the Leo Baeck Institute, 1* (1956), 360–69.

Lasher-Schlitt, Dorothy, "Heine's Unresolved Conflict and *Der Rabbi von Bacherach*," *Germanic Review, 27* (1952), 173–87.

Laube, Heinrich, *Erinnerungen 1841–1881 (Gesammelte Schriften, 16)*, Vienna, 1882.

Launay, Robert, *Figures Juives*, Paris, 1921.

Legras, Jules, *Henri Heine Poète*, Paris, 1897.

Leschnitzer, Adolf, "Vom Dichtermärtyrtum zur politischen Dichtung. Heines Weg zur Demokratie," *Zur Geschichte und Problematik der Demokratie. Festgabe für Hans Herzfeld* (Berlin, 1958), pp. 665–93.

Levy, Madeleine, *Victoire du Poète. Essay sur Henri Heine*, Paris and Geneva, 1960.

Levy, Sieg[mund], "In Heines Schöpfungsliedern," *Archiv für Litteraturgeschichte, 12* (1884), 482–83.

Lichtenberger, Henri, *Heinrich Heine als Denker*, Dresden, 1905.

Liebeschütz, Hans, "German Radicalism and the Formation of Jewish Political Attitudes During the Earlier Part of the Nineteenth Century," *Studies in Nineteenth-Century Jewish Intellectual History*, ed. Alexander Altmann (Cambridge, Mass., 1964), pp. 141–70.

Linde, Otto zur, *Heinrich Heine und die deutsche Romantik*, Freiburg im Breisgau, 1899.

Liptzin, Sol., *The English Legend of Heinrich Heine*, New York, 1954.

———, *Germany's Stepchildren*, New York, 1944.

———, "Heinrich Heine's Homecoming," *Jewish Book Annual, 13* (1955/56), 55–57.

L[odenstein], J. F., "'Indessen—man wird Sie nicht lieben'—Ein Heine-Denkmal in Düsseldorf? Das ist die Frage," *Die Volksbühne* (1951), no. 6, pp. 5–7.

Loewenthal, Erich, "Heines Gumpelino-Roman. Mit unveröffentlichten Stücken aus der Urschrift," *Bimini* (1924) no. 11, pp. 9–10.

———, "Heines Stellung zum antiken Vers (Heine als Vorgänger Andreas Heuslers)," *Archiv für das Studium der neueren Sprachen und Literaturen, 145* (1923), 168–70.

———, "Der Rabbi von Bacherach," *Heine-Jahrbuch 1964*, pp. 3–16.

———, *Studien zu Heines "Reisebildern,"* Palaestra, *138*, Berlin and Leipzig, 1922.

Longfellow, Henry W., "German Writers: Heinrich Heine," *Graham's Lady's and Gentleman's Magazine, 20* (Jan./June 1842), 134–37.

Lowenthal, Leo, "Heine's Religion: The Messianic Ideals of the Poet," *Commentary, 4* (July/Dec. 1947), 153–57.

Ludwig, Albert, "Eine Nichte der Frau von Stein in Heine's Buch Le Grand," *Zeitschrift für deutsche Philologie, 61* (1936), 309–14.
Lülsdorff, Isolde, "Salome. Die Wandlung einer Schöpfung Heines in der französischen Literatur," diss. Hamburg, 1953.
Lüth, Erich, *Hamburgs Juden in der Heine-Zeit,* Hamburg, 1961.
Lukács, Georg, "Heine und die ideologische Vorbereitung der achtundvierziger Revolution," *Aufbau, 12* (1956), 103–18.
———, "Heinrich Heine als nationaler Dichter," in Lukács, *Literatursoziologie,* (Neuwied, 1961), pp. 358–82.
Lumley, Benjamin, *Reminiscences of the Opera,* London, 1864.
Lytton, R[obert Bulwer-], "Heinrich Heine's Last Poems and Thoughts," *The Fortnightly Review,* n.s. *39* (Jan./June 1870), 257–77.
Maché, Ulrich, "Der Einfluß persönlicher Beziehungen auf die Literaturkritik des jungen Heine," M.A. thesis, University of British Columbia, 1961.
———, "Der junge Heine und Goethe. Eine Revision der Auffassung von Heines Verhältnis zu Goethe vor dem Besuch in Weimar (1824)," *Heine-Jahrbuch 1965,* pp. 42–47.
Maliniemi, Irja, "Über rhythmische Satzkadenzen in Heinrich Heines Prosaschriften," *Heine-Jahrbuch 1965,* pp. 33–37.
Mann, Golo, "Über Heines Gedichte," *Deutsche Rundschau, 82* (1956), 1300–09.
———, "Zur Geschichte der deutschen Juden," *Neue Rundschau, 77* (1966), 563–73.
Mann, Michael, "Heine-Handschriften als Quellenmaterial zu einem biographischen Revisionsbericht. Heines Musikberichte in der 'Allgemeinen Zeitung' und in der 'Lutezia,'" *Heine-Jahrbuch 1963,* pp. 85–101.
———, "Heinrich Heine und G. W. F. Hegel zur Musik," *Monatshefte, 54* (1962), 343–53.
———, ed., Heinrich Heine, *Zeitungsberichte über Musik und Malerei,* Frankfurt am Main, 1964.
Marcus, Friedrich, *Jean Paul und Heinrich Heine,* Marburg, 1919.
Marcuse, Ludwig, " 'Denk ich an Deutschland . . .' (Nachtgedanken)," *Die Zeit* (Aug. 19, 1960), p. 6.
———, "Geschichte des Heine-Denkmals in Deutschland, *Das goldene Tor, 1* (1946), 129–35.
———, *Heine: A Life Between Love and Hate,* New York, 1933.
———, "Heine and Marx: A History and a Legend," *Germanic Review, 30* (1955), 110–24.

———, *Heinrich Heine in Selbstzeugnissen und Bilddokumenten,* Rowohlts Monographien, *41,* Hamburg, 1960.

———, *Revolutionär und Patriot. Das Leben Ludwig Börnes,* Berlin, 1929.

Mayer, Hans, "Anmerkungen zu einem Gedicht von Heinrich Heine," *Sinn und Form, 3,* no. 4 (1951), 177–84.

Mayerhofer, Alfred, *Heinrich Heines Literaturkritik,* Munich, 1929.

Mehring, Franz, *Gesammelte Schriften,* ed. Thomas Höhle, et al. *10,* Berlin, 1961.

Meissner, Alfred, *Heinrich Heine. Erinnerungen,* 2d ed. New York, 1856.

Mende, Fritz, "Bekenntnisse 1837. Heinrich Heines 'Einleitung zum Don Quixote,'" *Heine-Jahrbuch 1967,* pp. 48–66.

———, *Heinrich Heine im Literaturunterricht,* Berlin, 1962.

———, "Heinrich Heines literarisches Persönlichkeitsideal," *Heine-Jahrbuch 1965,* pp. 3–17.

Meredith, Owen. See Lytton.

Meyer, André, "Parallelen zu Versen Heinrich Heines," *Archiv für das Studium der neueren Sprachen und Literaturen, 62* (1908), 283–86.

Meyer, Bertha, *Salon Sketches: Biographical Studies of Berlin Salons of the Emancipation,* New York, 1938.

Meyer, Richard M., "Motiv-Wanderungen," *Deutsche Dichtung, 25* (1898/99), 25–28.

———, "Nicht mehr als sechs Schüsseln. 2. Göttinger Würste," *Euphorion, 8* (1901), 706–09.

Miller, Philip L., *The Ring of Words,* Garden City, New York, 1963.

Milska, Anna, "Heine über Polen," *Sinn und Form, 8* (1956), 66–77.

Moenkemeyer, Heinz, "Die deutschen Erstdrucke von Heines 'Doktor Faust,'" *Heine-Jahrbuch 1966,* pp. 58–67.

Mollenauer, Robert Russell, "Three 'Spätromantiker' on Romanticism: Hoffmann, Heine, and Eichendorff," diss. Indiana University, 1960.

Moos, Eugen, *Heine und Düsseldorf* (*Beiträge zur Kritik von Heines "Memoiren" und "Buch Le Grand"*), Marburg, 1908.

Mücke, Georg, *Heinrich Heines Beziehungen zum deutschen Mittelalter,* Forschungen zur neueren Literaturgeschichte, *34* Berlin, 1908.

Müller, Joachim, "Heines Nordseegedichte. Eine Sprach- und Stilanalyse des ersten Teils," *Wissenschaftliche Zeitschrift der Friedrich-Schiller-Universität Jena. Gesellschafts- und Sprachwissenschaftliche Reihe, 6* (1956/57), 191–212.

———, "Romanze und Ballade, Die Frage ihrer Strukturen, an zwei

Gedichten von Heinrich Heine dargelegt," *Wissenschaftliche Zeitschrift der Friedrich-Schiller-Universität Jena. Gesellschafts- und Sprachwissenschaftliche Reihe, 7* (1957/58), 377–85. Reprinted in *Germanisch-romanische Monatsschrift, 40* (1959), 140–56.

———, *Wirklichkeit und Klassik,* Berlin, 1955.

Müller von Hausen, Ludwig, "Heinrich Heine bei jüdischer Beleuchtung," *Deutsche Tageszeitung,* Berlin, May 5, 1910.

Münchhausen, Börries Freiherr von, "Der Dichter Firdusi," in Münchhausen, *Meisterballaden* (2d ed. Stuttgart, 1958), pp. 55–66.

Mustard, Helen Meredith, *The Lyric Cycle in German Literature,* New York, 1946.

Mutzenbecher, Heinrich, *Heine und das Drama,* Hamburg, 1914.

Na'aman, Schlomo, "Heine und Lassalle. Ihre Beziehungen im Zeichen der Dämonie des Geldes," *Archiv für Sozialgeschichte, 4* (1964), 45–86.

Nassen, J., "Heinrich Heine und die sogenannte katholisierende Richtung seines Jünglingsalters," *Literarische Beilage der Kölner Volkszeitung, 44,* no. 16 (Apr. 21, 1904, 121–25.

———, *Neue Heinefunde,* Leipzig, 1898.

———, "Zu Heinrich Heines Salon IV und seinem Gedichtzyklus 'Katharina,'" *Euphorion, 10* (1903), 624–32.

Neumann, Robert, "Deutschland und Heinrich Heine," *C. V.-Zeitung, 6* (1927), 456–57.

———, "Heine-Dilettantismus," *Die Weltbühne, 25* (1929), 602–03.

Niehaus, Max, *Himmel Hölle und Trikot. Heinrich Heine und das Ballett,* Munich, 1959.

Noethlich, Werner, "Was geschah mit Heines Nachlaß?" *Heine-Jahrbuch 1966,* pp. 107–20.

Nordmeyer, George, "Some Notes on Heine's *Belsatzar,*" *West Virginia University Bulletin,* Ser. 40, no. 3–I (Sept. 1939), 60–64.

Ochsenbein, Wilhelm, *Die Aufnahme Lord Byrons in Deutschland und sein Einfluß auf den jungen Heine,* Bern, 1905.

Ott, Barthélemy, "Heine et l'Histoire dans le Romancero," *Revue de l'Enseignement des Langues Vivantes, 47* (1930), 193–200.

———, *La Querelle de Heine et de Börne. Contribution à l'étude des idées politiques et sociales en Allemagne de 1830 à 1840,* Lyons, [1936].

Owen, Claude R., "Charruas und Tacuabé. Interpretation zu einem dunklen Passus in Heinrich Heines 'Tableaux de Voyage,'" *Heine-Jahrbuch 1965,* pp. 38–41.

———, "Heinrich Heines Kenntnisse der Weltliteratur ohne Berück-

sichtigung der deutschen Literatur. Ein bibliographisches Verzeichnis," M.A. thesis, University of Alberta, 1961.
———, "Ramiro de Maeztu über Heinrich Heine," *Heine-Jahrbuch 1967*, pp. 90–98.
Pache, Alexander, *Die literaturhistorische Stellung von Heines Natursymbolik*, Hamburg and Leipzig, 1904.
Paul, Adolf, "Heinrich Heines 'Atta Troll'—eine literarisch-politische Satire," *Zeitschrift für deutsche Philologie*, *56* (1931), 244–69.
Pfeiffer, Johannes, *Wege zur Dichtung. Eine Einführung in die Kunst des Lesens*, Hamburg, 1952.
Pfeiffer, Sibilla, *George Eliots Beziehungen zu Deutschland*, Anglistische Forschungen, *60*, Heidelberg, 1925.
Pfizer, Gustav, "Heine's Schriften und Tendenz," *Deutsche Vierteljahrsschrift*, *1* (1838), 167–247.
Pissarev, D[mitri] I[vanovich], *Heinrich Heine. 10 Essays*, ed. Ernst Joseph Görlich, Sonderdruck des *Österreichischen Kulturwort*, Vienna, 1965.
Plotke, Georg J., *Heinrich Heine als Dichter des Judentums*, Dresden, 1913.
Polak, Léon, "En nogmaals Heine's Buch Legrand," *Revue des Langues Vivantes*, *15* (1949), 96–100.
———, "Heinrich Heines *Buch Legrand*," *Neophilologus*, 7 (1921/22), 260–72.
Politzer, Heinz, "Heinrich Heine," *Neue Rundschau*, *59* (1948), 1–29.
———, "Um einen Heine von innen bittend," *German Quarterly*, *34* (1961), 422–30.
Pongs, Hermann, "Neue Aufgaben der Literaturwissenschaft II. 1. Masse," *Dichtung und Volkstum*, *38* (1937), 274–77.
Porterfield, Allen Wilson, "Graf von Loeben and the Legend of the Lorelei," *Modern Philology*, *13*, no. 6 (Oct. 1915), 65–92.
Posener, S., "A propos de la subvention d'Henri Heine," *Mercure de France*, *235* (Apr./May 1932), 252–53.
———, "Les fonds secrets du quai d'Orsay en 1841," *Mercure de France*, *232* (Nov./Dec. 1931), 676–80.
Prang, Helmut, "Heine im Schatten Hölderlins," *Neue deutsche Hefte*, *2* (1955/56), 474–75.
Prawer, S. S., *Heine: Buch der Lieder*, London, 1960.
———, "Heine's Return," *German Life and Letters*, n.s. 9 (1955/56), 171–80.
———, "Heines Stimme," *Heine-Jahrbuch 1964*, pp. 56–62.

———, *Heine The Tragic Satirist: A Study of the Later Poetry, 1827–1856,* Cambridge, England, 1961.

———, [Review of Hans Kaufmann, *Politisches Gedicht und klassische Dichtung,* Berlin, 1959], *German Life and Letters,* n.s. *13* (1959), 76–77.

Preisendanz, Wolfgang, "Aufklärung und Verdinglichung in den Gedichten Georg Trakls," *Immanente Ästhetik. Ästhetische Reflexion. Lyrik als Paradigma der Moderne,* ed. W. Iser (Munich, 1966), pp. 227–61.

Pröhle, Heinrich, *Heinrich Heine und der Harz,* Hamburg, 1888.

Psaar, Werner, "Zur Deutung Heinescher Gedichte im Deutschunterricht. Probleme und Versuche," *Heine-Jahrbuch 1967,* pp. 99–123.

Putz, Karl, "Jean Paul und H. Heine," *Archiv für Litteraturgeschichte, 10* (1881), 585–88.

Rahmelow, Werner, "Zu den Anfängen des feuilletonistischen Stiles (Untersuchungen an Heine)," diss. Freiburg im Breisgau, 1936.

Rappaport, S., "Heinrich Heine," in Rappaport, *Jewish Horizons* (Johannesburg, 1959), pp. 186–95.

Ras, Gerard, *Börne und Heine als politische Schriftsteller,* The Hague, 1926.

Reinhard, L. J., *Heinrich Heine,* Reprint of the article in the *Great Soviet Encyclopedia,* Berlin, 1956.

Reiss, H. S., "The Criticism of Heine in the 'Heine-Jahr': A Survey," *German Life and Letters,* n.s. *11* (1957/58), 130–36.

———, "The Criticism of Heine Since the War: An Assessment," *German Life and Letters,* n.s. *9* (1955/56), 210–19.

———, "The Study of Heine: Retrospect and Prospect," *German Quarterly, 32* (1959), 3–10.

Reissner, H. G., "Heinrich Heine's Tale of the 'Captive Messiah,'" *Der Friede. Idee und Verwirklichung. The Search for Peace. Festgabe für Adolf Leschnitzer* (Heidelberg, 1961), pp. 327–40.

Remer, Paul, *Die freien Rhythmen in Heines Nordseebildern. Ein Beitrag zur neuen deutschen Metrik,* Heidelberg, 1889.

Reynaud, L., "La source française d' 'Atta Troll,'" *Revue germanique, 10* (1914), 145–59.

Riesel, Elise, "Sprache und Stil von Heines 'Harzreise,'" *Der Deutschunterricht, 9* (1956), 11–18, 79–95.

Rilla, Paul, "Heinrich Heine—heute," in Rilla, *Essays* (Berlin, 1955), pp. 133–41.

Robson-Scott, W. D., *The Literary Background of the Gothic Revival in Germany,* Oxford, 1965.

Roos, Carl, "Nordische Elemente im Werk Heinrich Heines," *Orbis Litterarum, 10* (1956), 150–65.

———, "Nordiske Elementer i Heinrich Heines Værk," *Festskrift til L. L. Hammerich* (Copenhagen, 1952), pp. 193–207.

Rose, William, "Ein biographischer Beitrag zu Heines Leben und Werk," *Weimarer Beiträge, 3* (1957), 586–97.

———, *The Early Love Poetry of Heinrich Heine: An Inquiry into Poetic Inspiration,* Oxford, 1962.

———, "Heine Conference at Weimar," *German Life and Letters,* n.s. *10* (1956/57), 162–63.

———, *Heinrich Heine: Two Studies of his Thought and Feeling: Heine's Political and Social Attitude; Heine's Jewish Feeling,* Oxford, 1956.

———, "Studies of Heine Since the War," *Orbis Litterarum, 10* (1956), 166–74.

Rudow, W., "Ein noch nicht erklärtes Werk Heines," *Internationale Litteraturberichte,* [illegible] (1895), 340–47.

Rüdiger, Gertrud von, "Die Zitate in 'Shakespeares Mädchen und Frauen' von Heine," *Euphorion, 19* (1912), 290–97.

Ruhrig, Helmut Ernst, "Heinrich Heine. Beiträge zur Bestimmung seines ironischen Humors," diss. Freiburg im Breisgau, 1953.

Saint-René Taillandier, René-Gaspard-Ernest, "Poètes Contemporains de l'Allemagne. Henri Heine, sa vie et ses écrits," *Revue des deux mondes, Nouvelle période, 14* (1852), 5–36.

Salinger, Herman, "Heine's 'Rote Pantoffeln': Wit and Autobiography," *Monatshefte, 33* (1941), 213–16.

———, "Heinrich Heine's Stature After a Century," *Monatshefte, 48* (1956), 309–16.

———, "Helping Heinrich Heine Explain his Archetypal 'Night Journey' Poem," *Literature and Psychology, 13* (1963), 30–36.

———, "Housman's *Last Poems,* XXX and Heine's *Lyrisches Intermezzo,* 62," *Modern Language Notes, 54* (1939), 288–90.

———, "The Riddle of the 'Kinderball' in Heine's 'Bäder von Lucca,' " *Monatshefte, 34* (1942), 145–52.

———, "Some Heine Notes," *Modern Language Notes, 53* (1938), 430–33.

Sammons, Jeffrey L., "Heine's Composition: Die Harzreise," *Heine-Jahrbuch 1967,* pp. 40–47.

———, "Heine's *Rabbi von Bacherach:* The Unresolved Tensions," *German Quarterly, 37* (1964), 26–38.

Santkin, Paul, *Ludwig Börnes Einfluß auf Heinrich Heine,* Betzdorf, 1913.

Schellenberg, Alfred, *Heinrich Heines französische Prosawerke,* Germanische Studien, *14,* Berlin, 1921.

Scher, Steven Paul, *Verbal Music: Literary Evocation of Music in Works by Wackenroder, Tieck, Hoffmann, Heine, and Thomas Mann,* New Haven, 1968.

Scherer, Wingolf, "Heinrich Heine und der Saint-Simonismus," diss. Bonn, 1950.

Schiff, Hermann, *Heinrich Heine und der Neuisraelitismus. Briefe an Adolf Strodtmann,* Hamburg and Leipzig, 1866.

Schlösser, Rudolf, "Kleinigkeiten aus dem Koheleth bei Klopstock und Heine," *Euphorion, 22* (1915), 89.

Schmid, Carlo, *"Denk ich an Deutschland in der Nacht." Eine Heinrich-Heine-Rede,* Berlin, 1956.

Schmidt, Erich, *Deutsche Reimstudien,* Sitzungsberichte der königlichen preußischen Akademie der Wissenschaften, *33,* Berlin, 1900.

Schmidt-Weissenfels, Eduard, *Über Heinrich Heine,* Berlin, 1857.

Schmitz, Gerhard, *Über die ökonomischen Anschauungen in Heines Werken,* Weimar, 1960.

Schmohl, Erika, "Der Streit um Heinrich Heine. Darstellung und Kritik der bisherigen Heine-Wertung," diss. Marburg, 1956.

Schneider, Wilhelm, "Heinrich Heine. *Seegespenst,"* in Schneider, *Liebe zum deutschen Gedicht* (Freiburg im Breisgau, 1952), pp. 256–65.

Schoeps, Hans-Joachim, "Ein unbekannter Agentenbericht über Heinrich Heine," *Heine-Jahrbuch 1967,* pp. 67–80.

Scholem, Gerschom, "Juden und Deutsche," *Neue Rundschau, 77* (1966), 547–62.

Schoolfield, George C., *The Figure of the Musician in German Literature,* University of North Carolina Studies in the Germanic Languages and Literatures, *19,* Chapel Hill, N.C., 1956.

Schüssler, Alexander J., "Die englischen Übersetzungen von Heinrich Heines *Buch der Lieder,"* diss. Mainz, 1953.

Schulte-Kemminghausen, Karl, "Tagebuchaufzeichnungen des westfälischen Freiherrn Ludwig von Diepenbrock-Grüter über Heinrich Heine," *Festschrift für Jost Trier,* ed. Benno von Wiese and Karl Heinz Borck (Meisenheim, 1954), pp. 277–96.

Schulze, Anneliese, "Johann Heinrich Voß—ein Vorgänger Heines im Kampf gegen Obskurantismus," *Der Deutschunterricht, 9* (1956), 689–703.

Seeger, Heinz, "Der Erzähler in Heines Balladen und Romanzen. Zur Deutung und Kritik seiner Dichtung," diss. Bonn, 1953.

Seelig, Max, *Die dichterische Sprache in Heines "Buch der Lieder,"* Halle, 1891.

Seifert, Siegfried, "Der unbewältigte Heine," *Neue deutsche Literatur, 13* (1965), 172–79.

Selden, Camille (pseud. for Elise Krinitz), *Les derniers jours de Henri Heine,* Paris, 1884.

Servières, Georges, "Les Scénarios de Ballets de Henri Heine," *Le Menestrel, 99* (1937), 17–20.

Seuffert, Bernhard, "Heines 'Heimkehr,'" *Vierteljahrschrift für Litteraturgeschichte, 3* (1890), 589–601.

Siebert, Wilhelm, *Heinrich Heines Beziehung zu E. T. A. Hoffmann,* Marburg, 1908.

Sieburg, Friedrich, "Beschwörung und Mitteilung. Zur Lyrik Heinrich Heines," *Jahresring, 3* (1956/57), 56–73.

———, "Karl Kraus' großer Augenblick," *Die Gegenwart, 8* (1953), 237–39.

Siegrist, Christoph, "Heines Traumbilder," *Heine-Jahrbuch 1965,* pp. 17–25.

Silz, Walter, "Heines Synaesthesia," *PMLA, 57* (1942), 469–88.

Simon, Ernst, "Heine und die Romantik," in Simon, *Brücken. Gesammelte Aufsätze* (Heidelberg, 1965), pp. 135–56.

Simon-Baumann, Lotte, "George Eliot über Heinrich Heine," *Anglia. Zeitschrift für englische Philologie, 55* (1931), 311–20.

Slochower, Harry, "Attitudes Towards Heine in German Literary Criticism," *Jewish Social Studies, 3* (1941), 355–74.

Söhn, Gerhart, *Heinrich Heine in seiner Vaterstadt Düsseldorf,* Düsseldorf, 1966.

Spann, Meno, "Exoticism and Heinrich Heine," *Studies in Philology, 30* (1933), 86–102.

———, *Heine,* Studies in Modern Literature and Thought, ed. Erich Heller and Anthony Thorlby, London, 1966.

Staarstecher, J., See Keiter, Heinrich.

Stamm, Friedrich, "Die Liebeszyklen in Heines 'Neuen Gedichten,'" *Euphorion, 23* (1921), 82–95.

Stein, Ernst, "Der spröde Klang. Zur Besonderheit der Lyrik Heines," *Aufbau, 12* (1956), 118–21.

Stein, Jack M., "Schubert's Heine Songs," *Journal of Aesthetics and Art Criticism, 24* (1965/66), 559–66.

Steinhauer, Harry, "Heinrich Heine," *Antioch Review, 16* (1956/57), 445–58.

Steinmann, Friedrich, *H. Heine. Denkwürdigkeiten aus meinem Zusammenleben mit ihm,* Prague and Leipzig, 1857.

Stern, Arthur, "Heinrich Heines Krankheit und seine Ärzte," *Heine-Jahrbuch 1964,* pp. 63–79.

Stern, J. P., "History and Prophecy: Heine," in Stern, *Re-Interpretations: Seven Studies in Nineteenth-Century German Literature* (New York, 1964), pp. 208–32.

Sternberg, Kurt, *Heinrich Heines geistige Gestalt und Welt,* Berlin, 1929.

Sternberger, Dolf, "Rede über Heinrich Heine," *Gestalt und Gedanke, 4* (1957), 148–70.

Stockhammer, Morris, "Heinrich Heine als Pessimist," *Schopenhauer-Jahrbuch, 43* (1962), 111–16.

Stössinger, Felix, "Heines Götter," *Neue Schweizer Rundschau,* n.s. *18* (1950/51), 412–18.

———, ed., Heine, *Mein wertvollstes Vermächtnis. Religion, Leben, Dichtung,* Zurich, 1950.

Strich, Fritz, "Goethe und Heine. Ein der Jüdischen Vereinigung Zürich 1947 gehaltener Vortrag zur Feier von Heines 150. Geburtstag," in Strich, *Der Dichter und die Zeit* (Bern, 1947), pp. 185–225.

———, "Heinrich Heine und sein Denkmal in Düsseldorf. Eine Deutung," *Das Tor, 19* (1953), 126–30.

Strodtmann, Adolf, *H. Heine's Leben und Werke,* Berlin, 1867–69; 2d ed. Berlin, 1873; 3d ed. Hamburg, 1884.

———, "Die Mutter H. Heine's, nach ihren Jugendbriefen geschildert," *Deutsche Rundschau, 12* (1877), 86–100.

Süskind, W. E., "Heinrich Heine nach hundert Jahren," *Neue deutsche Hefte, 2* (1955/56), 862–66.

T., W., "Die Taufe des deutschen Aristophanes," *Die Gartenlaube* (1877), pp. 18–20.

Tabak, Israel, *Judaic Lore in Heine: The Heritage of a Poet,* Baltimore, Md., 1948.

Teichgräber, Susanne, "Bild und Komposition in Heinrich Heines 'Buch der Lieder,' " diss. Freiburg im Breisgau, 1964.

Thalmann, Marianne, "Heinrich Heine. 'Die Nordsee,' eine Lesartenstudie," *Zeitschrift für deutsche Philologie, 52* (1927), 153–57.

Theunissen, G. H., "Vom Wesen des rheinischen Journalisten. Ein Versuch über Görres und Heine," *Dichtung und Volkstum, 39* (1938), 51–60.

———, "Wesen des Journalismus. Versuch über Görres und Heine," *Rheinischer Merkur* (Oct. 19, 1951), p. 7.

Trilse, Christoph, "Heine-Ausgabe kritisch betrachtet," *Der Morgen* (Berlin, Apr. 10, 1965), p. 4.

Untermeyer, Louis, *Heinrich Heine: Paradox and Poet: The Life,* New York, 1937.

Uyttersprot, H., *Heinrich Heine en zijn Invloed in de Nederlandse Letterkunde,* Oudenaarde, 1953.

———, "Nog eens Das Buch Le Grand," *Album Prof. Dr. Frank Baur* (Antwerp, Brussels, Ghent, and Leuven, 1948), *2,* 317–32.

Veit, Philipp F., "Heine's Birth: Illegitimate or Legitimate?" *Germanic Review, 33* (1958), 276–84.

———, "Heine's Imperfect Muses in *Atta Troll:* Biographical Romance or Literary Symbolism," *Germanic Review, 39* (1964), 262–80.

———, "Die Rätsel um Heines Geburt," *Heine-Jahrbuch 1962,* pp. 5–25.

Vermeil, Edmond, "Heine als Politiker," *Sinn und Form, 8* (1956), 407–14.

Victor, Walther, *Heine. Ein Lesebuch für unsere Zeit,* Weimar, 1963.

———, *Marx und Heine,* Berlin, 1953.

———, *Mathilde. Ein Leben um Heinrich Heine,* Leipzig and Vienna, 1931.

Vollmer, Clement, "Heine's Conservatism," *South Atlantic Quarterly, 45* (1946), 339–49.

Vontin, Walther, "Heinrich Heine und Hebbels 'Judith,' " *Heine-Jahrbuch 1963,* pp. 43–59.

W. T. See T., W.

Wadepuhl, Walter, "Heines Geburtsjahr," *PMLA, 61* (1946), 126–56.

———, *Heine-Studien,* Weimar, 1956.

———, "Heines Verhältnis zu Goethe," *Goethe. Neue Folge des Jahrbuchs der Goethe-Gesellschaft, 18* (1956), 121–31.

———, "Heines Vorrede zu den 'Französischen Zuständen.' Ein Beitrag zur Geschichte der preussischen Zensur," *PMLA, 58* (1943), 499–513.

———, "Eine ungedruckte Vorrede zu Heines *Reisebildern,*" *Philological Quarterly, 20* (1941), 74–81.

Wagner, Richard, *Das Judenthum in der Musik,* Leipzig, 1869.

Walden, Helen, "Gottfried Keller's 'Apotheker von Chamounix," *German Quarterly, 11* (1938), 21–29.

Walter, H., *Heinrich Heine,* London and Toronto, 1930.

Walzel, Oskar, *Gehalt und Gestalt im Kunstwerk des Dichters,* 2d ed. Darmstadt, 1957.

———, *Heines Tanzpoem Der Doktor Faust,* Weimar, 1917.
Warkentin, Roderich, "Gemeinsamkeit der Quellen für Goethes Paralipomena zur Walpurgnisnacht und Heines Faust," *Zeitschrift für vergleichende Litteraturgeschichte,* n.s. *11* (1897), 30–35.
Weber, Dietrich, " 'Gesetze des Standpunkts' in Heines Lyrik," *Jahrbuch des Freien Deutschen Hochstifts 1965,* pp. 369–99.
Weber, Heinrich, "Entlehnung oder Uebereinstimmung," *Deutsche Rundschau, 100* (July/Sept. 1899), 303–09.
Weber, Werner, "Heinrich Heine. Die Grenadiere," *Wege zum Gedicht,* ed. Rupert Hirschenauer and Albrecht Weber (Munich and Zurich, 1963), *2,* 267–69.
Weckmüller, Artur, *Heines Stil.* Sprache und Kultur der germanischen und romanischen Völker, Germanistische Reihe, *11,* Breslau, 1934.
Weidekampf, Ilse, *Traum und Wirklichkeit in der Romantik und bei Heine,* Palaestra, *182,* Leipzig, 1932.
Weigand, Hermann J., "The Double Love Tragedy in Heine's *Buch Le Grand:* a Literary Myth," *Germanic Review, 13* (1938), 121–26.
———, "Heine in Paris: Friedrich Hirth's Commentary on the Letters 1831–44," *Orbis Litterarum, 10* (1956), 175–83.
———, "Heine Manuscripts at Yale: Their Contribution Concerning him as Man and Artist," *Studies in Philology, 34* (1937), 65–90.
———, "Heine's Buch Le Grand," *Journal of English and Germanic Philology, 21* (1919), 102–35.
———, "Heine's Family Feud—The Culmination of his Struggle for Economic Security," *Journal of English and Germanic Philology, 21* (1922), 70–106.
———, "Heine's Return to God," *Modern Philology, 18* (1920/21), 309–42.
———, "How Censorship Worked in 1831. Heine's Amusing Bickerings and Baitings Sensationally Documented by an Unpublished Manuscript of the Kohut-Rutra Collection of Heineana," *Yale University Library Gazette, 10* (1935/36), 17–22.
Weinberg, Kurt, "Heine and French Poetry," *Yale French Studies,* no. 6 (1950), pp. 45–52.
———, *Henri Heine. "Romantique défroqué." Héraut du symbolisme français,* New Haven and Paris, 1954.
Weiss, Gerhard, "Die Aufnahme Heinrich Heines in Großbritannien und den Vereinigten Staaten von Amerika (1828–1856)," diss. Mainz, 1955.
———, "Die Entstehung von Heines 'Doktor Faust.' Ein Beispiel

deutsch-englisch-französischer Freundschaft," *Heine-Jahrbuch 1966,* pp. 41–57.

———, "Niederdeutsche Laute und rheinisches Wortgut bei Heinrich Heine," *Heine-Jahrbuch 1962,* pp. 39–49.

Weiss, Walter, *Enttäuschter Pantheismus. Zur Weltgestaltung der Dichtung in der Restaurationszeit,* Gesetz und Wandel. Innsbrucker literaturhistorische Arbeiten, *3,* Dornbirn, 1962.

Weitzmann, Siegfried, "Heine und die Emanzipation," *Mitteilungsblatt* (Tel Aviv, Jan. 27, 1961), p. 3.

Werner, Alfred, "Heinrich Heine: Jewish Nationalist," *Judaism, 5* (1956), 76–84.

Westra, P., "Heinrich Heines sogenannte '*Josepha-Lieder,*'" *Neophilologus, 40* (1956), 117–28.

———, "Henri Heine et le Judaïsme," *Revue des langues vivantes, 16* (1950), 30–39.

Wieland, Wolfgang, "Heinrich Heine und die Philosophie," *Deutsche Vierteljahrsschrift, 37* (1963), 232–48.

Wiese, Benno von, *Politische Dichtung Deutschlands,* Berlin, 1931.

Wilhelm, Friedrich, "Über drei Gedichte Heinrich Heines (Belsatzar, Der Hirtenknabe, Schelm von Bergen)," *Beilage zum Jahresbericht des Königlich Evangelischen Gymnasiums zu Ratibor,* Ratibor, 1905.

Wilhelm, Gottfried, and Eberhard Galley, *Heine Bibliographie,* 2 vols. Weimar, 1960.

Wille, François, "François Willes Erinnerungen an Heinrich Heine," ed. Eberhard Galley, *Heine-Jahrbuch 1967,* pp. 3–20.

Windfuhr, Manfred, "Heines Fragment eines Schelmenromans '*Aus den Memoiren des Herren von Schnabelewopski,*'" *Heine-Jahrbuch 1967,* pp. 21–39.

———, "Zu einer kritischen Gesamtausgabe von Heines Werken," *Heine-Jahrbuch 1962,* pp. 70–95.

Wolff, Max, *Heinrich Heine,* Munich, 1922.

Wood, Frank Higley, Jr., *Heine as a Critic of his Own Works,* New York, 1934.

Wulf, Josef, *Literatur und Dichtung im Dritten Reich. Eine Dokumentation,* Gütersloh, 1963.

Zagari, Luciano, "Heine in der italienischen Kritik," *Heine-Jahrbuch 1965,* pp. 51–63.

Zenker, Rudolf, "Heines achtes Traumbild und Burns' Jolly Beggars," *Zeitschrift für vergleichende Litteraturgeschichte,* n.s. 7 (1894), 245–51.

Supplementary Note

The revival of interest in Heine I spoke of in my preface has acquired much more momentum than I foresaw when this study was first conceived and begun. Six or seven years ago it was easy to keep track of the annual body of work; now this is beginning to be something of a challenge. Around 1962, when the *Heine-Jahrbuch* began publication, there was a suggestion in the air that a renewed concern with Heine was in the offing, but there was little concrete evidence that the situation would change so rapidly.

In order to complete this book, I closed the bibliography as of the summer of 1967. Consequently, my study does not have the benefit of the most recent researches, and I should like to mention briefly a few items as an indication of what has occurred in the short space of two years:

> Among a number of special studies, attention should be called particularly to Paul Konrad Kurz, *Künstler Tribun Apostel: Heinrich Heines Auffassung vom Beruf des Dichters* (Munich, 1967), an important and useful monograph to which I managed to slip in only one brief reference; and A. I. Sandor, *The Exile of Gods: Interpretation of a Theme and a Technique in the Work of Heinrich Heine* (The Hague, 1967), an unusual and imaginative interpretive effort. The last two years of the continuously improving *Heine-Jahrbuch* should also be mentioned with admiration. The East German authority Hans Kaufmann, whom I discuss in Appendix I, has meanwhile brought out a new book, *Heinrich Heine: Geistige Entwicklung und künstlerisches Werk* (Berlin and Weimar, 1967). The study by Robert Stiefel, said to be unpublished in the footnote on p. 340, has since appeared in *Germanic Review, 44* (1969), 187–98.
>
> Heine editions have at last begun to appear in West Germany. The Insel-Heine, edited by Christoph Siegrist, Wolfgang Preisendanz, Eberhard Galley, and Helmut Schanz

(Frankfurt am Main, 1968), consists of three excellently edited volumes of prose and one dubious volume of poetry, so permeated with distaste for *Buch der Lieder* that it is an interesting, if regrettable, sign of the times. The more ambitious Hanser-Heine, edited by Klaus Briegleb (Munich, 1968–), of which one volume has appeared at this writing, is full of information and rather problematic argument that would have had a bearing on some aspects of my own study. At least one more edition, in the Winkler Verlag, will probably begin to appear before this book is published.

Most important of all, the first scholarly book-length study by a West German professor is now available: Manfred Windfuhr, *Heinrich Heine: Reflexion und Revolution* (Stuttgart, 1968).

This two-year record represents more significant contributions than appeared during all the years I worked on my own book. By the end of 1969 the list will have become substantially longer.

The increased tempo of publication is an aspect of a highly charged and often tense atmosphere of critical revision in German intellectual life, the kind of atmosphere in which Heine may be expected to thrive. One example of this is two lectures on Heine, by Helmut Hartwig and Helmut Koopmann, delivered at the agitated conference of Germanists in Munich of October 1966; they appeared in the volume *Nationalismus in Germanistik und Dichtung,* ed. Benno von Wiese and Rudolf Henss (Berlin, 1967), which came to my attention too late to be considered here. Another is that the New Left periodical *Text + Kritik: Zeitschrift für Literatur,* published in Aachen, devoted its January 1968 issue to Heine. In other respects, too, the cause of Heine appears to improve. The Heine Archive, which was inadequately and obscurely housed when I worked there in 1966, has now moved to more spacious and attractive quarters within the Düsseldorf Library. On the other hand, the sad tales are not yet at an end; another chapter to the ancient *Denkmalstreit* has been written by the opposition to a proposal to name the new University of Düsseldorf after Heine.

All of this activity naturally has some relevance to what has been said in this book. There are a number of places where reference to the newest developments would have been appropriate, and I may have made an observation here and there that is now out of date. I think, too, that my basic attitude toward one or two fundamental issues may have shifted somewhat under the force of most recent argument. When a subject has become suddenly very much alive, the necessarily deliberate pace of scholarly publication makes such overlap inevitable. I hope my reader will be reasonably indulgent about this, and will share my delight that these problems are due to the current liveliness of the dialogue on Heinrich Heine.

June 1969

Index

1. Proper Names

2. Heine's Works

Poems contained in *Buch der Lieder, Neue Gedichte, Romanzero,* and *Gedichte 1853 und 1854* are listed under those headings in the order in which they appear in the collections. Paralipomena to *Buch der Lieder* are entered in alphabetical order at the end of that list. Other poems are alphabetized individually. Prose works from *Reisebilder, Der Salon,* and *Vermischte Schriften* are entered under their own titles.